The Investigative Reporter's Handbook

A Guide to Documents, Databases and Techniques

The Investigative Reporter's Handbook

A Guide to Documents, Databases and Techniques

Fifth Edition

Brant Houston
University of Illinois at Urbana-Champaign

Investigative Reporters and Editors, Inc.

BEDFORD/ST. MARTIN'S
Boston ◆ New York

For Bedford/St. Martin's

Executive Editor for Communication: Erika Gutierrez
Developmental Editor: Joanna Imm
Editorial Assistant: Mae Klinger
Production Supervisor: Sarah Ulicny
Marketing Manager: Adrienne Petsick
Project Management: Books By Design, Inc.
Text Design: Books By Design, Inc.
Cover Design: Billy Boardman
Composition: Books By Design, Inc.
Printing and Binding: RR Donnelley & Sons Company

President: Joan E. Feinberg
Editorial Director: Denise B. Wydra
Director of Marketing: Karen R. Soeltz
Director of Development: Erica T. Appel
Director of Editing, Design, and Production: Marcia Cohen
Assistant Director of Editing, Design, and Production: Elise S. Kaiser
Manager, Publishing Services: Emily Berleth

Library of Congress Control Number: 2008936834

Manufactured in the United States of America.

7 6 5
k jj i h

For information, write: Bedford/St. Martin's, 75 Arlington Street, Boston, MA 02116   (617-399-4000)

ISBN-10: 0-312-58997-2
ISBN-13: 978-0-312-58997-4

Preface

In the six years since Investigative Reporters and Editors produced the last edition of "The Investigative Reporter's Handbook," journalism has undergone a revolution. Newspapers and other news outlets have been shaken by massive shifts in ownership and drastic cuts in reporting staffs across the United States. Technology has brought exciting changes, including the rise of digital journalism, calls for more "citizen journalism," the increase in foundation-funded newsrooms and the creation of investigative blogs.

Despite the changes brought by the disastrous decreases in news industry revenues and the surge in new forms of journalism driven by technology, it remains essential to uphold the principles and methods that support all good reporting—and especially all good *investigative* reporting.

This book examines those fundamental guidelines—accuracy, multisourcing, documentation, fairness and a relentless pursuit of the truth—and serves as a road map for any journalist, student or citizen who wants to practice investigative journalism. It shows how obtaining authentic documents and conducting numerous interviews lead to good—and sometimes great—stories that serve the public well. This book explains how to embrace new techniques, approaches and technologies without abandoning the hard-earned knowledge of working journalists.

What Is Investigative Journalism?

Journalists and scholars have for many years debated the specific meaning of the term "investigative journalism." IRE defines it as "the reporting, through one's own initiative and work product, of matters of importance to readers, viewers or listeners. In many cases, the subjects of the reporting wish the matters under scrutiny to remain undisclosed." Over the years, journalists have expanded the definition to include analyzing and revealing the breakdown of social or justice systems and documenting the consequences.

Others have proposed a broader definition, suggesting that every journalist is an investigative journalist because they all ask questions and read documents, but this broader definition ignores the more rigorous requirements of credible investigative journalism. Every journalist *can* be an investigator, even if only for one story, if he or she is willing to put in the time. Investigative journalists ask more questions, go through more documents and spend more time thinking about a story than daily reporters do. Often, investigative journalists demand only the curiosity and desire to know the story behind the story—that is, to understand the circumstances of a situation and the real goals of a politician or businessperson.

Investigative journalists also spend more thought and time on deciding what is worthy of coverage. Instead of simply attending a city council meeting and filing a brief deadline story, a reporter could investigate by checking reports, property records, audits and city contracts, carefully reading the minutes of previous meetings and collecting and analyzing city databases. Or a reporter might cover the meeting just to get background for a larger project.

An investigative journalist wants to know how the world works—or fails to work—and takes the time to study it closely. But persistence and study must always be accompanied by a healthy skepticism, stopping short of cynicism. Investigative reporting must be accompanied by an outrage that expresses itself through the journalists' creed of comforting the afflicted and afflicting the comfortable. The traits of a good investigative reporter—curiosity, persistence, skepticism, a sense of outrage—lead to important exposés not because of luck but because chance favors those who have done the legwork. If a reporter has these traits, the rest can be learned.

About IRE

IRE, a grassroots nonprofit organization dedicated to improving the quality of investigative reporting, was formed in 1975 by leading investigative journalists in the United States. Its goal was to provide a network for those seeking to do investigative reporting and editing, to provide training at seminars and conferences and to provide resources and guidelines for the profession. It was incorporated in Indianapolis by founding reporters Myrta Pulliam and Harley Bierce and attorney Edward O. DeLaney.

The first IRE conference in June 1976 drew more than 300 journalists who shared tips and techniques. But the conference had an additional focus: Just days before, investigative journalist and IRE member Don Bolles was fatally injured by a car bomb while working on a story in Phoenix. In response, IRE formed a team of editors and reporters from around the country, known as the Arizona Project, to go to Phoenix to expand on Bolles' work on government corruption and organized crime and to create an "insurance policy" for investigative journalists. IRE wanted to show that no one could kill a story by killing a reporter because dozens of others would appear to continue the work.

The Arizona Project resulted in a 23-part series that was published nationwide. Although the series was criticized by some mainstream press leaders as presumptuous "gang-bang" journalism and IRE was unsuccessfully sued by some subjects of the investigation, the Arizona Project received a major national award and raised the profile of IRE as an organization that is crucial to the future of watchdog journalism.

Despite the cost of fighting the lawsuits, IRE survived and established its headquarters at the University of Missouri School of Journalism in 1978. The first full-time executive director was John Ullmann, who was a co-author of the first and second editions of this book. Those editions were published by St. Martin's Press, now Bedford/St. Martin's, in the 1980s. The third edition was written by Steve Weinberg for IRE, who followed Ullmann as executive director. The fourth edition was written for IRE by Brant Houston (then executive director of IRE), Len Bruzzese (then IRE deputy director) and Weinberg, who had continued as faculty member at Missouri School of Journalism.

About This Book

Since 1983, IRE has produced "The Reporter's Handbook," now "The Investigative Reporter's Handbook," to provide both students and professionals with a comprehensive guide to investigative journalism. In each edition, it has updated the story examples, delved into new hot topics such as transportation funding and health insurance and discussed new investigative techniques and resources. With this text, users can plan and carry out investigations on beats and topics of their choosing while building on the knowledge and stories of other reporters.

"The Investigative Reporter's Handbook" not only guides journalists to thousands of documents and databases, it also helps them find and cultivate human sources. It is both a primer of investigative techniques and a reference for investigations into particular topics; it is designed to be both a textbook and a practical guide for working journalists. In this edition, the text begins with an overview of the skills and knowledge needed for any investigative story. Then it focuses on particular topics and beats, covering government in Part Two, business in Part Three and specific issues in Part Four.

Although you can use the index or table of contents to find specific information, we suggest that you concentrate on the chapters that are most relevant to the story you are working on.

About the Fifth Edition

The topics and examples covered in this edition reflect both the suggestions of our reviewers and readers and the popular subjects commonly investigated today. We have expanded the coverage of religious organizations, testing in K-12 education, environmental issues, lobbyists and campaign finance reform and health care.

One of the major changes to this new edition is the addition of suggested exercises at the end of each chapter. This feature, called "Check It Out," will help you practice what you have learned in the chapter. The exercises are broad enough to be done in any U.S. community, allow a choice in focus and will help you delve into specific documents and sources from which dozens of story ideas might evolve.

This edition continues to emphasize the use of electronic information, whether it is Web sites, e-mail, social and professional groups on the Web, downloadable databases or electronic text reports.

Wherever appropriate, this new edition refers to the latest techniques and resources needed for superior investigative reporting. Like the previous edition, this book lists suggested resources and helpful Web sites at the end of each chapter; these lists will be updated periodically at the IRE Web site.

To keep this book affordable, we had to limit the number of pages, and that means that some topics—such as the military—did not receive as much attention as we might have wished. We made the choices based on what most journalists cover, combined with the areas that we think most need investigating. Second, many case studies are told in short form; for readers who want to know more, fuller accounts are available from the IRE Resource Center, commercial databases, the Web, public and newspaper libraries, bookstores, periodicals or the journalists themselves. Third, many resources are discussed only briefly, so we have included references to other texts and to the Web so readers can dig deeper if they want.

Contact Us

IRE's Web site is www.ire.org. Web site addresses in this book will be kept up-to-date at IRE's Resource Center, www.ire.org/resourcecenter. We would appreciate hearing about outdated or otherwise inaccurate information, as well as gaps in coverage. IRE can be reached at info@ire.org. The telephone number is (573) 882-2042, and the fax number is (573) 882-5431. The mailing address is 138 Neff Annex, Missouri School of Journalism, Columbia, MO 65211.

Acknowledgments

This book owes a large debt to the four previous editions. John Ullmann, then executive director of IRE, conceived the first edition. He served as primary editor with help from Steve Honeyman, then a graduate student at the University of Missouri School of Journalism. By the time of the second edition, Ullmann had left IRE but served as co-editor. Jan Colbert, an IRE staff member as well as a journalism professor at the University of Missouri, was the other co-editor.

For the third edition, Steve Weinberg changed the approach of the handbook, instilling more narrative into it. For the fourth edition, Brant Houston led the writing with much help from Steve Weinberg and Len Bruzzese. For this edition, we have relied extensively on the knowledge accumulated in the third and fourth editions and want to especially acknowledge the significant contributions by Steve Weinberg that remain in the fifth edition.

We would like to thank the fourteen journalism professors who teach and practice investigative reporting and whose reviews and comments helped shape this edition of "The Investigative Reporter's Handbook." They are Margaret E. Altizer, Suffolk Community College; Mary Beth Callie, Regis University; Matthew Cecil, University of Oklahoma; Ira H. Chinoy, University of Maryland; Richard Craig, San Jose State University; Holly Edgell, Florida A&M University; Bob M. Gassaway, University of New Mexico; Christopher Harper, Ithaca College; Deborah Huff, Liberty University; Christopher D. Karadjov, State University of New York at Oswego; James C. Landers, Colorado State University; Mead Loop, Ithaca College; Leonard Strazewski, Columbia College Chicago; and Sharon Crook West, Ohio State University.

Throughout the many revisions of this book, subject matter experts from government agencies, universities, trade associations and private-sector businesses agreed to read sections of the manuscript for errors of commission and omission.

Those responsible for bringing the fifth edition to fruition include Bedford/ St. Martin's president Joan Feinberg, editorial director Denise Wydra, executive editor Erika Gutierrez, director of development Erica Appel, editorial assistant Mae Klinger, and for earlier stages of the project, Vikram Mukijha and Michaela Garibaldi. For their excellence in production, design and manufacturing, we thank Emily Berleth and Sarah Ulicny at Bedford/St. Martin's and Nancy Benjamin and Janis Owens at Books By Design, Inc. Lastly, we especially want to thank Joanna Imm for her excellent editing during the long and winding journey to bring this edition to completion.

We also relied on the work done by journalists, particularly IRE members, in the past few years. Their stories, detailed comments about their work and tip sheets can be found at the IRE Resource Center (www.ire.org/resourcecenter), in The IRE Journal, in IRE contest entries, in IRE's Beat Book series and on audio recordings of speakers at IRE conferences.

About the Authors

Brant Houston is the Knight Chair in Investigative and Enterprise Reporting at the College of Media at the University of Illinois. He was the executive director of Investigative Reporters and Editors (IRE) and a professor at the University of Missouri School of Journalism for 10 years. The author of three editions of "Computer-Assisted Reporting: A Practical Guide," Houston served as managing director of the National Institute for Computer-Assisted Reporting for three years after working in daily journalism for 17 years. He was an award-winning investigative reporter at the Hartford Courant, The Kansas City Star and several news organizations in the Boston area.

Investigative Reporters and Editors, Inc. is a grassroots nonprofit organization dedicated to improving the quality of investigative reporting. IRE was formed in 1975 to create a forum in which journalists throughout the world could help each other by sharing story ideas, news-gathering techniques and news sources.

Contents

Preface   v

About the Authors   xi

PART I   Investigative Reporting Skills   1

1 The Investigative Process   3

The Investigative Process   4
Choosing an Investigation   *4*   ■   The Research Hypothesis   *4*   ■
Secondary Sources   *5*   ■   Having a "Documents State of Mind"   *5*   ■
Human Sources   *6*   ■   Research Techniques   *7*   ■   Organizing
the Information   *8*   ■   Questioning Conventional Wisdom   *8*

The Paul Williams Way   9
Step 1: Conception   *10*   ■   Step 2: Feasibility Study   *11*   ■
Step 3: Go/No-Go Decision   *12*   ■   Step 4: Base Building   *12*   ■
Step 5: Planning   *12*   ■   Step 6: Original Research   *13*   ■
Step 7: Re-Evaluation   *13*   ■   Step 8: Filling the Gaps   *13*   ■
Step 9: Final Evaluation   *13*   ■   Step 10: Writing and Rewriting   *13*   ■
Step 11: Publication or Airing of the Story and Follow-up Stories   *13*   ■
Examples of the Paul Williams Way   *14*

Check It Out   15
Resources for Reporting   16

2 Secondary Sources   19

Newspapers   20
Finding the Right Newspapers   *20*   ■   Stories and
Announcements   *21*   ■   Legal Notices, Police Reports and
Classified Ads   *23*

Non-Newspaper Secondary Sources   23
Broadcast and Cable Sources   *23*   ■   Magazines and
Newsletters   *23*   ■   Reference Books   *25*   ■   Dissertations
and Theses   *26*   ■   Books   *26*   ■   Libraries   *28*

Search Techniques   29
Key Word and Citation Searches   *29*   ■   Bibliographies   *30*   ■
Secondary Source Databases   *31*

Check It Out   32
Resources for Reporting   33

3 Primary Documents   34

Specific Primary Documents   35
Using Social Security Numbers   *35*   ■   Public Records   *36*   ■
Vital Records   *37*   ■   The Uniform Commercial Code   *38*   ■
Liens and Tax Documents   *39*

Primary Documents Databases   39
Commercial Databases   *39*   ■   Government Agency Records   *41*   ■
Government Databases   *42*   ■   Depository Libraries   *43*   ■
Technical and Scientific Sources   *43*   ■   The National Archives
System   *44*

Putting It All Together   45
Using Primary Documents: A Real-Life Example   *45*   ■   Using Primary
Documents: A Sample Investigation   *48*

Check It Out   51
Resources for Reporting   52

4 Computer-Assisted Reporting   53

Finding, Accessing and Using Computer Databases   54
The Tools of Computer-Assisted Reporting   *54*   ■   Finding Databases
and Deciding Which to Use   *55*   ■   Keeping Databases
on Hand   *56*   ■   Gaining Access   *57*

Local Data Sources   58
Politics   *59*   ■   Business and Economy   *59*   ■   Property and Tax
Records   *59*   ■   Crime and Guns   *60*   ■   Education   *60*   ■
Courts and Jails   *60*   ■   City and County Government   *60*   ■
Infrastructure   *61*   ■   Accidents   *61*   ■   The Environment   *61*

State Data Sources   62

Federal Data Sources   62
Demographic Data   *62*   ■   Other Federal Data Sources   *63*

Check It Out   63
Resources for Reporting   65

5 People Trails   67

Identifying and Evaluating Sources   68
"Currents" and "Formers"   *68*   ■   Whistleblowers   *69*   ■
Outside Experts   *70*

Locating Sources   71
Online Tools   *71*   ■   Telephone Directories   *72*   ■   City
Directories   *72*   ■   Workplace Directories   *72*   ■   Personal
Habits   *73*   ■   Useful Documents and Records   *73*   ■   Mapping
Power Structures   *74*

Interviewing Sources   76
Researching the Source   *77*   ▪   Looking for Credentials Fraud in
Résumés   *78*   ▪   Getting in the Door   *79*   ▪   Understanding
the Source's Motivations   *81*   ▪   Preparing Questions   *82*   ▪
Structuring the Interview   *83*   ▪   Taking Notes and Following Up   *85*

Check It Out   86
Resources for Reporting   87

6 Writing the Compelling Investigation   89

The Fundamentals   89
Writing an Effective Story   *90*   ▪   Getting the Details   *94*   ▪
Avoiding Clichés and Stereotypes   *95*   ▪   Writing From Chronologies
and Outlines   *95*

Story Structures   96
Focus and Resolution   *98*   ▪   Leads: The Opening Sentences   *99*   ▪
Middles: Flow and Momentum   *101*   ▪   Point of View and Tone   *103*   ▪
Endings   *104*

Check It Out   105
Resources for Reporting   106

7 Ethics of Investigative Reporting   108

Ethics and Accuracy   109
Fairness and the Law   *109*   ▪   The Golden Rule   *110*

Dilemmas in Reporting   110
Obtaining Information Covertly   *110*   ▪   Conducting Ambush
Interviews   *112*   ▪   Exposing Private Behaviors of Public
Figures   *113*   ▪   Using Unidentified and Paid Sources   *114*

Writing Ethical, Accurate Stories   115
Line-by-Line Accuracy Check   *115*   ▪   Prepublication Review   *116*

Check It Out   118
Resources for Reporting   119

PART II   Investigating the Government   121

8 Investigating the Executive Branch   123

The Players and Processes   124
Understanding Government Agencies   *124*   ▪   Using the Federal
Register   *125*   ▪   Making Sense of Agency Budgets   *126*   ▪
Consultants and Contractors   *128*   ▪   The Contracting Process   *130*   ▪
Budget and Management Watchdogs   *133*

Investigating Federal Affairs 134
The Top Executive *135* ▪ Cabinet Appointees *135* ▪ Conflicts of Interest *136* ▪ Inspectors General *138* ▪ The Permanent Bureaucracy *140* ▪ Civil Service *140* ▪ Public Affairs Personnel *141* ▪ Public Authorities and Self-Regulatory Organizations *143*

Investigating State and Local Affairs 144
The Governor *144* ▪ State and Local Employees *145* ▪ Campaign Finance Corruption *146* ▪ Using the State Register *147*

Check It Out 147
Resources for Reporting 148

9 Investigating the Legislative Branch   152

Investigating Legislators 153
Following the Money *153* ▪ Campaign Finance *155* ▪ Lobbyists *157* ▪ Financial Disclosure of Legislators *159* ▪ Resources and Perquisites in Office *161* ▪ Personal Character *163* ▪ Making Legislation *163* ▪ Authorizations and Appropriations *164* ▪ Committees and Oversight *166* ▪ The Government Accountability Office: The Research and Investigative Arm of Congress *167*

Investigating Local Legislatures 169
Following the Money *169* ▪ Lobbyists *170* ▪ Other Paper and People Sources *171*

Check It Out 172
Resources for Reporting 173

10 Investigating the Judicial System   179

Approaches to Investigating the Judicial System 180
The Judicial System as a Political System *180* ▪ Two Tracks: Civil Cases and Criminal Cases *182*

Tracking the Civil Case 183

Tracking the Criminal Case: From Arrest to Sentencing 184
Between Arrest and First Court Appearance *184* ▪ From Jail to Courthouse *185* ▪ Initial Appearance in Court *186* ▪ Pretrial Hearings *187* ▪ The Assignment of Judges *188* ▪ The Jury *188* ▪ Case Backlogs *189* ▪ Victims of Crime *190* ▪ Sentencing *191* ▪ Appeals *192*

Investigating Punishment: Prison, Probation, Parole, Commutations and Pardons 193
Gaining Access to Prisons *193* ▪ Prison Conditions *194* ▪ Probation *196* ▪ Parole *197* ▪ Commutations and Pardons *198*

Investigating Juvenile Cases and Family Court   198
Juvenile Cases   *198*   ▪   Family Court   *199*

Investigating Judicial Operations and Personnel   200
Court Budgets and Court Operations   *200*   ▪   Personnel   *201*   ▪
Wrongful Convictions   *204*

Investigating Specialized Courts   205
Traffic Court   *205*   ▪   Municipal Court   *205*   ▪   Divorce
Court   *206*   ▪   Probate Court   *206*   ▪   Small Claims Court   *207*   ▪
U.S. Tax Court   *208*   ▪   U.S. Bankruptcy Court   *208*   ▪   U.S. Court
of Appeals for the Federal Circuit   *210*   ▪   U.S. Military Courts   *210*

Check It Out   211
Resources for Reporting   213

11   Investigating Law Enforcement   218

Investigating Local Police   219
Monitoring Individual Law Enforcement Officers   *220*   ▪
Recruitment   *221*   ▪   Training   *221*   ▪   Raises, Promotions and
Pensions   *223*   ▪   The Top Command   *224*   ▪   Discipline of
Wayward Officers   *224*   ▪   Moonlighting   *227*   ▪   Police Reporter
Edna Buchanan's Tips   *227*

Delving Into Different Crimes   228
Murder   *228*   ▪   Rape   *231*   ▪   Domestic Violence   *232*   ▪
Narcotics   *233*   ▪   Vice   *236*   ▪   Missing Persons   *237*   ▪
Stolen Property   *238*   ▪   Arson   *239*   ▪   Bombings   *241*   ▪
Traffic Violations   *241*   ▪   Organized Crime and White-Collar
Crime   *242*   ▪   Juvenile Crime   *243*

Investigating Other Aspects of Law Enforcement   244
Patrol Officers, Dispatchers and 911 Operators   *244*   ▪   Crime Scene
Technicians and Crime Laboratories   *245*   ▪   Evidence Rooms   *246*   ▪
Coroners and Medical Examiners   *247*   ▪   Canine (K9) Corps   *247*   ▪
Civil Rights and Community Relations   *248*

Resources for Investigating Law Enforcement   249
Crime Statistics   *249*   ▪   Budgets and Contracts   *250*   ▪   Records
Divisions and Public Information Officers   *251*   ▪   People Trails   *252*   ▪
Paper Trails   *253*

Check It Out   254
Resources for Reporting   255

12   Investigating Education   261

Issues in K-12 Education   261
Student Test Scores   *262*   ▪   School Violence and Discipline   *264*   ▪
Student Retention   *266*   ▪   Curriculum   *267*   ▪   Class Size   *267*   ▪
Technology and Corporate Sponsorship   *268*   ▪   Special-Needs

Students *268* ▪ Race, Class and Gender Equity *269* ▪
School Choice *269*

Investigating School Personnel and Facilities   271
Teachers *271* ▪ Administrators *273* ▪ School Staff *273* ▪
School Buildings *274*

Approaches to Investigating the Schools   275
Following the Money *276* ▪ Private Schools *278* ▪
Homeschooling *279* ▪ Vocational and Trade Schools *279*

Issues in Higher Education   280
Document Trails *281* ▪ Public University Revenues and
Expenditures *281* ▪ Accreditation Documents *282* ▪
The Scorecard *283* ▪ University Catalogs *284* ▪ Enrollment
and Retention *284* ▪ Diversity, Disabilities and Affirmative
Action *284* ▪ In the Classroom *285* ▪ Outside the
Classroom *286* ▪ Athletics *287* ▪ Campus Safety *288* ▪
Faculty *288* ▪ Administrators *290* ▪ Support Staff *290* ▪
Governing Boards *291*

Check It Out   291
Resources for Reporting   293

PART III   Investigating Business   299

13   Investigating For-Profit Businesses   301

Investigating Companies   302
The U.S. Securities and Exchange Commission *302* ▪ Annual
Reports *302* ▪ Federal Regulatory Agencies *305* ▪ State
and Local Business Agencies *306* ▪ The Paper Trail: Public
Documents *308* ▪ The Paper Trail: Other Document Sources *309* ▪
Human Sources *311* ▪ The Overlooked Resource: Labor *312* ▪
Labor Lawyers and the Courts *312*

Investigating the Workplace   313
Labor Unions *313* ▪ Labor Relations Boards *315* ▪ Mediation,
Conciliation and Arbitration *316* ▪ Safety and Health *317* ▪
Wage Enforcement *318* ▪ Pensions *320* ▪ State Employment
Security Divisions *321*

Investigating Licensed Professionals   322
Finding Licensing Documents *324* ▪ The Licensing Process *325* ▪
Professional Associations as Sources *327* ▪ Investigating the
Protectors *328*

Check It Out   330
Resources for Reporting   331

14 Investigating Nonprofit and Religious Organizations   337

Investigating Charities and Foundations   338
Where to Begin: Questions and Documents   *339*   ▪   The Gaul and
Borowski Model   *340*   ▪   Form 990: The Annual Informational Tax
Return   *342*   ▪   Fund-Raising Techniques and Conundrums   *344*   ▪
Foundations   *345*   ▪   Federal, State and Local Government
Regulation   *347*

Investigating Religious Organizations   348

Check It Out   350
Resources for Reporting   351

15 Investigating Financial Institutions and Insurance   353

Investigating Financial Institutions   353
Government Regulators   *355*   ▪   Banks   *355*   ▪   Savings and
Loans   *358*   ▪   Credit Unions   *359*   ▪   Credit Card
Companies   *360*   ▪   Investment Companies and Mutual Funds   *361*

Investigating the Issues   362
Redlining and Community Reinvestment   *363*   ▪   Insider
Transactions   *365*   ▪   High-Risk Transactions   *365*   ▪   Money
Laundering   *366*

Investigating Insurance   367
Health and Disability Insurance   *369*   ▪   Life Insurance   *370*   ▪
Automobile Insurance   *371*   ▪   Homeowners' and Other Property
Insurance   *372*   ▪   Commercial and Professional Insurance   *373*

Investigating the Players   374
Companies and Their Finances   *374*   ▪   Agents   *376*   ▪
State Regulators   *377*   ▪   The Government as Insurer   *379*   ▪
Workers' Compensation   *381*

Check It Out   383
Resources for Reporting   384

16 Investigating Health Care   388

Investigating Hospitals   389
Accreditation and Regulation   *389*   ▪   Costs and Billing   *391*   ▪
Hospital Errors   *392*   ▪   Indigent Care   *394*   ▪   Ambulances
and Other Emergency Medical Services   *396*

Investigating Other Care Providers   397
Veterans Administration Hospitals   *397*   ▪   Nursing Homes   *398*   ▪
Mental Health Institutions   *400*   ▪   Home Health Care
Companies   *402*   ▪   Physicians, Nurses and Other Health Care
Workers   *403*

Investigating Suppliers and Services   404
Health Maintenance Organizations   *404*   ▪   Medical Research
and Journals   *405*   ▪   Pharmaceutical Companies   *406*   ▪
Pharmacies   *407*   ▪   Medical Device Companies   *407*   ▪
Medical Laboratories   *408*   ▪   Blood Banks   *408*

Check It Out   409
Resources for Reporting   410

PART IV   Investigative Issues   415

17   Investigating Energy and Utilities   417
Investigating Utilities   417
State Regulation   *418*   ▪   Federal Regulation   *419*   ▪   Gas and
Electricity   *422*   ▪   Nuclear Power   *423*   ▪   Water   *425*   ▪
Communications   *426*   ▪   Cable   *428*

Check It Out   430
Resources for Reporting   431

18   Investigating the Environment   434
Regulation: The Environmental Protection Agency   435

Other Federal Agencies   436

Using the Toxics Release Inventory   437

Investigating Air Pollution   439

Investigating Water Pollution   439

Investigating Soil Pollution and Hazardous Waste   442

Check It Out   444
Resources for Reporting   445

19   Investigating Transportation   449
Investigating Land Transportation   450
Cars   *450*   ▪   Motorcycles and All-Terrain Vehicles   *453*   ▪
Trucks   *453*   ▪   Buses   *455*   ▪   Taxis and Limousine Services   *457*   ▪
Roads   *457*   ▪   Railroads   *459*   ▪   Hazardous Waste   *460*   ▪
Mass Transit   *461*

Investigating Aviation   461
Pilots and Flight Crews   *463*   ▪   Air Controllers and Ground
Crews   *463*   ▪   Airlines   *464*   ▪   Security   *464*   ▪   Commuter
Planes, Cargo Planes and Government Flights   *465*   ▪   Airports   *466*   ▪
Using Air Databases   *467*

Investigating Water Transportation   467
Commercial Shipping   *467*   ■   The U.S. Coast Guard   *468*

Regulatory Agencies   469

Check It Out   470
Resources for Reporting   471

20 Investigating Real Estate   476

The Document Trail: Finding Real Estate Records   477
Ownership Records   *477*   ■   Government Documents   *478*   ■
Liens   *479*   ■   Mortgage Documents   *480*

Issues in Real Estate Investigations   482
Property Value and Tax Assessment   *482*   ■   Landlords and
Tenants   *483*   ■   Development, Zoning and Rezoning   *485*   ■
New Developments   *487*   ■   Low-Income Housing   *488*

Check It Out   490
Resources for Reporting   491

21 Investigating the World of the Disadvantaged   495

Investigating the Issues   495
Special Challenges for Reporters   *496*   ■   Financial
Exploitation   *498*   ■   Employment   *501*   ■   Children and
Families   *502*   ■   Homelessness   *503*   ■   Health Care   *503*

Investigating the Programs   504
Temporary Assistance for Needy Families   *505*   ■   Child-Support
Enforcement   *506*   ■   Food Stamps   *506*   ■   Other Child and Family
Nutrition Programs   *507*   ■   Other Assistance Programs   *508*   ■
Welfare Reform   *509*

Check It Out   510
Resources for Reporting   511

Index   515

PART
I

Investigative Reporting Skills

The Investigative Process

This chapter is about how investigative journalists think and the methodologies they have developed over recent decades. The chapter discusses how documents and interviews build on each other during the investigative process to deliver a more complete story. It also gives brief examples of classic approaches to conceiving of and carrying out investigative stories.

Investigative journalism is a critical part of creating an informed and democratic society. In addition to helping citizens make knowledgeable decisions, investigative journalism also reins in the excesses of the powerful and holds government and business organizations accountable for their actions. But to perform that service, investigative journalists must produce credible, original and illuminating stories that are thoroughly researched through documents — both paper and electronic — and interviews, often with the powerless members of society who are overlooked by daily journalists.

Most journalists feel comfortable doing interviews, but many feel lost when it comes to delving into documents or databases. But James Steele and Donald Barlett, a longtime investigative duo, emphasize that investigative journalists should have a "documents state of mind" if they want to produce compelling projects. Steele and Barlett define a "documents state of mind" as knowing that a document exists somewhere to explore, contradict or confirm each point of an investigation.

In addition, the best investigative journalists generally share a technique that can be best described as "working from the outside in." Rendered graphically, the approach would resemble concentric circles, with the outermost circle labeled "secondary sources," the middle circle called "primary documents," and the inner circle, "human sources." The main subject of the investigation is at the center.

Investigative stories can be daunting to the inexperienced journalist because of the amount of research and interviews, not to mention persistence and patience, required for an investigation. But the only way for journalists to discover whether they have the temperament and talent for investigations is to try one.

The Investigative Process

Choosing an Investigation

Before tackling an investigation, a journalist must choose an appropriate subject, although often it can seem the subject has chosen the journalist. That is, a major news event, a series of complaints or tips, or a natural follow-up to a daily story may steer the journalist into an investigation.

But if a journalist has the ability to think about what he or she might investigate, there are a number of topics that always present themselves: government corruption, unsafe workplaces, shoddy construction, medical malpractice, environmental hazards and abuse of children or the elderly.

An investigative journalist might begin a story with a tip from a longtime source or from a stranger. A news story done on general assignment or a regular beat might call for investigation to determine why a program isn't working. Sorting or grouping of information in a database might reveal a trend, reveal an unusual case or provide new context for an old problem. Sometimes curiosity about why something is the way it is spurs a reporter to dig deeper or sometimes just plain daily observation can lead to a story.

Daily reporting provides many investigative ideas. For example, the famous investigative reporter Bob Woodward started his career at a weekly newspaper in the Maryland suburbs of Washington, D.C. By using routine assignments to start building investigative projects, he worked his way to The Washington Post. There he combined ideas from his beat with his penchant for digging. Leonard Downie Jr., in his book "The New Muckrakers," describes how Woodward "assigned himself" to uncover "small-to-middling scandals," such as supermarkets selling fatty meat and pharmacies dispensing outdated drugs and mislabeled prescriptions. Those stories prepared Woodward for the Watergate exposé, which appeared to be no more than a minor burglary at first.

The Research Hypothesis

Beginning with a hypothesis is not the same as starting with a closed mind. The best investigative journalists collect both supporting and contradictory evidence for a story. They then weigh carefully what the evidence shows. For example, because of several tips a journalist might hypothesize that the elderly in a chain of nursing homes are being neglected and abused. But if inspection reports and interviews with relatives of the elderly demonstrate otherwise, then the journalist would reconsider the story.

Newspaper editor Tom Honig wrote in The IRE Journal that "most good investigations come down to one of two things—either a process did not work or people did not follow the guidelines. . . . If a baby dies, was it one Child Protective Service worker who screwed up, or is the whole system failing?"

Here are questions to ask on the way to launching a project:

- How is the system supposed to work?
- How well is the system working?
- Who is benefiting and who is suffering because of the way the system works?

Secondary Sources

When a journalist is working from the outside in, information already published or broadcast can serve as a starting point for answering basic questions. Such information is secondary source material. If independently verified, it can be a road map or a tip. For example, a newspaper article written six years ago on the passage of state legislation on prison reform mentions those who pushed for its passage and who testified in its favor. That article might lead a journalist who is today investigating the state of prison reform to seek a hearing transcript and to interview those who testified.

News organizations provide indexes and online versions of their stories from the past few years. They also provide an indexed clipping library going back many years or enter published stories into a database. If the news organization does not have online copies, the stories might be accessible for a fee on third-party databases. Secondary source materials from television and radio are increasingly available. (Chapter 2 provides details about secondary sources.)

Having a "Documents State of Mind"

Secondary sources are most useful when they lead to primary documents or databases. A legislative hearing transcript is a primary document, as are a real estate deed, a political candidate's electronic campaign finance report, a lawsuit filing, an insurance policy and a discharge certificate from the military. Documents and databases can lie just like human sources can lie, because, after all, documents and databases are prepared by humans. However, unlike humans, documents do not claim to have been misquoted.

The best journalists possess the "documents state of mind" articulated by Steele and Barlett: They assume that somewhere a document or documents exist on any topic. Primary documents are more readily available than many journalists realize. With the expansion and prevalence of the Internet, the possibilities of documents and databases on anything have become much more apparent and have presented investigative journalists the challenge of having an overwhelming amount of information.

If the "documents state of mind" is difficult to imagine, a journalist need only consider his or her own life. From birth, the journalist is followed by a document trail, including a birth certificate and hospital admission and discharge records. School records, from report cards to yearbook entries, are next in the trail. Then a driver's license and most likely the title and registration for a car in the journalist's name. The journalist goes to college and receives student loans and college scholarships. Many college students work part-time jobs and may get a food-server license. After graduation, there is a résumé and completed job applications.

The credit card charges begun in college continue. Hobbies like fishing or hunting require licenses. A journalist has a pet and the pet has a license with information about its owner. The journalist pays personal property taxes on a car and eventually may be able to afford a house and then pay real estate taxes. The journalist registers to vote and may marry, have a child and divorce. Every one of these stages results in a record.

Institutions—whether government agencies, private corporations, nonprofit charities or some hybrid—leave document trails much as individuals do. For example, the articles of incorporation for a business can be likened to an individual's birth certificate, its annual reports to records of daily life, and its dissolution to a death certificate. (Chapter 3 contains a fuller discussion of primary documents and databases.)

Human Sources

Documents and databases serve many purposes, one of which is helping locate human sources. Too many investigators contact only the obvious sources—those in current positions (such as current spouse and current neighbors)—while ignoring "formers" (the former spouse, former professional colleague, former accountant, former neighbor, former minister and so on). The "formers" often have scores to settle or outdated knowledge, but they can be candid, have had time to reflect and may have kept relevant documents.

Human sources are crucial because documents take on new meaning when explained or discussed by insiders or experts. This is one reason to refrain from key interviews until the document trail is nearly complete. Information in documents often serves as the basis for questions during the interview; because a journalist might get only one interview with a source, it is best to wait until most documents are in hand. When it comes to interviewing the main subject of the investigation, documents serve as a reality check, helping to determine if the subject is lying or is ignorant about certain matters.

At the same time, it can help to show documents to nonadversarial sources because those human sources can correct errors in the documents or can identify other documents to gather. (Chapter 5 contains more information about people trails.)

Research Techniques

During the information-gathering stage, longtime journalist Dennis King merged paper and people trails through what he called parallel backgrounding and indirect backgrounding. Other top investigative journalists work the same way, but few have explained it as well as King in his book "Get the Facts on Anyone."

About parallel backgrounding, King says that when the subject is connected to an institution, the organization will leave its own trails. By following those trails, investigators might locate new information about the subject. For example, personal documents about Mr. Smith may contain no negative information, but city public works files on his contracting firm might include information suggesting bid rigging.

"The same principle also works in reverse," King says. "If your main target is a business enterprise or nonprofit organization, you may gain startling insights by examining the personal backgrounds of its principals or officers. That seemingly innocuous annual report of your local community development corporation may appear in a different light once you learn that the city has padlocked two buildings owned by the executive director because of illegal gambling on the premises."

King defines indirect backgrounding as "parallel backgrounding on a grand scale." An investigative journalist might find that the subject is tied to economic or political interests. The way to understand the relationships is to analyze the larger environment. King's research on a West African nation visited often by a New York businessman helped identify the man's possible Libyan connections. In another case, King's journey into the history of the Teamsters Union and organized-crime families led to a better understanding of politician Lyndon LaRouche, the subject of a biography by King.

Organizing the Information

As a journalist collects primary documents and human sources, the information gathered can become overwhelming if it is left to stack up on a desk. It's best to prepare files and folders to catch the information as it comes in and then to evaluate the information often (perhaps weekly) and make preliminary decisions about what is valuable.

The potentially valuable material should be entered into a chronology, whether of a person's life, an institution's history or an issue's progression. Creating a chronology does not mean writing the story chronologically. Rather, the chronology is meant to organize large amounts of information in a linear way to help illuminate links among factors that might otherwise seem unrelated. It also helps you to step back and see the bigger view when you feel you are getting lost in the details.

For example, suppose a city council member tells you that he never participated in a closed-door session 18 months earlier about rezoning land owned by a partnership involving his wife. The council member tells you he was out of town at the time. You enter that detail in the chronology as a matter of good record keeping. Then, three months later, you read minutes of a long-past meeting held by a neighborhood association concerned about the rezoning. As you enter details from those minutes into the chronology, you read that the city council member spoke at the meeting—during the period he claimed to be out of town. You investigate further, discover that the council member lied and write that the council member did participate in the rezoning meeting. Without the chronology, you might never have discovered the lie. A chronology is best done in a spreadsheet or database. Private investigators have been using such software tools for years, and recently some journalists have picked up the practice. Doing a chronology this way allows quick identification of trends and relationships.

One caveat about chronologies: Information excluded from the chronology early in an investigation become relevant later. As a result, all information collected must be re-evaluated from time to time during the reporting stage. For example, long-time investigative journalist Mike McGraw of The Kansas City Star says he sets aside time to review all his files periodically while working on a story because recent interviews or documents can throw new light on what he has already collected.

Questioning Conventional Wisdom

Sound information-gathering, organizing and writing techniques mean little if the underlying logic of the investigation is faulty. Investigative journalists should always question the conventional wisdom about an individual, institution or issue.

Journalists should look for answers about how and why things are as they are. Mary Kay Blakely, while writing for the Los Angeles Times Magazine, practiced that kind of thinking as she considered the problem of homelessness in an affluent society. The homeless "were not dropped on our streets by a deus ex machina," she wrote. "They arrived through human actions and social choices," which included government urban renewal that destroyed low-income housing but failed to replace it with something desirable and affordable; elimination of unskilled jobs that supported families; and deinstitutionalization of the mentally ill along with the simultaneous reduction in funding for community-based mental health programs.

When the Star Tribune of Minneapolis decided to investigate whether rapists are punished effectively, the reporters and editors studied past research projects. The team determined that many of the previous projects had been flawed. John Ullmann, in his book "Investigative Reporting: Advanced Methods and Techniques," explained why:

> Short follow-up periods. Many studies followed sex criminals for only a year or two after their release, not enough time to draw meaningful conclusions. Faulty study groups. Much of the research has focused on only a handful of sex criminals — too few to draw conclusions. Others have lumped all types of sex criminals together — rapists with incest offenders, for example — even though their patterns are as different as apples and oranges. Poor counting techniques. Many studies noted only subsequent convictions or returns to prison, failing to count such reliable indicators as arrests. Erroneous time calculations. Many studies were sloppy in calculating the time frames in which sex criminals committed later offenses; for example, many didn't deduct the time a rapist was in prison and therefore unable to commit another rape.

The Star Tribune team grounded its investigation in accepted principles of sound social science research, such as studying a sample of adequate size.

Journalists must confront what they think and become aware of certain assumptions they have brought to their subject. During an investigation, everything should be questioned.

The Paul Williams Way

Paul N. Williams, an investigative journalist from Omaha and a theorist of the craft at Ohio State University until his death in 1976, set forth a landmark idealized description of investigative reporting.

Williams recognized that theorizing would be anathema to journalists:

> The fundamentally intellectual nature of the discipline eludes many would-be Bernsteins, Steffenses, Hershes and Tarbells. Because some reporters have a tip, can surround it with circumstantial evidence and can dash off a sensational story, they think they will blow the lid off the town. Instead, they come up with a one-day, one-source story that falls flat. They then complain about public apathy because nobody reacts. They have failed the test of finding everything their readers need to know. They have failed to pull everything together.

To pull everything together, Williams said, investigative journalists ought to follow a procedure of 11 major steps (and numerous substeps). Because Williams' posthumous book, "Investigative Reporting and Editing," is out of print, his thinking is summarized here.

Step 1: Conception

The search for investigative ideas is "unending," Williams said in his book. Ideas can come "from anywhere—legal advertisements, estate sales, bankruptcy notices, transfers of business executives, company and professional newsletters. The bulletin of the local dental society, for example, once provided one of my reporters . . . with a story. He read a one-paragraph item about disciplinary action being proposed against two dentists. Why? He asked questions, found some public records, and established that the two had been milking Medicaid with false billing, and that the local prosecutors were waffling about whether to file charges."

"Sit and stare at the wall and ask what things happen in this town that affect a lot of people but are never written about," Williams advised. "What institution—public, educational, nonprofit, corporate—manages to stay out of the news?" Banks, savings and loans, credit unions, insurance companies, law firms, accounting firms, hospitals and labor unions are usually among the institutions escaping scrutiny.

Today, the best journalists read local and national newspapers every day, check Web sites and blogs, watch television news and listen to radio stations that carry news, look at a range of magazines, read books, monitor newsgroups, and place their names on listservs maintained by government agencies, corporations, charities and other organizations.

In fact, a good investigative journalist will accumulate a thick file within a month simply by paying attention to breaking news and then asking why or how something described briefly in a story happened.

Williams said never to discard a tip without screening; it might be the kernel of a story. He looked for proof of facts that gave credence to the tipster's claim.

Often, checking a tip means visiting the courthouse, the library or some other records repository. It might also mean a few calls to reliable sources to determine whether the tip is plausible.

For general assignment and beat journalists, developing regular sources is necessary. Journalists need to leave the office, meet sources face to face, listen to conversations in elevators and hallways and cover government meetings that no other journalists attend. For freelance journalists who move from topic to topic, regular sources are likely to be friends or social acquaintances. Every person a journalist meets knows something the journalist does not and therefore is a potential source.

Williams related an example involving a reporter investigating a political kickback scheme. A source mentioned a young man being intimidated by a probation officer. The reporter made a note and then returned to the tip several months later. It turned out that the intimidator was more than a probation officer. He reported directly to the mayor and to a judge who was the mayor's former law partner. The reporter documented that the subject also drew $1,500 a month as a consultant to the police department and received questionable fees as a security consultant to a municipal agency. The subject was eventually convicted of income tax evasion.

Step 2: Feasibility Study

The first step of a feasibility study is questioning what obstacles might hinder the investigation.

In his book, Williams mentions some obstacles to consider:

- Are records available?
- Will sources talk about the subject?
- Is there time to do the job properly before, say, the next election or the next session of the legislature or the next meeting of the city planning board?
- Do you or your colleagues know how to interpret the technical material related to the story?
- Will the target of the investigative story apply pressure on people not to talk? Will he sue?

Williams also says to ask whether one reporter can do it all. If not, are resources available to assist? Those resources might be other reporters and editors (including one who is expert at computer-assisted reporting), a researcher, a student intern, a librarian who handles database searching or outside experts.

Next, consider whether there is a downside for the news organization. Is it likely there will be a lawsuit, withdrawn advertising, a readers' or viewers' boycott? Disturbing answers should not derail a planned investigation but should be thought through. Editors, and sometimes legal counsel, must be part of this discussion.

And last, Williams asks how feasible it is to keep the investigation quiet. Is there a strong possibility that competing news media might print or broadcast something before the project is ready?

Step 3: Go/No-Go Decision

In the next step, Williams advises journalists to question whether an investigation will yield at least a minimum story. Williams quotes Bob Greene, who was at Newsday at the time, on what it means to consider the minimum and maximum results of an investigation:

> We received information that the Metropolitan Transit Authority had bought an airport here on Long Island, then leased it out to a fixed-base operator at incredibly advantageous terms to the operator. We got a copy of the contract. . . . What had been run as a private business at a $250,000 annual profit . . . was running $600,000 in the red. So we said all right, we have a minimum and a maximum here — the minimum is that we can show there's been a huge waste of taxpayers' dollars . . . and the maximum is that we can show somebody's been paid off.

Step 4: Base Building

How will the investigator go about learning the norms of the individual, institution or issue to gain historical and contemporary perspectives? To understand how something works, it is necessary to learn how it is supposed to work. Williams tells how a reporter started looking at an insurance agency and found it had advanced $163,000 to finance one of its directors as a general agent for the company. "The transaction was listed in a state-required report and meant little . . . until he [the reporter] discussed it with an expert source," Williams comments. The expert said such an advance was unusual. "This discovery of self-dealing became a basic reference point for . . . subsequent stories about an ingenious circular hustle involving the insurance company and a small bank in Washington acquired by California promoters."

Step 5: Planning

A chronology of an individual's career, an institution's existence or an issue's evolution can be a powerful organizational tool. All documents and interview notes should be painstakingly cross-referenced among relevant topic files.

Today these tasks include

- Obtaining documents and databases, through Freedom of Information Act requests if necessary
- Finding and interviewing human sources
- Transcribing interviews
- Filing manually and electronically
- Writing
- Copyediting
- Photography
- Graphics
- Accuracy checking
- Readings for possible libel

Step 6: Original Research

For information on following the paper trail, see Chapters 2, 3 and 4 of this book. For information on following the people trail, see Chapter 5 of this book.

Step 7: Re-evaluation

Should the investigation continue to move ahead? Should it be filed for now? Or should it be dropped permanently?

Step 8: Filling the Gaps

Key interviews and additional document work should be targeted at answering the questions that have not yet been answered.

Step 9: Final Evaluation

See Chapter 7 of this book.

Step 10: Writing and Rewriting

See Chapter 6 of this book.

Step 11: Publication or Airing of the Story and Follow-up Stories

Some of the best stories are done as follow-up stories. When a story is published or aired it is crucial that the reporter or reporters be available to get new tips and comments that may come in at that time. In addition, journalists often have follow-up stories already developing as they finish the first investigation.

Examples of the Paul Williams Way

No single investigative project follows the Paul Williams Way, or any other method, in a perfect progression. That said, some projects come so close as to be timeless models. The one that follows, by Pat Stith of The (Raleigh) News & Observer, relies on thought patterns and research techniques that any investigator reading this far ought to grasp. (At the end of Chapter 3, we will present the conceptual thinking and research techniques undergirding an extremely difficult, inspiring project.)

At the request of the American Society of Newspaper Editors for the magazine The American, Pat Stith discussed his investigations for the News & Observer. In discussing one example, Stith began, "The copy of the thank-you note, from the manager of the North Carolina State Fair to a Florida carnival owner, had been boxed up in a state government warehouse for 20 years. It was exactly what I had hoped to find." Earlier that year, Stith and a colleague had started looking into a $100,000 annual bonus paid by the North Carolina Agriculture Department, which runs the state fair, to the carnival company. Stith already knew that the carnival company had benefited from a lucrative contract for many years, a contract awarded with no competition. Stith also knew that the carnival company had entertained North Carolina agriculture officials at a convention in Las Vegas.

Stith could not help wondering: How far back did this cozy relationship extend? Thanks to a "documents state of mind," Stith assumed that information could be extracted from a document or an interview. Documents first: "State officials save the darndest things, so I went to the records warehouse looking for proof of an old, friendly relationship between agriculture officials and [the company]. The copy of the 20-year-old note I found thanked the carnival owner for his hospitality in Las Vegas—for meeting the North Carolina officials at the airport, for the dinners, the 'free booze' and the chauffeur."

With documents in hand, interviews tend to go better; they complement one another. When Stith and a partner interviewed the chief enforcer of the North Carolina motor vehicle inspection program for another project, they had such a document. Near the beginning of the interview, the enforcer said, "I've never given anybody the direction to go back and give anybody a license without having a hearing. I've never changed one. No." At that juncture, Stith handed the source a letter he had signed returning a license to a safety inspection station in the town of Ellerbe.

Stith contrasts that successful episode with another during the same project. He and his reporting partner interviewed the Division of Motor Vehicles director about a service station that had escaped punishment after being nailed by an undercover agent for fraudulent inspections. Because the service station was in the director's hometown, Stith asked whether the director had ever done business there. No, the director said. Stith asked if the director's car had been inspected at that station. "I can't say whether it was or not," the director replied. Stith thought that answer sounded less than convincing, so he did after the interview what he should have done earlier: He found the inspection record. It said that on May 10 of the previous year, the director had taken his 1981 Mercedes to be inspected at that very service station. Confronted later with the document, the Division of Motor Vehicles director admitted the untruthfulness of his previous statement.

⊃ CHECK IT OUT

✓ Request and review the minutes from three recent local planning and zoning meetings, and come up with three topics for further investigation.

✓ Pick an ongoing controversial local issue, and create a chronology of it from the beginning until the most recent current event.

✓ Pick a local topic worth investigating, and come up with at least three secondary sources that have previously covered the story locally. Find the names of at least three people — either reporters, experts, or other sources — who would be worth contacting if you decide to investigate this issue further.

RESOURCES FOR REPORTING

Tips From the Web

The Resource Center of the Investigative Reporters and Editors Web site
(www.ire.org/resourcecenter) is the place to start for tips on investigations on
any topic.

For more help with investigations on particular beats, go to the Council of
National Journalism Organizations (www.cnjo.org), where you'll find links to
organizations of journalists who pursue particular beats. For example, the council
has links to the Society of Environmental Journalists (www.sej.org) and the Education Writers Association (www.ewa.org).

The Poynter Institute for Media Studies (www.poynter.org) also has information on delving into documents for any beat.

For getting a general "documents state of mind," consider visiting the U.S.
Bureau of Census (www.census.gov), the National Archives (www.archives.gov) or
the National Security Archives (www.gwu.edu/~nsarchiv).

Social Science Techniques

Perhaps the best book by a journalist for journalists on employing social science
techniques is the fourth edition of "Precision Journalism: A Reporter's Introduction to Social Science Methods" by Philip Meyer. Published by Rowman & Little-
field Publishers Inc. in 2002, it is available from the IRE Resource Center, which
also houses numerous tip sheets on the effective use of these techniques. IRE has
published a book on the subject by Sarah Cohen, a Washington Post database editor, called "Numbers in the Newsroom."

The Theory and Practice of Investigative Journalism

The Paul Williams book is an excellent classic, but there are many other books on
investigative journalism. The following list consists of books that convey the theory and practice of investigative journalism. Some are out of print but may be
available through your local library, at a used bookstore, or through the Internet.

- Jack Anderson with Daryl Gibson, "Peace, War and Politics: An Eyewitness
  Account" (Forge, 1999). This is the third memoir from the now deceased muckraking Washington, D.C., columnist. Anderson places himself at the center of
  controversial stories in all three books. In his personal accounts are countless
  lessons about developing sources by listening respectfully to every whistleblower
  and leaker and about trusting young, eager reporters to use their brains and
  untiring energy to track down information that more skilled, older, complacent
  journalists fail to obtain. Dozens of Anderson interns and column associates have
  used their training with him to succeed at newspapers, magazines and broadcast
  stations after leaving his office.

- James L. Aucoin, "The Evolution of American Investigative Journalism" (University of Missouri Press, 2006). This book tracks how investigative reporting
  developed over the past 50 years and how current practices and standards were

formulated. It also highlights the important role IRE played in the transformation of investigative reporting.

- Carl Bernstein and Bob Woodward, "All the President's Men" (Simon and Schuster, 1974). Two Washington Post reporters describe how their initial investigation into the Watergate break-in led to the resignation of President Richard Nixon and the prosecution of some of his aides. The book is filled with discussions of journalists' thought processes and techniques. It is probably the best-known book by investigative reporters about how they did what they did on a particular project, and it deserves to be.

- Leonard Downie Jr., "The New Muckrakers" (New Republic Books, 1976). This is the very best of the worthwhile books profiling reporters and editors to emerge from the mid-1970s' fascination with investigative journalism. It helps that Downie himself was an experienced investigative reporter when he researched and wrote the profiles for this book. He later became the top editor at The Washington Post.

- Seymour M. Hersh, "My Lai 4: A Report on the Massacre and Its Aftermath" (Random House, 1970). This account probably should have been given more credit than it has received for jump-starting widespread investigative reporting. Hersh received his acclaim for helping to expose a military scandal four years before Woodward and Bernstein exposed a White House scandal. Furthermore, Hersh did it without the backing of an influential news organization. Hersh's account of how he uncovered the Vietnam War atrocity is captivating and instructive.

- Dennis King, "Get the Facts on Anyone," 2nd ed. (Macmillan, 1999). This is a revised version of the best-selling handbook for journalists.

- Jessica Mitford, "Poison Penmanship: The Gentle Art of Muckraking" (Knopf, 1979). This collection of Mitford's magazine and book journalism includes Mitford's commentary after years of reflecting on each of her projects. Mitford updated one of her books, perhaps her greatest, "The American Way of Death" (1963), during the 1990s. Knopf reissued it as "The American Way of Death Revisited" in 1998, shortly after Mitford's death.

- Margaret Jones Patterson and Robert H. Russell, eds., "Behind the Lines: Case Studies in Investigative Reporting" (Columbia University Press, 1986). This is an excellent book of investigative case studies. The cases do not seem dated because the thought processes and information-gathering techniques are so universal.

- Stanley Penn, "Have I Got a Tip for You, and Other Tales of Dirty Secrets, Political Payoffs and Corporate Scams: A Guide to Investigative Reporting" (Dow Jones, 1994). This is a good book that describes how to investigate business.

- James B. Stewart, "Blind Eye: The Terrifying Story of a Doctor Who Got Away With Murder" (Simon and Schuster, 1999). This fascinating story about a serial killer doctor began with a tip that Stewart received from a friend who had become a judge. It provides valuable information on how Stewart traced his path and shows how the system meant to keep bad doctors out of medicine had failed.

- Ida M. Tarbell, "All in the Day's Work" (Macmillan, 1939). This autobiography, published when the author was 82 years old, explains how Tarbell became the unlikely original practitioner of modern investigative journalism. Besides being one of the most thoroughly researched autobiographies extant, the book is filled with reporting and writing techniques.

- John Ullmann, "Investigative Reporting: Advanced Methods and Techniques" (St. Martin's Press, 1995). This handbook comes from Pulitzer Prize–winning newspaper editor and former IRE executive director John Ullmann.

Secondary Sources

This chapter offers methodical approaches to finding the best secondary sources for any investigation on which a journalist might embark. It looks at common secondary sources, such as newspaper articles and periodical indexes, as well as less-used sources, such as theses and dissertations. The chapter also discusses productive approaches to using the Internet in your search for secondary sources.

In a classic investigation, journalist Mike Berens demonstrated the value of secondary sources while reporting on the death of a prostitute in Ohio. Berens, then a reporter at The Columbus Dispatch, began to wonder whether a serial killer might be at work. It was a hunch based on past stories Berens had read about murdered prostitutes, combined with a comment years earlier by an FBI agent that some serial killers prey on prostitutes because they tend to be transient and are therefore often not missed for weeks.

From his newsroom, Berens logged on to an online database containing the full text of daily newspapers across the country. Berens began with Ohio newspapers, keying in the words "prostitute" and "body." That search turned up 60 stories.

One of those stories piqued Berens' interest. An Associated Press story told of a woman's body found outside Cincinnati after she had last been seen alive at a Youngstown truck stop. That sounded similar to a case Berens already knew about. While pondering the similarity, Berens found another brief story about the disappearance of a different prostitute from the same Youngstown truck stop.

Because all the bodies had been found along Interstate 71, Berens expanded his search at the suggestion of a Dispatch librarian to include the words "highway" or "interstate." That search located references to three more murders in Ohio of truck-stop prostitutes; each showed characteristics similar to the three cases already in Berens' files. One characteristic was that the women's bodies apparently had been dumped directly from a truck cab, so Berens decided to exclude cases of murdered prostitutes where the victims had been dragged or concealed.

He expanded his online search to newspapers in other states, turning up references to similar murders, spanning six years, of prostitutes in Alabama, Illinois, Indiana and New York. With evidence in hand to back his hunch, Berens built on his findings by calling sources, visiting truck stops, and canvassing sheriffs in Ohio and elsewhere whose officers patrolled interstate highways. Law enforcement officers from widespread jurisdictions eventually formed a task force based on Berens' work and began investigating the murders as the probable work of a serial killer.

About the same time, reporters at the Hartford Courant were performing a similar analysis on the local level. A brief article toward the back pages of the newspaper had described the discovery of a woman's body. Police said they were investigating similarities between that case and one or two other murders. The reporters examined the Courant's hard-copy clips of every unsolved murder of a Connecticut woman going back five years and entered details of about 40 such murders into a database.

By simple sorting and grouping of those details, the reporters saw that at least six of the women had lived in a small area of Hartford. Information gathered through interviews and medical examiner reports filled out the database. Finally, the evidence that one or more serial killers might be at large led to the creation of a statewide police task force that investigated the crimes and eventually made an arrest.

Berens and the Hartford Courant reporters used secondary source material — that is, already-published information — to generate investigative pieces. Secondary sources, such as newspaper databases, magazines and books, provide leads to investigative stories and extensive background on any issue, institution or individual. With much of secondary sources being electronically archived, journalists can use secondary sources more easily, especially if they have some training in search techniques.

But journalists should independently verify all secondary-source information. A journalist must check later issues of the publication for corrections, letters to the editor and clarifying follow-up articles and then must confirm the accuracy of the information by seeking out the original sources. But secondary sources still can be an invaluable starting point.

Newspapers

Finding the Right Newspapers

To learn which publications cover which geographic areas, journalists can consult the Newslink Web site (http://newslink.org), which lists daily and weekly newspapers city by city, state by state and country by country. Editor & Publisher's online edition of its yearbook (www.editorpublisher.com) has a comprehensive list but charges for it, as does Bacon's News Directory (http://us.cision .com/products_services/bacons_media_directories_2008.asp), but a local library might carry the printed version.

In many cities, there has been a tremendous growth in newspapers for specific neighborhoods as well as newspapers aimed mainly at workplaces or at specific ethnic, cultural or religious groups. In St. Louis, for instance, there are newspapers aimed at Italian-Americans, Korean-Americans, blacks, Chinese-Americans, gays, Jews and Lutherans. Many of those can be found in the Editor & Publisher International Year Book, but the New American Media Web site (http://news.newamericamedia.org/news) or the New York Community Alliance, formerly known as the Independent Press Association (www.indypress ny.org) would also be good to check.

For newspaper archives, the News Archives (www.newspaperarchive.com) on the Web indexes newspaper archives and describes how to access them. Although many published articles are accessible through online services, older articles may have to be obtained through CD-ROMs, commercial databases, hard copy or microfiche. For current articles, Google News is especially good now.

While online services have made these searches much easier, always consider a visit to a newspaper's library for older materials. The library may have hard-copy clips with a file that might include unpublished material of value. For example, at some newspapers, parents were asked to fill out birth announcement forms, which are filed with published clippings about the father, mother and/or child. Engagement, wedding and anniversary sheets may also include unpublished material.

Members of Investigative Reporters and Editors use hard-copy and online membership directories when looking for stories from distant newspapers whose stories do not appear on databases. They check their IRE membership directory, then contact the appropriate person at the distant newsroom. One alternative is the distant local public library, where sometimes the staff clips the hometown newspaper, then files the clippings under topic headings. See "Resources for Reporting" at the end of this chapter for more information.

Stories and Announcements

With many stories, local newspapers are the best place to begin your search for secondary source information. Often, only local newspapers (and their Web sites) contain specific information about local banks, businesses and government leaders. Only local newspapers have investigations that uncover misdeeds by businesspeople or public officials.

In addition, stories in local newspapers have aided reporters in other states and at national newspapers in their investigations into stories about government subsidies to farmers, workers' compensation, and international con men bankrupting financial institutions nationwide.

Besides news stories, local papers publish routine information, such as wedding and funeral announcements, that can help journalists. Birth and marriage notices can help determine relationships that might not surface otherwise. The birth notices tell of new parents with different last names: Carla D. Crane and Michael R. Storm are the parents of a 7-pound girl born March 2 at Regional Hospital. Marriage license listings serve a similar purpose, connecting Leslie Anne Logan, 30, of Columbia, with George Jacob Tice, 33, of Columbia.

Some organized-crime reporters use newspaper announcements to establish undisclosed relationships within crime families. Journalists also use society columns telling who was seen with whom (such associations may prove helpful, as when the subject of an investigation denies knowing someone), rewritten news releases with details about individuals that give details of their job history or education, and advertisements placed by businesses and professionals that turn out to be false claims.

Letters to the editor can be referenced too. While investigating the background of a murder suspect, a Columbia Daily Tribune reporter recalled a letter to the editor written by the suspect while he was imprisoned for a previous offense. By searching the newspaper's files, the reporter found the letter from three years earlier; in it, ironically, the prisoner said his sentence was too harsh; he was no threat to society because he would never act violently.

The local newspaper contains many other resources. As noted earlier, obituaries can be checked for names of survivors. Those names can reveal connections among people who previously seemed unconnected. Journalists covering city, county and state government can methodically collect information that shows relationships revealing nepotism and patronage. Information from obituaries is especially helpful when blood relatives have different last names. If the deceased is Harold P. Burnside, a powerful low-profile businessman, a journalist might learn from the obituary that Gayle O'Connor is his sister. That in turn might lead to a story about how O'Connor, as a zoning board member, cast the deciding vote on a rezoning request from her brother's development company without revealing her conflict of interest.

Legal Notices, Police Reports and Classified Ads

The paid legal notices in the back of the newspaper or on its Web site are all tips for possible investigations. These include notices on wills, divorces, child custody disputes, personal name changes, foreclosures and auctions of property, and government requests for bids on products or services. In addition, government reporters should read the legal advertisements every day. Often, they will find bids, purchases and projects they have never heard about. Reports about seized property and unclaimed property can also lead to stories.

Journalists should always check lists of alleged and actual lawbreakers. With knowledge of the community and a good filing system, journalists might recognize that the person arrested for shoplifting is the financial officer for a community college. (That actually happened.) Or that the person arrested for drunken driving is a school bus driver.

Classified advertisements also should be checked. Quite often get-rich-quick schemes or escort services are listed. In fact, the classified ads of most publications—hard copy or online—can provide a road map to the illegal sex trade in any community, including telephone numbers to call.

Non-Newspaper Secondary Sources

Broadcast and Cable Sources

The subjects of some broadcast news programs are also sometimes indexed and available in databases, as well as on the Web. Television News Index and Abstracts—which covers the national evening news programs, including ABC's "Nightline" and CNN's "Primenews"—is run by Vanderbilt University's Television News Archive (http://tvnews.vanderbilt.edu). Public television's "The NewsHour with Jim Lehrer" is covered in a print index and is available on a commercial database. The Journal Graphics service offers television news transcripts from a range of stations and networks. Contact information is Journal Graphics Inc., 1535 Grant Street, Denver, Colo. 80203, (800) TALK-SHO. The full text of some news programs is available online from Burrelle's Luce at http://tapesandtranscripts.burrellesluce.com.

Magazines and Newsletters

Periodicals come in many forms: general-interest magazines, newsletters, newspapers, trade journals, in-house publications, association newsletters, and local-, state-, and federal-government-generated printings. Journalists mining secondary sources should search listings of periodicals to get an idea of the range of publications that cover a specific investigation subject. Ulrich's Periodicals Directory (www.ulrichsweb.com/ulrichsweb) has an online service that contains international bibliographic information on journals, magazines and newspapers and claims to be the most comprehensive directory available on periodicals.

Other guides to periodicals cover titles in a particular field; many of those are published by H.W. Wilson Company, including the Index to Legal Periodicals and Books, Business Periodicals Index and Education Index. Brand-new publications can be tracked through the Library of Congress's New Serial Titles at www.loc.gov/today/pr/2008/index.html. H.W. Wilson also publishes the Readers' Guide to Periodical Literature (www.hwwilson.com/Databases/Readersg.htm), the largest directory of U.S. and Canadian periodicals, covering more than 56,000 journals, newsletters, newspapers and directories.

Because the directories often list individual editors for each periodical, a journalist can request to talk to that specific editor. That editor will have years of experience overseeing coverage of the topic. Editors of specialized publications are often generous with their knowledge, sharing industry norms as well as specific tips. Journalists should always look at newsletters, which are normally distinguished from magazines by their lack of advertising. There are thousands of newsletters, some so specific that they cover just one law or one agency—newsletters with names like Inside Mortgage Finance, New Jersey Center for Biomaterials and Medical Devices, and Food Chemical News. The Oxbridge Directory of Newsletters (www.mediafinder.com) provides information for more than 23,000 U.S. and Canadian consumer, association and business newsletters in 254 categories. In addition, the Specialized Information Publishers Association (www.newsletters.org), based in McLean, Va., lists little-known dailies, weeklies and monthlies.

In her book "Poison Penmanship: The Gentle Art of Muckraking," Jessica Mitford emphasizes the importance of specialized publications but distinguishes between those intended for broad public consumption (such as the Journal of the American Medical Association) and those not (such as Medical Economics), about which Mitford says, "In its glossy pages, you will find many a crass and wonderfully quotable appeal to the avarice of the practitioners of the healing arts." Discussing her investigation of the funeral industry, Mitford points out the gap between funeral directors' public postures in advertisements aimed at customers and their trade publications such as Mortuary Management: "Here were undertakers . . . talking to each other, in the secure belief that no prying outsider would ever have access to their inner councils."

Reference Books

A good place to start with reference books is Gale Research (http://gale.cengage .com), which publishes numerous indexes. For example, its Encyclopedia of Associations contains details on thousands of trade and professional groups, social welfare and public affairs organizations, labor unions, fraternal and patriotic clubs, plus religious, sports and hobbyist groups. These associations are a treasure trove of potential sources and experts in almost every field. Like many of Gale's other books, the encyclopedia is now searchable online. Two reference volumes from Columbia Books are also useful: National Trade and Professional Associations of the United States and its companion, State and Regional Associations of the United States.

Reference works containing biographical information are so prevalent that there are indexes to the indexes. One of the best, Gale Research's Biography and Genealogy Master Index, contains hundreds of thousands of citations to biographical articles from biographical dictionaries and who's who directories. Gale says more than 600,000 citations a year are added to the database and existing citations "are never removed." It's updated two times a year.

Another reference work, the Biography Index from H.W. Wilson Company, covers profiles that have appeared in periodicals, obituaries, references in book-length biographies, autobiographies, diaries and collections of letters.

Author Dennis King says, "Never assume a person is not listed, no matter how humdrum his or her life might be." If a subject has been listed over a stretch of time, it is useful to compare the most recent information with older versions. The older entries might list previous addresses or former spouses dropped from recent editions or might show a gap of time.

Biographical listings less obvious than Who's Who include local, regional and national social registers for the socially prominent; government handbooks, as well as privately published versions, with biographies of elected and appointed officials and their top aides; college reunion directories; and regional, statewide and national listings of members sharing a trade or profession, such as those kept by medical organizations and their parent, the American Medical Association.

What appears to be an uncontroversial listing might contain a key tidbit. As King explains, "The date of birth might help you in ordering driver's license abstracts and other public records concerning the subject. The name of a parent or former spouse may lead you to court papers regarding a divorce or probate of a will. Information about [the] subject's educational background may guide you to college yearbooks, a master's thesis, or a doctoral dissertation."

Reference books that are directories can be located through Directories in Print. One example is the Private Fleet Directory, covering about 34,000 companies that transport their own freight. Journalists can use such directories to locate competitors of a company and to learn about the industry. Directories in Print covers 26 topics, including health care services, community services/ social concerns, philanthropy/religion/ethnic groups, biography/genealogy, arts/ entertainment, and retail/wholesale/consumer service industries.

Journalists also should check the American Reference Books Annual, published by Libraries Unlimited. An excellent alternative is the Guide to Reference Sources, published by the American Library Association.

Dissertations and Theses

University libraries house doctoral dissertations and master's theses, each of which are part secondary source, part primary source. Freelance reporter Jack Tobin said his project about low graduation rates of college athletes "was aided immeasurably when I discovered that a former UCLA fullback had written a doctoral dissertation at another school on that precise topic." Doctoral and master's students often receive unparalleled access to institutions because they are seen as nonthreatening. A journalist should assume a thesis or dissertation has been composed on the project at hand, then find it through the online versions of Dissertation Abstracts International, or Masters Abstracts International, published by ProQuest Company (formerly University Microfilms Inc.), now at www.umi.com/products_pq/descriptions/dai.shtml.

Books

Sometimes the key for a journalist is a good book because some of the best maps to good sources are in their appendixes, bibliographies and endnotes.

Scouting through a library can work well only if the journalist understands that books on the same topic are scattered throughout the building. For example, books about drug abuse have a home base in the HV5800 classification (social pathology) of the Library of Congress system. But drug abuse books also appear in AS35 (societies), BV4470 (pastoral theology), LB1044 (teaching), QP37 (human physiology), several H classes (social sciences) besides HV, several KF areas (U.S. law), several R classes (medical) and under Z (bibliographies about drug abuse).

But perhaps a better way to find books illuminating an individual, institution or issue is to figure out the best search terms by using controlled vocabulary subject headings. A journalist investigating the death penalty will miss uncountable sources if he or she simply searches under "death penalty." The most useful material might be found under "capital punishment," "legal execution" or some other phrase.

Once a researcher has found some useful books, the reverse side of the title page can be checked for something called a "tracing," the subject headings assigned to that title. It can be used to search for other books that might be equally or even more useful. For example, the subject headings assigned to the book "Home Town," Tracy Kidder's profile of Northampton, Mass., include "Northampton (Mass.) — Social conditions," "Northampton (Mass.) — History" and "City and town life — United States — Case studies."

The most systematic way of finding the right subject heading is to consult the five volumes of the Library of Congress Subject Headings, found in any major library, which contain more than 280 headings. "This is the list of acceptable terms, with cross-references from the ones that don't work to the ones that do. For example, 'death penalty' will tell you to see 'capital punishment' instead," says Thomas Mann, author of "A Guide to Library Research Methods" and "Library Research Models: A Guide to Classification, Cataloging and Computers." "Unfortunately, very few researchers . . . seem to know that these books exist. Most just jump into the catalog with whatever terms they happen to think of, rather than find the headings that are formally acceptable."

Entries for each term also include narrower terms. For example, the heading "divorce" yields a narrower heading "children of divorced parents." The heading "suicide" refers journalists to "youth — suicidal behavior." The holdings of many libraries can be searched simultaneously through online public access catalogs, such as the OPAC Directory, published by Mecklermedia. (Database searches are covered later in this chapter and in Chapter 3.)

To increase your chances of locating the most recent book on your subject, look beyond a library catalog search, because it may take some time for a new book to be cataloged. Guides to already published or about-to-be-published books include Bowker's Books in Print (www.bowker.com) and Books Out of Print from Reed Elsevier; the magazine Publishers Weekly, especially its compilation issues of upcoming books; Kirkus Reviews; Choice, from the Association of College and Research Libraries; and Book Review Digest from H.W. Wilson. The Reader's Adviser from Reed Elsevier lists the best of recent and older books in a multivolume set. Systematic browsing of online bookstores such as Barnes and Noble or Amazon can also turn up otherwise overlooked books.

When a journalist locates a useful book, it is wise to contact the author to request any relevant information that may not have found its way between covers and resides unpublished in a file drawer.

Libraries

The Library of Congress in Washington, D.C. (www.loc.gov) is the ultimate repository for secondary-source materials. From the library's various reading rooms, it is possible to request a large percentage of books and periodicals printed in English and other languages.

The library allows searches of Scorpio, the in-house database, which guides access to secondary sources as well as many primary documents. Scorpio contains most books written in English and published in the United States since 1978; periodical articles on thousands of topics, going back to 1976; congressional files by topic, bill number, committee, subcommittee or member of Congress; plus a list of experts from about 15,000 organizations. The library's information office handles requests for interviews of subject-matter experts at the library, as well as reports from the Congressional Research Service (http://opencrs.com). The Library of Congress is not the only national library useful to journalists. The United States National Library of Medicine in Bethesda, Md., and the National Agricultural Library in Beltsville, Md., house collections and experts rarely consulted by journalists.

Most federal agencies operate subject-specific libraries, which contain a mix of secondary and primary source information, in their Washington-area headquarters. In an Environmental Protection Agency library, a journalist might find previously unknown, privately published periodicals, as well as obscure EPA-generated information about hazardous waste sites. Federal agency libraries are listed in Thompson Gale Research's Subject Directory of Special Libraries and Information Centers. Volume one of the three-volume set lists business, government and law libraries; volume two covers computer, engineering and science libraries; and volume three is devoted to health sciences libraries. Such specialized libraries can also be located through Information Today's American Library Directory.

No matter what library you visit, Mann suggests checking with reference librarians, "especially if you think you already know what the best sources are.

We can almost always suggest additional sources you have never heard of, and that you would never find on your own."

Search Techniques

Overall, the Internet is obviously the broadest-ranging repository of electronic information, growing every day with new databases, Web pages, blogs, discussion groups and online companies. But journalists should remember that no Web search can find all the information on the Internet. In fact, a large amount of information—known as the Invisible Web—resides in layers below the information that search engines see. That information includes databases, scholarly papers and many other resources. However, researchers have begun indexing the Invisible Web at various sites such as http://aip.completeplanet.com.

In addition, sometimes the search strategy is flawed or the journalist uses the wrong terms or does not take the time to read tutorials that explain how to do advanced searches. It is absolutely necessary now for a journalist to understand how search engines work, to know reference books that disclose how to search for hard-to-find information and to consult research librarians frequently.

Whether involving the Internet or commercial databases like LexisNexis, online searches enhance deadline stories as well as long-term projects.

A novice searcher who cannot rely on an experienced librarian for help should look for training either in person or through online instruction, particularly through IRE and the National Institute for Computer-Assisted Reporting. NICAR's Net Tour and tip sheets from the IRE Resource Center will help any journalist get a jump start. In addition, the newest edition of "Computer-Assisted Research" by Nora Paul and Kathleen A. Hansen, published by IRE, is a logical next step after the Net Tour. It is an excellent guide for every kind of online searching.

Because of the extensive information and databases on the Web, a journalist can track everything from the service history of an aircraft that crashed to the history of supporters of a political candidate. And if it isn't online, then journalists should see if there is information, particularly decades-old information, stored on CD-ROMs or available at libraries or through commercial vendors. The same principles of searching can work for CD-ROMs.

Key Word and Citation Searches

Key word searches in online indexes can be productive too. "What do you do when you want sources on 'managing sociotechnical change' and there is no good subject heading that corresponds to this topic?" Mann asks. "Or on 'urban sprawl'? Some topics fall between the cracks of the formally approved subject headings; others represent subjects that are too new to have been established in the system. While browsing may work to some extent in circumventing the lack of such headings, key word indexes usually work better."

Mann says the best key word indexes are published by the Institute for Scientific Information, Philadelphia: the Science Citation Index, Social Sciences Citation Index and Arts and Humanities Citation Index. These indexes cover academic and professional journals, indexing articles by key words. "They enable you to look up any exact words to see if two or more of the precise terms you want have appeared in the title of a journal article," Mann says. "You can thus look for the exact word 'sociotechnical' to see if it is paired with 'management' or 'planning.' It is."

Citation searches in paper or online indexes can supplement key word searches. "With a citation search," Mann says, "you have to start with a known source. It can be a book, a magazine or journal article, a dissertation, a conference paper—whatever. It can date from last year or 200 years ago—that does not matter either. A citation search will tell you if someone has written a later journal article that cites the source in the footnote." While researching a biography, one of the authors looked up a book that the subject of the biography had written decades earlier. Learning who had cited it since led to information that quite likely would have escaped attention otherwise. The Thomas Scientific indexes offer the best sources for citation searches.

Bibliographies

Searching published bibliographies can also be revealing. They list hundreds of relevant published works that probably would take months for a journalist to compile. After finding the Library of Congress subject heading, a journalist can plug it into these two formats in the library's main catalog: "SUBJECT HEADING—Bibliography" (for example, "Education—Bibliography") or "SUBJECT HEADING—Geographic subdivision—Bibliography" (for example, "Homeless Persons—United States—Bibliography").

An alternative is to use the appropriate search term in the Bibliographic Index (www.hwwilson.com/databases/biblio.htm), published by H.W. Wilson Company, a listing of published bibliographies, including those with 50 or more citations at the ends of books and journal articles. The first cousin to the bibliography is the directory. About 16,000 directories are listed in Directories in Print (Gale Research).

Secondary Source Databases

Hundreds of U.S. and international daily newspapers are searchable in full text through one or more commercial computer databases and increasingly through the newspapers' own Web sites. Database vendors that allow you to search for newspaper stories offer other resources as well. Journalists can find information about 15,600 databases and data products by consulting the Gale Directory of Online, Portable and Internet Databases.

Database superstores, including Dialog, LexisNexis and Factiva.com, provide access to databases produced by hundreds of organizations. Each superstore offers access to some of the same resources — for example, The Washington Post is available through many of them — but each has traditionally enjoyed exclusive access to other resources. Full-text databases are usually preferable to those providing citations or abstracts only. Full text means that a search will look for your search term anywhere in the document, not just in the citations or abstract. A passing reference to your investigative subject might even hold the key to the investigation. A journalist could mine full-text databases for references to the subject of an investigation, finding his name in footnotes to judges' opinions and near the bottom of a feature story; similar references in footnotes and bottom paragraphs have become starting points for entire new sections of investigative projects. One reference work, Fulltext Sources Online (www.fso-online .com) helps sort out which resources are available online in full text.

The conventional wisdom that lots of information is free on the Web is not a myth; it is just overstated. There are lots of Web sites with free versions of a few publications in full text, but the majority of periodicals still cost money to access as full text online. Using an electronic version of a print publication can be problematic. Portions of the print text (such as sidebars and graphics) are routinely omitted online, and sometimes entire years of coverage are missing.

Whatever the time or cost involved, learning about online databases is vital. They are often superior to print indexes not only because of broader coverage and full text, but also because the searcher can combine terms, such as "organized crime" and "waste haulers," capturing only items mentioning those terms together. Increasingly, information available from databases cannot be found in print indexes. Furthermore, these resources are updated more frequently than in print. That is true not only for some secondary sources, such as privately published newsletters, but also for certain primary sources from government agencies. For example, the U.S. Geological Survey ceased producing its paper copy of Selected Water Resources Abstracts, now known as Water Resources Abstracts, which is produced only electronically by Cambridge Scientific Abstracts.

In another example, a search for the term "homeless" in the print index of the Encyclopedia of Associations would list only a dozen organizations whose names include the word "homeless." An online search, on the other hand, yields dozens of references because the text of the organizations' entries is included. The text lists areas of emphasis; "homeless" shows up in the text even when it is not part of the organization's name.

⊃ CHECK IT OUT

✓ Using local newspaper indexes, construct a profile of a local city or county official. Among the articles to use are news clippings, wedding announcements and obituary notices. Create a list of business relationships, a list of family members, and a list of social relationships. Then write a two-page report describing the person.

✓ Using newspaper legal ads, find one recent request for bids and one recent foreclosure announcement. Use the bid request as a starting point for any news stories having to do with similar kinds of work, whether it is roadwork, sewers or other construction. Use the foreclosure request as a starting point to look up more information on the lender and the individual. Write one page on each of your findings.

✓ Using the indexes mentioned earlier, find magazines and newsletters about the funeral home industry. Make a list of ongoing industry issues, and select three of those issues for stories. Write a memo describing how those stories might be pursued and listing other documents that might be sought.

RESOURCES FOR REPORTING

These resources and indexes change so often that it is best to check the links at the IRE Resource Center (www.ire.org) for the latest updates.

News Stories and Media Archives

Newslink (http://newslink.org) provides a free comprehensive index of newspapers throughout the world. In addition, New America Media (http://news .newamericamedia.org/news) provides links to ethnic media organizations in the United States for a low price.

- For newsletters, the Specialized Information Publishers Association (formerly Newsletter & Electronic Publishers Foundation) (www.newsletters.org) is one of the most helpful places to begin.

- For broadcast, the Vanderbilt Television News Archive (http://tvnews .vanderbilt.edu) offers the most extensive collection of TV news.

- For newspaper archives, News Archives on the Web (www.ibiblio.org/riverat/ internet/archives/html) has resources arranged by state.

U.S. Government Information

The Fed World (www.fedworld.gov) will lead you to thousands of government publications, including Supreme Court decisions and scientific and technical work. The Library of Congress (www.loc.gov) includes information on government publications, congressional actions and records, copyright information, and many other topics.

Academic Papers

To find scholarly papers, using Google Scholar is effective.

Science and Medicine

Mednews (www.newswise.com/menu-med.htm) offers a news service on the latest in research and academic papers on science and medicine. The U.S. National Library of Medicine (www.nlm.nih.gov) offers indexes and links to papers and studies in medicine.

Libraries

The subscription service of the American Library Directory (www.american librarydirectory.com) gives members information on more than 35,000 public, private, government and institutional libraries and library-related organizations across the country.

3

Primary Documents

This chapter is about original records, known as primary documents, which are often filed at government agencies. The chapter will review how to find these documents in paper and database format. The chapter will show how primary documents often provide the foundations for investigative stories.

Documents and databases, both online and offline, can be revealing in high-impact ways, and the best investigative reporting almost always relies on the collection of primary documents, whether they are licenses, birth certificates or property records.

Throughout the following chapters, this handbook will list an incredible number of primary documents, but no reference book lists every document and database available at every government agency and in every library. Good reporters, however, will find primary documents pertinent to any investigative topic, obtain those documents and have a portrait of a person or institution before the first interview. In fact, the best interviewers often compose a dossier on the subject before they set up the interview.

Lou Rose, author of "How to Investigate Your Friends and Enemies," says,

> There are people I've constructed who I've never met. I can tell them, totally from the public record, when and where they were born, the color of their eyes, how many cars they own, what they paid for them, where they borrowed the money for them, how often they trade cars, whether they have been divorced, whether they've gotten traffic tickets, how long they've owned their home, the whole history of their real property, what their credit reports are.

Starting in the 1990s, the ability to background an individual, institution or issue through databases rose dramatically. But it would be a mistake to assume that everything gathered through database research is complete and accurate. Nor should investigative journalists assume they can forego checking hard-copy documents. Nevertheless, for savvy journalists, the Internet and commercial databases are good starting points.

Specific Primary Documents

Which documents or databases a journalist seeks first depends on whether the story is mainly about an individual, an institution or an issue: the three I's. Every project falls primarily into one of those three categories or some combination of them.

During an investigation of an individual, a journalist should try to examine every public record concerning the individual, including property records, loans, property taxes, licenses, voter's registration, liens and lawsuits, including any divorce or probate court proceedings.

Using Social Security Numbers

Because it is a unique, quasi-national identifier, an individual's U.S. Social Security number can be of help in finding documents or databases with information about the individual within any level or branch of government. And although a Social Security number is supposed to be private, it often is listed on numerous public documents.

A Social Security number can open many doors for a journalist investigating one or more individuals. For example, the number tells where the person was living when they got their number. The first three digits show the state of issuance. For example, 001 through 003 designate New Hampshire, and 004 through 007 is Maine. Because so many people apply in their state of birth, knowing an individual's Social Security number can save a journalist time when searching for a birth certificate.

There are exceptions. Refugees entering the United States received California numbers 568-30 through 568-58 between 1975 and 1979. North Carolina received 232-30 from West Virginia. Before 1963, workers covered under the Railroad Retirement Act received 700 through 728 no matter what their state of residence at the time of application.

The fourth and fifth digits, called the group number, divide geographic areas into more manageable chunks for the Social Security Administration. In theory, a group number could range from 01 to 99, but some are intentionally unassigned; a journalist checking the validity of a number should ask the Social Security Administration whether the group number is false.

Former journalist Brad Goldstein wrote in Uplink, the newsletter of the National Institute for Computer-Assisted Reporting, about how he obtained a state government computer tape of area welfare recipients, complete with Social Security numbers. With that tape in house, he asked a different Massachusetts agency for a computer tape of workers' compensation awards. His intention was to learn how many welfare recipients winning workers' compensation claims illegally failed to tell the welfare office. But the second agency said it would have to omit Social Security numbers. Goldstein protested and the agency then said it would provide the Social Security numbers, but only after it removed names and dates of birth. Knowing he already possessed that information from the first agency, he agreed to the compromise. Eventually he was able to report that 99 percent of welfare recipients receiving workers' compensation were cheating.

Although Social Security numbers and other primary documents are usually valid, sometimes they are falsified or stolen. At KCBS-TV, Los Angeles, Joel Grover and Sylvia Teague uncovered a criminal network established to sell legitimate California driver's licenses to recipients who then used them illegally to obtain government benefits, board commercial airliners and perpetrate illegal activities tied to the licenses' role as de facto identification cards.

Military veterans who want to enhance their records and nonveterans who want to pose as wartime heroes have found ways to obtain or create falsified service records. Glenna Whitley of D Magazine in Dallas and B.G. Burkett, a Vietnam veteran upset at the widespread fraud and how often those frauds fooled journalists, collaborated on a book to expose the situation, entitled "Stolen Valor: How the Vietnam Generation Was Robbed of Its Heroes and Its History."

It is frequently difficult for investigative journalists to establish the validity of what seem to be legitimate primary documents. But the illicit nature of such documents is something to which investigative journalists must always be alert. In recent years, both CBS and the Los Angeles Times had major stories retracted because of unauthentic documents or questions about authenticity.

Public Records

If a Social Security number is unavailable, there are many other ways to gather information on an individual. For example, a voter's registration application in Missouri shows state of birth (helping an investigator narrow the search for a birth certificate), age, previous place of residence, length of residence at the current address and occupation. When Des Moines investigative journalists John P. Dolan Jr. and Lisa Lacher compiled the Guide to Public Records of Iowa Counties, the looseleaf notebook ran to thousands of pages. To unify the manual, Dolan and Lacher created Dr. Willoughby F. Wrighteous to act as a sample investigative subject. They show how almost every aspect of Wrighteous' life can be illuminated through documents.

Veteran journalist Duff Wilson has provided a guide to backgrounding an individual online at his Web site Reporter's Desktop under his "John Doe" section (www.reporter.org/desktop/tips/johndoe.htm).

Another example of this kind of manual is Access, a guide to documents in Boone County, Mo. A library science professor at the University of Missouri served as editor. Access has since been updated by the Freedom of Information Center at the Missouri School of Journalism. Investigative journalists anywhere might find a local guide, especially in a newsroom or at a journalism school. If none exists, guides from elsewhere can suggest records to be found locally. Joe Adams of The Florida Times-Union in Jacksonville compiled the 457-page Florida Public Records Handbook, available through his newspaper or through the First Amendment Foundation in Tallahassee.

Vital Records

Primary documents also include vital records such as birth, death, marriage and divorce certificates. These records can point to sources as well as provide information about subjects under investigation.

As with all other documents, the information contained in vital records might be misleading. After analyzing death certificates, a reporter from Harper's Magazine gave an example: The pianist Liberace's doctor had listed subacute encephalopathy, a brain disease, as the cause of death, but the coroner, citing autopsy findings of a form of pneumonia found in patients with AIDS, rejected the certificate; the coroner said Liberace's doctor had known the truth all along. The lesson: Investigative journalists must try to verify all information in primary documents.

In many states, vital records are kept at the county level and in the state capital. Access varies from state to state, and because of identity theft, some states have severely limited access to these records. The U.S. Department of Health and Human Services publishes a guide to birth and death record locations in the states, as do private publishers, including the Consumer Education Research Center. Private companies are crossing state lines to gather vital statistics in ways that make searching more efficient. For example, the National Institute for Computer-Assisted Reporting periodically acquires death records from Social Security master files. Although the database is massive and flawed, it can help when a state will not release its death records. For searches on a few individuals at a time, an easy-to-use Web site for Social Security death records is Ancestry.com.

In some cases, journalists will have to use online database pay services, such as Accurint or Intellius, for information on individuals.

The Uniform Commercial Code

When an individual or company borrows money and promises to repay on schedule, a lender that wants legal protection should file a Uniform Commercial Code financing statement. UCC recordings are to personal property—such as computers, yachts and automobiles—what mortgages are to real property like land and buildings. They are called "uniform" because they are used by every state. The statement, filed under the borrower's name, is now kept at the secretary of state's office in each state and can often be found at their Web sites. UCCs filed in the past might also be found at the offices of the county recorder of deeds.

Journalists use UCC statements to document who is doing business with whom. For example, while checking a rumor that a local politician voted to shift the city's money from one local bank to another in exchange for favorable personal loans, journalist Steve Weinberg found bank officials invoking confidentiality. Looking at UCC filings under the name of the politician turned out to be a first step in establishing a borrower-lender relationship.

UCC forms have revealed the address of a borrower unlisted in telephone directories; the names of a borrower's spouse or business partners; dates of transactions plugged into a chronology about a subject's rise or fall; and property owned by the borrower, listed as collateral.

UCC filings have also been used to track airplanes or yachts as collateral, and that can lead to property or registration documents. Journalists have tracked art fraud and inside deals among art dealers when paintings are used as collateral and have uncovered misuse of government funds such as loans from the Small Business Administration.

While investigating government contracts to supposedly minority-owned construction companies, reporters also have used UCC forms. One reporting team heard that companies owned by whites were using minority members as fronts to gain government contracts. So they looked for UCC filings by lenders who provided money to the minorities. Then they looked for follow-up transactions between minorities and white contractors suggesting the contractors were assuming financial responsibility for the original loans.

Liens and Tax Documents

Borrowers sometimes end up with liens placed against their property by the Internal Revenue Service or a state agency due to unpaid taxes. The lien is generally filed at the county or city recorder's office in the borrower's home county, although in some states, federal tax liens are filed in one office and state tax liens in another.

Some counties have records of tax liens online or a tax lien database that can be obtained inexpensively, used often and updated routinely as a basic newsroom reference source. In Columbia, Mo., a journalism graduate student obtained a tax lien database, then found leads for stories on the liens against a college coach and against a previously unreported-on defunct business in debt to the government for millions of dollars.

When longtime investigative journalists Donald Barlett and James Steele examined 20,000 tax liens during an investigation of the Internal Revenue Service, they found a physician who owed more than $900,000 in income taxes and an insurance executive who owed more than $2 million.

Debtors often end up paying far less than they owe. Settlements for reduced payments are filed at an IRS regional office or IRS headquarters. Settlements, liens and UCC filings can lead investigative journalists to tax cases that end up in court where many more documents can be found. (U.S. Tax Court, tax cases in district courts and bankruptcy courts are treated more fully in Chapter 10.)

If a borrower fails to pay local property taxes, the property can be foreclosed on and sold at auction. Every week in local newspapers and on Web sites, unpaid property auction notices appear, listing the borrower and the lender. Sometimes the debtor is prominent in the community. In addition to providing leads to stories on individuals, the notices also can indicate whether foreclosures are on the rise in the community.

Primary Documents Databases

Commercial Databases

Commercial database vendors like LexisNexis and Westlaw offer many primary documents—from the legislative, executive and judicial branches.

At The (Cleveland) Plain Dealer, reporter Tim Heider volunteered to perform a search on one of this book's previous authors, using a commercial database called Autotrack Plus. In two minutes, Heider learned the Social Security number of the subject; his height, weight, eye color, current address and driver's license status; property ownership going back three residences; names, addresses and telephone numbers of current neighbors; whether the subject held professional licenses; whether he was subject to tax liens, consumer loans, court judgments or bankruptcy proceedings; and whether he held licenses for controlled substances, airplanes or boats. Heider also learned the identities and Social Security numbers of his spouse, who retained her family name, and his children. Through the search, Heider even discovered the name of a relative with a criminal record who had used the subject's address as his own for a while.

Many reporters use Accurint, another online commercial service, to obtain the same kind of information.

Reporters who once faced the daunting prospect of traveling to records repositories in county after county, state after state, now find that much of what they seek is online. Journalists searching for documents from a distance because of time or money constraints can do just as well as if they were actually at the government agency.

To get an idea of what's online, they can go to sites like www.searchsystems .net, a site that indexes all the public records it can find online. Journalists may still have to travel to examine the complete files, but online searches of both commercial databases and government databases provide enough information for them to make intelligent decisions about which trips to schedule.

Database vendors publish state-by-state lists of documents available online. Westlaw, for example, offers these primary documents from Missouri alone: Supreme Court of Missouri cases (back to 1923), appellate court cases (back to 1944), attorney general opinions (1977), state taxation administrative cases (1979), public utilities reports (1953), required filings by corporations and partnerships, insurance regulation cases, all state statutes, the status of proposed legislation while the legislature is in session, and current Uniform Commercial Code filings, which show some of the loans made to businesses.

When it comes to the federal government, database services offer pending legislation in Congress, compilations of U.S. laws and regulations, plus decisions by many agencies, including attorney general opinions, U.S. Office of Government Ethics rulings and Federal Election Commission advisories. The Federal Internet Source, a reference book by the National Journal Group Inc., Washington, D.C., lists many of them.

LexisNexis and its competitor, Westlaw, are best known for their online state and federal judges' opinions. These include opinions not found in hard copy.

In one recent year, the 6th U.S. Circuit Court of Appeals issued 550 opinions in hard copy and digitally, but made 2,250 opinions available by computer only.

Government Agency Records

A journalist investigating an institution can examine records from government agencies, such as the National Labor Relations Board and the U.S. Equal Employment Opportunity Commission, if the institution is a major business in town. For example, filings from the U.S. Nuclear Regulatory Commission and records from congressional and state legislative hearings would be a good place to start when investigating the issue of nuclear waste disposal.

A journalist should consider which level of government records (federal, state, county, city or special district) to examine first. If investigating the issue of nuclear waste, for example, the journalist would start with the U.S. Nuclear Regulatory Commission, a federal agency with headquarters in Washington, D.C. The regulation of nuclear power plants is done primarily by the federal government. So the journalist would seek documents at the federal agency's Web site, headquarters and at its closest regional office.

On the other hand, if the investigation involves an insurance company, the journalist would start at the appropriate state insurance commission because the insurance industry is regulated by the states. Picking the correct level of government is a matter of research and experience. There is nothing inherently logical about nuclear power plants being regulated by the federal government or insurance companies by state governments.

To decide whether the federal government is involved, the quickest guide is the U.S. Government Manual, published by the U.S. Government Printing Office in Washington, D.C., and available online and at almost any library. If an agency's entry in the U.S. Government Manual looks promising, the next step is contacting a public affairs officer or going online to obtain the agency's annual report and studies relevant to the investigation, including those prepared because of congressional laws. It almost always helps to check recent reports from the General Accounting Office's Web site (www.gao.gov), which audits federal agencies and programs.

Having decided which level of government to try first, an investigator should search all branches of that level. Every level has three branches: legislative, executive and judiciary.

The Nuclear Regulatory Commission, for example, is an executive branch agency, but it implements laws approved by Congress, the legislative branch.

Thus it makes sense for a journalist to read the documents and debates leading to passage of the laws affecting the NRC as recounted in the Congressional Record, a daily account of activity in the U.S. Senate and House of Representatives. Furthermore, it is quite likely that laws and NRC rules have been challenged. So the investigator can look for lawsuits against the NRC, starting with U.S. district courts.

Government Databases

When a Midwest reporter received a tip from a college student that an immigration lawyer had left town with her money, he checked county records online. By doing so, he learned that the lawyer had recently purchased a $305,000 home with a $275,000 mortgage and more recently had taken out a $40,000 second mortgage. He had also bought a $40,000 automobile. It seemed he spent more than he could afford, because a federal tax lien of $36,825 had been placed on his home and a lien of $22,504 on his business. Creditors had sued him; the names of the lawyer's own attorneys showed up in the online county records. Because the county's database only summarized court records, the reporter telephoned the court clerk, gave her the case numbers and arrived at the courthouse later that day to pick up the complete records. The reporter was then able to start reporting how the lawyer had stolen his clients' money.

One of the best books published on government databases was Matthew Lesko's "The Federal Database Finder: A Directory of Free and Fee-Based Databases and Files Available From the Federal Government." Available on CD-ROM, it contained an index and descriptions of thousands of federal databases. Although it has not been updated since 1995, its entries are still relevant and useful.

The National Technical Information Service, part of the Technology Administration of the U.S. Department of Commerce, provides the Directory of U.S. Government Data Files for Mainframes and Microcomputers. This directory lists computerized record sets from federal agencies, divided into dozens of topics. For example, the Regional Air Pollution Studies documented emissions in selected cities hour by hour for three years.

The National Technical Information Service also manages FedWorld, a gateway to mostly free government agency bulletin boards. One of the most useful is the U.S. Department of Agriculture's Agricultural Library Forum, accessible on its own or through FedWorld. The forum offers bibliographies on topics of interest to journalists, such as rural health care, nutrition, cancer, poverty and toxic waste.

Depository Libraries

Federal and state depository libraries allow journalists to find lots of primary documents in one location. The U.S. Congress Joint Committee on Printing publishes "A Directory of U.S. Government Depository Libraries," which lists about 1,400 libraries. Depository libraries decide which documents to order from the government; those designated as regional depositories must carry certain items and provide interlibrary loan and reference services.

Every federal depository carries the federal budget, the census of housing and population, the Congressional Record, the U.S. Government Manual, the Federal Register, a monthly catalog of the Government Printing Office, subject bibliographies, the Weekly Compilation of Presidential Documents, U.S. Supreme Court decisions, the U.S. Code (laws divided by subject matter into 50 titles) and the Code of Federal Regulations (regulations meant to implement the laws).

There also are state government depository libraries. In Missouri, these libraries are operated by the secretary of state's office. Public libraries in St. Louis and Kansas City are full depositories, as are libraries on eight university campuses. Another 28 libraries, a mix of public and university sites, are partial depositories. The state depository library issues a monthly checklist of new publications, plus the cumulative Missouri State Government Serial Publications.

Congressional hearings and publications available at depository libraries are especially valuable for journalists — and not just those working in Washington, D.C. A hearing record might contain valuable information about a local program, for example. Depository libraries carry congressional committee hearings and reports in hard copy or on microform.

A superb guide is the Congressional Information Service Index. It allows investigative journalists to search by topic, congressional committee, institutions mentioned prominently or individuals testifying. It is available in hard copy or online. One of this book's authors found hearings in which members of Congress questioned the subject of a biography, plus additional references to him and his corporations.

Technical and Scientific Sources

Government technical reports are intended for experts but can be useful to journalists. Most are sponsored by three agencies: the U.S. Department of Defense, the U.S. Department of Energy and the National Aeronautics and Space Administration. They publish their own indexes, too: the Defense Technical

Information Center Digest, Energy Research Abstracts (supplemented by its computerized Energy Data Base) and Scientific and Technical Aerospace Reports, respectively.

The National Technical Information Service offers more than 3 million reports at any given time. They are divided into subject categories (such as health care and transportation), which in turn are divided into hundreds of topics. Many are derived from overseas research. Reports are available from the sponsoring agency, the funding recipient or NTIS, the U.S. Department of Commerce or online from Thompson Scientific.

Journalists should check the proceedings of technical and scientific conferences around the world; many proceedings break new ground. The Institute for Scientific Information publishes the Index to Scientific and Technical Proceedings online, covering thousands of meetings annually. Here is an example from the "Forestry" category: "International Symposium on Fire and the Environment—Ecological and Cultural Perspectives." The specific presentations listed would excite any journalist interested in covering natural resources. In addition, ISI publishes Current Contents, which reproduces contents pages from hundreds of scientific journals.

Scientific proceedings are often filled with statistics. The American Statistics Index, from the Congressional Information Service, details comprehensive federal sources; it even covers charts and tables appearing in largely nonstatistical government publications.

Journalists will find background, in the form of statistics or text, by consulting subject bibliographies compiled within agencies and distributed through the Government Printing Office. For example, the bibliography Water Pollution and Water Resources lists three pages of government publications, including "America's Wetlands: Our Vital Link Between Land and Water" and "Quality Criteria for Water."

The National Archives System

Besides the Library of Congress and its satellite depositories, a government repository filled with primary documents is maintained by the National Archives and Records Administration. Many of the records are recent and relevant for contemporary investigations and can be found at its Web site. The Guide to Federal Records in the National Archives of the United States, from the Government Printing Office, can help speed a journalist's research.

The main archives building is in downtown Washington, D.C., supplemented by a newer building in College Park, Md. The saying chiseled into the stone above the downtown entrance should be a watchword for journalists: "The Past Is Prologue."

While researching a biography, for example, journalist Steve Weinberg found documents showing how the subject—then still alive and therefore not "historical"—had sought favorable government rulings for his business ventures. One of those documents was a passport application that helped verify a crucial point made by a human source. The ins and outs of obtaining passport applications and other documents are explained in Prologue, the archives' quarterly magazine.

Documents of local interest are located in regional archives. With the exception of the archives in Anchorage, each region covers at least three states. Each state government operates its own archives, as do institutions such as universities.

NARA also administers military and some civilian personnel records centers, separately from regional records centers, in St. Louis. A thorough guide to military personnel records is "How to Locate Anyone Who Is or Has Been in the Military: Armed Forces Locator Guide," by Richard S. Johnson, an Army lieutenant colonel.

When reporter Joanna Kakissis wrote to the National Personnel Records Center to obtain as much historical information as possible about a career military officer killed by a terrorist bomb in Greece in 1988, she received detailed records, including date of birth, dates of military service, names and birthdates of his children, name of his wife, educational achievements, military decorations and a photograph.

Besides military records, the National Archives system encompasses the presidential libraries, from Herbert Hoover through George H.W. Bush, which contain documents of interest to contemporary journalists. An investigation into the closing of a local military base would benefit from records in each presidential library back to the year of the base's opening. "Records of the Presidency: Presidential Papers and Libraries From Washington to Reagan," by Frank L. Schick with Renee Schick and Mark Carroll, explains the evolution of the presidential library system.

Putting It All Together

Using Primary Documents: A Real-Life Example

Journalist Alan Green used to volunteer at the National Zoo in Washington, D.C. When a zoo insider wanted to complain to somebody about questionable animal-handling practices at Reston Animal Park in suburban Virginia, that insider contacted Green. Curious, Green started poking around, eventually finding a dozen boxes of court records derived from the divorce proceedings of the animal park's former owner. Mixed in with all sorts of documents, Green found receipts showing that the National Zoo had sent surplus animals to this little-known roadside menagerie. So had other big zoos, such as Lincoln Park Zoo in Chicago. Intrigued, Green decided to learn more about whether this discarding of animals was standard operating practice.

Like many other investigative reporters, Green knew he would have to find a focus for his story if his hunch turned out to be accurate. So he decided to maintain his focus on Reston Animal Park, in particular a pair of bear cubs housed there. He had located documents at the Virginia Department of Agriculture and Consumer Services showing that a Wisconsin animal dealer actually owned the bears. That dealer, Green discovered, had pleaded guilty to the federal offense of supplying bears to an exotic meat broker.

Suspecting the bears would be relocating after the Reston zoo closed for the winter, Green did some detective work. Learning the bears' departure time from an inside source, he followed the truck about 500 miles to northern Ohio. When Green looked for paperwork later about the bears' move, he experienced a defining moment in the project: There were no records about the move. Federal and state regulators knew nothing of the animals' whereabouts. Green wondered how many other exotic animals were disappearing from regulators' sight. For another three years, he pieced together the answers.

As Green learned about the exotic animal underworld, he realized that certificates of veterinary inspection, commonly known as health certificates, were the key document. Because he wanted to expose the means by which zoos, universities and other institutions laundered animals until their trail was obscured, Green knew that the records of any given institution would not be enough. Those institutional records would at best show the first leg of the journey — the sale of an animal to a dealer, for example — leaving the ultimate fate of the animals uncertain.

By gathering health certificates, Green believed he could create a trail from first sale to ultimate destination. But because animals are often moved from one state to another, only records from many state capitals would provide a complete picture. He eventually visited 27 state capitals himself, found paid or volunteer researchers in 11 others and used freedom-of-information laws in four states. He skipped the rest after determining they had virtually no exotic animal traffic.

As Green visited more states and added more transactions to the database he created, he found answers emerging. For example, documents in New Jersey showed that a safari park moved antelopes to a North Carolina dealer. Corresponding health certificates Green turned up in North Carolina showed that the dealer moved some of the antelopes to an address in Pennsylvania, others to an address in Texas. A magazine advertisement that Green clipped in his examination of secondary sources told him the Pennsylvania site was a privately operated shooting ground where customers receive assurances they will not leave empty-handed. An Internet search indicated the Texas address belonged to a private hunting preserve too.

Another trail: Green found a document in Des Moines showing that an Iowa woman sent six reindeer to a Missouri auction. So Green checked Jefferson City, where he found a document showing one of the reindeer had been sold to a Wisconsin man. Working backward, Green traced the five-year-old reindeer to its birth in the Yukon and sale to the Iowa woman. Working forward, Green determined the Wisconsin buyer to be the owner of a canned hunt. The annual report of a licensed deer farm to the Wisconsin Department of Natural Resources showed that a patron of the hunting preserve in the town of Almond shot the reindeer on October 10, 1996. Because Wisconsin game wardens were looking into the hunting preserve, they interviewed a taxidermist doing business with the man who shot the reindeer. An Internet search revealed more about the shooter, William Backman, including his appointment by Indiana's governor to the state Natural Resources Foundation—a group dedicated to conservation and thus seemingly opposed to for-pay hunting. Additional digging showed Backman to be an official scorer for Safari Club International, a pro-hunting organization with an ethics code opposing canned hunts. After repeated requests, Backman finally confirmed that he had in fact shot the reindeer that Green was studying.

Green obtained a CD-ROM, published by the International Species Information System, that chronicled thousands of transactions. Using the CD-ROM, Green cross-checked the movements of animals identified in other records and thus obtained fresh leads. Green created his own database from two years' worth of advertisements in Animal Finders' Guide, a trade publication for the private exotic animal trade. He determined the identities of advertisers using CD-ROM versions of reverse telephone directories and Web sites like www.infospace.com. But despite all the documentation, Green knew he would be missing the big picture without lots of help from human sources. State veterinarians told Green that, at most, 15 percent of exotic animals moving across state lines did so with the required paperwork. Green determined that records from one state or federal agency failed to match records from some other agency. When an individual showed up on a document as the recipient of an animal, Green learned to check the telephone number against the address. More than once, the phone number belonged to somebody in a faraway location.

With backing from the Center for Public Integrity, Green turned his research into a book, "Animal Underworld: Inside America's Black Market for Rare and Exotic Species."

Using Primary Documents: A Sample Investigation

The Green example is entirely taken from real life. Unfortunately, no real-life example can cover every document and every people trail or be the ultimate teaching tool. So a bit of enhancement is useful for educational purposes. In that spirit, this chapter ends with a timeless account by the late Patrick Riordan, based on a real project. While he was a Miami Herald reporter, Riordan wrote a chapter for an earlier edition of this book, published before the widespread availability of electronic information. It is reassuring that although technology has altered information-gathering techniques, many practices and theories never become outdated. Riordan's account is reprinted here, lightly edited from the original edition:

> You're methodically researching your project on the monorail the county wants to build at the new zoo, when your editor starts flailing her arms. The police have an update on a bust at a disco last night. They found marijuana, cocaine and Quaaludes. A Colombian citizen was among those arrested. The police are cooperating with the Drug Enforcement Administration, but not with you. They're giving out nothing beyond the arrest sheets. There are unanswered questions:
>
> - Who owns the disco?
> - What else does this person own—land, buildings, cars, boats, airplanes?
> - What's the disco owner's economic background?
> - Has the owner ever been accused of a crime?
> - Does the owner use corporations to hide behind?
> - Is there a limited partnership involved?
> - Who are the disco's investors?
> - How much did they invest?
>
> Public records could answer every one of those questions in a few hours. Let's suppose the police won't even tell you the name of the disco owner. You can still find it. You have the address of the disco from the arrest sheet or the phone book. Go to the office of the tax collector, or the office where deeds are kept on file, and convert the street address into a legal description of the property. In an urban area, that will be a block number and one or more lot numbers in a particular subdivision.

For example, suppose the disco is located at 3000 Coral Blvd. in Miami. Either by asking a clerk or by using the county real estate plat map yourself, you find that 3000 Coral Blvd. is in Miami's Urban Estates subdivision and that your particular address corresponds to Lots 5, 6 and 7 of Block 5. With that information, you can find the owner in one of two ways.

The easy way: If your county keeps abstract books, tract indexes or a property index, look up the book page, computer screen or microfilm reel for your subdivision until you come to Block 5. Then go to the last entry under Block 5 and work backward. The first entry you come to for Lots 5, 6 and 7 is the most recent. It reflects the current owner. The harder way: If you don't have abstract books for each subdivision, work through the tax roll. You may need to convert the legal description of the land into a folio number, composed of the block and lot numbers, a code number for the subdivision and municipality and other code numbers for section, range and township—terms you'll encounter more often when you're researching rural acreage. Each piece of property in your county has a unique folio number. The folio number shows who's paying the taxes. About 99 percent of the time, it is the owner. No matter how you get the name of the apparent owner, it is a good idea to double check. Go to the office where the deeds are kept. It is the recorder's office in some states; the registrar of deeds, clerk's office or official records office in others.

In this case, the current owner appears to be something called Taca Corp. Ask for the grantor and grantee indexes (also known as the official records index, the deed index or the index to real estate transfers). To find the owner's deed to the disco property, look up Taca Corp. in the grantee index. There you will find a reference to Book 289, page 34. Find Deed Book 289 on the shelf or in a microfilm drawer. Turn to page 34, and you've got the deed. Taca Corp., it appears, acquired title to the property from Charles Candyman, a name that's vaguely familiar. The corporation owes $50,000 on the property to First Smuggler's Bank and Trust Co. That is its first mortgage. It owes another $375,000 to Candyman, payable in quarterly installments over 10 years. That is the purchase-money second mortgage. You note in the grantor and grantee indexes that Taca Corp. seems to have several other deeds on file. But before proceeding, you decide to learn a little more about Taca other than its property holdings.

The courthouse office where licenses are kept sheds little light on the subject. Taca holds the local business license in its corporate name. You could check the utilities office to see who pays the water and electricity bills, but you decide to pass for the moment. You call the secretary of state in the capital to ask for the corporate information office. It will give you a lot of information on the phone and send you more by mail. [Since Riordan wrote this passage, many secretary of states' records have become available through commercial databases.]

Always ask for current officers and directors, including their addresses; the corporate address (also called the registered address); the name of the registered agent; the nature of the business in which the corporation engages; whether the corporation is up-to-date on its franchise tax; and the date of incorporation. From the original articles of incorporation, you can get the names of the people who formed the corporation, the attorney who handled the paperwork, the notary public who notarized the corporate charter and, sometimes, a more detailed statement about the business in which the corporation engages.

In this case, one name jumps out at you: It is Charles Candyman, who sold the disco to Taca. He turns out to be the president of Taca, its registered agent and one of its original incorporators three years ago. His lawyer, a well-known criminal defense attorney, is Taca's corporate secretary, though that's a little out of his line. Call another agency in the capital, the Uniform Commercial Code office. Taca, you discover, owes a restaurant supply company for its kitchen and bar equipment at the disco, but that's all. Now you call the Alcoholic Beverage Commission or whichever agency licenses bars in your state. The agency will have in its files a list of stockholders of the disco if it has a liquor license.

It turns out that there is only one stockholder—Candyman. A picture is emerging. The disco where the police found the drugs has a complicated corporate structure but only one man behind it all. That man receives large sums of money in the form of mortgage payments. This could be a clever scheme to steal from the business, then declare bankruptcy. Or it might be Candyman's way of establishing a large, on-the-record taxable income for IRS consumption, in order to conceal his real income from drug smuggling. Back to the deed books. Those other transactions involving Taca now become much more interesting than they were before. You get copies of all deeds involving the company. With each deed the pattern grows stronger. In your county alone, Taca owns 50 acres near the new free-trade zone, a key parcel next to the seaport and two old downtown hotels in the path of a new convention center, along with three condominium apartments and the disco where the drugs were found. You extend your research. The Uniform Commercial Code office does not have any record of loans on cars, airplanes or boats. Maybe that's because Candyman paid cash for his smuggling vehicles.

You call the motor vehicle records office in the capital and explain the general nature of the inquiry. A state employee looks up Candyman and Taca. Candyman owns a new Seville in his own name with no lien on it. He paid cash. Taca owns three large, straight-body trucks and a four-wheel-drive vehicle, all free and clear. The Department of Natural Resources (or the agency that licenses boats in your state) looks in its files for Candyman and Taca and discovers three Donzi speedboats, each capable of outrunning anything owned by the U.S. Customs Service. The state Department of Transportation looks up Candyman and Taca. The corporation, it seems, owns two aircraft: a plush, radar-equipped Piper Aztec, suitable for spotting ships at sea and hauling cocaine, and a Convair 220, capable of hauling 10,000-pound payloads. Taca begins to look like a smuggling conglomerate. At the local courthouse, you look up Taca in the index to see if anyone has ever sued it. There's only one case: a patron who slipped and fell on the dance floor and settled out of court.

You look up Candyman and find a divorce file. The property settlement contains a reference to Taca Investors, Ltd. You double back to the deeds office and look up Taca Investors, Ltd., kicking yourself for missing it the first time. You find three deeds and a limited partnership declaration. According to the deeds, the partnership owns an apartment building, rural acreage that includes a landing strip and some ocean-front land with a canal leading to a privately maintained channel where smugglers have been arrested before. Best of all, the declaration of partnership lists Candyman, his lawyer and a city council member as limited partners. The general partner is Taca.

According to the declaration, each investor put up one-third of the investment. But only the general partner, the corporation, can be held financially accountable, and its liability is limited by the state corporation laws. One last stop—at the criminal court building—confirms what you thought you remembered: Nine years ago, Candyman was convicted of selling 600 pounds of marijuana and a kilo of cocaine to an undercover cop. He's got a record as a dealer; he's tied to a public official; he owns boats, planes, trucks, a landing strip and a secluded harbor, all of which he paid cash for; and his criminal defense attorney is his business partner. You put it all together and call a friendly cop. You tell him what you have. The cop trades you a little information in return: Candyman is about to be arrested, along with five of his lieutenants. The officer asks you to hold the story until Candyman is arrested. You spend the time polishing the writing. Everything you have is tied to a public record. Everything is documented and almost certainly libel-proof.

⊃ CHECK IT OUT

✓ Choose a local politician who has been elected to office several times. Look up the politician's voter registration at the appropriate clerk's office and see whether the politician has voted in the last two elections. This will tell you if the politician is participating in the election process in addition to running for office.

✓ Continue your research on the local politician by going to the recorder's or registrar's office and researching whether there are any tax liens against the politician or the politician's business. Also, check at the tax collector's office to see if the politician owes taxes. This will tell you if the politician is paying taxes in a timely fashion.

✓ Continue your research on the politician by checking at the recorder's office and the secretary of state's office to see if there are any UCC filings in connection with the politician or the politician's businesses. Also, check at the recorder's office to see what mortgages there are on the politician's property by looking at the grantor/grantee index.

RESOURCES FOR REPORTING

The NICAR Net Tour (www.ire.org/training/nettour) provides a one-stop site to link to information on public records and databases and how to find them and obtain them.

Specific Sites for Finding Public Records

Use the ever-growing search index SearchSystems (www.searchsystems.net) to see what is available online at any level of government in the world. If you can't pay the monthly fee for direct links, you can see what is available and then use a search engine to find links to the records. You can also use the Public Record Finder (www.publicrecordfinder.com) to look for indexes on available public records.

Freedom of Information and Access to Government Records

The Freedom of Information Center at the Missouri School of Journalism (www.missouri.edu/~foiwww) is an excellent gateway to information on access to public records.

The National Freedom of Information Coalition (www.nfoic.org), which is also headquartered at the Missouri School of Journalism, provides links to state freedom-of-information issues and organizations around the country.

The Reporters Committee on Freedom of the Press (www.rcfp.org) has extensive information on federal and state FOI issues and also samples of open-record request letters.

The Brechner Center for Freedom of Information (www.brechner.org) also offers superb guidance on public records and access to them.

Backgrounding Individuals Through Primary Documents

The Reporter's Desktop by Duff Wilson (www.reporter.org/desktop) has practical suggestions on records searches on an individual. You'll learn how to find information on anyone at www.reporter.org/desktop/tips/johndoe.htm.

The IRE Resource Center (www.ire.org/resourcecenter) has many tip sheets on backgrounding individuals.

You can also use Ancestry.com (www.ancestry.com) to trace the genealogy of a person.

4

Computer-Assisted Reporting

This chapter shows the importance of data analysis to investigative reporting in the 21st century and how it has become an integral part of investigative stories by both reporters covering a beat and those working on long-term projects. This chapter describes the basic techniques of computer-assisted reporting and shows how to find and obtain federal and local government databases, particularly by using open-records laws. In addition, the chapter outlines the kinds of stories that can be done in any community using computer-assisted research.

Whether the story is about transportation safety, city hall, campaign contributions or government contracts, journalists everywhere are using databases for both quick and long-term stories. As we moved into the 21st century, many stories archived in the Investigative Reporters and Editors Resource Center involved database analysis as an integral part of their reporting. Consider the range of stories:

- The New York Times analyzed databases extensively while investigating what would become Pulitzer Prize–winning stories on dangerous and sometimes fatal conditions for workers in the United States and for stories on railway crossing accidents.
- Several newspapers used a U.S. database on dams to show that old and potentially dangerous dams were subjected to little or no inspection.
- Both local broadcast stations and local newspapers used databases in reporting on the ineffective placement of sirens that were supposed to warn of tornadoes.
- Many newspapers used nursing home records to show severe shortcomings in the care that nursing homes provided to the elderly.

In some of those stories, journalists acquired databases from government agencies under the Electronic Freedom of Information Act or under open records laws that require the government to release their information in electronic format. In other cases, reporters—particularly from outside the United States—built databases themselves by getting paper records and then entering the information into database software. All of these investigations used databases for context or depth or as a launching pad and tip sheet for the story. And each of these stories included old-fashioned shoe-leather reporting, such as interviewing sources and researching hard-copy documents.

Thus, database analysis—also known as computer-assisted reporting or CAR—has become an integral part of investigative reporting and has improved the accuracy, credibility and breadth of journalism.

Indeed, more journalists each year seek to learn the skills and techniques of CAR. The National Institute for Computer-Assisted Reporting, a joint program of Investigative Reporters and Editors and the University of Missouri School of Journalism, offers a broad range of training in CAR tools at the university, in on-the-road seminars and at the IRE Web site. To learn more about these tools, see "Computer-Assisted Reporting: A Practical Guide" by Brant Houston (Bedford/St. Martin's, 2004).

Finding, Accessing and Using Computer Databases

The Tools of Computer-Assisted Reporting

Many journalists are now using the tools of computer-assisted reporting: acquiring, reading and analyzing databases on a routine basis.

There are three basic tools of CAR and three advanced tools.

The first basic CAR tool is online databases. You might use online databases to find health, environmental or demographic data. Some of the more common downloaded databases include federal campaign finance reports, census data and crime statistics.

The second basic tool is spreadsheet software programs—such as Microsoft Excel—which are sophisticated calculators best used for databases with numbers, such as budgets or salaries.

The third basic tool is database manager software—such as Microsoft Access—which allows a journalist to sort, filter, summarize and compare hundreds of thousands of records quickly. For example, it is not uncommon for a journalist to obtain a database of 100,000 or more prison records to examine the early release rate for convicts.

The first advanced CAR tool is mapping software, which allows journalists to visualize extensive columns and rows of data through maps. For example, a journalist could create a map of votes to more quickly describe the geographic distribution of support for candidates in a congressional or presidential election. The most popular mapping software among journalists is ArcView.

The second advanced tool is statistical software—such as SAS or SPSS—which helps journalists search for patterns in major data sets and for possible causes of events. For example, statistical software has been widely used to examine racial disparity in the denial of home loans.

The third advanced tool is social network analysis software—such as UCINet—which helps journalists visualize connections and lines of influence between people or entities. It has been used to look at overlapping boards of directors of major corporations, charities associated with terrorists and the flow of money from political committees to candidates.

Finding Databases and Deciding Which to Use

Because governments have been using databases for decades, there are databases waiting to be analyzed for almost any story that comes to mind.

Here is a quick rundown of how to find out if a relevant government database exists for your story:

- Check the IRE Resource Center story index (www.ire.org/resourcecenter) with the key words "computer-assisted reporting" and the topic of your story to see if other news organizations found useful databases.
- Check with the NICAR database library (www.ire.org/datalibrary), which collects government databases for distribution to journalists.
- Check local, state and federal audit reports. Auditors frequently analyze an agency's databases as part of their audit and cite which databases they reviewed in the appendix of the audit.
- Check the Web site of a government agency. It often refers to databases and sometimes offers databases online that might be denied to a reporter in person.
- Check to see if there has been a recent inventory of the databases that a government administrative agency maintains. One inventory may be an agency's record-retention schedule. Agencies must keep track of the information they keep because laws stipulate how long an agency must wait before throwing out records.
- Check indexes of useful government databases. Two of those created by journalists are www.reporter.org/desktop and the NICAR Net Tour at www.ire.org/training/nettour. Another handy site is Search Systems (www.searchsystems.net), which is constantly indexing and updating data available online throughout the United States and the world.
- Using the advanced search tool of Google, specify the data type as "xls" when you search for your key words. This will find Microsoft Excel

spreadsheets associated with the key words. To find Microsoft Access databases, you can type the key word in the regular search box followed by "filetype:mdb." For example, to look for databases associated with hospitals, you would type "hospital filetype:mdb."

After a journalist ascertains that a certain database exists, there are several steps to follow before acquiring it.

First, the journalist should ask the agency for the record layout, the code sheet and the hard-copy form that is filled out for each record. The record layout shows what columns (that is, categories) of information are included in the database. A campaign contribution database, for example, would have columns for names of contributors, their addresses, amounts of contributions, kinds of contributions, dates of contributions and the names of those receiving the contributions. The code sheet translates any codes used in the database. The actual form filled out for the database is useful for checking whether all the information was entered into the database.

Second, the journalist should ask to see the actual data on a computer screen or on a printout. Just because there are columns listed in the record layout doesn't mean the data were entered. The database will be worthless if the data needed for a story aren't there.

Third, the journalist should determine what format the data are in and the size of the database. Format is important because it tells the journalist how difficult it will be for spreadsheet or database manager software to read or use the file. The size of the file allows a journalist to determine how large and fast a computer is needed to deal with the data analysis.

After receiving the database and beginning the analysis, it's always important to do an "outer integrity" check: Compare the electronic records against a sample of hard-copy records, and compare the totals of amounts in the database to totals in hard-copy reports. Also, other journalists or experts who have worked with the same database can explain its potential flaws or misleading data. Remember that every database is incomplete and imperfect—just like human sources.

Keeping Databases on Hand

Many news organizations have set up internal networked sites—intranets—that make data available to the entire newsroom or to those trained to handle data. One challenge of an intranet is determining the limitations of each database and making sure to warn reporters of those limitations. Another challenge is keeping the data sets updated.

When a newsroom wants to accumulate databases, it's difficult to choose among the huge electronic stacks that are available. Here are some general principles:

- Community databases come from more than local agencies. A multitude of regional, state, federal and commercial databases can be easily sliced to the local level.
- Whenever possible, a database should not be used for just one story. It will remain valuable for years, so it should be archived, be part of a reference library and, when appropriate, be distributed on the newsroom intranet.
- There should be a plan for the periodic updating of databases to keep them current and to provide the opportunity for trend stories.
- Journalists need to keep up with databases available online (particularly on the Internet) that can augment or update in-house databases. Make a schedule for downloading that information.
- When an electronic database doesn't exist, it's reasonable for a newsroom to consider building its own from hard copy if the database can produce a minimum story — that is, a story worthy of being published, aired or posted — and be maintained in a reference library for other stories.

Some of the newsroom databases that have been built from scratch include information on court records, local campaign finance records, police reports and government contracts. If reporters do build their own databases, they should carefully consider what information is needed for the story and do test analyses as the database is being constructed. You don't want to spend hours entering data into a database and then discover you left out a crucial column of information for the story.

Gaining Access

Elliot Jaspin, who taught many reporters how to use databases and did ground-breaking work while at The Providence Journal, once outlined his strategy for gaining access to databases. Unfortunately, even with changes in the law, much of his description still rings true:

> First thing I will do is get the paper records. For example, if I wanted to get driver's licenses, I would go in and get one person's driver's license record. Then I go back and say "How are your records kept on computer?" And generally they are pretty happy . . . to explain to me "Well, we have this thing here and whirls here and lights flash there and I take notes." . . . Then I come back and I say "Okay, I got the technical specs, and . . . I want it this way, and it's a public record because here's the

paper record I got from you folks. Now give it to me." Then they go through a period of fits and moaning at which point you say to them "Here's the state privilege of information act; it says you have got to give it to us." Now at that point they usually cave in. If they don't cave in — this is absolutely key to our operation — it is as certain as the sun comes up that we're going to file a lawsuit.

Today, obtaining a paper record first is not always possible. A Houston Chronicle series about access told of a local police department that entered crime reports into computer terminals with no paper backup. In the past, citizens could read reports at no charge. But citizens now had to pay, sight unseen, for computer printouts. Another police department no longer separated public information from private in computer printouts. Each had to be reviewed by a police lawyer.

David Armstrong, formerly of The Boston Globe and now at The Wall Street Journal, says money often is a sticking point, as when an agency agrees to provide information but at an enormous cost. Armstrong's response:

> In most instances, the agency attempts to take advantage of the reporter's perceived lack of computer knowledge. . . . Always require a detailed estimate. You want to know Central Processing Unit time cost per hour, the cost per hour of a programmer, and all other costs for which you are being billed. Now that you have that information, here are some favorite, and real, shenanigans to look for. . . . Agencies have attempted to bill the newspaper $60 per hour and up for the work of a government computer programmer. Just do some simple math and calculate the rate out to an annual salary ($117,000). . . . Obviously, no programmer in government is paid that much.

Local Data Sources

Before there were databases, good journalists kept contact Rolodexes, index cards and hard-copy reports as aids to understanding a community and to doing investigations. Much of the information in this chapter is simply instructions on how to obtain in electronic form what reporters formerly acquired on paper. What complicates this process is the availability of the local data, which varies because of state laws and which is sometimes withheld because of concerns about security or privacy.

Most states now have their open-records laws on the Web, but a helpful guide is also available through the Reporters Committee for Freedom of the Press. The committee's Web site (www.rcfp.org) also has the complete Electronic Freedom of Information Act and sample requests for electronic information. The IRE Web site (www.ire.org) also has sample freedom-of-information requests.

Newsrooms can now break down basic local databases into different categories based on a beat or topic.

Politics

A voter registration database is an excellent tool for finding and identifying people in the community. The tabulations of votes in previous elections are often kept in electronic form.

Campaign finance reports are critical. Make sure to get federal campaign contributions reports for local House and Senate seats, which are available electronically. For state legislators and municipal candidates, it's well worth building databases of contributions and expenditures in local elections if these data are not available in electronic form. These databases help to trace the lines of influence and the players in a community, and they provide yet another "people finder."

Most communities require some officeholders to file disclosures on their business and personal finances to prevent conflicts of interest. Sometimes these are electronic, but if not, a newsroom can build a database of these records.

Business and Economy

The federal and state governments may provide an overview of economic data, but the only place that a reporter can get the nitty-gritty data is at local offices. For a profile of businesses, a newsroom can begin with the database of business licenses issued by the city or county. Those records should have the names of the operators of the businesses and the addresses and types of businesses in the community. Other license databases to obtain include taxi licenses and liquor licenses. (Liquor licenses may be issued by the state.) To see loans obtained by businesses for equipment or other assets, look for the Uniform Commercial Code records, which are generally electronic. A database of building permits also helps gauge a community's economic health.

Property and Tax Records

A database of property-assessment records can reveal whether the taxes are fair for each property owner. This database is critical for looking at the equity of the property tax system because it shows the value of a piece of property as assessed by government officials. Taxes then are based on that assessed value. If two similar houses have very different assessed values, then one taxpayer is being unfairly taxed.

Tax delinquency records should be updated twice a year. The tax collector's office keeps these records, which frequently forecast business or personal bankruptcies. They can be checked against public officials' names too.

If a county maintains a database of tax liens, a newsroom should obtain it. Tax liens, filed by the Internal Revenue Service or the state against businesses or individuals, also forecast business or personal financial problems and offer numerous tips for stories.

Crime and Guns

The FBI's Uniform Crime Reports is a standard database to have. It should be supplemented by Bureau of Justice Statistics surveys and any local crime data sets that are available. The FBI excludes certain crimes if they do not fit into the FBI's definition. For example, the FBI's definition of rape doesn't match that of several states. Furthermore, a database of local incidents, arrests and charges gives a more detailed look at crime in the community.

Most communities have a database of gun permits issued, and the federal Bureau of Alcohol, Tobacco and Firearms maintains a database of registered gun dealers. The federal database can be cross-referenced with local business licenses to see whether local gun dealers have the proper licenses.

Education

Test score databases are available from both local and state agencies and are standard databases to have in the newsroom. School enrollment databases are good for education stories and for stories that show how a community is changing. Personnel information about school employees (name, title, salary, date of hire and other information) can be coupled with their time and attendance records.

Courts and Jails

Many courts have electronic civil and criminal dockets. A database of dockets for the preceding year can show patterns of litigation. The personnel database for courts is another must-have.

Local jails keep a database of prisoners and usually have data on race and ethnicity and whether individual inmates are awaiting trial or have been convicted.

City and County Government

Every newsroom should have a database on municipal employees that includes name, title, gender, race, department, salary and date of hire. This database should be updated every six months.

A vendor database—listing companies and individuals supplying goods and services to the municipality and revealing how much each of them was paid—should be updated twice a year. It can be compared to databases on campaign finance.

Databases of building and restaurant inspections should also be kept, along with actions and fines.

Infrastructure

Two good databases available from the federal government are the National Bridge Inventory and the Dam Inventory. NICAR has these databases and can inexpensively slice and distribute local data from them. NICAR also distributes many of the databases mentioned below in "Resources for Reporting." A list can be found on the IRE Web site (www.ire.org/datalibrary/databases) with descriptions of the information in those databases.

Accidents

If it collides, newsrooms want to report on it. There are several good federal databases to check for possible stories and to keep as references:

- *Highways.* FARS (Fatality Analysis Reporting System) is the federal database giving the location of accidents and the number of fatalities nationwide. State highway patrols generally have more detailed information on both fatal and nonfatal accidents.
- *Aircraft.* The Federal Aviation Administration, the National Transportation Safety Board and the National Aeronautics and Space Administration all have reports on maintenance problems and in-flight difficulties for specific aircraft.
- *Railroads.* The Federal Railroad Administration offers a downloadable database on its Web site (http://safetydata.fra.dot.gov/officeofsafety) that shows where railway crossing accidents occur.
- *Boating.* The Coast Guard keeps a database with detailed information on boating accidents—both in the ocean and on inland waterways in the United States.

The Environment

There are numerous environmental databases, but a good start is the Toxic Release Inventory kept by both state agencies and the U.S. Environmental Protection Agency. The database offers information on estimated pollution by manufacturers. Newsrooms should assume there is a database—and probably more than one—for any potential story relating to the environment.

State Data Sources

Even before looking for locally kept data, reporters should tap into key state agencies for online data and databases that can be brought in-house. Note that this list mirrors many of the hard-copy documents mentioned in this handbook. Furthermore, not every state has opened all these records, but most of these databases with local information are available.

A number of state agencies have valuable data:

- The tax department: income levels of individuals, businesses, homeowners and renters.
- The secretary of state: databases on for-profit and nonprofit corporations, partnerships and election information. (The IRS database on the financial filings of nonprofits is a good supplement to this information.)
- The labor department: employment by industry, wages and income.
- The judicial department or highway patrol: arrest and crime statistics.
- The education department: extensive information on schools, budgets and testing.
- The health department: data on medical facilities and health statistics.
- The transportation department: accidents, spending and infrastructure.
- The economic or finance department: state funding patterns.
- The housing department: data on public and private housing.
- The vital statistics department: birth and death records.
- Professional and occupational licensing boards: databases of the names and addresses of the professionals they license.
- Motor vehicles department: driver's licenses.

Yahoo! offers indexes on information available in the states and locally through their directory. Also, state agencies and municipalities are now making some of their databases available online.

Federal Data Sources

Demographic Data

Census data are a key component for a database library for community reporting. The census serves not only as a way to better understand the composition and change in a community, but also as a template for investigative stories.

Recently, the U.S. Census Bureau added a yearly survey to supplement its 10-year census report. The American Community Survey is a nationwide survey to provide communities with "a fresh look" at how they are changing. The survey collects updated information that includes age, race, income, and home value, and that information can be critical in looking at social injustice.

Census data generally comes out in several releases, with more detail with each release, so it is important to understand what each release offers. For more detailed information on the census, go to the U.S. Census Bureau Web site (www.census.gov). For more information on reporting on the census, go to www.2000census.org, which is operated by IRE and is a good one-stop Web site that also links to other sites, such as that of census expert and Arizona State University professor Steve Doig.

Journalists can use demographic information to gain greater understanding of information in databases on other topics. Reporters have matched lottery ticket sales to income data to show how the poor are gambling the most, house mortgage denials against racial data to show racial disparity, toxic waste sites against income data to show how toxic chemicals are being dumped in poor areas of town, and disallowed voter ballots against racial data to show that the oldest election technology is used in minority areas. To supplement federal census data, journalists should make contacts with state data centers and local demographers.

For profiling community demographics, the Census Bureau Web site provides other useful data sets that can be downloaded, as well as links to other sites. For detailed information on Census Bureau Web sites, see "Resources for Reporting" at the end of this chapter.

Other Federal Data Sources

There are many federal databases that can help journalists track the impact of federal money on the local economy. The Consolidated Federal Funds Report shows how much federal money is flowing into an area through expenditures, grants and loans. The entire database is available for purchase. The Small Business Administration offers databases that show which businesses in a community have received loans guaranteed by the government and which businesses or individuals have received loans after a disaster.

⊃ CHECK IT OUT

✓ Go to the Data Library page of the IRE Web site (www.ire.org/datalibrary), and review the file layouts and sample data of three transportation databases.

✓ At the Data Library page of the IRE Web site, download the Microsoft Excel file of fatal boating accidents. Using Excel's filter function, select all deaths caused by drowning in which boaters were not wearing a life jacket. (See the tutorial linked to the data set for help in filtering.)

✓ Go to the Web site of the Environmental Protection Agency (www.epa.gov), and download a local data set of the Toxic Release Inventory in an Excel worksheet. Sort the data set from high to low, based on total emissions by manufacturers. (See the tutorial linked to the data set at www.ire.org/datalibrary.)

RESOURCES FOR REPORTING

General CAR Web Sites

These organizations and Web sites offer a wide range of information about computer-assisted reporting:

- IRE Resource Center (www.ire.org/resourcecenter)
- IRE's NICAR Net Tour (www.ire.org/training/nettour)
- IRE and NICAR databases (www.ire.org/datalibrary/databases)
- The Reporter's Committee for Freedom of the Press (www.rcfp.org)
- The Reporter's Desktop (www.reporter.org/desktop)
- Right to Know Network (www.rtk.net/rtkdata.html)

Census Web Sites

Profiles of local economic sectors by city or ZIP code are available at www .census.gov/econ/census02. Databases on county business patterns that show employment, payroll and business size distribution can be obtained at www .census.gov/epcd/cbp/view/cbpview.html. But you can also build your own profiles using the American Factfinder tool at the Census site.

The Internal Revenue Service Migration data set also adds information to the census. You can buy county-to-county and state-to-state migration data at www.irs.gov/taxstats/productsandpubs.

The Bureau of Labor Statistics also has data on employment and unemployment (www.bls.gov/data), while the Bureau of Economic Analysis has data on personal income at its BEA Regional Facts Web site (BearFacts, www.bea.gov/ regional/bearfacts).

The IRE Web site offers workshops and training for journalists working with federal census data (www.2000census.org).

Commercial Demographic Databases

The information that can be gleaned from the following sites is a good, reliable starting point, but this listing is only a sample of the available demographic and economic data sets.

- RAND (www.rand.org)—demographic and real estate data
- Claritas (www.claritas.com)—demographic, wealth and income, and retail sales data
- Woods and Poole Economics (www.woodsandpoole.com)—economic and demographic data

- Global Insight (www.wefa.com)—economic and wealth data
- DataQuick (www.dataquick.com)—real estate data

Subject-Specific Databases

For local economic data:

- Census Bureau's County Business Patterns (www.census.gov/epcd/cbp/view/cbpview.html)

For transportation:

- Fatality Analysis Reporting System (FARS, www-fars.nhtsa.dot.gov)
- Federal Railroad Administration (http://safetydata.fra.dot.gov/officeofsafety)

For politics:

- IRE's Campaign Finance Information Center (www.campaignfinance.org)

For the environment:

- EPA's Toxic Release Inventory Program (www.epa.gov/tri)

5

People Trails

*This chapter examines how to find and develop sources — both on background
and on the record — while doing an investigation. There are many ways to find
sources today, both through face-to-face meetings and online search engines and
indexes. In addition, journalists' interviewing techniques have become more
sophisticated. This chapter will discuss both how to approach potential sources
and how to handle people when they do decide to talk.*

Learning about individuals, issues or institutions from secondary and primary
documents is a critical part of investigative journalism, but it goes hand in hand
with interviewing. Often, document searches come before interviews because
it is better to go into interviews having done the research. As noted earlier in
the book, you can ask far more penetrating and intelligent questions if you
have done your "homework" before sitting down to talk to a source. Sometimes, though, a preliminary informational interview with a source can provide
a journalist with a roadmap for asking for and finding the right documents.

In either case, despite the heavy emphasis in this book on document research, the document trail alone is seldom adequate. According to Steve Lux-
enberg, a long-time newspaper projects editor,

> Records are a means to an end, not the end in itself. A record is often conclusive
> proof of something, but records can also be wrong. They can lead you to a certain
> set of facts, but they can also lead you astray. What I'm saying is this — use your
> common sense. Think about what the records are saying. Above all, call the people
> who created or maintain the records, and ask them to explain them. Call the people
> whose lives are being described in the records, and give them a chance to say what
> the records mean. . . . Records don't tell you why something happened, they just tell
> you what happened.

Because interviewing is tied up with understanding human nature, there is
always more to learn. John Sawatsky is a legendary investigative reporter from
Ottawa and has become a widely regarded expert in interviewing techniques,
teaching journalists at the Canadian Broadcasting Corporation, doing regional
training, writing about interviewing and then becoming a consultant for ESPN.

His interviews are so productive that his name has become a verb, as in, "Have you been Sawatskyed?" That productivity comes from decades of study and application, from trying techniques that seem counterintuitive to routine journalism interviews.

Identifying and Evaluating Sources

"Currents" and "Formers"

Journalists frequently get advice and training on finding documents, but they don't get the training they need on finding sources. When beginning an investigation, a journalist can take one quick organizational step by dividing potential sources into "currents" and "formers."

"Currents" are those people currently dealing with an organization: current employees, current contractors, current consultants and so on. They are usually easy to find with directories, phone calls and e-mail. "Formers" are those who used to belong to or do business with the organization.

Experienced investigative journalists work to keep up with where "formers" go from an agency or business they are covering. They know that a "former" is much more likely to talk freely about their previous place of work. But finding "formers" can be difficult when you are starting an investigation of an agency you haven't covered before.

In each investigation, it's good to make a list of potential interviewees. Let's say a journalist is looking into alleged misconduct by a company president. Among the potential interviewees would be

- Current and former board directors of the company
- Current and former employees who have had routine contact with the president
- Current and former employees at past places of employment
- Current and former executives at competing companies
- Current and former labor union leaders, if there has been union activity
- Current and former in-house and outside lawyers, accountants, stockbrokers and so on
- Current and former licensed professionals providing services to the company
- Current and former neighbors
- Current and former leaders at the subject's place of worship

- Current and former colleagues from clubs or lodges
- Current and former social friends
- Current and former spouses
- Family members, including children, siblings, cousins, aunts, uncles, nieces, nephews and their families

We will list more ways later in the chapter, but good starting points for finding "formers" are checking newspaper archives for articles that deal with the comings and goings of people in government and business. Newspaper business sections often are packed with such items. Check press releases from the agency or business. Check industry magazines. And of course check with "currents" on where the "formers" have gone.

Whistleblowers

One type of source is the whistleblower. Whistleblowers are "currents" or "formers" who seek attention or find themselves unwillingly in the spotlight because they know of wrongdoing. Their importance in exposing wrongdoing is recognized by a federal law, the Whistleblower Protection Act, and by some state laws. Many state legislatures have approved whistleblower laws protecting public employees; some states also provide protections for private-sector employees. The federal government and states have public records not only about the individual whistleblower but also about the alleged corporate or government transgressions that led to the whistleblowing.

Many whistleblowers are sincere and correct in their assertions, having become whistleblowers reluctantly because they could not change the organization through regular channels. Some are correct but are seeking either publicity or payback because they are disgruntled. Others are sincere but ultimately incorrect, perhaps coming forward because of mental instability. Some may simply want money; whistleblowers can receive monetary awards under the federal False Claims Acts if the government collects a penalty from the company.

If a journalist is not contacted directly by a whistleblower, he or she can find whistleblowers through other people or documents. If the employer is unionized, union representatives can serve as a contact between the journalist and whistleblower. If the whistleblower has worked for the federal government, the Web sites of the federal Office of Special Counsel and the federal Merit Systems Protection Board are excellent sources of potential whistleblowers. An investigative journalist also can call watchdog groups such as the Government Accountability Project or go to the organization's Web site.

Outside Experts

Journalists can benefit by interviewing outside experts who, unlike whistle-blowers, do not have to worry about recognition leading to disciplinary action. Experts are especially prevalent at universities, which often publish directories of faculty members who are willing to talk to journalists. They often are what longtime investigative reporter Mike Berens calls "the detached source."

It is important to background outside experts to see if their knowledge is up-to-date and if they are respected in the field. Being an expert can be big business for some individuals. A journalist should check the résumé and newspaper articles on these sources before interviewing them. Also, several journalists have shared their indexes of reliable experts on the Web, and members of IRE frequently share their experience with experts with other members.

One place to start to find experts is the Research Centers and Services Directory (http://library.dialog.com/bluesheets/html/bl0115.html), which contains information on 27,500 organizations worldwide that are conducting research. Other sources to consult are the Washington Information Directory from Congressional Quarterly Inc. and the Encyclopedia of Associations, covering about 23,000 groups, from Gale Research. Specialized groups have their own organizations too, such as the American Society of Association Executives. PR Newswire runs ProfNet, a Web service that is a network of organizations with experts. When a journalist posts a query to the system, it goes to thousands of universities, corporations, nonprofits and public relations firms. The service is free to journalists.

Most organizations of significant size have public information officers with their own specialties. Sometimes journalists get what they need from public information officers. But it is not always useful to go to the publicists or their supervisors, because bosses are frequently unaware of what is happening in the ranks.

Think tanks are other valuable places to locate experts, although think tanks can have an ideological bias, and that bias must be identified in any story.

Many think tanks are located in Washington, D.C., including the American Enterprise Institute for Public Policy Research, the Heritage Foundation, and the Brookings Institution. A second geographic locale filled with think tanks is California; the Hoover Institution at Stanford University and the RAND Corporation in Santa Monica are examples. The Scientists' Institute for Public Information is a far-flung think tank whose experts have agreed to share their expertise with journalists. Some of the experts who reply to journalists' queries may have financial or ideological ties that journalists will need to evaluate.

When experts are used from these think tanks, it is critical that the journalist identify the think tank's ideology or politics.

Locating Sources

Once identified, sources must be located. When a source's whereabouts is not readily available, there are many resources that can help journalists in tracking him or her down.

Online Tools

Nora Paul and Kathleen A. Hansen, authors of the newly revised "Computer-Assisted Research: Information Strategies and Tools for Journalists," explain how much easier it is to locate a source, thanks to the Internet.

E-mail. They advise that finding an e-mail address for a source or subject might actually be easier than finding an unlisted telephone number. There are multiple sources for finding e-mail addresses, including www.whowhere.com, www.infospace.com and www.iaf.net, as well as online e-mail directories maintained by universities, corporations and other institutions.

Discussion groups, called listservs. There is an e-mail discussion list (or listserv) for just about every topic. As they say, "Anyone with a specific beat . . . should subscribe to at least one discussion list on that topic. This is a great way to keep up with what experts are talking about, solicit information, advice or contacts from them and to generally tap into a broad expert base." You can find listservs at www.tile.net/lists or www.lsoft.com/lists/listref.html.

Newsgroups. Newsgroups are collections of messages distributed through Usenet, a system invented to move information from network to network rather than individual to individual. One excellent newsgroup directory is Google Groups at http://groups.google.com.

Personal and professional Web sites or blogs. A journalist should check whether the source or subject has an individual Web page. More contact information might appear there. A journalist could start by simply typing the individual's name into a Web search engine like Google or using one of the many blog index sites like Quacktrack (www.quacktrack.com), Technorati (www.technorati.com) or Google Blogsearch (http://blogsearch.google.com).

Telephone Directories

Journalists should always consult phone directories, either online or in print.

Phone directories are effective for finding many "formers," who leave jobs but stay in the same geographic area. There are many online databases combining thousands of hard-copy telephone directories, making it easier than ever before to locate "formers."

The Internet offers many possibilities for locating individuals through telephone numbers and e-mail addresses. The IRE Web site lists the best of the current services. When looking for someone who is hard to find, be sure to use multiple online directories. An investigative journalist might find current and past addresses at www.zabasearch.com, www.switchboard.com, www.anywho .com, www.infospace.com or www.whitepages.com.

City Directories

Because so many telephone numbers in the United States are unlisted (as many as two-thirds in some cities), journalists must frequently go beyond telephone directories to locate sources. Commercial companies, most notably R.L. Polk, produce city directories for thousands of locales in the United States and Canada. Public and newsroom libraries often have current and past volumes.

Instead of using print versions, it's now easier to go to the Web to find reverse directories, such as www.411.com and www.infousa.com. In addition to the traditional alphabetical listing, these directories also list the names of adults at the same address, plus their occupations; telephone numbers in numerical order (so 874-2221 would follow 874-2220); and street-by-street, block-by-block listings. The Web site www.whitepages.com can show the name and phone number of a potential source's neighbor. A Sports Illustrated reporter found a former neighbor of a subject through this kind of directory. The building manager could not help and tenant records went back only five years, but the former neighbor knew where the target had gone.

Workplace Directories

One of the most useful directories is the workplace directory. Whenever a journalist begins an investigation, he or she should get the in-house directory, whether it's for a business, government agency, church, college or social organization. Alumni directories are particularly useful. For example, the Association of National Security Alumni, whose members are former employees of the Central Intelligence Agency and other security agencies, has its own publication called "Unclassified."

Many, if not most, internal directories are in databases. At the St. Paul Pioneer Press, the newsroom has in-house access to a computer database of all city employees. Other directories may be found on the Web in a spreadsheet format by just specifying the format as "xls" in the advanced search areas.

Personal Habits

Some seemingly hard-to-find individuals can be located through a combination of detective work and common sense. If somebody is known to fish or hunt regularly, for example, an address might show up on an application for a fishing or hunting license.

Most people live according to patterns. What are the potential source's habits? Does he frequent a diner at breakfast because of its famous biscuits? Does he normally have lunch downtown once a week with a men's empowerment group? Can he be found at a particular church for Sunday services? What about the Tuesday night bowling league that his former supervisor mentioned? Maybe calling the labor union he belongs to will yield a workplace shift.

Useful Documents and Records

Voter registration records can lead to a local address, as can pilot's licenses. Driver's license records used to be especially efficient for this purpose; driver's license databases are statewide (voter registration, in contrast, is county by county), and the majority of Americans age 16 or older have a license. The records are kept in the state capital; the agency in most states is named the Department of Motor Vehicles or something similar. However, in recent years some states have made the information in driver's licenses private.

Nevertheless, in some states it is still possible to request an individual's license information in person, by mail, by tapping into the agency's database online after an account has been established or by obtaining the full database from the agency. If the subject fails to show up in the driver's license database, the motor vehicles department might have information about transferred licenses, indicating which state received the records when the subject applied there.

When driver's license information is unobtainable, there are many potential alternatives. Pet licenses often contain otherwise unlisted numbers. When people are trying to escape detection, they sometimes leave clues by adopting a variation of their name, a nickname or their mother's maiden name. A Boston detective found a suspected murderer 25 years after the killing by starting with his given name, his nickname (Stacey) and his mother's maiden name (Griffin). The name the suspect was using? Stacey Griffin.

Mapping Power Structures

Whether investigating an agency, business or institution, it is often clear who has ultimate authority in the organization. But sometimes titles and organization charts can be deceptive. In some cities, the mayor is a figurehead, with major employers calling the shots from their closed weekly luncheons. In some universities, the chancellor is a rubber stamp for the board of regents. A journalist should be able to discern and then penetrate power structures. To this purpose, some journalists have used social network analysis—an accepted method of social science—to diagram networks of power.

In fact, as long ago as 1976, IRE's Arizona Project got the assistance of a university professor to diagram the informal power structure of Phoenix, Arizona. Members of the Arizona Project team were reporters who came to Arizona to finish the work of journalist Don Bolles, who had been murdered while reporting on public corruption. The power structure of Phoenix actually called themselves the "Phoenix 40," since they were 40 movers and shakers in business and government who often kept a low profile. The project resulted in a 23-part series that exposed an extensive web of organized crime, public corruption and land fraud in Arizona.

On a less ambitious scale, an investigative journalist might compose profiles of individuals in the power structure as a way of educating readers, listeners or viewers. A Seattle Times reporter did that when she wrote a feature about a consultant involved in opposing limits on downtown Seattle skyscrapers, keeping the professional baseball team from moving to another city and helping New York investors buy the landmark Pike Place Market without significant opposition. Despite his involvement in these activities, his name was little known to those outside the power structure.

Philip J. Trounstine, when at the San Jose Mercury News, wrote extensively about power structures. In an article he wrote for The IRE Journal, Trounstine described the "reputational model" he developed over the years, which asks the influential members of a community or organization who they believe are the most powerful. We've excerpted parts of the article that describe how a journalist might use this model:

> You start by pulling together every conceivable list you can get your hands on. Political organizations, corporations, banks, neighborhood groups, churches, civic organizations—absolutely any forum that you think plays some role in your community. Study local histories and back newspaper clips. Who surfaced in [controversies over] issues? Who led fights? Who founded businesses and philanthropic projects? Who ran campaigns? Be especially careful to seek minority group leaders

and women. They will seldom appear among the most powerful so you have to guard against bias at the outset by making sure you have included them in the original stages.

Create a [file] for each person, listing relevant information. . . . Be sure to check the country clubs and other exclusive groups; if your community has a social register, use it. . . . Do not be afraid to add or cut names if you are convinced it is the right thing to do. I try to be as inclusive as possible, working with about 200 names. . . . The next step . . . involves selecting about 15 initial judges to cut the list down to size. This is probably the most critical stage of the process and the step most fraught with subjectivity.

The idea is to choose people you . . . consider close to and knowledgeable about power and influence in your community. But the list must also be broad-based. Key city or county bureaucrats, chamber of commerce insiders, minority community leaders, United Way fund-raisers, socialites, grass-roots organizers, bankers, news media executives, education leaders, labor leaders, behind-the-scenes politicians, religious leaders, elected officials—all these should be considered. Be sure to have women [and minorities] among the initial judges.

Now you need to draw up a form to use as a questionnaire. . . . The first task for the judges, interviewed individually and confidentially, is to work from the list of names, placing the top 30 leaders in approximate rank order. The idea is to get them to think in terms of across-the-board power and influence—political, economic, cultural and social issues. Those in the top ten will get three points; those in the middle ten, two points; and those in the third ten, one point.

From [sociologist Floyd] Hunter's original work I have devised the following series of questions. You could come up with others:

- If a project were before the community that required decisions by a group of leaders, which ten could put it over?

- Name the ten persons most effective at initiating projects.

- Name the ten persons most effective at stopping projects.

In discussion with respondents, I explain that a project could be anything—political, social, economic or cultural. The idea is to think of those who individually and collectively best fit the category. They can overlap.

Be sure also to tell judges that they are not limited by the initial list of names. If someone they think of belongs on the list of 30 or on any list of ten, by all means include them. The study is open-ended and it is possible you may have overlooked someone.

I also ask judges to name the person who has the most power, the person who exercises the most power, the most influential person in town and the top leader in town. Each person named gets five points. By asking questions this way it is possible to distinguish subtle differences among leaders and power holders. After the judge has completed the form—this takes about 45 minutes to an hour—I generally discuss some of the choices with him. My experience is that only if you guarantee confidentiality will people openly discuss those named as powerful. But if you do, you will get remarkably candid insights. After the second stage is completed, tally the results. You should come up with a cluster of people—from 20 to 40 names—that appear to stand apart from the others.

Let us say it is 30 names. Alphabetize that list, draw up a new questionnaire and you are ready for round two of interviews. This time you want to narrow the choices more exactly. I ask each person to list, in precise rank order, the most powerful and influential persons in town. Be sure to tell them they are not bound by the list. Number one gets ten points, and number ten gets one point. This time I ask, If a project were before the community that required decisions by a group of leaders, which four could put it over? Each person named gets five points. (I then follow with the same questions as before.) I also throw in, Name the most underrated leader. Name the most overrated leader. Name the most trusted leader. Name the least trusted leader.

No points are assigned to the answers, but the questions yield new dimensions for the final stories. . . . After interviews with as many of the 30 as possible . . . you once again tally the results. In my experience, there is generally a small group that stands apart from the others.

. . . Often your readers will not know who some of the top ten are. I have found that many reporters have never heard of some of the people, or if they had heard of them, they had no idea they were influential. Both those situations are good reasons for doing power structure stories.

Understanding the power structure of any institution gives a journalist a road map for ferreting out secret sources and hidden motivations. Journalists should keep a directory of those who do not hold high official positions yet wield influence in the community.

Interviewing Sources

Once a journalist has located potential sources, the next steps are learning about the subjects, scheduling interviews in a logical order (if the schedules of those involved allow), eliciting information on the record and condensing it fairly and accurately, all without burning bridges for future investigations. The more you put into building relationships and lists of sources, the easier your reporting will become.

Information about obscure events and inner lives does not normally come that easily. Developing trusting, reliable sources can be hard work. Reporter Lisa Hoffman shared her techniques with the Missouri Group, authors of "News Reporting and Writing." One of her tips is to think of beat sources as extended family:

To become part of the family, you must convince your sources that you're a human being and that you're interested in them as people, too. I take them out to lunch or for drinks. I ask about their spouses and children and tell them about the fight I had with my boyfriend and the movie I saw Saturday night. I bitch about my editors and grumble about the play of a story. Many have only a "Front Page" perspective of the news business, and most are fascinated by how the process really works.

Hoffman ignores top-down protocol when it interferes with the quest for truth: "I check each morning with the secretaries who answer the phones, open the mail, prepare the dockets. Like most mothers, they're the ones who keep the household running. They also know first what is going on."

Researching the Source

An interview might focus on an issue, the person being interviewed or an institution or organization or a topic about which the person has special knowledge. Whatever the emphasis is, the interviewer needs to know as much as possible going into the interview. Author Walt Harrington has a specific goal: "To understand people as they understand themselves. One of my profile subjects . . . a man whose son had committed suicide, described better than I ever could what I hope to discover—'Your thoughts when you say your prayers in a quiet room.' Yes, exactly."

In his book "American Profiles: Somebodies and Nobodies Who Matter," Harrington writes,

> I try to approach each subject, whether a vice president or a retarded man, from the same cast of mind—the belief that each person, famous or obscure, is at once ordinary and extraordinary in his own way. My job is to discover those ways.
>
> Always, I begin my research looking for continuities or rifts in each person's life that might help clarify how he or she came to be the person he or she is. I look for the social context—how a subject's sex, race, age, religion, or social class might have shaped his or her life. I look for the individual context—how family and personal experiences might have shaped a subject.

Some potential subjects and sources have provided clues to the continuities and rifts by publishing autobiographical material, writing such material but never publishing it beyond circulating it to family members, or posting it to anonymous blogs. It is wise to search for published material (online and off) and unpublished material. After the capture of child molester and murderer Joseph Duncan in May 2005, journalists discovered his blog, where Duncan discussed his daily fight against succumbing to his violent fantasies and his sense of persecution as a registered sex offender.

Interviewers should know how to speak the language of their potential sources. If an outsider wanted to chronicle the work of journalists, it would be necessary to understand terms like "scoop," "lead," "managing editor," "field producer," and "computer-assisted reporting." Similarly, an interviewer speaking to a physicist should understand quarks; one looking into airline safety should understand stress fractures before asking questions of an engineer. Good preparation leads to productive interviews.

When preparing for interviews, an investigative journalist should look not only for lies but also for neutral and positive information. Some information can be used as an icebreaker, to show something common between the reporter's life and the interviewee's. Knowing the interviewee collects stamps is an icebreaker, especially if the interviewer is also a collector. Or perhaps the connection will be that the subject's daughter is attending the same college the journalist attended two decades earlier. A journalist knowledgeable about the interviewee's employer or specialty (such as nuclear waste disposal) will impress the source, whose prior experience with journalists may have left the impression that they tend to be inadequately prepared.

The positive information might relate to the interviewee's accomplishments. An interviewer should work into the conversation the interviewee's receipt of a local award or authorship of a book. Compliments can be a door opener; furthermore, mentioning positive information is one more way to demonstrate preparation.

Documents discovered during preparation can come in handy during the interview. In John Ullmann's book "Investigative Reporting: Advanced Methods and Techniques," the now-deceased journalist Jerry Uhrhammer said that reluctant witnesses are more willing to talk if they are being asked about documents and what those documents mean. This approach has an added advantage: If you get good documentation, it often obviates the need for a human source, named or unnamed, in the story. This can appeal to someone who may have key knowledge of what's happened but doesn't want to be publicly associated with the story.

Looking for Credentials Fraud in Résumés

An investigative journalist should check a source's résumé line by line for exaggerations or falsifications. Journalists have over the years found inflated or false résumés by school superintendents, academics, politicians and businesspeople. After Hurricane Katrina, reporters discovered that the head of the federal disaster agency had no real qualifications for his job and had even misstated his job title and duties when working for a city in Oklahoma.

Many assertions on a résumé can be checked easily. College degrees can be verified with a call to the campus registrar. If a subject mentions military service, a journalist should check the local courthouse for military discharge Form DD 214. As private investigator Edmund J. Pankau said in his book "Check It Out," "Personal references are almost always chosen by the job applicant, so if that person is a fraud, you had better not depend on those references, because they could even be an integral part of the scam. The telephone number of a supposed past employer might be the number of a friend or answering service that has been paid to lie."

False identities are so easy to create that when a Hartford Courant reporter set out to adopt one for himself as part of a newspaper project, he had little trouble becoming someone who had died 31 years earlier as a 4-day-old infant.

Getting in the Door

When time permits, some journalists try the old-fashioned way to set up an interview: They write a letter. Often, though, it is a phone call or an e-mail that begins the process. The timing of phone calls must be considered ahead of time. Knowing a person's work hours allows a journalist to call at the start of the workday; if the person is known to be a workaholic, the journalist can call after hours when there is no assistant to intercept the call.

But even when a journalist gets through by telephone, it still may be an inconvenient time for a source. A journalist should quickly arrange another time to call that is convenient for the source or should arrange a meeting away from the source's workplace.

E-mail is more frequently used now, but the subject heading needs to be precise so the e-mail won't get blocked as spam. It is wise to follow up the e-mail with a phone call.

Writing letters is one way to overcome the perils of phone and e-mail. Most sources see mail addressed to them. Furthermore, most people read their mail when they have time; letters are not as intrusive as telephone calls. They can reread the letter, too, mulling it over. The words do not disappear as in telephone calls.

The wording of the letter is crucial. Reporter Olive Talley says, "I formulate what is going to be my standard explanation of what the story is about, and I tell everybody the same thing. . . . That way, if people you talk to compare notes, they will have heard the same story."

While formulating your wording, journalist and author Steve Weinberg suggests avoiding words like "interview" and "investigation." "Instead," he says, "I use phrases such as, 'I would like to talk with you to fill gaps in my research.' When I have reason to believe sources are reluctant or hostile, I explain why it is in their interest to talk. That involves first guessing why a source would talk to any journalist, then figuring out why you."

On the matter of why a source would talk to any journalist, investigator Don Ray says, "She has to, it's her job; she believes strongly in her cause; she wants to defend herself against rumors; she hopes the exposure will help her career." People have many reasons to talk to journalists, sometimes just because they are curious about what the journalist is working on. On the matter of why a source would talk to a particular journalist, Ray lists these reasons: "She believes you really understand and care; she is impressed with your previous work; she believes you have information to share."

If a source is reluctant to talk, a journalist can use a third party to vouch for his or her integrity. The timing and order of interviews is often important. In difficult stories, always assume every question and statement you make in an interview might be repeated to the next person you interview. If a source refuses to talk to a journalist, then it's time for the journalist to appear at the person's home or office—depending on which is appropriate—and politely explain why it is important that the journalist speak with the source.

When contacted, some people may want to talk but feel they cannot for job-related or legal reasons. In those cases, an investigative journalist could ask where else information might be obtained. The source might reveal a specific person to talk to or the precise location of relevant files. The classic investigative book "All the President's Men," by Bob Woodward and Carl Bernstein, has many examples of this kind of technique.

In any case, a positive mental attitude might tip the balance. Reporter Eric Nalder says, "As a warm-up, maybe during your morning shower, imagine a successful interview. Reporters who don't believe they will get the interview . . . usually fail. As far as I'm concerned, no one should ever refuse to talk to me. It works."

The time and place of a potentially difficult interview are crucial. Meeting the source at home makes sense if the journalist knows that contacting the source at his or her workplace could be damaging to the source's career. But the office may make more sense if the source will be more comfortable there. If the journalist works in a newsroom, that might be the best place because a source won't be seen by chance in public with the reporter. If complete confidentiality is an issue, the journalist should be careful to prevent being seen by others.

Understanding the Source's Motivations

It is the journalist's responsibility to try to understand the motivation of an interviewee, whether a "current" or a "former." The journalist should also know what defects or shortcomings the "current" or "former" has, since any source may come under attack or criticism. After all, a "current" can be just as unreliable as a "former" who holds a grudge.

Mike Berens has put together a description of various kinds of interviewees and their motivations. Here is a summary of his list:

- The socially conscious source who wants to correct injustices and change the world.
- The disgruntled employee who wants to get even with the boss.
- The ignored source who can't get anyone's attention at his or her place of work and gets no respect from his or her colleagues.
- The stealth source who enjoys secretly brokering information to cause trouble at his or her place of work or in the hopes of gaining some kind of control over the reporter.
- The investment source, usually highly placed in an organization, who gives the reporter information in hopes that later the reporter will not do critical stories about the source.
- The detached source who is highly intelligent and generally looks down on the media but will talk to reporters who do their "homework" on the topic before the interview.
- The circumstantial source who is a victim or witness that a reporter needs to talk to in order to get the details of a story. This source may have little motivation to talk to a reporter except for the need to talk about the event or to be mentioned in a story.
- The belligerent source who hates reporters and has something to hide or believes the story may hurt someone or some entity that the source wants to protect. This source may believe he or she can bully the reporter into not doing the story.
- The principled source who talks to the media but whose loyalty lies with the institution he or she is a part of. Often, this kind of source believes he or she can hide the facts or can try to guide the reporter in another direction.
- The unsure source who doesn't know if he or she can trust the media but who will throw a reporter a small bit of information to see how he or she handles it.

There are strategies for dealing with each one of these sources, and a journalist needs to think about a source's motivation for speaking to the media, especially if the source approaches the journalist first. After judging the source's motivation, the journalist then can decide on the best approach to the interview.

Preparing Questions

The order in which the journalist asks questions also can be crucial, and so some time should be spent before the interview carefully ordering the questions. Sometimes chronological ordering makes the most sense. A chronological account helps a journalist fill in holes in the source's story.

Many interviewers move from neutral questions to more specific and worrisome ones. Good interviewers ask sources what they were wearing at the time of a key event, what they remember about the meeting room, whether it was storming or sunny outside. The details might help construct a compelling narrative when it is time to write, and they also allow the journalist to compare the source's story with existing facts. Because answers sometimes open up new avenues of inquiry, the journalist needs to stay flexible.

It's important to remember that even if the journalist has heard serious allegations of misconduct, he or she should be careful to maintain a balanced and neutral stance on whether the allegations are true—especially if they come from only one reliable source.

Leading questions are risky, but like most other risks, they occasionally yield results. Journalist Oriana Fallaci became well known for asking risky leading questions. When interviewing the Pakistani president, she alluded to antagonism between him and the Indian prime minister, then asked, "You two really can't stand each other, can you?" The president's intemperate response led to a story for Fallaci.

An investigative reporter should leave no easy out for the interviewee. Rather than ask whether the subject fired the whistleblower, ask why. That puts the subject in the position of explaining rather than issuing a simple, and perhaps disingenuous, denial.

Some of the best interviewers use silence to their advantage. Reporter Tad Bartimus says the pregnant pause is one of her favorite interviewing tools: "Most people abhor silence. It makes them nervous. . . . Often an interviewee, in an attempt to fill a silent void, will volunteer information that astounds both the talker and the listener. 'My God, I've never even told my husband that,' said one shocked interview subject. 'Good! Now we're getting somewhere,'" Bartimus remembers thinking.

It is important to figure out what is not being said, as well as what is. Reporter Bruce Selcraig notes, "It might be significant if the mayor speaks to you routinely about his family yet never mentions his wife, or a successful businessman talks for hours without crediting his partner." Selcraig tests for lies in confrontational interviews. He asks questions for which there is only one true answer. When interviewing sources who have good reason to be concerned about his questions, reporter Mike McGraw uses a three-phase approach. Phase one is the "time to lie" interview. He uses the opportunity to tell his subject (and related sources) about the proposed story, then asks what appear to be softball questions like, "How do things work here?" and "Is there anything wrong with the way things work?" The answer is often to the effect that everything is just fine, though McGraw suspects otherwise. "Okay," McGraw says, "I'll do some checking and get back to you." Phase two is the "interim" interview, when McGraw returns with some harder questions. By then, he has worked hard to adopt his subject's angle of vision, to see how things look from that side of the desk. McGraw has thought about ways his subject can gain power or money by abusing the system.

McGraw might appear naive, hoping to receive detailed responses from someone who can't help explaining himself. Phase three is the "come to Jesus" interview, in which he lets his subject know the results of all the research. "We both know a lot now," McGraw will state. "Have you told me everything you want to say? Are you sure that's your final answer to this question?" That approach often leads to confessions and then to explanations of the confession. Respect is part of the process. As reporter Pat Stith puts it, "You can say 'please' and 'thank you' and still ask, 'Did you steal the money?'"

Structuring the Interview

The first few minutes of the interview should be devoted to breaking the ice. This is the time to mention the small-world commonalities that were the fruit of preinterview research, to talk about the institution or issue at hand. It is also wise to explain where the investigation is headed and to go over any ground rules previously discussed. Such a review can minimize misunderstandings later.

Impressions created during the small talk are important. Nalder says, "Never approach your subjects as though they seem menacing or likely to clam up. Appear innocent, friendly, unafraid and curious. If you are a hard-boiled, cynical reporter who talks out of the side of your mouth, you will need acting lessons." From the other side, the journalist should never be seduced or turned off by first impressions. First impressions, after all, can be misguided.

While the source is talking, good interviewers make eye contact. They nod their head. They make reassuring noises such as "uh-huh" and "yes," and maybe they say "fascinating" or "how interesting." When appropriate, they ask, "How?" or "Why?" or "What do you mean by that?" Eventually, they ask for documentation in an indirect way, such as "How do you know that?" They hope such questions will produce a response along the lines of "I am going to tell you how I know."

When an interview becomes unproductive, the interviewer must know how to get back on track. Michael Schumacher, in a Writer's Digest article headlined "Creative Interviewing," uses this example from author Gary Provost:

> I'll let people go on for a while, and then I'll try to get them back to the point in a way that doesn't sound as if I'm saying "shut up and let's get back to the point." I try to make a question sound as if it's related to what they're talking about. For example, let's say I wanted to talk to Dan Wakefield about writing fiction, and he's telling me about a time when he was in Cuba, writing a nonfiction piece for The New York Times. I might say something like "Did you ever think of writing a novel about Cuba?" I'm really trying to get him back to a discussion about whether he prefers writing novels over nonfiction, but it sounds as if we're discussing Cuba.

To keep an interview moving productively, the structure of questions is vital. If the journalist wants full-blown answers, open-ended questions should be asked, and those that can be answered yes or no should be eliminated. If an open-ended question ("What are your plans after you retire from the Senate next year?") results in a useless response, the journalist can ask a second question that forces the source to focus ("What would it take for you to return to teaching at Harvard?"). To elicit feelings, the interviewer can ask, "Describe your state of mind when you decided to quit." To get details for local color, he or she might say, "Take me back to the day before the murder; walk me through the scene."

Sources are also frequently comfortable sharing what they consider anecdotal information. While recounting anecdotes, an interviewee may reveal previously unknown information—such as an ex-wife or a hobby. The journalist can use that information to identify additional sources to interview or new document searches to conduct.

The best interviewers suggest that as the interview is ending, it is always good to ask "Is there anything I didn't ask that you want to discuss?" Journalists also should ask whether there is anybody else they should interview and any books, articles or reports they should read.

Taking Notes and Following Up

A journalist who is a weak note taker or who wants proof of every word said should tape-record the session. Some sources are nervous about that and they should be offered a copy of the tape or be encouraged to do their own taping. In circumstances where taping is impractical or likely to stifle candor, the journalist should devise a personal shorthand that he or she can read later.

If the note taking still fails to keep up with the subject's words, the interviewer can ask from time to time for the source to repeat what was said, perhaps by saying, "That last point was so fascinating I want to make sure I have it word for word." Another tactic is to ask a throwaway question, completing the note taking from the previous answer while the source rattles on about an irrelevant matter. Or an interviewer can simply say that he or she can't keep up.

If the interviewer expects the interview to be on the record but the source says it off the record, offers not-to-be-quoted background or suggests some other unacceptable condition during the session, there are ways to reply.

One possibility is to listen respectfully, then later interject, "That information you shared earlier is fascinating. Is there any way I can quote you about that?" Another possibility is to find out from the source whether documents or other people might reveal the same information. A journalist can stand on principle, telling the source that everything must be on the record because that was the original verbal or implied contract, but recently lawyers have advised that a private person can come back and successfully argue that information given on the record can no longer be used.

When a story is likely to continue for months after an interview, the journalist should contact sources periodically to let them know about the story's progress and to check to see if anything has changed. This sometimes leads sources to call back with additional information.

On the beat, a journalist should not hesitate to contact sources after a critical story. It shows that the journalist is not worried or embarrassed about the story and sometimes can lead to more information gathered while the source berates the reporter or after the source cools down. Such a call might keep the source talking in the future. Interviewing is about building bridges, maintaining them and sometimes repairing them—all to get as much information as possible.

⊃ CHECK IT OUT

✓ Research an elected city official in preparation for an interview by reading news stories, searching the Web and examining documents. Make a list of interviewees to talk to for background.

✓ Decide in what order you will interview the sources. Include interviews with the city official, three friends, three opponents, two family members, one current employee and one former employee.

✓ Write the profile, and then analyze what interviews you are missing.

RESOURCES FOR REPORTING

Online People Finders

- Anonymous e-mail postings: www.anonymizer.com
- AT&T searchable database of 800 numbers: http://businessesales.att.com/products/lookup_toll_free_results.html
- E-mail addresses: www.whowhere.com, www.iaf.net, www.emailaddresses.com/email_find.htm
- Reverse directories: www.411.com, www.infousa.com
- Telephone directories: www.switchboard.com, www.anywho.com, www.infospace.com, www.longlostpeople.com

Internet Communication Tools

- Discussion lists: http://tile.net/lists
- Newsgroup directory: http://groups.google.com; also found at Yahoo! at http://groups.yahoo.com
- Web page directory: http://geocities.yahoo.com
- Blog directories: www.technorati.com, http://blogsearch.google.com, www.quacktrack.com

Whistleblowers

Accounts of whistleblowers by journalists include "Serpico," Peter Maas's book about a New York City police officer who talked openly about corruption.

Myron Peretz Glazer and Penina Migdal Glazer, in "The Whistleblowers: Exposing Corruption in Government and Industry," relate findings from their study of 64 ethical resisters and their spouses.

Web sites to consult about whistleblowers include

- Office of Special Counsel (www.osc.gov)
- Merit Systems Protection Board (www.mspb.gov)
- Government Accountability Project (www.whistleblower.org)

Outside Experts

Journalists interested in finding outside experts should start by consulting the Research Centers and Services Directory, the Washington Information Directory from Congressional Quarterly, and the Encyclopedia of Associations. The Web site ProfNet (www.profnet.com) allows journalists to connect with researchers, scholars, consultants and government officials.

For additional sources of outside experts, a journalist might consult one of the following think tanks:

- American Enterprise Institute for Public Policy Research (www.aei.org), Washington, D.C.
- Heritage Foundation (www.heritage.org), Washington, D.C.
- Brookings Institute (www.brookings.org), Washington, D.C.
- Hoover Institute (www.hoover.org), Stanford, Calif.
- Rand Corporation (www.rand.org), Santa Monica, Calif.

David M. Ricci describes the activities and uses of think tanks in "The Transformation of American Politics: The New Washington and the Rise of Think Tanks."

Power Structures

For those interested in the debate over power structures, one of the most interesting summaries is in "Who Rules America Now?" by G. William Domhoff. Information on social network analysis can be found at www.ire.org/sna.

Interviewing

There are entire books on techniques that will help an interview go smoothly. These are among the best:

- "Interviewing the Interviewers," a series of articles from The IRE Journal published in book form
- "Interview," by Claudia Dreifus
- "The Craft of Interviewing," by John Brady
- "Interviews That Work: A Practical Guide for Journalists," by Shirley Biagi
- "Creative Interviewing," by Ken Metzler
- "Before the Story," by George M. Killenberg and Rob Anderson

Credentials Fraud in Résumés

Reporter Glenna Whitley and military veteran B.G. Burkett teamed up to write "Stolen Valor: How the Vietnam Generation Was Robbed of Its Heroes and Its History," which was published in 1998 by Verity Press Publishing. They also wrote about the phenomenon in the July 1999 issue of The IRE Journal. The IRE Resource Center has related articles filed under the heading "Credentials Fraud."

6

Writing the Compelling Investigation

*There are many books on journalism and writing, but few deal solely with how
to write an in-depth investigative story. This chapter is aimed at helping investigative journalists present their stories in the most compelling way possible, no
matter what the medium in which they are presented.*

The writing and editing of investigative stories are going through a transformation, just as the profession of journalism itself is. It is becoming impossible to
think of presenting an investigative story in one medium. A story that is initially published in print might also appear on the Web with multimedia components. The same applies to broadcast stories, where the Web has expanded
the traditional limits of two- to five-minute investigative reports.

The investigative journalist now needs to take into account that the story
may include text, audio and video. He or she might even consider taking a
screenwriter's approach to the story. Nonetheless, many of the fundamentals of
writing a strong investigative piece still apply. Investigative stories must show
the impact of the issue on people, must speak to the issue or injustice in a direct
and understandable manner, and still must unfold in a way that draws the
reader or viewer into the story, no matter how complex it might be.

The Fundamentals

Newsroom managers tend to divide journalists into "reporters" and "writers."
Some journalists spend so much time on the reporting that when it comes time
to write the story, they are fatigued or lost in too many facts. At that point, the
editor wants to bring in a "writer" to shape the material and make it "sing."

While it is true that some journalists excel at reporting and others at writing,
it's best if a journalist works at being as strong as possible in both areas. A journalist's reporting will improve by knowing that attention to the details of a particular person's behavior and mannerisms may be key to telling a memorable

story. Similarly, a journalist's writing will be much stronger if it's based on thorough research that involves extensive interviews and reviews of documents.

Over the years, a series of adages has evolved in investigative journalism when it comes to writing the story, whether in print or broadcast:

- Start writing as soon as the reporting begins, whether that means jotting down a weekly memo or composing small sections of the story.
- Constantly work on summarizing your story in as few words as possible. Be able to tell an editor or manager what the story is about in 25 words or less. (Broadcast journalists are often told to tell what the story is about in three words.)
- If you have worked primarily in print, start thinking visually about the story from the day you start investigating. Involve photographers, graphic artists and Web staff at the beginning of your investigation to ensure you collect the necessary material for a strong visual presentation.
- Read colleagues' and other journalists' work — and read books on writing.

Writing an Effective Story

One of the best overviews on writing investigative stories is the classic article from Ron Meador, then projects editor at the Star Tribune in Minneapolis, entitled "Remembering the Outrage: How to Stop Drawing Indictments and Start Telling Stories." The article appeared years ago in The IRE Journal. Here is an excerpt:

Suppose you catch your state-run vocational schools putting out phony placement statistics, luring job-hungry hopefuls to courses that tout 90 percent success but deliver less than 50.

You prove this using the schools' own data, taken from computer tapes and analyzed with expert help. You find juicy examples of duplicated and wasteful programs that violate state efficiency rules but serve the pork-barrel interests of legislators and local school boards. You publish this in the paper with sidebars and pictures and color graphics in the very week the legislature is reviewing budgets for all college and vocational programs. And your story sinks like a set of car keys.

Legislators ask the program chiefs a few questions and let the budgets go forward. Dozens of vo-ed students write to thank you, and so do several academics, but nobody else pays much attention. The schools adopt a few internal reforms — but also stop collecting the data you used to prove their misdeeds. Can you imagine how this might feel? I know, because it happened at the Star Tribune, and it was my fault.

I've read this project many times since then. I'm always impressed. By all the usual measures, it was a very solid piece of work. The findings were important and presented authoritatively and were never challenged. The stories were clear and crisp even by the usual high standards of their author, David Peterson. Graphics and sidebars added depth and detail. I had assumed that readers would flock to a series showing that a $160 million-a-year, tax-financed educational system was ridden with waste and deception. But they didn't. Why? I can see now that many of the stories ran very long, covering multiple topics. We probed issues exhaustively, but said too little about people. Some graphics tried to make so many points that it was hard to see any of them. We took a tone of informing and educating our readers rather than talking to them, provoking them, engaging them. The lesson of this experience? We investigative types have to stop drawing up indictments and start telling stories. This is a big challenge, a continual struggle. I certainly don't have all the answers, but I have a few suggestions.

Keep the Outrage in Sight

There has been a transformation in investigative journalism in the last decade or so, a shift from nailing individual bad guys to dissecting failing systems. Sometimes in our absorption with documenting these dysfunctional systems, we forget that actual people are getting screwed, that other people are screwing them or letting it happen. We forget the outrage that first moved us, and we lose the aspect that can move our readers.

We ran a series by Joe Rigert and Maura Lerner showing that more than 200 nursing-home patients are strangling each year in vests and belts intended to keep them from harm. Worse, the primary manufacturer of these "protective restraints" had known about the deaths for years, and government regulators turned aside persistent signs of trouble. Documenting this indifference made the story much more compelling.

A different project contradicted the folk wisdom that readers are capable of outrage only over death, injury and wasted tax money. Rigert and Tom Hamburger did a quick project on the Federal Reserve Bank's efforts to replace its 18-year-old, state-of-the-art Minneapolis headquarters with a $110-million palace. They found that the bank had exaggerated the existing building's repair problems and used some questionable financial analysis to make a case for abandoning it.

Rather than count on readers to be outraged by the waste of semipublic money—$110 million is just a big abstraction—we built our lead on the threatened destruction of a unique, expensive architectural landmark that had become part of the soul of Minneapolis, where pride in such things runs high.

Put People in the Foreground

There is a tradition in project writing that puts the issues and findings in the main pieces, individual human stories in the sidebars. Our shop talk reflects that thinking: This is a Numbers Story, this is the Policy Story, these are the People Stories over here. Numbers are essential, people are optional. When people show up in a Numbers Story or a Policy Story, it is usually as a three-paragraph anecdote leading off the piece or one of its subsections. The idea is to use a bit of pungent humanity to lure readers into the hard stuff. This sort of journalistic bait-and-switch is cheap and cynical.

Readers deserve more respect. They care about issues but are impatient with abstraction. They want to see problems and conflicts in the flesh. They want to make a personal connection, to imagine how this outrage would feel to them.

I think we have to find ways to weave human experience throughout our stories. The heavier and harder a story is, the more humanity it needs. Allen Short and Donna Halvorsen wrote a three-day series about predatory sex offenders and how the courts fail to protect us from them. The main findings were about numbers and policies — high recidivism rates, lenient sentencing patterns, failed treatment programs — but each day's presentation gave equal prominence to powerful portrayals of sex crimes, of the men who commit them, of the women and children whose lives have been shredded by rape. That approach made us work harder to avoid redundancy, to give each story a unique identity. But we decided we did not want any reader to be able to lose sight, even for a moment, of the horrors being endured by women and children while the public policy debate drones on.

Talk to Readers — Do Not Lecture Them

Imagine sitting down on the bus, turning to your fellow commuter and saying, "A U.S. Air Force pilot shot down over Laos in 1968 and listed as missing in action, whose widow has repeatedly received evidence that he might still be alive, was almost certainly killed in the crash, the Star Tribune has learned after an exhaustive review of military records and interviews with the pilot's squadron commander, who acknowledged lying about the incident." I cannot say nobody will read a story that starts that way. All our newspapers keep running endurance tests like that, and we get enough calls and letters to know that some people keep reading past them. But there is a better way. We can write for our readers the way we talk to our neighbors. We can stop using newspaperese and start using conversational English. We can stop cramming sentences so full of facts and figures that we need to wrap them with bungee cord to keep them from bursting. We can kill all those wooden quotes, partial quotes and long-winded quotes that are paraphrased. We can get rid of jargon and other language that has meaning only for insiders and newspapers junkies. We can strip away clichés. We can introduce Bob Ehlert's MIA story by saying, "For nearly 22 years, Richard Walsh's family has waited for him to come home, alive or dead, from the jungles of Southeast Asia. All because of a lie."

That will get a few more sinners into the tent, I think.

Let Graphics Carry More of the Load

We are all using graphics these days. When they are good, they are very, very good. When they are bad, they say the same thing as the story, only not as clearly.

We have two rules for our graphics:

1. Each one has to make its own point. The point must be sharp enough to be conveyed in a short declarative sentence. This sentence focuses the content and design of the graphic, and often becomes the headline. Not "Patterns of Crime," but "Sex Criminals Commit Multiple Offenses." Not "Treatment and Recidivism Rates," but "Treatment Shows Little Benefit."

2. Graphics must stand on their own, just like sidebars. They exist to make or develop their own point, which may have been mentioned in a story only briefly, or not at all. They are not there to say in pictures what we have already said in words.

When Rigert and Bob Franklin wrote a series on cheating, skimming and theft in Minnesota's $1-billion-a-year charitable gambling industry, we faced a big challenge: How to expose the wrongdoing while simultaneously introducing the complicated, unfamiliar system that was being abused.

Our solution was a front-page graphic titled, "A Catalog of Cheating." It showed how the system worked, with pull-tabs moving from distributors to bars to players, as money flowed from players to gambling operators to charities. At the same time, it showed how crooks siphoned off a share at each stage. . . .

At Every Step, Remember the Interested, Impatient Reader
Perhaps there was a day when we could throw our evidence of waste and fraud and wrongdoing before our readers like so much raw meat, then sit back and watch them feed. If so, it certainly is long gone. Readers are much more demanding now, and they're getting more sophisticated all the time. I do not believe, as some journalists do, that readers are losing interest in issues these days. I do believe they are losing patience with newspapers that force them to work too hard and make them care too little. Readers do not like dense, endless stories. They do not like graphics that read like income-tax forms. They do not like getting the same point over and over in a story, sidebar, graphic, cutline, blurb. They do not like to be lectured.

I do not have a prescription for styling investigative stories. Some demand a narrative. Some need a more traditional, newslike structure. Some require an analytical approach, some rest squarely on the facts.

But I do have one last tip. When you have got the project drafted, ask a half-dozen uninitiated readers to look it over and react. You can use people from around the newsroom, or people from outside who can be trusted with the secrets. We have done it both ways, with good results.

Odds are they will show you a lot of things that could be done better. This is not always welcome news in the last weeks of getting a project ready for print. But if you are turning off your readers, it is better to know it before the papers are out the door.

All of this may sound terribly obvious and ordinary, the kind of thing everybody already knows and everybody already does.

I wish that were so. I really do. But the mail brings a lot of projects to my office, from a lot of great newspapers, and a lot of them are long and dull. Gray. Preachy. Too hard. Too complicated. Too dry.

I cannot get through these projects. That makes me sad, because I know there is good work in them. If I cannot read them, on a Thursday afternoon, in my office, when I am hungry for ideas and scouting for techniques to steal—well then, imagine how these projects fare with Mr. or Mrs. Average Reader on a Sunday morning, when the kids are fighting or brunch is arriving or the yard work has to get done.

Our work is too important to be laid aside.

Getting the Details

An investigative story should answer the "so what?" as well as the who, what, when, where, why and how. The answers are usually in the details. The reporter and editor should think about collecting details not only for their content, but also for how those details can illustrate the project's theme and make audience members angry, sad, relieved or more informed about a topic that touches their lives.

Throughout this book, investigative journalists are encouraged to notice details on their own, as well as ask questions of sources that will elicit details. Rather than ignoring the obvious, top investigative journalists are perpetually amazed by it. They collect details that nobody else does.

Edna Buchanan of The Miami Herald once wrote about a man who had been murdered and whose body was dumped into the street by the driver of a pickup truck. It was only later, after publication, that Buchanan learned that the dead man was wearing a black taffeta cocktail dress and red high heels. When she questioned the detectives about why they never told her this, they replied, "You didn't ask." She started asking after that.

Writer and journalism professor Walt Harrington, who made his name at The Washington Post Magazine, tells of an incident in which a reporter who wanted to portray a country doctor was in the car with the doctor driving to the scene of an accident where a tree had fallen on a man. Several miles away from the accident scene, the doctor began beeping his car horn at short intervals. The noise could be heard throughout the countryside. An observer might have assumed that the doctor was emulating, as best he could, an ambulance siren, hoping other motorists would clear the way. The investigative journalist assumed nothing. The journalist asked the doctor, Why were you beeping your horn? The doctor answered that the man pinned by the tree might hear it, know help is on the way, be filled with hope and thus hang on to life. As Harrington explains, "The doctor's motive tells us a great deal about the doctor—his sensitivity and empathy, his desire to grasp even the slimmest advantage in his effort to save a life. Yet it is easy to imagine any fairly good journalist describing that scene, but missing its dramatic and fully subjective meaning by forgetting to ask the last simple and obvious question—what does it mean?" If the pinned man lived, the reporter could ask if he heard the horn and what he thought. A journalist should think of these details as the heart of the story, not just nice stylistic touches.

To capture details, Harrington uses his handwritten notes, his memory, a tape recorder and photographs from the interviewee, his own camera, or a professional photographer. Only details that move the story forward should survive the writing and rewriting, though. The surviving details should form a chain of facts rather than a stack of facts.

Avoiding Clichés and Stereotypes

Screening out inappropriate or misleading details is difficult. It means contradicting the natural tendency for journalists to see what they expect to see. Newsroom coach Donald Murray, author of "Writing for Your Readers," warns against clichés of vision:

> The more professional we become the greater the danger that we will see what we expect to see. Experience, of course, is an advantage, but it has a dark side. It may keep us from seeing the real story—the cause that does not fit the stereotype, the effect that is not predictable, the quote that we do not hear before our question is answered. The effective writer must always have an essential naiveté; skepticism must be balanced by innocence. The reporter must be capable of seeing what is new.

Murray illustrates his point with an example:

> A young man has run amok in the neighborhood, killing eight and maiming 15. The man is described as quiet, studious, polite to the neighbors, good to his mother, neat, mild-mannered and the last person in the world you would have expected to do anything like that. . . . He is the cliché killer, and the reporter is happy to find him. There is no problem writing the story; it has been written before, and before, and before. The neighbors all fall into the stereotype. They are not lying, but they are shocked; they do like the mother; they want to avoid responsibility for what they have overlooked the last twenty years.

If readers are lucky, at least one reporter will refuse to be blinded by such clichés of vision. Murray says, "Some good, hard-edged reporting will discover that neighborhood pets have been disappearing for years, the nice young man was seen cooking pigeons when he was three years old . . . , that his father, two brothers and three sisters have refused to live at home with him; that the studious young man has the reading level of a nine-year-old; and that his mother has fought a guerrilla war against getting psychiatric help for him since he was three years old."

The investigative reporter who refuses to be trapped by clichés is also likely to chronicle the larger context and universal themes.

Writing From Chronologies and Outlines

As the details accumulate, an experienced journalist will find that building a chronology is an effective way to manage the information. The virtues of a chronology are explained in Chapter 1. A chronology is more than a way to keep track of information. It is also a writing tool.

Whether investigating an individual, institution or issue, an experienced journalist will start building a chronology from the first week. After each interview, the journalist decides what to include in the chronology and what to file away at this point without mention. A chronology should also include revealing direct quotations and relevant descriptions and other facts that might help make the story compelling as well as accurate. Experienced journalists will use the chronology as a basic text as they write their first drafts to check the original thesis, identify gaps in reporting, and look for new angles. This approach saves time by avoiding rereading massive files.

Some journalists compose a draft without their chronology or any other notes when they know there are holes to be filled. Writers should trust the subconscious. Sometimes what the subconscious remembers is worth including and what it forgets perhaps should be forgotten.

Writing a draft from a chronology or from memory, though, is no substitute for an outline for many writers. One way to test the logic of a draft is to outline it after composition. Does each major point of the project deserve its own Roman numeral? If not, something is awry. Do the secondary points, designated by capital letters and grouped together under each Roman numeral, derive in a natural way from the major point? Do those secondary points fit together naturally in a grouping, or do they need to be separated, perhaps placed elsewhere in the outline?

Some journalists construct their outline first and then compose their text, Roman numeral by Roman numeral, capital letter by capital letter. Some find that writing from a chronology first (but not necessarily chronologically) gives projects a more natural flow; the outline comes later, as a check on the work rather than the ruling document.

Story Structures

When first sitting down to write, an investigative journalist should consider what structure the story should take.

In her textbook "Writing and Reporting News," Carole Rich describes six different possibilities for story structures.

- The *inverted pyramid* organizes information from most important to least important. The advantage for audience members is that they receive the highlights quickly. The disadvantage is that audience members have little incentive to finish the story.

- The *high fives formula* is a variation on the Inverted Pyramid. Its five elements are the News (what happened or is happening), Context (the background of the event or trend), Scope (the local event as part of a national event or trend), Edge (where the news is leading, what happens next) and Impact (why anyone should care).
- Rich next describes *The Wall Street Journal formula*, which goes from the specific to the general. There is a soft lead, a summary paragraph, a backup for those two elements, supporting points, explanations and an ending that ties back to the lead.
- The *hourglass story* provides the most important news at the top, and then proceeds chronologically.
- The *pyramid structure* frequently is the most appropriate for an investigative piece, as it consists of a lead, foreshadowing, chronological storytelling and the climax.
- The *sections structure* is akin to a book with well-crafted chapters, each with a lead, body and kicker. At the end of each section, readers should be compelled to move to the next section. The beginning of each section uses a list technique to introduce and summarize key points.

Other structures, not specifically identified by Rich, are the functional and organic structures.

- *Functional structure.* An investigative reporter examining a massive institution like the U.S. Agriculture Department might dissect it function by function. For the Agriculture Department, that might mean part one focuses on meat inspection, part two on farm supports and part three on rural housing assistance.
- *Organic structure.* Jon Franklin says dramatic stories usually consist of three major parts. In an organic structure, the opening focus in part one is the complication. The three focuses in the middle part describe developments of the main "character" as he or she tries to resolve the complication. And the final focus, in part three, is the resolution.

    An example:

    Complication: Company fires Joe.
    Development: Depression paralyzes Joe; Joe regains confidence; Joe sues company.
    Resolution: Joe regains job.

Whatever the structure of the in-depth piece, writers and editors must decide whether to present the material all at once or divide it into a series of articles appearing on separate days. Bruce DeSilva, a journalism writing coach, suggests avoiding series except "when you have a tightly focused question that you can express in a sentence, but which has an answer too complex to be expressed in a single story." DeSilva uses an example of a project that started out as a "condition of higher education" assignment. The reporters and editors finally decided to narrow the question to "How are recent changes in finances and demographics affecting college teaching, research and access to higher education?" Each part of the three-part series focused on one aspect of that question.

Focus and Resolution

Even the best outline cannot overcome fuzzy thinking. Journalists should hone their focus by writing and rewriting a one-sentence summary of no more than 25 words. When Laura Sessions Stepp of The Charlotte Observer was trying to identify an appropriate lead for a series on occupational hazards in the textile industry, she found herself struggling. Her supervisor asked her to summarize the months-long project. "Cotton dust is killing people," Stepp said. She had just verbalized the focus, which eventually came out in print as "Cotton dust is a killer in Carolina's mills."

Inherent in any focus statement should be tension and resolution. The tension might be between individuals, between an individual and an institution (such as an employer), an individual and the larger society, an entrenched belief and a newly discovered fact, or what is being done versus what should be done.

Walt Harrington says, "Introduce tensions early that will be resolved by the end. If possible, let your subjects seem to gain insight and self-awareness in the course of your story. This sounds impossible, but with proper in-depth interviewing, it happens most of the time. Of course, it will not just happen if you have not anticipated and chronicled this growth or change while reporting."

Sometimes resolution is real, but other times it is an imposed dramatic device. In Madeleine Blais' story "Zepp's Last Stand," one of Walt Harrington's favorites, the resolution is real: The old man wins the honorable military discharge he had sought for decades. But if he had not received it, Blais still could have brought dramatic closure to her story. Harrington's guess is that she would have argued that by failing to clear his name, Zepp continued to have reason to live.

Perhaps the best-known apostle of the complication-tension-resolution model is Jon Franklin, author of "Writing for Story: Craft Secrets of Dramatic Nonfiction by a Two-Time Pulitzer Prize Winner." He says almost any compelling story can be described like this: "a sequence of actions that occur when a sympathetic character encounters a complicating situation that he confronts and solves."

Franklin suggests avoiding projects that lack a basic complication of significance to the audience. A stolen car is not much of a complication to a wealthy person who can pay cash the next day for a new vehicle. But it is a complication to a poverty-stricken, single mother who depends on the car to drop her children at day care before driving from one house-cleaning job to another.

Franklin also suggests that journalists avoid stories that have no resolution, but that is not realistic for many investigative journalists. After all, the discovery of safety violations in an apartment building may not have a resolution until several stories later. And then there may be resolutions to choose from: A corrupt city employee is removed from his position or a federal investigation is launched into the bankrupt property management business that left creditors impoverished.

Leads: The Opening Sentences

Although the first paragraph is the most important part of an investigative report, Franklin suggests writing the ending first: "The story doesn't pivot on the beginning, it pivots on the ending. So write that first. That way you know exactly what it is that you need to foreshadow." Another important adage for writers to remember is that we tend to bury our leads and write past our endings.

When journalists are finally ready to craft their openings, they will find that sometimes hard-news leads are best on complicated projects.

The veteran investigative journalist Paul Williams believed a hard-news summary lead worked on a complex project if an overwhelming revelation, supported by unequivocal evidence, stood out after the reporting had been completed. For example, after Tom Braden looked into the public housing authority for the Columbia Missourian, his opening sentence read: "The city's biggest landlord also may be the worst."

But when that kind of straightforward lead is impractical, there are other possibilities that are generally viewed as softer leads: the descriptive, the narrative and the anecdotal.

- The *descriptive lead* paints a picture of what is going on. For example, it can detail the living conditions in a housing project by noticing the details such as peeling paint, vomit in the hallways and the occasional sound of gunfire.

- The *narrative lead* recounts the action of a particular person or an event, such as a terrorist trying to cross into the United States from Canada to carry out a bombing, and uses that narrative to launch the investigative story into a larger issue or subject, such as the terrorist group itself.
- The *anecdotal lead* might detail the story of an uninsured person who was denied treatment at a hospital to show in human terms the shortcomings of a health care system.

Journalists might have difficulty deciding between a news feature lead and a softer lead, such as what you see in a feature story. Walt Harrington says, "The difference between news features and features is the difference between the humanized overview takeout on, say, mainstreaming handicapped children in the public schools, versus telling the in-depth bittersweet story of one handicapped child who has been mainstreamed for the first time."

Leads that focus on a person can be anecdotal or narrative or both. The key element, however, is the use of one person as the connecting thread for the entire project. That is different from opening with one person, using her as a symbol for a few paragraphs, moving to the summary (sometimes called the "so what?" or the "nut") paragraph, then dropping all mention of that person for good or until a tie-back ending.

Skillful project journalists can tell a sweeping story through a particular person by including context. As author Tracy Kidder says, "You pluck a guitar string and another one vibrates." Maureen Dowd of The New York Times explains how a sweeping story can be told through delineating one person's character:

> I have always thought that covering the person—I would not call it character, really—is as important as the policies, because politicians change their policies. I mean, with [President George] Bush, you knew he had made a sort of Faustian bargain to be president, and he had no compass in terms of principles, and he had traded away a lot of what he believed in. So you could hang on to that, and that would help you explain a lot of what he did. And with [President Bill] Clinton I think it is the same. Every time the country has gotten into really deep trouble—the Bay of Pigs, Vietnam, Watergate—all these things have come from the president's personal characteristics.

Occasionally, a project can open with a direct quotation. Thomas G. Duffy, in his book "Let's Write a Feature," uses an example from an investigation about substandard student housing in a university town. It begins with this quotation: "'I stay at the library until it closes,' the woman said, shivering. 'Then I come home and go to bed fully dressed.'" The relevance of the quotation? The woman's dingy student apartment had a defective heating system that left tenants nearly freezing during winter.

Whatever type of lead you choose, you can use Donald Murray's 30 questions (from his book "Writing to Deadline: The Journalist at Work") to gauge its effectiveness. Here are some of the most pertinent questions for investigative projects:

- What one thing does the reader need to know more than any other?
- What surprised me when I was reporting the story?
- Where is the conflict?
- What is the appropriate voice for this story?
- What point of view should the story be told from?
- Can the essence of the story be captured by an anecdote, image, metaphor, quotation?

Middles: Flow and Momentum

Middles of stories receive little attention in many writing books, overshadowed by discussions of leads and endings. A punster might say that too many projects consist of a beginning, a muddle and an end. But it's essential that a writing project filled with dense information does not flag in the middle.

Part of the trick is grounded more in common sense than literary skill. For example, handling numbers with skill can keep a project from losing momentum. When discussing a federal agency boondoggle as part of an overall budget topping $1 trillion, a writer should never assume that amount can be understood without help. Readers are much more likely to understand if the story explains that it would take 31,688 years to produce a trillion dollars at the rate of a dollar per second. If there is a 250-square-mile oil slick off the California coast, a writer can explain that the slick is about twice the size of San Francisco.

Using the Franklin formula, the middle of the story can be built around the actions that the main "character" (which might be an institution) takes on the way to resolving the complication, the changes in the character wrestling with the problem, the insight (perhaps a flash, perhaps a slow unfolding) that leads eventually to the resolution. Broadcast journalists, in particular, excel at building the story around a character.

One technique for maintaining interest during the middle portions is writing in scenes. Scenes that are done skillfully show rather than tell, entertain as well as explain, and involve readers or audience members as if they were there. A project about unsafe bridges could include a scene of a school bus filled to capacity crossing one of those unsafe bridges every day. To make readers or audience members feel as if they are on the bus, the reporter would make the trip multiple times before composing the scene.

Whatever techniques journalists use to craft effective middles, transitions are mandatory. Transitioning from sentence to sentence and from paragraph to paragraph is taught in almost every university journalism course and is illustrated in almost every book on effective nonfiction writing. Writers implicitly know why they place sentence B after sentence A, paragraph D after paragraph C, but the logic might be less obvious to the audience. Transitions make the logic clear. A transition can be accomplished by repeating a word or phrase in paragraph D that appeared in paragraph C. A transition can be as simple as one word (a connector such as "however" or "then") or as complex as several sentences. Each transition is a conscious act by the writer but should appear seamless and effortless to the audience.

Pacing is another key element in writing effective middles. Varying the lengths of sentences improves readability generally and can help set the appropriate tone for the events described. The lead-in to paragraphs describing an act of murder might consist of mostly long sentences (35 to 50 words) explaining the backgrounds of the killer and the victim as well as how they came together. But the paragraphs depicting the violent act will almost surely be more effective if the sentences are short (10 to 15 words). Harrington and other stylists read their work aloud, looking for pacing problems and, Harrington says, for the following:

- Words that do not roll off the tongue
- Rhythms that clash
- Clichés that must be rephrased
- Language that is encrusted with the made-up words of bureaucrats and social scientists
- Attributions that give long, meaningless job titles instead of conversational job descriptions

Several editors have said they can go into a newsroom and pick out the best writers by watching whose lips move as they type.

Skillfully rendered dialogue is another tool for making an engaging middle. Harrington says that such dialogue creates the sense of real life, while quotations from sources speaking to no one but the reporter work against the sense of real life. In novels, subjects do not talk to the omniscient narrator; they talk to one another, in their own special language.

When using dialogue, handling attribution gracefully is one of those "little things" that matters. When one source dominates an extended portion, "he said" and "she said" should be used as little as possible. If your source says during an interview that she hitchhiked from Connecticut to California at age 16 and that fact can be verified, there is no reason to write, "She says she hitch-hiked." Instead write, "She hitchhiked." The same is true of factual material; there is no reason to write, "He says the condemned building has broken windows," unless the investigator is unable to verify that the building is condemned or cannot see that the windows are broken.

Foreshadowing and flashbacks are helpful but must be used carefully. Foreshadowing is a literary device that gives the audience a taste of what is to come, while simultaneously promising more than a taste later. Broadcast investigative journalists frequently use foreshadowing.

For example, in a story about a crime, a writer might show how Jill talked regularly about committing suicide; her cousin Betty preached against it. Angry about the preaching, Jill threw a wine bottle at Betty, narrowly missing her; the full bottle shattered against the wall, and Jill said something menacing. The writer could end that section of the story like this: "That was when Betty began to be scared of her own cousin." The audience ought to be hooked at that point.

Flashbacks, unlike foreshadowing, are rarely imbued with such drama, but they can serve a purpose. A writer might tell of a black man who has lost his job because of workplace bias despite his unquestioned capability. Throughout the story, the writer flashes back to the man as a child, struggling in classrooms where teachers continually underestimated his abilities.

Occasionally, straight chronology—eliminating literary devices like foreshadowing and flashbacks—is the best way to handle an investigative project. Many readers naturally think chronologically. That approach also has the virtue of making cause and effect clear, because the cause appears unambiguously before the effect. Beware, however, of falling into a post hoc fallacy, where you assume (or suggest) that X caused Y just because Y occurred directly after X. Cause and effect is a way of emphasizing the "why" in the how, what, when, where, who and why formula of journalistic writing. But chronology can be effective even when there is no cause and effect.

Point of View and Tone

Point of view has a dual meaning. It can describe the conclusions reached by the reporter after gathering information, but it can also signify from whose vantage point the story will be narrated. Walt Harrington warns against taking on the stance of the judgmental journalist, the self-righteous crusader. He prefers to come to a story with the motivation of an anthropologist or a novelist. Tracy Kidder describes his battle with point of view as he worked on "Among Schoolchildren," his book about an inner-city elementary classroom:

I had spent a year inside her classroom. I intended, vaguely, to fold into my account of events . . . a great deal about the lives of particular children and about the problems of education in America. I tried every point of view that I had used in previous books, and every page I wrote felt lifeless and remote. Finally, I hit on a restricted third-person narrative.

That approach seemed to work. The world of that classroom seemed to come alive when the view of it was restricted mainly to observations of the teacher and to accounts of what the teacher saw and heard and smelled and felt. This choice narrowed my options. I ended up writing something less comprehensive than I had planned. The book became essentially an account of a year in the emotional life of a schoolteacher.

My choice of the restricted third person also obliged me to write parts of the book as if from within the teacher's mind. I wrote many sentences that contained the phrase "she thought." I felt I could do so because the teacher had told me how she felt and what she thought about almost everything that happened in her classroom. And her descriptions of her thoughts and feelings never seemed self-serving. Believing in them myself, I thought that I could make them believable on the page.

Point of view can be chosen before you decide on the story's tone. Possibilities for tone include formal, conversational, dramatic, skeptical, and ironic. Don't underestimate the importance of tone. Choosing the right tone means the difference between a reader feeling manipulated by your emotional rendering of a single mother's plight with cancer or empathizing through your more objective but honest portrayal of her.

Endings

If possible, an ending should leave deep thoughts and emotions in the minds of readers, without editorializing or preaching. Some investigative journalists end with a punchy quotation from their notes, letting somebody else's words do all the work. Others work hard to close a circle: They begin the story with an anecdote involving one person. That person then drops from sight until the final paragraph, when the character is resurrected as a tie-back to the lead.

Some reporters work hard to find clever endings, reaching into their files for a moment of surprise. But too often they overreach or make mistakes in judgment. For example, in a project about the unjustly convicted that focused on a woman who advocates for their release, the writer saved a surprise for the end—the woman had turned in her own son for selling drugs. He served eight years alongside some of the inmates his mother was trying to assist. Wow! But why did the writer fail to develop that point? Should it have been the lead rather than the ending? Probably.

When there is a tie-back to the lead, it should be natural. Walt Harrington opened and closed his inquiry into the career and personal life of investigative journalist Jack Anderson with a focus that neither expected when the research began: Anderson's relationship with his father. As the story opens, Anderson is showing Harrington through his family home in Utah. His father had bought a home so big they could not pay the mortgage, so the Andersons lived in the basement while renting the rest of the home. The opening anecdote ends with Anderson thinking about his now elderly father and saying, "He was a weird guy." Throughout the story, Harrington refers to the rocky father-son relationship as an ambiguous motivation for Anderson's career.

At the end, Harrington shows Anderson making a rare visit to his father, who after a lifetime of finding his famous son lacking, compliments him and cries in his presence for the first time. Anderson hugs his father, trying to comfort him. Harrington's final sentence about Jack Anderson, perceived as a champion hard-boiled muckraker: "Then Jack falls silent, fighting back his own deep tears."

⊃ CHECK IT OUT

✓ Select three Wall Street Journal front-page stories. Compare all three by determining their story structure and analyzing the effectiveness of their leads, middles and ends.

✓ Watch a recent award-winning investigative broadcast piece from the IRE Resource Center (www.ire.org/resourcecenter), and take notes on its story structure. Then examine the transcript, and compare it to your notes.

✓ Pick a recent newspaper investigative story that has a significant Web component. Detail how the Web component added to the story, whether through graphics, an interactive database or additional photos and text.

RESOURCES FOR REPORTING

Online Writing Resources

- Dictionary.com (www.dictionary.com)
- Bartleby.com (www.bartleby.com), Great Books Online. This site contains numerous reference books, such as Strunk and White's Elements of Style, The American Heritage Dictionary, Roget's Thesaurus and The Columbia Guide to Standard American English.
- Poynter Institute (www.poynter.org), Writing/Editing section.

Books About Writing and Investigative Journalism

"Custodians of Conscience," by Steven Ettema and Theodore Glasser, has pertinent sections on the approach to investigative stories and the use of irony.

Walt Harrington's "American Profiles: Somebodies and Nobodies Who Matter" and "Intimate Journalism" offer ideas on writing and story structures.

"The IRE Collection: Interviewing the Interviewers" offers some of the most renowned interviewers sharing their experiences, techniques and advice. The book includes chapters on dealing with sensitive issues, cross-cultural interviewing, confrontational interviews, handling whistleblowers, technical interviews and finding and cultivating sources. Each chapter includes "Tips from the Pros," with specific time-tested techniques. The book also includes a list of tipsheets and tapes taken from IRE conferences to provide additional help.

Anne Lamott's "Bird by Bird" talks about writing in ways that have proved valuable to journalists.

In his book "Follow the Story: How to Write Successful Nonfiction," James Stewart explains how he turned potentially boring topics into compelling stories at The Wall Street Journal, at The New Yorker and as a book author. Much of Stewart's wisdom is summarized in the September 2000 issue of The IRE Journal.

Donald Murray's "Writing to Deadline: The Journalist at Work" contains all 30 questions to ask to gauge the effectiveness of a lead.

Books About Literary Journalism as a Discipline

Franklin and several dozen other practitioners and scholars have created a body of work that could be called the literature of literary journalism. Besides reading the books already mentioned in this chapter, print and broadcast journalists can benefit from the theories, explanations and examples found in these titles, among others:

- "The Literary Journalists," edited by Norman Sims
- "The Art of Fact," by Barbara Lounsberry
- "The New Journalism," by Tom Wolfe

- "The Art and Craft of Feature Writing," by William E. Blundell
- "The Writer Within," by Lary Bloom
- "The Heart Is an Instrument: Portraits in Journalism," by Madeleine Blais
- "Coaching Writers: The Essential Guide for Editors and Reporters," by Roy Peter Clark and Don Fry

7

Ethics of Investigative Reporting

*This chapter provides guidelines and discussion points on how to maintain accu-
racy and credibility while doing investigations. The topics include how to do line-
by-line fact checking for stories, how to deal with anonymous sources and how to
approach sensitive stories. The chapter also reviews some of the common ethical
dilemmas that investigative journalists face.*

Investigative reporting not only demands the highest standards of accuracy, but
also delivers more ethical dilemmas on a daily basis than almost any other form
of journalism. This means that as investigative journalists gather information,
they need to ensure they are investigating fairly, with factual accuracy, with
contextual accuracy and without any ethical breaches. They must be concerned
that the story that eventually appears is fair and not libelous. But they also
must be concerned about how they report and how they conduct themselves
during the reporting.

In journalism, solutions to many ethical lapses are covered by a consensus.
For example, it is agreed that journalists should never accept tangible gifts, travel
or free meals from sources. Journalists should never invent facts, quotations or
entire stories. They should not plagiarize. They should not make promises to
sources that cannot be kept.

Journalists working in newsrooms with ethics codes should review and discuss those codes, and if they have questions about, or disagreements with,
newsroom-specific codes, they should bring them up. Journalists working in
newsrooms without codes can read the model codes from the Society of Professional Journalists, the Associated Press Managing Editors or the Radio and Television News Directors Association.

There are many ethical questions and dilemmas in investigative journalism
that are not easily dealt with, and these require thought, consideration and
discussion.

Ethics and Accuracy

Fairness and the Law

A journalistic practice may be legal, but the question may still be asked: Is it ethical? That question can arise both in everyday matters and on larger issues of whether to publish or broadcast particular information.

For example, in some states, it is legal to tape-record someone during a phone conversation without telling that person. But some journalists will say that the practice is deceptive and that they would want to know if they themselves were being tape-recorded. They say a reporter should tell an interviewee they intend to record them. Other journalists will say that anyone talking to a reporter should expect that the reporter will be taking notes and possibly tape-recording the conversation.

In another example involving the issue of whether to publish information, two newspapers in Minneapolis–St. Paul handled the same story in very different ways. The story involved a high school athlete who hanged himself in a school building. One newspaper published the story but withheld the name of the student on the grounds that the suicide was a private act. The other newspaper published the name, partly because of a similar previous incident and partly because the editors considered the hanging a public act in a public place. Both decisions were legal. Could both be considered ethical? The point should be obvious: Just because something is legal does not mean it is ethical. Journalists cite the law so often because it is usually more clear-cut than ethical codes.

Nevertheless, it is important that investigative journalists know the laws applying to libel, privacy and the infliction of emotional distress. It is wise to review some of the dozens of books about the statutory and case laws that apply to journalists. Those books contain warnings that ought to be considered. In particular, every reporter should review the "Briefing on Media Law" contained in The Associated Press Stylebook. (See "Resources for Reporting" at the end of the chapter.) That said, journalists should not refrain from investigating individuals, institutions and issues for fear of being sued.

Unfortunately, anyone can file a lawsuit against journalists. Even if the lawsuit is obviously frivolous, journalists and their organizations can spend a few months and thousands of dollars to win a summary judgment. Sometimes, successfully defending against a lawsuit can take years and hundreds of thousands of dollars. But investigative journalists especially must accept that risk. If plaintiffs can stifle investigative journalism by threatening or filing litigation, they have won their objective even if they eventually lose the case.

The Golden Rule

In making judgments about the ethics of investigative practices, journalists should consider applying the golden rule. They can ask these questions:

- How would they feel if a media critic obtained a newsroom reporting job with the express deceptive purpose of collecting information about the decision-making process — information that would end up in a report critical of the news organization?
- How would they react if the infiltrator made and used copies of internal memos between reporters and editors working on a sensitive investigation?
- How would they feel about being criticized by unnamed sources in, say, the Columbia Journalism Review for their inaccuracies?

Besides applying the golden rule, journalists should consider the harm they could cause when deciding whether to begin an investigation and how to conduct it. These questions might guide that process:

- Can the potential harm to an individual, institution or society be justified because it benefits society?
- Can the potential damage to a journalism organization or to journalists in general be justified by the public service rendered from broadcast or publication of the exposé?

Edmund B. Lambeth, a University of Missouri School of Journalism professor, addressed these questions and many more in his book "Committed Journalism: An Ethic for the Profession." Lambeth's book reviews the ethical quandaries in investigative journalism and puts them in context by applying classical ethical theory to contemporary journalism. Lambeth's book can help journalists navigate their way through many of the challenges in investigative journalism.

Dilemmas in Reporting

Obtaining Information Covertly

In a classic story, the Chicago Sun-Times received a tip from a government official who refused to be identified in print or to help further. The source said that some medical clinics were falsely telling women they were pregnant, then charging them for phony abortions. The newspaper could have informed health or law enforcement authorities at that point but did not. It could have limited itself to seeking evidence from current and former clinic employees but did not.

Instead, the newspaper practiced deception by sending female investigative journalists as "patients" to the clinics. The patients carried urine samples from male colleagues. When the clinic claimed that those samples showed pregnancy, the newspaper heightened its deception by placing journalists in jobs at the clinics—as receptionists, counselors and nurses' aides. The investigative journalists provided no false information in their job interviews but omitted references to their journalism connections. For months, the journalists knew women were being harmed through phony abortions but kept collecting evidence without informing authorities. The collection of evidence included illegally photocopying patient files. When the series of stories was published on the clinic's misconduct, the public was outraged. State prosecutors opened investigations into the clinics, and federal regulators initiated a crackdown.

On another project, the Chicago Sun-Times set up a phony bar, ironically named the Mirage, to document corrupt behavior by public officials who were allegedly asking for bribes from small businesspeople to keep their businesses running. In recent years, some broadcast stations have worked with private groups on the Internet to lure child sexual predators to houses where they think they are meeting a child. Instead, the broadcasters do surprise on-camera interviews with the alleged predators.

Journalists routinely debate whether this practice protects the public or is entrapment. In the Mirage bar case, the journalists involved denied charges of entrapment, saying that they were giving officials a chance to demonstrate their normal talent for lawbreaking. In the sexual predator stories, the journalists said they were preventing the predators from continuing to prey on children, but some critics question the collaboration with the advocacy group and the aggressive acts to encourage the men to come to the home.

There are hundreds of other examples involving journalists going undercover; some of the examples include hidden video or audio recorders. Does that behavior harm the credibility of a specific story or of journalists in general? Some journalists would say that going undercover is never justified, although the history of investigative journalism contains groundbreaking work in the late 1800s and early 1900s by the early muckrakers that continues to be admired.

More recently, in the 1990s, two reporters from ABC falsely filled out employment application forms and were hired as workers in the meat-preparation area at Food Lion stores. After their story aired on unsafe and unsanitary practices at the stores, the company sued them not for defamation or falsehoods in the story, but for trespass and for falsely filling out the employment applications. After a civil trial, a jury found in favor of Food Lion and awarded hefty damages.

During the appeal of the case, Investigative Reporters and Editors filed an amicus brief in which IRE defended the undercover practice because of the public good that resulted. The brief, written by IRE pro bono attorney David B. Smallman, stated:

> The history of investigative and undercover reporting shows that such practices are valuable to the public—especially, as here, during a dangerous bacteriological outbreak affecting the safety of the nation's food supply. Such reporting also contributes to the functioning of a democracy, and is within the mainstream of American journalism. Press practices antedating and attending the adoption of the press clause indicate that broad protection was intended for the right to gather and publish news, show that the Founding Fathers and Framers of the Constitution routinely concealed their identities when reporting news and opinions anonymously, and also show that they essentially functioned as undercover political reporters, although they did not themselves describe their activities as such.

When considering undercover or surveillance work, journalists should ask these questions:

- Is it possible to get convincing evidence through documents and interviews instead?
- What significant points will undercover work or surveillance add to the story in terms of accuracy and credibility?
- Will the results of the story be important and alarming enough to overshadow the deceptive practices?

Conducting Ambush Interviews

Sometimes journalists identify themselves accurately and have their recording equipment in plain sight but still spawn ethical dilemmas by catching sources unaware, usually in a public place, and then acting aggressively. The shorthand for this phenomenon is the loaded term "ambush interview."

Ethical dilemmas can be alleviated if a journalist has been persistent in requesting interviews of the source in more traditional (and polite) ways: office or home visits, telephone calls, letters, faxes, and e-mails.

The attempts to contact a person should be thoroughly documented. For example, a letter can be sent by registered mail, with a return receipt requested. Only when all those attempts fail to produce an interview with a key source does it make sense to attempt a surprise interview. If the ambush produces no more than a "no comment" or a rude rejection from the source, why broadcast that footage? Some audience members will attribute broadcasting it to sensationalism, and they might be correct. Others might see it as convincing evidence that the person refuses comment on a matter for which he or she has responsibility. When journalists broadcast ambush interviews, they should at minimum explain to the audience all of the previous, more traditional attempts made to reach the source.

Another ethically debated interviewing technique is to contact a source an unreasonably brief time before publication or broadcast. Most projects take weeks or months of reporting and writing. The question of fairness in giving a source such a short time to respond may overshadow the substance of the story.

Exposing Private Behaviors of Public Figures

The public exposure of President Clinton's affair with Monica Lewinsky brought again to the forefront the question of how much of a public figure's private life should be open to public disclosure. Since then, the debate has only continued and continues to be revived every election season. Here are some questions a journalist might ask when investigating a public figure:

- Does it matter if an elected official is involved in an extramarital sexual affair?
- What if the official is involved but with the permission of one or both spouses?
- Does it matter if the extramarital affair involves not an elected official but an appointed agency head, such as a Cabinet secretary? What about a police chief, a judge, a university president, a high school principal or the chief executive of a local employer?
- What if the private behavior at issue involves not sex but rather alcohol consumption, drug use, failure to pay bills on time, divorce or personal bankruptcy?
- What if the errant behavior involves not the powerful figure but that person's spouse, child or parent?

The easy answer to all those questions is to publish or broadcast the information only if the private behavior clearly affects public performance or the larger society in some demonstrable way. But like all other seemingly easy answers, it is usually difficult to document the behavior without invading someone's privacy, and it is just as difficult to show its impact in an unambiguous manner. Yet investigative journalists cannot always look the other way simply because it is less complicated to do so.

Using Unidentified and Paid Sources

The sensitive matter of publishing accusations based on information from sources who refuse to be identified publicly will never go away. Concern over the use of anonymous sources has led many newsrooms to try to curtail the practice and ensure that reporters check with supervisors before promising anonymity. In addition, publications are going much further in explaining in a story why anonymity was granted. After the Jayson Blair scandal, The New York Times changed its rules in 2004 to give readers a better idea of why a source was granted anonymity. And in 2005, Newsweek revised its standards for using unidentified sources after an international backlash against a questionable story about a Koran being flushed down a toilet at the Guantanamo Bay detention camp.

In general, journalists can take three steps to lessen the controversy:

- First, they should try hard to obtain the information from on-the-record human sources and from documents. Quite often, the information is available from more than one source.
- Second, they should try hard to persuade the original off-the-record source to go public; many will when asked the right way or when the reporter carefully explains how the credibility of the story will be significantly improved.
- Third, when nothing else works, journalists should explain fully why the source has requested and been granted anonymity.

Bob Woodward, book author and Washington Post staff member, is probably the most successful and best-known investigative journalist of the past three decades. His extensive, largely unquestioning use of anonymous sources in sensitive situations has been repeatedly debated, especially when it was recently revealed that the source known as "Deep Throat" in the Watergate investigation was a highly placed FBI official. Critics want to know why government officials who are paid with tax dollars should ever be granted anonymity and why they shouldn't be held accountable to the citizenry for their thoughts and actions. Woodward would answer that the information would never come to light otherwise and that he does not use any information unless it is independently verified through other sources. Another question that arises is whether it is ever ethically defensible to pay a source for information, with cash or noncash material goods. Some journalists say yes, as long as the payment is disclosed. Other journalists say no, not ever. There is also disagreement about other journalist-source transactions, such as accepting stolen or leaked information from sources or using information from children or others who are not legally capable of consent.

Writing Ethical, Accurate Stories

Line-by-Line Accuracy Check

While at the Star Tribune in Minneapolis, projects editor John Ullmann refined the line-by-line accuracy check to near perfection. Here is an explanation of Ullmann's procedure from his book "Investigative Reporting: Advanced Methods and Techniques":

> Near the end of each project, we go over every word of every line to check for accuracy, fairness and context. . . . I take a draft of the first story, starting at the top, and the reporter goes back to the original documentation to check out each fact. When we come to quotes, the reporter reads the quotes from the computer where the transcribed interviews reside. This is our last chance to make sure everything is right and it is a much more thorough method than any lawyer's. We wait until near the end because most problems arise not from the facts we use but in the words used to characterize them, as in adverbs and adjectives. How we say something is as important as what we say. . . . We are not just looking for simple things, such as is the name spelled correctly or is the date of birth right.

Ullmann explains that the line-by-line procedure is also meant to spot logical inconsistencies or information gaps. He provides three extended examples. Here is an adapted version of one, involving an investigation of 22 children who had died from abuse or neglect or under suspicious circumstances:

> All of the children had been known to authorities as being in problem homes, but the system had failed to protect them. Most did not live to their first birthday. The project team concluded that these deaths showed a system out of control. But against what standard?
>
> It can be argued that the death of one child is one child too many, but can we conclude the system is a failure? During this same period, the system handled some 20,000 cases. Did 22 deaths make the system a failure? Looked at another way, did the 20,000 or so child survivors make the system a success? How about another measure—the success/failure rate of other states? Depending on how it is measured, Minnesota was about average or among the best. What, then, could reasonably be concluded from the facts we had dug up?
>
> By taking the cases and poring over them anew, a different pattern emerged. In every case, when the person taking care of the child wanted to avoid supervision, it had been ridiculously easy for him or her to do so. The parent would move a lot. Or, in at least one case, when the social worker came to the door and was told to come back because the child was sleeping, the compliant and overworked case officer failed to return before the child's death.

Another clear pattern showed that the system failed to integrate observations of doctors, police and case workers until after the death, thus severely reducing the chance, in many cases, of exposing the danger to the child. This was coupled with some underused research the team had dug up. A researcher in Chicago had compiled a statistical profile of the child most likely to be at risk, a profile that fit most of our children like a glove. That is, these were children who should have benefited from the most aggressive intervention, but had not. This was a system seriously out of kilter and in need of reform.

Ullmann ends his discussion with this thought: "No one I ever worked with likes going through the line-by-line procedure, including me, but they and I like the feeling before publication that every single thing we published has a reason to be believed."

Prepublication Review

One practice that continues to be debated is prepublication review by subjects of investigations. Many journalists read quotes or passages back to sources or show them paragraphs on complex or technical topics. But most journalists shudder at the thought of showing the entire story to sources or to the targets of investigations. They do not worry that inaccuracies may be pointed out, but that the subject may take action to pre-empt the impact of the story, use the material to threaten legal action and hold up the story or demand misleading changes. They also worry that editors or producers may make independent changes to the story after it is shown to a subject that could undercut the journalist's defense if the subject later sues.

Steve Weinberg, a previous author of this book and a longtime and respected investigative journalist, makes a strong argument for allowing subjects to review the text of stories. He wrote in previous editions of this book:

> It was in 1978 that I began to question the conventional wisdom about prepublication review. I was investigating wrongdoing at a large law firm. Understandably, some of my key sources were reluctant to be quoted by name. Some were nervous about providing details even off the record. Some worried about losing their jobs if they talked. So I asked them if I could do anything to reduce their apprehensions.
>
> We trust your work, they responded, but this project might place our livelihoods in jeopardy no matter how good a job you do. We would like to read what you write before it goes into the newspaper. I decided to find out if I could satisfy them without compromising the story.
>
> When the experiment worked, I decided to expand its usage. Gingerly at first, more confidently later, I began offering the privilege of review—for accuracy only—to a variety of sources involved in my newspaper, magazine and book projects.
>
> Before expanding on the benefits of the procedure, I will convey the objections I have heard, accompanied by rebuttals.

- Objection One: Sources will have the chance to deny the quotations attributed to them, or shoot down other information.
- Rebuttal: Before I conduct prepublication review, I make it clear, in writing, that the source is checking for accuracy only. If something is demonstrably inaccurate, I change it. All other requests for change are just that—requests. I make the decision. If a source denies a quotation attributed to him, I have it either on tape or in my verbatim notes. After any objection, I recheck the tape and the notes. If I have made a mistake, I correct it. If I am correct, I share the recording or the notes with the source. Sometimes the words are correct, but the source objects to the context. I am willing to engage in that dialogue. We regularly miscommunicate with our spouse, our children, our parents. So why should we expect perfect communication with a source we barely know?

  If the context needs changing, I change it. If the source is acting in a self-serving way that impedes rather than serves truth, I change nothing. In any case, discussion before publication is preferable to publishing an out-of-context remark. It is also preferable to hearing from an angry source after publication—a source who had no opportunity to review the manuscript and is now threatening a lawsuit. Never has a source who had an opportunity to review the manuscript threatened to sue me after publication. Furthermore, not once have I made a change against my better judgment.

- Objection Two: Sources might successfully pressure higher-ups in the news organization to revise or kill a piece.
- Rebuttal: Yes, that could happen. If my editor or publisher betrayed the truth that way, I would never work for that person again. I would also use journalism magazines and organizations such as IRE to publicize their shameful conduct.
- Objection Three: Sources might threaten to sue after reading the manuscript.
- Rebuttal: So what? Courts have almost always refused to engage in prepublication suppression. Besides, if a source is angry enough to make such a threat, the same source will quite likely sue after publication—whether or not there was a prepublication review. Should that occur, I suspect most judges and jurors would be impressed by a reporter so eager to be accurate that he or she conducted a prepublication check.
- Objection Four: Prepublication review is unprofessional. Competent journalists get their information right the first time.
- Rebuttal: This is wishful thinking. Look at the corrections appearing in the best newspapers and magazines. (Most broadcast outlets almost never air corrections, but that is a result of arrogance, not inerrancy.) Listen to people who are experts on a subject or have attended an event in the news. Almost without exception, they complain about errors and out-of-context information. I once interviewed 40 newspaper editors about how mistakes occur. Every one of them said they had been misquoted—often in their own publications. While I was researching my Armand Hammer biography, I found errors of fact and interpretation in almost everything written about him, covering thousands of newspaper articles, magazine pieces, broadcast clips and books.

The benefits of prepublication review might be clear by now. First, it sometimes catches errors—the primary purpose of the exercise. Second, it builds trust with sources. The next time I go to those sources, their doors are likely to be open. Furthermore, they will tell future sources about my desire for accuracy, opening additional doors. Third, previously cooperative sources recall new information while reading the manuscript. One such source wrote me an eight-page single-spaced letter filled with gems while reading a manuscript chapter on Armand Hammer. I had interviewed him multiple times; he had been a fount of information. But reading the manuscript opened a section of his memory that had been closed until that point. Fourth, previously uncooperative sources are so impressed by the procedure that they warm up.

All journalists should know their organization's policy on prepublication review and should consult the organization's attorney. Freelance investigative journalists should consult a media attorney if they are considering that kind of review so that they are up to date on the advantages and risks of the practice.

⟳ CHECK IT OUT

✓ A public employee tells you that she has had a consensual affair with a male superior. She says the affair has ended, but the superior is now sexually harassing her. What guidelines do you apply in deciding whether to report on the matter?

✓ You have promised anonymity to a private defense attorney who agrees to supply you with confidential legal documents on grand jury testimony. After you publish a story based on the information, the source claims in court that the case against his client has been tainted by the release of secret grand jury information. Should you continue to get documents from this source? Should you continue to grant the source anonymity?

✓ You are reporting on illegal drug use in an impoverished area of your community. During your reporting, you see that children are being exposed to the drug use and sometimes given drugs. Do you alert the authorities to the situation, or do you wait and publish the story and rely on the authorities to take action?

RESOURCES FOR REPORTING

Books on Ethics and Journalism

The following books include discussions and thoughts on journalism ethics and libel:

- "Sack on Defamation: Libel, Slander and Related Problems," by Robert David Sack
- "Elements of Journalism," by Bill Kovach and Tom Rosenstiel
- "Feeding Frenzy: How Attack Journalism Has Transformed American Politics," by Larry J. Sabato
- "Ethical Journalism," by Philip Meyer
- "Media Ethics: Issues and Cases," edited by Philip Patterson and Lee Wilkins
- "The News at Any Cost: How Journalists Compromise Their Ethics to Shape the News," by Tom Goldstein
- "Doing Ethics in Journalism," by Jay Black, Bob Steele and Ralph Barney
- "Responsible Journalism," edited by Deni Elliott
- "Secrets: On the Ethics of Concealment and Revelation," by Sissela Bok
- "Journalism Ethics: Arguments and Cases," by Martin Hirst and Roger Patching
- "The Journalist and the Murderer," by Janet Malcolm
- "Committed Journalism: An Ethic for the Profession," by Edmund B. Lambeth
- The Associated Press Stylebook

Organizations and Web Sites

The following organizations discuss ethics in journalism. More information can be found on their Web sites.

- Associated Press Managing Editors (APME) Code of Ethics (www.apme.com/ethics)
- Journal of Mass Media Ethics (http://jmme.byu.edu)
- Poynter Online, Tip Sheets: Ethics (www.poynter.org/content/content _view.asp?id=31889)
- Poynter Online, Ethics Bibliography (www.poynter.org/content/content _view.asp?id=1208)
- Radio and Television News Directors Association (RTNDA) Code of Ethics (www.rtnda.org/pages/media_items/code-of-ethics-and-professional-conduct48 .php)
- Society of Professional Journalists (SPJ): Ethics (www.spj.org/ethics)

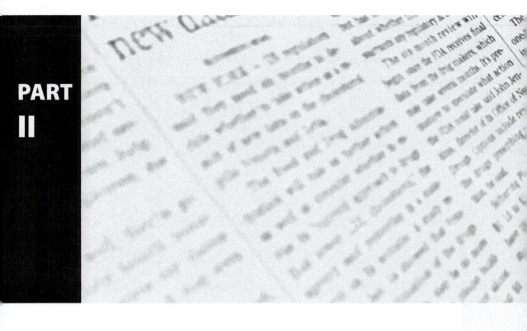

PART

II

Investigating
the Government

8

Investigating the Executive Branch

This chapter covers how to probe corruption and misdeeds in the executive branches of governments, whether they are local, state or federal. It will show how to "follow the money" in spending by offices and agencies in the executive branch, including spending on contracts, personnel and services. The chapter also reviews the parts of government that journalists do not always cover thoroughly, such as public authorities and special districts.

Many journalists focus their investigations on executive-branch agencies, performing a watchdog role by monitoring how public employees spend the public's money and how they conduct their business. Public employees affect a huge number of lives every day, whether they work at the federal, state or local level. The techniques for investigating the executive branch and the trails of documents, databases and people are similar at each level, from the White House to the mayor's office.

In most cases, the investigative journalist is measuring the employees' or agency's performance against well-articulated and understood standards, regulations and laws. For example, a public official is not supposed to favor anyone for a job or a service; the official is supposed to hire the best employee for the position or the best company for a publicly funded job.

But the influence of money—from an outright bribe to a cheap price for a summer condo—can corrupt an official into favoring a poor job candidate or an incompetent company. So too can political pressure from campaign contributors or from a public employee's boss who needs those contributors to get re-elected.

In "Investigative Reporting and Editing," Paul Williams wrote:

> To be a successful investigative reporter, you need to assume that the institutions of government are under constant and pernicious attack by both external forces seeking special advantage and internal operators who figure that graft is one of the perquisites of office. . . . You need also to assume that within these institutions, most of the people are still either essentially honest, unaware of what's going on, or merely jealous of the grafters and graftees. This majority comprises your best resource, your best hope for doing reporting that will effectively describe our systemic problems.

123

Longtime investigative reporter David Burnham also wrote about approaches to investigating bureaucracies in The IRE Journal while writing his book "A Law Unto Itself: Power, Politics and the IRS":

> I had decided [years earlier] that my principal role as the New York Times reporter assigned to cover the system of criminal justice was to describe the reasons why the agencies within this system often failed to achieve their stated goals. This approach to reporting about the police worked equally well with the IRS. The stated goal of the NYPD — to make the streets safe for all New Yorkers — was terrific. But like all human institutions, the NYPD frequently came up short. People were mugged. Houses were burgled. Women were raped. Why? Was it because the department had been given an impossible mission? Was it because the department had been given inadequate resources? Was it because many police officers cared more about receiving their weekly paycheck than providing public service? Was it because a large number of cops were corrupt? Quite obviously, the failures of the department can be blamed on all of the above and a number of other factors, too.
>
> My game plan — trying to tell readers why the NYPD did not achieve its stated goals — was the rationale behind my decision to write an article about "cooping," the widely accepted practice of sleeping while on duty, especially while working the midnight to 8 a.m. shift. . . . Like the NYPD, the IRS has been given an impossible mission and inadequate resources. Like the NYPD, the IRS suffers from a number of lazy, poorly trained, underpaid and incompetent managers. Like the NYPD, the IRS always is vulnerable to corruption and political fixes. The inevitability of these problems in large organizations does not mean society can afford to shrug its collective shoulders and accept them.

The Players and Processes

Understanding Government Agencies

To find agency standards, goals and performances, an investigative journalist can examine government Web sites where agencies post their mission statements, reports, statistics and audits about their activities. Journalists also can review government manuals and guides.

Reading about each agency, a reporter can see the agency's mission, whether it's granting licenses, setting rates, establishing industrywide rules or inspecting and imposing sanctions on individuals and institutions. Agencies can act like governments in themselves, with quasi-legislative and judicial powers to complement their executive duties. With such wide authority, agencies have the potential to commit large abuses of power.

Before checking out a tip or planning a methodical investigation into a city or agency, an investigative journalist can begin collecting basic information that will provide context, if not story ideas.

Among the documents, or preferably databases, to collect are these:

- The list of all employees, with their name, department, title, date of hire, salary and, if possible, their date of birth for the purpose of verifying identity
- The list of all those appointed to commissions and boards and other appointed positions
- The list of all vendors who supply materials and services and how much they receive in public funds annually
- Campaign finance reports from the last four years
- The list of any grants given out
- Any required statements of potential conflicts of interest and financial disclosures by officials
- The last three years of the budget and any audits

There are many more documents to obtain, but these form the basis of a good library of information for following people or paper trails at government agencies.

Using the Federal Register

Journalists should read the documents that those in power publish to establish the rules governing daily life. On the national level, the Federal Register is a tool for investigative journalists interested in monitoring the executive branch, much as the Congressional Record is for the legislative branch (see Chapter 9). The Register appears every workday; some issues contain up to 1,000 pages of small type. It is searchable online through the Government Printing Office. (See "Resources for Reporting" at the end of this chapter.) It is not only useful for national level stories, but also can help a journalist understand how federal agencies and funds are affecting local communities.

A Federal Register notice can lead to an immediate story. The Chronicle of Higher Education used a Federal Register notice as the basis for an article headlined "New Policy of Naming Scientists Who Are Found Guilty of Fraud Renews Debate on Federal Role." The story noted that the Public Health Service used the Federal Register to publish the names of 14 scientists found guilty of misconduct since the creation of the Office of Research Integrity.

For documents-minded investigative journalists, Register notices from the Office of Management and Budget can be especially useful. Under the Paperwork Reduction Act, every document that an agency uses to collect information must be approved by OMB on Standard Form 83. The Federal Register designation for such approvals is "Public Information Collection Requirements Submitted to the Office of Management and Budget for Clearance." For instance, IRS Form 211, "Application for Reward for Original Information," filed by citizens who want a reward for supplying information that "led to the collection of taxes, penalties, fines and forfeitures," carries OMB Clearance Number 1545-0409.

In a Register submission from the Health Care Financing Administration (HCFA), the agency told OMB it wanted to collect information for a study of nursing home and home health care needs of Medicare and Medicaid patients; the annual form would be completed by state and local governments. An investigative journalist wanting to know more could call an HCFA telephone number in the Federal Register notice or the person named at OMB's Reports Management Branch. OMB publishes a list of approved forms in a monthly inventory. It is arranged in alphabetical order by agency name, then broken down further according to the agency's internal units.

A particularly valuable issue of the Federal Register is the semiannual agenda of regulations published by each agency. Each agency lists a contact person and a direct telephone number. The agenda items are organized by program office (for example, Office of Public and Indian Housing; Office of Fair Housing and Equal Opportunity), then divided by stage of development (pre-rulemaking actions, proposed rules that have been published, recent final rules that have been published or recent completed actions).

The Register has codes for different topics and each title is broken out into chapters, which usually have the name of the issuing agency. Chapters are divided into parts covering specific regulatory areas, and parts are divided into sections. Here's an example: Title 8, Aliens and Nationality; Chapter 1, Immigration and Naturalization Service, Department of Justice; Part 235, Inspection of Persons Applying for Admission; Section 235.10, U.S. Citizen Identification Card. The U.S. government's booklet "The Federal Register: What It Is and How to Use It" contains a useful example of how to trace a brief reference in a newspaper article to the actual law and regulations.

Making Sense of Agency Budgets

A budget is a key document for looking into waste, fraud and abuse in government. Budgets show where the money comes from (revenue) and where the money goes (expenditures), and they also reveal what and who are important to the government. (One useful maxim to remember is "Budget is policy, policy is budget.")

Budgets can be misleading, however, because some expenditures may be contained in another program or, in the federal government, may be "off-budget" —

that is, contained in an entirely different financial accounting report. This is one way governments avoid showing that they are actually running deficits by spending or obligating more money than they have.

For example, some governments do not make clear the future pension liabilities in current budgets, even though the money will have to be paid out as employees retire. That means large obligations that would drive up deficits go unnoticed.

Overall, governments use three kinds of budgets:

- The general operating budget, which covers day-to-day commitments
- The capital improvements budget, which covers long-term, tangible items like buildings and streets
- The debt service budget, which covers payments to investors and lenders on financial obligations incurred in previous years

Tracking a budget effectively is a year-round job. In a guide for journalists at the Memphis Commercial Appeal, Walter Dawson and Jimmie Covington wrote,

> Don't wait for the new budget to come out. Get started now with the current budget so you'll become familiar with it and be ready to address any changes from it to the new budget. The current budget also gives you a chance to practice your knowledge and questions on your sources. . . .
>
> Find a mid-level person in the budget office and take him to lunch to find out how he helps put the budget together. . . . Talk to the finance director, the person who is in charge of the budget process. Ask her about the bigger picture—is it financially wise for the city to keep property taxes low while increasing the city's debt through bonds? . . . Most states have an auditing division with some oversight responsibilities on local budgets. If possible, travel to the capital and get to know these people face to face.

At the local agency level, revenue usually comes from

- Taxes on property, income and retail sales
- Fees for garbage pickup and other services to individuals
- Fees collected from businesses for licenses
- Fees paid by utilities and other monopoly franchises
- Penalties, such as parking tickets, traffic tickets and court fines
- State and federal funds
- Sales of tax-exempt bonds to investors
- Interest on investments

Each category presents investigation opportunities for journalists. For example, rather than being invested at a good rate, revenue might be in a low-interest-bearing account at a local bank controlled by a supporter of the mayor.

In "Investigative Reporting and Editing," Paul Williams quoted New York City budget director Frederick O'Reilly Hayes about avoiding the simplistic "compared to last year" budget story. As Hayes said,

> This approach has obvious limitations. Usually the increases . . . account for only 5 to 10 percent of the total budget, and reductions are even smaller. . . . [If we] only look at these pluses and minuses, we are accepting on faith the other, larger part of the budget—for example, our attention might be directed to a police chief's request for ten additional detectives and a proposed 5 percent pay increase, but not to the uses of the 900 officers already on duty. Like an iceberg, the largest part of the budget escapes our gaze.

In almost every government's budget there often is a major project that is questionable. The projects can range from building roads and sewers for shopping malls that benefit only developers to the construction of sports stadiums and convention centers.

But governments that issue bonds in order to finance projects like convention centers are required to release annual financial updates to supplement information provided at the time of sale. These financial updates can provide story tips and outright revelations.

Issuers are also supposed to release information on "material events," such as the closing of a major employer or the withdrawing of a large airline from the local airport. And the Securities and Exchange Commission (www.sec.gov) requires more municipal bond disclosure than in previous decades.

Expenditures should not be the only focus for journalists on the lookout for waste, fraud and abuse. Journalists should scrutinize agencies for what they sell as well as what they buy. Government agencies regularly dispose of surplus equipment at prices that may benefit purchasers rather than the general taxpaying public. To get an idea of how much can be auctioned off, journalists can go to the Web site www.usa.gov, run by the U.S. General Services Administration. In addition, journalists should take a particularly close look at sales and auctions by local governments.

Consultants and Contractors

Over the past decade, governments have allocated a significant portion of their budgets to paying private consultants and contractors to perform government activities. Since the war in Iraq began, the issue of contracting out services such as troop support and security for government officials has resulted in numerous stories. An investigative journalist can ask questions that include these:

- Is the agency understaffed?
- Is the agency adequately staffed but operating inefficiently?
- Do contractors and consultants fall under the same agency rules as staff members?
- Are contractors or consultants hired because of their political or personal connections instead of their skills?

When Washington Post reporters Ted Gup and Jonathan Neumann delved into consulting contracts given by the federal government, they learned that more than two-thirds had been awarded without competitive bidding. Commerce Business Daily, the official government publication that advertises contract opportunities, went largely unread in the private sector because so many awards had been decided before the notification appeared. By looking at lists of government contracts (which now is much more easily done through databases), Gup and Neumann found that government officials who awarded and monitored contracts accepted favors from contractors. In one case, the contractor lived with the government employee heading the office that supervised the contract. In another instance, a contractor hired prostitutes for the official who monitored the firm's troubled contracts.

Many corporations are dependent on government contracts. Despite the large amounts of money to be earned, those who try to follow the rules sometimes give up. The chief executive officer of one supplier explained in The Washington Post why he would no longer seek contracts after 20 years of selling paint to the government. According to the article, he blamed the General Services Administration, the purchasing arm of government:

> The officers responsible for procuring paint are separate from those involved in contract administration, thus ensuring turf wars and lack of accountability for results. . . . These contract administration officers know almost nothing about the paint they are purchasing, since they lack any chemical or engineering background.
> The executive said overly specific 20-year-old government specifications were irrelevant to military paint applications, where technological advances occur continually. As a result, the government denies itself newer, better products.

Investigative journalists trying to explain contracts for $400 hammers should explore not only corruption and inefficiency by the agency and contractor but also built-in factors. Those could include government accounting standards (it might be that all the long-distance telephone calls necessary to close the contract were included in the cost) and socioeconomic policies (such as accepting a higher unit price from a minority contractor).

Contracting problems at all levels of government are so rampant that they should be a full-time beat. In Oklahoma, commissioners in dozens of counties accepted kickbacks from suppliers on road-building projects. Harry Holloway and Frank S. Meyers chronicled the case in their book "Bad Times for Good Ol' Boys: The Oklahoma County Commissioner Scandal." The section on the anatomy of corruption is a road map for investigative journalists looking at suspicious contracts anywhere:

> A commissioner would act as his own purchasing agent and conduct the purchase of materials for the road and bridge program. Orders involved such things as gravel, sand, culvert pipe and lumber. . . . The requirement that the counties buy from a bid list was no barrier to the kickback system for two reasons. First, the "lowest and best bid" loophole would allow commissioners to contract the favored supplier, even if that supplier was not the low bidder, on the grounds that the supplier was the lowest and best bidder. Second, the suppliers jacked up their bids to cover the cost of their kickbacks. . . . In this perverse system the commissioners even had an incentive to use poor-quality materials. Frequent breakdowns meant frequent opportunities to order supplies, with their accompanying kickbacks.

The Contracting Process

The best tactic for a journalist unfamiliar with contracting is to take a well-defined government task—for example, the awarding of an office supply contract by the school system or the hiring of an architectural consultant by the city council—and examine it step-by-step. The investigator should begin with the enabling law and the executive-branch regulation implementing the law. Ted Wendling of The (Cleveland) Plain Dealer did just that while looking at food bids solicited by seven school districts. Writing in The IRE Journal about finding $1 million of excessive food costs, Wendling said school administrators "were engaging in bidsplitting, in which they were paying different prices for the same foods." That was not all: "We found [cases] in which the district accepted the low bid, even though it didn't meet specifications and was lower only because it didn't include sauce, an essential ingredient."

Experienced investigative journalists know there are well established procedures to examine. Some reporters, particularly at The Washington Post, have actually taken a university course to understand federal contract procedures. Here is how the process often works:

Informal Cost Estimates Government officials somewhere write down estimates, even on nonbid items, and can get an idea of a reasonable estimate by searching the Web for the going prices. An investigative journalist should obtain the estimate and then determine whether the awarded contract was below, at or above the estimate. The journalist can also perform a similar search for prices on the Web.

Other times a government official is expected to get three quotes — that is, prices from three different vendors.

If there is a significant discrepancy between the estimate and the actual cost, the journalist ought to figure out why. If there is never an advertisement for bids, the journalist should inquire whether the government agency is violating rules. Sometimes an agency will divide a bulk purchase into units small enough to avoid competitive bidding, A review of small purchases during previous years might reveal a deliberate plan to shift nonbid business to a political contributor, a friend or a company in which the government administrator or a relative has a financial interest.

Notice of Bid Local, state and federal rules prescribe how much notice is given to potential bidders, as well as the media through which word must be spread. The most common medium is a general-circulation newspaper or a national daily.

Requests for Proposals Governments sometimes use requests for proposals instead of bid notices when seeking flexible, open-ended contracts, especially for consulting services from such professionals as engineers and architects. That flexibility can benefit taxpayers, but it also leaves room for abuse. Reporters in Kansas City found by reviewing county RFPs that a county engineer was awarding all outside engineering work to a former business partner to whom the county engineer owed money.

Examination of Bids An investigative journalist can check each company that bids or wins a bid and ask these questions:

- Does it owe back taxes to the city, county, state or the federal government?
- Do its officers, directors, stockholders, lawyers, accountants or other key players have links to members of the government awarding the contract?
- Has the company failed to finish jobs satisfactorily in the past?
- Are there postcontract audits that document past problems or has it been barred from other public business?
- Have any lawsuits resulted from the company's alleged poor performance?

Investigative journalists should also determine whether specifications favor a particular supplier by excluding all but one brand of equipment. Narrowly drawn specifications ought to be a red flag. Journalists can check to see if the potential supplier helped the agency write the terms or if the supplier is a political contributor.

Product Preferences Rules often mandate that governments select locally produced goods if the local bids are equal to, or maybe even higher than, those of distant suppliers. Journalists can look at whether the local preferences are being used to award contracts to friends or supporters.

Minority Contracting Requirements Government rules often require that agencies make reasonable efforts to contract with minority-owned businesses. But white-owned contractors have been caught placing minorities as fronts in subcontracting firms and then using those illegally planted fronts to win the overall job.

Audit Requirements Rules call for government contracts to be audited at intervals during the job and at completion. Sometimes the audit is performed by an independent outside firm; sometimes internal government auditors are allowed to do the checking. Journalists should obtain any and all audits to check whether taxpayer money is being spent legally and wisely.

Bid and Performance Bonds A bond posted by the prospective supplier is supposed to assure the government that the supplier will accept the contract if its bid is selected. The bond is forfeited if the supplier rejects the contract offer. Later, a performance bond covers the agency if the supplier fails to fulfill the contract. The bonds usually cost the supplier a percentage of the contract's dollar value.

Journalists should ask whether the bonding company is monitoring contractors and whether it is paying the government if default occurs. Journalists should also check courthouses for lawsuits over disputes between bond companies and governments.

A journalist tracking contracts has to be alert to all manner of scams. For example, the apparent low bidder might turn out to be a bad deal for taxpayers. A reporter for the Rocky Mountain News looked into a company that had won a Denver computer services contract. Bid documents showed that firms competing for the contract promised to pay property taxes on the hardware they supplied. But the winning company never paid those taxes. Companies that planned to pay the taxes lost to a company that failed to pay. It turned out that the supposed low bid was costing taxpayers money.

Change Orders Another scam often involves change orders. While change orders can be justified, it is one way for a contractor that made the lowest bid to earn more money.

For example, a low-bid contractor hired to remove concrete from a city street suddenly "discovers" that it is six inches thicker than premised in the bid. As a result, he convinces the city to issue a change order allowing an extra charge. The potential for dishonesty is especially high with change orders because they are not subjected to competitive bidding. Even when the change orders are for relatively small dollar amounts, they can add up quickly as a percentage of the total contract.

Budget and Management Watchdogs

Every agency and government has a budget staff. Keeping track of each agency is an executive-branch superagency like the White House Office of Management and Budget or its counterpart in state and local government executive branches. The agency recommends which individual agencies receive budget increases and which budgets are cut. Those decisions reveal priorities and sometimes the influence of special interests. After all, as the saying goes, budget is policy and policy is budget.

The superagency also tracks whether individual agency expenditures during the year are consistent with administration policy. Sometimes a superagency will discover illegal or unethical practices, but the scrutiny of individual agency budgets is often minimal; the agencies can overwhelm the relatively understaffed watchdog.

In his book "How Washington Really Works," Charles Peters says if overmatched OMB examiners manage to cut through obfuscation, agencies have "yet another way of dealing with the problem—offering the OMB investigator a higher salary to come work for the agency. When this is done by a private government contractor, the impropriety is obvious. But it's done all the time within the government."

One situation that a journalist should look for is an agency's spending spree during the last month of the fiscal year. The reason is to prevent a budget reduction next year on the grounds that the agency did not need its full allocation.

Investigating Federal Affairs

Investigations into the executive branch fill the IRE Resource Center. One of them provides a longtime model for the kind of digging and research that pays off.

In a classic example, journalists at The Miami Herald began their probe of a state agency after seeing a listing in The Miami Herald's Sunday real estate column: notice of a $100,000 mortgage loan on generous terms to the director of the regional Federal Housing Administration office. The reporters, Mike Baxter and Jim Savage, looked into the loan, writing a brief story about the connection between the favorable terms and approval of a questionable housing project proposal by the federal administrator. Little did they know the story would evolve into a scandal about the operations of an entire agency, bringing down a U.S. senator along the way. Their exposé became the basis for a chapter in the book "The New Muckrakers," by Leonard Downie Jr.

As a result of their original real estate story, Baxter and Savage received an anonymous tip: The federal regional office was giving favored treatment to one developer of government-subsidized single-family housing. The reporters asked their builder sources about the alleged favored treatment. To their surprise, nobody knew anything about the builder who was allegedly benefiting from the deal. A check of the city directory showed him only as proprietor of a hearing aid business.

Some reporters would have given up then, but an inner sense, fed by agency stonewalling about releasing documents, prompted Baxter and Savage to continue. When The Herald finally obtained the documents, though, the alleged kingpin builder barely showed up in them. Still, the investigation continued. As Downie relates, Baxter and Savage "became convinced, as their real estate contacts had told them, that [the builder] was somehow hidden in several places on that FHA list in the disguises of several unfamiliar corporations." While Savage explored other angles, Baxter visited the courthouse to run the paper trail on corporations receiving FHA money.

> It was work that many journalists avoid because they perceive it as boring, but Baxter became caught up in his sleuthing through the courthouse records. He began finding real estate corporations that the builder was on record as controlling, although none of these corporations turned up on the FHA list of subsidy commitments. At the same time, he found that many of the corporations on the FHA list did not turn up in the telephone book, other city directories or the courthouse corporation records.

These mysterious companies did appear from time to time in the land records, however. They bought land for the projects that the FHA office had approved. . . . The names signed as officers of these corporations were unfamiliar, but Baxter noticed that the notaries used by all the mysterious corporations were the same.

What Baxter and Savage had uncovered was a sophisticated scheme of corruption involving an executive-branch agency, a developer and—it turned out— a U.S. senator from Florida.

Delving into executive-branch conduct does not always yield such blatant corruption. In fact, if a taxpayer-supported agency is performing well, that can easily be a story since there is so much skepticism about government.

The Top Executive

Effective investigations of the government's chief executive depend on gaining access to the policy-makers and support staff. These include the aides who are liaisons to the legislature; staff members who recommend political appointees; and political operatives who go in and out of any executive office on a routine basis. In addition, secretaries, custodians and other lower level staffers—both current and former—often can offer unfiltered information about the inner workings of the office.

Paying attention to what's happening in the executive office is another way for an investigative journalist to scrutinize agencies. At the least, that is where the tone is set for the rest of the executive branch.

The chief executive's pronouncements are a starting point. For example, presidential executive orders, which are legally binding despite never receiving congressional approval, appear first in the Federal Register, the Monday through Friday publication of the executive branch. Even obscure orders can have far-reaching impact.

For example, Charles Savage of The Boston Globe won a Pulitzer Prize for exposing President George W. Bush's practice of using so-called "signing statements" to bypass laws passed by Congress instead of using his veto power. Using obscure "signing statements" meant that the practice was generally hidden from the public and Congress.

Cabinet Appointees

At the federal level, the most visible are the Cabinet departments, and many state governments are organized similarly. Because many such appointees are already public figures before they are tapped by the chief executive, investigative journalists can find useful background information about them. Cabinet appointees often have a lengthy record of public service or of experience in the business world that has never been examined thoroughly. In addition, some have written books that can be mined for insights; for instance, when President Clinton took office Publishers Weekly magazine printed a list of books by his Cabinet nominees.

At the federal level top executive-branch appointees require Senate confirmation, and the confirmation hearing record is filled with information about nominees. At lower levels of government, the executive may simply announce the appointments.

Conflicts of Interest

Investigative journalists can begin a corruption check by examining financial disclosures by executive-branch supervisors. The disclosures must be filed with the designated agency ethics official under the federal Ethics in Government Act. Many states have similar laws, as do counties and cities.

When journalists at the Center for Public Integrity in Washington, D.C., started digging into the Office of the U.S. Trade Representative, they learned from disclosure forms that two top officials held stock in tobacco companies while pushing to open foreign markets to tobacco. A savvy investigative journalist will also examine disclosures in search of corporate directorships. When an agency official is a bank director, for example, it is legitimate to ask whether the bank has interests pending before the agency. From a different perspective, a journalist might ask what is in the directorship for the official: cash payments, perhaps, or a lucrative job after leaving government.

At the federal level, the Office of Government Ethics can help with inquiries about executive-branch conduct. The agency requires journalists to provide written requests for information, but disclosure forms filed there allowed The New York Times to report on the personal wealth of President Bill Clinton and Hillary Rodham Clinton, identifying specific bond, stock and mutual fund holdings.

Sometimes conflicts are disclosed in places other than annual financial forms. A careful reader of the Congressional Record will spot disclosures by executive-branch officials, as mandated in various laws. For example, the Interior Department secretary supplies Congress with disclosures of bureaucrats who have responsibilities under the Energy Policy and Conservation Act. A separate Congressional Record notice reveals campaign contributions by presidential nominees for ambassadorships; a law requires such disclosures to guard against wealthy citizens' secretly buying ambassadorships.

The Federal Register contains equally informative disclosures, and it can be searched on the Web, saving journalists an incredible amount of time. For example, when a new secretary took over the Energy Department, the Federal Register contained a notice explaining that agency officials are prohibited from "knowingly receiving compensation from, holding any official relation with, or having any pecuniary interest in any energy concern." The appointee, it turned out, received a survivor annuity through her husband's employment at a utilities company. But Energy Department ethics officials allowed her to keep the annuity as long as she excused herself from decisions involving the particular utility.

Most state governments have similar disclosure requirements and reports that can produce strong stories both at the state and the local level. If the state or local government does not have disclosure requirements—or has weak requirements—that can be a story in itself.

One common conflict is the revolving door between government positions and those in the private sector. These are difficult to monitor because the comings and goings are frequent and intentionally low-profile. Some of the conflicting interests are so egregious, however, that journalists need to make the effort to uncover them.

When Bill Clinton became president, he vowed to stop the use of government as a steppingstone to riches in the private sector. But less than a year into the Clinton administration, The Wall Street Journal reported that the White House deputy chief of staff was departing for a $500,000 annual salary at the U.S. Telephone Association. The article said that the president required some senior appointees to sign a pledge promising not to lobby the offices where they work for five years, but that pledge did little to prevent officials from joining organizations that lobby Congress.

For example, the Defense Department's Standards of Conduct Office supplies the Senate and House Armed Services committees with a list of military retirees or former civilian employees who are taking jobs with defense contractors. Title 10, Section 2397, of the U.S. Code requires Defense Department military and civilian employees above certain levels to file a report if hired by a major defense contractor above a certain pay rate. In one year, one of the authors of this book found 1,623 defense officials had moved to private-industry jobs. Only 79 had moved from private industry to government defense employment.

On the state and local level, journalists can find many other examples of the revolving door, whether it's the banking industry, the utility industry or any other industry that the official has been regulating.

Inspectors General

Executive-branch agencies are more likely to perform efficiently and honestly if they are audited from inside. Most federal agencies, plus many state and local agencies, house such an office. At the federal level, there are not only auditors, but also the inspector general, who does both audits and investigations. Inspectors general produce semiannual reports. As prescribed by Congress in the Inspector General Act, the report is supposed to

- Discuss deficiencies in agency programs, along with proposals for corrective action.
- Identify previous proposals that have not been implemented.
- Summarize items referred to prosecutors.
- List audits issued during the six-month reporting period.

Inspectors general often concentrate on programs with large dollar values (e.g., the U.S. Department of Agriculture's $24 billion food stamp program) or that are especially vulnerable because guidelines have changed recently or are new or have a reputation for weak management.

Journalists should look for wrongdoing more urgent than what is mentioned in the semiannual report; in cases of "particularly serious or flagrant problems, abuses or deficiencies," inspectors general are supposed to contact the relevant agency head immediately, who must inform the appropriate congressional committees within seven days. Every federal agency's inspector general has a Web page, where journalists can search indexes and press releases for reports and get electronic copies.

When Leslie Henderson wrote about inspectors general in The IRE Journal, she mentioned the value of their reports to investigations in four newsrooms. The Des Moines Register used Agriculture Department inspector general information while delving into sanitation violations by a company supplying 42 percent of the meat for the school lunch program. The Washington Post cited Environmental Protection Agency inspector general audits in an investigation of wastewater treatment plants and their failure to prevent pollution in drinking water. At the Milwaukee Journal, reporters used an inspector general's audit of the Department of Housing and Urban Development to show that the agency was running its local programs poorly. The Chicago Sun-Times found information in inspector general files showing that the Farmers Home Administration had reversed loan rejections after members of Congress intervened on behalf of unqualified applicants.

Audits generally contain two sections: the *management advisory report* and the *financial statement*. The first section shows compliance (or noncompliance) with laws and regulations, deviations from sound business practices, and the program's degree of effectiveness. The financial statement includes

- The balance sheet, which lists assets, liabilities and fund balances on a particular date (usually the final day of the fiscal year)
- A statement of revenues, expenditures and encumbrances during the year
- A statement of changes in financial position during the year

There are four kinds of opinions an auditor can render about an agency's financial books.

There is the *unqualified*, or *clean, opinion*; the *qualified opinion*, which includes observations on weaknesses in handling money; the *adverse opinion*, which points to serious and possibly criminal problems; and *no opinion* because records do not permit the auditor to make an adequate judgment.

Most federal grants awarded to localities are audited locally. At the Department of Housing and Urban Development, for instance, only 10 percent of 40,000 grants might be done by the inspector general. The others were contracted out to local accounting firms.

Journalists need not wait for audit reports to investigate federal grants. There are documents and people to consult every step of the way. What follows is the chronology of one $600,000 federal grant, used to restore a city's abandoned cotton mill for use as a community center.

The first document to get is the city's application, which includes a contact person, a list of other grants already received from the federal agency and a budget separating expenses into nine categories. The second document is the federal agency's approval, with a proviso that at least 10 percent of the grant will go to minority-owned businesses and that at least 26 percent of the laborers hired will belong to a minority group.

After receiving approval, the city advertised for bids, studied the bids received and made an award. As renovation progressed, the city filed monthly employment utilization reports documenting the breakout of the work force, plus minority business enterprise utilization reports providing details of contracts and subcontracts to minority-owned businesses. Periodically, the city asked for permission to amend the project, such as using money to demolish a building separate from the old mill. At various stages, the city submitted a project performance report. The reports told of progress, but also outlined problems with specific subcontractors. Eighteen months after renovation began, the city christened its community center. But it was three years before the city submitted its final report, showing a cost overrun of $240,000, funded with other than federal money. The independent auditor completed its report two months later, and the federal agency inspector general reviewed the independent audit five months after that.

The Permanent Bureaucracy

Below the highest levels of government, many officials remain in the bureaucracy their entire working lives. The careerists often know more than the presidential appointees and use that knowledge to resist change, whether it would be good or bad.

As noted earlier, in the permanent bureaucracy, a journalist should cultivate low-level employees on the organization charts, such as clerks and custodial workers. They hear and see much, can supply copies of documents if they want to and sometimes have little loyalty because of their low pay and status.

Agency telephone directories can lead to such sources. For example, the directory for the U.S. Department of Housing and Urban Development contains a section for the general counsel. In that section are names of secretaries to the general counsel, with their direct telephone numbers, as well as names and direct lines of every secretary to every deputy general counsel. The directory lists personnel in HUD's 10 regional offices too. The importance of regional office personnel entered public consciousness during investigations of President Clinton's role in the Whitewater-related land dealings. Three government employees of the now defunct Resolution Trust Corp.'s Kansas City regional office received suspensions because of their activities in the Whitewater affair. At massive agencies like the Agricultural Stabilization and Conservation Service, decisions on how to spend billions annually are made at the grassroots level by committees of farmers who decide who will receive payments. The Wall Street Journal exposed a local farmer ASCS committee in Georgia that doled out huge amounts to those who grew and then destroyed squash to qualify for payments under a crop disaster program.

Civil Service

As vacancies occur, personnel officers try to hire competent people but often face political pressure or do not have the funds to hire the best. When investigative journalists are checking inefficiency or corruption within an agency, part of the inquiry ought to focus on hiring and firing practices:

- Does the agency offer salary and benefits in line with comparable private-sector jobs?
- If not, what does the agency say to the brightest applicants — those who have a choice between government and industry?

- Once somebody is working within the agency, what incentives exist to encourage peak performance?
- When an employee is inefficient or corrupt, how do higher-ups find out about the problem? How do they handle it?

If an especially egregious incident causes the manager to act, the worker's file may fail to reflect serious past incompetence, causing union officials or hearing judges to question the agency's case. Journalists should look for inept management handling of legitimate cases, just as they should look for valid charges by workers of unfair treatment. Neither situation benefits taxpayers.

An enlightening discussion about the permanent bureaucracy of one government agency occurred in the Cato Institute's Regulation Magazine in an article written by Wendy L. Gramm, former chair of the Commodity Futures Trading Commission, and Gerald D. Gay, CFTC chief economist during Gramm's tenure. Gramm and Gay explain how they changed the agency's overall culture more readily than their counterparts at other agencies had been able to do. The reasons for their success included a staff that was young and therefore not so entrenched; a relatively small work force, making communication easier; a receptive, intelligent mix of backgrounds, including lawyers, economists and accountants; a regulated sector with the option of escaping CFTC scrutiny by relocating offshore, thus causing the agency to examine all decisions with special care; and congressional committees with little interest in micromanaging an agency whose mission they barely understood.

Many government agencies are so convinced that traditional employees are inefficient and corrupt that they have moved to award operations to private businesses. When journalists have delved into specific privatization operations, though, they sometimes find less service for more money. The San Francisco Bay Guardian determined that animals in the local zoo were suffering from neglect because the private company that was managing the zoo on a lucrative contract was laying off experienced zookeepers who had worked for the city. The bottom line had taken precedence over the animals. Employee labor unions often oppose privatization, making union members and officials potentially talkative.

Public Affairs Personnel

Investigative journalists should use public affairs personnel for basic information gathering. They have their own organization, the National Association of Government Communicators, located in Alexandria, Va. News releases, despite spin meant to make the agency look good, can contain valuable information.

That is especially true if the release mentions action against an individual or institution, such as the Missouri Department of Natural Resources release headed "Confirmed or Uncontrolled Hazardous Waste Disposal Sites." Accompanying the release was a multipage description of each site, plus maps.

Agency libraries and reading rooms are filled with in-house periodicals, specialized outside periodicals and summary documents, such as the agency's annual report to the legislature. Public affairs staff work with agency statisticians and economists to produce documents like "Residential Electric Bills in Major Cities"; some agencies house number-crunching subdivisions, such as the Bureau of Labor Statistics and National Center for Health Statistics.

Through public affairs staff, investigative journalists can identify the unofficial lobbyists within agencies: the employees in the office of legislative liaison. Their mission is to convince the legislature that the agency is doing a good job and is therefore entitled to more money to do an even better job. Some legislators become dependent on the liaisons, asking them to draft bills affecting the agency. That dependence raises questions about the statutory independence of the legislature and so ought to be reported. It certainly has the potential to compromise meaningful legislative monitoring of programs that might result from the bills.

Agency liaisons sometimes influence legislators when it comes to advisory committee appointments. Some advisory bodies to executive-branch agencies are for show; others influence policy. Either way, they are good stories, but many journalists never think about them. Gale Research's Encyclopedia of Governmental Advisory Organizations contains thousands of such bodies at the federal level alone. The Federal Advisory Committee Act requires the president to submit an annual report to the House and Senate on each body.

Public affairs staff also serve as spokespeople for lawyers from the general counsel's office, publicizing some of the legal battles — as plaintiff and defendant, civil and criminal — that typically engage a government agency. One fertile area for investigation is how often the agency settles cases on terms favorable to the other side rather than to the majority of taxpayers. If settlements are frequent, why is that so? If settlements are rare, what is the record of the general counsel when cases go to trial?

The Orange County (Calif.) Register started by examining one case: a lawsuit by a prisoner in the county jail. The county government's lawyers settled confidentially. The reporter pursued the story until he learned the settlement terms. He then started researching what turned out to be a 17-part examination of lawsuits against the government. The Public Agency Risk Managers Association, based in Arlington, Va., and made up of local and state government officials, says budget cutbacks make it harder to fund prevention activities, such as street repairs, that could reduce court awards and settlements.

Some legal disputes are heard within agencies before reaching the judicial branch of government. Administrative law judges are executive-branch employees with a great deal of independence, as a Legal Times story demonstrated. It explained how the U.S. Mine Safety and Health Administration had penalized operators of 800 mines for tampering with equipment that measures hazardous airborne particles in the shafts, thus endangering worker safety. The fines levied by the agency totaled $5 million. The operators appealed to the Federal Mine Safety and Health Review Commission, which has administrative law judges who can uphold or overturn the regulatory arm. The story reported that one of those judges ruled that the agency had to prove that "intentional tampering was the only reasonable explanation for the altered sample[s] . . . not just the most probable." The ruling meant that the agency had to split the aggregate case into 800 separate trials to meet the new burden of proof, a costly enterprise that pretty much guaranteed the suit would not be pursued.

Public Authorities and Self-Regulatory Organizations

When it comes to monitoring the executive branch, perhaps the hardest type of agency to track is the public authority or special district. The U.S. Census Bureau lists more than 34,000 special districts across the nation in a spreadsheet that can be downloaded from the Census Web site. Kevin Johnson of the Los Angeles Times explained their reach:

> When even the simplest things in life become too expensive, unmanageable or just too much trouble, Californians for generations have responded with heavy doses of government. When swarms of disease-carrying mosquitoes accompanied soldiers home from World War II, mosquito abatement districts became the bureaucratic rage. The early solution to a shortage of hospital beds in 1945 — hospital districts. Even in death, government has been able to find new life. In the 1920s, upset by the deterioration of local cemeteries, residents throughout the state worked to guarantee a future of respect for their burial grounds. How? Special cemetery districts, of course.

Johnson counted 3,000 public authorities in California, with a collective annual budget of $14 billion.

In addition, there are self-regulatory organizations that, depending on the viewpoint of the observer, can be either the essence of capitalistic democracy or self-serving organizations concocted by powerful industries in concert with corrupt government agencies. A prominent example is the New York Stock Exchange, which the Securities and Exchange Commission allows to manage its own affairs, including disciplining stockbrokers. The Commodity Futures Trading Commission, with congressional consent, has given self-regulatory authority to the National Futures Association in Chicago.

Investigating State and Local Affairs

While investigations into the executive branch of the federal government are critically important, most investigative journalists monitor the performance of governors, state agencies, county commissioners, mayors and city government. Often, investigative journalists can serve the public best—and prevent waste and fraud in government at the local level—by acting as ever-vigilant watchdogs on a daily basis.

For example, in an award-winning and dramatic investigation in 2004, reporters from the Chicago Sun-Times exposed waste and corruption in the city's Hired Truck program. Under the program, the city hired dump trucks and low-wage drivers to haul away debris and construction material from city work sites.

The investigation started when a reporter noticed one of those idle trucks near his home. Working from that observation, the newspaper discovered not only that the city had such a program, but that many of one company's trucks sat idle while the company continued to receive large payments from the city. The newspaper then found a trucking company owner who admitted to paying bribes to city officials and discovered that other companies had made large campaign contributions to city officials.

This kind of local investigation is common and within the reach of most reporters.

The Governor

In recent years, investigative journalists have exposed a governor in Connecticut who received gifts from state contractors (which led to the governor's conviction on corruption charges), governors in several states who misused state airplanes and cars for personal or political trips, and governors who favored political contributors with contracts, grants and appointments.

These stories are initiated by a close scrutiny of public documents, such as legal ads for state bids in newspapers, state vendor records, civil lawsuits, conflict-of-interest statements by state officials, governor's calendars and both political campaign contributions and expenditures. Journalists should also review expenditures in the governor's office and track campaign contributions and lobbyist spending and compare those documents to political appointments, legislation and the awarding of contracts.

It is also worth a reporter's time to scrutinize the political aides to the governor and their involvement in the awarding of executive-level appointments and contracts. In the case of appointments, an investigative journalist should make sure to check the résumés and qualifications of all appointees.

State and Local Employees

The IRE Resource Center contains numerous projects involving journalistic surveillance of state government employees. Reporters identified employees who took four-hour lunches, went shopping or fishing while on the clock and neglected important duties, such as safety inspections of bridges and commercial buildings.

Tracey Kaplan of the Los Angeles Times explained how Los Angeles County created an eight-person office to ferret out fraud among its 84,000 employees by randomly auditing selected telephone extensions, going through trash cans and conducting photographic surveillance:

> No fraud is too small to ferret out, it seems. A health department employee was counseled recently for stealing newspapers from a vending machine. But interviews with the investigators and their official reports show the other end of the spectrum. . . . There was the manager in the Department of Children's Services who resigned after investigators discovered he spent more than $500,000 on unauthorized computer services for the department and falsified records. . . . Then there was the "paper caper." Investigators tailed a Department of Mental Health employee and took photographs of him selling boxes of county-owned photocopy paper to local printers. He was fired.

Two areas to look at routinely are nepotism and patronage. A reporting team at the Beaver County Times in Pennsylvania noticed people with familiar last names being hired by a city government and a school district. The names were the same as those sitting on the city council and board of education. The team also found relatives with dissimilar names who were hired due to nepotism: daughters using married names, sons-in-law, brothers-in-law, cousins. In its IRE awards entry, the team said few of the government bodies "advertised job openings, reserving them instead for family members." Many news organizations have investigated such "family affairs." They also have looked for unqualified political supporters and friends who have been moved into jobs for which they never show up.

A Hartford Courant investigation found that a top aide to the governor was making calls on his government phone to his mistress as soon as he left his wife each morning. Many public officials carry credit cards, billing travel expenses directly to the government. Hotel bills charged to the government often contain telephone numbers called from the room. Expense reimbursement vouchers help a journalist determine an official's whereabouts on a specific date.

Absenteeism is at the center of some public employee scams. Employees might call in sick regularly while feeling fine or might be marked as at work all day when they showed up for the first 30 minutes only. Government agencies in a national survey reported absenteeism rates that were more than twice those of private-sector businesses.

Campaign Finance Corruption

An especially ingenious state campaign contributions scam occurred in Jefferson City, the capital of Missouri. After Terry Ganey of the St. Louis Post-Dispatch broke the news, he wrote for The IRE Journal that "what started out as an obscure workers' compensation fund had become a gold mine for a few insiders. An exclusive club of lawyers and doctors had learned how to milk a system known as Missouri's Second Injury Fund. Their trail led to the doorstep of the state attorney general . . . the Republican candidate for governor." Almost every state maintains a similar fund to supplement compensation for on-the-job injuries. Ganey explained the scam:

> Lawyers specializing in workers' compensation cases filed claims against the fund on behalf of injured workers. Defending the fund against these claims were special assistant state attorneys general. . . . Because thousands of claims were filed each year and because the expense of litigation often exceeded the value of the claim, 95 percent of the claims were settled by the lawyers involved. The Post-Dispatch first looked at the fund because unusually large contributions were flowing to [the] attorney general's . . . campaign from a small group of St. Louis lawyers filing claims against the fund. Soliciting the contributions from the claimants' lawyers was . . . one of [the attorney general's] appointees assigned to defend the fund. . . .
>
> The Post-Dispatch requested Second Injury Fund settlement documents from the state Division of Workers' Compensation. After some resistance from the state attorney general's office, a computer tape containing 11,647 settlements became available. The analysis showed that lawyers who contributed to [the attorney general] obtained substantially larger settlements from the fund for their clients than those lawyers who did not contribute. Larger settlements meant larger fees, since the lawyers' compensation was always 25 percent of the settlement amount. . . . The data-analysis story touched a raw nerve among a group of lawyers in St. Louis. They knew about specific claims with problems. Requesting anonymity, they began to tell their stories: How [a] workers' compensation attorney [who was the] largest individual campaign contributor obtained $65,000 in settlements for himself for a fall in his office and for hurting his shoulder while closing a file cabinet drawer.

On the local level, The Advocate in Baton Rouge determined that two-thirds of the contributors to the incumbent mayor were doing direct business with the city government. The newspaper's investigative journalists made the determination by matching campaign contributions with payout vouchers.

Many states have campaign finance disclosures patterned after federal law, and contribution reports for political candidates are filed at state election offices, often in the capital city. Each contributor is identified by name (individual or committee), town, state, ZIP code, amount given, date given, which election given for (primary or regular), occupation and place of employment. The Campaign Finance Information Center's Web site (www.campaignfinance.org/states/index.html) offers information on how to find state campaign finance data in every state. Much of the information these days is available online and can be searched and downloaded.

Using the State Register

The federal government system of records is generally duplicated by state governments. In Missouri, for example, the Missouri Register is published twice monthly by the Administrative Rules Division in the secretary of state's office; 154 agencies publish regulations for implementing legislative actions. The Missouri Code of State Regulations is actually thicker than the compilation of the state's laws. The Bureau of National Affairs, Washington, D.C., publishes the Directory of State Administrative Codes and Registers to guide an investigative journalist through each of the 50 systems.

↺ CHECK IT OUT

✓ Request a database or list of your town's, city's or county's vendors — the companies and individuals that your community pays for goods and services. Identify the 20 companies or individuals that get paid the most. Then check the campaign contribution records of your community's elected officials to see if they are receiving contributions from those companies or individuals.

✓ Ask for a database or list of your town's, city's or county's employees. Compare that database to political contributors to your community's officials.

✓ Obtain the last three years of your town's, city's or county's budget, and find the largest actual increases in the budget. Compare the actual increases with the projected increases, and find the widest differences.

Understanding Government Agencies

To find executive-branch Web sites, go to the FedWorld site (www.fedworld.gov) or the Villanova Center for Information Law and Policy's Federal Web Locator (www.lib.auburn.edu/madd/docs/fedloc.html).

To find state and local executive-branch Web sites (and others), you can go to www.statelocalgov.net, where you can search for county and city Web sites.

Scholars who see executive-branch misbehavior as institutionalized include Peter deLeon in his book "Thinking About Political Corruption" and John T. Noonan Jr. in "Bribes." An alternate view — that corruption is particularized, not generalized — can be found in Charles T. Goodsell's "The Case for Bureaucracy: A Public Administration Polemic."

Using the Federal Register

The Federal Register is published by the Office of the Federal Register, National Archives and Records Administration and is available online at www.gpoaccess .gov/fr/. Before using it, it's best to look at the search hints provided at www .gpoaccess.gov/fr/tips.html.

Books about executive-branch rule making can make the Federal Register come alive. "Smoking and Politics: Policymaking and the Federal Bureaucracy," by A. Lee Fritschler, is a study of a regulation from start to finish. Overviews of the process include George C. Edwards III's "Implementing Public Policy" and Cornelius M. Kerwin's "Rulemaking: How Government Agencies Write Law and Make Policy."

You can download the U.S. government's online tutorial "The Federal Register: What It Is and How to Use It" or read it online at www.archives.gov/federal-register/tutorial/index.html.

Consultants and Contractors

One case study that documents fraud across government branches and agencies is "Feeding Frenzy: The Inside Story of Wedtech." This book, about a manufacturer that bilked government agencies, is a collaboration between Washington correspondent William Sternberg and one-time Wedtech vice president Matthew C. Harrison Jr.

Government Executive magazine (www.govexec.com) publishes a helpful booklet called "The Top 200 Federal Contractors." Commerce Business Daily (http://cbdnet.access.gpo.gov) lists government notices of proposed actions, contract awards and sales in an online searchable database.

The Contracting Process

Journalists tracking contracts can study completed projects in the IRE Resource Center under headings such as "Bids," "Bribery," "Conflicts of Interests," "City Government," "County Government," "State Government" and "Contractors."

The Public Contracts Law section of the American Bar Association can provide perspective through its publications Public Contract Law Journal and Procurement Lawyer, as well as through members who are willing to talk.

Budget and Management Watchdogs

Advancing Governmental Accountability (www.agacgfm.org) of Alexandria, Va., and the Governmental Accounting Standards Board (www.gasb.org) of Norwalk, Conn., can provide resources for understanding budgets and questionable practices.

Books that can assist understanding include "The Federal Budget: Politics, Policy, Process," by Allen Schick, and "The Budget Puzzle: Understanding Federal Spending," by John F. Cogan, Timothy J. Muris and Allen Schick.

The Top Executive

Executive orders, speeches, news conference transcripts, proclamations and remarks to White House visitors appear in the Weekly Compilation of Presidential Documents (www.access.gpo.gov/nara/nara003.html).

These official documents can be supplemented with insider memoirs; independently researched biographies of past presidents, vice presidents, Cabinet secretaries and regulators; and exposés. Two overviews of the executive branch over the years are "Fall From Grace: Sex, Scandal and Corruption in American Politics from 1702 to the Present," by Shelley Ross, and "Presidential Saints and Sinners," by Thomas A. Bailey.

Cabinet Appointees

For more on Cabinet positions, see Stephen L. Carter's book "The Confirmation Mess: Cleaning Up the Federal Appointments Process." James Bamford's two books about the National Security Agency, "Body of Secrets" and "The Puzzle Palace," may be the best of the genre.

Biographies of former FBI director J. Edgar Hoover, with their timeless lessons about management, demonstrate how an investigative journalist can explicate executive-branch conduct in ways that transcend one agency.

Memoirs of Cabinet secretaries and other high-ranking executive-branch officials contain insight into policy-making. One example is "The Price of Loyalty: George W. Bush, the White House, and the Education of Paul O'Neill," by Ron Suskind, which offers insight and criticism by a former secretary of the treasury into the administration of President George W. Bush. Another example is "Taking Care of the Law" by former Attorney General Griffin Bell of the Carter administration.

Conflicts of Interest

Robert N. Roberts' book "White House Ethics: The History of the Politics of Conflict of Interest Regulation" offers a good overview.

Other resources include

- The Library of Congress's Congressional Links (http://thomas.loc.gov)
- National Active and Retired Federal Employees Association (www.narfe.org)
- The Council for Excellence in Government (www.excelgov.org)
- The Office of Government Ethics (www.usoge.gov), which is supposed to oversee federal postemployment conflicts but is largely toothless

Inspectors General

In his book "Monitoring Government: Inspectors General and the Search for Accountability," Paul C. Light writes about the large amounts of information that journalists can seek but cautions that inspectors general are not always unbiased, unrestrained investigators.

The Permanent Bureaucracy

The IRE Resource Center contains numerous projects involving journalistic surveillance of government employees. Many of those investigations are filed under "Public Workers."

Publications that cover executive-branch activities and cultures include these:

- Federal Times (www.federaltimes.com), Springfield, Va.
- Governing (www.governing.com), Washington, D.C.
- Government Executive (www.govexec.com), Washington, D.C.

Some Web sites focus coverage on one agency; an example is OMB Watch, www.ombwatch.org.

The Federal Staff Directory, Mount Vernon, Va., lists tens of thousands of "key federal executives," with profiles of nearly 3,000 of them. Carroll Publishing Co., Washington, D.C., publishes executive-branch directories for all levels of government. Details about personnel can be gained in many ways. After a Hartford Courant reporter sought information from the employment applications of city workers, a judge ruled that the city had to grant the request.

Agency publications, such as Scientific and Technical Aerospace Reports and the ERIC Database, are filled with names of "currents" and "formers" who could help nail down an investigation; in fact, that publication (and similar publications in other agencies) has a column headed "Retirements," which lists the name, specialty and years of service of each retiree.

You can browse a list of federal agency publications at www.gpoaccess.gov/api/index.html.

Public Affairs Personnel

The National Association of Government Communicators (www.nagc.com) and the Public Agency Risk Managers Association (www.parma.com) are two organizations whose Web sites might be of help to journalists.

Gale Research's Encyclopedia of Governmental Advisory Organizations contains thousands of such bodies at the federal level alone.

The Federal Administrative Law Judges Conference (www.faljc.org), Washington, D.C., can provide perspective about lawsuits against the government, as can the American Bar Association sections on Administrative Law and Regulatory Practice, plus Government and Public-Sector Lawyers.

Public Authorities and Self-Regulatory Organizations

The U.S. Census Bureau lists more than 34,000 special districts across the nation. The list can be downloaded from www.census.gov/ftp/pub/govs/www/gid.html.

Robert Caro's biography of Robert Moses, "The Power Broker," shows how one bureaucrat took public authorities to new heights (or new depths). Donald Axelrod's book "Shadow Government: The Hidden World of Public Authorities and How They Control Over $1 Trillion of Your Money" shows how Moses' concept spread. The most practical primer for journalists is by Diana B. Henriques. "The Machinery of Greed: Public Authority Abuse and What to Do About It" contains accounts of her own investigations (for example, of the New Jersey Housing Finance Agency) and investigations by other journalists. Thomas H. Stanton's book "A State of Risk," about costly but off-budget government-sponsored enterprises like the Farm Credit System, explains similarities and differences between the enterprises and public authorities.

Examples akin to those cited by Henriques are in the IRE Resource Center under "Public Authorities."

Investigating State and Local Affairs

Books by and about governors include Robert S. McElvaine's biography of New York Governor Mario Cuomo, a biography of Texas Governor Ann Richards by Mike Shropshire and Frank Schaeffer, Dwayne Yancey's biography of Virginia Governor Douglas Wilder, and Thad L. Beyle's "Governors and Hard Times." Book-length studies of local chief executives include a biography of Los Angeles Mayor Tom Bradley by J. Gregory Payne and Scott C. Ratzan, plus memoirs by New York City Mayor Ed Koch and Detroit Mayor Coleman Young.

Entries in the IRE Resource Center under "Governors," "State Government," "Mayors" and "City Government" are worth consulting. There are also resources for placing current state and local government actions in context, including the National Governors' Association, National Association of Counties, National League of Cities and U.S. Conference of Mayors, all in Washington, D.C., plus the Council of State Governments, in Lexington, Ky.

The National Association of State Auditors, Comptrollers and Treasurers (www.nasact.org) in Lexington, Ky., can also provide perspective.

Independently written books such as "County Governments in an Era of Change," edited by David R. Berman, can supplement information from the national associations.

9

Investigating the Legislative Branch

This chapter covers how to investigate the major aspects of the legislative branches, whether they are federal, state or local. It discusses how lobbying and campaign contributions can push legislators to make decisions contrary to the public's interest. The chapter explains how to follow the money trail in legislatures, including how to track campaign contributions that are funneled through committees and nonprofit organizations to circumvent campaign limits. In addition, this chapter shows the overall approaches and techniques that will help journalists understand and document paths of access, influence and corruption in the legislative branch.

Legislators at the federal, state and local level have great power. They allocate millions of dollars, benefit or harm businesses and individuals, and create laws governing the conduct of citizens. Investigative journalists need to constantly scrutinize the conduct and policy-making role of elected representatives, whether part of the U.S. Senate or House of Representatives, state legislatures, county commissions or city councils.

In recent years, the U.S. Congress has been wracked with scandals that have led to indictments, convictions and resignations of U.S. legislators on both sides of the aisle. The scandals have included the steering of contracts in exchange for bribes, the sexual harassment of congressional pages, campaign election abuses, and the misuse of legislative "earmarks," which are special clauses in appropriation bills to fund specific projects.

One scandal involved lobbyist Jack Abramoff, who received tens of millions of dollars in fees, including large sums of money from American Indian tribes and foreign entities. In its Pulitzer Prize–winning coverage, The Washington Post reported that Abramoff, who was well-connected to conservative Republicans in Congress, received millions of dollars in lobbying and public affairs fees from American Indian tribes and other clients, including foreign entities. During the same period, he advised the tribes to make $2.9 million in federal political contributions and donations to foundations linked to politicians.

Later stories revealed that he had provided trips and other favors to certain congressmen in hopes of favorable legislation for his clients. Abramoff later pleaded guilty to fraud, tax evasion and conspiracy to bribe public officials in a deal that required him to provide evidence about members of Congress. The scandal led to the indictment of others, including two congressmen.

And in every decade, state legislators and local officials have also been accused and convicted of wrongdoing in connection with government contracts and other public expenditures throughout the country.

The possibilities for investigations of elected representatives are endless, partly because the real scandal is what is legal. Paul Williams, speaking of state legislators, put it well in his book "Investigative Reporting and Editing":

> Because their salaries are rarely above those of skilled blue-collar workers, [state legislators] are subject to temptation and leverage from well-funded lobbyists and their corporate, professional or union backers. A financially hard-pressed legislator may suddenly find credit easy to get when banking bills are before his committee; if he is on the health and welfare committee, he may find his doctor making house calls and then staying to talk about medical-insurance legislation; or members of the house painters' union may want to show their gratitude by redoing his house free of charge, with paint donated by a major wholesaler. In examining the legislative process, your major problem is one of tracing subtle or ephemeral relationships that are kept secret. The use of public records to build personal profiles is a key.

If a U.S. representative pushes through a big public works project, such as a dam for his or her district, should the representative be praised for bringing jobs and safety from floods to constituents—or criticized for wasting tax dollars on a narrow segment of the population and harming the natural environment? When that legislator takes money from dam construction lobbyists, is he accepting support from like-minded individuals or selling favors to special interests? More than ever, journalists need to look at how effectively legislators represent their constituents and must decide how to measure that effectiveness.

Investigating Legislators

Following the Money

Following the money from outside interests to legislators is a good way to start an investigation. Campaign contribution and expenditure reports are more accessible than ever before, and on the federal level and often on the state level they are in databases that can be quickly searched, sorted and grouped.

In addition, nonprofit, nonpartisan organizations that help track campaign finances and expose political influence can give any journalist a jump start. The Center for Responsive Politics (www.opensecrets.org), the Center for Public Integrity (www.publicintegrity.org) and the National Institute on Money in State Politics (www.followthemoney.org) are good starting points for many investigations into money and politics at the federal and state level.

As veteran journalist Brooks Jackson, author of "Honest Graft: Big Money and the American Political Process," said, "The influence of big money on American politics is nothing new, as I was reminded by Louise Overacker's classic volume 'Money in Elections,' published in 1932. . . . She concluded that spending limits were futile and only encouraged concealment, that efforts to raise enough money in small donations usually didn't work and that public financing was the best solution."

In his book "How Washington Really Works," Charles Peters describes the insidious special access money can buy. He writes,

> If the other side can't get similar access, a lobbyist's views may be all the official ever hears. Especially on smaller issues, where a decision either way won't rock the ship of state too much, whichever side gets to the congressman usually wins. . . . Even when the congressman hears other views, the voice of a friend is likely to stand out in the cacophony of opinions. More insidiously, the psychology of access plays on the fact that most government officials are basically decent people who want to be . . . liked. Faced with a . . . fellow human being who wants something very much, with perhaps only an abstract argument on the other side, the natural reaction is to be obliging. That's why if you are a lobbyist, just getting through to a high official and presenting your case . . . no favors involved . . . gives you a good chance for success.

Journalists can find the impact of special-interest money everywhere. The result might be as obvious as a vote favoring the contributor's wished-for tax loophole. Or it might be more subtle, such as a bill that becomes stuck in subcommittee by a chairman paid through an industry's political action committees or a speech supporting an issue that is suddenly shelved when its opponents offer to send a senator on a trip.

Despite many investigations, the fact of legislators needing money and special interests wanting access has made fund raising a major industry in Washington, D.C., and in state capitals. If a legislator serves on the Agriculture Committee and favors sugar price supports, the lobbyist organizing the fundraiser will invite sugar producers. If the legislator opposes sugar price supports, the candy manufacturers will be on the guest list instead. Fund-raising events have become grist for investigative journalists more than ever. Those events can provide raw material for stories about influence peddling.

Journalists may not get invited to fund-raisers, but they can put out the word to sources, particularly the opposition, of their interest in tracking those fund-raisers. Investigative journalists can document the effect of fund-raisers by looking for Federal Election Commission reports or state campaign finance filings to see contributions on the same day from multiple donors in the same industry.

Still, the best stories go beyond raw dollars to look at why an individual or institution donates and what they get in return. For example, whenever a candidate receives a contribution from outside the district, journalists should be asking why a nonconstituent cares enough to give. If individuals and corporations within the same industry are donating to the same member of Congress, it is vital to ask some questions:

- What does the industry do, and how does it earn its money?
- Do the companies in the industry often receive government contracts, grants or subsidies?
- Is there legislation the industry is pushing that could increase its profits?

Campaign Finance

Before looking at campaign finance either at the national or local level, a journalist must first understand the system. Investigative journalists can track campaign dollars by studying the contribution and expenditure reports that are required at every level of government.

The contribution reports for congressional and presidential candidates are submitted to the Federal Election Commission in Washington, D.C., and are often filed at state capitals. Each contributor is identified by name (individual or committee), town, state, ZIP code, amount given, date given, which election given for (primary or regular), occupation and place of employment.

On the federal level, the raw contribution databases are available from the Federal Election Commission, the Center for Responsive Politics and the National Institute for Computer-Assisted Reporting. (See "Resources for Reporting" at the end of this chapter for more information.) Electronic databases of expenditures for Congress are now available, but on a state level most journalists have to build databases themselves to find how much candidates are spending on transportation, advertising, staff members who happen to be family members and other items.

In most campaign finance systems, there are limits on how much individuals or organizations can give. A journalist needs to know those limits so that when looking through contribution lists he or she can see if someone has blatantly violated those limits.

The journalist also should be aware of loopholes and lax laws that allow contributors to circumvent those limits. Often those kinds of donations are known as soft money. Large contributions that are actually intended for one candidate or a small group of candidates may be steered to state political parties or to ideological groups that are registered as nonprofits (known as 527s because of the statute that allowed their creation). Those parties or groups then buy ads, campaign on a particular candidate's issues or attack the candidate's opponent. To track the nonprofit 527 groups, a journalist actually has to go to another set of documents, known as Form 990s, which nonprofits must file with the IRS. (See Chapter 14 for more on 990s.)

Contribution limits are often challenged or changed, so it is best to consult the FEC Web site and state laws to stay current on limits.

Another way that contribution limits can be exceeded is through "bundling." For example, an organization might encourage its employees to write a check for the maximum amount allowable to a candidate, but a manager in the firm collects all the checks and hands them over to the candidate's committee in a "bundle." An investigative journalist can examine the dates on campaign contributions to see if employees of one company all gave on the same day or same week. A journalist can also look for contributions from the same ZIP code in a short time period. The practice is legal as long as the employer does not reimburse the employees—as did a supporter of Sen. Bob Dole when he ran for president. The employer and a Dole campaign official were convicted because of the reimbursements.

In a comprehensive study in the early 1990s, Dwight Morris, then of the Los Angeles Times, showed that contrary to candidate statements, campaign spending was not increasing primarily because of the high cost of TV advertising. He found that candidates' spending on TV advertising remained relatively constant as a percentage of total expenditures, but that candidates spent more money "on office overhead—rent, staff costs, telephones, leased automobiles, travel, etc.—than they spent on their commercials, staff, consultants, and polling."

Corporations cannot give directly to candidates. Instead, they form political action committees, which can give a limited amount to each candidate. Every PAC must identify a treasurer in its filings. The treasurer is a potential source; if the treasurer is prominent or unsavory, that might be a story in itself. Many treasurers are not politically savvy Washington types used to dodging journalists and therefore might talk candidly about FEC investigations or other sensitive matters.

The Center for Responsive Politics in Washington, D.C., assigns codes to every PAC based on its legislative interest: agriculture, highway construction and so on. By matching those codes to congressional committees, the center makes it easier to determine whether political action committees are donating to legislators because of committee assignments.

Despite the nonpartisan watchdogs, election law violations often go unpunished. The FEC's strength is compiling contribution and spending records. Its weakness (partly because it is headed by political appointees) is enforcement. One type of incumbent violation rarely policed is the use of personal staff from the House or Senate office—staff paid with taxpayer dollars—in a re-election campaign. The violation most common among challengers is the failure to file timely, complete reports.

To monitor enforcement, a journalist can examine the FEC's advisory opinions, audits and completed actions. Investigative journalists should examine the index of FEC rulings on alleged violations. Large contributors have often violated federal campaign laws; an alert reporter can find out what they did and how the FEC handled it.

Letters from contributors' attorneys might be part of the public record. When a Washington correspondent from Thomson Newspapers looked at large individual contributors from Pennsylvania, he found that several had violated the $25,000 annual limit. Why had the FEC failed to discipline the violators, he wondered. When he asked the agency's vice chair, she said that the FEC lacked resources.

Another practice involves legislators acquiring unsecured or favorable-rate loans from financial institutions, other corporations or individuals. Such loans are difficult to detect unless they are disclosed voluntarily. The loans are not always initiated by outsiders determined to wield influence. Frequently, legislators solicit the special treatment. Wealthy legislators and challengers probably do less soliciting—many have few reservations about contributing their own money instead of relying on outsiders.

Lobbyists

Beyond looking at campaign contributions, a journalist can examine other methods that lobbyists employ to reach legislators. Often it makes sense for a journalist to start at the beginning by learning how newsworthy lobbyists arrived at their calling and how they built and consolidated their influence.

In Public Citizen magazine, Nancy Watzman explained the 10 stages on the road to becoming an effective lobbyist:

- Get experience in the legislature or executive branch.
- Become especially knowledgeable about a specific issue.

- Find wealthy international clients to supplement domestic accounts.
- Skirt revolving-door rules.
- Raise lots of money for legislators.
- Give lots of gifts to policy-makers.
- Form coalitions with impressive (and often misleading) names.
- Manufacture what appears to be grassroots support.
- Disclose as little as possible.
- Renew contacts and reputation by re-entering government periodically.

It helps to know who is defined as a lobbyist and who is not. At the federal level and in many state capitals, there are concrete definitions of who must file regular reports. In Washington, D.C., lobbyists are defined as those who receive or expend money to influence legislation or who otherwise seek to push or block bills. Lobbyists trying to influence Congress are supposed to register with the secretary of the Senate or the clerk of the House. Thousands are registered at any given time; they are supported by thousands of secretaries, administrative assistants and others whose names never show up on registration forms. The form asks for a business address, the name and address of the employer in whose interest the lobbyist is working, the duration of employment, the amount of salary or retainer and expenses allowed by the employer.

Many corporations employ full-time lobbyists (almost always called by some other term, such as "vice president for government relations"). So do labor unions, universities, professional organizations and government units. Other groups hire lawyers and public relations firms to lobby part-time. In addition, special interests are frequently represented in Washington, D.C., or state capitals by trade associations, such as the American Petroleum Institute.

The law is so riddled with loopholes and so poorly enforced that lobbyists themselves estimate that many lobbyists never register; almost no one is punished for that failure. Despite the loopholes, it makes sense to check registrations to learn which individuals and groups are active in supporting or opposing legislation.

A look through just one month of lobbyists' registrations with the Senate turns up dozens of businesses, trade associations, labor groups, local governments and citizens' groups. One particular entry could spawn a project for either a Texas journalist, a higher education reporter or an environmental journalist: the University of Texas' registration as a lobbyist on a crude oil windfall profits tax.

Former members of Congress (who have their own association based in Washington) can be especially effective lobbyists because of their special access to the floor of the chamber, favors they did for other legislators while still in office, and their adeptness at appealing to the pet projects of current legislators. Larry Van Dyne, writing in The Washingtonian magazine, captured the personal side of legislating; for example, if a legislator's spouse develops Parkinson's disease, the legislator is suddenly willing to sponsor a bill increasing funding for research. Says Van Dyne, "Nobody in Washington understands this sentimental side of politics better than lobbyists, who stand ready to exploit even the smallest advantage. Which congressmen have arthritis? Whose wife has breast cancer? Who rides a bike to work? Whose child is dyslexic? He who knows these secrets about the lives of politicians knows where to find the soft spots in their hearts."

Lobbyists working on behalf of international governments are supposed to file separately under the Foreign Agents Registration Act, regulated by the U.S. Justice Department. Investigative journalists have found former U.S. representatives and senators, Cabinet members and a director of the Central Intelligence Agency lobbying for governments whose interests appear to be at odds with those of the American citizenry.

Charles Lewis and his colleagues at the Center for Public Integrity used the foreign registrations while researching "The Trading Game: Inside Lobbying for the North American Free Trade Agreement." Lewis commented,

> We have publicly criticized the way in which [the] records are collected and the way in which disclosure is enforced. . . . Nonetheless, the imperfect FARA documents are an invaluable resource. . . . Thousands of pages . . . were broken down into tens of thousands of facts—names, numbers, contacts made. . . . These facts were then entered into a database. . . . In this way, we were able to glean intriguing new insights. . . . We were, for example, able to . . . ascertain the top ten U.S. officials most frequently contacted by Mexican officials or their paid representatives.

One way to understand how lobbying can lead to corruption is to study the Abramoff scandal, in which the lobbyist gave favors to members of Congress in exchange for support for his clients. A review of articles about the scandal, particularly those from The Washington Post, can serve as a tutorial for an investigation into lobbyists.

Financial Disclosures of Legislators

When investigative journalists are investigating legislators and their staffs, they should consult required annual financial disclosures. The Capitol Hill publication Roll Call began with required disclosures to document that a leader of the U.S. House had received special treatment while buying and selling stocks that were part of corporate initial public offerings.

Financial disclosure forms will not answer every question. Jean Cobb reminds fellow journalists that "sometimes what is omitted from the forms is of greater interest than what appears. One U.S. senator failed to disclose loans he received from a California businessman, and also failed to mention debts forgiven by the same businessman." To fill in the gaps, a journalist needs to do basic research into a member of Congress by looking at local property records, business loan records like the Uniform Commercial Code records and any litigation.

U.S. Senate financial disclosures are filed with the Office of Public Records. The reports come from incumbent senators, candidates, officers and employees of the legislative branch; principal assistants to senators; employees designated to handle political funds; and some other highly paid employees. Most categories require disclosure of financial dealings affecting spouses or dependents. House of Representatives financial disclosures are filed by members, candidates, officers or employees making more than the GS-16 government salary, plus any employee designated as a principal assistant to a representative. Reports are filed with the Office of Records and Registration.

At all levels of government, journalists should ask legislators to go beyond the limited disclosure in the forms by supplying federal and state income tax returns.

An obvious question is whether a legislator's lifestyle appears to surpass what his or her stated income suggests is reasonable. Simply comparing a representative's latest financial disclosures with his or her first as a member of Congress can be enlightening.

Financial disclosures also can illuminate a senator's conflicts of interest with his or her committee assignments. At one point, a third of House Agriculture Committee members owned farms. Could they be objective about federal farm policy when personal enrichment was at stake? From one viewpoint, it makes sense for, say, a banker to sit on a banking committee. Why not bring the legislator's real-world experience into play? From another viewpoint, such a committee appointment is an obvious conflict. Journalists need to uncover these potential conflicts. After that, voters can decide how much they think it all matters.

A journalist should also check whether incumbents continue to receive income from previous jobs and how many hours they spend at that job. The time taken by the job could affect performance in office, or it could be that the job is a fiction, providing the employer with access to an influential legislator. A journalist should not stop with the legislator but should find out whether his or her friends and relatives have been benefiting from legislative decisions. For example, is the politician's sibling a lawyer whose clients win government contracts due to favoritism?

Journalists tracking special interests at the state level should also look into honoraria, which are monetary payments or anything with a resale value given to a legislator for an appearance or speech connected with his or her political appointment. Honoraria are often connected with travel sponsored by special interests. Because honoraria can be quantified accurately (as opposed to some other income), such payments are a sensible category to explore. Public Citizen magazine examined reports of privately funded trips for U.S. senators and then wrote a study about the abuses, "On the Road Again." One senator characterized such travel as an attempt by special interests "to get you on the airplane, to get you at the dinner table, to get you on the golf course. It's to be able to peddle a message."

Since then, honoraria have been eliminated, and since the Abramoff scandal, limitations have been placed on many kinds of favors for members of Congress and their staffs. But efforts like these will continue as long as lobbyists and corporations continue to try to influence Congress.

Senators and representatives once could keep honoraria for personal use; now they are supposed to donate them to charities. Investigative journalists should ask why one charity and not another gets the donations. As Jean Cobb noted in Common Cause, "While giving to the needy is a worthwhile cause, it can also be used as a source for building support. You may want to check which causes a member gives to and whether there are any relatives or business associates on these boards." And in a new twist, lobbyists or influence peddlers now give donations directly to a senator's or representative's favorite charity.

Resources and Perquisites in Office

Legislators are not totally dependent on special interests, outside jobs and investments. Their election to office brings resources that include salaries and office allowances. Members of Congress receive an annual salary ($165,200 as of 2006), and when they leave office, they receive generous taxpayer-funded pensions.

Their personal income, however, is dwarfed by their office allowances, which also come from the taxpayers. Each House member currently receives hundreds of thousands of dollars annually to run their office. Part of that total can be devoted to salaries for full-time and temporary assistants. Each senator receives funds for personal staff, plus additional money for staff assigned to legislative committees. Depending on the state's population, the annual amount for personal staff plus committee assistance can run into the millions of dollars. Both House members and senators are allowed to hire relatives, which provides an opportunity for journalists to determine whether such legal nepotism is being abused.

PART II   Investigating
the Government

Staff members, especially administrative and legislative assistants and committee staff, are often knowledgeable sources and should be cultivated. Some senators receive 10,000 constituent letters and e-mails daily, in addition to mass mailings from special-interest groups. Complaint letters about the same problem might take a journalist down paths that would never have been discovered otherwise. Or an individual letter might provide a journalist with the case needed to tell a story in a compelling, convincing manner.

Staff sources might be especially helpful during re-election campaigns, pointing out improper deployment of aides. As Knight-Ridder national correspondent Frank Greve wrote in the Washington Monthly,

> At least 70 incumbents summoned two or more federally paid Washington aides to their districts late in their campaigns, House expense records indicate. Typically, lawmakers claimed, "official business" required their aides' presence. Just as typically, that business ended on election day. . . . Because publication of House office expense records lags three months or longer behind outlays, it is impossible for challengers, or reporters, to learn during a campaign's heat whether aides remain on the federal payroll. The ethics manual states that [members of Congress] "should keep careful records documenting that campaign work was not done on official time." But many don't, and some lawmakers . . . refuse to disclose what leave or vacation time aides took for campaign work.

Between elections, as well as during campaigns, spending practices that are out of touch with commonsense ethics pervade Capitol Hill. Journalist Ward Sinclair said that looking through congressional expense records is like "tripping through a great mail-order catalog of life's amenities. If it exists, it's almost certain that a member of the House bought it—under the rubric of 'official purpose,' of course."

Some journalists consider perquisites to involve such small sums of money that they prefer to ignore them to concentrate on corrupt policy-making. Other journalists, believing the perquisites are a moral outrage, write regular exposés. They rely on the reports of members' expenditures published by the clerk of the House and the secretary of the Senate.

Disclosure of travel is required by legislators, officers or employees who accept trips or travel expenses outside the United States from a foreign government. Some foreign travel is underwritten by U.S. taxpayers as representatives and senators venture overseas in connection with their committee assignments. Supporters of such travel call the trips "fact-finding missions"; opponents call the trips "junkets." The word "junket" seems appropriate when an already defeated member of Congress is the traveler, billing taxpayers before leaving the House or Senate. By consulting the travel forms, Roll Call determined that 13 of 76 lame-duck U.S. representatives took a foreign trip—a higher percentage than legislators who had won re-election. Journalists who cultivate travel agents as sources might receive advance notice of interesting journeys.

Congressional Quarterly Weekly Report found that the true cost of foreign travel is often higher than what House and Senate members report. The official reports often exclude air transport and escort officers provided by the Defense Department or some other government agency. Furthermore, overseas travel is often absorbed into the expense reports of House and Senate committees, making it difficult to determine which individual members of Congress should be linked to the expenditure of taxpayer funds.

Personal Character

Scrutiny of legislators must go beyond campaign finances and conflicts of interest that affect legislating. Personal character must be explored too. The fact that a candidate is having extramarital affairs may or may not be worthy of publication. But if the politician lies about it what other lies might he or she tell—perhaps ones directly related to political agenda or performance?

Journalists have often investigated sex-related scandals in Congress because of the reflection on the character of the candidate. From the Sen. Gary Hart–Donna Rice scandal of the 1980s to Rep. Mark Foley's sexual advances to congressional pages in 2006, journalists have continuously exposed questionable conduct in Congress. Until the early 1970s, journalists almost always refused to disclose illicit sex or drug use by legislators unless the conduct was so egregious that it led to criminal charges. In retrospect, the past standard seems wrong as it becomes clear, for example, how John F. Kennedy's sexual conduct affected his performance in the U.S. Senate and in the White House.

In addition to checks on personal character, a journalist should check every line on the politician's résumé, looking for exaggerations or outright fabrications. If a would-be legislator is running for the first time, a journalist can examine the candidate's reputation in past jobs. If the past job was in the public sector (including a lower-level legislature), reports might be available from an agency inspector general, a state auditor or the like. The journalist can talk to fellow employees, employers, family members, neighbors, ministers, school classmates and teachers—the usual range of "currents" and "formers" set out in Chapter 5.

Making Legislation

Although many members of Congress pride themselves on constituent service, the most obvious part of elective office is legislating. Although the process sometimes strays from the paths described by books, certain steps are normally completed. Congress publishes booklets about the process, including "Enactment of a Law: Procedural Steps in the Legislative Process." Every bill introduced in a legislature has a primary sponsor; many carry the names of co-sponsors. Every day of publication, the Congressional Record and some state legislatures' services run a list of bills introduced. Sponsorship might be meaningful, although many bills are introduced for show—to satisfy campaign contributors or to assuage popular sentiment at home.

A journalist can ask around to learn whether a sponsor really believes in a proposal or introduced it halfheartedly, maybe even hypocritically. In her book "Senator," Elizabeth Drew says of one legislator, "He does not take on a large number of issues, and those that he takes on tend to be ones that make an important point—and also ones on which he feels he has a reasonable chance of winning." Drew contrasts him with a senator of whom it is said, "If 25 of the 50 bills he introduced were never heard of again, he didn't give it another thought."

Whether a legislator is serious about bills introduced is usually related to why the legislator sought particular committee assignments. Some legislators seek seats on the Armed Services Committee or a military appropriations subcommittee to protect military bases in their districts. They see their role as essentially local. Other legislators try to avoid selfish local politics, being more interested in setting broad policy. Some Armed Services Committee members, for example, do not have military bases in their districts.

Authorizations and Appropriations

Policy can be influenced from appropriations committees as well as from subject-specific committees. Legislatures usually separate policy-making from funding when establishing committees. The authorizing committees prepare grocery lists; the appropriations committees decide what will be purchased—one new hydroelectric dam or four, eight new bombers or 15—and at what price. Sometimes the appropriators strike an item from the list altogether or provide only minimal seed money. A seat on an appropriations committee is perceived as unglamorous by outsiders who think budgets are boring, but insiders understand the influence attached to such an assignment. A program might be authorized only once every several years, but money must be spent every year, with supplemental appropriations requested if the original amount turns out to be inadequate.

Sometimes appropriations come through a side door through a formula rather than a clear dollar allocation. For example, a New England senator might offer a seemingly innocuous amendment making "degree heat days" a criterion for heating oil aid to low-income families. In effect, the senator is trying to take part of the allocation from another region and channel it to his or her own. Journalist Spencer Rich said the appropriations formula game hides "a grubby reality. The formula that seemed fairest and most equitable to each senator usually turned out to be the formula that helped his state to a bigger slice of the pie."

Much of legislating consists of elected representatives' grabbing as much funding and special consideration as possible for their districts, and damn the overall consequences. The term for such behavior is "pork-barrel politics." As one member of Congress said, "Angels in heaven don't decide where highways are going to be built. It's a political process."

But because voters at home benefit from the deals, they tend to re-elect their legislators while simultaneously crying about the big deficits and higher taxes that flow from those deals. Almost all legislators try to win pork for their districts; an overlooked truism is that there are no fiscal conservatives in Congress. The reality, though, is that some legislators have more integrity or power than others when it comes to pork, so the costs and benefits are distributed unequally.

Another type of often irrational spending is the entitlement program, indexed to the rate of inflation or some other indicators beyond legislative control. Examples of entitlement programs include Social Security, Medicare, unemployment compensation, veterans benefits and federal employee pensions. The details of hundreds of billions of dollars in government budgets are not reviewed annually because they consist of entitlement programs. Journalists can try to match benefits and needs; many programs seem to ignore the truly needy.

Overall, there is much sleight of hand in the legislative budget processes, as legislators place spending off the books in transparent attempts to make deficits look smaller. One common tactic is the loan guarantee, a government obligation to pick up the cost of a program if private-sector financing fails. Despite their invisibility, off-budget programs "are as real as the Washington Monument," Robert Samuelson of the National Journal says. "They certify the ingenuity of politicians and bureaucrats, who crave the best of both worlds — extra plums for constituents without the extra pain of higher taxes."

Journalists who understand the process look not only for how power is used or abused in authorization and appropriations, but also for hypocritical legislators who approve the authorization (satisfying proponents of the program) but oppose funding (satisfying detractors of the program while hoping proponents will fail to notice).

Numerous groups keep tabs on legislators' voting records — particularly on the Web now — in an attempt to ferret out such hypocrisy. Voting scorecards are available from all sorts of groups, from the U.S. Chamber of Commerce to

Americans for Democratic Action. Rarely do groups keep track of every vote, instead choosing issues of importance to their membership. Sometimes the ratings that result are intellectually dishonest. A special-interest group will choose votes that make members of one political party appear to be anti-business, anti-labor or something else. As a result, journalists might need to check legislators' complete voting record by using the Congressional Record or tabulations in Congressional Quarterly Weekly Report, or new nonprofit Web sites that are using sophisticated data-mining tools to collect all votes.

Committees and Oversight

Besides looking for hypocrisy in the authorization and appropriations cycles, journalists look for hypocrisy in legislative hearings, whether in Congress or in the state house. Hearings records can be unparalleled resources for information gatherers. But sometimes the hearing is stacked to reflect the views of the chair. If the tobacco subcommittee of the Agriculture Committee holds a hearing on whether cigarette smoke is dangerous to nonsmokers and the witnesses discount the dangers, a journalist should check whether tobacco interests are contributors to subcommittee legislators or whether constituents are dependent on tobacco industry jobs or both.

The placement of witnesses on the hearing schedule can be a tip-off. Witnesses appearing in the morning tend to receive more attention from legislators and journalists. Later in the day, legislators drift to other duties, and journalists leave to file daily stories. Near the end of the witness list is the likely placement if the committee chair disagrees with the views to be expressed.

Legislative hearings can be shams in many other ways. For instance, Congress has an intentionally inefficient delineation of committee and subcommittee jurisdictions. Dozens of committees and subcommittees have some voice over surface transportation legislation, making it difficult for any one committee to act definitively. The blurring of jurisdictional lines provides more members of Congress a chance to grab publicity on any issue.

If a bill starts moving through overlapping jurisdictions in both the House and Senate, there are many stages that bear scrutiny by journalists, including these:

- Committee markup
- Committee report
- Setting of debate rules
- Discussion on the chamber floor
- Conference committee to iron out House-Senate differences

Each of these stages yields useful documents.

No matter how effective a legislator might be in pushing bills, serving on committees is supposed to be about more than getting laws approved. It is also supposed to be about monitoring the impact of laws, a function called "oversight," as in "overseeing" the results. When oversight hearings are conducted honestly, they can be forums for truth telling.

But "oversight" has a second, unintended, meaning—as in failing to do anything at all. Oversight does not necessarily win many votes at home. It requires penetrating the bureaucracy, which will fight back or cause delay. Besides, the subcommittee chair with responsibility for oversight is often the person who most strongly supports the program in question.

Executive-branch agencies run thousands of programs, but few per agency receive in-depth congressional oversight. When subject to scrutiny, program directors will work hard to obscure any information that shows shortcomings. Charles Peters, a one-time bureaucrat, admitted in his book "How Washington Really Works" that "I felt it was my duty to conceal from Congress any fact that might reflect adversely on my agency. The congressmen . . . were usually ill-prepared . . . and seldom asked me the right questions. When they did, it appeared to be accidental, and they failed to ask the right follow-up questions."

The Government Accountability Office: The Research and Investigative Arm of Congress

The research units of legislatures can be invaluable resources. Best known to journalists is the Government Accountability Office (prior to 2004, the General Accounting Office), frequently identified as the "watchdog arm of Congress." Its staff (many of them lawyers, engineers and accountants) write about 1,000 reports annually on public policy issues. The reports are indexed and available at the GAO Web site and should be routine resources for reporters working on local and national stories.

Although GAO reports are treated by many daily journalists as self-contained stories, they should be a starting point. That is especially true for the reports initiated at the request of a member of Congress. Although GAO employees are generally candid in person, their reports are sometimes couched in language so low-key it muffles the outrageousness of the misconduct.

One value of GAO reports is the description of the agency or program goals and the specificity of recommendations for reform. A journalist delving into an issue can report on failures to comply with GAO recommendations. One recent four-volume GAO report mentioned 2,334 unresolved recommendations.

Annotated bibliographies of GAO documents on numerous controvertains hundreds of references, such as "Hazardous Waste: Status of Private Party

Efforts to Clean Up Hazardous Waste Sites." A quarterly magazine, the GAO Review, is useful for its explanations of how the agency operates and for its mentions of hirings, promotions and departures among staff members. These staffers have an advantage over even the most talented investigative journalist: subpoena power.

Another helpful agency is the Congressional Budget Office. The CBO is the legislative branch counterpart to the White House Office of Management and Budget. The CBO was created to provide objective, nonpartisan and timely analyses to aid in economic and budgetary decisions on the wide array of programs covered by the federal budget and the information and estimates required for the congressional budget process.

The Budget Enforcement Act sets caps on discretionary spending and contains pay-as-you-go rules for entitlements and taxes. So if the CBO's projections are more conservative than OMB's, Congress must live within the CBO's limits. The director is appointed by Congress and can be removed by resolution of either chamber.

The director's first responsibility is to help the Senate and House Budget Committees. The next priority is to aid appropriations committees in both chambers, as well as the Senate Finance Committee and the House Ways and Means Committee. Many of the CBO studies transcend cost analysis to discuss policy implications. Examples are "Federal Options for Reducing Waste Disposal," "Rising Health Care Costs: Causes, Implications, Strategies" and "The Economic Effects of the Savings and Loan Crisis."

At the beginning of each congressional session, the Congressional Research Service provides each committee with a list of programs under its jurisdiction that are ready to expire, along with a companion list of topics the committees might want to examine in depth. During each session, CRS compiles major legislation of Congress. Some topics are singled out for in-depth treatment called legislative histories. The Congressional Research Service, part of the Library of Congress, is funded with tax dollars, but staff members will not release their research to the public unless authorized by the member of Congress or the committee requesting the information. A number of Web sites, profit and nonprofit, offer electronic copies of many reports. For example, OpenCRS works to publish as many reports as possible; the University of North Texas Libraries offers a database of public CRS reports. Also, Penny Hill Press, a private supplier of all CRS publications, makes them available individually and by subscription at its Web site and promises same-day delivery. Its public index will tell if there is a report on a topic.

Another way around the obstacle is to request specific issue briefs from a member of Congress. The briefs are listed in the CRS publication Update. (OpenCRS encourages the public to do this and then post to its site.) The magazine CRS Review provides highlights from CRS analyses that tend to be the talk of Congress.

Investigating Local Legislatures

While Congress gets most of the national headlines, it is the local legislatures— whether at the state or the county level—that pass laws and budgets that can affect citizens directly and adversely. State legislatures can decide in one session to cut the rolls of Medicaid by changing eligibility requirements, leaving thousands of poor people without health care. They can chop spending for higher education because they don't like a college program they think is too conservative or too liberal. They can pass open-records laws that set the fees for public records beyond the means of the average taxpayer. In a similar fashion, elected officials at the county or city level can set exorbitant fees for services, pass unreasonable taxes, or construct laws that limit free speech.

And at all levels of local government, local officials can give in to the temptation to feather their own nest or to enjoy the perks of power. Thus, monitoring is needed at all levels of government, and the routine check of documents is a must.

When nonsalaried city council members travel on legislative business, they often request a travel advance, which is documented on a pretravel authorization-request form. Upon returning, the local legislator files a travel expense voucher. In Columbia, Mo., an examination of such forms by journalists led to resignations and reprimands of council members due to travel expense abuse, including reimbursement for a spouse. In Florida, the Fort Myers News-Press found that 15 local officials had traveled to five hurricane conferences in one year, then profited on reimbursements because of lax accounting. In Torrance, Calif., the mayor was found to be spending tens of thousands of dollars to go to Europe on trips he said were for city business.

Following the Money

Coverage of how state legislators, county commissioners and city council members raise and spend money has become increasingly important. Excellent articles looking in detail at the state level have been published by newspapers in

Philadelphia, Syracuse, Indianapolis, Washington, D.C., Raleigh, Miami, Hartford, Los Angeles and Minneapolis/St. Paul. The Tennessean in Nashville found a congressman using campaign contributions to pay rent on a building he owned. He also created two computer companies, which then leased equipment to the campaign. The campaign treasury bought him a luxury automobile, a pickup truck, a mobile phone and furniture for his home, and paid his sister's salary.

In another example, the Asbury Park Press in Neptune, N.J., published a stunning eight-day series called "Profiting From Public Service: How Many N.J. Legislators Exploit the System." The investigation found that a third of New Jersey's 120 Senate and Assembly members held at least one other public job in addition to their $49,000-a-year legislative post, which allowed them to qualify for yearly state pensions as high as $100,000 when they retired.

The investigation discovered that state agencies awarded no-bid state contracts for bond sales to politically connected law firms that then put the money back into political campaigns for legislators. The investigation also found that almost one in five lawmakers had at least one family member on the payroll. And the paper reported that the legislature's financial disclosure laws, among the weakest in the nation, allowed members "to hide their business clients" and that there were virtually no laws to prevent ethics violations.

There are many ways to track state and local political money. Many states have campaign finance disclosure laws patterned after federal law. State election offices are in the capital city. They are sometimes complemented by obscure agencies that journalists can mine for information. For example, the state capital bureau chief for the St. Louis Post-Dispatch reported that the Missouri Ethics Commission levied substantial fines and ordered 16 candidates off the ballot during its first year of existence.

Journalists should also consult state legislators' annual financial disclosures. Starting in the 1990s, researchers from the Center for Public Integrity's 50 States Project "methodically evaluated financial-disclosure laws that apply to members of the legislatures in all 50 states, and ranked the states on basic disclosure components and access to public records. The report showed that nearly half of the states' disclosure systems fail to provide the public with basic information on state lawmakers' private interests."

Lobbyists

Many states require lobbyists to register, but as at the federal level, the definitions contain loopholes. Tens of thousands of lobbyists are registered in state capitals. Yet much of the money they spend on travel, gifts and entertainment goes unreported. The lobby disclosure laws often are so confusing that it is hard to figure out who should report what. The Washingtonian magazine discovered such discrepancies in Illinois, where "representatives from Las Vegas descended on the state capital for rounds of meetings with state legislators. Casino operators told reporters they spent $5.3 million lobbying for a pro-gambling bill. Lobby disclosure reports, however, indicated expenditures of just $24,000."

The (Raleigh) News & Observer made good use of lobbyist registrations, however imperfect, in North Carolina. A story by Van Denton opened like this:

> At Vinnie's Steakhouse and Tavern, it's easy to tell when the General Assembly is in town. "The bar is packed full," says [the] general manager of the North Raleigh restaurant. Inside . . . state legislators can fancy themselves a part of the capital's power clique to which Vinnie's caters. . . . If legislators don't want to pay a nickel, they don't have to. Because just as much as legislators enjoy going to Vinnie's and other classy Raleigh restaurants, lobbyists hired to influence them enjoy buying them steaks and Scotch. Vinnie's was the most popular spot in town on expense reports filed . . . by 486 corporations, trade associations and other interest groups that spent $3.3 million lobbying the General Assembly. . . . One legislator, . . . chairman of the House Commerce Committee, dined there at least 12 times before and during the legislative session as a guest of lobbyists for banks, savings and loans and mortgage companies.

A book showing how influence peddlers can poison a state legislature is "What's in It for Me?" by Joseph Stedino with journalist Dary Matera. Stedino, a convict turned government agent, posed as a mobster wanting to legalize casino gambling in Arizona. Working a sting through the Phoenix district attorney's office, Stedino's payoffs to legislators resulted in criminal charges. A more subdued account is "The Art of Legislative Politics" by Tom Loftus, former speaker of the Wisconsin General Assembly.

Other Paper and People Sources

The National Conference of State Legislatures in Denver publishes Inside the Legislative Process, which contains comparative data, state by state, on legislative organization, committee procedures and bill processing. Numerous publications by the conference help journalists put seemingly localized issues in perspective. The organization's catalog lists reports about the arts, tourism, cultural resources, corrections, criminal justice, economic development, education, employment, labor, insurance, fiscal affairs, health, human services, natural resources and the environment.

Names of key legislative staff can be found in each state's government manual and in the State Legislative Staff Directory, published by the National Conference of State Legislatures in Denver. Campaign consultants for each candidate will probably have some knowledge of strategy, aboveboard or otherwise. In state legislatures, staff members tend to accumulate lots of power, because those elected serve only part time. Journalists investigating their local legislators would be advised to cultivate these staff members as sources.

Just like at the federal level, state legislatures have support arms too, but these are usually more sparsely staffed than those of Congress. In Missouri, for example, the Committee on Legislative Research combines with the House of Representatives Computer Service to provide an index of bills organized by chronological number and name of sponsor. Wakeman/Walwort Inc. of Alexandria, Va., publishes numerous newsletters tracking issues in state legislatures. Some are as narrow as alcoholic beverage control. Others are as broad as taxation and revenue policy. Journalists can use these documents to more closely follow bills and issues that otherwise might be obscured in the deluge of proposed bills and the noise of political infighting.

⊃ CHECK IT OUT

✓ Get the campaign contributions from the last election for your local mayor, county commissioner or most powerful city councilor and his or her opponents. Determine the occupations of the contributors, and see which industries or professions favored the winners.

✓ Get the financial disclosure statements for your local legislators, and see what potential conflicts of interest they have. Then see if they sponsored legislation that could benefit themselves or their industries.

✓ Using locally available records or data available at the Center for Responsive Politics, track and detail which industries and special interests support your representative in Congress and then see if they are the same ones that supported that representative before he or she was elected.

✓ Perform the same investigation on your representative, but this time see how the ratio of in-state and out-of-state contributions changed after the representative became an incumbent.

RESOURCES FOR REPORTING

General Web Sites

- American Association of Political Consultants (www.theaapc.org)
- Center for Public Integrity (www.publicintegrity.org)
- Center for Responsive Politics (www.opensecrets.org)
- Center for Responsive Politics, lobbyist database (www.opensecrets.org/lobbyists)
- Congressional Budget Office (www.cbo.gov)
- CPI's "In Your State," a searchable database of state legislators' disclosure forms (www.icij.org/iys)
- Department of Justice, Foreign Agents Registration Act (www.usdoj.gov/criminal/fara)
- Federal Election Commission (www.fec.gov)
- General Accounting Office (www.gao.gov)
- Library of Congress, Congressional Links (http://thomas.loc.gov)
- National Conference of State Legislatures (www.ncsl.org)
- National Institute for Computer-Assisted Reporting (NICAR) Database Library (www.ire.org/datalibrary)
- Office of Technology Assessment (National Academy Press maintains archive) (www.wws.princeton.edu/~ota)
- Penny Hill Press, Congressional Research Service (CRS) (www.pennyhill.com)
- Sunlight Foundation, a nonprofit specializing in examining Congress and creating databases on it (www.sunlightfoundation.com)
- University of California gateway for the Government Printing Office (www.gpo.ucop.edu/crs)
- White House Office of Management and Budget (www.whitehouse.gov/omb)

Following the Dollar

Brooks Jackson, in "Honest Graft: Big Money and the American Political Process," describes in this classic work the influence of special interests and their money on elections.

Charles Peters stresses the insidious special access money can buy in his book "How Washington Really Works."

"The Buying of the Congress: How Special Interests Have Stolen Your Right to Life, Liberty, and the Pursuit of Happiness," by Charles Lewis and The Center for Public Integrity, dissects the effect of special interests admirably. The Center for Responsive Politics (www.opensecrets.org) tracks the influence of special interests every day through analyses of federal election databases. Larry Makinson, who has led the analysis for years, has written numerous times about the subject, including "Follow the Money Handbook," which provides solid advice in tracking this money. The investigative team of Donald Barlett and James Steele has tracked how Congress takes care of special interests, particularly the rich and the corporations, in their work at The Philadelphia Inquirer and at Time magazine.

Sunlight Foundation (www.sunlightfoundation.com) is a nonprofit that does monitoring and investigations of Congress with cutting-edge technology and should be bookmarked by everyone interested in Congress.

Some of the sharpest stories are in the IRE Resource Center (www.ire.org/resourcecenter) under "Campaign Finance," "Congress," "Elections," "Political Action Committees," "Politicians" and "State Government/Legislatures."

Campaign Finance Records

Federal Election Commission (www.fec.gov), the Center for Responsive Politics (www.opensecrets.org) and the National Institute for Computer-Assisted Reporting (www.ire.org/datalibrary) are good resources on this topic.

Lobbyists

The Center for Responsive Politics offers a wonderful database of lobbyists and expenditures that is searchable at www.opensecrets.org/lobbyists. It allows journalists and the public to search by individual or industry or lobbying firm. The magazine Congressional Quarterly Weekly Report and the official Congressional Record publish registrations on an occasional basis. In addition to the registration document, an investigator can check quarterly reports of income and expenditures.

The Center for Public Integrity (www.publicintegrity.org) has done major investigations of lobbyists with additional database, as has Sunlight Foundation.

To determine lobbyists not registered, it might help to check with the American League of Lobbyists, in Alexandria, Va.

A list of registered foreign agents (lobbyists representing foreign governments) can be found at www.usdoj.gov/criminal/fara.

Washington Representatives, published by Columbia Books, with more than 15,000 listings of special-interest advocates, is considered a more reliable guide to lobbyists than the official filings with the government. Another frequently consulted volume is Gale Research's American Lobbyists Directory. "Public Interest Profiles," from the Foundation for Public Affairs, lists individuals who consider themselves more altruistic than corporate lobbyists but are lobbyists nonetheless.

Financial Disclosures of Legislators

The Center for Public Integrity (www.publicintegrity.org) is a good place for reporters to start.

Another resource is "The Opposition Research Handbook: A Guide to Political Investigations" by Larry Zilliox Jr. of Investigative Research Specialists, McLean, Va.

Resources and Perquisites in Office

Details about staffing are available from the House Administration Committee and the Senate Rules and Administration Committee. Perspective is available from "Congressional Pay and Perquisites: History, Facts, and Controversy," published by Congressional Quarterly Books. If the knowledge of staff members is power, then there are some mighty powerful staffers. That is the premise of Michael J. Malbin's book "Unelected Representatives: Congressional Staff and the Future of Representative Government," and Harrison W. Fox Jr. and Susan W. Hammond's "Congressional Staffs: The Invisible Force in American Lawmaking." An insider account comes from John L. Jackley, "Hill Rat: Blowing the Lid Off Congress."

Staff turnover on the Hill is heavy, so journalists have little trouble finding "formers" to talk to. Many are disgruntled. Journalists can keep up with "formers" and "currents" on personal and committee staff by consulting the Congressional Staff Directory, Mount Vernon, Va., or The Almanac of the Unelected: Staff of the U.S. Congress, Almanac Publishing. Journalists can also check staffers' own organizations, such as the House Administrative Assistants Alumni Association, House Legislative Assistants Association and Senate Press Secretaries Association. The American Association of Political Consultants (www.theaapc.org) might be able to supply potential sources.

The American Society of Travel Agents, in Alexandria, Va., can provide names of its members broken out by location of business.

Making Legislation

A few books have captured the intricacy, mundaneness and occasional drama of legislating, especially "The Dance of Legislation" by Eric Redman (about a national health service bill); "Congressional Odyssey: The Saga of a Senate Bill" by T.R. Reid (about waterway user fees); "Blue Skies, Green Politics: The Clean Air Act of 1990" by Gary Bryner; "Lessons From the Hill: The Legislative Journey of an Education Program" by Janet M. Martin; and "The Bill: How Legislation Really Becomes a Law" by Steven Waldman (about President Clinton's national service program).

Memoirs by current or former members of Congress, while rarely devoid of self-serving passages, can provide insights into the process. Some of the most educational are by Tip O'Neill, John Tower, Jim Wright, Morris Udall and Donald Riegle. Biographies of contemporary legislators can provide insights too. Examples are Nadine Cohodas' biography of Sen. Strom Thurmond, Mark Kirchmeier's examination of Sen. Robert Packwood, Jerry Roberts' chronicle of Sen. Dianne Feinstein and Lee Roderick's life of Sen. Orrin Hatch. Political scientist Richard F. Fenno Jr. has specialized in the genre, writing "When Incumbency Fails: The Senate Career of Mark Andrews," "Learning to Legislate: The Senate Education of Arlen Specter," "The Emergence of a Senate Leader: Pete Domenici and the Senate Budget" and "The Making of a Senator: Dan Quayle."

Authorizations and Appropriations

Richard Munson's book "The Cardinals of Capitol Hill" demonstrates the power of the appropriations subcommittee chairs in the House and Senate.

R. Douglas Arnold's book "Congress and the Bureaucracy: A Theory of Influence" explains geographic allocation from a scholarly perspective.

Journalists have filled books with egregious examples of wasteful spending. They include Brian Kelly's "Adventures in Porkland: How Washington Wastes Your Money and Why They Won't Stop," and Martin L. Gross' "The Government Racket: Washington Waste from A to Z."

A book to stimulate thought about the relative equity of entitlements is "Who Gets What From Government," by Benjamin I. Page.

Richard Forgette's book "The Power of the Purse Strings: Do Congressional Budget Procedures Restrain?" provides detailed insights.

Committees and Oversight

The occasional books on congressional hearings provide rich detail. One bird's-eye account is "Men of Zeal: A Candid Inside Story of the Iran-Contra Hearings," by Senators William S. Cohen and George J. Mitchell. Overviews include "Congressmen in Committees," by Richard F. Fenno Jr., and "The Politics of Finance: The House Committee on Ways and Means," by John F. Manley.

"Congress Today," by Edward V. Schneier and Bertram Gross, describes the stages clearly.

Congress' in-house bill tracking arm, the Legislative Information Service, is available to outsiders by telephone or online. Legi-Slate, an online service in Washington, D.C., provides prepared testimony from every hearing and verbatim coverage of selected hearings.

James Hamilton includes such examples in his book "The Power to Probe: A Study of Congressional Investigations."

Joel D. Aberbach captures the essentials in his book "Keeping a Watchful Eye: The Politics of Congressional Oversight." A more specific treatment is Frank J. Smist Jr.'s "Congress Oversees the United States Intelligence Community, 1947–1989." David Schoenbrod explains the increased need for oversight as Congress abdicates on the specifics of legislation in "Power Without Responsibility: How Congress Abuses the People Through Delegation."

Personal Character

"Congressional Ethics: History, Facts, and Controversy" from Congressional Quarterly Press examines the consequences of such behavior for legislators within their chambers and among the voters. More theoretical approaches can be found in "Political Ethics and Public Office," by Dennis F. Thompson, and "Thinking About Political Corruption," by Peter DeLeon.

Two reference books establish the conventional wisdom about a legislator's character and its connection to his or her job performance: "The Almanac of

American Politics" (National Journal, Washington, D.C.) and "Politics in America" (Congressional Quarterly Press, Washington, D.C.).

Standards have obviously changed over the years, as explained by Larry J. Sabato in "Feeding Frenzy: How Attack Journalism Has Transformed American Politics."

Research Arms

Context is available in Frederick C. Mosher's books, "The GAO: The Quest for Accountability in American Government" and "A Tale of Two Agencies: A Comparative Analysis of the General Accounting Office and the Office of Management and Budget."

Journalists can ask GAO public affairs staff for regular mailings of full reports or monthly summaries, but it is just as easy to use the agency's Web site (www .gao.gov) when on deadline. It is useful to get the hardcopy reports too, because it is easy to overlook reports while browsing.

Annotated bibliographies of GAO documents on numerous controversies are available; for example, the bibliography on environmental protection contains hundreds of references, such as "Hazardous Waste: Status of Private Party Efforts to Clean Up Hazardous Waste Sites." A quarterly magazine, the GAO Review, is useful for its explanations of how the agency operates and for its mentions of hirings, promotions and departures among staff members who have an advantage over even the most talented investigative journalist: subpoena power.

The Congressional Research Service, part of the Library of Congress, is funded with tax dollars, but staff members will not release their research to the public unless authorized by the member of Congress or the committee requesting the information.

A number of Web sites, profit and nonprofit, offer electronic copies of many reports such as www.opencrs.org. Another way around the obstacle is to request specific issue briefs from a member of Congress. The briefs are listed in the CRS publication Update. The magazine CRS Review provides highlights from CRS analyses that tend to be the talk of Congress.

For example, www.gpo.ucop.edu/crs is a University of California gateway for the Government Printing Office. Also, Penny Hill Press says it is the only private supplier of all Congressional Research Service (CRS) publications and makes them available individually and by subscription at its Web site, www.pennyhill.com. Its public index will tell if there is a report on a topic. Those can be found through the privately published Congressional Information Service Index or the Monthly Catalog of U.S. Government Publications.

The Congressional Budget Office (www.cbo.gov) is the legislative branch counterpart to the White House Office of Management and Budget (www .whitehouse.gov/omb).

Using Congressional Information

In addition to being stories in themselves, legislatures and legislators can be marvelous sources of information for investigations about individuals, institutions and issues.

One of the most incredibly useful Web sites for Congress is Thomas (named for Thomas Jefferson). The Web site, run by the Library of Congress (http://thomas.loc.gov), has easily accessible, well-indexed information including the Congressional Record, proposed bills, passed bills, committee reports and budget appropriations.

Congressional committee documents and the Congressional Record are helpful for all inquiries as are committee reports.

An example is the House Ways and Means Committee's "Overview of Entitlement Programs." Nicknamed the "Green Book," the report tells reporters much of what they need to know about Social Security, Medicare, adoption assistance and other federal programs covering large subgroups of the U.S. population. To keep up with the release of hearing books and other committee publications, reporters can subscribe to Congress in Print from Congressional Quarterly Inc. or check investigative Web sites.

The Congressional Record is especially useful for its word-by-word transcription of House and Senate floor debates.

When a bill does become law, it enters the U.S. Code, where it is placed into one of 50 subject-matter chapters called "titles."

Investigating State Legislatures

Names of key legislative staff can be found in each state's government manual and in the State Legislative Staff Directory, from the National Conference of State Legislatures in Denver.

The center also has made a searchable database of state legislators' disclosure forms at www.icij.org/iys.

But a first place to check is stateline.org, a nonprofit that monitors statehouse reporting. Also, check the Web site of state capitol reporters at http://capitolbeat.wordpress.com and the IRE Resource Center for stories.

Also, check National Money and Politics (www.followthemoney.org/index.phtml), a nonprofit that tracks statehouse campaign finance.

10

Investigating the Judicial System

Experienced journalists have long valued the courthouse as the place to find records that will provide the underpinnings of their investigations. This chapter is about investigating the court system. It recounts the efforts of the journalists who report on the judicial system, but it includes much more than that. It is also about understanding and revealing how justice is dispensed and where to look if it fails, in big cities or little towns, in large or small systems. In addition, court documents, especially the ones in civil court, provide information and stories for many beats outside the courthouse.

Investigations of the justice system can be the most rewarding work a journalist can do. A reporter can help free an innocent person, expose lax prosecution of the guilty, reveal harsh and unfair prison sentences, or disclose misconduct by the very officials and employees running the justice system. Yet the challenges of doing these investigations are among the most difficult. The system encompasses numerous "players" and stages. The language of the system is filled with Latin phrases, and the rules are complex and Byzantine from a layperson's perspective.

Then there is the intimidating size of the system. Robert E. Dreschel, author of "News Making in the Trial Courts," conveyed the immensity of the task of covering—let alone investigating—the justice system as a daily beat in just one state:

> [The beat of one court reporter] includes 36 state and local judges and their staffs; 72 attorneys in the county attorney's office and 20 in the city attorney's office; 50 public defenders; about 20 private criminal defense attorneys . . . court administration staff; the U.S. attorney's office (12 prosecutors); four federal judges and their staffs; three federal magistrates; bankruptcy court; the FBI; the Drug Enforcement Administration; the Secret Service; the Minnesota Supreme Court . . . the state Lawyers Professional Responsibility Board; and the state Board on Judicial Standards.

But there is an effective way to approach investigations of the justice system and produce meaningful work. This approach uses the same methods—document trails and people trails—suggested in earlier chapters.

The justice system has clear junctures where documents are produced, decisions are made, and the roles of individuals are sharply defined. At each one of these junctures, there are numerous investigative possibilities and previous stories from which to learn and build new stories.

Beyond telling the story of how the judicial system performs, it cannot be stressed enough that court files also provide documents and data that can be used in stories that go far beyond the judicial system.

In an earlier edition of this book, Jack Tobin explained how wealthy, influential, reclusive billionaire businessman Howard Hughes had no driver's license, never voted and owned almost nothing in his own name. But a former aide sued Hughes for slander, and the trial unleashed a torrent of documents.

The aide won at trial, lost on appeal and settled out of court, but "the real winners," Tobin wrote, "were all those who hungered for details of the life of the world's most famous recluse. The exhibits in the case filled a room. They amounted to millions of pages of testimony, depositions, accounting reports and tape-recorded conversations." Thus any reporter studying an individual or institution always should check state and federal court cases for background and story leads.

In this chapter, we will look at the various approaches to investigating the judicial system, as well as the people and document trails in civil and criminal cases, prisons, parole and probation systems, juvenile cases and family court, the administration of the judicial system and the special court systems. At the end of this chapter, take a look at "Resources for Reporting" for more resources and tips for investigating the courts.

Approaches to Investigating the Judicial System

The judicial system is multifaceted. It is not composed just of court cases; it is also a government administrative agency involved with professional associations and nonprofit independent organizations. It is influenced by informal personal relations among attorneys, judges and other employees. When you start looking into courts, you need to be aware of the system's complexity and study it as closely as you would individual court cases.

The Judicial System as a Political System

"Just like city hall or presidential politics, the courts are a political system," said veteran investigative reporter Frederic Tulsky. The accuracy of that statement has been proven over and over again in the past decade. Throughout the

United States, elections for local judges have become as divisive and as expensive and donation-ridden as other elections. Disputes in Congress over the appointment of federal judges have led to filibusters and deep animosity between political parties.

To begin investigating the courts, a journalist should understand the process of how judges and prosecutors are chosen. However impartial that process seems, judges can still be politicians in robes. Similarly, prosecutors can be politicians who serve as officers of the court. In the federal system, judges and prosecutors, known as U.S. attorneys, are appointed by the president and confirmed by the U.S. Senate, often with the backing of the state's U.S. senators, representatives, and officials of the political party holding the White House.

After they're confirmed, federal judges and prosecutors play a role in appointing subordinates, such as bankruptcy court judges and assistant prosecuting attorneys, who also exercise power. Reporters should cultivate sources throughout the U.S. Department of Justice because that agency is involved in almost every portion of the criminal and civil case processes. Those sources can tip off reporters to important investigations and point them to public documents.

In state judicial systems, judges and prosecutors are either elected by voters or appointed (usually by the governor, with legislative approval). Supporters of the elective system say it allows greater opportunities for minorities and women to gain office. Supporters of the appointive system say it minimizes politicization of the courts and leads to higher-quality officials. Either way, the potential for politics to take precedence is there.

In an elective system, a candidate must raise money, often from lawyers who will later bring cases to a judge they supported. Sometimes lawyers will contribute to both candidates to hedge their bets.

Judges' campaign finance reports are public, but only recently have journalists begun examining those reports routinely. When Sheila Kaplan was at Common Cause magazine, she wrote that judgeship races were "once the Kmart of political elections," but that lawyers and other special interests had begun contributing large sums. Kaplan described a Florida lawyer solicited for a contribution on behalf of an incumbent judge running for re-election, just days before trying a nonjury case before that judge. She also reported that as two huge oil companies were pitted against each other in a multimillion-dollar Texas lawsuit, the law firms representing the oil giants contributed almost $400,000 to various Texas judges, including state supreme court justices who were not even standing for re-election.

Other journalists have documented connections between campaign contributions and attorneys who receive lucrative case assignments as trustees, guardians or arbitrators from judges. An Indianapolis Star investigation found cronyism at work in the bankruptcy court as judges awarded $14 million of professional fees over a four-year period. Much of that money went to attorneys with political ties to or financial relationships with the judges.

Journalists also can examine what lawyers actually accomplish for those professional fees. Detroit News reporters studying attorneys appointed to represent indigent defendants on their appeals found vouchers submitted by those lawyers that showed charges for visits to incarcerated clients. Comparing the vouchers to visitor cards on file at the state prison, the reporters found that the lawyers were paid for dozens of consultations that never took place.

When judges are appointed rather than elected, campaign contributions still can be an issue. A Los Angeles Times team reported that 118 lawyers who contributed to a California gubernatorial campaign became judges after the candidate won. Those 118 made up one-fifth of the governor's judicial appointments.

The court system also provides additional political rewards. The courts sometimes escape civil service regulations and can be repositories of patronage positions for judges and the political parties to which they belong. In Philadelphia, for example, reporters identified more than 2,000 court jobs that were excluded from civil service requirements. Journalists should ask how court workers got their jobs, if there are minimum qualifications, and whether tests are required and administered fairly.

For example, a Philadelphia Inquirer series showed the city's $55 million annual court payroll included relatives of at least 30 of the city's 120 judges, as well as relatives of court administrators. The deputy court administrator, with four relatives on the payroll, said, "I'm just sorry I can't get more of my family members on the court."

Two Tracks: Civil Cases and Criminal Cases

Adding to the challenges of covering the judicial system is the fact that there are two major kinds of cases—civil and criminal. The two kinds of cases might have different schedules, standards of evidence, procedures, lawyers, kinds of rulings and experts.

In civil cases, one party seeks compensation or penalties for damages allegedly inflicted by another party. In criminal cases, prosecutors seek to fine or imprison defendants for breaking the law.

Making it more complex is that a defendant can be found not guilty in a criminal trial and yet lose a civil trial based on the same evidence. This is what happened in the famous case of former football star and actor O.J. Simpson, who was accused of killing his ex-wife and her friend. The jury in his criminal trial found him not guilty, but a jury in his civil trial found he had committed the crime and would have to pay millions of dollars to the victims' families.

Tracking the Civil Case

Over the past decade, journalists have recognized the importance of civil suits and made them a part of their coverage. While some civil suits can be frivolous, others can serve as the impetus for investigative projects. Civil suits shed light on product safety, misconduct by doctors and other professionals, financial scams, organized crime, corporate misdeeds, poor performance by contractors, failures in prison systems and many other issues. No matter what beat or topic you are covering, you should always check civil cases in your county and federal courts.

Learning about cases is relatively easy, and they deserve daily checks of the files since they are added to throughout the life of a case. Dockets and new filings are often online and available to the public at courthouses. Court clerks are often helpful for finding files. Daily legal newspapers publish dates and places of upcoming cases, recently released opinions, disciplinary proceedings against lawyers and other information.

Civil case files can be obtained from the court clerk, the lawyers, the plaintiffs or the defendants. These paper trails are a journalist's dream, and they are usually more extensive than in criminal cases. The docket sheet is the best place to begin. It includes all filings by both parties and all actions of the court, listed chronologically. A complaint, also called a petition, is the first document filed.

Common early motions include those seeking dismissal before trial (referred to as summary judgment), alleging factual deficiencies, suggesting the plaintiff has no standing to sue at all (or at least not in that locale) and asking the court to reject evidence.

Each side learns about the other side's case through a process called discovery. Discovery materials can include office memoranda, in hard copy or electronic form, and depositions, which are sworn oral statements in question-and-answer format taken from a witness before trial. Fraud in civil cases sometimes surfaces during discovery: phony claims, staged accidents and the like. Journalists can go beyond the court record to seek paper trails and people trails that might help prove fraud.

Plaintiffs and defendants sometimes ask the judge to issue a pretrial protective order, sealing certain documents from public view. Journalists have sometimes successfully challenged protective orders. At other times, a judge might allow a case to be settled and seal all information as part of the settlement agreement.

Occasionally, civil cases are filed as class actions, involving hundreds or thousands of plaintiffs who claim to have been wronged in the same way by the same party, usually a large corporation. Class actions might be more lucrative for lawyers than for those allegedly injured after the award, if any, is split into many small pieces.

Sometimes settlement talks between lawyers occur as part of the court proceeding, with the judge's knowledge; in other cases, the parties seek extralegal help outside the court through arbitration, mediation or some different form of alternative dispute resolution. Journalists can inquire with local sources whether significant cases are going through arbitration and mediation outside the regular court system.

Some judges leave the bench to join private mediation or arbitration companies at salaries higher than their government pay. The nonprofit American Arbitration Association, New York City, is the largest alternative to the courts; it now faces competition from profit-making private arbitration corporations. One downside of the private system is unreported decisions and secret resolutions on matters of public importance.

The U.S. Department of Justice Civil Division sometimes becomes involved with civil litigation, suggesting regulations or getting involved with cases. Much of its concern centers on commercial litigation, especially federal contracts for goods and services. Its involvement in consumer litigation is usually tied to consumer protection and public health laws.

Tracking the Criminal Case: From Arrest to Sentencing

A criminal case can be a long and complicated trail of events and documents, but attention to detail can make all the difference in the quality and impact of the investigative story. Remember that each step in the case produces motions and records that deserve close scrutiny and often reveal injustices when they occur.

Between Arrest and First Court Appearance

In the criminal system, the people and paper trails begin with the arrest, when police take a suspect to the police station to be fingerprinted. Police conduct a criminal records check and may begin interviewing the suspect. Jails keep logbooks that record inmates and visitors and can help journalists keep track of arrests.

In many U.S. communities, the interview has become more complicated because the defendant, the victim or others may not speak English. At the very beginning of—and throughout—the process, a journalist can investigate possible inequities if a professional or volunteer translator is not on hand.

After the booking, a suspect may spend time in a holding cell. Journalists should

- Check if there have been official inspections, audits, reviews or lawsuits involving conditions at the jail
- Interview the defense lawyers, current and former jailers, and former prisoners and their relatives about the conditions, including medical care, food and especially how the mentally or physically disabled are treated
- Check jail logs to see how long a prisoner is held before seeing a magistrate and whether this time meets the standards established by court rulings

Brutal beatings and other abuse can take place in jails, and both those who are presumed innocent and those who have been found guilty can be the victims.

From Jail to Courthouse

After arrest, prisoners may be transported to the courthouse, another jail or a crime scene. In recent years, violent crimes have been committed by prisoners during these trips. By reviewing the standards for security and comparing them to actual procedures, a reporter can produce an investigative story that could save lives. Journalists should look at

- Staffing levels for security
- Qualifications of those providing security
- Incidents during transportation to the courthouse and in the courthouse and any disciplinary action against staff for lax supervision

After a person is charged, police may initially set bail, but a judge determines the bail for the length of the proceedings. Bail is intended to ensure that criminal defendants appear for their court proceedings. The bail system allows defendants to get out of jail while awaiting trial by posting a bond. A bond is insurance, usually offered by a bail bondsmen. The defendant pays the bail bondsman a portion of the total bond, often 10 percent—which the defendant never gets back—and puts up collateral that the bondsman can take if the defendant does not show up for his or her court date.

A judge sets bail at an amount deemed reasonable based on the likelihood that the defendant will flee. A defendant who cannot raise the money for bail stays in jail until trial. The defense attorney can ask that the amount be lowered or that the suspect be released without paying.

The prosecutor can oppose bail on the basis of danger to the community, the possibility that witnesses may be threatened, or the risk of flight—or can ask for a higher amount than the judge has set. With so many variables, this system can be flawed on either side of the equation.

For example, the Sarasota Herald-Tribune found judges releasing numerous defendants on their own recognizance—meaning they had to pay nothing—in cases in which the defendants had prior criminal records. WDIV-TV in Detroit determined that even criminals who paid bond could skip their court dates without fear of being pursued by the court because 12 law enforcement officials were expected to handle 22,000 fugitive cases statewide.

On the other hand, the bail system can imprison people before trial because of ineptitude or because defendants have little money. WCAU-TV in Philadelphia found that, because of bureaucratic backlogs, poor suspects had to wait days to see a bail judge, although many had not been charged with committing a crime. The Hartford Courant discovered that, on average, black and Hispanic male suspects paid twice as much as whites to be released on bail—although they had similar records and backgrounds. That also led to a much higher number of minority defendants in jail while awaiting trial.

Bail bondsmen offer other possibilities for investigation. Journalists do not scrutinize often enough the conduct of bail bondsmen and their companies to see whether they are properly licensed and whether they follow state laws. (In some states, bail bondsmen have been eliminated and the courthouses handle bail.)

The Oklahoman reviewed court records and found that an Oklahoma County special judge issued orders that improperly allowed bail bondsmen to avoid paying the court more than $800,000 in bond forfeitures. Other investigations have found serious and fatal flaws in the system in which bail bondsmen hire contractors—known as bounty hunters—to find defendants and bring them back to court. The bounty hunters can legally use violent methods to catch and subdue defendants, and investigators have uncovered cases in which they used brutal tactics, sometimes seriously injuring or killing innocent people.

Initial Appearance in Court

The preliminary hearing or the arraignment is the first court appearance after the filing of a criminal charge. The criminal charge might come directly from police working with the prosecutor, in which case a judge is supposed to decide if enough evidence exists to charge the defendant.

Prosecutors sometimes prefer to avoid a preliminary hearing by going directly to a grand jury, which consists of citizens. That is because the evidence presented in open court during a preliminary hearing might tip off the defense to the prosecution's strategy. If the grand jury believes the evidence is sufficient, it will issue an indictment. It can be easy for the prosecutor to steer a grand jury to the decision he wants since the grand jury hears only the prosecutor's side. Some states require prosecutors to seek grand jury indictments; other states make grand juries optional.

Defendants sometimes waive the right to a grand jury to limit media exposure. Laws governing grand jury activity vary from state to state, and federal grand juries operate under yet another set of rules, but all grand jury proceedings are held behind closed doors. Although journalists cannot observe grand juries in person, they can observe comings and goings, make telephone calls to lawyers and talk to law enforcement sources. Reporters can sit outside grand jury rooms to identify witnesses and ask them what they said. Subpoenas issued for witnesses may also be public. If witnesses are reimbursed for their expenses from public funds, their names might be available through a voucher system.

In many states, the law forbids witnesses from talking about what went on in the grand jury room. Grand jurors are almost always legally restrained from talking, although there are exceptions. In California state courts, for example, grand jury transcripts are available after an indictment. Furthermore, some prosecutors, jurors or judges do talk on background.

Journalists should try to determine what evidence was presented to the grand jury and whether the evidence was skewed to lead to an indictment. Journalists should also look for signs that there might be political motivation behind the convening of a grand jury.

Grand juries sometimes issue reports that go beyond the criminal conduct of an individual. The reports, called presentments, deal with government malfeasance. For example, a report could discuss the extent of organized crime's influence in the city or unsanitary conditions at the county jail.

When charged, a suspect can plead not guilty, guilty or nolo contendere (meaning "I do not want to contest it"). One reason for pleading nolo contendere is to avoid liability in the civil courts.

Pretrial Hearings

Before the trial, the defendant might file a suppression motion claiming that the state improperly obtained evidence. The motion will be heard at a pretrial hearing. At this stage, allegations of police misconduct are commonplace.

The Philadelphia Inquirer reporters who studied transcripts of pretrial hearings from homicide cases documented a pattern of police beating confessions out of suspects. The Inquirer found 80 cases during a three-year period in which judges refused to allow confessions into evidence. Judges and lawyers often know the reputations of certain police officers, and through interviews journalists can find out which officers are suspected of extracting confessions through heavy-handed tactics. Journalists then can examine transcripts and other records to determine whether the reputations are deserved.

Other pretrial motions might include requests to dismiss the case, move the trial to another locale, reconsider bail or determine whether a defendant is competent to stand trial. Attending pretrial hearings and examining court documents prepared for the hearing can provide key information for investigations.

The Assignment of Judges

In the federal courts and some local systems, cases are assigned by lottery to judges in roughly equal numbers. This system discourages "judge shopping," in which attorneys use their influence to place their cases before a favored judge. It can also cause backlogs. Some judges will be idle if any of their scheduled cases settle or break down unexpectedly.

When the system allows "judge shopping," a journalist can determine whether certain lawyers appear before certain judges more often than chance would suggest. The journalist can look at which lawyers win rulings or cases often before particular judges and determine whether there are business connections or social ties between judge and lawyer.

The Jury

Prosecutors and defense lawyers in criminal cases must decide whether their chances of victory would be helped or hurt by a jury trial. In most felony cases, the accused has a right to a jury, which usually has six or 12 jurors. In most states, plaintiffs and defendants in civil cases must also choose between jury trial and a bench trial (judge only). In most jurisdictions, reporters can calculate whether conviction rates are higher in jury trials or in bench trials and whether juries tend to favor plaintiffs or defendants in civil cases.

In some jurisdictions, judges ask all the questions during jury selection, which is called voir dire. In other jurisdictions, lawyers for both sides pose the questions. Journalists are often allowed to watch jury selection or to read questionnaires filled out by prospective jurors.

Racial, ethnic, or religious discrimination is sometimes present in jury selection, and consultants who study juries for lawyers can suggest that certain prospective jurors be excluded to favor their side. For example, The Dallas Morning News found that local prosecutors excluded 90 percent of eligible blacks from jury service in felony and capital murder cases. In general, the jury's makeup can be a good predictor of its decision.

People can be excluded from the jury for two reasons: cause or peremptory challenge. "Cause" means that the judge grants permission to a challenging attorney to exclude a potential juror because of discernible bias; for example, the person may say he or she distrusts all prosecutors or believes most defendants are guilty. Lawyers can make unlimited challenges for cause as long as the judge believes the challenges are valid. Lawyers on both sides are allowed to exclude a certain number of potential jurors without stating reasons to the judge; this is known as a peremptory challenge.

Ralph Frammalino of the Los Angeles Times made a database of juror questionnaires during the famous O.J. Simpson trial and found that most jurors who believed DNA evidence was credible—a point that was critical to the case—were not selected for the jury because they were deemed too media conscious.

The makeup of a jury is beyond the total control of the judge and the lawyers, especially when the pool of jurors comes solely from lists of registered voters. In some locales, a large percentage of citizens have not registered to vote. Journalists should see whether a significant percentage of nonregistered citizens come from ethnic or racial groups that are frequently underrepresented on juries.

Reporters at WHDH-TV in Boston analyzed the racial makeup of federal juries in Massachusetts and found that, in some cases, jury pools had no people of color whatsoever. According to their investigation, minorities remained underrepresented in the justice system as much as 50 percent of the time because jury pools are chosen according to who responds to the town census. Because the census was an unfunded mandate, many low-income neighborhoods did a bad job of responding to the census.

Although jurors can illuminate their decisions after a trial, some judges try to forbid reporters from contacting jurors even after the verdict is in. In many cases, jurors' names and addresses are withheld from the media. But the Legal Times reported that "some defense lawyers and jury consultants . . . say that veiling the identity of the jurors strips the defendant of the presumption of innocence" because the unusual policy injects a fear factor leading to conviction. Rules and laws vary from state to state. Journalists have circumvented the attempt to limit access to jurors by contacting the lawyers in the case or family members of the jurors.

Case Backlogs

As is often said, justice delayed can be justice denied. Criminal suspects have constitutional protection on this issue: In the federal system and in many state

PART II   Investigating
the Government

systems, defendants have the right to a speedy trial. However, high numbers of criminal and civil cases can overwhelm a court system, creating case backlogs and prison overcrowding.

The Courier-Journal in Louisville found that more than 650 cases in Franklin County, Kentucky, had to be dismissed because of lack of prosecution. The problem was a continual backlog of cases, as well as a general mismanagement of the system as a whole. In a few cases, prosecutors and judges debated whose responsibility it was to track the number of pending cases.

Court administrators are concerned with the raw numbers on backlogs. After all, their job is to see that backlogs diminish or at least appear to be diminishing. But achieving justice and disposing of cases are not always synonymous.

The push to resolve backlogs without proper resources has its downside. Lawyers need enough time to prepare adequately, and that is especially true for a public defender with a heavy caseload who meets the accused for the first time at the preliminary hearing.

Most journalists are used to covering trials, but watching the trial with an eye to attorney preparation, exhibits and witnesses is key to understanding whether there has been incompetent representation or misconduct by officials.

Victims of Crime

When prosecutors fail to win a conviction, a common reason is uncooperative victims. David C. Anderson, in his book "Crimes of Justice," noted that about 70 percent of dismissed charges in some jurisdictions stem from complainants refusing to testify.

Although victims must be scrutinized, they can be victimized twice: first by the assailant and then by the criminal justice system.

One type of revictimization occurs when victims of a crime are not notified about dropped charges, probation, parole or expungement of the perpetrator's criminal record. Suddenly the assailant is back in their lives without warning. In some jurisdictions, victims have the right to see their assailants tried speedily, can make a statement at the time of sentencing and parole hearings and are generally allowed to participate at any other stage. Journalists can study the impact of such participation on trial outcomes, probation proceedings and other aspects of the process.

Another type of revictimization occurs when restitution payments fail to benefit victims. The San Jose Mercury News discovered that two-thirds of court-ordered restitution payments never reached victims. The (Provo) Daily Herald found that Utah's Crime Victims Reparation Fund was accumulating a large reserve through investments while the intended recipients received nothing.

The irony of uncompensated victims is obvious. Taxpayers support imprisoned criminals at a cost of $20,000 or more annually, supplying meals, education and health care that might be superior to anything the prisoner previously experienced. Meanwhile, the victim, who may have been injured or incapacitated, receives nothing.

Sentencing

Before imposing a sentence in a criminal case, the judge normally orders a presentencing investigation by a probation officer, social worker or psychologist. The big question is, Is the accused going to commit another crime? Because it is difficult to know for sure, even the most effective, equitable sentence is partly educated guesswork.

Presentencing reports are normally closed to reporters without the aid of a source. Sometimes the convicted person will open the report to a journalist on request. It also might be possible to view the prosecutor's sentencing memorandum, which is supplied to the judge. It is well worth pursuing these reports since they can provide critical insights for investigations of the system.

In some jurisdictions, judges can impose varying prison terms within a range (for example, one to 10 years for aggravated assault), based on a defendant's history, the nature of the crime and any peculiar circumstances. This indeterminate sentencing model is grounded in a belief that prison rehabilitation can succeed and does so at varying rates. If rehabilitation seems to have succeeded, in, say, two years, the judge in some jurisdictions has the discretion to release the criminal. If there is no indication of rehabilitation, the judge can refuse early release.

Detroit Free Press reporters found that sentences varied widely for similar manslaughter convictions across Michigan. Two similar killings would earn one defendant probation and another six years in prison. Many similar projects document shocking discrimination in the judicial process. The Florida Times-Union, for example, determined that defendants who killed whites received much longer prison sentences than defendants who killed blacks.

For less serious crimes, the judge may institute a monetary fine (perhaps including restitution to the victim), community service, a suspended sentence, a jail term, probation or a combination of these. Evaluating the effectiveness of these programs should be a standard procedure for any investigative journalist.

There are other laws that give judicial officials extraordinary leeway. Manny Garcia and Jason Grotto of The Miami Herald found the practice of "withholding adjudication" or clearing charges changed "into a handy tool to close cases that, in many instances, appears anything but just. Rapists, child molesters, child abusers, wife beaters, burglars, cocaine traffickers, repeat offenders, even corrupt public officials got the break." They also found another law that allowed judges to block the first-time convictions of felons so they wouldn't have the stigma of being a felon.

Journalists should compare the sentencing patterns of individual judges with those of the entire court. WAGA-TV, Atlanta, found a judge forcing defendants to attend $70 counseling sessions with a therapist who was treating the judge for his own disorders. Many courts now have databases that track each case so a journalist can more easily look for patterns.

To eliminate inconsistencies, including racial discrimination in sentencing, some state and federal laws specify maximum and minimum terms. For federal crimes, the U.S. Sentencing Commission, Washington, D.C., is supposed to determine sentence ranges. The agency, which considers revisions annually, instructs judges on how to consider each convict's criminal history as part of the mix of factors.

When no flexibility is allowed, it might be because the crime falls into a category requiring mandatory sentencing. However, mandatory sentencing has drawbacks. First, it does not eliminate disparities, because many defendants subject to mandatory sentences plea-bargain instead. That shifts decision making from the judge, who exercises it publicly from the bench, to prosecutors, who exercise it in closed conferences. Second, when a prisoner's mandatory sentence has been served, the prisoner must be released, even if the prisoner remains a menace to an individual or group.

Appeals

State courts handle several hundred thousand appeals annually; federal courts handle about one-tenth the amount, still a considerable number. Journalists should ask which prosecutors engage in questionable tactics or outright misconduct, which often wins convictions but leads to reversals. Another compelling story is which judges' decisions are overturned most often. Because about 80 percent of civil appeals and 90 percent of criminal appeals fail, it is especially significant if a trial court judge's rulings are repeatedly overturned.

When an appeals court reviews a jury verdict, the Seventh Amendment comes into play: "No fact tried by a jury shall be otherwise reexamined than according to the rules of common law." An appeal usually includes claims that the judge mistakenly interpreted the law at trial. Because appeals normally deal only with matters raised at trial, journalists must study the written record from the lower court.

Once the appeal is argued by the lawyers who are appealing and those who are opposing the appeal, the case is decided by a panel of judges. The questions to each side and statements of appellate judges during oral argument are usually significant. The function of written briefs by lawyers appearing before the panel is to show the court *how* to decide in their favor; the function of oral arguments is to make the court *want* to decide in their favor.

Journalists should check prisoners' appeals. A prisoner who has been convicted and sentenced does not have many options; direct appeals and collateral attacks on the conviction (maybe because new evidence has surfaced) represent their last hope.

A journalist can get started on a potentially good story by examining which cases are appealed from the courthouse being covered and which decisions are overturned. By focusing on the overturned cases, a journalist can see which judges or prosecutors most often have cases overturned and begin digging into why they have the poorest records.

Investigating Punishment: Prison, Probation, Parole, Commutations and Pardons

Journalists who first write about individual prisoners or prisons as institutions are generally shocked when they delve into the system. An increasing problem has been access to documents and people, making it hard to portray conditions and reveal abuses and injustices.

A defendant who is convicted of a crime can become part of several other systems: probation, which can be a substitute for prison time; parole; or pardons. Each system has it own potential defects and injustices and should receive the same examination as the prison system.

Gaining Access to Prisons

When it comes to gaining access, the warden, who oversees the prison, and the guards reign supreme.

Wardens are powerful because they not only control access to prisoners, but also oversee all the punishment within the prison. Thus they ought to be scrutinized closely. At the same time, all prison personnel should be carefully looked at. Unionized or not, the hiring system is sometimes a failure because the job description is so unattractive. When shortages occur, guards might be recruited from the street in nearby towns, without job references or aptitude checks.

Some state governments have turned prison construction and management over to private companies, making wardens even less accessible.

Although prisons keep records on inmates, those records are usually denied to journalists on grounds of personal privacy and administrative efficiency. An inside source, such as an inmate or a prison guard, is usually necessary. A journalist can find specific federal prisoners by using the Federal Prison Locator telephone service; some state prison systems offer similar locator services.

Poor access to prisoners is a complaint among journalists in almost every state. When prisoners can get to a telephone at all, their time is usually limited, and the cost of the collect call to the party on the other end is usually hefty. Journalists can find out whether telephone calls are monitored; they often are because some inmates have used their calls to arrange crimes, including the intimidation of witnesses for the prosecution.

Prison Conditions

To find out about prison conditions, journalists can examine prison complaint files, interview recently released prisoners and check lawsuits filed by prisoners in federal and state courts. In many such lawsuits, the plaintiffs represent themselves (*pro se* is the legal term), using law books in the prison library for reference.

Journalists also can contact former employees, defense lawyers and the family members of prisoners to increase their knowledge of prison conditions. One common rights violation involves the use of a restraint chair when an arrestee being detained in a local jail or a convict in a prison allegedly misbehaves. Another is prison rape.

In a classic story, Loretta Tofani of The Washington Post was covering a suburban courthouse when she wandered into a sentencing proceeding. She heard a lawyer say a prisoner had been gang-raped in the county jail. The result, months later, was a three-part series. To locate jail guards, Tofani obtained names and addresses from sheriffs' deputies who transported prisoners, court depositions in lawsuits filed by rape victims and an internal jail personnel list supplied by a friendly source.

Tofani cultivated jail medical workers, whose names she got from guards. When she called on the medical workers at home, they refused to talk. "I kept going back to those houses, each time with a slightly different pitch. Eventually the door slammers turned into my most valuable sources. . . . The reason medical workers risked their jobs and decided to help me mainly was because they were troubled about the rapes." Tofani next convinced victims and rapists to talk, most of them on the record—proof that investigators should never assume a potential source will say no.

Journalists also should examine the number of suspects who die in local jails before being convicted or even formally charged. If an inmate commits suicide, the journalist should see if there is flawed supervision. Danielle Gordon of The Chicago Reporter found that in an eight-year span, 177 blacks, 80 whites and one Asian-American had died in Cook County Jail.

Probing into health care at prisons can result in compelling investigations, too. The Dallas Morning News found the federal prison system to be a haven "for doctors of dangerous backgrounds, foreign doctors who had trouble with English and doctors too inexperienced or untrained to perform the tasks demanded of them."

State prisons and local jails are often just as grim. A KPRC-TV team uncovered at least seven deaths in Houston's Harris County Jail that probably would have been prevented if the doctor-patient ratio had been better than one to 4,000.

Another key question about prisons is whether anybody is being rehabilitated. Journalists can inquire about

- In-prison educational programs, including those that could lead to a high school diploma or a college degree
- Facilities for physical conditioning
- Spiritual guidance, no matter the choice of religion
- Psychological counseling for habitual sex offenders
- Treatment to alleviate drug addictions and control alcoholism
- Vocational training, including help with job placement

One trend, boot camps for younger offenders, also known as shock incarceration units, has not shown success but is still prevalent. Studies have found that long days of physical conditioning and verbal abuse generally have little positive impact on recidivism.

Prison industries are not boot camps, but they do employ forced labor. Enterprising journalists will examine whether work programs meet the goals of rehabilitation and eventual job placement. That is especially relevant now that more prisons are charging inmates a daily fee for cell and board, a fee due soon after release if it is not paid during incarceration. Privately operated prisons, concerned about maximizing profits, are often willing to accept inmates from other states beset by overcrowding—for a fee.

Prison overcrowding also leads to the court-ordered release of convicted criminals. Overcrowding can be blamed in part on the overcriminalization of certain behaviors. Journalists should question why legislators and executive branch bureaucrats underestimate the need for prison cells so that criminals end up back in the community prematurely.

Journalists also can do a better job of showing prison conditions and the need for early releases for overcriminalized cases by describing the mixing of violent hardened criminals with nonviolent offenders and the spread of tuberculosis and AIDS among those incarcerated.

The federal prison system categorizes its facilities according to the types of prisoners incarcerated there: penitentiaries, correctional institutions, prison camps, detention centers and medical and administrative facilities. Convicts can ask to be imprisoned near family members; such requests are often granted if the nearest facility has space available.

State prison agencies do not usually oversee such a variety of facilities, but they do usually produce publications, annual reports and directories similar to those of the federal system. The state agencies adopt some suggestions from the National Institute of Corrections, a federal agency think tank. The National Prison Project, part of the American Civil Liberties Union Foundation, Washington, D.C., is a private organization interested in prisoners' rights and prison conditions.

Probation

Even after a defendant has lost all hope of overturning a conviction, imprisonment is still not a certainty. Being sentenced to probation is usually the preferred alternative, though not the victim's preference, because probation means relative freedom. For the judge, a defendant's relative freedom poses a dilemma.

Ideally, probation officers act as social worker, employment counselor and teacher all in one. Lawbreakers assigned to probation officers try to keep contact minimal, because a probation violation that gets noticed might mean they will go to prison.

Most probation officers are so overloaded that supervision of probationers can be almost nonexistent, which is why journalists should inquire about caseloads. If a probation officer is supposed to supervise more than 50 probationers, the journalist should explore the defects in the system that are almost sure to exist. Journalists can document the officer-probationer ratio, compare it to similar jurisdictions and follow an officer to understand what that kind of caseload really means day to day.

Journalists should see

- Whether probation officers can actually keep track of all their clients
- What kind of training the officers receive

- Whether the pay for officers is reasonable
- What kind of turnover rate there is among officers

In many jurisdictions, more than half of probationers commit new crimes. Despite its failures, judges impose probation more often when they have to consider prison overcrowding in their jurisdictions and the success of rehabilitation efforts.

Parole

Unlike probation, release on parole comes only after a portion of a prison sentence has been served. Parole boards, at the state and federal levels, can be secretive, inefficient or corrupt—or all of those. They are often filled by political appointees without the experience or the desire to do a good job. Because they can be politically sensitive, parole boards can release prisoners too soon as a result of well-connected lawyers who represent the prisoner, or the boards can clamp down too tightly as a result of a publicized case in which one parolee commits more crimes.

Looking at the Michigan system, the Detroit Free Press found that 6 percent of felons served full sentences, compared to 17 percent nationally. The Free Press found the parole board violated state law by releasing prisoners without jobs or educational plans because budget reductions had led to fewer parole officers.

A classic investigation of parole and pardon corruption, "Marie," by Peter Maas, chronicles the appointment of a woman to head the Tennessee Board of Probation and Parole. Her discovery of wrongdoing led first to her dismissal and then to her decision to become a whistleblower against the governor. Not all states have parole boards. Journalists in states with them can compare the effectiveness of their state's system with states that handle matters differently. One objection to the elimination of parole is that it leads to loss of hope among prisoners, who then are more likely to be troublesome while incarcerated and who prepare less vigorously for their release. The U.S. Parole Commission produces an annual report that can provide perspective.

Under the current system, it is inevitable there will be a high level of recidivism among parolees since most face job discrimination and lack bank accounts. Often, they are released from prison with only a bus ticket and a small amount of money. Many have no support network of family or friends. Quite a few are addicted to alcohol and other drugs. Some investigations have shown recidivism to be as high as 90 percent.

Commutations and Pardons

When a prisoner has exhausted parole possibilities but is politically connected or retains a politically connected lawyer, there is always a chance the U.S. president or a governor will commute the sentence or issue a pardon. When this occurs, there is sometimes a scandalous reason. The high number of pardons, many of them controversial, that President Bill Clinton made as he left office brought the issue to the forefront.

Journalists should look closely at controversial pardons by examining possible political connections and comparing them to similar cases in which pardons were not granted.

Investigating Juvenile Cases and Family Court

Like probation, parole and pardons, juvenile cases are governed by their own set of standards and practices. But when examining crimes committed by juveniles, it's good to keep in mind that those cases and family court are often intertwined and that despite the barriers of confidentiality you can get inside both of these systems.

Juvenile Cases

The juvenile justice system deserves special attention by journalists despite the extraordinary difficulties in getting access to records, court hearings and other information. Each time a journalist has devoted the time to examining the system, he or she has found a system rife with serious problems.

"The main reason journalists ignore juvenile justice is its confounding secrecy," wrote Pittsburgh Post-Gazette reporters Steve Twedt and Barbara White Stack in The IRE Journal. "Many hearings are closed. Dockets and records are sealed. Officials are forbidden to talk."

The sealing or expungement of juvenile records when a subject reaches adulthood results in further complications. Some scholars have questioned the practice of giving juveniles a clean slate as they enter adulthood because of the number of juveniles who are repeat offenders—in some instances, serial killers—before reaching adulthood. However, in some jurisdictions, juvenile records—at least those documenting serious crimes—are available to school officials, employers, social workers, police and prosecutors to help them make more fully informed decisions.

In addition, when a defendant is tried as a juvenile, the case is normally heard in a separate court, and the defendant has no constitutional right to bail, a jury trial or a public proceeding. The standard of proof is less rigid than that which prevails in the adult justice system ("beyond a reasonable doubt"). Those traditions might make it seem as if the system is stacked against youthful offenders, but often the system deals with juveniles leniently.

Journalists who have investigated the juvenile justice system, including Twedt and Stack, have found that programs lack sufficient staff and money, juveniles with mental illnesses languish untreated in institutions for months, harsh prison sentences show racial disparity, juveniles with less serious charges are pushed into adult court, and juveniles placed in adult prisons are more likely to reoffend.

Investigating the juvenile justice system is an arduous task as long as police and court records about juveniles are closed to the media, but there are some exceptions. The exceptions normally occur in one of two ways: A judge allows access to files and hearings if the reporter agrees to withhold identification of the youth, or a judge rules that the youth should be tried as an adult.

In addition, journalists can find other sources, including

- Juvenile divisions of police departments
- Domestic abuse divisions within prosecutors' offices; local and state social service departments
- Officials of juvenile institutions, attorneys in private practice or in a public defender's office and child advocacy groups

Family Court

Closely related to juvenile court is family court, which handles cases of child and spousal neglect and abuse. Family court, called domestic relations court in some jurisdictions, is designed to follow a family for many years. That way, the judge can make decisions based on an understanding of the family's history. New York City Judge Richard Ross shares his observations in his book "A Day in Part 15: Law and Order in Family Court."

WFAA-TV in Dallas reported that "traditionally, Family Court has received little scrutiny from the media. The underlying feeling has been that when divorcing parents wage bitter custody battles over their children those are personal matters best left in the dusty files of the courthouse basement."

In their eight-month investigation into the family court system in North Texas, reporters from WFAA found a legal system filled with political corruption on the part of judges, lawyers and even psychologists. In one instance, they discovered that a court-appointed psychologist used outdated psychological tests to falsely label some parents unfit to care for their children.

In addition, judges are frequently dependent on court-appointed investigators or private lawyers serving as guardians ad litem in cases involving the termination of biological parents' rights through foster care and adoption. A guardian ad litem is someone appointed by the court to take legal action on behalf of a minor.

But the system of a guardian ad litem can have its flaws. The Boston Globe Magazine exposed greedy and incompetent investigators and guardians ad litem who hurry their cases in order to get paid more quickly, give credence to unreliable hearsay and generally act in ways that fail to place children's interests first. When lawyers serve as guardians ad litem, they rarely have training in mental health evaluation; however, when mental health professionals accept the assignment, they often are baffled by the workings of the legal system.

Delays in family courts are common, recidivism prevails and judges may make snap decisions without adequate information. Poor handling of child abuse cases — first by executive-branch social welfare agencies, later by courts — is sadly common, sometimes with fatal consequences. Other stories have shown that family court has also failed to significantly reduce problems between spouses over timely child-support payments.

Investigating Judicial Operations and Personnel

Court Budgets and Court Operations

Journalists should treat the courts like any other government agency and investigate how the taxpayers' money is spent by the court on personnel, equipment, services, supplies and other items. Every court has a budget based on legislative appropriations, filing fees and fines collected. State supreme courts supervise lower courts, and some states also have agencies to provide administrative support for local courts. Courts often seek bids for building new courthouses, renovating old ones or constructing annexes. They need to have lawns mowed, floors and offices cleaned, and their offices' heating and cooling systems serviced. All these needs can create opportunities for favoritism or mismanagement. Courts also must handle money from fines and penalties, and those financial operations must be audited and the audits made public.

In addition, all court employees, including judges, are expected to earn their salaries and work full days. Several news organizations, including The Boston

Globe and the San Jose Mercury News, have caught judges taking time off—for example, playing golf—when they should have been dealing with large caseloads.

Personnel

Understanding people in any system and how they work together is key to good investigative reporting. In this section, we will look at judges, prosecutors and defense attorneys and the impact of their behavior and their political network on the judicial system.

Judges A relatively simple-to-document story involves a judge's work habits. Many hold court a few hours in the morning, take long lunch recesses, then leave early, perhaps to play golf, as documented over the years by many news organizations. Meanwhile, plaintiffs and defendants wait months or years for rulings or trials because of a supposedly overcrowded court docket.

By talking to lawyers, law professors, clerks and fellow judges, a journalist can gauge whether a judge is considered to favor plaintiffs or defendants.

The animosity between judges and certain lawyers can be a fruitful area for inquiry. Journalists should know which judges issue more contempt citations than average and then inquire why. Similarly, journalists can examine whether a judge abuses his or her authority by refusing to step aside from a case (that is, recuse himself or herself) when evidence of a conflict of interest is presented by the plaintiff or defendant. Examining motions in court proceedings can reveal these refusals to step aside.

Many states require both candidates for judgeships and sitting judges to file reports detailing their personal finances. A check with the state elections commission or other appropriate state agency could be the start of a story about conflicts of interest.

The financial disclosures of federal judges, except for U.S. Supreme Court justices, are handled by the Administrative Office of the U.S. Courts, Washington, D.C. Each state is home to at least one federal court, and each of those courts employs from two to 28 judges. The reports for U.S. Supreme Court justices are available from the Court's public information office. These reports were impressively used by The Kansas City Star when it showed that federal judges had numerous conflicts of interest in civil trials because they held interests in companies they were ruling about. Meanwhile, Texas Lawyer found a judge who had extensive business dealings with a bank that appeared before him in court as plaintiff and defendant.

Other conflicts might arise from a judge's past affiliations. Insights into the dilemmas that judges face can be gained from reading what they read, including Judges' Journal, published by the American Bar Association's Judicial Division.

When a judge's behavior seems to be out of line, the state bar association, a quasi-governmental body like the Missouri Commission on Retirement, Removal and Discipline of Judges or the U.S. Department of Justice might investigate. After the investigation, a report might be available at the state supreme court or through the U.S. Congress. A ratings story, such as one identifying the jurisdiction's 10 worst judges (or the 10 best), can enlighten as well as get the community talking.

Prosecutors   The obligation of a prosecutor in representing the state is ostensibly to seek justice, not just convictions, but prosecutors are politicians too. Federal prosecutors are appointed by the administration in power with the consent of the U.S. Senate, and most local prosecutors (known in some jurisdictions as district attorneys and in others as circuit attorneys) are elected. Everything significant they do or fail to do ought to be examined in a political as well as legal context.

When federal prosecutors or their assistant attorneys misbehave, the U.S. Department of Justice's Office of Professional Responsibility is supposed to investigate. Many allegations come from defense attorneys who believe they are being harassed to discourage vigorous representation of their clients, especially in drug and white-collar crime cases. The Washington Post found that the OPR tended to treat misconduct charges against federal prosecutors lightly.

Local prosecutors might be disciplined by the state attorney general, who is usually an elected official. Local prosecutors and the state attorney general are frequently from different political parties or subscribe to different philosophies. Journalists should examine the backgrounds and performances of prosecutors and assistant prosecutors by looking at

- Whether the prosecutor hires from his former law firm or hires former business associates
- What kind of success rate he or she has in prosecutions
- Whether prosecutions are often overturned when appealed

Citizens who believe they have been abused by the awesome power of the prosecutor's office have virtually no recourse; the almost unanimous view among legislators and judges is that prosecutors cannot be sued for their job-related performance.

One measure of a prosecutor's performance is how many cases go to trial. There is no magic percentage that makes a prosecutor capable. But if almost every case goes to trial, something is amiss, because some cases brought to prosecutors by police are flawed and ought to be dismissed. On the other hand, if almost no cases go to trial, it is possible that too many defendants are getting off too lightly with plea bargains. Plea bargains take many forms: dropping charges, refraining from filing additional charges, making a generous sentencing recommendation or agreeing to stipulate a certain set of facts at sentencing.

Journalists should not assume that plea bargaining is unwise, but the more a system depends on closed-door dealing, the more likely it is someone with connections is receiving special treatment.

Journalists should also look for cases that go to trial but end in convictions on something less than the original charge, which is called undercharging. Another technique involves filing multiple charges against a defendant, then dropping one or more in exchange for a guilty plea to an outstanding charge. Defense attorneys are a good source for information about this phenomenon.

Defense Attorneys In criminal cases, a journalist should distinguish whether the accused is represented by a court-appointed public defender or by a private practice attorney chosen and paid by the accused. If the accused has been certified as indigent, then he or she is entitled to a public defender.

A good investigation for a journalist is whether public defenders are less competent or less successful than private practice attorneys. The stereotype of a public defender is that of a young, idealistic lawyer with a disdain for high pay. One quantifiable measure that can affect quality of representation is the lawyer's caseload. The private practice defense attorney might be handling a half dozen criminal cases simultaneously, while the public defender might have dozens or hundreds.

Journalists also should inquire about whether clients are being overcharged. Sometimes private attorneys bilk the court itself. The Miami Herald found bill padding and other types of fraud among lawyers appointed to represent indigent defendants whom the public defender's office could not accommodate. Some bills to the court claimed more than 24 hours of work in a single day.

Defense attorneys sometimes file motions that fly in the face of social order and common sense. The St. Petersburg Times and The Ann Arbor News, among other media outlets, discovered that with the help of defense attorneys and judges, clients could use state laws to wipe out their criminal records, even for crimes like murder, drug trafficking and rape. A successful expungement means a convicted rapist can teach school without having to tell the district about his past criminal conduct.

Wrongful Convictions

Journalists must be alert to guilty verdicts that are miscarriages of justice. It is not easy to second-guess a jury or judge, but some defendants do get railroaded, and by re-examining the facts journalists might be able to right a wrong.

Even if the wrongful conviction rate is just 1 percent, that could mean thousands of people each year are imprisoned for something they did not do. It also means thousands of perpetrators are still free, maybe killing, stealing or raping again. Journalists across the nation have repeatedly shown that they can do a more thorough job of investigating cases without subpoenas than law enforcement officers and prosecutors can do with subpoenas.

In a series of stories, the Winston-Salem (N.C.) Journal showed that it was likely that the wrong man was serving 29 years for assault because of flaws in the criminal justice system. The reporters found that time and again law enforcers pursued their own theories of what happened and ignored the obvious inconsistencies.

An investigative trio at the Chicago Tribune—Maurice Possley, Ken Armstrong and Steve Mills—was especially successful at finding many wrongful convictions of men who were on death row. Their award-winning series led to the release of several men from death row and a moratorium on all executions in 2000.

But there is no reason for a journalist to wait until after trial to examine a criminal case. From the time of the arrest, there are paper trails (police reports) and people trails (the accused, accusatory witnesses, alibi witnesses) to check.

Signs of potential problems include

- Coerced confessions
- Failure to run DNA tests, when it's practical, and failure to conduct careful analyses of them
- Information from paid jailhouse informants
- Inadequate lineup procedures that lead victims and witnesses to identify the wrong person
- Other unreliable eyewitness testimony
- Prosecutors and sheriffs looking for more convictions when they're worried about election returns
- Prejudicial statements by the prosecutor during trial
- Inept defense counsel

Investigating Specialized Courts

Besides general civil courts, criminal courts (sometimes with a separate drug court) and juvenile courts (sometimes with a related family court), there are other specialized courts to investigate. The local courts are traffic, municipal, divorce, probate and small claims courts. The specialized federal courts handle tax, bankruptcy, appeals and military matters.

Journalists should especially look at the management and workloads at local courts since numerous investigations have uncovered financial misdeeds or an overwhelming workload.

Traffic Court

Examinations of traffic courts have produced a wide range of findings, including ticket fixing, lax enforcement against drunken drivers, and quick and unfair hearings intended to raise revenue for a small city or county.

Fixed tickets cost taxpayers revenue but are not life-threatening. Mishandled drunken driving cases, however, can lead to fatalities. For example, The Virginian-Pilot found that a circuit judge reduced driving-under-the-influence convictions "to reckless driving in almost two out of every three DUI appeals he heard from 1999 through 2002." That rate was far higher than any of the judge's three colleagues on the bench, and the judge's DUI cases were appealed 40 percent of the time. The newspaper noted, "The judge knocked down DUI convictions even when evidence revealed that drivers had been drunk or had been involved in crashes that endangered others."

In other states, journalists have discovered that many drivers had cases thrown out by simply appealing or because the arresting officer did not appear in court.

Municipal Court

In some jurisdictions, traffic cases are heard separately, as are other specific types of cases, such as those involving landlord-tenant disputes. Many jurisdictions, however, mix all sorts of cases in municipal court. Because they are limited to violations of local ordinances, with the punishment minimal, municipal court would seem an unlikely place for major injustices to occur, but the Milwaukee Journal Sentinel found that poor people were held in jail for extended periods, often without hearings, because they were unable to pay fines for jaywalking and disorderly conduct.

Other investigations have found slumlords failing to pay millions of dollars in fines because of a court's backlog or a lack of strong enforcement.

Divorce Court

Divorce files can yield details about individuals embroiled in the fallout from a dissolving marriage. Even no-fault cases (only about 10 percent of divorces go to trial) accompanied by thin files can contain useful information on finances or assets. However, allegations by one spouse against another should be handled carefully and corroborated with other evidence.

More important, divorce court should be scrutinized as a system. Domestic relations cases account for about one-third of all civil filings in state courts, and that number calls for more scrutiny. Some investigations have found that one gender suffers because of the way the law is written or the bias of a particular judge. Journalists can probe to see whether judges are fair and considerate overall, whether they favor one gender, whether they consider the children, and whether they use mediation.

The Charlotte Observer, after analyzing hundreds of divorce cases with property at issue, concluded that the wealthier spouse sometimes dragged out the proceedings for years as the other party scrimped and sometimes approached grinding poverty. The Daily News, meanwhile, concluded that New York's divorce court is among the most secretive and disorganized in the country and that the average contested divorce stretched out for 640 days. An investigation of divorce court in Chicago Magazine emphasized the arbitrariness of the judges. Experienced divorce lawyers agreed with a colleague who said, "I could argue the same case before five different judges and get five different decisions."

Probate Court

When wealthy or newsworthy people die, journalists should check probate court (sometimes called surrogate's court or some other name). If the deceased left a will that has been filed with the court, it is normally a matter of public record. If the deceased died without a will, heirs sometimes battle over the assets in court.

Probating a will is frequently a simple job of gathering the assets of the deceased, paying bills (including taxes owed), investing the remaining assets temporarily while the case is being decided and then paying out those assets (plus money earned while invested) according to the will as validated by a probate court judge.

Lawyers, who are named to handle the estate—by either the deceased before dying or a probate judge after death—can earn huge fees. With the client dead and the beneficiaries distracted by grief and often unschooled in the ways of probate, there may be nobody to protest legal looting of the estate.

Journalists should learn whether the state regulates fees across the board by law or whether probate fees are privately negotiated case by case. At the same time, journalists can look for cozy arrangements between probate lawyers and judges. The judges and lawyers, who are sometimes known as public administrators, are supposed to protect the families and the public, but corrupt officials will set up deals that enrich one or both while cheating the estate.

The Gazette in Colorado Springs examined the probate court case of 80-year-old Josie Copmann and, at the same time, the probate court system in general. Copmann's case typified much of what critics say is wrong with probate court. Fees to attorneys, guardians, and residential care facilities can drain the estates of wards of the court. In Copmann's case, her $800,000 estate had shrunk to about $600,000 within two years after she was declared a ward. They also found that the probate court system awarded lucrative cases to only a small circle of probate attorneys, took too long to resolve cases, and failed to offer proper oversight of cases.

Legal notices in local newspapers, often required to be published, can help investigators identify estates about to be probated. When a famous or powerful person dies, reporters ought to check with the probate court automatically.

Probate court records can be valuable for stories on many topics. With probate records, journalists at The Kansas City Star were able to track the misdeeds of a banker who had killed himself, which led to an insurance investigator's report that outlined a nationwide bank fraud scheme.

In a more famous case, journalists James P. Cole and Charles C. Thompson explained in The IRE Journal how a $142 bill filed by a Memphis pharmacy in probate court against Elvis Presley's estate helped them prove the rock star died after mixing various drugs.

Small Claims Court

Disputes in small claims court involve so little money that journalists tend to overlook the court. Yet some disputes involve influential citizens or major businesses. Even when a journalist has no interest in a small claims case, the court can be a place to check to establish a relationship between two parties or to learn something about the holdings of a subject under investigation.

It is traditional to enter small claims court without a lawyer, so how disputants fare on their own—and how they are treated by the judge—can be a story in itself. Paperwork is minimal, rules are streamlined, there are no juries and the judge often rules quickly. Journalists looking into the court's performance should determine whether winners are able to collect their judgments.

U.S. Tax Court

Tens of thousands of cases are filed annually in U.S. Tax Court. Most involve income tax disputes, but the court also deals with estate, gift, excise, pension plan and Individual Retirement Account tax cases. Journalists should always check tax court when backgrounding individuals and corporations. All cases involve the Internal Revenue Service on one side and an individual or corporate taxpayer on the other side.

Each case begins with a notice of taxes owed and a decision by the taxpayer to dispute the assessment. Taxpayers who decide to pay the disputed amount and then contest it often end up in a U.S. district court. Their motive for paying first is avoiding penalties if they eventually lose.

Even a local investigative reporter should periodically check the docket of the U.S. Tax Court for the names of the wealthy in his or her community for possible stories.

U.S. Tax Court judges are in Washington, D.C., and hear cases in other locales from time to time. The judges are suggested by the U.S. Treasury secretary, appointed by the president and confirmed by the Senate's Finance Committee for 15-year terms. Associate judges hear the smaller cases, involving amounts of less than $10,000. To help with the caseload, the chief judge can appoint retirees as senior judges. There are no jury trials.

Filings, including normally confidential tax returns and final decisions, are available by visiting the court. Decisions are also available in law libraries and online. Commerce Clearing House's Tax Court Reporter is a private service that updates filings weekly. The "Tax Report" on page 1 of the Wednesday edition of The Wall Street Journal frequently contains briefs based on U.S. Tax Court decisions.

U.S. Bankruptcy Court

Bankruptcies filed by individuals or corporations provide detailed information about the party in question. Journalists should check for past bankruptcies of any subject. They can be checked on the PACER system, mentioned earlier in this chapter. From the records at the court, they might get the subject's Social Security number, bank account balances, landholdings, personal property (such as jewelry), stocks, bonds and income. Bankruptcy forms also can contain information about gambling debts.

The most significant story can be how an individual or business wound up bankrupt and who suffers from the bankruptcy. Sometimes the bankrupt firm is defrauded. Sometimes the firm defrauds others. Sometimes it is mismanagement, but in many cases it's the taxpayers and government who are owed money.

Among the best sources are creditors—those owed money—although they are potentially biased. One way to meet creditors, or at least their lawyers, is to attend a creditors' meeting.

Rick Desloge of the St. Louis Business Journal concentrated on unsecured creditors—those in the last group to receive payment; office supply and photocopier companies are often among them. Desloge has used bankruptcy court files in imaginative ways. After the arrest of a fugitive St. Louis business executive, Desloge found a document in Bankruptcy Court showing that the executive's children rented a truck before the capture and used it to remove property from the South Carolina apartment where the arrest eventually occurred, indicating that the businessman suspected law enforcement agencies were closing in.

Journalists should look at the performance of the court, too. The Indianapolis Star found cronyism and payoffs surrounding appointments of supervising lawyers by judges; unethical private contacts between lawyers and judges; and lax oversight of bankrupt firms, as assets that should have been used for creditors dissipated.

One source on fraud is the executive office of the U.S. Trustee, an arm of the U.S. Department of Justice. That office is supposed to ensure creditors are fairly represented as cases move through the courts. Some Chapter 11 filings come from solvent corporations seeking the court's protection from product liability or environmental claims. If a company is worried about having to pay millions of dollars because of a defective birth control device or harmful asbestos in buildings, it will ask a bankruptcy judge to limit or delay the claims.

Other companies have chosen to break a union contract or escape pension obligations. Not all questionable filings involve corporations. WJXT-TV, Jacksonville, Fla., demonstrated how individuals retained lavish homes and lifestyles while refusing to pay creditors. Each state has its own rules on what assets a debtor can shield from creditors.

Journalists should pay close attention to bankruptcy dockets, and when a significant or notable bankruptcy is filed, they should immediately look at the assets and liabilities and get the list of creditors to begin an inquiry.

PART II Investigating the Government

U.S. Court of Appeals for the Federal Circuit

This 12-judge court, located near the White House, listens to appeals of patent cases from all over the nation. Established by Congress in 1982, it is the only federal appeals court with specific subject-matter jurisdiction. Its creation regularized highly technical patent rulings and ended "forum shopping" in patent disputes.

The remainder of the court's docket consists of appeals from agency rulings of the Patent and Trademark Office, International Trade Commission, Secretary of Commerce, Department of Veterans Affairs and Merit Systems Protection Board, plus appeals from the U.S. Court of International Trade, U.S. Court of Federal Claims and U.S. Court of Appeals for Veterans Claims.

U.S. Military Courts

Although they've been around for centuries, military courts have gained the attention of journalists since the Iraq War. From the alleged abuse of prisoners to attacks on fellow soldiers, the military courts attained new relevance. But cases involving the military services have always been relevant to those whose communities have military bases or citizens serving in the military.

The Dallas Morning News studied hundreds of cases before the Iraq War and concluded, "The U.S. military disregards its own laws to convict service members of crimes—and sends a disproportionate number of minorities to its toughest prison." The Journal of the American Bar Association took another path, explaining the military justice system through an exposé of a military lawyer who had falsified his legal credentials.

A general court-martial is akin to a felony trial in civilian courts. The judges are officers who are senior in rank to the defendant; nonofficer defendants can ask that enlisted service members sit on the judges' panel.

A special court-martial is convened for offenses that involve less incarceration than offenses brought to a general court-martial. A summary court-martial is for less serious offenses still. The U.S. Court of Appeals for the Armed Forces, Washington, D.C., with judges appointed by the president and confirmed by the Senate, handles cases involving dishonorable or bad-conduct discharges carrying more than a year of imprisonment.

Because the prosecutor for each military service, known as the judge advocate general, evaluates the judges, critics of the system say independence is compromised. John Murawski of the Legal Times explained the controversy like this: "Imagine a court system where the judge owes his job—and his next assignment—to the office prosecuting the case." Journalists trying to determine if a military judge is sufficiently independent will have to examine rulings case by case and contact lots of sources. Each service (Army, Air Force, Coast Guard and Navy–Marine Corps) has its own mechanism for handling first-level appeals, clemency and parole requests. The judges on such cases can be military officers or civilians.

There is also a U.S. Court of Appeals for the Armed Forces, the final tribunal reviewing court-martial convictions. There are five civilian judges appointed by the U.S. president for 15-year terms, with Senate confirmation necessary.

⊃ CHECK IT OUT

✓ Visit the local court administrator and request the last three years of the budget for your local courthouse. Compare these expenditures over the last three years: personnel, supplies and services and capital expenditures. Look for large differences, examine the details of those parts of the budget and then interview courthouse administrators about increases and decreases. This will familiarize you with the operations of the court and at the very least produce a story about the financial challenges for the courthouse.

✓ Visit the courthouse administrator and request the last three years of statistics on criminal cases and civil cases, particularly the statistics on each kind of disposition—found guilty, dismissed, etc. Also, ask about the number of judges and other court personnel to determine caseload per judge and per employee. Interview judges, prosecutors and defense attorneys. At the very least, this will produce a story about how the court is handling its caseload and whether it is overwhelmed.

✓ Visit the local jail administrator and ask for statistics for the last three years about inmates, including whether the inmates are serving time after being convicted, while awaiting trial, or while awaiting their first court appearance. The statistics should also list the inmates' ethnicity and the crime or charge for which each inmate is imprisoned. Also, ask about the number of beds in the jail and the daily average and median capacity. Interview the jail warden, prison guards, defense attorneys, public defenders, and inmates or those recently released. This will produce a minimum story on the changes at the jail and potentially a story on overcrowding or on the number of inmates who have not been convicted but are imprisoned because they cannot pay the bail set for them.

✓ Visit the county court and obtain a list of lawsuits against your town or city and their dispositions for the last three years. Request the same list from the town or city and ask them to include all monetary settlement figures. Also, request the budget for the town's or city's legal department for the last three years and find out whether the city has an insurer or is self-insured. Ask how much the town or city has spent on nonhealth insurance each year. Interview local lawyers, municipal attorneys and the city or town finance director about how lawsuits against the town or city are handled. This will produce a minimum story on lawsuits against the city, whether they are frivolous and whether the city settles too easily.

Using court records used to be time-consuming and frustrating because the records were localized and journalists had to visit dozens of scattered courthouses. Today, electronic databases like Lexis/Nexis, Westlaw and other commercial resources (discussed more fully in Chapters 1 and 2) have made searching for records easier, and the Internet has increased the accessibility of many court documents.

Most online databases on court cases are free, such as those maintained by cities or counties, or inexpensive, such as the Public Access to Court Electronic Records system. PACER (http://pacer.psc.uscourts.gov) allows journalists to search recently issued and older opinions and cases from all federal courthouses, including U.S. Bankruptcy Court.

There also are numerous official hard-copy resources at public libraries, law schools and law firms. If cases are not included in those volumes, then information often can be found in narrative publications kept at other institutions. With these resources, there is little excuse not to make court records one of the first checks on any story.

Clearly, you can be overwhelmed by all the documents relating to a criminal or civil case. But the more you know about indexes and procedures in a courthouse, the easier it is to follow the document trail. This section is intended to make it easier to maneuver through all this information by breaking it down into sections on the different kinds of courts and documents.

The U.S. Sentencing Commission (www.ussc.gov) can also help.

Tracking Cases

Chronological indexes for civil and criminal cases can be found on the Web and at local courthouses. The indexes give the most complete information except for the files themselves.

The indexes include the complaint in a civil case or the charge in a criminal case, the names of defendants and plaintiffs in a civil case, the names of their attorneys, the date of the filing, the case number and the disposition, if one has been reached.

Among the free online sites that help you find cases are the following:

- FindLaw (www.findlaw.com), which searches for federal and state cases in the United States
- PACER (http://pacer.psc.uscourts.gov), which allows you to look up federal cases in any courthouse, including criminal, civil and bankruptcy courts
- SearchSystems (www.searchsystems.net), which indexes public records online by nation and state and can link you to courthouse databases

Court Procedures

There are several excellent guides and Web sites that explain legal terms and court procedures. The American Bar Association's (www.abanet.org) booklets are a good place to start. Another place is FindLaw, which lists U.S. District Court procedures by state (http://public.findlaw.com/library/state-laws.html) and gives a thorough overview of state courts (www.uscourts.gov/courtlinks/index.html).

Civil Case Files

Civil case files contain information on lawsuits against individuals or businesses that seek payments or actions to correct alleged damages incurred by those suing. They include the complaint or petition, which begins the lawsuit, answers to the complaint, all other motions, depositions and interrogatories (interviews and questioning of individuals before trial) and the verdict or final disposition of the case. With electronic databases, you can look up the names of plaintiffs or defendants and get the case number. With the case number, you can get an individual file from the court clerk.

Always check these files when backgrounding an individual or company. You may discover facts about the person or business that until then have been private, giving you new angles or sources for stories. But remember that the files can contain false allegations or incorrect information and must always be cross-checked.

Civil actions cover divorces, property disputes, accidents, business transactions, legality of ordinances, insurance and government enforcement actions.

Criminal Case Files

A criminal case file contains the charge or charges against the defendant, information about the alleged crime, motions and evidence involved in the case, and the disposition of the case when it is over.

Criminal files are generally open to reporters when the cases are current. You can obtain the case file from the court clerk if you have the case file number. Often, you can get a case file number and summary information of the case online through the indexes, whether the case is federal or local.

Criminal case files help you track a specific case and provide information for backgrounding defendants. You can use criminal case files to cover a specific case or to look for trends in how the system is working. Many jurisdictions have databases on criminal cases that summarize the file information, but you should always look at the complete case file when reporting on an individual case.

The Federal Justice System

The federal justice system is packed with statistics that can provide the underpinnings and context for many stories, and it is well worth looking through many of the federal Web sites. A starting point is the Bureau of Justice Statistics (www.ojp .usdoj.gov/bjs), which has information, studies and analyses of every aspect of the federal system.

The Federal Offenders in the U.S. District Courts is an annual statistical report about the disposition, sentence, type of counsel, age, sex and prior records of federal criminal defendants. It can be especially useful for measuring the consistency and quality of justice dispensed in a given geographic area or in connection with a

category of crime. The report can be found at several sites, including www.albany
.edu/sourcebook/ind/SENTENCES.Federal_offenders.1.html.

Local and State Courts

To be able to use local and state court records, which provide a rich source of
information on every element of society and many investigative story ideas, you
need to get familiar with them. In addition to FindLaw.com, these sites can help:

- The National Center for State Courts (www.ncsconline.org), which provides
  resources and information about state courts.

- In many states, a court clerk must report monthly to the state judicial overview
  agency on financial matters. This report details the amount, date and reason for
  expenses.

- State courts also submit annual reports to state judicial commissions on the number of civil, criminal and juvenile cases disposed and other pertinent statistics.

The Prison System

Prisons are difficult to report on because of limited access to prisoners and information, but there are many statistics that can provide context and story ideas.

- The Federal Bureau of Prisons (www.bop.gov) has information and statistics on
  federal prisons.

- The National Institute of Corrections (www.nicic.org) is an independent group
  that investigates prison rights and conditions.

- The American Civil Liberties Union (www.aclu.org), which can connect you to
  the National Prison Project, is a private organization interested in prison rights
  and conditions.

- The American Correctional Association (www.aca.org) provides information and
  support for those working in the correctional field. Such practices are explained
  in "The Perpetual Prisoner Machine: How America Profits From Crime," by Joel
  Dyer, and "Private Prisons and Public Accountability," by Richard Harding.

The Probation System

Several Web sites and publications provide an overview of statistics and issues
relating to probation:

- The Federal Probation publication (www.uscourts.gov/library/fpcontents.html)
  from the U.S. government contains articles about every aspect of the probation
  system.

- The American Probation and Parole Association, Lexington, Ky. (www.appa-net
  .org), represents prison administrators and staffs and has extensive information
  on issues concerning that group.

- The U.S. Parole Commission (www.usdoj.gov/uspc) oversees the early release and
  supervision of federal parolees and issues reports on its activities.

Juvenile and Family Court Issues

Another difficult court system to penetrate is the juvenile and family court system, which limits access to court records. However, the following Web sites provide information that will allow you to get started on stories:

- The National Court-Appointed Special Advocates Association (www.nationalcasa .org) has resources for advocates for abused children.

- The National Council of Juvenile and Family Court Judges (www.ncjfcj.org) provides information not only for judges, but for anyone interested in the system.

- The National Center for Juvenile Justice, Pittsburgh, Pa. (www.ncjj.org), has resources on child and family caseloads in the juvenile justice system.

- The National Conference of State Legislatures (www.ncsl.org) provides valuable information, especially in the report "Comprehensive Juvenile Justice: A Legislator's Guide."

Judges

Given the great powers that judges have in society, it is useful and necessary to understand what procedures they are supposed to follow and to know how to background them. Here are some useful resources:

- The Judicial Staff Directory (www.jsd.cq.com/original_index.html), run by Congressional Quarterly, is a good starting place for researching judges' biographies, appointments and other information.

- The Judge Advocates Association, Bloomsburg, Pa. (www.jaa.org), can provide perspective on the differences between the military courts and civilian courts.

Prosecutors and Defense Attorneys

Check these sites when backgrounding prosecutors and defense attorneys:

- The National Association of Criminal Defense Lawyers, Washington, D.C. (www.criminaljustice.org), provides an overview of issues, concerns and other information about defense lawyers.

- The Association of Trial Lawyers of America (www.atlanet.org) provides resources particularly about lawyers who litigate civil cases.

- The Martindale-Hubbell Law Directory (www.martindale.com/locator/home .html) organizes the names of almost every lawyer and law firm alphabetically by state and city.

- State bar associations receive and investigate complaints against attorneys, prosecutors and judges. The records are generally open if the case resulted in disciplinary action. You can find bar association information through searchsystems.net or the American Bar Association (www.abanet.org).

- The American Bar Association (www.abanet.org) keeps a national database of complaints against attorneys.

Specialized Courts

Specialized courts have different rules and their own unique vocabulary. For backgrounding, these resources can be helpful:

- For Traffic Courts, the Missouri Bar Center put out a useful guide a few years ago. It can found at http://library.findlaw.com/1999/May/25/130034.html.

- To learn about Probate Court, FindLaw offers excellent resources at http://estate.findlaw.com/probate/probate-court-laws.html.

- Most states have a guide on how small claims courts work. For example, you can check out Oregon's guide at www.osbar.org/public/pamphlets/smallclaims.html.

- "Everybody's Guide to Small Claims Court" from Nolo Press, Berkeley, Calif., can also provide perspective.

- You can visit the U.S. Tax Court at www.ustaxcourt.gov.

- For Bankruptcy Courts, you can consult do-it-yourself books like "How to File for Bankruptcy" by Stephen Elias, Albin Renauer and Robin Leonard; "Personal Bankruptcy: What Every Debtor and Creditor Needs to Know" by William C. Hillman, a bankruptcy judge who was commissioned to write the book by the Practicing Law Institute, New York City; and "The Bankruptcy Law Reporter" from the Bureau of National Affairs, Washington, D.C. The Administrative Office of the U.S. Courts publishes overviews of bankruptcy proceedings. The American Bankruptcy Institute, Washington, D.C., can help provide context and perspective.

- You can find information about the parlance of military courts at www.dtic.mil/doctrine/jel/new_pubs/jp1_02.pdf.

Investigating Law Enforcement

This chapter suggests ways to do investigative stories by scrutinizing police offi-cers' actions and behavior, by looking at how well law enforcement agencies pre-vent and investigate crimes, and by examining other aspects of law enforcement, such as crime statistics, crime labs and emergency response times.

For years, journalists at the San Francisco Chronicle had done critical reporting on problems in the city's police department. But in 2005, the newspaper de-cided to dig deeper and take a systematic look at which officers were using excessive force and what the department did about them.

A team of reporters began the investigation by collecting information from police logs across the city to create a database that tracked the use of force by officers. After constructing and examining the database, the reporters were able to see the problem with clarity. They wrote, "For years, the police department failed to control officers who repeatedly resorted to force, hitting, choking, clubbing and pepper-spraying citizens at rates far higher than fellow officers who patrolled the same streets."

By doing what the department had never done, the reporters identified a core group of fewer than 100 officers who accounted for most of the incidents. They simply tallied the incidents that were kept in paper records at individual police stations. They further reported, "The department lags far behind many other major cities in developing an effective system for identifying problem officers. And it has failed, over and over, to take steps to get these officers off the streets."

The newspaper also found that officers with questionable records were pro-moted to supervisory positions or were assigned to train rookies, "putting them in position to carry forward a culture that tolerates or rewards the use of force."

Such stories are not easy to do. Beyond the grunt work of collecting paper and doing data entry, many reporters face barriers at every turn because jour-nalists who criticize individual officers or entire departments are frequently cut off from the official police spokespeople, shunned, misled or even harassed.

Law enforcement is one of the most difficult and challenging topics for jour-nalists to investigate. Officials often use privacy and security concerns to resist releasing records. Police officers, who often experience severe stress on the job, are reluctant to give interviews and can be belligerent and threatening. Law enforcement issues can be complex, and the reasons for any shortcomings in the system are many and varied. Yet many journalists do excellent public-service journalism on this topic and expose departments and employees who are threatening and endangering the public rather than protecting it. Because law enforcement agencies tend to be run like the military, members also tend to close ranks against outsiders more emphatically than bureaucrats inside other institutions do. Even a journalist who writes about a crime increase based on the police department's own statistics may be perceived as attacking the integrity of law enforcement.

Adding to the difficulty police reporters face is their inability to get the other side of the story. Often suspects will not talk for fear of retaliation by the police. Even if they want to talk, they may be dissuaded by family members or lawyers. Many members of the public automatically side with the police, too, because of the belief that extreme tactics are warranted against criminals to keep the public safe. Nonetheless, it is necessary for journalists to monitor and report on the police because they are entrusted with great power and are a part of daily life.

In the United States alone, there are about 18,000 local and state law enforcement agencies and dozens of federal government law enforcement units, plus thousands of specialized police departments for universities, subway systems, airports, parks and public housing complexes.

It is important to see the police as part of an entire justice system that includes courts and prisons. Chapter 10, on investigating the judicial system, deals with other integral parts of the system.

In his book "Crimes of Justice: Improving the Police, the Courts, the Prisons," David C. Anderson, a journalist specializing in law enforcement, likens the system to a funnel: "At the top a broad flood of crimes challenges and mobilizes the police, courts and correctional system. At the bottom is the apparent result of all their labors — a relative trickle of convicted felons actually sent to prison."

Investigating Local Police

It is easy for reporters on the daily police beat to simply report on who has been arrested, what the charges are, and when the accused is scheduled to appear in court. In all but the smallest communities, there is plenty to report on each day, and a journalist can feed the hunger for breaking news and stop at that. But as the San Francisco Chronicle investigation showed, taking the time to look for the causes and patterns of what lies behind the daily incidents is just as crucial a part of the reporter's job, if not more so.

Monitoring Individual Law Enforcement Officers

As in most other occupations, the majority of law enforcement officers and civilian employees are honest and efficient. When a significant minority are not, however, the consequences can be serious and even fatal.

It is not easy for a journalist to determine how good a police officer or department is. The same is true when it comes to assessing any other bureaucrat or bureaucracy, but journalists should monitor police officers from recruitment to retirement. The following techniques apply:

- Observing officers directly
- Studying incident and arrest (and eventual conviction) records and rates
- Tracking day-to-day prevention efforts
- Talking regularly to citizens in neighborhoods
- Knowing the leaders of the police union
- Studying budgets and expenditures
- Reading personnel files when available
- Checking for investigations by the police department's Internal Affairs Unit
- Following lawsuits in the local courts
- Checking to see if the agency is accredited by the Commission on Accreditation for Law Enforcement Agencies or any other commission

The measures of individual performance are numerous. For example, do individual officers miss court appearances? Or do individual officers spend more time around the courthouse than necessary as a method of ringing up lucrative overtime?

The Miami Herald found that more police officers than necessary showed up at driving-while-intoxicated hearings in a scheme to collect overtime. Normally, a maximum of three officers is needed at such a court hearing: the officer making the traffic stop, the officer administering the roadside sobriety test and the officer administering the breath alcohol test. The Herald found that officers' names appeared on arrest reports seemingly for the sole purpose of allowing them to appear in court. The published stories, under the headline "Collars for Dollars," reported that the scam sometimes led to arrests of innocent motorists.

Recruitment

The (Fort Lauderdale) Sun-Sentinel wrote about an officer with five arrests in his past, not an ideal candidate for police work. But Florida's police certification commission granted him a license nevertheless. More than a decade later, the officer in question was still on the force, despite 11 acts of serious misconduct.

The state of the economy sometimes influences the tolerance of law enforcement agencies when considering candidates with criminal backgrounds. When higher salaries are available outside law enforcement, it can be difficult for governments to hire police officers for the salaries that departments can afford. That problem raises questions not only about applicants' backgrounds but also about why starting salaries for police are set so low.

Reporters should check screening protocols at the local police department. Are résumés checked carefully? Do applicants undergo lie detector tests about their backgrounds? Drug testing? Psychological testing? A Wall Street Journal investigation carried the headline "Psychological Tests Designed to Weed Out Rogue Cops Get a 'D': Critics Say They Fail to Halt Racial and Other Abuse; Questions Easily Evaded."

Journalists should be especially alert for problems at the hiring stage when the department is expanding. Rapid expansions are usually a political response to public fear about crime or to court-ordered affirmative action meant to remedy shortages of female and minority-group officers. After a rapid expansion in Miami, about 10 percent of all officers ended up imprisoned, fired or otherwise disciplined.

Sometimes there are limitations on recruitment and eventual hiring—such as residency requirements—that have little to do with fitness for the job. How should an agency balance the importance of having an officer living in the jurisdiction where he or she works versus losing promising recruits because they want to live outside the jurisdiction for family or other personal reasons?

Training

A police officer's competence is determined partly by the training received in a police academy. Yet journalists seldom inquire about the local academy. It makes sense to write a feature about the academy to become familiar with the training, perhaps saving the tougher questions for a follow-up story when there is time to research it adequately.

Many states have a central academy; in some states, individual police departments run certified academies. Small departments contract with private companies for training and certification courses. Those private companies can be fruitful topics for investigation, and it's worth looking at whether contracts have been terminated or whether they have been sued.

Academy training might last six months, followed by six months of field training before assignment to a precinct. As always, it's important to compare various jurisdictions and ask some questions:

- Why do some jurisdictions require so much more or less time for training than other jurisdictions?
- How do the curricula compare across jurisdictions?
- What is the background of the trainers?
- How effective is the training?

For example, San Francisco Chronicle reporters Susan Sward and Bill Wallace found that of 298 training officers designated by the police department, 102 had been sued for alleged misconduct on the job.

Physical conditioning is one part of training. Reporters should be alert for conditioning trainers who demand too much of novices. The Home News Tribune in central New Jersey found abusive conditions at an academy after a recruit collapsed and died. New York magazine found the other extreme. Standards had dropped so low that the prevalence of obesity among recruits had increased. The magazine found that some recruits were too weak to pull the trigger of a revolver. Poor initial physical conditioning is almost sure to spawn out-of-shape police as they gain seniority.

Besides physical conditioning, a sound curriculum covers

- Investigation procedures for specific types of crime at the scene and afterward
- Use of force, including guns and high-speed chases
- Report writing
- Interrogation techniques
- Constitutional law
- Undercover work
- Counseling in domestic violence and hostage situations
- Sensitivity training to help officers understand the opposite gender and other racial, religious and ethnic groups

Without first-rate academy training, officers may pose a danger to society. For example, if they do not learn in the academy how to handle their car during a high-speed chase, they will have to learn during a chase. Through an analysis of 947 police pursuits in 2005, The Indianapolis Star found that people were dying for largely inconsequential crimes as a result of police car chases that reached speeds of up to 170 mph.

Continuing education, or the lack of it, can spawn trouble. When an officer is taken off the street and given an administrative job, is there any internal training? Outside continuing education programs can go awry. The Boston Globe found police taking advantage of a statewide program to get better education. The reporting team said, "The noble idea of encouraging police to seek higher education has turned into a much abused, $12 million-a-year program in Massachusetts, providing hefty pay increases to many officers for securing quick and easy college degrees." One small school was issuing more graduate degrees in criminal justice than any major university in the country; it required little reading or writing in its courses. At another school, police officers were falsifying attendance records to cover for absent colleagues.

Raises, Promotions and Pensions

Like every other bureaucracy, law enforcement agencies may be riddled with personal favoritism, political intrigue, inefficiency and corruption. A journalist should check whether deserving officers are receiving raises and promotions, or whether factors like friendship and affirmative action are inordinately influencing decisions.

The Chicago Sun-Times found that the Chicago Police Department based its performance evaluations more on quantitative criteria — the number of arrests — than on qualitative measures, such as effective crime fighting. The Village Voice found that a New York City police union had the power to influence raises and promotions, power that often worked against the public good, given the union leadership's ties to criminal elements.

While delving into job-related benefits, journalists should examine workers' compensation claims. Police suffer many legitimate injuries, physical and mental, on the job. But some take advantage of the workers' compensation insurance system by filing false claims, maybe with the help of a corrupt physician or lawyer. Reporters for the Hartford Courant and the Boston Herald found that some claims qualified police for 100 percent of their wages, tax-free, meaning they could increase their pay by staying off the job. Newsday won a Pulitzer Prize for stories in which it found that lifetime payments were awarded to "disabled" officers who nevertheless were able to work as lifeguards, lift weights and play softball.

Police pensions tend to be generous, with taxpayers footing the bill. Journalists should ask whether retirement after 20 years is counterproductive if the retired officers then double-dip by moving to a police agency elsewhere.

The Top Command

When journalists delve into the background and current performance of the police chief, they almost always end up with an informative story. How the top person got the job may be revealing. It's worth checking these items:

- Did the chief come up through the ranks?
- What were the chief's performance evaluations?
- If the chief was hired from the outside, what was his or her track record in the previous jurisdiction?
- Who really chose the chief? A city manager or a city council or political patrons?
- To what extent did patronage or nepotism play a role in the selection? Years ago, the St. Louis Post-Dispatch found that a new police chief took office after secretive lobbying by business leaders. That story led to a look at the department's entire top management, and previously confidential evaluations indicated that political connections mattered more than policing skills.
- In situations where the top person is elected — the case with many county sheriffs — is appropriate law enforcement experience a factor? Journalists also can check on whether the agency is used as a center for patronage and nepotism.

U.S. marshals in each state are chosen on a patronage basis by the senior senator of the president's political party or the senior U.S. House member of that party. A journalist can check on how many marshals and their deputies have previous law enforcement experience.

Not all the attention should be paid to the top person. Assistant chiefs, district commanders and station house sergeants usually escape journalists' scrutiny, even though those middle managers can have a significant impact on a neighborhood or an entire city.

Discipline of Wayward Officers

Because police wield life-and-death powers, weeding out irresponsible officers is vital, but there's a dilemma. Honest officers are reluctant to speak up for fear of being shunned. No bureaucracy is good at investigating itself; as a result, departmental internal affairs divisions are prone to cover-ups. The local prosecutor is unlikely to pursue a case of police misconduct aggressively because such aggressiveness might have negative consequences for the prosecutor, who depends heavily on police crime-scene investigators. Yet an outside investigator is unlikely to receive cooperation from clannish officers; that is one reason citizen review commissions are also often ineffective.

The Chicago Reporter studied the Chicago Police Board, made up of nine civilians appointed by the mayor and paid a part-time salary. Of 8,000 allegations of misconduct made against police officers in the year studied, just 49 reached the board, and 29 resulted in dismissals. The other thousands of cases—usually involving excessive force, drug or alcohol violations or theft or bribery—ended up being dismissed or handled internally before reaching the board. One of many problems with the system as established is that the city's lawyers prosecute wayward police officers in front of the board, then sometimes defend the actions of those same police officers in civil lawsuits against the city.

Sometimes brutality occurs during interrogation of suspects. Journalists should ask whether local police departments have instituted a policy of videotaping interrogations to minimize mistreatment. When tapes are made, journalists should seek to view them regularly, just as they make a regular practice of seeking and reading arrest reports. Another way of tracking problem officers is to examine transfers within departments to lower-profile or less desirable assignments.

Examining the Florida system, The Palm Beach Post found that the state licensing-disciplinary commission had only six staff members to review cases and three lawyers to consider prosecution. Before the commission, consisting of 17 unpaid appointees, could consider a complaint prepared by the staff, a state administrative law judge had to rule independently on the quality and quantity of evidence. Because the administrative judges heard cases from other state agencies too, there was often a backlog. Meanwhile, officers accused of brutality or other dangerous behaviors—sometimes more than once—remained on the job. The commission's open caseload stood at 1,200.

Fred Schulte and Margo Harakas looked at errant police in great detail in the (Fort Lauderdale) Sun-Sentinel series "Above the Law: Cops Who Betray the Badge." The reporters obtained computer tapes from the commission with information on more than 100,000 current and former officers. The data originated with the state's 400 police agencies, which are supposed to notify the commission when officers are fired or when any of 70 types of police misconduct are confirmed.

"Commission tapes contain a termination code for each job," Schulte explained in The IRE Journal.

> The codes tell us that about 10 percent of departures . . . came amid misconduct or evidence that the officer was unfit. We also picked out scores of cops fired more than once, or reported to the commission for revocation twice or more. Knowing the

names of problem officers saved us time later when we visited police departments to review personnel files.

[A] second database enabled us to review 1,600 police commission cases since the early 1980s. . . . We found the commission took no action in 60 percent of its cases, which typically dragged on for two years; about 40 percent of 223 cop crimes weren't reviewed by prosecutors; sex crimes were the most common reason for license revocations; other violence against women was occurring regularly; blacks appeared to be singled out for disciplinary action. Margo Harakas and I spent a week in Tallahassee reviewing commission evidence.

The files gave us dozens of horror stories to wrap around our statistics. Our next step was to find bad cops who had not been reported to the licensing commission. We reviewed hundreds of yellowed newspaper clips naming troubled officers and had a librarian search electronic clips. We found 400 accused cops not known to the commission. Many had been suspended or fired by a city, prompting a news story. Some didn't stay fired. A few agreed not to sue to get their job back if officials would expunge records of their misdeeds and say they had resigned. Several police departments admitted that they failed to report bad colleagues despite laws requiring them to do so.

Documents about individual police officers are frequently closed to journalists because of personnel exemptions in open-records laws. But sometimes courts rule that the interest of the public in disclosure outweighs the privacy rights of an individual law enforcement officer.

Internal affairs units, usually less open than even the most secretive outside state or local citizens' commission, conduct brutality investigations and others involving less violent forms of misconduct.

Journalists do not always have to wait to hear from state disciplinary agencies or departmental internal affairs units to investigate police misconduct. "Cadging" is a common offense that journalists can document themselves. It occurs when police officers stop at fast-food restaurants, grocery stores and other businesses, especially those open around the clock. On one level, store managers welcome the visits because a police presence discourages robbers. The visits are less welcome when police expect free merchandise in return. Honest officers discuss cadgers among themselves. Journalists who have good sources among officers can learn names.

There is no national registry of bad law enforcement officers, meaning that an officer who runs amok can move to another city or state and find a job in another police department. To make matters worse, prosecutors are reluctant to bring charges against police officers because they worry about harming their long-term relationship with the officers they need to work with.

Furthermore, when citizens—tired of waiting for prosecutors—enter the court system with excessive-force lawsuits of their own, they lose two of three cases on average. Brutality is hard to prove without sympathetic witnesses, and many potential witnesses worry about retaliation from the police. Jurors—mostly citizens who put their hopes in the police to stop crime and protect them and their families—want to believe the best about officers and so are reluctant to convict.

Moonlighting

Many law enforcement officers work as bar bouncers or security guards or in other quasi-police positions while off the clock at the police department. Journalists can check the policies of local law enforcement agencies about moonlighting and locate actual cases that seem to violate the policies.

The Press of Atlantic City, N.J., investigated a police program that allowed officers to moonlight as security guards. In its review of payroll records, the newspaper revealed that officers often called in sick and then worked as security guards for more than eight hours, thereby collecting sick pay and compensation for working security.

And security guard firms themselves deserve scrutiny. Private-sector security agencies do not fit under the government umbrella. But their function in the community is similar, they deal with police often and they provide plenty of investigative opportunities.

Private security agencies are shadow police forces in certain neighborhoods—but their employees often lack the civil rights or weapons training of officers on the public payroll. A Time magazine investigation found the security guard industry to be a dumping ground for unstable, violent people, some with criminal records. On the local level, KSEE-TV of Fresno, Calif., reached similar conclusions, as did Willy Stern in the weekly newspaper Nashville Scene and Mary Zahn at the Milwaukee Journal Sentinel.

Police Reporter Edna Buchanan's Tips

Longtime police reporter Edna Buchanan provided a set of classic tips on tracking excessive force for the American Society of Newspaper Editors. She suggests keeping an especially close watch on the midnight to 8 a.m. shift, which is where problem officers are often assigned. Although they might be the officers most in need of supervision, that is exactly what they fail to get because the most talented administrators are off duty then. The cover of darkness is an added temptation. Furthermore, a city is often relatively quiet on the midnight shift, allowing officers from around the area to converge on a trouble call; as they congregate, they may play off each others' fears and aggressiveness, creating what is in effect a police mob.

Buchanan warns journalists to be skeptical, but not dismissive, of excessive-force complaints registered by career criminals, who could be eager to deflect charges against them by accusing those who made the arrest. Another warning sign could be an alleged victim who contacts lawyers and journalists before filing a complaint with the police department's internal affairs division. For such questionable victims, Buchanan suggests asking if they will submit to a lie detector test or examination by a neutral physician.

Use of force does not always mean brutality, Buchanan says: "Good cops doing their jobs and stepping on toes will generate complaints; many lousy cops putting in time until the pension never do a thing and have clean records." The proficient officers who use force to subdue suspects manage to keep from crossing the line, Buchanan says: "The difference between the force necessary to subdue and force that maims, breaks bones and sometimes kills is easily discernible."

Delving Into Different Crimes

Each type of crime has different roots, different types of perpetrators and victims and different investigation techniques. Federal laws alone identify about 3,000 crimes. All that makes the challenge of covering law enforcement even greater for journalists.

Murder

The Washington Post conducted an investigation of 1,286 homicides in Washington, D.C., committed during a three-year stretch. Trying to figure out how many ended in apprehension and conviction, the newspaper found that the major difficulty encountered in its investigation was the separate record-keeping systems of police, prosecutors and courts.

For example, victims' names from police files were useless at the courthouse, where record keeping was by defendant's name. When the newspaper finally finished compiling the information, it found no arrests in 40 percent of the homicides; in cases with arrests, charges were dropped in one-third; of defendants going to trial, one-third were acquitted. Half the murders occurred on the midnight shift, which is staffed by fewer detectives than the other two shifts.

When reporters chronicle murder investigations, they need to explain the "why" behind the progress, or lack of it, in the case. They can get a better understanding of police investigative procedure by enrolling in police administration courses (offered by colleges with criminal justice degree programs); studying police manuals; and reading books like "Homicide: A Year on the Killing Streets," by Baltimore Sun police reporter David Simon, or "Criminal Investigation," by James W. Osterburg and Richard H. Ward, former New York City policemen-turned-academics.

Reporters should ask:

- How well did police record the crime scene through photographs, sketches and notes?
- How well did they collect and preserve physical evidence, allowing them to reconstruct the crime, identify the substance or object used to kill and link a suspect to the victim or crime scene?
- Have police considered all possible motives, including financial gain, sex and self-protection (during an interrupted burglary, for instance)?
- With evidence in hand and motive in mind, how thoroughly have detectives followed people trails and paper trails to gather further information?
- Does the police department turn to psychics when it reaches a dead end? The main question for journalists is "Why?"—as in, "Why did you decide to bring in a psychic?" or "Why did you decide against bringing in a psychic?" Backgrounds of psychics can be checked with other law enforcement agencies, the families of crime victims and researchers into extrasensory phenomena.
- Do homicide detectives refuse to ask for help, even when they need it? Detectives are considered the elite within the department, and often work long hours and earn overtime pay.
- Do they use profilers? Profilers can be wrong, of course, but at times their educated guesses are uncannily accurate. FBI profiler Bill Tafoya contradicted his colleagues about the characteristics of the famous Unabomber, who sent bombs in the mail and turned out to be Theodore Kaczynski. Tafoya concluded that the Unabomber was in his 50s rather than much younger, as the FBI team believed. Tafoya added the strong possibility that he had a Ph.D. in engineering or math. If the investigators had trusted Tafoya's profile, they could have narrowed the suspect list drastically.

The substance of homicide reports can make a difference on public perceptions. Are police reports written in a way that shows how many murders are committed by strangers to the victim? This is vital information to a populace terrified, perhaps unjustifiably, of random shootings. The (Tacoma) News Tribune was troubled that police records failed to designate drive-by shootings, leaving journalists to rely on possibly unreliable anecdotal evidence. The police wanted to know more about these crimes too, so they began collecting the information. Analysis of the first year's worth of data found that drive-bys occurred about once every other night, not three or four times a night, as the anecdotal evidence suggested. Furthermore, the data showed that drive-by shootings were concentrated in a few parts of the city, usually near crack houses or where gangs hung out. In other words, the bullets were rarely aimed at strangers. Then again, police in some jurisdictions suggest that at least 18 unreported drive-by shootings occur for every one that is reported.

Guns and murders tend to go together. Members of IRE and reporters in many newsrooms can search a national gun dealers database in-house. Some law enforcement departments contribute to the gun problem by selling or trading older weapons, supposedly to avoid high disposal costs. The licensed dealers who end up with the old weapons then sell them to the public. Some of those weapons later become involved in murders.

The use of the term "vehicular homicide" could change public perceptions as well. Automobiles and trucks can be just as deadly as guns. But a police report styled as a "traffic fatality" sounds less menacing than a loss of life labeled as "murder."

The Philadelphia Inquirer examined 400 murder cases and found that in about 80 cases, judges ruled that detectives had acted illegally by beating confessions out of suspects. Court records yielded medical reports and eyewitness testimony to suggest that those beatings had indeed occurred.

Every murder is major to the victim's relatives, friends, neighbors, schoolmates and co-workers. Veteran police reporter Cheryl Reed suggests spending time in the deceased's neighborhood, talking to neighbors, asking whether the victim had a criminal record. She also suggests asking about the virtues of the accused.

Autopsy reports and death certificates can provide detail for stories. The local coroner or medical examiner therefore should be cultivated as an adjunct to police. Deborah Cenziper at The Charlotte Observer studied 394,600 deaths in North Carolina during a five-year span. Of those, 51,250 deaths were referred to medical examiners. In 69 percent of those cases, no autopsy ever occurred, despite the suspicious nature of the deaths.

When murders remain unsolved, it is legitimate to ask whether a specific law enforcement agency, perhaps working with medical examiners and other experts, can send those murders to a cold-case squad. There are examples throughout the nation of cold-case detectives solving long-ago crimes by looking at evidence with a fresh perspective.

Rape

Rape is a devastating crime for the victim and can end in homicide. Catching rapists should be a top priority for law enforcement officers. But for many reasons, rape cases do not always seem to be a priority, and some police departments intentionally underreport them to keep crime statistics lower.

Jeremy Kohler of the St. Louis Post-Dispatch noticed St. Louis' low number of reported rapes compared with other cities. After a lengthy public records battle, Kohler reported in 2005 that St. Louis police had failed to file official reports on many sex crimes over the past 20 years. Instead, police wrote informal memos on cases so the rapes would not be counted in the city's crime statistics. In analyzing many of the records of cases, the Post-Dispatch discovered that police "often discounted claims by women who were reluctant to testify, easy to discredit or difficult to locate."

Author James Neff wrote in The IRE Journal about how to evaluate rape investigations. His advice is reprinted here with minor changes:

> What percent of your city's rape reports are deemed unfounded? FBI statistics say the national average is 9 percent; a significantly higher number is cause for alarm. For instance, Oakland police showed a 24 percent unfounded rate until an exposé by San Francisco Examiner reporter Candy Cooper revealed that detectives wrote off the complaints of victims who were drug abusers, prostitutes and others whom police felt had inappropriate lifestyles. Victims were not even given the courtesy of an initial interview. These women were the very group most vulnerable to sexual violence. Are the overworked sex crimes detectives in your city doing likewise?
>
> As sex crimes soar, so has the number of therapists. There are now more than 1,100 therapists specializing in working with sex offenders, says the head of the Association of the Behavioral Treatment of Sex Abuse, an organization of therapists based in Portland. He says only 20 percent are qualified. Most therapists are not required by state laws to have any sort of academic degree or accreditation. Which raises the question — are your local courts sending sex offenders to qualified therapists? How are court referrals handled? Who gets the work? What are the ties to the referring judges?
>
> See if a correlation exists between the time victims take to report rapes and the subsequent rates of indictment. Among some law enforcers, a persistent stereotype exists of the distraught, emotional victim being the "good victim." Often law enforcers don't take seriously a three-day-old complaint of a somewhat emotionless victim, even though this is quite normal.
>
> Eliminating treatment of sex offenders is a trend today; it is a good move if you want more rape victims. Look for a correlation.
>
> When faced with serial rapists, are police working together in a task force to apprehend a criminal crossing districts, precincts and city lines? Or are they playing politics, hoarding information, impeding the investigation? Have the detectives been trained, especially in victim interviewing methods? What are the staff turnover rates in the unit, its caseload and clearance rates? How do they compare to those of

other cities' sex crime units? When detectives are stumped by a serial rapist, have they checked the neighborhood police blotter for reports of suspicious persons, trespassers, peeping toms, nearby break-ins—all characteristics of stranger rapists? Voyeurism very often is the gateway crime for rapists. Check the blotter or field investigation cards yourself to see what turns up. With an in-house arrest database obtained from police, as exists in the St. Paul Pioneer Press newsroom and many others, journalists can do some of the checking themselves.

Journalists have investigated how many rape kits available to law enforcement investigators and DNA samples are actually analyzed. An ABC News 20/20 investigation in 2002 revealed that although DNA is often the best evidence to catch a rapist, hundreds of thousands of rape evidence kits were sitting unprocessed in police storage rooms across the country. Police said many rape kits remain unanalyzed simply because there is no money to process them. On average, it costs $500 per kit. ABC actually paid to have some of the kits processed.

Those convicted of sexual assault are generally released into the community, where they are supposed to register as sex offenders. Most jurisdictions now aggressively publicize the names and addresses of such offenders through the Internet, and journalists have done extensive investigations mapping where offenders are said to live to see how close to schools, school bus stops and day care centers the offenders are living.

Journalists can examine the benefits and drawbacks of requiring convicted sex offenders to register. Parents and other members of the community understandably want to know if a convicted sex offender is living among them. On the other hand, violence against convicted offenders and the stigmatization associated with the conviction could be considered a form of double jeopardy. Some convictions are the result of consensual sex between young teenagers for which the boy was prosecuted.

Some offenders go underground due to their fear of reprisal. As a result, they do not receive treatment that might make them less dangerous to society, and they might be more likely to become repeat offenders.

Domestic Violence

Domestic violence is one of the toughest crimes police and the criminal justice system must deal with. Journalists can delve into the training police officers receive and the procedures they follow in domestic violence cases.

The 1994 arrest of former football star and actor O.J. Simpson on murder charges directed the public's attention to the issue of domestic violence. As journalists delved into Simpson's past, they learned that five years before the murder of his former wife, he had been arrested on a battering charge. Prior to that, there had been at least eight domestic violence calls, none of which ended in an arrest. Such incidents seldom become stories until somebody dies or until an arrest is made. But the failure of police to make an arrest after many calls suggests an approach that is not working.

Police usually fear domestic violence calls because of their volatility. Hostage situations are sometimes connected to domestic violence, as the perpetrator holds a weapon on the spouse, a significant other or a child. Even when no hostage is involved, a common occurrence is for a family member to call the police, who expose themselves to danger by responding to the incident, and then refuse to press charges.

The (Raleigh) News & Observer reported in 2003 that in cases where women were killed by an intimate partner, almost half of the killers had been in district court before on domestic violence allegations, which were often dismissed. The News & Observer also reported that North Carolina's laws weren't adequate for dealing with domestic violence crimes and that there were wide disparities in how North Carolina prosecutors handled domestic violence cases.

Narcotics

The war on drugs has been fought for decades without any clear resolution. Although it has recently been overshadowed by the war on terror, huge amounts of money and effort continue to be poured into the drug war, particularly on the southern border of the United States.

In documenting how domestic law enforcement agencies are dealing with drug-related crime, journalists should look at their tactics, which tend to fall within these 10 categories:

- Observation arrests
- Undercover operations
- Examination of physical evidence
- Electronic surveillance
- Community-based intelligence gathering
- User-control programs
- Drug education by police officers
- Asset forfeiture
- Historical conspiracy investigations
- Ancillary approaches, such as traffic enforcement or housing code violations

Because so many local drug crimes involve interstate movement and thus become federalized at the prosecution stage, journalists everywhere are wise to develop contacts at the Drug Enforcement Administration, which is part of the U.S. Justice Department.

Drugs are mainly a cash business. Anyone trying to figure out how the cash reaches its ultimate destination has to understand money laundering through banks, otherwise legitimate retail businesses (which falsify receipts to account for the cash flow) and offshore entities. The job of law enforcement, with support from the U.S. Justice Department's Criminal Division specialist prosecutors, is to detect money-laundering techniques so criminals have difficulty enjoying their illegal proceeds.

Journalists can explore how law enforcement agencies are handling the emergence of new narcotics while trying to combat the standbys. In recent years, many investigations have focused on methamphetamine. For example, The (Portland) Oregonian has devoted extensive time and resources to probing the spread of methamphetamine throughout the western United States.

In 2004, The Oregonian showed that Congress and the Drug Enforcement Administration could have stopped methamphetamine growth across the West during the 1990s, and that it still could. The newspaper explained how the drug can be controlled because it relies on chemical ingredients produced by only a handful of factories worldwide. The newspaper disclosed that two clampdowns on the legal trade of the chemicals caused meth shortages, prompting users to quit and meth-related property crime to fall. But, the newspaper said, the drug trade survived because of loopholes and lax enforcement.

As part of the investigation, The Oregonian examined DEA drug seizures, DEA-registered sellers of the drug, ephedrine drug shipments, ephedrine seizures, congressional records, the federal budget, federal audits, property tax records, patents, academic studies and public policy. In a story in 2005, Oregonian reporter Steve Suo found that Mexico allowed drug companies to import twice as much pseudoephedrine as they needed to produce cold medicines and that the surplus was leading to a massive increase in methamphetamine production by drug cartels.

Suo reported that Mexican cartels remain the dominant source of meth in the United States, and U.S. officials have failed to curb the cartels' access to pseudoephedrine. The supply of meth is at a near-record high, addiction is unabated and the purity of meth has doubled since 1999, reaching its highest level in a decade.

In general, illegal drugs continue to flourish despite huge numbers of imprisoned dealers and users (about 60 percent of all federal prisoners and 20 percent of state prisoners).

Law enforcement officials often are frustrated by the lack of progress in the drug war and sometimes will share information that allows journalists to more clearly see the network of drug trafficking. Some journalists also have successfully mapped drug raids in a particular jurisdiction, looking especially for repeat visits by law enforcement officers to the same site.

The Detroit News studied 300 addresses that had been scenes for at least three felony arrests each over a three-year span. It turned out that the city of Detroit owned one-fifth of those properties. The journalists found that a law allowing the padlocking of such properties had been poorly used. In addition, the journalists learned that absentee landlords who could have helped clean up the problem often had never been notified about the arrests on their properties.

On the other hand, police have been found to make unfounded drug accusations or overly aggressive arrests, enabling them to seize property in a proceeding known as forfeiture. A forfeiture law might allow an entire farm to be seized because marijuana plants are growing there, and it can be done before the grower is convicted or acquitted. A forfeiture law might allow seizure of an automobile after a routine traffic stop simply because the driver is carrying lots of cash and the police assume, however arbitrarily, that the cash is the fruit of a drug sale.

Some forfeiture laws and practices seem to operate on the assumption of guilty until proven innocent. Reliable nationwide statistics on forfeiture are nowhere to be found, although the U.S. Marshals Service houses a seized-assets division that makes educated guesses, broken out state by state. The incentive for an overzealous seizure policy is clear: Law enforcement agencies use the assets thus acquired to fatten their budgets. Dishonest officers might fill their own pockets with cash or make personal use of seized goods.

At The Kansas City Star, reporter Karen Dillon discovered that local law enforcement officers were calling in federal agents for the arrests to make a bust look like a joint operation. The federal agents would retain some of the seized assets, then quietly return the remainder to the local department. The purpose of the maneuver? To avoid a Missouri law requiring seized assets to help fund education instead of law enforcement.

Drug cases are worthy of scrutiny for yet another reason: They rely heavily on the police use of informants. That is always risky; informants tend to be unreliable. Many have criminal records and receive a reduced prison sentence in exchange for their information. The Columbus Dispatch found that informants who faced drug trafficking and related murder charges fabricated evidence in exchange for favorable judicial dispensation, cash payments or both. "Professional" informants, especially those who are incarcerated and thus in a position to report jailhouse talk, finger cellmates. Judges, despite knowledge of the questionable arrangements, often look the other way. The trouble is that many of the accusations, made for mercenary reasons, lead to wrongful convictions. (The phenomenon of wrongful convictions, and what journalists can do about them, is covered in Chapter 10.)

Vice

Because drug transactions involve willing parties, legalization advocates sometimes refer to them as victimless crimes. Prostitution is also frequently referred to as a victimless crime; talk of legalization is common. But vice officers see the situation differently. They see prostitutes forced into the business by bullying pimps, sometimes to support drug and alcohol addictions. They see those infected with HIV engaging in sex for money without warning their paying customers. They see prostitutes beaten and robbed by customers. They see the prostitutes' customers (already lawbreakers by definition) beaten and robbed by prostitutes and pimps. Some of the altercations end in murder.

Prostitutes, pimps and johns are also vulnerable to corrupt or brutal police officers. Some officers squeeze prostitutes on the beat, taking a percentage of their earnings in exchange for freedom from arrest. Others demand free sex. By working human sources and looking for complaints filed with a police internal affairs unit, a citizens' review board, a licensing or disciplinary agency or in court, journalists might uncover officers taking advantage of their vice assignments. To supplement people and paper trails, journalists can observe the life of the streets firsthand. They will see how prostitutes sometimes organize their soliciting around the schedules of vice officers.

One of the most controversial duties of vice officers is policing pornography. When does a book, Web site, video or live show cross the line of constitutionally protected free expression to become illegal?

Combating pornography that features children is less controversial and has become a significant issue in the Internet age. The criminals who produce and the pedophiles who consume the material are despised by all segments of society, providing widespread support for their apprehension. At the federal level, the Justice Department's Criminal Division helps investigate and prosecute sexual exploitation of minors, including the possession, manufacture and distribution of child pornography, plus the often related crimes of selling, buying and transporting children to engage in sexually explicit conduct.

The Arkansas Democrat-Gazette examined the spread of child pornography on the Web and reported that one in five children had been sexually solicited on the Web and one in four children had visited pornographic sites.

In 2004, in a controversial investigation, KCTV in Kansas City looked at the tactics of a group called Perverted Justice, which exposed men who use the Internet to prey on children. A member of Perverted Justice would pose as a minor in an Internet chat room and wait for an adult man to inquire about sex. The "minor" would then arrange to meet the man at a home rented by KCTV. After four days, 30 men made appointments to meet the "minor" for sex. Sixteen came to the door and were confronted by the news crew. The station said the investigation showed how prevalent and serious the problem of Internet predators is.

Since then, NBC Dateline signed a contract with Perverted Justice and has come under strong criticism for doing so because of issues of possible entrapment.

Missing Persons

The topic of missing persons is fraught with statistical peril. In a groundbreaking story in the 1980s, The Denver Post did an award-winning investigation that showed that the statistics put out by missing children's groups were greatly exaggerated and in many cases involved custody disputes.

But there are still numerous cases of missing persons that deserve attention. Families of missing persons are almost always upset at police. In the early stages of the investigation, family members perceive police as overly skeptical that foul play is involved. During later stages, if police believe the missing person might indeed have met with violence, family members become upset that the case remains unsolved.

A 10-part series by the Seattle Post-Intelligencer in 2003 showed that "because of ignorance or poor training, police in Washington state and around the nation routinely fumble missing-person reports." The newspaper built one database of missing person cases using reports from more than 270 police agencies in the state and built another database of unidentified bodies from autopsy records and other reports to show how police track down critical information.

Journalists can explore police policy on missing persons cases by asking these questions:

• Do police always wait at least 24 hours before initiating a missing persons case, based on the unvarying assumption that the person might have disappeared voluntarily?

- If that is the policy, is the assumption behind it sometimes counter-productive?
- At what age does the policy kick in: 16, 18 or 21?
- When police receive a missing person report about a child, they usually operate differently. Should that mode of operation be the norm for missing adults, too?
- When the missing person turns out to be a runaway under legal age, to whom do police refer the juvenile?

Stolen Property

Crimes against persons are a higher priority for police than crimes against property. But property crimes might outnumber violent crimes by 10 to 1 in a jurisdiction. Property crimes are rarely solved, which can leave negative impressions about police among the citizenry.

Stolen property crimes leave police in a dilemma and lead to these questions:

- If the department is overworked, does it make sense to respond promptly to every call, especially when the amount of stolen property is small and nobody has been injured?
- Do police feel they must respond immediately to every burglar alarm at a private home or business, when studies indicate that as many as 97 percent are false, triggered by bad weather, faulty equipment, forgetful homeowners or roaming pets?
- Has the locality instituted fines or jail time for the property owner when a false alarm sounds?
- Do the police refuse to respond unless the alarm company verifies the trouble first? It often makes sense for law enforcement agencies to focus their resources on stolen property cases in which the criminal has threatened the owner of the property with violence or has acted violently.

In a story for Worth magazine, Mike Mallowe used a technique that law enforcement officers sometimes use to learn: He asked a professional burglar to explain the nuances of the job. Journalists everywhere can learn from a show-and-tell by an ex-convict, then use that newly acquired knowledge to predict or decipher criminal activity.

One type of property crime of special interest to journalists working in large cities and resort areas involves thefts from hotels and motels. Are the buildings staffed by private security guards as well as covered by city police? If so, how effectively do they share their jurisdiction? Do they undercount or completely suppress crime reports to avoid damaging tourism? ABC-TV News aired an investigation showing lapses in hotel security, increasing the vulnerability of guests.

Property crimes in all kinds of locales are sometimes inside jobs. If a business or home is protected by a private security firm, that firm might use its knowledge of the premises and its ability to disconnect the alarm system temporarily from the main office to perpetrate the crime. Some property crimes are staged so the purported victims can file false insurance claims.

Another angle on such crimes is the destination of the stolen property. Journalists should examine pawnshops, flea markets and street-corner vendors. At the Sun-Sentinel, reporters Scott Glover and Evelyn Larrubia established a linkage between Fort Lauderdale's high burglary rate and the high concentration of pawnshops. The reporters obtained about 70,000 pawn slips collected by police from the shops over a year's span. Those slips showed several individuals visiting pawnshops more than 100 times during a year. Almost all the frequent pawnshop customers had criminal records.

In some states, including California, pawnshop owners must report every transaction to a statewide police database. If police are looking for an item stolen from a crime scene, the linked database should make discovery of the item possible within minutes, instead of the days, weeks or months it used to take police to search the hundreds of pawnshops in the state.

Automobile theft is one category of burglary with a high recovery rate when the motive is only a joy ride. An aggressive approach to seeking and checking abandoned vehicles can improve arrest rates because the thieves will have less time to cover their tracks.

A persistent reporter can uncover the locations of the chop shops, which are often in league with salvage yards, auto salesrooms, auto auctioneers, body repair garages and insurance companies.

Arson

As journalists examine suspicious fires, they should consider all possible motives. They should ask the following:

- Has the owner incurred unexpected financial obligations: back taxes, alimony or child support payments, for example?
- Has the owner lost a business license, zoning case, property tax appeal or major investor?

- Is the building in violation of code? Have city building inspectors or fire department inspectors ordered expensive renovations?
- Were the owners planning to go out of business anyway?
- Is there reason to believe a disgruntled current or former employee set the fire?
- If the fire occurred at a personal residence, is it possible the owner planned to apply insurance proceeds to business debts?

Witnesses — neighbors, tenants, competitors, business partners — who saw the owner remove items from the building shortly before the fire could provide valuable information.

Not all cases of arson are connected to business difficulties. Other motives include pyromania, vandalism, revenge against an unfaithful spouse or concealment of another crime, such as incineration of a body after a murder. In a classic story, the (Minneapolis) Star Tribune documented an arson ring led by a fire chief, his brother, plus 15 associates (including an insurance adjuster and construction company executive), who had reported 51 fires during a 25-year span.

A project by The Providence Journal showed that of 6,033 arsons reported in one year, only 19 resulted in prison sentences. Those statistics on their face suggest either corrupt or inept investigators and prosecutors.

Police officers do not always know much about arson. Police academy trainers may assume the fire department will take the lead in such cases. But because police are often the first on the scene of a suspicious fire, they should know how to handle evidence of arson. Arson is usually a property crime foremost, but it always harbors the potential of maiming or killing human beings.

A journalist can document the cooperation or dissension between police and fire department investigators, often known as fire marshals. The journalist can study police and fire department arson reports going back several years. If disagreement exists, might it stem from inadequate training of police or payoffs to fire inspectors by the beneficiaries of the arson?

Fire departments can be difficult to investigate because of the heroic work their members do. Yet some departments are poorly administered, offer inadequate training and are hotbeds of racism and sexism (much like some police departments). While some police departments have lost their reputations, most fire departments have not. Detroit News reporters Melvin Claxton and Charles Hurt explained in a 2001 issue of The IRE Journal how they equated poor equipment maintenance, understaffing of firehouses and second-rate training of firefighters with fire-related deaths that could have been avoided.

Bombings

Since the Oklahoma City bombing in 1995, the terrorist attacks on the United States in September 2001, and the attacks on transportation systems in other cities worldwide, investigations into bombings have taken on greater significance.

Journalists must be more prepared than ever to cover bombings. They should know the police procedures for handling bomb threats and the protocol of investigations into bombings and bomb threats by local police and federal authorities, such as the Bureau of Alcohol, Tobacco, Firearms and Explosives.

Bombs are generally the weapons of choice by the perpetrators of terrorism and hate crimes. Such crimes are not only violent in nature but also clearly violate civil rights laws, adding another dimension to the investigation. These are a few of the questions to ask:

- Who keeps records on bomb threats locally?
- Who are the best contacts in the police and fire departments on bomb threats and bombings?
- Who is licensed locally to sell explosives?
- What are the ATF's investigative procedures for tracking explosives and investigating bombings?

Traffic Violations

In an issue of The IRE Journal, Jim Lewers of The Wichita Eagle wrote that when his newspaper "asked the Kansas Department of Transportation for all the Kansas traffic accident data for the 1990s, reporters and editors had mostly vague ideas about what stories would result." Stories that did result included a three-part series on nearly 2,000 drivers involved in five or more serious accidents during the 1990s, a piece about the increasing number of car-deer collisions, one about seat belt use and another about motorcycle safety problems.

In addition, journalists should scrutinize police on traffic patrol. For example, journalists should examine how police recruits are taught in the academy to handle traffic stops, then determine whether officers are following the procedures to minimize dangers.

Catching drunken drivers is also part of the traffic patrol's work. Questions surrounding enforcement of driving-under-the-influence laws include whether police should set up sobriety checkpoints at which every passing driver is pulled over and tested and whether the blood-alcohol test being used by the police is the most accurate available. (The handling of drunken driving cases is mentioned in Chapters 10 and 18.)

Police scandals sometimes have their roots in traffic patrol. Officers might work out a sweetheart deal with a towing company. When the traffic patrol sees an accident requiring a tow truck, the same company gets the call every time. WJZ-TV in Baltimore found such a questionable relationship between police and a towing company, plus one between the towing service and a body shop charging exorbitant prices.

Speed traps set to ensnare motorists going too fast sometimes lead to ticketing of motorists who were obeying the law, as police realize they can abuse their authority to raise revenue, not to mention harass or sexually abuse those they stop in an exercise of raw power. Journalists can examine the number of tickets written per year by each officer. Is there a quota system?

Another potential story revolves around the targeting of minority motorists for traffic violations, even when they are not breaking any law. Racial profiling is the term used to describe such activity. Newsrooms throughout the United States have done numerous stories on racial profiling, and some states have mandated the creation of databases on traffic stops as a way of combating racial profiling.

In one classic example of profiling, a reporter at The Belleville (Ill.) News-Democrat examined nearly 19,000 tickets that indicated the driver's race to document the allegations, after receiving a tip from a former Illinois policeman. Blacks received tickets five times more frequently than whites in the locale, most likely to deter them from entering the city. The situation was aggravated by the percentage of black police officers — zero — and the proximity of Belleville to East St. Louis, an almost all-black city.

If a traffic stop leads to an arrest for a nontraffic offense, journalists can ask whether police had legitimate reasons for their search. What is police policy? Journalists can also check to see whether judges regularly set defendants free as a result of traffic stops that result in nontraffic charges.

Organized Crime and White-Collar Crime

Organized-crime syndicates are often involved in drugs and vice. Seemingly legitimate businesses controlled by Mafia families and other syndicates should be the focus of coverage, in accord with the maxim "Follow the dollar."

Organized-crime operations in the United States with roots in Colombia, China, Russia and Vietnam tend to be less diversified than their historical Italian counterparts. The Colombian cartels, for example, are well known for buying and selling illegal drugs. Some organized-crime enterprises know no ethnic or national boundaries, making it especially challenging for journalists to identify them with precision. Much of the effort to combat organized crime is federalized, which means journalists are wise to develop sources within the U.S. Justice Department's Criminal Division, as well as the Federal Bureau of Investigation.

Not all organized crime involves guns and physical threats. White-collar criminals practice organized crime in the financial markets, stealing millions of dollars while misleading investors and the public.

White-collar crime, sometimes called enterprise crime, involves a network of individuals linked together in an illegal relationship. With white-collar crime frequently emanating from corporate suites, the crime can consist of manipulating energy prices, avoiding taxes, selling sham products or violating environmental laws.

The policing of white-collar crimes usually comes from a government agency not normally associated with law enforcement, such as the U.S. Securities and Exchange Commission or the National Association of Security Dealers, or from divisions of other departments. (This topic will be discussed further in Chapter 15.)

Some of the policing is regulatory. For example, the SEC enforcement files sometimes lead to criminal investigations and can tip off a reporter to businesspeople or businesses that should be scrutinized.

The criminal investigations are led by state attorneys general or U.S. Attorney offices, and the filings by those offices often outline and make clear the alleged criminal wrongdoing.

Journalists should ask law enforcement agencies what is being done about white-collar crime, especially now that it frequently occurs via computers in cyberspace:

- Does the agency have a detection policy, or does it simply wait for disgruntled insiders to blow the whistle?
- Are any officers trained in uncovering enterprise crime?
- Is surveillance—through undercover infiltration, wiretapping, neighborhood stakeouts and the like—part of the crime-fighting strategy?
- Are investigators using a powerful law, the Racketeer Influenced and Corrupt Organizations Act, as well as laws aimed at money laundering, to full advantage?

Juvenile Crime

About one-third of arrests for violent crimes nationwide have historically involved young people under age 18. Unless police, prosecutors and judges agree that a youthful perpetrator should be tried as an adult, the name of the accused is normally kept confidential. The idea is to give juveniles a chance to turn their lives around before being publicly labeled as criminals.

But journalists need to determine if the juvenile is a habitual offender and find out how the law enforcement system deals with that kind of offender and juvenile crime. (Chapter 10 explains the juvenile justice system in more depth.)

Sometimes juvenile criminals are part of gangs. Some law enforcement agencies train officers as gang specialists and place them in an anti-gang unit. That can be a useful tactic, but a journalist needs to look at the entire approach to juvenile crime and how law enforcement is working with parents, schools, social workers and other agencies.

Investigating Other Aspects of Law Enforcement

There are numerous other areas of law enforcement to investigate. Those areas range from administration and budget, medical examiners and evidence rooms to civil rights violations. Good journalists can find investigative stories in the areas that seem the most rudimentary and routine.

Patrol Officers, Dispatchers and 911 Operators

The Fort Worth Star-Telegram reported that the Fort Worth Police Department received a call every 39 seconds—what some law enforcement officials term "the tyranny of 911" because so many of the calls are not emergencies or are phony. With 942 officers, the department had a ratio of 2.1 officers to every 1,000 citizens, which was then below average for large cities. As a result, some calls labeled "emergency" failed to receive the desired emergency response. The story tracked one emergency call, from a woman with a two-year-old daughter who rang 911 to report four men trying to break into her home. When the call arrived, the 911 operator (one of seven then on duty) sent the information to one of four police dispatchers working that shift, but no on-duty patrol officer was available.

The Star-Telegram's investigation found that one-third of all calls received did not meet the police department's own response-time goals. Response times are often excellent in some parts of the city (usually the most affluent) and substandard in other parts (usually the poorest and most crime-ridden). Overall response time is determined by a variety of factors, and thus consists of multiple data sets. The now-defunct Pittsburgh Press documented response time disparities by analyzing computerized records of 911 calls after listening to complaints from neighborhood groups who offered anecdotal evidence about slow police responses.

Many law enforcement agencies erase 911 tapes after a month or two, so journalists must move quickly if they want data from tapes to explore a specific case or overall response quality.

But even the best response times cannot help a caller whose location is unknown. Journalists can examine the quality of the local 911 system, asking whether it is enhanced so it does not have to rely on callers to provide their location, an especially important matter with the proliferation of cell phones, whose calls can be easily tracked now.

Journalists who learn about police patrol will discover how patrolling means hours of routine interspersed by minutes of action. They will learn whether patrol officers are using ineffective techniques, such as arriving at the scene with sirens and lights on, warning suspects of their arrival.

Journalists can learn why some responsible patrol officers take time away from the street after each dispatched call. This gives them a chance to do preventive work—looking in on local drug dealers, for example. Many arrests come from such initiative. Although it makes response time statistics look bad, some officers think it is necessary to achieve maximum effectiveness. They also have to find time during their shift to write reports. If reports are dashed off, their poor quality might make it more difficult or impossible to obtain convictions.

In some jurisdictions, a prosecutor is based at a local police station and visits crime scenes along with officers. On-the-spot legal advice from that prosecutor can mean the difference between a botched investigation and an eventual conviction.

Quick response is mostly about apprehension, but police set up patrols to maximize prevention. There is constant debate on the manner of patrol: motorized vehicles (cars, motorcycles) that have the virtue of speed but that separate officers from their communities, or slower means that increase contact (bicycles, horses, foot patrol). Closer contact has been at the core of the community policing movement, a movement officially advocated by the Office of Community Oriented Policing Services within the U.S. Justice Department.

Community policing, even when carried out enthusiastically, is not necessarily a panacea because it does not automatically reach into private places away from street view. Robberies in office suites, rapes in public housing elevators and drug deals in the basement of a home can escape notice. There are ways for police to address crime in private places, but those take planning.

Crime Scene Technicians and Crime Laboratories

In "What Cops Know," Connie Fletcher quotes an officer saying, "Policemen are notorious for screwing up crime scenes. The first thing they do is pick up the gun — in order to prevent the victim from killing anyone else, I guess. It's inherent in the policeman. I wish I could tell every cop who ever gets called to a scene, 'The best place for your hands at a scene is in your pockets.'"

To minimize evidence contamination, every officer should have specialized training. It also helps to have professional fingerprint lifters, sketch artists, computer artists and photographers at the crime scene. After the evidence has been collected at the scene, it may go to a crime lab. An inefficient or ineffective laboratory might mean failure to convict.

WCCO-TV, Minneapolis, investigated a vehicular homicide in which poor work by the state crime lab caused trouble for the prosecution. The Seattle Times found crime labs with such huge backlogs that they had stopped accepting samples for analysis, leaving police and prosecutors unable to proceed against suspected criminals.

In a few jurisdictions, crime lab personnel serving as witnesses for the prosecution have been exposed as occasional or habitual liars, willing to say whatever serves the prosecution's case. Unfair trials and some wrongful convictions have occurred as a result of such behavior.

Polygraph operators might be attached to the crime lab. Wherever they fall within the organization chart, their capabilities and the use to which their lie detector results are put should be grist for journalists. The same is true for DNA analysts, who are an important factor in police work. Journalists need to check that DNA analysis is done correctly and prevents errors due to inexact equipment or poorly trained, overworked technicians.

Evidence Rooms

If evidence is misplaced, destroyed or stolen, a guilty person might go free. Yet journalists almost never inquire about the handling of evidence. A Kansas City Star story told of 13,000 guns jutting from shelves and dangling from hangers in a police subbasement. The story also noted "evidence bags stuffed with pills, pot, speed and LSD spilling from shelves in a long, store-sized room." Kansas City police were trying to control internal theft from the storage areas, but without total success.

Journalists can ask these questions:

- How often do officers take evidence for personal use?
- Whose responsibility is it to track down mishandled evidence?
- What happens to officers who are caught stealing evidence?

The Seattle Times documented the mishandling of a cotton swab carrying evidence of child molestation. As a result of the mishandling, the swab became contaminated, and the alleged molester was acquitted due to the lack of physical evidence.

Coroners and Medical Examiners

In some counties, coroners are elected; they are often funeral home directors or other people without medical training. Funeral directors have an especially poignant conflict of interests: They want to sell a funeral to the family, making it tempting to rule a death natural.

In urban areas, there may be an appointed medical examiner, often a physician trained in forensic pathology, rather than an elected coroner. Journalists should inquire whether a medical examiner has other specialized training that might help increase the certainty of the autopsy results.

In Colorado, where any registered voter can run for coroner, Megan Hall of the Denver alternative weekly Westword found that coroners frequently could not be reached by police when needed at a crime scene. Hall exposed a deputy coroner, appointed by his elected boss, who worked as a bartender and sometimes arrived at crime scenes drunk.

Reporters can check whether the findings of the coroner or medical examiner at the early stage of an investigation disagree with the preliminary findings police have announced. Medical examiners and coroners are in a peculiar position, balancing on the tightrope between law and medicine. They are responsible for determining the deceased's identity, plus the time and cause of death, which are medical questions; they also determine the legal issue of the manner of death. The cause of death refers to the medical reason for death, such as heart failure or a knife wound. The manner of death refers to the circumstances—natural, accidental, homicidal or suicidal. Despite many successes by coroners and medical examiners, investigations in the IRE Resource Center show incompetence and corruption too. As a result, killers literally got away with murder, or innocent people were convicted.

Canine (K9) Corps

Police dogs can be valuable law enforcement tools, but in some jurisdictions, police use dogs to harass and even harm citizens. In the relatively rare instances when journalists have delved into the use of police dogs, they have found an inordinate number of unleashings against minority citizens.

Journalists can easily check whether police departments in their jurisdiction use dogs and whether their training is sufficient. Brutality complaints sometimes cite dogs and their police handlers. In fact, one of the most wrenching police brutality investigations ever done by a journalist involved dogs. William Marimow of The Philadelphia Inquirer was the investigator. His colleague David Preston wrote about it in The IRE Journal: "Marimow received a telephone call from a law enforcement official who alleged that a handful of the K9 unit's 125 officers were ordering their dogs to attack innocent, unarmed citizens without justification. . . . He tracked down victims and witnesses of K9 attacks, pored over court testimony and medical records and traced cases through the criminal justice system."

After receiving the original tip, Marimow heard from a local attorney who said that two other lawyers had witnessed a K9 attack. Then a newsroom colleague told Marimow about an attack on the son of a family friend. After four months of digging, Marimow published a story. Calls about other attacks then poured in. Before Marimow had finished, he knew of more than 350 apparently unwarranted attacks. Two officers and their dogs accounted for 50 of those attacks.

Civil Rights and Community Relations

Many police departments have negative images in black and other minority neighborhoods. Journalists can look into what law enforcement agencies are doing to alleviate those negative images and whether the image is justified. Some questions to ask are these:

- Is the department hiring officers who reflect the diversity of the jurisdiction where they work?
- Are officers from all ethnic, racial and religious backgrounds trained in dealing with sensitive, sensitized portions of the population?
- How do police deal with panhandlers, transients, squatters in vacant buildings and other down-and-out citizens who are not breaking any laws?
- If community relations positions exist, are the officers assigned to them full time? Or is the community relations work an additional, occasional responsibility?

When trouble refuses to die down, do local police ever consult the Community Relations Service of the U.S. Justice Department? Its mission is to support communities in preventing racial and ethnic tensions. The U.S. Department of Justice's Civil Rights Division often enters locales far from Washington, D.C., to investigate and prosecute discrimination in any program receiving federal financial assistance. The division's investigators and prosecutors can extend their reach even when no federal money is involved, as in cases when intimidation is used to deprive citizens of specific rights, such as voting, housing, employment, education, health care, use of public facilities, exercising religious preference or receiving an abortion.

After the race riots in Cincinnati in 2001, NBC Dateline probed deeper into community problems across the nation and showed how racial profiling played a strong role in those problems. In an award-winning investigation called "A Pattern of Suspicion," Dateline analyzed data from more than four million traffic stops in a dozen cities. It found that in almost every city, blacks were at least twice as likely as whites to be stopped or ticketed for nonmoving violations. As IRE contest judges noted, the story put into focus the subtle ways that police target nonwhite "suspects."

Resources for Investigating Law Enforcement

There are numerous resources for every kind of investigation into law enforcement. The suggestions below touch on just a few of them.

Crime Statistics

The U.S. Justice Department's Sourcebook of Criminal Justice Statistics often supplements or contradicts the Federal Bureau of Investigation's Uniform Crime Reports because the Justice Department tries to account for unreported as well as reported crimes. The FBI data exclude unreported crimes. If an automobile is stolen but never reported, statistically it is as if the theft never happened. Furthermore, the FBI data cover only eight categories: murder and non-negligent manslaughter, rape, robbery, aggravated assault, burglary, larceny/theft, motor vehicle theft and arson.

Another problem with the data is that law enforcement agencies that funnel information to the FBI have varying systems of crime statistics management. In some states, certain police departments refuse to provide thorough data to the state police or the FBI. The reasons for the lack of cooperation include ignorance, laziness, budget shortfalls and a desire to portray the community as safer than it really is. The lack of cooperation can render law enforcement ineffective, as when police fail to catch a serial rapist because they are unaware of an unreported sexual assault with the same modus operandi in a nearby community. Inadequate statistics also mean that police within the jurisdiction may be unable to deploy their patrol officers and specialized units efficiently.

Numbers can lie locally as well as nationally. Pam Zekman, of WBBM-TV, Chicago, found police departments wrongly taking credit for lowered crime rates. It made no sense to Zekman that crime was decreasing in Chicago when so many people she knew had been victimized. Zekman's hunch turned out to be correct. Officers, anxious to please their superiors, were marking legitimate crime reports—especially rapes, robberies and burglaries—as "unfounded." By comparing that "unfounded" designation to statistics from departments in other cities, Zekman determined that Chicago police had used the term up to 50 times more frequently than police in New York, Los Angeles and St. Louis. In some areas, police discourage citizens from reporting minor crimes. This makes the geographic area appear safer than it actually is and reduces police paperwork. Journalists can inquire into police practices that discourage citizen reporting, such as refusing to accept complaints by telephone.

The (Tacoma) News Tribune performed a computer analysis of violent crime data that shattered myths. For example, the assumption that military personnel were more likely to commit crimes turned out to be mistaken: They had half the level of reported violent crime as the rest of the population. Even local police expressed surprise at which neighborhoods had the highest number of reported crimes. Adam Berliant, a computer-assisted reporting expert at the News Tribune, suggested starting with computerized information at the local, not the state, level because the most appropriate local agency is probably the one that submits statistics to the FBI.

A reported crime is considered cleared by police if it results in an arrest or in the gathering of enough evidence that an arrest could have been made if not for external factors. But a high clearance rate is not necessarily cause for celebration among the citizenry. When the emphasis is on clearing crimes for statistical reasons, quite a few arrested suspects turn out to be innocent. If they are eventually freed due to lack of evidence, the line on the statistical chart might still read "crime solved."

Budgets and Contracts

As mentioned in previous chapters, journalists can learn a lot by scrutinizing budgets. In the case of police, overtime payments might indicate the shifts on which additional officers are needed to combat crime increases or on which specialists are spending extra hours combating a particular type of crime that has spiraled out of control.

As another example, journalists might be able to determine from the budget how much money is used to pay informers and then ask, when informers are used, whether they are already in prison or under threat of imprisonment. Does their potentially tainted testimony hold up often enough to make payment sensible?

Contracts should be scrutinized too, as at any other taxpayer-supported agency. The Grapevine Sun in Texas received a tip from a police officer resulting in a story describing questionable spending for repair and maintenance of city police vehicles. The stories told how the chief funneled business to a local garage where his son-in-law worked, paying excessive prices for parts and labor. The reporter relied on repair shop invoices, vehicle maintenance logs, request-for-repair forms filed by police and monthly department expenditure reports.

Sometimes agencies operate outside their budgets because of circumstances they could not have predicted, such as the sudden increased availability of a particular street drug like methamphetamine, or "crank." A concerted effort to fight meth sales can bust a budget quickly, but police administrators might believe they have no choice but to accumulate a deficit.

Records Divisions and Public Information Officers

Journalists are by definition interested in the accessibility and completeness of police records. Complaints initiated by citizens and those initiated by police themselves ought to be organized logically. Too many departments organize them only by date and time of day. That is of little help to journalists or other citizens who have only the name of the complainant or the alleged offender.

Journalists can help themselves and the general public by scrutinizing the logic of reporting forms. Do they capture the relationship between the victim and the offender? If not, how can police know in a systematic way whether they are more often fighting crimes involving people who know each other or crimes involving strangers? Because acquaintance crimes and stranger crimes are handled differently in both the prevention and apprehension stages, such information ought to be considered vital.

Are crime statistics charted by neighborhood rather than citywide only? Relying on citywide statistics does not allow police to plan their crime fighting according to each precinct where officers are stationed. For example, a citywide drop in aggravated assaults might mask an increase in knife fights between Chinese-American and Vietnamese-American gangs within a particular precinct.

Public information officers can help journalists figure out how reports are organized and can assist with accessibility to the documents or databases. Public information officers ought to be consulted and trusted unless they prove themselves untrustworthy. Crimes on campuses of colleges that accept federal money are covered by a specific federal law that requires annual reports in a specific format. Many campuses post and update the data on a Web site. (The higher education section in Chapter 12 covers this topic more fully.)

People Trails

As in any other bureaucracy, current and former employees should be culti-vated as much as possible. Sources in other law enforcement agencies can pro-vide perspective, especially if the agencies have worked together on solving crimes that cross jurisdictional lines. Journalists can meet connected sources simply by hanging out in police station waiting areas. Private detectives, also known as private investigators, can be sources about what is going on inside police departments. Many are former police officers. They do favors for police and sometimes receive favors in return. Private detectives sometimes help jour-nalists by obtaining unlisted telephone numbers, running credit checks and finding missing persons. Journalists should expect to pay expenses for such assistance some of the time.

Prosecutors can help journalists too. If the prosecutor's office or the police department is in need of reform, there is always the chance one will blow the whistle on the other. Police often dislike prosecutors because they will not file charges without question. Prosecutors often become angry at police for bring-ing poorly prepared cases or for violating suspects' rights. Each side possesses files on specific cases that journalists would not normally see. The same is true for public defenders and defense attorneys in private practice. (Prosecutors and defense attorneys as sources are treated more fully in Chapter 10.)

Victims, witnesses and those arrested can be interviewed even without police cooperation. Cheryl Reed of the Dayton Daily News checked the criminal rec-ord of a 20-year-old murder victim after hearing he had been found in a known drug area. She obtained his rap sheet through a newsroom computer hookup to a local law enforcement network. The rap sheet showed the victim's criminal his-tory as well as the name and telephone number of his mother. Reed interviewed the victim's family before police had even released his name to the public.

Victims' compensation programs mandated by federal or state law might be a conversation starter if a victim's family members are reluctant to talk about the crime itself. The National Organization for Victim Assistance and the National Association of Crime Victim Compensation Boards might be able to provide specifics about local programs (benefits vary widely), as well as tech-niques for gaining access to reluctant potential sources. The U.S. Department of Justice's Office for Victims of Crime tries to ensure respectful treatment of victims throughout the nation.

The St. Louis Post-Dispatch asked a convicted murderer for access to his records, which contained insights into the crime. The 31-year-old man, who first killed when he was 14, signed a release giving the newspaper medical and conduct records that had accumulated during his 16 years in prison.

Other types of sources who get closeup views of police conduct include coroners, medical examiners, funeral home directors, emergency room doctors, nurses, ambulance personnel, citizens crime commissions, scholars in university criminal justice departments, psychologists and psychiatrists who examine the accused, informants, pawnshop employees and gun dealers.

Journalists can connect with news sources by covering crime, especially violent crime, as a public health issue instead of covering it as a series of disconnected incidents. These are some of the questions journalists can address:

- How typical is this type of violent crime in this community?
- What is the relationship of the people involved?
- Have those people been in trouble with the law before?
- Do they have jobs? Do they earn enough to support a family above the poverty level?
- If a gun is involved, how did it come into the possession of the accused? Is it legally registered?
- Is alcohol involved? What about narcotics? If they are involved, how did they come into the possession of the accused? Is it easy to obtain alcohol nearby? Narcotics?
- After a crime, who pays medical expenses, law enforcement investigative expenses and salaries of courthouse personnel? Put another way, what is the tangible cost to the larger society?

Paper Trails

If they read carefully, journalists might find that police department organization manuals spell out established paper trails. After studying such a manual, a journalist might know precisely what form to request and thus might get it by dint of that knowledge.

The National Crime Information Center, coordinated by the FBI, contains a wealth of data. Records are entered by local law enforcement agencies. Each state maintains a control terminal, which is supposed to help with data input and retrieval. The NCIC files include missing persons; wanted fugitives; stolen and retrieved but unidentified guns; and missing stocks, bonds, cash, license plates and boats. The computer system is off limits to journalists, but sometimes an insider leaks information from it.

Search warrants filed in local courthouses are not off limits and can help journalists break open a case. The San Francisco Bay Guardian used search warrants while investigating the apparently unnecessary fatal shooting by police of an Oakland, Calif., resident in his home. "According to the seven-page warrant," the story said, "police were looking for equipment used to alter the encoded magnetic strip on credit cards and any goods purchased with the stolen or altered cards." The warrant named the man's wife, who was not home at the time of the fatal raid. The raid turned up no such evidence as listed on the search warrant, and the dead man's wife never was arrested.

If police conduct a warrantless search, that is a story in itself. The Las Vegas Review-Journal investigated incidents in which the police failed to obtain search warrants. Three officers eventually faced criminal charges in connection with the death of a man during a warrantless search. Local jails maintain books listing people who have been incarcerated there. The books contain such information as the person's name, date of birth, address, gender, race and physical description; the name of the arresting agency; the date of commitment to the county jail; who made bond and how; the discharge date; and the suspected offense. The book usually is indexed chronologically. Read carefully; it can lead to previously unreported stories. For instance, a prisoner who is admitted in battered physical condition and is soon given medical attention might have been a victim of excessive force by police.

⊃ CHECK IT OUT

✓ Obtain the last five years of crime reports issued by your community's police department, preferably organized by patrol area. Compare the reports, and determine where the largest changes have occurred.

✓ Obtain the last three years of salaries for your community's police department, and compare them with state and national median salaries. Also, obtain the requirements from the department for being a police officer, and see whether they have changed over the past three years.

✓ Obtain the last three years of arson reports for your community. Interview both police and fire investigators to determine whether arson is increasing in your community.

RESOURCES FOR REPORTING

General Resources

The Bureau of Alcohol, Tobacco, Firearms and Explosives (http://atf.treas.gov) investigates and keeps numerous reports and records in these four areas. They particularly get involved with bombings.

The Commission on Accreditation for Law Enforcement Agencies (www.calea .org) contains extensive information on the standards and performance of police departments.

The Department of Education, Office of Postsecondary Education, Campus Security Statistics (www.ope.ed.gov/security) is especially useful for tracking campus crime.

The National Coalition Against Domestic Violence (www.ncadv.org) has a wealth of information on domestic violence issues.

The Office of Community Oriented Policing Services (www.cops.usdoj.gov) provides resources on improving community policing.

The U.S. Marshals Service (www.usdoj.gov/marshals) bills itself as "the nation's primary fugitive hunting organization" and provides the names of federal fugitives and information on its work.

The Web site www.officer.com is aimed mainly at law enforcement officers.

Books About Policing

Edna Buchanan of The Miami Herald is the author of such classic works as "The Corpse Had a Familiar Face" and "Never Let Them See You Cry."

Here are several other books that offer an inside look at police departments:

- "The Killing Season: A Summer Inside a Los Angeles Police Department Homicide Division," by Miles Corwin of the Los Angeles Times
- "Crime Scene," by Mitch Gelman of Newsday
- "The Cop Shop," by Robert Blau of the Chicago Tribune
- "Police and Policing: Contemporary Issues," edited by Dennis J. Kenney and Robert P. McNamara

Accreditation of Law Enforcement Agencies

The Commission on Accreditation for Law Enforcement Agencies (www.calea.org) in Fairfax, Va., can supply guidelines to journalists who want to know what separates the accredited from the unaccredited agencies.

Recruitment

Alan W. Benner's essay "Psychological Screening of Police Applicants" is a starting point for journalists delving into recruitment. It is part of the book "Critical Issues in Policing," edited by Roger G. Dunham and Geoffrey P. Alpert.

PART II   Investigating the Government

Groups like the National Black Police Association (www.blackpolice.org) in Washington, D.C.; the National Fraternal Order of Police (www.fop.net) in Nashville, Tenn.; and the International Association of Women Police (www.iawp .org) in Decatur, Ga., also have information on personnel issues.

Training

The National Tactical Officers Association (www.ntoa.org) in Doylestown, Pa., has information on training.

The essay "Learning the Skills of Policing," by David H. Bayley and Egon Bittner in the Dunham and Alpert anthology "Critical Issues in Policing," is a useful starting point. A good supplement is the career guide "Police Officer," by Hugh O'Neill, Hy Hammer and E.P. Steinberg, and another perspective is available from William Dunn in his book "Boot: An LAPD Officer's Rookie Year."

The Federal Law Enforcement Training Center (www.ustreas.gov/fletc), part of the U.S. Treasury Department, concentrates on raising the competence level of personnel employed by the 70 or so police forces within the federal government's Cabinet departments and commissions. But sources at the Center also promote training of local police and so can serve as dispassionate sources about local law enforcement preparation to handle just about any type of crime.

The Top Command

To learn about management in police departments, a reporter can check numerous sources, including the International Association of Chiefs of Police (www .theiacp.org), Alexandria, Va., and its magazine, Police Chief (www.policechief magazine.org); the Alexandria-based National Sheriffs' Association (www.sherrifs .org); and the Police Executive Research Forum (www.policeforum.org), Washington, D.C. From time to time, chiefs talk more or less candidly about the problems and pressures they face. See, for example, Anthony V. Bouza's "Police Unbound: Corruption, Abuse and Heroism by the Boys in Blue." Bouza served as chief in Minneapolis and as a commander in the Bronx.

Police Brutality and Discipline of Wayward Officers

Discipline issues are discussed in Douglas W. Perez's book "Common Sense About Police Review." The Reporters Committee for Freedom of the Press (www.rcfp.org) comments regularly on access to police disciplinary records in its magazine The News Media and the Law (www.rcfp.org/news/mag/index.php).

At the federal level, agencies have professional associations and unions that might provide information about specific cases from the viewpoint of those being disciplined. One example is the FBI Agents Association (www.fbiaa.org).

Overviews of the problem of police brutality are provided by Jerome H. Skolnick and James J. Fyfe in their book "Above the Law: Police and the Excessive Use of Force" and by Jill Nelson in her edited book "Police Brutality: An Anthology."

Despite the difficulty of proving brutality, the IRE Resource Center is filled with investigations on the topic. Some cases have become the subject of books:

- "Murderer With a Badge: The Secret Life of a Rogue Cop," by Edward Humes
- "The Dark Side of the Force: A True Story of Corruption and Murder in the Los Angeles Police Department," by Jan Golab
- "Deliberate Indifference: A Story of Murder and Racial Injustice," by Howard Swindle

Murder

Among the books on this topic are "Homicide: A Year on the Killing Streets," by Baltimore Sun police reporter David Simon, and "Criminal Investigation," by James W. Osterburg and Richard H. Ward, former New York City policemen-turned-academics.

The IRE Resource Center contains a "Medical Examiner" heading that encompasses coroners. The center can be searched by key word within the story summaries created by IRE staff. The book "Coroner" by Thomas T. Noguchi, former Los Angeles County medical examiner, contains useful insights. In her book "The Corpse Had a Familiar Face," journalist Edna Buchanan provides fascinating examples of how the Dade County–Miami medical examiner solved two murders through a combination of scientific knowledge, common sense and intuition.

The April 2000 issue of Uplink and the July–August 2000 issue of The IRE Journal explain the uses of the national gun dealers database.

The American Academy for Forensic Sciences (www.aafs.org) in Colorado Springs, Colo., and the International Association for Identification (www.theiai .org) in Alameda, Calif., can provide many resources.

Juvenile Crime

The Youth Law Center (www.youthlawcenter.com) in Washington, D.C., and the National Center for Juvenile Justice (www.ncjj.org) in Pittsburgh are good starting points for journalists interested in juvenile crime.

Journalist Douglas Century captures the culture of youth gangs in his book "Street Kingdom: Five Years Inside the Franklin Avenue Posse." Mark Fleisher looks at the phenomenon from a more academic perspective in his book "Dead End Kids: Gang Girls and the Boys They Know."

The National Youth Gang Center (www.iir.com/nygc), Tallahassee, Fla., focuses on gang activity.

Rape

Besides Jim Neff's tips in The IRE Journal, suggestions can be found in "Practical Aspects of Rape Investigation," edited by Robert R. Hazelwood and Ann Wolbert Burgess, as well as Chapter 22 of "Criminal Investigation" by James W. Osterburg and Richard H. Ward.

Nancy Ziegenmeyer explains the perspective of the raped woman in "Taking Back My Life," written with Larkin Warren. Helen Benedict explains the traps of insensitivity journalists enter in her book "Virgin or Vamp: How the Press Covers Sex Crimes."

Domestic Violence

The Dunham and Alpert anthology "Critical Issues in Policing" contains a helpful essay by Joel Garner and Elizabeth Clemmer, "Danger to Police in Domestic Disturbances—A New Look." Lawrence W. Sherman's "Policing Domestic Violence: Experiments and Dilemmas" further examines the law enforcement challenges in this area.

More information is available at the National Coalition Against Domestic Violence (www.ncadv.org) in Denver and from the U.S. Justice Department's Violence Against Women Office (www.usdoj.gov/ovw).

Narcotics

The National Association of State Alcohol and Drug Abuse Directors (www.nasadad.org), Washington, D.C., is a helpful source, as are the National Institute on Drug Abuse (part of the National Institutes of Health, www.nida.nih.gov), the White House Office of National Drug Control Policy (www.whitehousedrugpolicy.gov) and the U.S. Justice Department's Drug-Free Communities Support Program (www.ondcp.gov/dfc).

Hundreds of books about the national and international drug wars have been published. These books by former U.S. Drug Enforcement Administration officials provide different perspectives:

- "Dead on Delivery: Inside the Drug Wars, Straight From the Street," by Robert M. Stutman
- "Deep Cover: The Inside Story of How DEA Infighting, Incompetence and Subterfuge Lost Us the Biggest Battle of the Drug War," by Michael Levine

One of the many scholarly books that shed light on the fight against illegal drugs is Steven R. Belenko's "Crack and the Evolution of Anti-Drug Policy."

Vice

Tamar Hosansky and Pat Sparling's book "Working Vice," essentially a biography of Cleveland police officer Lucie J. Duvall, looks at almost every type of vice investigation possible. The section about the connection between bars and crime explains why police in some geographic areas spend so much time trying to find liquor license violations as a way to close the bars, thus reducing neighborhood vice crime.

Organized Crime

Books that examine organized crime include Jonathan Kwitny's classic "Vicious Circles: The Mafia in the Marketplace." William Kleinknecht's "The New Ethnic Mobs: The Changing Face of Organized Crime in America" looks at new organized-crime groups.

White-Collar Crime

Books that explain enterprise crime include "The Criminal Elite: Professional and Organized Crime," by Howard Abadinsky; the similarly titled "The Criminal Elite: The Sociology of White-Collar Crime," by James William Coleman; and "Masters of Deception: The White-Collar Crime Crisis and Ways to Protect Yourself," by Louis R. Mizell Jr. The U.S. Department of Justice's National White Collar Crime Center can provide perspective.

Stolen Property

The National Burglar and Fire Alarm Association (www.alarm.org) in Bethesda, Md., is a good first stop on the topic. Connie Fletcher's book "What Cops Know" contains additional insights in the property crimes chapter. Another insightful insider account is "Burglars on the Job: Streetlife and Residential Break-ins," by Richard T. Wright and Scott Decker. The same authors collaborated on the book "Armed Robbers in Action: Stick-ups and Street Culture."

Private companies like Carfax of Fairfax, Va., can help journalists track a vehicle's history if the vehicle identification number is known. The history will indicate odometer fraud, undisclosed rebuilding resulting from salvage and other suspicious activity. Carfax pieces together its histories from state motor vehicle department title documents and odometer readings registered at vehicle auctions.

Another resource is the International Association of Auto Theft Investigators (www.iaati.org) in Horseshoe Beach, Fla.

Arson

Organizations to contact include the National Association of Fire Investigators (www.nafi.org) in Hoffman Estates, Ill., and the Insurance Committee for Arson Control (www.arsoncontrol.org) in Washington, D.C. The International Association of Fire Chiefs (www.iafc.org) and the International Association of Firefighters (www.iaff.org) can help too.

Chapter 24 of the Osterburg and Ward book "Criminal Investigation" is a starting point for understanding how an arson investigation should be conducted. A book by Peter A. Micheels, "Heat: The Fire Investigators and Their War on Arson and Murder," provides an education through interviews with eight fire marshals. "Last American Heroes: Today's Firefighters," by Charles W. Sasser and

Michael W. Sasser, is based on observations of one Miami Beach firehouse. The newsletter Public Safety and Justice Policies (www.statecapitals.com/publicsafety .html), Alexandria, Va., tracks fire department issues. The IRE Resource Center contains projects under the headings "Arson" and "Fire Departments."

Bombings

Organizations like the Anti-Defamation League (www.adl.org) track hate crimes, including bombings, around the nation. The Bureau of Alcohol, Tobacco, Firearms and Explosives has information on investigations.

911 and Patrol Officers

The National Emergency Number Association (www.nena9-1-1.org) is a good resource, as is the Office of Community Oriented Policing Services (www.cops .usdoj.gov). A useful book is "Community Policing: How to Get Started," by Robert Trojanowicz and Bonnie Bucqueroux.

Crime Scene Investigation

The Osterburg and Ward book "Criminal Investigation" includes a chapter, "Physical Evidence: Discovery, Preservation, Collection, Transmission," that should help journalists formulate questions. The FBI publication "Crime Laboratory Digest" can provide leads and context, as can the American Society of Crime Lab Directors (www.ascld.org).

Crime Statistics

Uplink has published numerous articles by journalists about how they cracked crime statistics. The first issue of the newsletter discussed that topic, as did the issues of December 1997, January 1999 and June 1999. Almost every important technique journalists use is explained in "Understanding Crime Statistics: A Reporter's Guide," which is part of IRE's Beat Book Series.

Tracking Victim Issues

Among the organizations to use on this topic are the National Organization for Victim Assistance (www.trynova.org), the National Association of Crime Victim Compensation Boards (www.nacvcb.org) and the U.S. Department of Justice's Office for Victims of Crime (www.ojp.usdoj.gov/ovc). A helpful book is Leslie Sebba's "Third Parties: Victims and the Criminal Justice System."

12

Investigating Education

This chapter covers investigation into the major aspects of education, from early childhood education to the university campus. It addresses issues not only of testing and discipline, but also of administration, teacher competence, contracts and budgets. The education beat is an endless source of ideas and stories for the enterprising journalist. While the beat is challenging, a dedicated journalist will be rewarded with stories that are wide-ranging and deeply meaningful to the public. In addition, this chapter shows the approaches and techniques that will help a journalist navigate the statistics, reports, studies and often secretive bureaucracies of education.

Over the past decade, journalists have been steadily improving their scrutiny of education. They have probed teacher certification, deteriorating facilities, faulty test scores, school discipline, campus crime, academic fraud, tuition loans, questionable contracts, fraternity misdeeds and the influence of corporations on education.

But as they have delved deeper into education issues, journalists have had to supplement their traditional reporting with the use of databases and social science methods. These newer methods help journalists sort out and examine the numerous reports and studies that educators produce, whether it is for K-12 or higher education.

While there are many intersections between secondary education and higher education—such as SAT issues—this chapter will look first at compulsory education and then move on to higher education, since most resources and publications are split along those lines. For tips and resources for investigating education, turn to "Resources for Reporting" at the end of this chapter.

Issues in K-12 Education

Education reporters should focus first on the quality of learning. A reporter in the back of the classroom should be constantly asking whether the education of children is being hindered by tradition, politics, prejudice, bad teachers, or poor administration.

Many news organizations have found public school systems placing politics ahead of children's needs, with nepotism prevailing over merit, old classroom methods being adhered to despite research showing better ways to teach, a misuse of public funds to reward cronies, and an inattention to students that leads to poor performance and high dropout rates.

Although measuring the quality of a school system is challenging, there are many basic topics to look at.

Student Test Scores

Test scores are being emphasized more than ever in the United States because of the No Child Left Behind initiative, which links federal funding for school systems to students' success on standardized tests. The pressure to ensure that students pass tests, however, has led to the reporting of questionable test scores.

Holly Hacker and Joshua Benton of The Dallas Morning News expanded a story about one school's alleged cheating on standardized tests into a piece about cheating across the state. Measuring performance over time, Hacker used regression analysis to show suspicious improvements among historically low-performing schools. She and Benton pinpointed one impoverished school where the fourth-graders had trouble adding and subtracting yet nearly all the fifth-graders got perfect scores on the math portion of the Texas Assessment of Knowledge and Skills.

In another story, the two reporters used Texas reading test scores to show that the top school in terms of third-grade test scores was an unlikely champion. They wrote, "Wilmer Elementary—a perennial underachiever in a district many consider the state's worst—beat out the scores of 3,212 other elementary schools. But substantial evidence, including a Dallas Morning News data analysis, indicates that cheating may be behind that success."

Hacker and Benton noted that the school's high scores for third-graders were not repeated in higher grade levels: "The amazing scores came only in the one grade where poor test scores have severe consequences—and, according to cheating experts, educators have a greater incentive to fudge."

A year earlier, Diana Jean Schemo and Ford Fessenden of The New York Times examined the Texas "education miracle" in Houston in 2003, where school officials boasted of higher test scores and academic proficiency.

They reported that "an examination of the performance of students in Houston by The New York Times raises serious doubts about the magnitude of those gains. Scores on a national exam that Houston students took alongside the Texas exam from 1999 to 2002 showed much smaller gains and falling scores in high school reading."

No matter what the testing results are, questions must always be asked:

- Who decides which tests to use and which to reject?
- How much do the tests cost to acquire and score?
- Are comparable school districts using tests that yield more sophisticated results?

In addition, Hacker gives these tips about testing:

- Find out how scores get reported—often, it's in more than one way. No Child Left Behind, the sweeping federal education law, puts the focus on passing rates.
- Also look for scale scores, which are based on raw test scores and can be added, subtracted or averaged.
- Look at your data graphically. What's the distribution of school test scores? Of poverty rates?
- Search for context when reporting and analyzing scores. What makes high-scoring schools different from low-scoring ones? With the SAT, a big factor is the percent of students taking the test. With state scores, it's often the poverty level of students, mobility rates (how often kids change schools), teacher experience or a combination of factors.
- Examine results over time. Any school can have a big jump in test scores from one year to the next. Look at results over three or more years. Sometimes the school that made that big gain one year loses a lot of ground the next.
- Pay attention to the number of students taking the test. If only a few students take the test at one school, one or two scores can skew the results. For example, a chart could show that the greater the number of test takers in a school, the less swing in the results. This also goes for looking at gains or losses from one year to the next.
- Try different ways of reporting scores. Scale scores may be helpful for analysis, but it might also help to explain scores as percentiles—for instance, that a school went from the bottom 25 percent of schools one year to the top 5 percent the next.
- Check your findings with an expert, such as a professor at a local university. You want people to poke holes in the analysis before it's in print or on the air—not after.

- If you're comfortable with basic statistics, try learning regression analysis. It lets you see the relationship between variables—say, test scores and poverty—and make predictions based on that relationship.

Some investigations by newsrooms have found that the low income of a family can sometimes predict low test scores, but others have found that other factors can come into play that instead shift responsibility to teachers and district administrators.

In addition to local experts, there are experts in distant universities who can help, as well as sources at the International Test and Evaluation Association in Fairfax, Va., and other groups that serve as watchdogs of the testing industry, including FairTest in Cambridge, Mass. The Education Writers Association also can point to many groups and resources on No Child Left Behind issues.

While it is important to report on the test results, keep in mind that the placement of children in classes on the basis of standardized tests has itself been questioned. Professor Stanley Greenspan and Washington Post reporter Jacqueline L. Salmon, co-authors of the book "Playground Politics," wrote that standardized testing is unfair and ineffective: "Most standardized tests don't pick up on many of the skills that really count in the 'real world'—creativity, persistence, dedication, problem-solving abilities, the ability to think on your feet even when tense and anxious, a gift for seeing the 'big picture' and a gut-level instinct for making the right move."

School Violence and Discipline

In city after city, schools have been putting new security plans and measures into effect because of school shootings, student violence and gang activity. Yet journalists have found many flaws in those strategies.

Chris Halsne of KIRO-Seattle used records kept by schools to find that violent incidents in high schools were not being reported to the police. In five Tacoma high schools that KIRO looked at, "there were 468 students disciplined for fights, 180 assaults and 123 violent threats," yet police were called just 13 times for fights, 95 times for assaults and 29 times for threatening behavior. "District policy mandates police get called whenever a student gets assaulted or hurt in a fight, but that doesn't usually happen," he reported.

David Olinger and Jeffrey A. Roberts of The Denver Post also found inconsistent reporting when they examined records on violent incidents in Colorado schools. They said the disclosures of school violence vary wildly from one district to another. Some schools reported every punch thrown on the playground, they wrote, but others did not include incidents that police classified as assaults. School guidelines lead some officials to report only those incidents that cause severe injuries. "How accountable are the accountability reports?" Olinger and Roberts asked.

As more schools look for answers to discipline problems, journalists should be asking these questions:

- How effective are security measures in discouraging violence?
- Who chooses the values to stress in the classroom, and how? Can such a theoretical approach possibly improve discipline?
- How do individual teachers keep order in the classroom?
- Is there a written policy adhered to uniformly throughout the school district?
- Are teachers receiving support from parents, or are parents and teachers working at counter purposes?
- Does the Individuals with Disabilities Education Act, a federal law, prevent certain children from being shunted from school to school because of disruptive behavior, or does it keep potentially dangerous students from being removed, due to claims such as attention deficit disorder?

One sensitive question to explore is whether some teachers and administrators abuse authority by singling out students of particular racial or ethnic groups for punishment.

Charlotte Observer reporters Peter Smolowitz and Adam Bell pried data out of the Charlotte-Mecklenburg School District to highlight the district's problems with repeat troublemakers: Some 450 students were suspended more than 10 times each last year; one child was suspended a whopping 31 times, and some kids missed a third of the school year because of suspensions. The district had put out its own analysis of the data, which shed little light on the complex issue.

Misbehavior often is related to trouble at home. When teachers and administrators hear rumors about sexual abuse, domestic violence, divorce and extreme poverty during the school day, do they ignore it or intervene in the family's problems? Do they follow laws that require the reporting of suspected abuse?

Some misbehavior is tied to alcohol and other drug abuse. Police officers in the narcotics division might discuss their perceptions of the school drug problem. It is necessary to verify the alleged problem with arrest reports, records of overdoses, results of locker searches and interviews with students in treatment.

Student Retention

In many schools, students automatically progress to the next grade no matter how poor their academic performance or how disruptive their behavior. In other schools, such students must repeat grades. A journalist can compare a high school's pass-on, repeat and dropout rates, daily attendance and graduation percentages with national and state averages.

One compelling topic to look at is whether poor-performing students are being promoted to the next grade to make the school look good. Such students are compelling subjects for profiles.

At The (Cleveland) Plain Dealer, Ebony Reed and Thomas Gaumer analyzed state education data in 2005 and found that more than 95 percent of Cleveland fourth- and sixth-graders had been promoted at the end of the previous school year, although more than half the students in those grades had failed state reading or math exams. Promotion rates varied among schools and grades, but Reed and Gaumer found that the gap between promotion rates and test scores was more pronounced for black and Hispanic students, who failed the tests more often than their white classmates.

Meanwhile, putting faces on the dropouts and the perpetual absentees will be illuminating no matter what the explanation. Among the questions to explore are these:

- Are talented students leaving school because classes fail to challenge them?
- Are overworked student counselors allowing students to slip through the cracks?

Many lower-income children doubt that good grades and other signs of learning pay off in society. The Wall Street Journal captured the culture of failure at a Washington, D.C., high school by focusing on a few high-achieving students who were ostracized by classmates and peers who had already dropped out.

Knowing dropout rates can lead to other questions: For those who leave, is there any hope later, such as an easily accessible program leading to a high school equivalency diploma?

Many school districts ask students why they drop out in order to provide statistics about the reasons. But investigative journalists have found dropout statistics to be confusing, unreliable or outright false. Education Week reported that states, school districts and federal researchers may all use different methods and definitions to tally up how many students have dropped out of high school. Thus the results can vary enormously—which is why high school dropout numbers can be notoriously unreliable.

The LA Weekly reported on how an inner-city Los Angeles high school masked its dropout rate by keeping "ghost" students on its enrollment list. The fraud gave the school "a breather from chronic overcrowding" and allowed it to keep its funding. It pointed to the larger problem that the state of California does not conform to widely accepted standards for counting dropouts honestly and accurately.

Curriculum

Most schools track students by placing them in classes based on ability, but the prevalence of this policy has failed to diminish the debate over it. Journalists who look at tracking should ask these questions:

- Does placement seem to be based on race, ethnicity or class?
- Are students in the lower tracks given the opportunity to move to college preparatory classes if it turns out the original placement was mistaken?
- Does tracking benefit gifted children and hinder slower learners?

Journalists also should investigate textbooks when considering a school's choice of curriculum. In many districts, teachers, administrators, parents or school board members may sit behind closed doors to choose textbooks. Despite their deliberation, they may choose books that are factually inaccurate, poorly written or biased. In some school districts, religious and ideological groups pressure school boards and publishers to delete or change the text. By understanding the selection process and seeking documents related to it, a journalist can ferret out which books were chosen and which rejected, and why.

Even when textbooks are chosen openly and honestly, controversies abound. For instance, how do reading teachers choose among textbooks that rely on completely different theories? Each academic discipline has its own philosophical disagreements about how and what to teach. One ongoing controversy is over Darwinism and the theory of evolution. Debate about Darwinism versus creationism or intelligent design gets mixed into the controversy about religion in the classroom, as it did in 2005 in Kansas, Pennsylvania and other states. In those states, parents and politicians have pushed to include curriculum that is not science-based to refute theories of evolution.

Class Size

Investigating class size is not complicated because it is a quantitative matter. Journalists writing about class size should know about state laws, district policies and national guidelines for class size. When class sizes are larger than allowed by law, who is responsible?

Technology and Corporate Sponsorship

As schools become increasingly dependent on computers, committees created to choose hardware and software will hold the same type of power as those choosing textbooks. Schools attended by wealthy families and with parent-teacher associations that are good at raising money tend to have more computers than schools in low-income areas. Why do those disparities exist, and what are the effects on the students?

If a computer manufacturer offers machines at little or no cost, should the school board accept, thereby helping the company build its customer base to the exclusion of competitors? Corporations are influencing the availability and content of instructional materials in classrooms by supplying them free in times of tight budgets. Local businesses get their messages into schools through the noblest sounding of programs, such as "Partners in Education." A business "adopts" a school. The arrangement seems sincerely altruistic, but in some cases the motivation is building goodwill on the way to increasing corporate profits or influencing the content of classroom instruction. Journalists should find out what the school's policies are on accepting corporate sponsorship.

Sometimes, there is misspending on computer equipment not because of closeness to a corporation, but because a school system wants to modernize its technology too quickly. The Atlanta Journal-Constitution did an investigation into the amount of funds wasted on expensive technology in Atlanta public schools. The school system purchased pricey equipment and installed an unnecessary, expensive network for the Internet. The district purchased everything in response to a national program called E-rate, which helps schools initiate an Internet infrastructure but does not purchase the actual computers. Reporters discovered that the school district spent a lot of money on equipment it didn't need or couldn't use. Because the schools did not take bids, they were often overcharged and chose the most expensive Internet and network components.

Special-Needs Students

In most schools, the term special needs is used to refer to children who are mentally or physically disabled. Federal regulations identify more than a dozen disabilities.

An investigative journalist should inquire whether the school district neglects special-needs children, forcing them into distant state schools, private schools or home schooling. If the local school district does have special-education programs, a journalist can find out whether the special-needs students are segregated or mainstreamed. Mainstreaming, sometimes called inclusion, means that the special-needs children take classes with nondisabled students of the same age at the neighborhood school. Both approaches—segregation and inclusion—raise difficult issues. If a school district chooses inclusion, how does it afford the extra costs associated with it, and how do teachers and other students respond?

In a classic story, U.S. News and World Report found too many students being placed in special education because of financial incentives from the federal government. The results: students with relatively minor learning disabilities being unfairly labeled as impaired learners, a bloated bureaucracy with a separate transportation system and angry parents and teachers.

An investigation by Wisconsin Public Television found that children with special learning needs in Wisconsin were not being educated adequately. To establish that the system was flawed, the reporter used federal and state court records, complaints filed at the Office of Civil Rights, state and federal regulations covering special education and articles in academic journals.

Because the federal government requires extensive documentation for every special-needs student, schools should have plenty of material for journalists to examine. Parents can be good sources too if they are willing to share student records.

Racial, Class and Gender Equity

Although many school districts are considered officially desegregated, minority students sometimes end up clustered in certain schools. A journalist should look closely at the student numbers by school to see whether the school is truly desegregated. Where the public schools are open to all, white children may attend all-white private schools, creating de facto segregation. The white children remaining in the public schools may come from low-income families, creating segregation by economic class. Journalists should also study whether busing students outside their neighborhoods, often over long distances, has a negative impact on their learning.

In schools with significant racial diversity, a journalist can determine through observation if desegregation means true integration. For instance, do students from different races and ethnic groups mix in the lunchroom, or do they cluster exclusively at race-specific tables? If they cluster, what role, if any, should teachers and administrators play in encouraging mixing? The journalist also can look at whether faculty and administrators are racially and culturally diverse.

Whatever the level of integration, government agencies expect schools to promote multiculturalism in the classroom and in extracurricular activities. A journalist can examine whether multiculturalism has become de facto resegregation, in which every race and ethnic group has its own curriculum and its own extracurricular clubs. An observant journalist will check such details as whether all students are encouraged to attend events by extracurricular ethnic student clubs.

When investigating gender equity, journalists should explore these issues:

- In physical education classes and after-school athletics, are female students given the same options as male students?
- Do interscholastic sports for females receive as much funding as sports for males?
- Are females encouraged or required to enroll in industrial arts?
- Are males encouraged or required to enroll in home economics?

School Choice

As noted, sometimes students attend schools outside their neighborhoods because of mandatory busing to achieve desegregation or because of centralized special-needs classes. Other times, the reasons are questionable or skirt the rules, as when parents use permits to get their children into schools outside their neighborhoods because of alleged child care arrangements or by claiming medical problems. Beyond such individual situations, school choice has become a sociopolitical movement. In his book "School Choice: The Struggle for the Soul of American Education," Peter W. Cookson Jr. asks and answers questions like these:

- Should families be able to decide which schools their children attend on the basis of any factor except neighborhood?
- Does increased competition among schools for students really lead to higher-quality education?
- Are school choice laws logistically feasible and economically viable?
- What happens to schools not chosen by many families?

Charter schools are on the rise. As the Education Writers Association says, charter schools are public schools that are freed from most local, state and federal mandates but nevertheless receive public funds.

The EWA named charter schools a hot topic at the beginning of this decade and cited two studies as helpful. A report by Bruce Fuller and the staff of the Policy Analysis for California Education at the University of California–Berkeley estimated that one out of five children is attending a school outside his or her assigned one. The U.S. Department of Education commissioned a study to track charter schools' growth and impact and showed that the number of schools continues to proliferate.

As the number of charter schools has risen, so have press inquiries into them. The East Valley Tribune in Mesa, Ariz., found that Arizona's charter school movement had experienced serious problems. People with criminal backgrounds and little education were teaching, schools were closing from financial mismanagement and the charter schools, which are supposed to be held more accountable than public schools, were actually less accountable.

The Philadelphia Inquirer's Connie Langland and Dale Mezzacappa reported on a charter school's manager "who has turned Chester Community Charter School into a profitable, expanding business in the heart of the virtually bankrupt school district." The reporters found that the management company had a 20-year contract with the school's board of trustees that both refused to make public, although the county has paid the company about $10 million over a six-year period, with a large percent of that going toward the company's management fee. The Inquirer's examination of the school's finances was based on state data and financial reports and six years of federal tax filings.

Investigating School Personnel and Facilities

Teachers

When Chicago Tribune team members examined the city's schools, they found a fourth-grade classroom in which all 22 students had to attend summer school. The reason? Their teacher was so incompetent that the children failed to learn enough to move to fifth grade. Four previous schools had tried unsuccessfully to remove the teacher from classroom work.

Obviously, it pays for journalists to examine the quality of teaching. States set a minimum score to pass the National Teacher Examinations, prepared by the Educational Testing Service in Princeton, N.J. A journalist can check a state's certification standards, including how they compare with other states. In Mississippi, reporters found that the required score was so low that only 3 percent of those taking the test nationally would have failed.

About half the states allow certification without a degree from an education college. Teacher fellowship programs have been created in New York and other states, and the outcome of those programs deserves scrutiny. Journalists can ask if any of this is working to improve the quality of education. Many education colleges themselves are not accredited by the National Council for Accreditation of Teacher Education, Washington, D.C., whose accreditation is probably the most recognized. Journalists should see whether training is demonstrably inferior at unaccredited schools than in those institutions that have won accreditation. However teachers prepare, journalists should question what they actually learn about how children acquire knowledge and how to manage a classroom. Investigators can interview current and past education professors, classroom teachers, administrators, parents and students for some answers.

In Florida, a series of articles in the Sarasota Herald-Tribune examined equality among schools by looking specifically at teacher qualifications. The reporters found that thousands of teachers struggled to pass basic skills tests and that one in three teachers failed an exam at least one time. Furthermore, the reporters found that the teachers who struggled the most on the tests were funneled into poor and minority schools, while those who did well went to wealthier white schools.

Interviews should be supplemented with extended observation in education colleges and children's classrooms. In a Columbia Journalism Review article headlined "The Beat Nobody Wants," Mary Ellen Schoonmaker quoted a principal: "Teachers and the complexities of their lives are not represented. People don't know what it's like to have 170 kids in a high school each week. It's a backbreaking, bonebreaking job."

Teacher burnout, as this principal suggests, is an underreported problem. Some advocates say low teacher salaries are a factor causing burnout and affecting the overall quality of instruction.

In addition to teachers who never achieve competence, journalists have found working teachers who are convicted felons or of questionable character by comparing a database of teachers with prison records.

Teachers who also coach should be scrutinized with extra care because they have more opportunities for taking advantage of students than the average teacher does. Furthermore, their sins tend to be overlooked or forgiven in an atmosphere of winning at all costs.

The Seattle Times found dozens of public school coaches who had been disciplined for sexual misconduct with students being passed on to other schools despite their dangerous records. As the paper's stories showed, administrators often try to keep disciplinary proceedings secret, whether they involve a coach or a teacher. A journalist should delve into a district's procedures for checking potential teachers and should also find out how the district handles requests for information about former problem teachers who are seeking employment elsewhere.

Administrators

Many principals and districtwide superintendents served as teachers (and often coaches) before becoming administrators. A journalist should check whether they received any training in administration before or after they were promoted. Furthermore, a journalist should check to see whether a local or national search was conducted and whether an excellent local candidate was ignored during the excitement of conducting a high-profile, high-cost national search. In addition, a journalist must always check on the accuracy of an administrator's résumé. There is much pressure in education to exaggerate credentials.

The ultimate supervisors of principals and superintendents are usually elected, unsalaried school board members. They are likely to be dependent on the administrators for information, a system that often reduces board members to nothing more than rubber stamps for everything from curriculum changes to salary increases. On the other hand, individual board members may be extremely ideological or disruptive.

One study of school boards found that although 30 percent of public school students are nonwhite, only a small percentage of local board members are nonwhite. In an increasing number of school board races, candidates are running on single-issue platforms, with low voter turnouts making it more likely they will be elected. Board members are being sued more often by students, teachers and staff; those lawsuits are discouraging some of the best people from serving.

Some districts have already shifted to school-based management, allowing a council of teachers, staff and parents to choose principals and vote on policy questions. In these cases, journalists should ask if the councils represent the diversity of the student body and the community at large.

Where traditionally chosen boards exist, journalists should research whether members are steering school district contracts, administrative jobs and teaching positions to business partners, friends and relatives. Do they have instructional agendas they would like to impose on classroom teachers? These are not theoretical situations; the IRE Resource Center contains examples of each of these abuses.

School Staff

It takes more than teachers and administrators to make a school work. But because support personnel tend to be poorly paid, schools often attract less than the cream of the labor force. Journalists have obtained lists of bus drivers from school districts or transportation companies, matched names with state motor vehicles databases, and found speeding tickets, alcohol-related offenses and other violations, including child molestation.

Even if the drivers are safe, the buses may not be. An investigation by WCBD-TV in Charleston, S.C., revealed "safety problems on school buses . . . including bad brakes and tires, dangerous seats, windshields recalled for safety problems and faulty governors designed to keep bus speed down as required by law. . . . Maintenance shop staff were performing shoddy workmanship and the supervisor was using the garage for his personal projects." That situation raises questions about why the bus company received a transportation contract in the first place and whether the district administration was monitoring the contract.

School lunch programs sometimes present an opportunity for board members and administrators to hire family members or others suggested by local politicians. In a story that can be easily localized, NBC Dateline found widespread problems in school food programs around the country.

Custodians, playground supervisors, secretaries and other support personnel also should be scrutinized for efficiency and to make sure they want to be around children for the proper reasons. No reporter can check the record of every such employee, but spot checks are practical. At the least, a reporter can write about the school district's own system of checking.

School Buildings

The title of a study from the Education Writers Association says it well: "Wolves at the Schoolhouse Door—An Investigation of the Condition of Public School Buildings." An investigator who looks at buildings from the inside will often notice significant problems. Why did administrators allow such deterioration? Where will the money come from for repairs? If repairs are left undone, what physical dangers might result? What harm to learning is likely in such an environment? What is the status of air-conditioning and heating systems?

By examining a billion-dollar bond program to repair schools, The Detroit News found that many district officials paid for work that was never performed, hired inexperienced companies to manage the construction work and awarded contracts without competitive bids.

Jason Grotto and Deborah Cenziper at The Miami Herald analyzed data from Miami-Dade's school construction program and found that the school district "has routinely covered the signs of sloppy and incomplete construction by demanding that its own maintenance force fix sweeping deficiencies in new schools, diverting crucial dollars from aging campuses waiting for repairs and upgrades."

Overcrowding is a common building problem. Journalists should visit as many schools in the district as possible, looking for tangible evidence of overcrowding. One rough but objective measure is square feet per student. In general, newer schools are less cramped than older buildings.

Fire safety is another issue journalists may want to investigate. Nate Carlisle and Jessica Ravitz of The Salt Lake Tribune reported on the state of fire inspections in public schools, following a fire that destroyed a junior high school that was old and did not have modern fire safety features. They wrote that state records show that some Utah schools have no record of fire inspections since the 1980s.

Asbestos within schools has been a continuing problem. The federal Asbestos Hazard Emergency Response Act requires districts to inspect for asbestos and then devise a removal or abatement plan. Some state laws were in place before the federal law, but many were more lax. Journalists can ask whether their state has been granted a waiver because the state law is as stringent as the federal law.

KTHI-TV in Fargo, N.D., found that not a single local school had been inspected for asbestos and that the government had done nothing to punish the schools for violating the law. On the other hand, some schools are not given adequate time and money to deal with the problem. Amid the controversy, journalists should ask whether asbestos hazards have been overstated. Is covering exposed asbestos an adequate response, rather than the far more expensive, and hazardous, process of removal?

Radon is another issue that journalists can explore. WBNS in Columbus, Ohio, discovered that the radon levels in Ohio schools were almost three times the national average, meaning that many schoolchildren were put at greater risk for lung cancer through daily exposure to the radioactive gas. Reporters found that of all of Ohio's public schools, only 11 percent even tested for radon. Of those that did tests, many did not fix the problems.

Approaches to Investigating the Schools

When at the Lansing (Mich.) State Journal, Lisa Gutierrez noted that it rarely makes sense to cover education in the traditional way: by attending school board meetings. "Meetings reveal what administrators want the public to know, not necessarily what it should know," she wrote. "Meetings don't tell you that the budget cuts being discussed mean students will keep using history books written in the 1960s." It is the "why" that interests Gutierrez the most: "Why can't Johnny or Jane read when they graduate? Why do children need middle schools?" To learn the why, Gutierrez cultivated teachers as sources: "The most important books I own are school district directories with home phone numbers for employees."

Gutierrez cultivated parents as sources, too, and attended the opening PTA meeting of each school year, making sure to hand out business cards. "They won't always call you first, but you can count on a few good whistleblowers in the bunch," she said. Another locale for sources is the state department of education. Gutierrez suggested getting to know the numbers people—the ones who conduct opinion polls on education and keep statistics about dropouts and test scores.

Her favorite sources, however, were the students. "If you can't talk to young children and teenagers, stay away from education reporting," she said. Gutierrez was able to find stories in what other reporters might consider fluff: Her assigned feature on a Hispanic graduation ceremony became a way to discuss why Hispanics drop out of high school at almost twice the district average.

While making sure to work the human resources, it is equally important to gather all the reports and studies possible. Story ideas flow from the materials collected by schools as they prepare for accreditation, a process almost all schools—elementary, secondary and postsecondary—are required to complete. The state government sets accreditation standards for public elementary and secondary schools. If accreditation is granted provisionally or is denied, the school has to submit follow-up reports about problems. The Council of Chief State School Officers, Washington, D.C., can sort out state-by-state rules.

Accrediting agencies are not the only ones evaluating schools. Government advisory committees, blue-ribbon private panels and public-spirited foundations make recommendations every year on improving quality.

Following the Money

Schools are big-money operations, which means that they can be scrutinized like other government programs: by following the money. A journalist can begin with the budget, comparing line items and totals with previous years to see what shifts in funding have occurred. All educational institutions purchase goods and services, from test tubes for chemistry class to drug abuse workshops for high school teachers. A journalist should look at what goods or services require bids (see Chapter 8) and then monitor the process. Most of all, money in education is supposed to be a means to an end: learning.

Keeping buildings safe, reducing class sizes and supplying up-to-date text-books require money. A district's revenue stream affects what occurs in the classroom, even if there is no direct correlation between dollars spent and quality of education. While wrestling with the relationships among revenue, expenditures and quality of education, an investigative journalist must first determine how much money schools have available to educate students.

One approach is to break out expenditures school by school. Many journalists do their calculating at the district level rather than the individual school level. The trouble with that approach is that many districts allocate expenditures unequally from school to school. Whether this is done intentionally or not, schools in well-to-do neighborhoods can fare better than schools in lower-income neighborhoods, an equation that favors political clout over need.

In some states, courts have ruled that the property tax system violates principles of fairness. But few states have found an alternative that makes a clear majority happy. State lotteries have been one of the most highly touted solutions, but lotteries may shift some of the burden to the poor.

School districts often sell bonds to generate money, and the most complete view of income and expenditures often can be obtained from information about these transactions. An offering statement, called a prospectus, discloses the district's finances to members of the public who are considering buying the bonds. Bond-rating agencies establish the creditworthiness of the district, thus influencing how well the bonds sell. Journalists should investigate any drop in a district's bond rating and investigate its cause. The principal independent bond-rating agencies are Standard & Poor's Corp. and Moody's Investors Services, both in New York City.

Besides cash from property taxes and bond sales, a school district might generate revenue from landholdings. A reporter can find out about school-owned property by running the name of the institution through the county assessor's or recorder's office. Reporters from The (Jackson, Miss.) Clarion-Ledger found that school districts were failing to take advantage of state land set aside to be leased out for their benefit. The reporters showed that thousands of acres were under lease for pennies an acre annually. That was great for the leaseholder but not for the school district's treasury.

In some locales, the largest percentage of funding comes from a central appropriation (usually tax revenue allocated by the legislature to state education agencies), supplemented by the federal government (funds usually earmarked by Congress to be channeled through executive branch agencies to local districts). The nature of funding sources can point to many possible stories. For example, a school district can be overly dependent on federal funds, making it especially susceptible to unforeseen budget cuts. Another school district may fail to take advantage of federal money, depriving its students of opportunities.

While studying the revenue flow, a journalist should also explore the other side of the ledger, concentrating on expenses that seem unrelated to quality education. Any budget entry might be interesting. In West Virginia, The Charleston Gazette reported that the superintendent misused thousands of dollars in public and private funds, making more than 1,700 personal phone calls on a state-issued credit card and accepting more than $99,000 from a nonprofit organization whose contributors included some of the largest corporations in the state.

Contracts awarded by elected or appointed school boards include those for construction, transportation of students, teacher training, food for the lunchroom and supplies. As with any other contract, the journalist should check whether those in charge are skirting the law by awarding no-bid contracts or tailoring the bid for a specific vendor.

In New York City, a contract for construction of a high school went $50 million over budget. State officials found evidence of bid rigging, bribes and phony construction company invoices paid by board of education employees who apparently were parties to the falsification. At the time that arrests took place, a New York Times reporter quoted an investigator explaining why the inquiry took nine years. The board of education, she said, "has loads of bureaus and lots of people with titles that don't match their jobs. There were officials with very important sounding titles that did not have much real power and others with lowly titles but a lot of important responsibility. It was very hard to figure out."

Private Schools

Private schools are tougher to investigate than public schools. Most states do provide information about accredited private schools, allowing an investigator to compare class sizes, test scores, teacher salaries and elective offerings. But finding out about unaccredited private schools can be more difficult. A local private school association might supply some information. County health and fire departments should share information about the school buildings. Many private schools are nonprofit and tax exempt. That means they might file a Form 990 informational tax return with the Internal Revenue Service, a document that must be checked. A journalist should also check to see whether there are any lawsuits involving the school.

Homeschooling

Many parents who school their children at home do so because of religious beliefs. Others are motivated less by religion and more by the fear of secular humanism. Still others have no specific religion or ideology to promote but turn to homeschooling because they believe the public schools provide second-rate education.

Investigators can check whether the state education department issues guidelines for homeschooling. Some states treat home schools similarly to private schools, with no certification required for teachers. The states' lack of common guidelines for homeschooling raises questions:

- If a homeschooler wants to enroll in public school or plans to enter college, what documentation must parents show about the coverage of certain subjects?
- What if a homeschooled student appears to be way ahead of his public school peer group but does poorly on standardized tests because of inexperience with such tests?
- If parents are teaching racial discrimination, hatred of homosexuals or other doctrines that would be unacceptable in public school classrooms, should authorities be able to intervene?

Vocational and Trade Schools

An investigative journalist should research how well public vocational schools and private trade schools provide vocational training. Here are some questions to ask:

- Are the programs set up so that participants avoid the label of "low achiever"?
- Do the programs offer employers the quality and quantity of workers needed?
- Are students prepared for high-technology industries as well as for traditional manual-labor jobs?

State employment agency officials can be interviewed, as can employers themselves.

Overall, journalists tend to overlook public vocational high schools, even though they deserve scrutiny. Reporters who have looked into these schools sometimes have discovered school officials having free work done on their cars and houses and funds being diverted for unnecessary travel. Trade schools for high school dropouts and graduates also deserve more scrutiny.

The Sacramento Bee found that students who signed up for vocational schools—seeking training in computers, health care and cosmetology, among other fields of study—filed 1,177 complaints to California's Bureau for Post-secondary and Vocational Education in a two-year period. The newspaper found that bureau administrators admitted to being passive regarding student complaints, which were most often about school fraud, false advertising and failure to make refunds. It also found that schools failed, with impunity, to report satisfactory graduation and job-placement records, as required by law. Indeed, the federal regulators opened an investigation of one company for possible falsified attendance records, grades and job-placement statistics, none of which was caught by California's bureau.

Issues in Higher Education

Billions of tax dollars and other public support go to higher education because the public depends on its colleges and universities to prepare students for jobs and vocations that keep the country healthy and moving forward.

But colleges and universities are often resistant to scrutiny, reluctant to release information and have open discussions, and more tempted to create educational policies and practices based on politics or government and corporate funding than on students and educational philosophy.

Because of these shortcomings—real or potential—journalists and student journalists need to routinely perform watchdog journalism on campuses. Such investigations touch on numerous areas: campus crime, research grants, annual spending, the influence of donors and corporations, misconduct in sports programs, fraternities, alcoholism, courses, and nonprofit institutes associated with the university.

We will review many different kinds of investigations (but not nearly all) in the remainder of this chapter. For mid-career journalists, some of these investigations will be easier than others. In addition, they will not face the same kinds of pressures or possible censorship that student journalists or their faculty advisers could face.

Document Trails

No matter how a school tries to keep its activities private, an abundance of information is available, including a long trail of documents revealing how the school functions.

Whether it is a public university, a private college or a community college, each school has its own associations, accrediting bodies, publications and books written about it. Its Web site will be full of information about the school. Its revenues and expenditures will be public in one format or another. Its property will be listed in local county offices. Many of its contracts will go out to bid. The lawsuits in which it is involved will be at the local courthouse.

For tips and resources for investigating issues in higher education, see the "Resources for Reporting" section at the end of this chapter. No matter what the issue, a good starting place is The Chronicle of Higher Education.

Public University Revenues and Expenditures

As mentioned throughout this book, a useful way to start an investigation is by following the money. Universities are big-budget enterprises. Income arrives from state legislative appropriations, congressional funding funneled through the U.S. Department of Education and other federal agencies, tuition and fees from students, gifts from institutional and individual donors, athletic revenues and sales by university-owned businesses. Much of this income can be tracked, even when the university is uncooperative. For example, gifts from overseas must be reported to the Department of Education as part of legislation intended to track foreign influence.

A large part of funding involves athletics programs, which may or may not be the big moneymaker a university says it is. Reporters often have to file freedom-of-information requests to obtain athletic department budgets, and sometimes separate independent funds are not included in response to those requests.

Local universities sometimes take money that legislators have earmarked for a specific project that escapes competitive merit reviews. It is common for public universities to employ lobbyists at the state level or even the federal level or to help fund lobbyists for a group of universities. Just following the activities of the university lobbyists can lead to fascinating stories.

At the same time, universities seek to establish or increase large endowments from which they use investment income to fund programs. Endowments give universities independence from political meddling by legislators and also sometimes independence from public scrutiny of how they invest or use the money.

Tracking how the endowment money is invested and spent can be another productive route for journalists. Activists have criticized universities for what they considered morally incorrect investments, and investigative journalists have looked at the cost of managing the money. The Wall Street Journal, for example, looked into who manages university endowments and found that some managers are paid more than anyone else on campus, sometimes more than a million dollars a year.

Journalists also can examine the compensation of high-level administrators and some professors. Universities will say they are simply being competitive with private industry, but a reporter should check that assertion. Some university officials fail to understand how perceived lavishness will upset students, faculty, staff and taxpayers. They fail to see the anger that their high salaries, subsidized mansions, and chauffeured limousines will produce when contrasted with financially strapped students who are taking full course loads, simultaneously working one or two jobs and accumulating significant debt from student loans.

Accreditation Documents

A university's accreditation process can provide a journalist with vast resources on the quality of its education. The University of Missouri, for example, is examined by the North Central Association of Colleges and Schools, Commission on Institutions of Higher Education, Chicago, one of six such regional organizations. Specific academic programs receive accreditation separately. The Missouri School of Journalism, for instance, is accredited by the Association for Education in Journalism and Mass Communication. When dealing with public institutions, obtaining the accrediting body's full report, sometimes running to hundreds of pages, should pose few problems because of access laws. If a private university refuses to provide a copy, the state agency for higher education may have a copy. If the university operates a teaching program on a military base, the base commander or educational liaison officer may also have a copy.

The following documents often emerge during the accreditation process.

The Self-Study   Compiled by the university's faculty-administration committee, the self-study provides an internal look at strengths and weaknesses in curricula, faculty credentials, administrative operations, financial stability and the gamut of other issues that the university faces. Self-studies usually must be obtained from the university.

The Visiting Team Report This report is likely to be more objective and hard-hitting than the self-study and should include the following:

- A recommendation on accreditation status
- A statement on the university's mission and whether it has been achieved
- An evaluation of the short- and long-range planning mechanisms at the school
- An assessment of administrative performance, particularly if the school faces morale or financial problems
- An assessment of general education patterns
- A judgment on financial stability
- An analysis of development activity
- An analysis of faculty credentials overall
- A comparison of faculty salary levels with those at competing institutions
- The role of faculty in governing
- An analysis of students' academic credentials, geographic spread, educational interests and retention rates
- Evaluation of the physical plant

The Final Action The final action of the accrediting association's governing body may be obtained from the accrediting association or the individual school. The final action accredits the school while suggesting improvements or may withhold full accreditation until changes are made.

Follow-up Reports Accrediting associations might require universities to submit follow-up reports on trouble spots, such as a weak core curriculum or financial instability, within a year to three years after accreditation is extended. A university may receive full accreditation for 10 years, but a follow-up report may prompt downgrading to provisional accreditation or withholding of further accreditation.

The Scorecard

An alternative to accreditation reports is the scorecard required by legislatures as part of the accountability movement. The Chronicle of Higher Education once noted that the West Virginia report card "offers 275 pages of information on public colleges, including narratives on each college, statistics on enrollment over the past six years, the age of undergraduates and college budgets. Then the report compares the institutions according to several criteria, including scores on college entrance exams, students' cumulative grade-point averages, campus crime rates, and, where applicable, the amount of sponsored research."

University Catalogs

Sometimes the most comprehensive document is a university's catalog, which amounts to a prospectus. A catalog usually contains the following:

- The accreditation status
- A mission statement
- Admissions procedures, including approximate high school rank and standardized test scores
- Policies on the release of student information
- Requirements for majors and graduation
- Tuition, room, board, book and other fees
- Financial aid and eligibility requirements
- Information on counseling, advising services, and health care
- Student organizations
- Residence hall policies
- Descriptions of the campus physical plant
- Officers and trustees
- Faculty and their academic background
- Alumni association information

Enrollment and Retention

With the budget information and accreditation report, a reporter can start to focus on different areas of the school, particularly the students and how they are selected and encouraged to finish their degrees.

A good place to begin is to look at admission policies. Here are some questions:

- What goals in student test scores and scholarship does the university have?
- What is the disparity in tuition for in-state and out-of-state students?
- What are the policies on encouraging diversity and affirmative action?
- What is the acceptance rate of students by the university and the acceptance rate by the students of the university?

Diversity, Disabilities and Affirmative Action

The Chronicle of Higher Education publishes online many statistics on enrollment by ethnicity and by gender for about 4,200 colleges and universities. But diversity and affirmative action programs mean more than consideration for students with certain ethnicities.

The Chronicle of Higher Education once learned that universities that were violating the rights of women and the disabled were requesting "letters of finding" from the Department of Education's Office for Civil Rights. In each case, The Chronicle found, the federal government reached an agreement to bring the college into compliance with the law. The Chronicle noted that the colleges generally did not have to acknowledge guilt as part of the agreements but had to promise to make certain changes in policies by specific dates. Once accepted, students from disadvantaged backgrounds are less likely to enroll if financial aid is unavailable. Financial aid falls into three general categories: grants (including scholarships and tuition waivers), part-time employment and low-interest loans. An investigative journalist can ask these questions:

- Is financial assistance available to all needy students?
- If so, how is assistance allocated?
- If not, how is the scarce money allocated?
- How many students have loans tied to the Student Loan Marketing Association (Sallie Mae), a private company chartered by the U.S. Congress as a government-sponsored enterprise?
- What is the default rate on student loans?
- Does the school effectively collect delinquent loans?
- Does the school get federal money by misrepresenting the qualifications of students?

Each type of financial aid has its procedures, which a journalist can learn by reading the legislation that created the aid and regulations implementing it. Then the journalist has the guidelines and laws against which to measure the school's performance.

A savvy journalist will take the next step by examining retention and graduation rates. If the rates are low or surprisingly high when compared to similar institutions, then it's time to do an in-depth investigation on admission policies, grading policies, and special programs to retain students.

In the Classroom

Most class syllabuses are published on the Web now but are seldom scrutinized by journalists, even though syllabuses present a clear outline of what's being taught on campuses. Among the questions journalists should be asking are these:

- Is the reading list current?
- Who decides what values are taught?
- Do the course materials reflect multiculturalism or some kind of bias?
- Do the course materials avoid certain facts because of fear of controversy?

Journalists can look at how student or faculty conduct affects education and also how a school deals with fraud and plagiarism. When questions about student conduct come up, universities sometimes convene disciplinary boards, consisting of faculty, students and administrators. These groups deal with questions of cheating and are often confidential. Nonetheless, they should keep aggregate numbers each year on the cases they deal with.

Grading policies are worthy of inquiry. Journalists can look at the number of A's and B's given and consider whether the school is devaluing grades or just ensuring that students have a chance at graduate schools that ignore students who receive C's. Journalists can ask whether, in a time of overall grade inflation, educators are considering whether it is better to just have high pass/fail standards.

The grades of student athletes often come under scrutiny, especially given scandals in higher education where administrators have fraudulently allowed athletes to pass classes so they would be eligible to play sports.

Outside the Classroom

Many universities are major property owners, not just on the campus, but throughout town. During the past decade, newsrooms at colleges have often reported on fire code violations at dorms and off-campus housing, especially after fires have killed one or more students. For example, a year after three students were killed in a Seton Hall dorm fire in New Jersey, journalists found that most dorms at the university lacked sprinklers. But journalists can perform an important public service by methodically examining building and fire inspections before a tragedy occurs.

Journalists should examine the condition of private rental properties for students and determine whether landlords are following the laws regarding evictions and security deposits. In addition, journalists should scrutinize not only the living conditions and code violations at fraternities and sororities, but also the issues of hazing, underage drinking and violent activities at some houses.

Another area to scrutinize is the health services provided for students. Questions can be asked and documents checked about accessibility, services offered, the cost and the professional qualifications of the staff at student health clinics.

Athletics

Improprieties in sports programs have become a staple of investigative reporters who now look at the money required for these programs, the influence of boosters, the prevalence of special tutors for the athletes and the program's general management.

Since the athletes are also supposed to be students, a journalist can explore these issues:

- Do athletes graduate at much lower rates than other students, and what are the graduation rates for student athletes in each sport?
- Do the athletes receive special treatment to keep them eligible for competition?
- Did the athletes attend a community college before going to the university, and what were their academic records at those colleges?
- Are professors and teaching assistants pressured to pass star athletes?
- Do athletes get donated cars to drive and special parking privileges? (An investigation in California revealed that football players were using disability tags to get prime parking spots.)

Rick Linsk was one of the St. Paul Pioneer Press reporters who worked on the University of Minnesota men's basketball academic fraud scandal in 1999, a story that won a Pulitzer Prize in 2000. The St. Paul Pioneer Press team reported that University of Minnesota basketball team staff members wrote more than 400 papers for at least 18 players over a five-year period. The story led to a nine-month, $2.2 million investigation by the university, the departure of the coach and staff members and NCAA sanctions against the university.

In a tip sheet for investigating college athletics, Linsk suggested that investigative journalists acquire these documents:

- The university's course catalog, which lists the course name, days scheduled, instructor and credits. Some universities publish their catalogs on the Web, but Linsk suggests actually getting the source data behind what's on the Web since it might be more complete.
- The university's staff directory, which includes phone numbers and e-mail addresses for faculty members, their department and perhaps the courses they teach.
- Sports program budget data. (Comparisons may be available at the NCAA Web site.)
- Team and coaches' travel and expense records.

- Student housing subsidies.
- Graduation data for athletes, such as the data available at www.ncaa.org/grad_rates.
- Nonprofit institutional data from the IRS on "exempt organizations" at www.irs.gov/taxstats/charitablestats/article/0,,id=97186,00.html.
- Information on previous NCAA investigations from the searchable database, available through a link at www.ncaa.org/wps/portal.

Campus Safety

A recent national investigation by ABC's Prime Time show, using the publicly available data on campus crime from the FBI, revealed how prevalent violent crime on campuses was and how school administrators downplayed it and failed to take significant action to prevent it. In addition, the ABC investigation was dealing with data that generally underreport incidents.

A classic investigation by the newspapers referred to as the Bees (The Fresno Bee, The Modesto Bee and The Sacramento Bee) examined the reporting of sexual assaults and rapes at University of California campuses and found that the rapes and assaults were seldom made public despite a federal law created to force colleges to report those crimes. "The result: annual crime reports provided to students and parents that create a misleading portrayal of safety at UC campuses," the newspapers said. Similar stories have been done across the country by other newspapers and by USA Today, using statistics reported and released by the FBI as a starting point.

Journalists can investigate the following safety issues on campuses:

- How easy is it to walk in and out of classrooms and dorms?
- When crime occurs, does jurisdiction belong to the university's security force? Is it made up of competent law enforcement officers? Do they carry guns? What training do they receive?
- How often are students the criminals instead of the victims?
- Does the university keep and release information about campus crime, as required by federal law?

Faculty

Journalists should look at the quality of the personnel at universities and colleges, just as they would for any corporation or institution. It is important to realize that universities and colleges do have a different personnel culture that is full of tradition and hierarchy and the idea of permanent job security—tenure—for some.

Starting with faculty, here are some questions to explore:

- How are faculty recruited and hired?
- How are faculty evaluated by staff, deans and administrators?
- Do faculty show up for their classes? How often do assistants teach their classes?
- How do salaries and benefits compare with those of other schools and the private sector?
- How are faculty disciplined, and is discipline overly influenced by politics or ideology?
- How much outside work and consulting are faculty permitted to do?

Journalists should pay close attention to tenure, including the process of getting tenure and the number of faculty on tenure. A tenured professor is a large investment by a school since it is extremely difficult to remove a tenured professor if they become incompetent.

Journalists should also look at adjunct faculty members who are hired to supplement or substitute for regular faculty members. Good adjunct faculty members who are working in the field can be a great boon to a school because they have up-to-date knowledge. But they often are paid very little and sometimes have little extra time for students.

Larger universities may rely heavily on teaching assistants. These questions should be asked if teaching assistants are used:

- How qualified are they?
- Are they screened and trained before teaching?
- Do they speak the same language as the majority of their students?

A growing area of concern in higher education is faculty research. There should be extensive information—from newsletters to databases to press releases—available on what research a university is conducting, how it is funded, who is doing the research and how the research benefits the university and its students.

If research grants come from the government, universities may charge exorbitant overhead costs to cover administrative expenditures that auditors later question. Journalists should always request all federal, state and university audits on grants.

If human subjects are involved, the researcher must file forms showing consent and alleviating concerns about mental or physical harm. Like other universities, the Institutional Review Board at the University of Missouri, consisting of faculty members appointed by the administration, scrutinizes the documentation. Animal research often spawns controversy and internal review as well. A reporter should ask whether research projects involve financial conflicts of interests or pressures from supervisors or sponsors to produce inaccurate data. University faculty members often have to file consulting reports.

Sometimes the money goes for unnecessary projects. The Chronicle of Higher Education has looked at "pork-barrel funds" steered to specific colleges and universities by Congress. One analysis a few years ago showed that Congress directed government agencies to spend more than $1 billion for such projects, a record amount at the time.

Journalists should be alert for professors taking advantage of students psychologically, sexually or professionally. Journalists should see if the university keeps records on cases and should look at the outcome of those investigations and whether they were fairly conducted. Faculty are sometimes unfairly accused; the American Association of University Professors in Washington, D.C., places universities on its censured list for mistreating professors.

Administrators

Several recent journalism investigations of university and college administrators have turned up questionable travel, expenditures and cronyism. An award-winning Nashville TV station found the president of the University of Tennessee taking lavish trips and misspending state money.

Among the documents that journalists can search are account ledgers, invoices, audits, minutes of regents' meetings and college credit card reports.

More broadly, journalists should look at whether a university is top-heavy with academicians-turned-administrators who never enter classrooms or research laboratories. One way to do this is by comparing administrator-faculty ratios with other similar universities.

Like examinations of faculty, journalists should look at the hiring practices of administrators and what extra benefits they receive, such as housing and cars.

The Chronicle of Higher Education polls universities to document administrative salaries. Universities and colleges with nonprofit status might report their highest salaries to the Internal Revenue Service on Form 990.

Support Staff

Secretaries, administrative assistants, custodians, laboratory technicians, computer programmers, bookkeepers, building supervisors, locksmiths, groundskeepers, power plant operators, parking attendants, campus police, and librarians: Without them, a university could barely function, yet journalists usually overlook them when they should be cultivating them as sources. Some questions journalists should ask are these:

- Are support staff paid a living wage? Are they treated with respect? Have staff members found it necessary to unionize because of perceived or actual second-class treatment? (If so, officials of the union locals might be good sources.)
- Are staff given enough money to keep the physical plant from deteriorating? If not, is the short-term neglect penny-wise and pound-foolish for taxpayers?
- What do support staff know about teaching, research, administration and other university functions that those in power may have a reason to hide?

Governing Boards

Finally, there are the governing boards of regents, curators or trustees that oversee universities and colleges. These boards meet only periodically and can easily be buffeted by politics or overly influenced by administrators.

Some governing boards are rubber stamps for the campus president or chancellor. As rubber stamps, they grant huge compensation packages and golden severance parachutes. Sometimes board members are disengaged from the school and only hold their seats because they have made large donations.

Among the issues to explore are these:

- How and why are the members of an institution's board chosen? In many states, the governor appoints curators of public universities, placing them in the political realm.
- Why do they serve? Are they directing university business to friends, or are they promoting their own careers?
- Do they ever mingle with students, faculty, administrators and staff?
- Do they have private business dealings with the school?

⊃ CHECK IT OUT

✓ Get the last three years of your local school system's budget. Find the three largest increases and the three largest decreases in the budget, and determine the reasons for them.

✓ Get a list (preferably a database) of federal grants coming into your local school system, and check into how they are being spent and whether any of them have been audited.

✓ Ask for documents on all school bus accidents over the past three years in your local school system, and determine whether they are increasing or decreasing and whether seat belts would have made a difference in accidents that caused injuries.

✓ Get the graduation rates in athletics for your local college or state university for the past five years. Determine the highest and lowest rates and the biggest change found on one sport team.

RESOURCES FOR REPORTING

General Resources

Education Week, based in Washington, D.C., covers elementary and secondary schooling, while The Chronicle of Higher Education, also based in Washington, D.C., concentrates on the postsecondary world.

Check out the U.S. Department of Education (www.ed.gov) and its statistics pages (www.ed.gov/stats.html). The Web site of the Education Writers Association (www.ewa.org), Washington, D.C., points to recent education stories, hot topics and tips on education reporting. The IRE Resource Center (www.ire.org/resource center) has tip sheets and copies of hundreds of investigations into education.

Other organizations to consult include the American Association for Adult and Continuing Education (www.aaace.org) in Washington, D.C., the National Clearinghouse on Literacy Education (www.ncela.gwu.edu) in Washington, D.C., and the National Middle School Association (www.nmsa.org) in Columbus, Ohio.

The Educational Resources Information Center (www.eric.ed.gov/index.html), a federally funded national information system, is a clearinghouse for 16 different educational topics, including the National Library of Education (www.ed.gov/NLE). AskERIC (http://ericir.syr.edu), a Web site run by Syracuse University, allows users to search more than 1 million abstracts of documents and journal articles on education research and practice.

Barbara White Stack at the Pittsburgh Post-Gazette put together a list of other Web sites helpful to local reporters. Public Agenda's Web site provides links to many education sources and story ideas at www.publicagenda.org/issues/frontdoor.cfm?issue_type=education. Also check out the links to state education agencies at www.ccsso.org/seamenu.html and the Education Commission on States at www.ecs.org.

The following books are good places to start general research:

- "A Guide to Sources of Educational Information," by Marda Woodbury

- "American Higher Education: A Guide to Reference Sources," by Peter P. Olevnik et al.

- "South of Heaven: Welcome to High School at the End of the 20th Century," by Thomas French

- "Small Victories: The Real World of a Teacher, Her Students and Their High School," by Samuel G. Freedman

- "Horace's School: Redesigning the American High School," by Theodore R. Sizer

- "Schooling Without Labels: Parents, Educators and Inclusive Education," by Douglas Biklen

- "All of Us Together: The Story of Inclusion at the Kinzie School," by Jeri Banks

- "Succeeding Against the Odds," by Sally L. Smith

Student Test Scores

These books about testing might prove helpful:

- "Testing, Testing: Social Consequences of the Examined Life," by F. Allan Hanson
- "Underachievers in Secondary School: Education Off the Mark," by Robert S. Griffin
- "None of the Above: Behind the Myth of Scholastic Aptitude," by David Owen
- "The Validity Issue: What Should Teacher Certification Tests Measure?" by Michael L. Chernoff, Paula M. Nassif and William P. Gorth

The organization often criticized in such books, the Educational Testing Service (www.ets.org), Princeton, N.J., has its own body of evidence supporting tests, which should be looked at to ensure balance and fairness. Also consult the Web site of FairTest (www.fairtest.org), Cambridge, Mass.

School Violence and Discipline

The Education Writers Association (www.ewa.org) has set up a Web page with links to materials and organizations on school violence, including the Center for the Prevention of School Violence (www.ncsu.edu/cpsv).

A book to read is Irwin A. Hyman's "Reading, Writing and the Hickory Stick: The Appalling Story of Physical and Psychological Abuse in American Schools."

Additional resources are available from the American Counseling Association (www.counseling.org), Alexandria, Va., and the National Association of School Psychologists (www.nasponline.org), Silver Spring, Md.

Curriculum

The following books discuss curriculum in American schools:

- "Religion and American Education: Rethinking a National Dilemma," by Warren A. Nord
- "The Censors and the Schools," by journalists Jack Nelson and Gene Roberts Jr. In this 1962 book, the team examined textbook controversies before each became among the most celebrated investigators of their era.
- "A Conspiracy of Good Intentions: America's Textbook Fiasco," by Harriet Tyson
- "Lies My Teacher Told Me: Everything Your American History Textbook Got Wrong," by James W. Loewen
- "Crossing the Tracks: How Untracking Can Save America's Schools," by Anne Wheelock

Consult these resources for more information on the curricula of specific disciplines:

- The National Council of Teachers of Mathematics (www.nctm.org), Reston, Va.
- The National Art Education Association (www.naea-reston.org), Reston, Va.

- American Biology Teacher magazine from the National Association of Biology Teachers (www.nabt.org), Reston, Va.
- The American Council on the Teaching of Foreign Languages (www.actfl.org), Yonkers, N.Y.

Special-Needs Students

When researching special education, consult the National Association of State Directors of Special Education (www.nasdse.org), Alexandria, Va., and the Council for Exceptional Children (www.cec.sped.org), Reston, Va.

Links to the publications of the U.S. Department of Education's Office of Special Education and Rehabilitative Services are located at www.ed.gov/about/offices/list/osers/osep/products.html.

Michael S. Rosenberg and Irene Edmond-Rosenberg's book "The Special Education Sourcebook: A Teacher's Guide to Programs, Materials and Information Sources" is a good source for reporters.

Racial, Class and Gender Equity

Here are some books to check out:

- "Simple Justice," by Richard Kluger
- "The Carrot or the Stick for School Desegregation Policy: Magnet Schools or Forced Busing," by Christine H. Rossell
- "Failing at Fairness: How America's Schools Cheat Girls," by Myra Sadker and David Sadker
- "Multicultural Education: Issues and Perspectives," by James A. Banks and Cherry A. McGee Banks

Also contact the National Association for Girls and Women in Sports (www.aahperd.org/nagws), Reston, Va.

School Choice

Peter W. Cookson's book "School Choice: The Struggle for the Soul of American Education" is a good overview of the subject.

Investigating School Personnel and Facilities

Teachers The two major teachers' unions, the National Education Association (www.nea.org) and the American Federation of Teachers (www.aft.org), both based in Washington, D.C., compile national salary data. Also consult the American Association of Colleges for Teacher Education (www.aacte.org), Washington, D.C.

Teachers' perspectives are related by Catherine Collins and Douglas Frantz in their book "Teachers Talking Out of School." To understand the pressures facing teachers, author Tracy Kidder immersed himself in an elementary school classroom for a year to write his book "Among Schoolchildren." Emily Sachar of Newsday did her extended observation from the teacher's desk, spending a year in front of an eighth-grade mathematics classroom. She chronicled that year in her book "Shut Up and Let the Lady Teach." Another valuable book is Barry A. Farber's "Crisis in Education: Stress and Burnout in the American Teacher."

Administrators The following organizations may aid in your research:

- National Association of Secondary School Principals (www.nassp.org), Reston, Va.
- National Association of Elementary School Principals (www.naesp.org), Alexandria, Va.
- National School Boards Association (www.nsba.org), Alexandria, Va.

Approaches to Investigating the Schools

Following the Money Consult Richard Lehne's book "The Quest for Justice: The Politics of School Finance Reform" and the National Association of State Budget Officers, Washington, D.C.

Private Schools These groups can provide perspective on private schools:

- National Association of Independent Schools (www.nais.org), Boston, Mass.
- Council for American Private Education (www.capenet.org), Washington, D.C.
- National Catholic Education Association (www.ncea.org), Washington, D.C.

About half of the private schools in the United States are affiliated with the Catholic Church. The rest are affiliated with other religions, military academies and college preparatory institutes or are specifically for disabled children.

Homeschooling Resources on homeschooling include the following:

- National Center for Home Education (http://nche.hslda.org), Purcellville, Va.
- Home School Legal Defense Association (www.hslda.org), Purcellville, Va.
- Home Education magazine (www.homeedmag.com), Tonasket, Wash.

Issues in Higher Education

National and state-by-state statistics are available in The Chronicle of Higher Education's annual "Almanac Issue" and at http://chronicle.com/stats/archive/archive.htm.

Another source of overview information is the Higher Education Directory, from Higher Education Publications Inc., Falls Church, Va.

At the local level, every campus is teeming with secondary and primary documentary sources, not to mention hundreds of articulate human sources. One resource that too many investigators overlook is the student newspaper. It might be amateurish and less accurate than a professional newspaper, but it is almost always filled with tips unavailable elsewhere.

Some writers have entered the attack mode. Broadsides against higher education include Roger Kimball's book "Tenured Radicals: How Politics Has Corrupted Our Higher Education" and Charles J. Sykes' "ProfScam: Professors and the Demise of Higher Education." The credibility behind their indictments varies from point to point, but their books, and others that have attracted less attention, are worth reading for an understanding of why many university graduates are disenchanted with higher education. There are also hundreds of books presenting less outraged but nonetheless critical overviews of universities. Every week, The Chronicle of Higher Education publishes a listing headlined "New Books on Higher Education."

Journalists investigating trade schools might begin with the Career College Association (www.career.org), Washington, D.C. Those looking into community colleges should consult the American Association of Community Colleges (www .aacc.nche.edu), Washington, D.C., which publishes the Community College Journal. Perspective can also be gained from the book "The Diverted Dream: Community Colleges and the Promise of Educational Opportunity in America," by Steven Brint and Jerome Karabel.

Admissions and Retention More information on admission and retention can be obtained through the National Association of College Admissions Counselors (www.nacacnet.org) in Alexandria, Va., the American Association of Collegiate Registrars and Admissions Officers (www.aacrao.org) in Washington, D.C., and the National Association of Student Financial Aid Administrators (www.nasfaa.org) in Washington, D.C.

Campus Safety The Student Press Law Center publishes a booklet "Covering Campus Crime," which includes suggestions on how to deal with universities that refuse to cooperate with inquiries about crime. Additional resources include the International Association of Campus Law Enforcement Administrators (www .iaclea.org), Hartford, Conn., and "Campus Security and Law Enforcement," by John W. Powell, Michael S. Pander and Robert C. Nielsen.

Outside the Classroom Consult the United States Student Association (www .usstudents.org), Washington, D.C.

Faculty Academe (www.aaup.org/AAUP/pubsres/academe), the magazine of the American Association of University Professors, tips off journalists to many disputes between faculty and administration. The American Association of University Women (www.aauw.org), Washington, D.C., can also add a valuable perspective.

The National Education Association and the American Federation of Teachers, better known for representing faculty below the college level, have organized numerous campuses as well.

Governing Boards The Association of Governing Boards of Universities and Colleges (www.agb.org), Washington, D.C., and Clark Kerr and Marian L. Gade's book "The Guardians: Boards of Trustees of American Colleges and Universities" are both valuable resources.

PART
III

Investigating Business

13

Investigating For-Profit Businesses

This chapter gives an overview of how to investigate businesses, from large publicly traded companies to smaller local businesses to licensed professionals. This chapter is intended to help journalists investigate not just corporations, but local businesses, worker safety, pension funds and product safety. Some projects that could be categorized as business investigations are also in other chapters, such as the bankruptcy court section of Chapter 10.

In 2000, longtime business journalist Diana Henriques of The New York Times wrote a column for The IRE Journal about the necessity of every journalist knowing how to investigate business:

> Although business has been a very powerful force in American society for at least the past 100 years, for much of that time, the influence of business was balanced by other hefty cultural and political forces.
>
> But over the past 20 years, business has quietly survived most of its natural predators. It has entered the bloodstream of the nation. Businessmen were the 20th century's heroes, from J.P. Morgan to Bill Gates. I don't mean to suggest that business is bad. It isn't. Business has produced some extraordinary products that have made our lives easier and healthier and a lot more comfortable.
>
> But business is enormously powerful. And the old rule about how power can be corrupting hasn't been repealed. Since business has outlasted most of the other forces that once curbed its power, the muckraker is left standing pretty much alone in the field. If we don't keep business under intelligent scrutiny and hold it accountable for how it uses the power it has, then almost no one else will — because almost no one else can.

Some types of business failings have such a huge impact on readers, viewers and listeners that they are treated in separate chapters of this book: utilities, financial institutions, insurance companies, health care providers and non-profit organizations. But many sources and strategies in this chapter are useful for investigating all types of businesses, including these.

This chapter emphasizes resources not mentioned earlier in the book. Nevertheless, it is important to reread Chapters 1 through 7 because most of the paper, people and database trails apply to private-sector investigations just as much as they do to government investigations. Like government investigations, business investigations go beyond stories about institutions to encompass individuals and issues. And often government and business investigations intermingle when business exerts a corrupting influence on legislation and the awarding of government contracts and grants.

Investigating Companies

The U.S. Securities and Exchange Commission

Publicly traded companies are easier businesses to examine because of federal and state laws and regulations that require the filing of a wide-ranging assortment of documents. The starting point for an investigation into a publicly traded company is the U.S. Securities and Exchange Commission; much of the information you need is a click or two away on the SEC's Web site (www .sec.gov). You can find rules, enforcement actions and numerous filings by publicly traded companies. Often the companies are multinational and not always based in the United States, so the site also is a useful resource for business journalists in any country.

If the company's stock is listed on a U.S. national exchange — such as the New York Stock Exchange or NASDAQ — or if there are more than 500 stockholders and assets are above $5 million, the company generally must file extensive electronic documents with the SEC.

More than 11,000 companies must file, and many of them are among the nation's largest private-sector employers that operate locally — such as Wal-Mart. (Millions of businesses do not fall within the SEC's jurisdiction, but they are covered more fully later in this chapter.)

Beginning in 1997, all public companies were required to file their documents for the SEC electronically through EDGAR, the SEC's database. With this database, it is easy for a reporter to find details about the largest local businesses. For more information on EDGAR, see "Resources for Reporting" at the end of this chapter.

Annual Reports

A key corporate document is the annual report, which is often posted on a corporation's Web site. Even the report's physical attributes might reflect the financial health of the company. One year it might be in black and white and the next year it might be a slick multicolor package.

But more important is that the annual report is filed as a 10-K report electronically with the SEC, and it can be conveniently searched by key words. Reporters frequently find the annual report's most interesting information, whether in hard copy or electronic form, in its footnotes. A typical annual report to the SEC contains at least a dozen pages of footnotes, many of them revealing to a knowledgeable journalist.

For example, companies can improve their bottom line without earning a cent by revising upward the assumed rate of return on their pension funds. That means they need less cash to fund pensions and therefore can claim profit. That practice is revealed in financial statement footnotes toward the back of the annual report, not in the text at the front.

In one case, a banking corporation's annual report referred in a footnote to "certain related parties"—officers of its banks—who had received millions of dollars in loans that the company was writing off as delinquent. A separate document—the bank company's proxy statement to stockholders sent before the annual meeting—filled in the missing information with two and a half pages of explanation, the names of the relevant officers and the amounts of their loans.

And that is just one filing.

At an annual conference of Investigative Reporters and Editors, David Armstrong of The Wall Street Journal and David Dietz of Bloomberg Markets put together a straightforward approach to using not only 10-K filings but many other filings for investigative stories. Here is a condensed version of their presentation:

- *The S-1.* Filed by private companies selling shares to the public for the first time through an initial public offering, or by companies that have been public less than three years and are making additional sales of stocks or bonds. (Foreign companies file an F-1.) It includes items like company history, financial results, description of business risks, backgrounds of executives, details on early shareholders and what they paid for their shares, and document exhibits. The S-1 can be used to show who will get rich from the IPO or to undercut prior optimistic predictions by a company.
- *10-K.* The official version of the company's annual report. (Foreign companies must file Form 20-F.) The form contains the company's full year and last quarter results; audited financial statements; descriptions of business and key customers; and details about top executives, directors, shareholders and litigation.
- *10-Q.* A quarterly report of financial results that details more than a company press release. It contains financial statements (unaudited, unlike the

10-K), important news since the company's last quarterly filing, information about market risks, disclosure of lawsuits and regulatory investigations, details about business transactions with officers and directors and attachments that can include employment contracts.

Both the 10-K and 10-Q can be used to find out about disputes between the company and its board members, investigations by federal regulators and lawsuits over products.

- *DEF 14A* (also known as a proxy). A company's notice to shareholders of its annual meeting or a special meeting that gives stockholders a chance to vote on such matters as a merger or the election of officers. It contains pay details of the chief executive officer and four other highest-paid officers; disclosure of how much stock is owned by top executives, directors and shareholders owning at least 5 percent of the company shares; details on whether that group does business with the company; how much the company auditor is paid; and details on board meetings and attendance.

  Nearly every story on outrageous or questionable executive pay has used the proxy. Reporters have also used it to show how executives are exploiting loopholes in a law intended to tighten corporate governance and still have close business ties to companies and contractors.

- *Form 4.* Discloses purchase or sale of stock by officers, directors, and large shareholders. This reveals "insider" trading and can provide an early sign that something might be wrong at the company because executives are starting to sell off stock. Form 4 sometimes reveals information about executive benefits that is not found in other forms.

- *Form 13-F.* Quarterly filings by money managers holding more than $100 million in stock, including pension funds and hedge funds. Bloomberg Markets magazine used these filings to show how mutual funds bought up stocks of their banking clients during the boom years of the 1990s and continued to hang on to the stocks after they collapsed — thus hurting investors who were counting on good performance in their mutual funds.

These are just a few of the filings available electronically, but this list shows how a journalist can background a company, looking for possible problems or questionable conduct to examine.

In addition to the SEC site, journalists can subscribe to the Web site www.10kwizard.com, which makes it easier to use the 10-K and other disclosures, puts out alerts on financial information, cross-references company information and puts some data into an easy-to-download spreadsheet format that is easier to search and analyze.

Another useful Web site is www.footnoted.org. It is run by financial journalist Michelle Leder, who looks at issues concerning both corporations and investors. She and other financial journalists—like Andrew Leckey, who runs a nonprofit training center for business journalists, and Henry Dubroff, a well-respected financial journalist who founded the Pacific Coast Business Times—offer many tips on finding warning signs that a company is in trouble. Among those warning signs are these:

- Big changes in corporate structures without a clear explanation. The corporation may be trying to hide a financial shortfall.
- Optimistic company press releases that are contradicted by a 10-K containing more sobering financial numbers.
- Substantial deals between executives or directors with the company.
- Footnotes on company reports that reveal huge debt or investigations, as mentioned before, or that are simply written in an obscure or incomprehensible way.
- Failure of the independent audit committee to meet frequently.
- Frequent amendments to reports, particularly the 10-K and 10-Q.

Federal Regulatory Agencies

Some federal agencies other than the SEC regulate public companies and also most private companies. Part of the mission of these regulatory agencies is to prevent fraud and questionable business practices and to promote social responsibility by businesses.

Among the agencies regulating businesses are these:

- The Federal Trade Commission, which was created to guard against anticompetitive behavior and deceptive business practices. For example, the commission might investigate whether the takeover of a small company by a larger one would increase chances that the small company would later be shut down.
- The Consumer Product Safety Commission, which was created to guard against injuries from dangerous products.
- The Small Business Administration, which offers grants and guarantees loans to small businesses that can't otherwise get loans—including those owned by women and racial and ethnic minorities—and then monitors

compliance with the terms of the grant or loan. The SBA's performance is generally judged by the volume of loans and not their success, so it's always worth checking which businesses received loans and whether they still exist or have gone bankrupt.

- The Equal Employment Opportunity Commission, which was created to protect employees from discrimination on the basis of race, ethnicity, gender, age and physical or mental disability. The sweeping Americans with Disabilities Act has kept the agency busier than ever before and has caused consternation among some employers. Alcohol use, smoking, poor eyesight and difficulties handling stress are among the conditions employees have claimed as disabling under the law. Employers are responding that sometimes those should indeed be disqualifying conditions.

  Journalists can find stories by tracking both the agency's activities and discrimination lawsuits against corporations. They should also delve into how employers are implementing ADA provisions for reasonably accommodating worker disabilities.

- The Environmental Protection Agency (covered in Chapter 18), which was created to reduce pollution of the land, air and water by institutions and individuals. Information disclosed to the EPA by individual businesses in almost every industry can help journalists learn not only about pollution but about work-force safety, corporate investments and manufacturing processes.

- The Federal Election Commission (covered in Chapter 9), which oversees political action committees formed by businesses and labor unions to support or oppose candidates for the U.S. Senate, House of Representatives and presidency. Many individuals employed by businesses or belonging to labor unions make contributions in their own names, in addition to funneling money through the committees. Individual contributions are also subject to FEC scrutiny.

- The Labor Department, which regulates the treatment and pay of employees. Its Occupational Safety and Health Administration oversees worker safety.

These and many other federal agencies can provide a wealth of material on businesses that otherwise couldn't be found on the public record.

State and Local Business Agencies

States and cities require varying degrees of disclosure from businesses, and the intensity of monitoring those businesses varies from state to state.

In many states, the attorney general collects information from consumer complaints but may move slowly on those complaints. The states receive tens of thousands of consumer complaints annually, and these can generate numerous investigative stories. Journalists can also check in with the National Association of Attorneys General and the National Association of Consumer Agency Administrators, both in Washington, D.C.

Many state agencies collect information before a complaint arises. For example, sales of securities within a particular state require registration with its securities commissioner. Journalists can get more information from the North American Securities Administrators Association, Washington, D.C., which is an alliance of state commissioners.

State agencies tend to regulate many businesses and their performances through required filings and licensing. One way to find a document trail is to find out what filings and licenses a business or an individual would have to get to open and continue to operate. By cross-referencing information and databases, a journalist might be able to arrive at an informed approximation of how much even the most secretive company is taking in. In Missouri, for example, for-profit corporations with assets over $200,000 pay a state franchise tax, and retail companies also pay tax based on a percentage of sales.

States also target specific kinds of businesses for licensing and regulation. These include alcoholic beverage manufacturers and retailers, hospitals, nursing homes and insurance companies.

On the local level, city business licenses, property taxes, tax liens, lawsuits and filings under the Uniform Commercial Code made by lenders to businesses for equipment and other property can help background a local business and can aid in an investigation. Sometimes a private company's revenue can be calculated by how much a company's city license fee was.

In addition, construction permits and fire and health inspections of the buildings housing private businesses can provide information. Traditionally, cities have heavily regulated certain types of private-sector activity, including restaurants (subject to special health inspections as well as rules cutting across all lines of business), street vendors, rental units and hotels and motels.

In an article in The IRE Journal, longtime business and investigative reporter Ron Campbell offered a list of basic documents to consider collecting when looking into a local business. Here is a condensed version:

> State secretaries of state or corporate commissioners register corporations, limited liability corporations, partnerships and limited partnerships. Corporation commissioners in many states police offerings of securities. They occasionally ban particularly abusive offerings. While the SEC focuses solely on disclosure (did the offering

disclose all material facts?), many states focus on fairness—whether a particular deal treats investors fairly. So shady operators who design their deals to avoid federal scrutiny sometimes run afoul of the states.

Each state maintains copies of corporate charters, bylaws and the name of each corporation's agent for service of process—the guy authorized to accept lawsuits on behalf of the corporation. Many also list current officers and boards of directors. Documents on limited partnerships are spotty.

Key documents at the secretary of state's office include the following:

- Articles of incorporation, which contain the name of the company, the date it was incorporated and the names of the incorporators. Often, these are just attorneys who represent the real incorporators.
- Officers and directors, the people who run the corporation.
- Partnership records, including the names of the partners. Each member of a partnership holds unlimited liability for the partnership. In other words, if a jury awards a $1 million verdict against the partnership, and partnership assets are insufficient, the partners are personally liable.
- Limited partnership records, including the names of the partners in a limited partnership. Some states provide this; others do not. In a limited partnership, the limited partners are liable only for the money they invested. The general (or managing) partner has unlimited liability.
- Enforcement records, including cease and desist (or desist and refrain) orders, which require sellers of a security to stop what they're doing within the state lines. Years ago, Campbell documented a series of wireless cable TV scams by matching C&D orders from several states; the same names appeared in many of the C&Ds.

The Paper Trail: Public Documents

County courthouses and city halls are repositories for an enormous number of business documents. It is literally impossible to open or operate a business without creating a paper trail at the nearest county or city office. The quantity and quality of public records varies widely from jurisdiction to jurisdiction, however. Key business records—for example, revenue-based local business taxes—may be considered secret. Consult your state public records law for guidance.

Coverage varies dramatically by jurisdiction. Certain widely used public records, particularly real estate transactions, routinely are filed online. The Reporters' Committee for Freedom of the Press (www.rcfp.org) has a useful online guide to public records laws in all 50 states entitled "Tapping Official Secrets."

Key documents from the county and city include these:

- Business licenses and fictitious business name records. Many jurisdictions require businesses to obtain a license before opening. Businesses also must register their names; the fictitious business name filing tells you the names of the people behind the business, the form the business takes (sole proprietorship, partnership, corporation), and the date it was formed.
- Property assessment — the value, for tax purposes, of land or buildings owned by a business. Property assessment records usually include the mailing address for the person who pays the tax bill. Assessment appeals will tell you what a business says its property is really worth.
- Local tax collection records — how much in property taxes were levied and whether they were paid.
- State and federal tax liens — how much a business or individual owes in unpaid taxes and when the taxes were due. One of the first signs that a business is in trouble comes when it fails to pay income tax withholding on behalf of its employees to the state and federal tax collectors.

Sometimes local governments possess information about businesses through tax breaks. David Lindorff, writing in the Columbia Knight-Bagehot Guide to Business Journalism, said this about business relocation incentives from local governments:

> Some jurisdictions will offer property tax holidays, others access to subsidized land, others job training tax credits. Still others have set up new business incubators in conjunction with local university research centers. Besides the fact that such programs invite corruption because of the amounts of money involved, typically the lack of public involvement in the decision-making process raises serious questions about whether the community gets what it pays for. Companies that get tax holidays often pick up and leave when the holiday is over. And even when a business stays, the cost per job to the community can be extraordinary.

The Paper Trail: Other Document Sources

When beginning a business investigation, journalists can find basic corporate financial data regularly updated in reports from Standard & Poor's, Moody's and Dun & Bradstreet. You can buy a credit rating and other summary information about a business online from Dun & Bradstreet, as well as purchasing information that analyzes how quickly the business pays its bills and its likelihood of paying a supplier on time. As with all credit reports, you need to confirm their validity and make sure they are current. You can do that by cross-referencing them with other business documents or simply by running the numbers by the business itself.

Updated reports can also be found in university and public libraries. InfoUSA's business profiles can help. For $5, you can get a rudimentary analysis of a business, including the names of the principals, local competitors, approximate revenues and years in business. Be skeptical of any credit rating you see on the list; it's a probability of paying, rather than any reflection of actual credit history. Hoover's, a commercial Web site (www.hoovers.com), offers profiles of big companies.

Reports on companies and industries are issued by securities analysts with brokerage houses, such as Merrill Lynch, UBS (which bought Paine Webber), and Morgan Stanley. Because stockbrokers are reluctant to criticize corporations publicly, the analyses tend to be bullish, but they frequently contain industry data unavailable elsewhere. The best analysts in each industry are chosen each year by Institutional Investor magazine, New York City, as well as other publications. Recently, the potential conflicts of interest that stockbrokers may have because they have an interest in stock they are recommending have surfaced in many stories. Gretchen Morgenson, a veteran financial reporter at The New York Times, has written extensively on those kinds of conflicts of interest and how investors have been misled.

The 400-page IRS book "Financial Investigations: A Financial Approach to Detecting and Resolving Crimes" is useful when businesses cross the line from legal but questionable accounting to lawbreaking. It is available through the Government Printing Office, Washington, D.C.

Overlooked sources of information include public relations releases and advertisements. For larger companies, a journalist can see what a company is saying about itself at PR Newswire, which has a searchable database of press releases (at prnewswire.com). PR Newswire also has a separate section for journalists only: the PRN Press Room, a free service that has a deeper archive of press releases, additional contact information and other features. Business Wire is another searchable database of business press releases.

Advertisements sometimes deliver detailed documentation. An advertisement to buy acreage in Colorado appeared in Forbes magazine; one of its own divisions was the seller. At the bottom of the enticing, promise-the-moon sales pitch was a dense paragraph of tiny type, reprinted here in full to illustrate all of the available documentation:

> Obtain the Property Report required by federal law and read it before signing anything. No federal agency has judged the merits or value, if any, of this property. Equal credit and housing opportunity. A statement and offering statement has been

filed with the secretary of state of the state of New York. The filing does not constitute approval of the sale or lease or offer for sale or lease by the secretary of state or
that the secretary of state has in any way passed upon the merits of such offering. A
copy of the offering statement is available, upon request, from Sangre de Cristo
Ranches. A statement of record filed with the New Jersey Real Estate Commission
permits this property to be offered to New Jersey residents, but does not pass upon
its merits or value. Obtain the New Jersey Public Offering Statement and read it
before signing anything.

Human Sources

Written records lay the foundation for a business story, but human sources are
essential to provide the detail and road maps for stories. The discussion on
using "currents" and "formers" in Chapter 5 shows how to delve into private-
sector institutions.

Even the best books sometimes give little attention to the range of people
who allow businesses to function. For example, private-sector corporations employ people to perform the same types of functions as in government: public
affairs, budgeting, accounting, auditing, contracting, legal affairs, personnel,
internal security, secretarial and maintenance. As in government, people performing those functions band together to form national associations that
might help journalists, such as the American Corporate Counsel Association or
the Institute of Internet Auditors.

Academics can be good sources. Most universities have faculty members
with varied areas of business and economics expertise. They can provide good
comments and perspective for local reaction to national developments or
analysis of economic trends. Some of the professors might have worked at or
consulted for the business being scrutinized. Think tanks, covered in Chapter
5, are worth checking on many business and labor topics.

Many businesses place at least one person from outside the company on the
board, ostensibly because outsiders have more independence than a corporate
owner or manager, and these outside directors can be good sources for journalists.
Although outside directors are paid for their service, they also assume legal and
moral responsibilities on behalf of the public. If there is trouble, they may share
their views with journalists. Outside directors are quite likely to have strong
views, one way or another, about whether the chief executive should be receiving
millions of dollars in bonuses on top of a $1 million base salary. They also can be
privy to information about illegal or troubling activities within the company.

Journalists may find that executives from the Chamber of Commerce and
the Better Business Bureau will open up and offer story ideas. Local business

association executives tend to be protective of their members, but with patience, a reporter can win their confidence so they will talk candidly about troubled businesses.

Trade associations are another valuable source for covering specific types of businesses and workers. Nearly every industry and every type of employee is represented by an association, such as the National Association of Convenience Stores and the International Brotherhood of Teamsters union, in Washington, D.C., and state capitals.

Other outside sources could include a company's current and former customers, suppliers, competitors, franchise holders, advertising agency executives, lawyers, accountants, bankers, institutional investors and lobbyists, as well as legislators and regulators concentrating on business issues.

The Overlooked Resource: Labor

With the end of most labor beats in the 1980s, many reporters today do not get a chance to become familiar with labor documents.

If a business is unionized, the officers of the local will know many things about their employer and will often share their knowledge. Union leaders will know which current and former employees are the most knowledgeable. When there is no union to consult, a reporter can locate current and former employees in other ways.

One method is to get current and old internal phone directories and compare them to see who has left. Other ideas are to do Internet searches on databases that keep histories of a person's addresses or employment and to visit a restaurant, bar or other establishment where employees gather after work hours.

Labor Lawyers and the Courts

Labor law has undergone so many fundamental changes in recent years — and changes are still occurring — that the courts and labor lawyers have become excellent sources. Journalists should always check the courts for lawsuits involving corporations and other types of businesses as plaintiffs or defendants.

Journalists should also contact the state bar association for a listing of its labor law section, as well as the American Bar Association membership list for its section on Labor and Employment Law. Employment law newsletters published by law firms for their corporate clients can be an excellent source for keeping up with local decisions. A journalist can go online in most states to check for employment-related lawsuits by the names of individual workers, companies or unions.

As Mike McGraw of The Kansas City Star, who is an expert in labor issues, says "The way workplace law has been expanding, you're likely to find almost any kind of claim in the courts these days."

Investigating the Workplace

The need for investigating the workplace is obviously everywhere.

For example, a building under construction collapses and kills several workers. Using records from the Occupational Safety and Health Administration, a journalist might find that the construction companies involved had horrible safety records, including numerous previous accidents, and that past dangerous practices were never corrected. The journalist might find that government safety inspectors had been to the site but had failed to catch problems that might have contributed to the collapse. A union official responsible for safety on the job might have had a conflict of interest because his son was the top officer of one of the contracting companies.

In another example, a military plane crashes halfway around the world, killing the entire crew. The Air Force blames the plane's avionics system, which was made in the reporter's hometown. By looking in the right places, the reporter finds that the company fired all its quality control inspectors the previous year to save money, that other employees had been complaining about flawed parts and that Pentagon auditors had given the company poor marks in previous site visits.

Not all workplace stories are this dramatic and dependent on one event. A journalist can examine work conditions and salaries at any kind of business through interviews and documents to see whether workers are being exploited.

When workplace dissidents complain openly about problems, they are supposed to be protected by federal and state whistleblower laws. (Whistleblowing is discussed more fully in Chapter 5 of this book.) One investigation that combined a corporation's finances, workplace ethics and whistleblowers in a near-perfect mix appeared in The Philadelphia Inquirer. The investigation exposed a scheme by a national convenience store chain to extort money from poorly paid employees by falsely accusing them of stealing.

Labor Unions

Some labor unions need as much scrutiny as employers. Although union membership has declined nationally in recent decades, about 15.4 million workers were union members in 2006. Local government had the highest membership rate at 36 percent. The most highly unionized occupations—although none had more than 40 percent unionization—were education, training and librarians. Among the major private industries, transportation and utilities had the highest union membership rate, at 23.2 percent, followed by construction at 13 percent.

Here are a few of the documents used most heavily by the journalists who do union-related stories:

- *Form LM-1* is a union's initial filing, which should include its constitution and bylaws, the composition of members, the name of the parent body, the expected annual receipts, the names and titles of officers, the date of the next union election, any fees or dues required and whether work permits are needed.

- Depending on its annual receipts, a union files an annual financial report on *Form LM-2, LM-3* or *LM-4*. The form contains the names and salaries of officers and most employees, receipts and disbursements, including those to charities, real estate purchases, trust funds and whether losses of funds or property were discovered. These reports can also be used to notify the government about the termination of a union through merger, consolidation or dissolution.

- *Form LM-15* must be filed by a parent union 30 days after it suspends autonomy of a union local by putting it under trusteeship or supervision. That might result from election irregularities, an attempt to control dissident members and officers or financial irregularities. Follow-up reports are required every six months explaining why the trusteeship was continued.

- *Form LM-16* is required when the trusteeship is lifted and includes the method of selecting the officers left in charge. Reporters should watch such a development closely. Trusteeships can be abused by officials of parent unions who dislike leaders chosen by the local union or who want to bring members of a certain local in line with other locals.

Racketeering investigations by the U.S. Labor Department, sometimes in conjunction with the Justice Department, often involve unions. Federal agents, for example, might explore shakedowns in which construction companies pay off a union official before certain work is performed. A journalist with good sources can investigate rumors of such activities long before the federal agents arrive.

Labor Relations Boards

The National Labor Relations Board is a federal agency that investigates and prosecutes unfair practices involving unions and employers, unions and their individual members as well as employers and their employees—both union and nonunion workers. The NLRB has broad jurisdiction in the private sector, intervening in situations such as a corporation's cutting off pension credits of striking workers in the middle of the dispute. Disputes involving state and municipal employees (including schoolteachers) are handled by the individual states.

The board also tries to ensure the integrity of elections in which workers can choose to unionize or throw out a union. It is frequently useful for a journalist to know whether workers have attempted to unionize an employer. For an NLRB-sponsored election to occur, 30 percent of eligible workers must sign a petition. (The agency does not have jurisdiction over all employers that could be unionized; for example, a retail business has to take in at least $500,000 annually and receive or send merchandise across state lines.)

A more or less typical case involved an employee of a chain discount store who tried to organize a union local in Hinsdale, N.H. When store supervisors found out, they offered the employee a raise if she would desist. She persisted. She said she was then harassed, fired and challenged by her former employer when she tried to receive unemployment compensation. The worker filed an unfair labor practices challenge against the company. After hearing evidence, the agency issued a formal complaint to have the worker reinstated, with back pay.

The process of filing a charge with the NLRB works like this: An aggrieved member who feels discriminated against because of union activity or feels the union is not providing fair representation files at the regional NLRB office. This can be done without the aid of a lawyer. The charge is a public document containing the employee's name, home phone number, employer, union local and a description of the complaint. It is assigned to an NLRB investigator, who interviews all parties and witnesses. The investigator recommends to the regional director whether the charge has merit. If the board investigator finds no merit in the claim and the regional director agrees, the charge is dropped. The charging party can appeal the regional director's decision to the general counsel in Washington, D.C. If the regional director believes the charge has merit, a complaint is issued, which is much like an indictment. The regional director then gives the other party a chance to settle the matter informally. If a settlement cannot be reached, a hearing before an administrative law judge is scheduled. The hearings are public; transcripts are available at board offices. The law judge issues a decision, also public, and either party can request a review of the decision by the National Labor Relations Board in Washington, D.C. In turn, the NLRB's findings can be appealed to the courts and eventually to the U.S. Supreme Court.

The best NLRB sources are the regional director and regional attorney. Individual investigators might be excellent sources who can say, for example, if internal board decisions about whether to pursue specific cases represent pro-union or pro-management biases. One method of contacting investigators is through local officials of the union that represents them: the independent National Labor Relations Board Professional Association. Board clerical workers can also be helpful; one way to get to know them is regular visits to board offices to check docket sheets for pending cases that might make good stories.

The Federal Labor Relations Authority and state public employee relations boards provide the same services for federal, state and local government workers. The Federal Labor Relations Authority also makes its decisions available by subscription through the Government Printing Office.

When federal construction projects run into labor-management strife, there are special tribunals to issue decisions. An example is the Wage Appeals Board within the U.S. Labor Department. If contractors are trying to avoid paying the prevailing local wage on projects, the board might intervene.

Mediation, Conciliation and Arbitration

When labor-management disputes mean work slowdowns or stoppages, journalists should look for the involvement of outside negotiators. The Federal Mediation and Conciliation Service is an independent federal agency—separate from the National Labor Relations Board and the Labor Department—that is supposed to be notified by unions at least 30 days before the expiration of labor contracts. The agency might assign commissioners based in Washington, D.C., or a regional office to help resolve disputes before or after strike deadlines. These commissioners, usually former management or union negotiators or officials, vary widely in background and ability.

The Merit Protection System Board has an online searchable database (at www.mpsb.gov) where a journalist can search for cases in any federal agency.

Arbitration services—some government-run, some private-sector—are available to settle disputes. Although hearings by arbitrators are not normally open to the public, reporters can attend with permission. Accounts of past arbitration hearings can often be found in published volumes.

There are two types of arbitration. Grievance arbitration occurs when an employee challenges an action of management through the union contract and the matter cannot be settled by union and management officials. It is appealed to a third-party arbitrator who hears evidence and issues a decision. These hearings sometimes are public, but few reporters ask to attend. Interest arbitration, which usually occurs in the public sector, takes place when labor and management cannot agree on a new contract. If strikes are prohibited by law (often the case with public employees) or both sides want to avoid a strike, they can turn to an arbitrator who will hold hearings and issue a decision.

Many states offer arbitration services to government employee unions; these decisions are often public. For example, an arbitration award may be the only document available detailing the disciplinary action of a police officer alleged to have stopped and sexually harassed young female drivers.

Safety and Health

Safety and health disputes are often at the center of labor-management disagreements.

Because the problems are so pervasive, one of the most important U.S. Labor Department agencies is the Occupational Safety and Health Administration. OSHA is divided into regional offices around the country, with area offices under them. Each area office is divided between safety inspectors (often former union construction workers or management safety experts), who investigate physical hazards, and health inspectors (often recently graduated industrial hygienists), who investigate health matters, such as injuries from toxic chemicals.

States have the option of enforcing private industry safety and health rules themselves, as long as the rules are at least as stringent as the federal rules. Sometimes the responsibilities are shared. For example, OSHA conducts inspections of businesses based in Missouri, but so do state agencies under certain conditions; the Department of Health's Bureau of Environmental Epidemiology focuses on diseases associated with exposure to workplace chemicals. Because OSHA has no jurisdiction over federal government workplaces, some states have similar agencies to cover municipal and state workers. Federal workers are covered by the workplace rules of their given agency.

OSHA conducts three types of inspections:

- Those that are programmed (companies in especially dangerous industries are randomly picked by computers for wall-to-wall scrutiny)
- Those that result from a signed complaint by a worker or union official
- Those that are triggered by accidents, especially if someone is killed, at least five people are hospitalized or the accident attracts public attention

PART III Investigating Business

Inspections frequently result in no citations. If a problem is found, the citation categories are "other than serious," "serious" and "willful." OSHA can request that the U.S. Justice Department conduct an investigation, but it usually depends on fines—based on the company's size, past record and maybe other factors—for serious or willful citations. The company has 15 days to contest the citation, request an informal conference or pay the fine. An informal conference, usually held with the OSHA area director, often results in reductions of fines by as much as 80 percent in return for a promise by the company to abate the safety hazards. The agency's regional administrator might become involved if the proposed reduction is more than 50 percent.

If no settlement is reached, the company can appeal to the Occupational Safety and Health Review Commission, which assigns administrative law judges to hear arguments from OSHA and the company. When the commission upholds a law judge's ruling against a company, that decision can be appealed to the courts. The commission's decisions are available by subscription through the Government Printing Office.

After an accident, journalists should request the OSHA inspection report, including the inspector's handwritten notes. Note that mining conditions and accidents are covered by a separate agency, the Mining Safety and Health Administration.

Journalists should not wait for accidents to happen before they begin an investigation. Instead, they should request employers' inspection histories from OSHA and then visit the work sites to see if the current situation is better or worse.

In-person visits can determine how accurate the OSHA reports are. Many workers suffer injuries that are never reported because of employer pressure. A journalist touring the workplace can look for a posting of OSHA Form 200, listing a summary of all injuries and illnesses. If the form is not posted, a journalist can ask why and request to see it. If the journalist has trouble obtaining any reports from the employer or from the OSHA area director, he or she can appeal to the regional director before invoking the federal Freedom of Information Act.

Most regional OSHA offices have a labor liaison (usually a former union official). A reporter should cultivate a relationship with the liaison.

Wage Enforcement

The (Fort Lauderdale) Sun-Sentinel found that local garment manufacturers were cheating employees by the thousands out of the minimum wage, overtime, medical benefits and compensation for job-related injuries. Similar investigations can be completed almost anywhere if journalists just focus their attention.

Overseeing minimum and overtime wage provisions falls to the U.S. Labor Department's Wage and Hour Division within the Employment Standards Administration. Reports available to journalists show employers fined for failing to pay federally required minimum wages or premiums (time and a half after 40 hours) in any one week. The reports can show a pattern of illegality, such as companies that deduct from workers' paychecks to make up for cash drawer shortages.

Journalists who examine complaints filed at the Labor Department under the 1931 Davis-Bacon Act might be amazed at the detail of the information. The original law was meant to please labor unions that wanted contractors disqualified from construction projects involving federal money unless they paid the prevailing union wage. The law shut out workers who were willing to work for less, many of them blacks, who had been denied union membership. Enforcement of the law still excludes many minorities and drives up costs to taxpayers on many federal projects. Journalists should look for local employers who want to pay less than minimum wage to workers deemed incapable of producing at the same rate as a "normal" worker. These usually include mentally retarded people whose work can be considered therapeutic. But abuses abound; the federal agency has granted permission to state agencies to pay less than the minimum wage to clients, such as veterans, producing at normal levels. Journalists can learn about what constitutes a reasonable wage by subscribing to the published federal occupational compensation surveys.

The Employment Standards Administration, sometimes working with state agencies, investigates violations of child labor laws. When reporters for The Boston Globe looked for usually invisible child workers, they found them in sweatshop garment factories and on farms, where they were in danger of being maimed by dangerous heavy equipment. But when employers employ and abuse underage workers or illegal immigrants, they are rarely caught. Regulators are outnumbered and often are unable to assign anybody full time to violations involving children. In the few instances when fines are levied against employers, the amounts are so low that they have little or no deterrent value.

Federal and state agencies try to watch over migrant and seasonal workers, but journalists should not wait for understaffed and sometimes uncaring agencies to visit the fields. KGW-TV in Portland, Ore., found migrant workers in substandard housing being paid less than minimum wage for backbreaking work near pesticides that were causing serious illnesses.

Government agencies are becoming increasingly aware of abuses involving corporations that are replacing regular employees with temporary or part-time workers to save money on wages and benefits. To discover such situations, journalists can develop sources at local employment agencies and temporary worker pools. Hanging around the entrances of those places early each morning is one way to meet talkative workers.

When regular employees leave a job temporarily for sound family reasons, there is supposed to be a position available when they return. The federal Family Medical Leave Act applies to companies with 50 or more employees within a 75-mile radius; it is supposed to guarantee up to 12 penalty-free weeks of unpaid leave because of a birth, adoption or serious illness involving the worker or the immediate family. Journalists have found that many employers are ignoring the law by refusing leave requests, granting them but then failing to guarantee a job upon return or cutting off benefits.

Pensions

As the U.S. population ages and corporations strive to please Wall Street investors, pensions have become an enormous issue. Throughout the United States, companies are eliminating or cutting back on pensions, and journalists everywhere should check into local companies' activities in this area.

Most of the pension-related investigations in the IRE Resource Center look at government employees who are being cheated or are doing the cheating. Those are important stories, involving as they do billions of dollars of taxpayer money. But the emphasis on public employee pensions inexplicably gives short shrift to private-sector pensions. Every year, millions of workers find they will receive little or nothing at retirement due to corporate ineptness or fraud combined with ineffective government regulation of business.

The Pension and Welfare Benefits Administration, part of the Labor Department, collects information about company plans for workers on Form 5500. Required under the Employee Retirement Income Security Act, the form details assets of the pension, health or welfare plan, the number of participants, the names of trustees who handle the assets, administrative costs and a breakdown of investments.

The law, approved as a result of corporate pension funds going bankrupt, limits the kinds of investments trustees can make. Only about 30 percent of retirees are covered by work-related pensions.

The reports on Form 5500 are meant to provide information that will point out trouble before it is too late to intervene. The forms are sent first to the Internal Revenue Service, which evaluates them for continuing tax-exempt status, and then to the Labor Department. Journalists interested in a specific company's pension should find out whether the Labor Department has audited the information disclosed. Because the Labor Department assigns just a few hundred auditors to track nearly a million pension plans, fraud has run rampant. For example, a bank invested $727,000 of its pension plan assets in securities issued by one of its affiliates. That was an improper investment that jeopardized future payments to retirees.

Journalists who examine local companies' pension-reporting forms will often detect problems that the responsible government agency missed. Besides providing clues about how unions and management can steal dollars from such funds (hiring a brother-in-law to administer funds at inflated costs or investing in a friend's venture), the forms are valuable for other stories. Some companies have declared pensions "overfunded" under federal regulations; they dissolved them, purchasing less reliable annuities for the remaining workers and using the leftover assets as operating capital. Workers' future retirement funds are then dependent on the financial health of the insurance company providing the annuities. Many pension funds, to the detriment of workers, have played a part in reducing the sales price of a dying company. For example, Company A owes millions of dollars to its underfunded pension plan but agrees to a sale to Company B for cash and an agreement that Company B make good on the debt to the pension fund. Company B gets a bargain-basement price, fails to make good on the pension fund debt, then files bankruptcy and dumps the ailing plan on the government's taxpayer-financed Pension Benefit Guaranty Corporation.

Pension Reporter, Chicago, and Pension World, Atlanta, are two of many publications that can help journalists understand the issues, institutions and individuals involved in pensions.

State Employment Security Divisions

A valuable source on companies, unions and individuals is the state unemployment office, sometimes called the employment security division. A reporter can use unemployment records to find former company employees or former union members, to look for local employment trends and to determine why workers got fired or quit. The records can help plumb the depths of alcohol or drug-abuse problems among local employers. With help from unemployment records, reporters have told the stories of an employee who was fired for sitting on the copying machine and selling the results to co-workers and a slightly mentally disabled dishwasher who was fired from a restaurant for dropping a small stack of dishes.

The system works this way: When workers are fired, laid off or quit for what they feel are valid reasons, they can claim unemployment benefits, which are paid out of the state's unemployment trust fund, financed by employer taxes. Validity might turn on whether the employer has issued an employee handbook and, if so, whether the employer violated any provisions of that handbook. It is always worthwhile for a journalist to find out whether a handbook exists, and then obtain a copy if it does. Some courts have ruled that the practices and policies in a handbook constitute an implied binding employment contract.

Workers may be disqualified from receiving benefits if state examiners disagree that a worker quit for good cause. How each state defines "good cause," and the cases arising from those definitions, might be the genesis of interesting articles.

For example, some states consider sexual harassment in the workplace good cause, but most do not believe sexual harassment allegations solely on the alleged victim's say-so. Some workers fail to qualify for unemployment insurance on the face of it, including self-employed individuals and those working on a commission arrangement, such as insurance and real estate agents. Some unemployed workers are denied government insurance payments because they are judged to be seeking work haphazardly rather than systematically. In each of these kinds of cases, a journalist can check through documents and interviews to see if the system is working fairly.

Journalists also should check state government files and sources to determine whether any local employers are refusing to pay the required amount into the unemployment insurance fund. Those that do cheat and get caught usually benefit from no publicity because journalists don't systematically track these cases.

An increasingly common situation is the unemployment that occurs when businesses close their plants so they can move elsewhere in the country or out of the country. Frequently, employers that make these moves hope to pay lower wages, offer fewer benefits and escape certain government regulations, without regard for the damage their move will do to the community.

Investigating Licensed Professionals

Simply by checking on whether a person is licensed can lead to an important story. For example, California Lawyer magazine unmasked a self-proclaimed lawyer. He fooled not only his clients but also the six attorneys he had hired to work alongside him day after day. When the San Francisco Chronicle printed the article, its headline said: "Everyone thought Fred Sebastian was a do-gooder lawyer until he was arrested. Then they discovered he wasn't a lawyer. He wasn't even Fred Sebastian." Chapter 5 of this book discusses résumé fraud. Checking the résumé of a person in a licensed occupation will often uncover fraud. Checking with the licensing agency should be part of the résumé verification.

Sometimes the courts help professionals hide the past. The St. Petersburg Times produced a series, "Hiding the Past," in which it discovered licensed professionals who had used the courts to wipe out records of guilty pleas and convictions. The newspaper found teachers, day care workers, bus drivers, child psychologists, physicians, nurses, pharmacists, veterinarians, lawyers, police officers, security guards and private detectives all working with sealed convictions.

The Times reporters wrote stories about case after case, including that of a title company president who had a criminal record resulting from the theft of $88,000 from her customers' accounts. When she petitioned to have that felony erased from her record, a judge did so. Two months later, she sought a state license to run a new title company. On her application, she said she had no felony record; the expungement law allowed her to do that. Knowing nothing about her record, Florida's insurance regulators granted her a license. When those regulators later learned the truth from the Times, they said they never would have issued the license if they had known.

While K. Connie Kang was covering the legal beat for The San Francisco Examiner, she kept hearing about lawyers who were breaking rules set for the profession by the state supreme court. She decided to investigate systematically. Reporters James A. Finefrock and Alex Neill joined the project. Following paper and people trails, the team pieced together "The Brotherhood: Justice for Lawyers," a series demonstrating that the state's lawyer discipline system was slow, lenient and secretive. Eleven lawyers lost their licenses in California in the same year that nearly 9,000 complaints came to the attention of legal disciplinary organizations. Convicted felons continued to practice law without their clients learning of their convictions. The reporters looked at 70 cases in detail, naming names, to illustrate the larger themes.

Among the professionals for journalists to investigate are lawyers; doctors; police officers; accountants; teachers and other school personnel; real estate salespeople; insurance agents; stockbrokers; social workers; bus drivers, airplane pilots and other transportation carriers; funeral home directors; nurses; and pharmacists.

This section provides a systematic way of thinking about obtaining information from the licensing process. It also suggests investigations of the process itself and the players in it.

Finding Licensing Documents

Many businesses are run by licensed professionals, and journalists can learn much about the business and its owners by examining licensing documents. One easy way to find where those documents are kept is to use Search Systems (www.searchsystems.net), a Web site that indexes all public records available on the Web, whether federal, state or municipal. It also indexes public records in countries around the world.

Licensing records include applications, reviews, and regulatory and disciplinary action. Often the oversight boards of licensees keep complaints secret unless they result in disciplinary action, but those complaints sometimes become public in lawsuits. In addition, the boards are composed of those in the same field as those they license and often reluctant to move quickly or harshly against colleagues.

Journalists must determine first if an occupation is licensed or otherwise regulated in a way that information on individuals will be accessible. Many states have much information on their Web sites on professional licensees.

For example, in Missouri the Secretary of State's office oversees dozens of boards that license or otherwise regulate hundreds of thousands of individuals in specific occupations. On its Web site, a journalist can look up individual licensees, relevant statutes, news from the various boards and sometimes occupational newsletters. Although there are many boards under the agency, there are some professions that aren't found there. Insurance agents are one example. In Missouri and other states, insurance agents fall under the jurisdiction of an insurance department, which is often part of the governor's cabinet. Lawyers are another example. They are licensed by their professional association, the Missouri Bar, under the general supervision of the state supreme court.

Studying the small print in the state manual on boards can lead to investigative leads. For example, every board consists of professionals from the occupation being licensed; at most, there is one "public member" per board. This means that the profession is left to police itself, which could include colleagues, former colleagues and friends. Board members may be reluctant to move quickly or harshly against people they know.

Journalists should also consider how money can create a conflict of interest, since boards earn all or much of their operating budget through licensing and renewal fees. Does that encourage disciplinary laxness, because more licenses and renewals mean more revenue?

Officially, appointments to the licensing boards are made by the governor with the consent of the state senate. Journalists should ask these questions:

- What role does the professional association play?
- Are the governor and the senate likely to name members whom the association leaders dislike?
- Does political affiliation or political philosophy play a role in what should be a nonpolitical activity?

Most of the boards are part of a national network. The Missouri State Board of Accountancy, for example, is a member of the National Association of State Boards of Accountancy. Journalists should inquire about what the benefits and drawbacks are for making licensing of occupations national rather than state-by-state.

If an occupation is not licensed by a state government, it may be licensed in another way. Maybe that occupation is licensed in other states. Journalists should also check with the local government (which often is the exclusive licensing body for taxi drivers, to take one example) or the federal government. (The U.S. Securities and Exchange Commission, for example, licenses stockbrokers, investment advisers and other financial professionals, in conjunction with their professional organization, the National Association of Securities Dealers, or the stock exchange where they do business.)

Sometimes institutions or businesses are licensed (bars and liquor stores, for example) even when the owner is not. The application for a permit to operate a bar, granted by the local government, is likely to contain personal information about the owner. As another example, states license employment agencies even though they do not license the owners. By requesting a blank licensing form from the Missouri board regulating employment agencies, a reporter would learn that owners must supply a signed employment history.

The Licensing Process

Step 1: Licensing To be licensed, a professional must meet certain standards. These might include age, citizenship, residency, level and type of education, examination scores, field experience and moral character. State or federal statutes or municipal ordinances set the standards. For example, to find out what the state legislature requires of accountants in Missouri, a journalist can read Chapter 326 of the codified statutes in the state law, which is online.

Some states also have reciprocity agreements, allowing professionals to practice if they are licensed in another state with similar standards. In such cases, a journalist can look for public files in one state that are closed in the other. Journalists must also be alert to disciplinary action in one state that is never conveyed to another.

Assuming that certain occupations require licensing might be a mistake. Most states do not license income tax preparers, and neither does the Internal Revenue Service. Some tax preparers may be licensed accountants, however, and state licensing boards for accountants maintain lists of disciplinary actions. But the lists are often inaccessible to the general public, and many tax preparers are not accountants anyway. Using a variety of resources—lawsuits, professional networks, word of mouth, placing newspaper and magazine ads requesting horror stories, or checking online newsgroups or blogs—a journalist can piece together a list of dishonest or incompetent tax preparers.

Step 2: Performance Standards Having received a license, professionals must adhere to performance standards or face losing the license through suspension or revocation. Again, journalists should first turn to the statutes. Most often, grounds for license revocation or suspension fall into the following areas:

- Felony conviction
- Obtaining fees by misrepresentation
- Drug or alcohol abuse
- Mental incompetence (as judged by a court)
- Physical abuse of patients
- Other dishonorable or unethical conduct that harms the public

For example, real estate brokers in some states can lose their licenses for employing unlicensed salespeople, issuing an appraisal report on real property in which they have an interest without disclosing that interest or violating federal fair housing laws, civil rights laws or local ordinances of a similar nature.

Those within the occupation know performance standards, but often outside groups contain sources every bit as knowledgeable. For example, AARP has an interest in monitoring funeral home operators. As a result, the association hires staff members who become experts about undertaker conduct and misconduct.

Step 3: Complaints and Investigations A complaint by a fellow professional or a member of the public usually initiates an investigation. In some states, licensing boards have the power to start an investigation on their own initiative. For instance, the state association of engineers may investigate a member and submit its findings to the licensing authority, the state attorney general's office or the local district attorney's office for action.

When disciplinary bodies refuse to discuss individual cases, a journalist can ask for aggregate data. Such information can help lead a journalist to a good story. For example, divorce lawyers are the subject of more complaints than any other type of lawyer. Knowing that, a journalist might want to begin by talking to divorce lawyers and their clients. When checking court indexes for legal malpractice suits, the names of local divorce lawyers might be the most sensible to run first.

Many licensing boards release complaint files, but only after the case has reached an advanced stage. In Missouri, a journalist can keep track of the boards' disclosures on its Web site or at a nearby university law library. The law library receives all disciplinary notices and files them in binders placed on open shelves. Furthermore, a journalist can check filings at the Administrative Hearing Commission in the state capital. This quasi-judicial agency examines preliminary findings by the boards to determine whether there is adequate evidence for a license suspension or revocation to proceed.

The right of privacy is at work here, which makes the issue difficult. But journalists must make difficult determinations about when a professional's privacy is being protected at the expense of public safety.

Newsday, the Hartford Courant and the (New York) Daily News all recently looked at the flaws in the medical system. In some cases, health maintenance organizations were recommending doctors who had been disciplined. The National Practitioners Database was set up to prevent bad doctors from going from hospital to hospital or from state to state, but as the newspapers have shown, the database can be flawed or not used by the profession.

Being alert to disciplinary actions from unexpected quarters can pay off in an important story. A North Carolina real estate agent became a convicted felon not because her licensing agency took action, but because a federal prosecutor charged her with violating a money-laundering statute after she allowed a client to pay part of a home purchase with $60,000 of undisclosed cash. The prosecutor said the agent should have figured out that the cash came from illegal drug profits.

Professional Associations as Sources

Professional associations can help reporters obtain information about individual members and about professional standards. Sometimes the information will come from paid staff, sometimes from volunteer board members, sometimes from publications. The CPA Journal, a national magazine disseminated by the New York State Society of Certified Public Accountants, is just one example of an in-house publication that may be useful to journalists. Independent specialized publications, such as the Public Accounting Report, based in

Minneapolis, and the Journal of Accountancy, Jersey City, N.J., are covered in Chapter 1 and should be consulted as well.

Most organizations are set up to help their members or to promote a cause. There is usually no law or regulation compelling an association to release information about its members, but many will at least confirm whether a particular person is a member and, if so, supply standard biographical data about that person.

Large national and regional associations, such as those of lawyers, doctors and engineers, sometimes have state and local chapters, both of which should be consulted. Some associations produce membership directories, available from their headquarters (or from a friendly local member). Journalists must remember, however, that information in directories is supplied by the member and thus can be self-serving or even fictitious.

Many associations work with governments to develop standards and then act as the primary policing body for the profession. A few examples — of hundreds that could be listed — are the American Institute of Certified Public Accountants, New York City, and the National Association of Realtors, Chicago.

Even if the association has no authority to sanction its members, it might have ethical guidelines, often called codes of professional responsibility, that can inform a journalist's investigation.

Some licensed workers, such as electricians and plumbers, are more likely to belong to a labor union than to a trade association. When nonunion workers try for certain jobs, they are often frozen out. For example, when a nuclear power plant is being built, the immensity of the job means hundreds of out-of-state plumbers and pipe fitters will be brought in. Because all are required to pass a state proficiency exam, copies of the tests may show up on the job site, may be sold through the operator of the local lunch wagon or may end up in the hands of union officials.

Investigating the Protectors

When investigating licensed professionals, it pays to look at the state board too. The place to start is with the law that created the board. Questions to ask about the board itself include these:

- What is the board supposed to be doing?
- Does it have an adequate budget?
- What regulations has the board approved to achieve the legislative mandates?
- Who are the board members, and what are their backgrounds?

- Were they once, or are they still, members of the regulated profession, and do they have a vested interest in lackadaisical enforcement?
- How are staff investigators trained, and on what are they told to focus?
- How do their counterparts around the country go about their jobs?
- How do the cases fare that they take to court?

While inquiring about waste in the District of Columbia government, the Washington City Paper entered the thicket of licensing boards. The investigation revealed that the Barber and Cosmetology Board had been at odds for a decade with a hair-braiding salon it wanted to regulate. The owner said procedures for cutting and shampooing hair had no relevance to braiding; the board disagreed and fined the owner, who took the fine to court. As that legal battle unfolded, the owner convinced the city council to set up a separate licensing board for braiders.

The article also chronicled the Board of Interior Designers saga. In its first eight years of existence, the board had received only one complaint, about overcharging for rugs. So the question arose, why license and oversee interior designers? The answer seemed to be twofold: First, interior designers appreciated the prestige of being a licensed profession whose entry could be controlled. Second, the local government appreciated the fees generated by the licensing procedure.

As journalists look at a board's effectiveness, they should ask whether the board pursues certain types of violations while ignoring other types. Useful categories to consider, no matter what the profession, are misrepresentation of qualifications, practicing without a valid license, hiring unqualified assistants, functioning outside the area of competence, impairment due to alcohol or drugs, overtreating a problem, undertreating a problem, overcharging, sexual assault or other sexual abuse and malpractice leading to injury.

Boards tend to inflate the number of disciplinary actions they handle by taking credit for suspensions or revocations initiated by sister agencies in other states. The boards play down their reluctance to discipline for substandard performance, which is vital but subjective. It is easier to evaluate cases of stealing, drunkenness or a felony conviction in the courts (all of which can be proven by using objective criteria).

Sometimes the boards have attorneys on staff; sometimes they retain outside lawyers from the private sector or receive help from government-paid lawyers in the attorney general's office. It's good to get comparative information from the national Federation of State Medical Boards, based in Fort Worth, Tex. The information tells whether an agency has had more or fewer

PART III Investigating Business

than the average number of investigations per 1,000 physicians, a higher budget than comparable boards, more or less quasi-judicial authority than average to discipline wayward doctors and much more.

Occasionally outside groups try to police the boards. Their data, comprehensive or anecdotal, can be a good starting point. For instance, the Public Citizen Health Research Group in Washington, D.C., ranks disciplinary boards state by state and publishes the names of every known physician disciplined by the state or federal governments.

⊃ CHECK IT OUT

✓ Examine a local business, such as a bar or restaurant. Get as many documents about it as possible, including its business license, liquor license, food-serving license and building permits. Also, acquire any inspection records of the business.

✓ Pick a local publicly traded company, and look at its most recent 10-K filing with the Securities and Exchange Commission. Check the compensation of its executives, and check for any litigation it is involved in.

✓ Check the Web site of the state regulatory board overseeing funeral home directors and embalmers. Find out which directors and embalmers have been disciplined, and examine the files of one.

RESOURCES FOR REPORTING

General Resources

You can find relevant stories in the IRE Resource Center under the key words "Business," "Corporations," "Employment," "Job Training," "Labor Unions," "Product Safety" and "Unemployment."

"Writing About Business: The New Columbia Knight-Bagehot Guide to Economic and Business Journalism," edited by Terri Thompson, provides a useful overview of writing about business, as did the earlier version, "The Columbia Knight-Bagehot Guide to Business and Economics Journalism," edited by Pamela Hollie Kluge. Also helpful is Business Journalist, the magazine produced by the Society of American Business Editors and Writers at the University of Missouri Journalism School.

Publicly Traded Companies

The document trail for publicly traded companies starts at the Securities and Exchange Commission (www.sec.gov). At the SEC Web site, consult the EDGAR database at www.sec.gov/edaux/searches.htm.

Two organizations that might be useful to journalists include the Association of Publicly Traded Companies, Washington, D.C., and the American Association of Individual Investors (www.aaii.com), Chicago, Ill.

Annual Reports, Proxy Statements and Prospectuses

SEC Today is a daily summary of major filings and actions involving individuals and institutions regulated by the commission. SEC Docket is a weekly compilation of new rules, changes to old rules and reports of disciplinary actions. Outside publications, such as SEC Compliance, Englewood Cliffs, N.J., can provide leads for journalists. SEC filings and other business information make up the heart of many online computer databases and CD-ROMs, including ABI/Inform, Business Index and Disclosure.

Federal Business-Related Agencies

Here are just a few of the business-related agencies of the federal government:

- Environmental Protection Agency (www.epa.gov)
- Equal Employment Opportunity Commission (www.eeoc.gov)
- Federal Trade Commission (www.ftc.gov)
- U.S. Consumer Product Safety Commission (www.cpsc.gov)
- Federal Election Commission (www.fec.gov)
- Federal Reserve (www.federalreserve.gov)
- Occupational Safety and Health Administration (www.osha.gov)
- Small Business Administration (www.sba.gov)

Consult magazines like Business Ethics, Minneapolis; read books like "Rating America's Corporate Conscience" from the Council on Economic Priorities, New York City; develop ties with watchdog groups like the Investor Responsibility Research Center, Washington, D.C.; document the amount and direction of charitable contributions; and determine which politicians receive contributions from corporate political action committees.

State and Local Business Agencies

Here are three national organizations of state and local business agencies:

- National Association of Attorneys General (www.naag.org)
- National Association of Consumer Agency Administrators (www.nacaa.net)
- North American Security Administrators Association (www.nasaa.org)

Other Business Resources

For basic financial information on businesses, consult the Web sites of Dun & Bradstreet (www.dnb.com), InfoUSA (www.infousa.com/partner/profile.htm?402) and Hoover's (www.hoovers.com).

The PR Newswire (www.prnewswire.com) offers the PRN Press Room (www.prnmedia.com), a free service that has a deeper archive of press releases, additional contact information and other features. Business Wire (www.businesswire.com) is another searchable database of business press releases.

Some good general resources include the following:

- "Business Information Sources," by Lorna M. Daniells
- "Understanding Wall Street," from the New York Stock Exchange
- "How to Read a Financial Report," from Merrill Lynch
- "Financial Investigations: A Financial Approach to Detecting and Resolving Crimes," available through the Government Printing Office (www.gpo.gov), Washington, D.C.
- "The Big Eight" and "The Accounting Wars," Mark Stevens' exposés of accounting firms
- "Financial Shenanigans: How to Detect Accounting Gimmicks and Fraud in Financial Reports," by Howard Schilit

Human Sources

These are just a few of the national organizations useful to journalists investigating businesses:

- Association of Corporate Counsel (www.acc.com), Washington, D.C.
- Financial Executives International (www.financialexecutives.org), Morristown, N.J.
- Institute of Internal Auditors (www.theiia.org), Altamonte Springs, Fla.

- National Association of Corporate Treasurers (www.nact.org), Washington, D.C.
- Employee Assistance Professionals Association (www.eapassn.org), Arlington, Va.

Local chambers of commerce have a national organization in Washington, D.C.; local better business bureaus have their national organization in Arlington, Va.

Two books that examine whole industries are "Brokers, Bagmen and Moles: Fraud and Corruption in the Chicago Futures Markets," by David Greising and Laurie Morse, and "Merchants of Grain," by Dan Morgan. It is instructive to compare Morgan's book, which features Cargill Inc., with the authorized history of Cargill by Wayne G. Broehl Jr.

Ralph Nader and William Taylor's "The Big Boys: Power and Position in American Business" and Dorman L. Commons' "Tender Offer: The Sneak Attack in Corporate Takeovers" are worth reading.

The National Association of Corporate Directors is in Washington, D.C. Directors and Boards magazine is one of many publications that journalists can read to gain insight.

And for basic information, the Dictionary of Occupational Titles, published by the U.S. Labor Department, is a listing of almost every job imaginable—more than 20,000—including salary ranges, descriptions and future prospects. When journalists are unsure whether they have found and interviewed all types of employees relevant to an investigative project, this reference book can be invaluable.

Labor Lawyers and the Court

The School of Industrial and Labor Relations at Cornell University, Ithaca, N.Y., operates a book publishing company offering many relevant titles that mesh well with information from labor lawyers and lawsuits. An example is "Mutual Gains: A Guide to Union-Management Cooperation," by Edward Cohen-Rosenthal and Cynthia Burton.

A rare book detailing management tactics from the inside is "Confessions of a Union Buster," by Martin Jay Levitt with Terry Conrow. Modern union strategies are the subject of Hector L. Delgado's book "New Immigrants, Old Unions: Organizing Undocumented Workers in Los Angeles."

The Journal of Labor Research, Fairfax, Va., is one of many periodicals with useful articles. General-circulation publications like Business Week, Forbes and Fortune regularly publish articles that are worth reading. The Wall Street Journal is unmatched among national newspapers for its labor-management coverage. The Labor Relations Reporter from the Bureau of National Affairs, Washington, D.C., and Labor Law Reporter from Commerce Clearing House, Chicago, keep up with court cases, government agency rulings and other developments.

Investigating the Workplace

Some books to consider are Juliet B. Schor's "The Overworked American: The Unexpected Decline of Leisure" and the more comprehensive "Every Employee's

Guide to the Law," by Lewin G. Joel III, and "The Employee Rights Handbook," by Steven Mitchell Sack.

The U.S. government's Monthly Labor Review is a good source for big-picture stories and trends, as is the statistics-based government publication "Compensation and Working Conditions."

Labor Unions

For investigating labor unions, start with the National Labor Relations Board (www.nlrb.gov) and the Federal Labor Relations Authority (www.flra.gov).

Books about labor leaders and unions are weighted toward coverage of corruption, with the Teamsters Union the most exposed. "The Teamsters," by Steven Brill, is a classic. Kenneth C. Crowe brought it up to date in "Collision: How the Rank and File Took Back the Teamsters." James Neff's biography of Teamsters leader Jackie Presser ("Mobbed Up") and Arthur A. Sloane's biography of Teamsters leader Jimmy Hoffa ("Hoffa") show what can be done given persistence and talent.

The Bureau of National Affairs Inc. (www.bna.com), Washington, D.C., publishes the annual Source Book on Collective Bargaining and Employee Relations and the Directory of U.S. Labor Organizations — two of many reference books that can help journalists see the big picture. Charles J. Coleman and Theodora T. Haynes are editors of the annotated bibliography Labor Arbitration, with hundreds of references useful to journalists.

Many unions publish informative newspapers and magazines. Some of the best have traditionally come from the United Auto Workers, United Mine Workers, Service Employees International Union and American Federation of State, County and Municipal Employees. Print journalists might already be familiar with the Guild Reporter. The National Right to Work Committee, Springfield, Va., an anti-union organization, is one of many potential sources on union excesses.

Safety and Health

Two classic exposés are "Expendable Americans," by Paul Brodeur, and "Bitter Wages," by Joseph A. Page and Mary-Win O'Brien, about Ralph Nader's Study Group on Disease and Injury on the Job.

OSHA data are available from the National Institute for Computer-Assisted Reporting.

Other sources include university safety or health programs and occupational medicine clinics; specialized publications like the Occupational Safety and Health Reporter, Washington, D.C.; and statistical services like OSHA Data, Maplewood, N.J., which sells computerized enforcement and compliance data back to 1972.

Russell Mokhiber's book "Corporate Crime and Violence: Big Business and the Abuse of the Public Trust" emphasizes criminality surrounding workplace health and safety. The book contains a 50-point program to fight corporate crime. Discussion of those points (for example, enactment of a federal homicide statute to be used against officers, directors and the corporation itself in certain cases of workplace death) could yield an educational sidebar for an investigative series.

Temporary Employment

The National Association of Temporary Services, Alexandria, Va., can help journalists locate the biggest or oldest local suppliers of workers.

Robert E. Parker's book "Flesh Peddlers and Warm Bodies: The Temporary Help Industry and Its Workers" contains useful examples and theories.

Pensions

Pension Reporter, Chicago, and Pension World, Atlanta, are two of the many publications that can help journalists understand the issues, institutions and individuals involved in pensions.

John A. Turner's book "Pension Policy for a Mobile Labor Force" is a good resource.

Every interested party has its own advocacy organizations. Examples based in the Washington, D.C., area include the Association of Private Pension and Welfare Plans (for employers), Pension Rights Center (for employees) and the Society of Professional Benefit Administrators (for third-party managers).

Unemployment Claims

Resources for tracking local and regional employment trends include three U.S. government publications available by subscription: "Area Trends in Employment and Unemployment," "Unemployment in States and Local Areas" and "Employment and Earnings."

A helpful guide is the book "How to Maximize Your Unemployment Benefits," by Raymond Avrutis and Geraldine S. Wulff. The U.S. government guide Comparison of State Unemployment Insurance Laws provides useful detail; the newsletter Employee Policy for the Private and Public Sectors, Alexandria, Va., can also be helpful.

Licensing: General Resources

The Council on Licensure Enforcement and Regulation (www.clearhq.org), Lexington, Ky., and The American Society of Notaries, Washington, D.C., might be able to put individual cases into perspective.

Stanley L. Gross's book "Of Foxes and Henhouses" focuses on licensing and the health professions.

The Licensing Process

A good Web site to check is Search Systems (www.searchsystems.net). This regularly updated site has a collection of thousands of links to free, searchable online databases, most operated by government entities. The site includes separate sections linking to resources in each state and can provide a shortcut to licensing information on the Web.

Professional Associations as Sources

Journalists seeking information on accounting should look at The CPA Journal, by the New York State Society of Certified Public Accountants, the Public Accounting Report, based in Minneapolis, and the Journal of Accountancy, based in Jersey City, N.J.

The Guide to National Professional Certification Programs, compiled by Phillip A. Barnhart, includes hundreds of entries.

Rena A. Gorlin edited a compilation, "Codes of Professional Responsibility," for the Bureau of National Affairs. It covers lawyers, doctors (including psychiatrists), accountants, engineers, real estate agents, insurance underwriters, arbitrators, architects, financial planners and social workers.

Numerous books place ethical codes in a larger societal context. An example is "Ethics and Professionalism," by John Kultgen. A philosopher, Kultgen studied ethics codes from 19 professional associations to illuminate his thinking. Some ethics books focus on one profession, such as Philip G. Cottell's "Accounting Ethics: A Practical Guide for Professionals."

The Federation of State Medical Boards (www.fsmb.org) and Public Citizen Health Research Group (www.citizen.org/hrg) are two resources for licensing in the health profession.

14

Investigating Nonprofit and Religious Organizations

This chapter provides an overview of how to investigate nonprofit and religious organizations, especially through documents specifically useful in such investigations. It is intended to help journalists examine the sources from which nonprofits receive their revenues and how they spend those funds. The chapter also helps guide journalists looking into the finances and activities of religious organizations.

Paul Williams was an editor at the Sun Newspapers in metropolitan Omaha. In 1972, he decided that his tiny staff should scrutinize Boys Town, the sprawling, famous home away from home in Omaha for wayward boys.

For decades, Boys Town had operated in financial secrecy, keeping regulators and journalists at a distance. Nobody was inclined to push very hard to pierce the veil—until Williams. He believed that all major institutions—governmental and private sector—ought to be examined in depth.

As the Sun staff slowly pieced together the puzzle, it became increasingly obvious that Boys Town had more money than it could use. How to learn the exact amount of the institution's assets was eluding Williams, though.

As the staff discussed how to proceed, a local financier who served as chairman of the Sun Newspapers board mentioned IRS Form 990. He guessed Boys Town would be exempt from filing the form because of its church affiliation, but it might be worth checking.

When Williams received the document, he was amazed to find the institution's net worth listed—and even more amazed to see what it was: $191 million, and growing by about $17 million annually. That sum could run Boys Town for years and years. Williams had his story and eventually a Pulitzer Prize.

Over the past decade, journalists' scrutiny of nonprofit businesses and religious organizations has sharply increased. Nonprofits are prevalent now in many professions and industries and do work around the globe, whether it's addressing environmental problems, fighting poverty or providing disaster relief. At the same time, probes into religious institutions have become more frequent as such problems as child abuse by Catholic priests, financial mismanagement of Christian church funds, and the funneling of money to Islamic terrorists through religious charities have become public.

More than a decade ago the idea of approaching nonprofits with the same attitude as for approaching for-profit businesses was outlined by Gilbert Gaul and Neil Borowski when they did a groundbreaking series in The Philadelphia Inquirer on nonprofits in the United States. They noted that "many nonprofits operate just like for-profit businesses. They make huge profits, pay handsome salaries, build office towers, invest billions of dollars in stocks and bonds, employ lobbyists and use political action committees to influence legislation. And increasingly they compete with tax-paying businesses."

The same attitude can also apply to the coverage of religious institutions both in the United States and abroad—institutions that perform duties associated with nonprofits.

This chapter looks at the documents and sources that an investigative journalist can use to closely examine nonprofits and religious groups and to determine whether they are carrying out the mission for which they have been exempted from taxes.

Investigating Charities and Foundations

One of the primary reasons for the success of nonprofit organizations is the advantage they possess by not paying taxes. Under tax law, they can accumulate surpluses as long as they do not distribute them as stock or dividends. Instead, they can spend surpluses on building construction, large salaries and new commercial ventures.

More than a decade ago, veteran reporter David Cay Johnston created a nonprofits beat at the Los Angeles Times and investigated the local United Way. He found secret low-interest loans to five of the organization's executives. He also found an authoritarian executive director pulling down a huge salary, riding around in a Cadillac and socializing at an all-white, all-male country club paid for by donors' charitable contributions.

Johnston wrote an influential article for the Columbia Journalism Review calling for greater scrutiny of nonprofits—and explaining the techniques for applying such scrutiny. Since then, investigation of the local United Way has become nearly routine with journalists focusing on abuses by executive directors, distribution of funds and general financial mismanagement.

Where to Begin: Questions and Documents

Some nonprofits—the Salvation Army is an example—have become a leading provider of social services in the community. Other groups, known as 527s, have become the latest influential political and ideological groups. Wherever a journalist looks, nonprofits have proliferated in both presence and influence in society. Accompanying their growth has been an increase in abuses.

The big questions about nonprofits are obvious, yet journalists don't ask them often enough:

- What percentage of the funds raised by a nonprofit goes to administrative costs?
- How much money does a nonprofit spend to raise funds?
- What percentage of total donations is spent on charitable activities?
- Is the nonprofit helping the people it says it will help?
- How well is the nonprofit managing its money?

Journalists should routinely check to see if audited financial statements and other financial reports are immediately available upon request.

In any investigation, a journalist should find out what section of the Internal Revenue Code an organization used to gain its tax exemption. Most nonprofits fall under Section 501(c), which is detailed at the IRS Web site (www.irs.gov). There are approximately 1.9 million such groups today, having doubled in the past 25 years. There are 28 types of 501(c) designations; the standard nonprofit organization, such as the Red Cross or the Humane Society, is exempt under Section 501(c)(3), while AARP and MoveOn.org operate as political education organizations under Section 501(c)(4).

Nonprofit organizations in the 501(c)(3) category are referred to as public charities, meaning that they operate by raising money from the public and using these funds for the direct benefit of the public. Donations to these groups are tax deductible, which is not generally the case with other types of exempt groups. Because public charities receive the most tax breaks, they are limited in the kinds of activity they are permitted to do, such as lobbying. Many charities get around this by setting up affiliate groups. For example, under the Sierra Club umbrella are different groups: the Sierra Club Foundation, a public nonprofit exempt under Section 501(c)(3); the Sierra Club Fund, a 501(c)(3) private foundation; and the Sierra Club political committee, a 501(c)(4) and a political action committee (527).

It's a good idea to check for affiliate groups—which are listed in a 990 form that must be filed with the IRS annually—when reporting on nonprofits. It gives a more complete picture of the holdings, activities and reach of the nonprofit. It also gives a better idea of how donations can be channeled, because tax deductions will vary from 100 percent with a 501(c)(3) to zero with a 527 designation.

The Gaul and Borowski Model

In their pioneering 1993 series, Gaul and Borowski conducted a massive investigation of the nonprofit sector by identifying about 1.2 million tax-exempt organizations nationwide, excluding churches. Their estimated total annual revenue topped $500 billion, which meant that the economy gave up an estimated $40 billion in revenue due to tax exemptions. Meanwhile, Congress and the Internal Revenue Service keep adding tax-exempt categories, including mutual life insurance companies, health insurers, labor unions, credit unions, cemeteries, fraternal groups and trade associations. A professional football league that paid its commissioner more than $1.5 million annually had tax-exempt status.

Gaul and Borowski's investigation, the subject of their book "Free Ride: The Tax-Exempt Economy," began with Gaul's curiosity. He had covered the changing nature of supposedly nonprofit hospitals for a decade. Benefiting from tax exemptions, hospitals were becoming more and more involved in commercial activities while providing little nonprofit care. Gaul proposed a major study of the entire nonprofit economy. Borowski, curious about an increase in tax-exempt real estate, joined Gaul. The paper trail the two men followed provides a good outline showing how to investigate nonprofits.

- *Form 990 informational tax returns.* These are filed annually with the IRS. Most IRS-recognized tax-exempt organizations (using Form 1023 or Form 1024) incur a legal obligation to file an informational tax return, even though they do not have to pay taxes. The only blanket exemptions are for churches and for nonprofit groups with less than $25,000 in annual revenues. Gaul and Borowski obtained some of the forms from the IRS, some from state attorneys general and some from the organizations themselves. Today, most of the forms can be obtained from GuideStar (www.guidestar.org), which collects 990s and other financial information. Furthermore, federal law has changed, and nonprofits are supposed to allow interested parties to inspect their 990s and to make copies and to make their operations more transparent.
- *Audited financial statements of nonprofits.* Gaul and Borowski said in their IRE contest entry form that the audited statements "were valuable supple-

ments to the tax returns because they contained additional financial information, so could be used as a check against the Form 990s. Hospitals, for instance, often report smaller profits on their 990s than they do on their financial audits through the use of accounting methods that allow them to 'reserve' income against future charges." Such audited statements are generally easy to obtain from nonprofits that are operating responsibly. Fund-raising appeals might include audited statements or might explain how to obtain copies. However, be cautious when making comparisons. Form 990s and audited statements do not always match exactly because of accounting definitions, different fiscal years or other reasons.

- *Unrelated business income tax.* UBIT results from revenue not directly related to the group's charitable purpose. This income is supposed to be reported on Form 990T. Some nonprofits fail to report such income at all or underreport it by overallocating expenses against revenues. This is done to minimize corporate income tax payments associated with UBIT.

- *Offering statements for tax-exempt bonds.* The offering statements for tax-exempt bonds sold by hospitals, universities and other organizations often contain historical and biographical information. Gaul and Borowski used bond sale filings to show how a Texas financier used charities to buy and dispose of Iowa nursing homes with tax-exempt bonds, making a profit of more than $6 million. Bonds are issued by quasi-governmental authorities like the New Jersey Economic Development Authority and the Health Care Facilities Finance Authority. Thus tax-exempt groups drain government treasuries even more by receiving tax breaks from bond sales.

- *Local, state and federal court cases.* The Inquirer team reviewed about 150 court cases involving nonprofit organizations. In many cases, the tax-exempt status of the organizations was being challenged. Federal bankruptcy court records contained revelations in some instances. So did cases on file at U.S. Tax Court.

- *IRS studies of the tax-exempt sector.* These studies are available, as are statistics on IRS audits and revocations of organizations' tax-exempt status. The IRS also publishes a database identifying all organizations that are tax exempt according to its records. The data reported, however, are considered very "dirty," as almost no follow-up goes into maintaining these records.

- *Sales tax exemptions.* The reporters obtained information from state revenue agencies to determine the extent of lost sales tax revenue. They obtained and analyzed real estate assessment records kept at the county level in a similar fashion. (The same sort of legwork goes into determining how much in property taxes is lost due to ownership by nonprofit groups.)

- *Educational records from tax-exempt colleges.* These records are compiled by the U.S. Department of Education. The reporters compared the amount of charitable scholarships granted by colleges against the revenue lost to the greater society because of the institutions' tax exemptions.
- *Congressional hearings involving tax-exempt organizations.* Gaul and Borowski followed people trails as well, interviewing about 400 sources, including executives of tax-exempt groups, IRS bureaucrats, economists, state and county government regulators, legislators, academic experts, tax lawyers and health, education and welfare officials.

Generally, watchdog groups recommend that charities make available an audited annual report, spend at least 60 percent of annual expenses on the activities donors think they are supporting, keep net assets at a fiscally sound level but not more than twice the current year's expenses or the next year's budget, and find otherwise unaffiliated board members who will volunteer their time to meet at least twice a year. But a journalist should remember that these are guidelines and that the percentages can vary widely.

Form 990: The Annual Informational Tax Return

The Form 990 is considered the standard starting place for journalists looking at nonprofits.

When the Orlando Sentinel began investigating the temples of a charitable organization, the staff knew it was examining a sacred cow. Who could find fault with a fraternal organization that was raising money to operate orthopedic and burn hospitals for children? The year the newspaper conducted the investigation, the local chapter made an $81,000 profit—and, the journalists discovered, not a penny went to children's hospitals. Instead, it helped pay for members' entertainment, including the upkeep of their private bar and restaurant.

The story began with a tip from an insider. But it was the Form 990s that brought the story home. The forms showed that in most years, members spent more money on conventions and parties than on hospital operations. A fund containing money contributed for hospital endowments was making no-interest or low-interest loans to top officials. The organization's board of directors received free trips to exotic locales and had expense accounts running into the tens of thousands of dollars apiece. Directors of nonprofits are usually volunteers, but they sometimes benefit by accepting perquisites or providing services to the organizations for a fee. When too much of that dealing occurs, the board of directors can lose its effectiveness as a watchdog.

Here are some tips on how to read Form 990, the annual informational return for tax-exempt groups, and Form 1023 or 1024, the application for exemption. (These public documents should be made available on request.)

- *Review all sources of revenue.* What percentage comes from charitable donations? From government grants and contracts? From fees for services? The basic numbers are on the first page of Form 990.
- *Examine the net assets.* Go to the bottom line on the first page, and look at whether the net assets at the end of the year have fallen significantly from the beginning of the year. Excessive net assets and dramatic changes are signals to look further.
- *Review where the funds go.* Nonprofits will list their net incomes on their 990s as excesses or surpluses. Is this money parked in a reserve, earning interest but not helping anybody directly? Line 20 on Form 990, "Other Changes in Net Assets," shows whether a nonprofit transfers funds in or out of its organization. A schedule is required that provides additional details. This is one way of uncovering whether an organization is diverting assets to finance other activities.

    Some nonprofits understate their profits by playing accounting games that make them appear poorer than they really are. An organization can make it look as if it is spending more on its legitimate activities than it really is by using an accounting tactic called joint cost allocation. Fundraising costs are allocated to program expenses on the grounds that the solicitation letters contain educational material. The educational material, however, might be as sparse as one sentence with statistics about cancer deaths if the nonprofit is in the business of fighting cancer. Accounting rules exist to prevent such misstatements, but poor judgment or willful bending of the rules can result in misleading numbers.
- *Put together a corporate profile of the nonprofit.* 990s will list all the related organizations of the nonprofit, both tax exempt and for profit. This is useful for putting together a corporate profile of a nonprofit network. It's also useful for determining whether a nonprofit is parking huge sums in another company or in a 527, which is basically a political action committee.
- *Determine the actual wealth of the organization.* A Form 990 shows investments in stocks and bonds. It also shows the funds that a nonprofit has available for any purpose it chooses — the "Current Unrestricted" fund. It

offers one indication of the wealth and discretionary cash that the non-profit is holding.
- *Review business transactions between insiders.* 990s provide details of business transactions between board members and the nonprofit.

Journalists can get copies of 990s from the nonprofit organization itself or from GuideStar, a nonprofit that collects 990s and puts a great deal of information up on its Web site. Journalists also can request copies of 990s from the IRS or from the state government agency that oversees tax-exempt groups. This office varies from state to state. For example, in Alabama and in many other states, it is the attorney general, but elsewhere it might be the Department of Commerce or some other agency.

Some states have put a great deal of information online to make it easier for consumers and reporters to background nonprofits and to determine how much professional fund-raisers have raised for particular organizations.

Fund-Raising Techniques and Conundrums

If a nonprofit uses volunteer fund-raisers, their labor is free. When volunteer fund-raisers are not used, the organization probably hires professional fund-raisers who may rely on telephone solicitations. Charities that use telephone solicitations only should be checked thoroughly because many other charities ask for donations in writing. Professional fund-raising firms might lie to potential donors about how the money will be used (even when a legitimate nonprofit has hired them), might say they represent legitimate charities when they do not or might use names so similar to well-known charities that donors are almost certain to be confused.

In a stellar investigation, Ronald Campbell of The Orange County Register reviewed more than 10,000 pages of court records, financial reports and other documents and found that former associates of charity telemarketing king Mitch Gold raised more than $83 million in four years for dubious charities. Fund-raisers and managers kept almost all the cash, leaving just 7 cents on the dollar for charity. "A typical Gold-style contract guarantees a charity a set amount or a fixed percentage of the take—seldom more than 15 percent and sometimes far less," he wrote.

Even honest fund-raising firms might cause distress for donors because of the percentages they take from the donations. Journalists should find out if the fund-raising firm is working on a flat-fee basis or is taking a percentage of the money raised. A percentage arrangement might lead a fund-raising firm to use high-pressure tactics, since there is a direct linkage between what donors pledge and what the firm clears.

Journalists should find out which options are being presented to potential donors. There should be lots of choices. For example, most universities tell potential donors about the many ways to give, including cash gifts, securities, real estate, tangible personal property, bequests, charitable remainder trusts, pooled income funds, charitable lead trusts and gifts of life insurance proceeds.

If the fund-raising agency being scrutinized is the local United Way, journalists should question donors. Are they giving with the understanding that their contributions are being channeled only to specific recipient charities within the United Way circle or instead to groups traditionally outside the circle? Such widespread earmarking is a possible indication that local donors have lost their faith in the United Way to make appropriate decisions.

Foundations

Foundations are a type of nonprofit organization. There are several different kinds of foundations, but all have two things in common. First, they are generally deposits of money from wealthy individuals or companies that will fund charitable efforts, usually in the form of grants to other organizations. Second, less than one-third of the foundation's money comes from public donations, fees or government grants.

Foundations perform some functions of a nonprofit but are different in many ways. Although many charities file an annual Form 990 with the IRS, foundations — especially those dominated by a wealthy individual — file a Form 990-PF, which discloses similar kinds of information. Disclosure rules require that the main office of an exempt 501(c) group make its three most recent 990s, or 990-PFs, as the case may be, available for viewing during normal business hours.

Foundations are frequently associated with wealthy, prominent philanthropists. They can be financial shelters for the wealthy, spending tiny amounts to benefit society while hoarding the rest, much of it tax-free. Some foundations — those not set up and controlled by individuals — are spin-offs from hospitals and other organizations that originally did lots of nonprofit work. Often begun with donated corporate stock, they are still under the control of huge profit-making companies.

Foundations sometimes spend donations unwisely, even crossing the line from inefficiency into the realm of corruption.

In 2005, The Boston Globe's Spotlight Team reviewed tax records from some of the nation's wealthiest private foundations to find that the kinds of perks that corporate executives have been criticized for enjoying are not uncommon among foundation trustees. "Yet private planes and other big-ticket expenses go virtually unnoticed in the world of philanthropy, even though foundations are publicly subsidized through huge tax breaks for the wealthy donors who set them up," they wrote. "A Globe review of foundation tax returns revealed numerous instances of money earmarked for charity being used to fund travel and lavish perks for foundation trustees—the people charged with protecting foundation assets."

Even when run efficiently and honestly, foundations might still fail the populations they want to help. Increasingly, they charge fees for their services, violating the concept of nonprofit that originally earned them their tax exemptions.

The Foundation Center in New York City can be especially helpful to journalists. It keeps individual forms on file, publishes The Foundation Directory and offers many resources online. It covers thousands of groups that have at least $2 million in assets or that give grants totaling more than $200,000 annually. Journalists can use the center's resources to learn about a foundation that is already under scrutiny, or they can troll the directory's geographic section to identify local foundations that might be worthy of scrutiny.

By consulting the directory, for example, a Milwaukee journalist would find a local foundation with more than $400 million in assets and a reputation as the leading funder of conservative political intellectual activity. A Minneapolis/ St. Paul magazine found that local foundations have become the lead players in the power structure as government budgets atrophied and for-profit corporations cut back on philanthropy in hard times. The magazine documented construction projects and social policies emanating from foundation boardrooms.

Interlocking directorships might be a tip-off to questionable transfers. Donors who give more than 2 percent of the foundation's annual income are called substantial contributors. A private foundation cannot enter into certain business transactions with disqualified persons: substantial contributors and members of their immediate families, foundation officials and their families, companies owned by disqualified persons and government officials. Breaking the rule is called self-dealing. Banned transactions include property sales, leases or rentals, loans, transfers of foundation assets and sales of stocks, bonds or other securities.

A private foundation must limit its investment in any company in which disqualified persons also have an interest. If disqualified persons have a controlling interest, their holdings and the foundation's holdings cannot equal more than 20 percent of the company's voting stock. If disqualified persons do not exercise control, the combined ownership can equal 35 percent.

Foundations are required to give away at least 5 percent of their total assets each year (based on a complicated formula of percentage points averaged over a five-year period). The payouts can be in the form of program spending or grants to other charities. A 15 percent penalty tax is imposed on any shortfall. Gaul and Borowski found that many give away the minimum 5 percent "while earning much more on investments. With $163 billion in assets, they are operated like private banks, with elite, self-perpetuating boards of directors."

A private foundation cannot spend its money on certain things. It cannot lobby for or against legislation, and it cannot give grants to noncharitable organizations unless the foundation oversees how the money is spent.

Federal, State and Local Government Regulation

In some states, the regulation of charities and other nonprofits is handled exclusively by the attorney general's office. Other states have established more targeted units, such as a consumer protection division — sometimes freestanding and sometimes within the secretary of state's office. Many state agencies require IRS Form 990 to be filed along with a state form. Journalists can check with the National Association of Attorneys General and the National Association of State Nonprofit Officials, both in Washington, D.C.

Many states require professional fund-raisers who work the phones for nonprofits to register as well. Phone solicitors are sometimes dishonest, as KPRC-TV discovered using hidden cameras. They found telemarketers pretending to be disabled to generate extra sympathy from potential donors.

At the local government level, revocation of property tax exemptions is occurring more frequently, as cash-strapped agencies question whether tax-exempt organizations deserve that exemption. Gaul and Borowski estimated that in Philadelphia alone, nonprofit organizations owned property that would have generated close to $100 million annually for the city government if taxed. In some cases, tax-exempt groups negotiate a payment in lieu of taxes in an effort to find a middle ground without setting costly long-term precedents. When tax exemptions are revoked, organizations sometimes threaten to move elsewhere, taking jobs with them. Some carry through with the threat.

The IRS traditionally has done little to examine the truthfulness of a tax-exempt organization's stated mission, although the agency has become aggressive about looking for unrelated business income and determining whether groups continue to deserve their tax-exempt status. Most are never scrutinized beyond seeing whether the blanks are filled in, and those who fail to file often escape notice. After a federal tax exemption is granted, groups can usually gain exemptions from local property taxes, state income taxes and local and state sales taxes. They can borrow money through tax-exempt bonds and can use the U.S. mail at reduced rates. Those who make donations to tax-exempt groups generally do not have to pay taxes on those donations.

Given all the potential abuses that are possible and the lack of sufficient government oversight, the need for journalists to perform a watchdog role on non-profits is greater than ever.

Investigating Religious Organizations

"God Is My Landlord," a Village Voice investigation, showed how a once-small, pure nonprofit—in this case a religious organization and its related housing operations for the needy—can grow into an almost entirely unregulated big business. The religious organization at the heart of the Voice article could almost be called a slumlord, but despite its unsavory practices it was still exempt from most taxes, rent control ordinances and labor laws.

Some tax-exempt organizations escape regulation altogether, especially the estimated 300,000 to 400,000 churches and religious-based groups in the United States. Their unreported, unregulated activities range from local bingo games—a form of gambling often allowed in jurisdictions where other types of gambling are illegal—to the multimillion-dollar operations of television evangelists.

Over the past decade, investigative reporters have used business records, court records, government contracts, property records and many other public documents to stitch together portraits of abuse or malfeasance.

The Boston Globe, in particular, excelled in tracking and documenting through interviews and court documents the molestation of children by Catholic priests, winning a Pulitzer Prize for its efforts in 2003.

Later, reporters at the Los Angeles Times tracked the assignments of 228 priests from 1950 through 2003 who had been named or identified as the subject of abuse complaints. Their analysis showed that because the accused priests moved around the archdiocese on average every 4.5 years, the total number of parishes in which alleged abusers served was far larger than previously reported—more than three-fourths of the 288 parishes. In other investigations, reporters have dug into evangelists' business dealings over the years and have discovered questionable management practices and outrageous sexual conduct.

For example, Carolyn Tuft of the St. Louis Post-Dispatch used the Missouri Sunshine Law to get documents showing that "TV evangelist Joyce Meyer and her family received millions in salary and benefits from her worldwide ministry in recent years." The details were included in a dispute involving the tax status of the ministry's headquarters. The evangelist earned a $900,000 annual salary, and her husband received $450,000.

The Tampa Tribune and WFLA-Tampa teamed up to report that a central Florida church was actually "an elaborate money-making machine that generates revenue three ways." According to the report, the Deeper Life Christian Church sent people seeking food and shelter out on dangerous fund-raising missions, pushed its congregants to donate heavily and received money from satellite churches in other states.

Other journalists have looked into the activities of Muslim-related charities that allegedly steered money — sometimes U.S. government aid funds — to terrorists.

David E. Kaplan of U.S. News and World Report spent five months tracing the relationship between Saudi Arabian money and terrorism, finding that "over the past 25 years, the desert kingdom has been the single greatest force in spreading Islamic fundamentalism, while its huge, unregulated charities funneled hundreds of millions of dollars to jihad groups and al Qaeda cells around the world."

He found that Saudi charities played an important role in a $70 billion campaign to spread the message of the ruling Wahhabi sect, but that Saudi "largess" encouraged U.S. officials to look the other way, according to some veteran intelligence officers. He further discovered that "billions of dollars in contracts, grants, and salaries have gone to a broad range of former U.S. officials who had dealt with the Saudis: ambassadors, CIA station chiefs, even cabinet secretaries."

Tracking this kind of broad activity requires the cultivation of sources, access to government reports, and attention to litigation records. But it can be done on a local level, as The Kansas City Star showed when it revealed that a Missouri Islamic charity directed millions of dollars in U.S. aid money to terrorist networks.

Investigations into religious organizations can be especially difficult not only because of the lack of regulation, but also because of the sensitivity of the topic and the depth of emotions investigations can evoke. Nonetheless, journalists should not be dissuaded from examining the conduct of religious leaders, the finances of religious institutions or their political activities.

PART III Investigating Business

⊃ CHECK IT OUT

✓ Go to GuideStar (www.guidestar.org), and download the last three years of the 990s for the nearest humane society. Compare the years to see if the net assets are going up or down. Check to see if the public donations are going up or down.

✓ Go to GuideStar (www.guidestar.org), download the last three years of the 990s for the local United Way and examine the changes in revenues and expenditures. Go to the local United Way's Web site, and see if it posts its annual reports and audits. If the audits are not posted, request the last three audits, and then see what recommendations, if any, the auditors have made.

✓ Pick a local foundation, and download its 990 filings from the last three years. Examine the changes in its net assets and contributions. Also, search for news articles on the foundation to see what activities it publicizes.

RESOURCES FOR REPORTING

General Resources

Books about the United Way can inform journalists about this large charity, as well as about the charitable world in general: "The United Way: Dilemmas of Organized Charity," by Eleanor L. Brilliant, and "The United Way Scandal: An Insider's Account of What Went Wrong and Why," by John S. Glaser. Other books focus on other groups but make many of the same points. One such book is "Unhealthy Charities: Hazardous to Your Health and Wealth," by James T. Bennett and Thomas J. DiLorenzo, which focuses on the American Heart Association, the American Lung Association and the American Cancer Society.

The following are useful Web sites for general research:

- American Bar Association (www.abanet.org)

- American Institute of Philanthropy (www.nonprofitwatch.org)

- BBB Wise Giving Alliance (www.give.org)

- NonprofitWatch.org (www.nonprofitwatch.org)

- Capital Research Center (www.capitalresearch.org)

- GuideStar (www.guidestar.org)

- BoardSource (formerly the National Center for Nonprofit Boards) (www.boardsource.org)

- National Directory of Non-Profit Organizations from Taft Group Publishing (www.galegroup.com/taft)

Fund Raising

The following insider groups can be invaluable in answering questions about fund raising:

- Giving Institute (formerly the American Association of Fundraising Counsel) (www.aafrc.org)

- Association of Fundraising Professionals (www.nsfre.org)

- Independent Sector (www.indepsec.org)

- Council on Foundations (www.cof.org)

- National Committee for Responsible Philanthropy (www.ncrp.org)

- Capital Research Center (www.capitalresearch.org)

Guidelines are available from nonpartisan watchdog groups like the BBB Wise Giving Alliance (www.give.org) and the American Institute of Philanthropy (www.nonprofitwatch.org).

Following the Paper Trail

Conscientious journalists can study the rules, available from the American Institute of Certified Public Accountants, and carrying headings like "Accounting for Joint Costs of Informational Materials and Activities of Not-for-Profit Organizations That Include a Fund-Raising Appeal."

The following books and pamphlets aimed at nonprofit insiders can inform journalists:

- "Completing Your IRS Form 990: A Guide for Tax-Exempt Organizations," by Michael I. Sanders and Celia Roady
- "The Law of Tax-Exempt Organizations," by Bruce R. Hopkins
- "Protecting Your Organization's Tax-Exempt Status: A Guide for Nonprofit Managers," by Mark Bookman
- "Accounting for Governmental and Nonprofit Entities," by Earl Wilson
- "Unfair Competition: The Profits of Nonprofits," by James T. Bennett and Thomas J. DiLorenzo

For more information on reporting on nonprofits, see the IRE beat book by Sarah Wright, "Covering Nonprofits: Understanding the Tax-Exempt Organization."

"The Guidebook for Directors of Nonprofit Corporations," by the American Bar Association (published in 1993 and available through www.abanet.org), can provide benchmarks for journalists to study, as can information from BoardSource, formerly the National Center for Nonprofit Boards (www.boardsource.org), Washington, D.C.

Journalists can check with the National Association of Attorneys General (www.naag.org) and the National Association of State Charity Officials (www.nasconet.org).

Foundations

Among the numerous groups that can provide perspective on foundations are the Council on Foundations (www.cof.org) in Washington, D.C., the Association of Black Foundation Executives (www.abfe.org) also in Washington, D.C., and the Foundation Center (www.fdncenter.org) in New York City.

Religious Institutions

Books by journalists that can shed light on religious institutions include Charles E. Shepard's "Forgiven: The Rise and Fall of Jim Bakker and the PTL Ministry," Charles M. Sennott's "Broken Covenant" and Samuel G. Freedman's "Upon This Rock: The Miracles of a Black Church."

Some organizations that can help provide perspective are the Evangelical Council for Financial Accountability (www.ecfa.org) and the National Council of Churches (www.ncccusa.org). The Religion Newswriters Association (www.rna.org) also offers many resources.

15

Investigating Financial Institutions and Insurance

This chapter explains how to research and investigate both financial institutions and the insurance industry. It gives examples of investigations and lists both human sources and documents for examining the performance of banks and other lenders. It also covers the kinds of documents and sources needed for probes into insurers.

In recent years, financial institutions and the insurance industry have overlapped more and more. Although each has its own distinct language, expertise and documents, an investigation into one industry can easily include the other. As one consumer leader noted in a recent investigation, some insurers are "looking to shed their purpose as a risk bearer and become financial institutions."

Investigating Financial Institutions

In 2005, The Charlotte Observer reported that across America blacks who bought homes were "four times more likely than whites to get high interest rates for mortgage loans." Despite years of scrutiny and reform, The Observer found that deep racial disparities in home loans persisted throughout the nation. Reporters analyzed tens of thousands of records contained in the database created by the Home Mortgage Disclosure Act, focusing on 25 of the largest lenders in the United States. They discovered that blacks with annual incomes above $100,000 were charged high rates more often than whites with incomes below $40,000.

The Observer noted that blacks had attempted to get loans at any price, only to have lenders ignore entire black neighborhoods, a practice called redlining. They found that the nation's 10 largest banks denied black applicants twice as often as whites. On average they made only 5 percent of their home loans to blacks. The reasons cited in The Observer investigation were that discrimination can occur throughout the lending process and that blacks were on average less knowledgeable about the home-buying process than were whites. Lenders told The Observer that they don't consider race in lending decisions and that the availability of loans to blacks, even at high rates, constitutes progress.

In an eerie precursor to the so-called subprime lending crisis that emerged in 2006, The Observer pointed out that new companies that were not banks were making higher-risk loans at higher interest rates. These "subprime" lenders, companies like Ameriquest and New Century, charged higher interest rates than banks. Critics said the industry was now discriminating in a new way: "reverse redlining," in which lenders targeted black neighborhoods for the sale of high-rate loans.

Clearly, financial institutions have a much bigger impact on local communities and on their residents than many other private-sector businesses or any governmental agencies do. Banks, savings and loan associations, credit unions, mortgage brokers, and investment companies decide whether they will make money available for a business to begin or expand, for a family to buy or repair a home, for an individual to acquire an automobile, for one company to purchase another or for residents in a largely minority subdivision to join the mainstream of society.

Journalists and newsrooms need to cover financial institutions in a routine and meaningful way. By doing so, they can discover whether a lending institution is illegally discriminating in its loan policies, making dangerous loans to its own directors, laundering money for criminals or charging exorbitant fees or interest rates.

Covering financial institutions can be difficult because of the complexities of the language and practices. Furthermore, following ever-changing regulations could be a full-time job. For example, the Gramm-Leach-Bliley Act of 1999 is the most sweeping piece of bank legislation since the Great Depression. The law repeals key provisions of the Glass-Steagall Act, which prohibited banks, securities firms and insurance companies from affiliating. Among other things, the Gramm-Leach-Bliley Act allows for the creation of financial holding companies, which can engage in securities underwriting and dealing, insurance agency and underwriting activities and merchant banking activities.

But much information is available about financial institutions through regulatory documents, databases and people trails, as specialized publications like American Banker and National Thrift News have demonstrated for decades.

Government Regulators

Every bank, savings and loan association and credit union is supervised by at least one state or federal agency. Many state-chartered banks are scrutinized by a state agency. In addition, the Federal Reserve Board and its 12 district banks regulate state-chartered banks that are members of its system. The U.S. Office of the Comptroller of the Currency, part of the Treasury Department, regulates the several thousand nationally chartered banks and regulates credit card companies. The Federal Deposit Insurance Corp. tries to guarantee that depositors will be protected against total loss if a bank or savings and loan fails. The agency also possesses some supervisory powers.

If a particular financial institution is part of a holding company or a corporation selling stock broadly, the U.S. Securities and Exchange Commission and state securities departments might require filings. Savings and loans are usually regulated by the U.S. Office of Thrift Supervision. Credit unions fall under the jurisdiction of the National Credit Union Administration. These federal agencies have regional offices, and documentation is often more readily available there than in the agency's headquarters in Washington, D.C.

Examiners tend to look at similar criteria no matter what type of financial institutions they are inspecting. A useful acronym for journalists is CAMEL:

- Does the financial institution have adequate and stable Capital,
- high quality of Assets,
- a Management with competency and integrity,
- high-quality and sufficient Earnings,
- plus the necessary Liquidity?

Many news stories, such as those about discriminatory mortgage lending, cut across regulatory lines and apply equally to banks, savings and loans, credit unions and even nonbank financial institutions. Other stories are more about one type of financial institution than others because of different traditions and regulatory treatments. This chapter concentrates first on the stories that relate to each type of financial institution and then moves to the stories that cut across all of them.

Banks

Federal regulators rate banks in one of five categories: well capitalized, adequately capitalized, undercapitalized, significantly undercapitalized and critically undercapitalized. Banks in the last category are likely to be seized by the government or merged with a healthier bank. Sometimes the rankings are available directly from regulators through leaks or documents filed in a legal proceeding; other times private-sector bank-rating services will know in which category a bank falls. Some journalists have used data collected by the FDIC and sold by the National Technical Information Service or private vendors (such as Sheshunoff Information Systems) when reporting on the health of banks. (See "Resources for Reporting" at the end of this chapter for more information.)

Federally regulated banks are supposed to be inspected at least once a year by one or more examiners working from Washington, D.C., or a district office. Although objective criteria play a major role in the examination, to some extent a bank's report will reflect the personality of the individual federal examiner. There are informal discussions among financial institutions about which examiners are lenient, which are strict but fair, and which are considered unreasonably demanding. By developing sources over time, a journalist will learn which examiner is at the local bank during a given week and how that examiner is viewed by the industry.

Even the most secretive banks must make some financial information public. Journalists make a habit of getting and studying the call reports, or consolidated reports of condition and income required quarterly (available at the FDIC Web site). Major changes in any figures from quarter to quarter should be questioned.

Some of the key statistics subject to fluctuation are net interest income, provision for loan losses, quantity of insider loans, net profit or loss, net income per share, amount of investments in real estate and U.S. Treasury instruments and other securities. Shorter versions of the call report are embedded in the balance sheet and the income statement.

Knowing such figures allows a journalist to ask meaningful questions (most of which also apply to savings and loans and credit unions):

- What percentage of a bank's loans are nonperforming, meaning at least 90 days overdue and otherwise not in compliance with contract language? If the figure is higher than 5 percent, perhaps there is reason to be wary.
- How many loans have already been written off as uncollectible? What other assets are nonperforming? If the aggregate is higher than 3 percent, there might be cause for concern among depositors and borrowers.
- Is the bank lending enough of its deposits locally to keep the community healthy? If local loans are a relatively low percentage of deposits, the bank is perhaps too conservative. If the percentage is much higher, the bank

might face cash-flow difficulties. Some experts believe 80 percent is a sensible level in most circumstances.

- How many loans are being made outside the area? Such loans, especially on real estate, can be difficult to monitor adequately.
- Is the fair market value of current loans equal to the value of the loans when originally made? If loan values are declining, why?
- Have some real estate loans been made on the basis of inflated values, perhaps because the borrower and a land appraiser are collaborating?
- Is the bank offering interest rates higher than those of its local competitors? If so, that might indicate a need for cash.

Besides financial statements, journalists should ask regulators or banks themselves for the following documents, when relevant:

- Examination reports, available about once a year
- Supervisory letters warning management to change its ways
- Supervisory agreements, in which a bank signs binding terms to make changes mentioned in supervisory letters
- Cease-and-desist orders, stated in stronger terms than supervisory agreements
- Announcements that officers and directors have been removed
- Applications to open new branches or to buy subsidiary companies

Here is an excerpt of a cease-and-desist order available from the FDIC Web site. It would be an excellent starting point for a story.

FEDERAL DEPOSIT INSURANCE CORPORATION
WASHINGTON, D.C.

In the Matter of
BEARDSTOWN SAVINGS, S.B. BEARDSTOWN, ILLINOIS
(Insured State Nonmember Bank)

ORDER TO CEASE AND DESIST
FDIC-07-063b

Beardstown Savings S.B., Beardstown, Illinois ("Bank"), having been advised of its right to a NOTICE OF CHARGES AND OF HEARING detailing the unsafe or unsound banking practices and violations of law, rule, or regulation alleged to have been committed by the Bank, and of its right to a hearing on the charges under section 8(b) of the Federal Deposit Insurance Act ("Act"), 12 U.S.C. § 1818(b), and having waived those rights, entered into a STIPULATION AND CONSENT TO

THE ISSUANCE OF AN ORDER TO CEASE AND DESIST ("CONSENT AGREEMENT") with representatives of the Federal Deposit Insurance Corporation ("FDIC") dated April 26, 2007, whereby, solely for the purpose of this proceeding and without admitting or denying the charges of unsafe or unsound banking practices and violations of law, rule, or regulation, the Bank consented to the issuance of an ORDER TO CEASE AND DESIST ("ORDER") by the FDIC.

The FDIC considered the matter and determined that it had reason to believe that the Bank had engaged in unsafe or unsound banking practices and had violated laws, rules, or regulations. The FDIC, therefore, accepted the CONSENT AGREEMENT and issued the following:
ORDER TO CEASE AND DESIST

IT IS HEREBY ORDERED, that the Bank, its institution-affiliated parties, as that term is defined in section 3(u) of the Act, 12 U.S.C. § 1813(u), and its successors and assigns, cease and desist from the following unsafe or unsound banking practices and violations of law, rule, or regulation:

A. Engaging in hazardous lending and lax collection practices, including, but not limited to:

- The failure to obtain proper loan documentation;
- The failure to obtain adequate collateral;
- The failure to establish and monitor collateral margins of secured borrowers;
- The failure to establish and enforce adequate loan repayment programs;
- The failure to obtain current and complete financial information;
- The failure to maintain an effective watch list and loan grading system;
- The failure to enforce loan policy guidelines;
- The failure to properly report all new loans to the Board; and
- The failure to enter Contracts for Deed on reasonable terms.

B. Operating with an inadequate level of capital protection for the kind and quality of assets held.

C. Violating law, rule, or regulation, including . . .

Savings and Loans

Information about savings and loans is available from the Office of Thrift Supervision, part of the Treasury Department. The information is almost the same as that which can be obtained from the regulators of commercial banks: summaries of cease-and-desist orders, quarterly reports and applications, challenges, exhibits and so on. OTS has jurisdiction over several thousand federal and state-chartered savings and loans whose deposits are guaranteed by the Savings Association Insurance Fund, which is now part of the Federal Deposit Insurance Corp.

State regulators play a role as well. In Missouri, for instance, the Division of Savings and Loan Supervision, part of the Department of Economic Development, oversees a few dozen financial institutions as well as licensed mortgage brokers.

The increase in recent years of savings associations converting from mutual form (ostensibly owned by the depositors) to stock form has resulted in more savings and loans being subject to SEC filing requirements. Many SEC reports, such as the 10-Ks and 8-Ks (see Chapter 13), may be on file with OTS. Savings and loans are required to file certain reports with the FDIC, including applications for deposit insurance, mergers with noninsured institutions and insurance fund conversions.

Credit Unions

Credit unions were first created in the 1930s during the Great Depression as cooperatives to promote savings and provide loans for homes and personal property. They are likely to be regulated at one or both of two levels: the National Credit Union Administration—with main offices in Washington, D.C., and regional branches—or a state regulatory agency. The NCUA oversees federally chartered or federally insured credit unions, and the National Credit Union Share Insurance Fund is financed by fees charged to the credit unions.

The NCUA describes a credit union as "a nonprofit, cooperative financial institution owned and run by its members. Organized to serve, democratically controlled credit unions provide their members with a safe place to save and borrow at reasonable rates. Members pool their funds to make loans to one another. The volunteer board that runs each credit union is elected by the members."

The NCUA's Web site contains information on credit unions nationwide. State agencies are the primary regulators of a much smaller number of state-chartered credit unions—that is, those that are granted the right to operate by the state—and credit unions that carry no federal insurance. (The NCUA estimates that there are fewer than 500 credit unions that do not have federal insurance.) In Missouri, for instance, the Division of Credit Unions in the Department of Economic Development oversees a couple of hundred state-chartered groups.

Banks and savings and loans increasingly compete with credit unions, although local credit unions are limited by geographic area, type of employment or other well-defined boundaries.

Possible stories might be found in the credit union's call report, the same report required of banks. A credit union submits its financial reports to federal

PART III Investigating Business

or state regulators every three or six months, depending on its size and state. Federally insured state credit unions are supposed to supply a financial statement, income and expense statement, statistical loan information, statistical share information, line of credit information and miscellaneous data. Federally chartered credit unions supply essentially the same information but in a different format.

The financial statement includes information about loans to members; loans purchased from liquidating credit unions; allowances for loan losses; net loans outstanding; cash and petty cash; investments broken down by passbook accounts, certificates of deposit and government obligations; loans to other credit unions; land, buildings and other fixed assets; accounts payable; statutory reserve; special reserve for losses; and reserves for contingencies. The income and expenses statement includes interest on loans, income from loans, interest on real estate loans, income from investments, employee compensation, employee benefits, travel and conference expenses, association dues, office rent and supply expenses, educational and promotional expenses, professional and outside services costs, insurance costs, annual meeting expenses and the allocation of net gains or losses that year to dividends, statutory reserves and undivided earnings.

Regulators often add requirements for additional disclosure to obtain information they deem necessary to address emerging problems in the industry.

Credit Card Companies

In recent years, journalists have been digging into credit card scams and problems with legitimate credit card companies. The Sun-Sentinel, for example, looked at two entrepreneurs who owned or controlled three Fort Lauderdale companies that ran the credit card program for BestBank in Colorado. BestBank had closed, saying that it had bad credit card debts, and the Sun-Sentinel's investigation showed that the two entrepreneurs had issued cards to people with bad credit. The story also examined the impact of the bank's closing.

WFAA-TV in Dallas reported on how billions of dollars may have been wrongly taken from millions of credit card consumers. In its investigation of First USA, it reported that industry analysts estimated one-third of First USA's annual revenue came from the penalties and interest rate hikes it improperly assessed against customers, an amount totaling nearly $20 billion.

Through freedom-of-information requests, WFAA obtained from the Office of the Comptroller of the Currency the number of complaints against the 10 largest credit card companies in the United States. The station found that there were far more complaints against First USA than against the others. Working with consumers, WFAA found that credit card holders were being improperly charged late fees and improper interest rate hikes even though they were paying on time.

In another example, the Riverfront Times in St. Louis examined the Heartland Bank, which billed itself as "a paragon of Midwestern values." The newspaper found that the bank's impressive growth came at a price to thousands of credit card holders. According to the Federal Trade Commission, the bank did business with Internet pornographers who cheated consumers by charging credit card accounts without permission. In this case, the reporter used FTC documents, court documents from lawsuits and documents from the Office of Thrift Supervision, which regulated Heartland.

Investment Companies and Mutual Funds

Investment companies, especially mutual funds, are a powerful force in the business world. More and more middle-class individuals are entrusting their money to these companies, which pour that accumulated money into a variety of investments. Because mutual fund investments are not insured by the federal government—unlike deposits in banks, savings and loans and credit unions—citizens are at greater risk when they place money there. Some of these investors have no idea that their funds are uninsured. Their vulnerability is reduced only somewhat by the Securities Investor Protection Corporation, a nonprofit organization created by Congress to serve as a safety net for the public. The SIPC notes that it acts either "as trustee or works with an independent court-appointed trustee in a missing assets case to recover funds. . . . SIPC provides that customers of a failed brokerage firm receive all non-negotiable securities that are already registered in their names or in the process of being registered. All other so-called "street name" securities are distributed on a pro rata basis. The SIPC has a reserve that can be used to pay customer claims up to a maximum of $500,000. Recovered funds are used to pay investors whose claims exceed the SIPC's protection limit of $500,000. SIPC often draws down its reserve to aid investors.

Investment companies have two theoretical advantages over individual investors trying to profit on their own: professional research and enough money to diversify broadly as a hedge against a few poor performing choices. Their critics, however, point out that these companies often do no better than individual investors making educated guesses.

Because of financial market uncertainties affecting mutual funds combined with the potential for out-of-control management fees, the Securities and Exchange Commission requires investment companies to file extensive reports, starting with a detailed prospectus for potential investors.

PART III Investigating Business

The mutual fund industry suggests that potential investors look for as many as 17 important pieces of information in a prospectus, which includes a fund's statement of investment objectives. There are three main objectives: stability, defined as protecting the amount invested from the risk of loss; growth, defined as increasing the value of principal through capital gains; and income, defined as a steady stream of income payments through dividends.

Another of the 17 pieces is the fee table. All fees charged by a mutual fund to an investor are summarized in a table at the front of the prospectus. The first section of the table summarizes an investor's transaction expenses for purchases, exchanges or redemptions. The second section summarizes the mutual fund's operating expenses. The third section is a hypothetical example of how such fees reduce earnings over periods of one, three, five and 10 years. Located near the fee table is the per-share table, actually a condensed financial statement that illustrates how well the fund has been doing with investors' money for the past 10 years. In addition to overseeing the prospectus, the SEC regulates the activities of investment advisers to mutual funds and conflicts of interest involving fund managers.

Potential and real conflicts are receiving more attention from mainstream investigative journalists. As Diana B. Henriques wrote in her New York Times investigative series on mutual funds, "Fund managers, operating with little oversight by regulators, are investing in companies that employ executives, advisors or underwriters with whom they have close ties. Often, those deals have left the funds holding securities of dubious value."

As mutual funds take more and more money away from savings institutions, those institutions are seeking legislative and regulatory authority to compete. Journalists should inquire whether traditional financial institutions like banks make it clear to consumers that the funds are not federally insured against loss or collapse when they sell mutual funds in their lobbies. Some mutual fund industry sources believe that if banks are going to enter the fray, then their trust departments ought to be scrutinized under federal securities laws. The same could be said for insurance companies. In other words, the same rules should apply to every institution with decision-making power over pooled investments.

Investigating the Issues

Often, investigations into financial lenders focus on the kinds of services the institutions are providing to the community. Over the years, much federal regulation has been passed to ensure that lenders treat their customers fairly and reinvest in the community, rather than using the funds in another region.

Redlining and Community Reinvestment

In addition to the Fair Housing Act and the Equal Credit Opportunity Act, journalists have relied on two other laws to study redlining (the deliberate action of insurers and agents to exclude from coverage certain people in low-income neighborhoods, often blacks or other minorities). As noted earlier, the Home Mortgage Disclosure Act pinpoints one type of loan. The law requires depository institutions with assets of more than $10 million and at least one branch in an urban area to disclose the number and total dollar amount of mortgage loans made, in addition to keeping application data by race, gender and income level. Part A of the statement reports loans written, organized by census tract and listed by type of loan, number of loans and total dollar amount. Types of loans include those from the Farmers Home Administration and the Department of Veterans Affairs, as well as home improvement, nonoccupant, multifamily dwelling and conventional loans. If the financial institution has redlined any neighborhoods, the first indication might show up in Part A as portions of census tracts in which it has made few or no loans. Part B reports on mortgages purchased from other institutions. It tells how much business a particular financial institution is doing in the secondary market.

The Community Reinvestment Act (CRA), which is broader than the Home Mortgage Disclosure Act, requires financial institutions to ascertain and meet the credit needs of minority and low-income areas near their branch locations. Financial institutions must make available a list that identifies loans for one- to four-dwelling residential units, small businesses, housing rehabilitation, farmers and commercial property. The CRA statement is available on request from the financial institution. A file must be kept by the bank of signed comments received from the public within the previous two years that specifically relate to the CRA statement or to the lender's performance in meeting the credit needs of the community, together with any responses the lender wishes to make.

The CRA encourages lenders to include a description of its efforts to evaluate and meet community credit needs, including efforts to offer and publicize special credit-related programs. Although these activities are encouraged rather than required, government examiners take the lender's efforts into consideration when deciding whether to grant approval on applications for facility expansion or new services.

Critics say the CRA's effectiveness has been diluted in recent years. In fact, a journalist who searches the database of examinations of the CRA at the FDIC Web site will find that nearly every bank received a satisfactory or higher rating. But the statements are still valuable because they contain a wide range of information about the institutions and the communities they serve.

PART III Investigating Business

Also, because lots of mortgage lending is now done by nonbank financial institutions, including huge brokerages like Merrill Lynch, information available under current banking laws fails to provide a complete picture, if any, of redlining in a community. Lawmakers and regulators are considering whether all lenders ought to report their practices. Meanwhile, journalists will have to obtain whatever data they can from lenders that are exempt from disclosure.

The HMDA database is available from the federal government (and from the National Institute for Computer-Assisted Reporting), and as a result, computer-assisted reporting has been employed for many years on redlining projects. A 1988 computer-assisted project at The Atlanta Journal-Constitution ignited interest in the database, which has changed over the years but has continued to be a valuable tool for measuring lending practices, particularly in the subprime market.

Lenders generally say that higher percentages of rejections or higher interest rates for blacks or Hispanics have nothing to do with race or neighborhood and everything to do with creditworthiness.

But many journalists, including those from The Charlotte Observer, have found deep disparities in lending practices. The Orange County Register also documented that black and other minority neighborhoods tend to lack loan offices, while white areas have easy accessibility to such facilities.

Most investigations have focused on loan rejection rates because they are the most readily available. A better test might be to combine loan rejections with loan applications. After all, raw rejection rates tell nothing about applicants' credit or income histories (and nobody is advocating that lenders provide mortgages that are almost sure to go into default). Loan application statistics have their flaws too. But if a financial institution is receiving proportionally equal numbers of applications from all races and ethnic groups, it is probably trying to do the right thing.

A Wall Street Journal investigation used such a technique. In an explanation of its methodology, The Journal said it merged information from 2.25 million loan applications and U.S. census data on the racial makeup of neighborhoods:

> The Journal first counted the number of applications each lender received on property in all U.S. census tracts. It also calculated the number of applications a lender received on property in census tracts where blacks make up at least 75 percent of the population. The Journal next computed the percentage, or share, of applications a lender garnered in all states in which it operated, and then the share of applications a lender received from census tracts with a black population of 75 percent or more.
>
> For each lender, a share ratio was derived by dividing its percentage of predominantly black-area applications by its overall share of applications. A ratio of one indicates equal penetration in black and non-black areas. A ratio less than one shows less

marketing penetration in black areas than white, and a ratio greater than one shows more penetration in black areas.

Blacks submitted just 128,000 (5.6 percent) of the 2.25 million applications; only 25,000 came from blacks in mostly black neighborhoods. Unlike most previous investigations, The Journal's investigation—which found substantial disparities in rejection rates—covered largely unregulated nonbank mortgage lenders as well as traditional commercial banks and savings and loans. Some of the nonbank mortgage lenders, though, are the unregulated subsidiaries of commercial banks and savings and loans.

Insider Transactions

Investigative journalists can find out if officers, directors, major customers, politicians and other powerful people benefit from a financial institution in ways unavailable to the average customer. Using documents filed with regulators, plus human sources, journalists can piece together salaries paid to officers, fees paid to inside and outside directors, loans made to officers and directors or their companies, rent paid to insiders who own the financial institution's building or land, remuneration to insiders who broker loans and mortgages and legal, accounting or other professional fees paid to insiders.

Because financial institutions control so much money, they can attract criminals and con men. Even when insiders look clean on paper, they might have a history of greed that will show up in civil lawsuits or emerge through extensive interviewing.

In a classic example, The Detroit News looked at the directors of a savings and loan. The newspaper discovered one director who had voted in favor of lending money to a business partner for a housing development, other directors who made real estate deals with officers and borrowers, public officials who served on the board while accepting campaign contributions from borrowers, a lease for a yacht to be used by the institution's president and a rent agreement between the institution and a director who eventually sold the space to the savings and loan for a profit. The Resource Center of Investigative Reporters and Editors is filled with other projects documenting the activities of greedy insiders at financial institutions.

High-Risk Transactions

Journalists can also investigate how financial institutions can decrease their exposure on risky loans by getting guarantees from federal agencies. Despite regulatory changes and reforms, investigative journalists have found U.S. Small

Business Administration loan guarantees that allowed financial institutions to make loans they should have avoided.

Several news organizations have used SBA databases, bankruptcy records, and civil court documents to look at the use of SBA loans by banks. They have discovered higher loan default rates than expected and millions of dollars in losses covered by taxpayers.

Journalists also can look at investments in U.S. Treasury securities that would seem to carry little risk but contain risks nevertheless. Financial institutions sometimes fail to set aside capital to cover losses from Treasury securities, so when interest rates rise and the value of the securities drops, an institution's reserves might be significantly diminished. Furthermore, the losses might be masked because the institutions do not have to report losses unless they actually sell the securities. So, it is worthwhile to look at whether local financial institutions are overextended in U.S. Treasury securities.

Another area to examine is derivatives. Derivatives are complicated financial instruments that banks, savings and loans and other trusted institutions buy and sell. They are contracts that derive their value from an underlying stock, commodity or financial instrument. Banks have to report their derivative holdings on special schedules in their call reports. They must list the dollar amount of their holdings in collateralized mortgage obligations, interest rate contracts and foreign exchange rate contracts.

Journalists should determine what percentage of a financial institution's assets is tied up in derivatives, and then ask the following questions:

- How well do the institution's officers understand the derivatives they have bought?
- Have they been conned by securities dealers who are looking to dump derivatives that more sophisticated investors avoid?
- What is the long-term earnings record of the derivatives owned by the financial institution?
- Have they traditionally earned well in early years and then fallen dramatically?

Money Laundering

Not all money laundering involves banks or other financial institutions, but sometimes they are accomplices in helping drug dealers and other criminals move the huge amounts of cash they accumulate. An investigation by the Center for Public Integrity revealed a Bank of New York money-laundering scandal involving billions of dollars from the former Soviet Union.

By law, regulated financial institutions are supposed to complete IRS Form 4789 every time a depositor brings in cash of $10,000 or more. Those currency-transaction reports have discouraged the kind of brazen money laundering that used to occur. But financial institutions that care little about the law will work with launderers to break up the cash deposits into amounts under $10,000. Some dishonest bankers will also look the other way when huge amounts of cash come in from retail businesses that realistically could not generate that amount of money.

A typical scenario would be for a drug ring to buy a jewelry store and create fake invoices, allowing dirty money to be disguised as revenue from jewelry sales. Business Week magazine summarized other scenarios:

- Launderers buy money orders locally, which are then deposited in a bank or wired across the country to a fellow launderer who does not need identification to cash them.
- Dishonest offshore insurance brokers accept cash from launderers, buy large annuities from U.S. insurance companies, cancel the annuities and obtain cash in the form of a refund check.
- Launderers buy postal money orders, which are exempt from currency transaction reporting rules, and then redeem them at foreign banks.
- Currency exchange shops, sometimes called *casas de cambios*, take cash from launderers and then deposit the money in regulated financial institutions. When the institutions file currency transaction reports, the exchange shops show up, not the launderers.

Journalists should be alert for such dishonest players. Furthermore, if a local bank has a correspondent relationship with an offshore bank, especially in the Caribbean, journalists should explore why.

Investigating Insurance

To guard against economic devastation, individuals pay for personal insurance—life, health, automobile, homeowners' insurance—or wish they could. Businesses buy insurance too—for workers' compensation and unemployment, as well as for protection against natural disasters, crop failures, equipment failures, malpractice claims, libel and more.

Federal and state governments pay for Medicare and Medicaid insurance coverage, and they contract with insurance companies to provide care for the employees who staff the government.

Insurance companies, part of the private sector already covered in Chapter 13, provide three types of coverage: life, health and property-casualty (liability) insurance. Some companies form subsidiaries to sell every kind of insurance. This chapter focuses on how investigative reporters can scrutinize insurance companies and their agents.

Following the disastrous damage caused by Hurricane Katrina in New Orleans and the frequent destructive wildfires in California, the insurance industry's handling and denial of consumer claims came under closer scrutiny by investigative journalists than ever before.

One model investigative series by Bloomberg Markets magazine entitled "The Insurance Hoax" explored how insurers use secret tactics to cheat homeowners. Using insurance industry filings and documents from court cases, Bloomberg found that the industry had, with a major consulting company's guidance, developed methods to aggressively deny legitimate claims or to lower payouts in order to increase profits. In its investigation, Bloomberg found numerous examples of people who encountered adjusters and claims handlers who refused to give them a fair payout.

Several news organizations also conducted major investigations. Dateline NBC won awards for its probe into the denial of claims by State Farm Insurance. The Sun-Sentinel in Ft. Lauderdale showed the other side of the story, revealing an underground network of people staging accidents to cheat insurance companies and consumers. Inside Edition revealed the ugly practices of door-to-door salesmen persuading poor clients to purchase insurance at high prices. The Sacramento Bee looked at what it means for nearly 7 million Californians—more than 20 percent of the state's population—to rely on emergency rooms or their own finances when they get sick because they are uninsured. U.S. News and World Report and the Wisconsin State Journal revealed possible redlining by insurers, and KCBS-TV in Los Angeles revealed insurance scams. And many news organizations have dug deeply into stories about the impact of insurance on medical care.

Insurance is clearly a rewarding area for inquiry. The stories involve people from all walks of life, usually in moments of suffering. It is nearly impossible to live or do business without insurance, and when people are uninsured, that in itself is an important story.

Individuals and businesses have many complaints about the hundreds of billions of dollars they spend on premiums each year and how the insurance companies respond to claims. In 2006 and 2007, The Kansas City Star did a series examining the insurance industry from the consumers' viewpoint. Reporters examined nearly 35 million electronic records from the National Association of

Insurance Commissioners about consumer complaints and gathered thousands of specific complaints from all 50 states.

The Star found numerous legitimate complaints from consumers and uncovered billions of dollars in fraud, which raised premiums for everyone. But the Star also found heavy lobbying of federal officials by the insurance industry and discovered that many regulators had worked in the industry.

The average U.S. family spends at least a tenth of its income on insurance. Many families buy on the basis of name brand or a reassuring-sounding promise ("You're in good hands" and "Like a good neighbor") or because they know a local insurance agent or are swayed by high-pressure sales tactics.

Regulation by state agencies tends to be lax, and federal regulation is minimal since insurance companies have successfully lobbied against nationwide regulation. The potential for fraud is great. In that way, the insurance industry is like the banking and savings and loan industry: There is so much money coming in every day that it is going to attract people who intend to misuse it.

Health and Disability Insurance

Of all types of insurance worth investigating, health coverage is frequently the most compelling. The stories literally involve life and death.

Because so much health insurance is employment based, journalists should be delving into the coverage provided by local employers. Do they offer adequate and equal coverage for all employees at a reasonable price? Inadequate coverage might exclude some of the very illnesses usually associated with that type of workplace—for example, repetitive motion injuries in a meatpacking plant. Unequal coverage might mean that an employer excludes a worker with a pre-existing kidney problem or charges that worker higher rates than others covered by the group policy are charged. An unreasonable price might mean that some workers cannot afford their share of the premium and so go without coverage.

More than 45 million Americans lack health insurance; they are likely to be unemployed or part-time workers, minorities or foreign born. A journalist should locate local residents who are uninsured and seek documentation of any steps they have taken in an attempt to obtain insurance. Questions to ask include these:

- Have employers and insurers acted illegally or unethically in denying coverage?
- Is there a government program for those unable to obtain coverage any other way? Are the policies offered through the program affordable and adequate?

PART III Investigating Business

- Are procedures routinely performed by doctors and hospitals being denied coverage?
- And if coverage is finally approved by the insurer affiliated with the HMO, does it come only after delays, during which the patient's condition deteriorates?
- If, according to high-technology testing, a patient has a tendency toward a genetic disease but shows no overt signs of it, should an insurer be able to deny coverage without penalty?

Disability insurance is a more limited health policy, designed mainly to replace lost income. In scrutinizing disability coverage, a journalist should ask whether it excludes certain causes of injury, especially those most likely to happen in a particular workplace.

Other questions should be explored:

- Will the insurance company pay benefits if the policyholder can do some work but not his or her previous occupation?
- Will it pay benefits for enough weeks or months to matter?
- Will it begin paying only after a certain number of months or years, leaving the policyholder with no income during the waiting period?

As insurance companies become more aggressive in fighting disability claims, journalists will find more complaints filed by policyholders with state insurance commissioners, as well as more lawsuits pitting disability insurers against individuals trying to collect after being injured. Insurers believe a large number of disability claims are fraudulent, and they receive large numbers of claims for disabilities that were once uncommon, including carpal tunnel syndrome, Epstein-Barr virus, stress-related disorders and AIDS.

Life Insurance

Life insurance is often advertised as a savings tool. But journalists should determine whether the investment and savings features really pay, or whether the policyholder would be better off putting the money in a lower-risk investment than buying term life insurance for its death benefit.

The variations on life insurance seem endless. Universal life insurance was popular as agents promised huge earnings tied to rising interest rates. But when interest rates fell, policyholders had to pay additional premiums. Next came variable life insurance, tied to mutual fund performance. That meant policyholders became dependent on stock market performance. Other forms of life insurance offerings can be simply ludicrous, such as when agents have offered policies whose eventual payout is significantly less than the premiums paid.

On the other hand, consumers can defraud life insurers. When they do, the cases are often dramatic and high-profile because they involve economically motivated murders or staged deaths. The book "Death Benefit," by David Heilbroner, explains how a lawyer helping a fellow church member collect a death benefit on her daughter uncovered a serial killer who collected life insurance benefits on her victims.

Automobile Insurance

In a classic investigation into the underground world of insurance scams, Fred Schulte and Jenni Bergal of the Sun-Sentinel in Fort Lauderdale exposed a network of scam artists staging fake automobile accidents and submitting false bills to care clinics. Their seven-month investigation identified more than 4,000 Florida residents who played roles in at least 1,400 suspicious auto accidents statewide during the 1990s.

In an IRE Journal article, Schulte and Bergal identified public records that could help reporters get an inside look at the multibillion-dollar criminal enterprise:

- *Civil court files.* Increasingly, auto insurers are refusing to pay bills they believe are inflated or bogus and are pressing their cases in court. Records of these civil lawsuits, especially depositions of doctors and clinic owners, are invaluable, both for locating patients and for establishing questionable billing practices and medical testing abuses.
- *Disciplinary and criminal case files.* We obtained a list of all Florida Board of Chiropractic Medicine disciplinary cases in the last five years and requested hard copies of cases that involved insurance fraud or patient solicitation, including penalties imposed.
- *State Department of Insurance files.* To our surprise, the Florida Division of Insurance Fraud allowed us to visit five of their offices around the state, where we inspected more than 500 closed cases, dating to 1995. Most had been closed without an arrest.
- *Department of Highway Safety and Motor Vehicles.* We accessed driving histories and accident records for people investigated for insurance fraud, accident staging or possessing a phony driver's license. The latter is the criminal charge that often gets filed against those who stage accidents.

States generally require proof of auto insurance to issue driver's licenses or to register cars. But if coverage is supposedly mandatory, why are there so many uninsured motorists driving? There is no way to obtain precise numbers of uninsured drivers, but journalists can talk to sources at the state insurance department, state motor vehicles division, state highway patrol, other agencies and insurance companies and then supplement what they learn from those sources by looking for accident reports and lawsuits involving uninsured drivers.

Geographic distinctions, type of car driven, number of miles driven in an average week for what purposes, age of the driver and driver's health might all be factors in determining rates. Journalists can look into whether it's fair that a motorist with a perfect driving record in, say, Massachusetts has to pay a much higher premium than a comparable driver in Kansas.

Because of such rate differentials, journalists on the borders of two states can look at where cars are insured. How many motorists live in, say, New York, but insure their car in New Jersey to get lower rates?

Journalists who understand the anatomy of fraud in auto insurance will look for suspicious circumstances in police reports and lawsuits. Those journalists will also talk regularly to insurance company investigators who can direct them to compelling stories. The insurance industry established the National Insurance Crime Bureau in Palos Hills, Ill., to help investigators uncover policyholder fraud, as well as to aid in auto theft prevention and recovery. (Stolen car fraud is handled more fully in Chapter 11 of this book.) Several hundred NICB agents work with law enforcement agencies to solve cases. The group's computer databases can help detect fraud by spotting false claim patterns.

Homeowners' and Other Property Insurance

Homeowners' policies usually cover damage to the home, theft of its contents and legal liability for bodily injury or property damage of others. As Hurricane Katrina proved, journalists should look closely at exclusions that mean the policyholder has less coverage than he or she expects. When damage occurs to the structure or contents are stolen, does the policy provide enough coverage to rebuild or replace the home with comparable quality, thanks to inflation protection combined with a replacement-value provision? Or will the policyholder be surprised to learn that the insurer will pay only the original cost minus depreciation because the contract contains an actual cash value clause?

Other issues journalists should explore about homeowners' insurance include these:

- Should people who live in high-risk weather or high-crime areas be excluded from coverage by insurers or have to pay higher premiums than they would for the same coverage in a different locale?
- In high-risk weather areas or high-crime areas, should insurers be able to pull out of the market or charge policyholders more?
- If the local building code is lax in its standards or its enforcement, are homes (and commercial buildings) more likely to suffer damage than if they were more soundly constructed and more rigorously inspected?
- Should insurers be allowed to avoid all applicants from certain ZIP codes or census tracts?
- Should they be allowed to reject all applicants who live in homes that are 50 years old or older, even if the homes are in good condition?
- Are some of these conditions meant to exclude applicants on the basis of race or ethnicity?

As with other types of policies, house and property fraud against insurance companies is common. Journalists should be alert for civil lawsuits and criminal cases aimed at policyholders trying to bilk insurers by staging burglaries, overvaluing stolen contents, claiming money for pre-existing damages, backdating policies, inflating property repair costs and paying somebody to fake an injury on the property, collect damages and then split the award. The most insidious fraud involves arson because it often results in death, serious injury and damage to the property of innocent parties. (Arson investigations are treated more fully in Chapter 11.)

Commercial and Professional Insurance

In Florida, insurance companies writing medical malpractice policies were pushing for the authority to charge higher premiums. But the Orlando Sentinel showed that insurers were misleading the public about a widespread medical malpractice crisis. It turned out that 3 percent of all doctors in Florida accounted for half the malpractice claims paid by insurers. Instead of dealing with that tiny minority, insurers wanted to raise rates for all doctors.

Another type of professional liability insurance for journalists to monitor covers officers and directors of businesses. Journalists can find out how much local employers pay for that coverage and whether local employers have had to use their officers' and directors' coverage as the result of lawsuits filed against them. Journalists should also check on the costs of commercial insurance coverage to insurers. There are dozens of types of commercial insurance, including ocean marine, inland marine, earthquake, glass and machinery policies. Journalists can read state insurance departments' reports on specific lines of commercial and professional liability insurance. For example, one Missouri report showed a substantial profit on medical malpractice insurance for most insurers during the period studied.

Commercial and professional liability insurance policies for business constitute a large part of overall insurance fraud because these policies generally involve more money than personal insurance policies. These frauds can include corrupt adjusters, although the adjusters are employed by the insurers. One clue to fraud is the involvement of outside "public" adjusters who receive a percentage of the eventual insurance settlement. Their participation might signal inflated monetary claims, an unusually large number of water-damage reports and so on.

Investigating the Players

Companies and Their Finances

Because life and health insurance company insolvencies have increased in recent years, investigative journalists should scrutinize the financial reports of these companies. Many technically solvent companies have been shown to be in weak condition, especially a substantial percentage of Blue Cross health plans, which collectively make up the country's largest health insurer.

An investigation of Empire Blue Cross and Blue Shield by The New York Times showed that Empire's filings with state regulators seemed to inflate losses on policies for high-risk individuals and small groups; rates on those policies came under state control, and the supposedly nonprofit insurer wanted to charge more. At the same time, the insurer appeared to understate losses on large business accounts, which were unregulated and desirable from Empire's standpoint. The legislature, believing all the figures, did Empire's bidding by requiring for-profit insurers to write health policies for high-risk applicants or to stop selling in the state.

It is still a challenge to determine the true state of a particular company's financial health. Insurers use accounting rules to mask their profits, thereby avoiding price decreases when state regulators mention the possibility. In trying to interpret the insurers' own numbers, journalists can rely on examinations conducted by state insurance departments at routine intervals or in response to perceived problems.

State insurance regulators are supposed to share information among the states, but many news organizations reported on a pyramid scam run by a Connecticut financier that took advantage of the fractured regulation system, which depends on each state individually overseeing insurance within its jurisdiction.

Furthermore, an insurance company might in fact be solvent, but that doesn't mean its practices are acceptable. State regulators must keep track of and investigate complaints against insurers. Journalists can read through those complaints—as The Kansas City Star did—which can lead to a larger story. Multiple complaints against the same company about the same practice might be the first step in documenting a pattern of illegal or unethical behavior.

A journalist wandering around a county government building one day decided to sit in on a court case of a large insurance company challenging its $31 million property tax assessment for a downtown building. The insurer wanted the assessment reduced to $20 million. The journalist checked with the state insurance commissioner and discovered that the company considered the building to be worth $27.4 million.

Journalists also should look for insurance companies involved in lines of business unrelated to insurance, such as computer software or real estate development. Do such subsidiaries yield financial gains for insurance company executives who are charging the main company outrageous management and equipment fees to line their own pockets? As with any other business, journalists should check for inflated executive salaries and benefits and favored treatment for directors, such as millions of dollars of company-related legal work that go to the lawyer on the board.

Journalists should also be on the lookout for redlining. The worst problems seem to be with automobile and homeowners' insurance. To investigate redlining allegations, journalists should check sales and claims data by ZIP code. They then should check whether agents' offices are absent from certain neighborhoods, but located in more affluent sections.

Another factor to check is whether a black person pays a premium comparable to that paid by whites. Also, look at whether a black person, who lives in a mostly white neighborhood, pays more for less coverage when the black person moves to a mostly black neighborhood.

Electronic data are not available in every state; when they are, news organizations can use insurance data and census data to show the sales patterns by ZIP code and income level, as U.S. News and World Report did nationally and the Wisconsin State Journal did statewide. CNN also pulled together evidence

PART III Investigating Business

of redlining for the cable network's projects reports. One irony is that insurance companies and agents might be hurting themselves financially while breaking the law by redlining. The Missouri Insurance Department conducted a study showing much higher percentage payouts to white policyholders than to blacks, because whites were more likely to file claims.

Agents

Journalists also should look at agents. Some agents sell exclusively for one company as employees. Others are independents representing numerous insurers. In one investigation of insurance agents, Forbes magazine priced 250 term life insurance policies for a 45-year-old male nonsmoker who wanted $1 million of coverage. The 10-year total bill ranged from $16,200 to $94,100. Inside Edition in its investigation in the South found that door-to-door insurance salesmen were selling insurance that had premiums higher than any potential payout.

Journalists should determine how much commission agents receive on each type of policy sold and then explore whether the level of commission influences what they try to sell to customers. By selling a certain whole-life policy, an agent can earn $550 on a $1,000 premium; an annuity policy, on the other hand, will earn only a $20 commission. When checking agents, journalists should ask whether they have achieved the rank of chartered life underwriter, chartered financial consultant, chartered property-casualty underwriter or certified financial planner. These ranks do not guarantee honesty, but their attainment shows that the agents sought advanced training.

State insurance departments, which license agents, might issue a notice of regulatory activity against a specific agent based on investigations of outside complaints or suspicions within the department. The notice shows the reason for disciplinary action and the disposition. A monetary fine, license suspension or license revocation are the most common penalties. The process tends to be reactive. In Missouri, for example, which has about 68,000 insurance agents, there is no individual review at license renewal time. That gives journalists all the more reason to initiate investigations. Some state insurance departments will release complaints against agents even when no discipline resulted.

The New York Times investigated sales pitches by agents from a major insurer who pushed term life to every customer, no matter how varied their situations. The reporter determined that some of the agents were improperly licensed and used misleading comparisons. For example, in denigrating whole-life policies, the agents showed no dividends, arguing that was fair because dividends were not guaranteed. But the whole-life policy in question had paid dividends every year.

When agent deception occurs, journalists should document whether individual agents are at fault or if the company encourages the deception. What happens to the insured if an agent embezzles the premium or misplaces the application, which then never gets to the home office? As journalists interview sources and review documents, they should determine whether checks are payable to the company or, at their insistence, to the agents, which can be an indicator of fraud.

State Regulators

Individual states regulate the insurance companies that do business in their state. Fraud is so rampant and state insurance departments are usually so understaffed that the regulators are forced to be reactive. Because they cannot investigate all complaints thoroughly, they sometimes fail to detect patterns of fraud. Knowing that, journalists should eagerly and regularly seek access to complaint files.

The annual statements that insurance companies file with state insurance departments are probably the most detailed disclosure of income, expenditures and assets required of any institution by any government agency. Investigators who read every page carefully will find kernels of many stories concerning the vast real estate holdings of the company, how it invests money from policyholders, whether its reserves are adequate to pay claims in a timely manner and much more.

Some state insurance commissioners are appointed by the governor with legislative consent; others are elected. Each system has strengths and weaknesses. Appointed commissioners might feel less accountable to policyholders, who are unable to vote them out of office directly. On the other hand, elected commissioners tend to be in the debt of campaign contributors from the insurance industry. How many commissioners have come from the industry or go to work for insurers immediately after leaving their state job? How many of their assistants do the same? How many state regulators came from the industry originally? That path is a way to gain intimate knowledge of the industry, but it might also lead to a pro-insurer, anti-policyholder mind-set.

As journalists explore the regulatory side of the industry, they should ask these questions:

- What is the appropriate level of regulation?
- Should states be able to force insurers to write policies for all applicants, require renewals and micromanage rates?
- Are consumers at large represented by a public advocate on rate increase requests? If so, how effective is the public advocate? If there is no public advocate, why not?

Noting that the Kansas City–based National Association of Insurance Commissioners lacks enforcement power as an organization, Newsweek finance writer Jane Bryant Quinn commented, "If the NAIC approves a paragraph [in insurance legislation] that key insurance companies hate, they will turn loose their lobbyists in the state capitals to excise the offending words." That is especially easy for insurers to accomplish when a significant number of state legislators are insurance agents, as is the case in many capitals. As an example, Quinn noted a model NAIC regulation that companies writing credit insurance pay out at least 60 cents in claims for every dollar collected. Only four jurisdictions met that standard.

Health insurance is barely policed by state agencies, especially if the insurance is provided by employers. That is because court rulings have held that employer-sponsored health insurance falls under the federal Employee Retirement Income Security Act. Unfortunately for employees, ERISA is a 1974 law that never contemplated the importance of health insurance as a benefit and so lacks regulatory bite. The National Journal reported a case of an employee insured by her employer who checked out of a hospital after learning her health insurance would not pay for care during a difficult pregnancy. Instead, the insurer said, it would pay for less costly monitoring at home. Two weeks later, the fetus died. The insurer had ignored the advice of two doctors, but when the patient sued the insurer for wrongful death, the court held that she had no right to sue under state law. And under ERISA, she was not allowed to sue in federal court either. There is almost no federal monitoring of insurance unless Medicare is involved. At the state level, monitoring is often split among several agencies; the state insurance department is supposed to oversee insurance companies, while state medical boards are supposed to oversee physicians. Health maintenance organizations often fall through the cracks of regulation, even though they might be controlled by insurance companies.

Sometimes the best that consumers—and journalists—can hope for is statistics rather than regulation. State insurance departments report on the number of complaints by company, type of insurance and reasons for the complaints, which number in the dozens. While studying complaints, journalists can try to determine whether the state department is handling even a small percentage of them effectively. One measure is the department's budget per complaint investigation (an average of $250, according to one study) or per company examination (an average of $4,000). Can the job be done properly with such budgets?

When an insurance company's insolvency occurs on the state's watch, journalists should review the regulators' monitoring and examination of that company.

- Had the regulators conducted a thorough examination of the company within the past few years, as prescribed by law?
- If so, what warning signs did the examination uncover? If none, why not?
- If regulators identified trouble spots, what action did they take? Did they feel constrained by a lack of jurisdiction?
- After the insolvency, did the state department work effectively to provide restitution for the maximum number of policyholders?
- Did the federal and state governments receive priority over other creditors, leaving individual policyholders impoverished?

Unless insurance commissioners in every state agree on new rules, there will be gaps and loopholes that allow the insurance industry to circumvent reform.

The Government as Insurer

When a government agency steps in to supplement or pre-empt the private insurance market, it often provides broader coverage at affordable prices. But at the same time, fraud and inefficiency can run rampant while taxpayers carry large burdens to support targeted segments of the populace.

The National Flood Insurance Program is an example. Most private insurers sensibly stay away from writing policies for people who insist on building homes and businesses in floodplains. But the federal government decided that the residential and commercial development of floodplains was worth certain risks. As a result, it pays certain policyholders again and again as water washes over their structures and fields. Newsweek told of an Illinois resident along the Mississippi River who had paid $6,000 in premiums over two decades but had collected payouts totaling $24,000 after four different floods.

Veterans' benefits are another example; they are discussed in Chapter 16 in the section on veterans' hospitals. Unemployment insurance, another program with heavy government involvement, is dealt with largely in Chapter 13.

Medicare, one of the federal government's largest insurance programs, is in essence partial universal health insurance for people 65 or older. Medicare Part A covers inpatient hospital expenses; it is financed by payments from workers and employers, based on a percentage of gross income. Elderly recipients pay no premiums and incur just one annual deductible. Part B covers other health care expenses, financed 75 percent by general tax revenues and 25 percent by individual premiums upon application; recipients pay a bit more through a deductible.

Journalists should begin their inquiries into Medicare by examining cases of fraud and abuse filed by the federal government against specific health care providers. The Federal Register will contain notices of specific cases; other sources could include the General Accounting Office, the U.S. attorney, the Medicare legal staff, congressional committees with jurisdiction over Medicare appropriations and state medical licensing boards.

Because Medicare is such a huge part of the federal budget, journalists have plenty of reason to ask questions. Payments for in-hospital care are limited to amounts set by the government according to 491 diagnostic-related groups (commonly called DRGs). They are usually below the rates charged to non-Medicare patients, so taxpayers are not being victimized often. So far, though, outpatient expenses have escaped DRG limits. Journalists should question whether private-practice physicians are charging Medicare for patients they have not seen or for treatments they have not administered. Are medical equipment suppliers (those providing wheelchairs, oxygen tanks and the like) submitting padded or otherwise fraudulent bills?

What about local physicians who refuse to participate? Their complaints usually include inadequate compensation, retroactive denial of claims and insurer interference with medical decisions. Are those complaints justified? Journalists should listen carefully and then investigate. If the physicians are correct, that could lead to a good story about an overbearing government. If the physicians are exaggerating, their failure to participate on the basis of mistaken perceptions is a good story too.

Another federal insurance program, Medicaid, paid by federal funds and governed by federal rules but operated by state governments, is meant to help the low-income and disabled. In many areas, Medicaid is hemorrhaging money through inefficiency and fraud, providing poor-quality care for those it reaches and failing to reach many people who need help. The Congressional Research Service summarized some of the problems in the preface to its Medicaid Source Book, prepared for the U.S. House Subcommittee on Health and the Environment:

> To many, the program is an enigma. The program's complexity surrounding who is eligible, what services will be paid for and how those services can be paid is one source of confusion. State Medicaid plan variability is the rule rather than the excep-

tion. For example, income eligibility levels vary, the services covered vary, and the amount of reimbursement for the services varies from state to state.

The program acts as a form of health insurance providing access to health services traditionally covered by private health insurance. However, it also provides payment for services such as nursing homes and community-based long-term care, services that have traditionally been outside the umbrella of private insurance. Furthermore, Medicaid is a program that is targeted at individuals with low incomes. But not all the poor are covered, and not all who are covered are poor.

The Chicago Tribune spent years investigating the Medicaid system and produced a nine-part series covering nearly every angle that journalists should be examining. Some of the issues they found included incompetent doctors, limited service in rural areas, administrators blindly accepting questionable charges, patients selling medication and equipment paid for by Medicaid, limited transportation for patients, and out-of-control Medicaid budgets taking money from other needed social programs.

Workers' Compensation

Workers' compensation insurance provides health care for job-related injuries. It started out as a no-fault system: The worker received payments underwritten by the employer after agreeing to refrain from suing the employer. Although it was a system pushed by business and employers, workers started hearing from lawyers wanting to represent them. The lawyers started filing litigation against employers and the state based on pain and suffering, rejected or delayed payments and inefficient, ineffective medical care. Gradually, a no-fault system turned into a plaintiff lawyer's dream. The litigation, combined with endemic fraud, has led to out-of-control insurance programs in many states that are ripe for exposure by journalists. At the same time, the system often fails those who have been seriously hurt. Compensation systems for injuries and disabilities claimed by municipal and state workers are particularly open to abuse. After The Hartford Courant and the Boston Herald exposed workers' compensation frauds in systems for government workers in separate locales, they combined to write an article for The IRE Journal.

They noted, "While workers' compensation systems differ from state to state and involve arcane insurance terms, each system ultimately boils down to blood, money and justice. Workers' compensation is supposed to pay medical expenses and replace the lost wages of an employee injured on the job. Sometimes, though, the system delays or denies fair benefits to legitimately injured workers while letting fakers collect from employers and taxpayers. In your state, both of those problems quite likely exist."

They offer these tips:

- Look at increases over the years in the state or municipal budget for workers' compensation.
- Talk to the administrators of the local or state program. They can point you to compensation case files of employees—at least part of those files should be public—showing the kinds of injuries claimed, the money spent and the contesting of the injury claims.
- If the case files are partially closed, there should be some documentation at the compensation board, usually in the state capital, where contested cases are heard. In addition, there may be labor-relations documents in which injury claim information is revealed when the government tries to fire an employee.
- When looking at state employees, keep an eye out for unusual benefits. For instance, in Connecticut and Massachusetts state employees who are injured by an inmate or a patient are entitled to 100 percent of their wages tax-free while out with an injury. That means they can earn 20 percent to 30 percent more by not returning to work.
- Numerous injuries do not necessarily mean bad employees. They also can mean that employers and managers do not care about the employees. Ask for documents on accident-prevention programs (also known as loss control) and programs to reduce dangers in the workplace (also known as risk management).
- Often the commissioners who hear disputed cases are politically appointed. Are they qualified? Can they be arbitrary, even crazy, in their decisions? Do they often let cases drag on? Do they fail to penalize insurers or employers who fight legitimate claims? Furthermore, these offices are generally understaffed and underfunded, meaning that employees lose their cars and houses while waiting for their cases to be heard.

On the private sector side, journalists can explore whether participation in the state plan is compulsory. When it is, employers frequently complain about high premiums, usually calculated in cost per $100 of payroll. But sometimes costs have risen in part because employers are cheating the system by understating payrolls (on which rates are based), misclassifying the type of business (claiming that roofers, for whom rates are expensive, are actually clerical workers, for whom rates are lower) and underreporting losses.

If participation in the state system is not compulsory, how many employers have decided to self-insure? Have the arrangements led to safer workplaces, fewer injuries and monetary savings? A key to companies' succeeding as self-insurers, they say, is deciding which doctors an allegedly injured worker can consult. That restriction will indeed cut the number of fraudulent claims approved by dishonest physicians taking kickbacks from patients. On the other hand, will the approved doctors refuse to certify legitimate injuries to stay in the employer's good graces?

Journalists can also look for doctor and diagnosis shopping. If a worker seeks medical care under an employer's health plan, the worker must pay for part of the bill because of deductibles. But workers' compensation often has no deductibles or other copayments, which encourages patients to undergo multiple medical tests. Such shopping around means it will be easier to find a physician or a chiropractor who will validate an injury, even though it is concocted.

A journalist should examine the original disability claims to see whether they are too easily granted by entry-level processors working for the government. When granted, is the level of benefits too high considering that the claimant is also receiving workers' compensation payments and money from a job-related or personal disability insurance policy? Journalists can often consult a fuller record when claims are rejected at the first level, because the allegedly disabled person often appeals. That might mean a full on-the-record hearing before a Social Security administrative law judge. When a claim is granted at the first level or on appeal, is the Social Security Administration reviewing cases to determine if claimants can return to their jobs? Or do disability payments continue long after the disabled person's health is restored?

⊃ CHECK IT OUT

✓ Visit a local bank. See how many regulatory postings are on the walls of the lobby, and make notes on what they are.

✓ Go to the FDIC Web site, and download a Call Report on the bank you visited. Examine the Call Report to find out how many bad loans the bank wrote off in the last quarter.

✓ Pick a local federally insured credit union, and see how much information is available about it at the National Credit Union Administration.

✓ Find out where consumer complaints are filed against insurers in your state. Try to obtain statistics on complaints filed over the past three years.

RESOURCES FOR REPORTING

Government Regulators as Sources

The FDIC's Web site (www.fdic.gov) offers searchable databases and has numerous individual institution reports, studies and statistics.

Banks

Some of the best books exposing banking practices are "Funny Money," by Mark Singer; "In Banks We Trust," by Penny Lernoux; and "False Profits," by Peter Truell and Larry Gurwin. Every issue of American Banker newspaper, New York City, is filled with useful stories.

Private-sector bank-ranking services include Veribanc Inc., Woonsocket, R.I.; Sheshunoff Information Services Inc., Austin, Tex.; Bauer Financial Reports, Coral Gables, Fla.; Weiss Research Inc., West Palm Beach, Fla.; W.C. Ferguson Inc., Irving, Tex.; and SNL Securities, Charlottesville, Va. The National Technical Information Service offers reports on the health of banks.

More information is available from these organizations:

- American Bankers Association (www.aba.com), Washington, D.C.
- Bankers Association for Finance and Trade (www.baft.org), Washington, D.C.
- Conference of State Bank Supervisors (www.csbs.org), Washington, D.C.
- Consumer Bankers Association (www.cbanet.org), Arlington, Va.
- Independent Community Bankers of America (www.icba.org), Washington, D.C.
- National Bankers Association (www.nationalbankers.org), Washington, D.C.
- Mortgage Bankers Association of America (www.mbaa.org), Washington, D.C.
- Bank Administration Institute (www.bai.org), Chicago, Ill.

Savings and Loans

Numerous books by investigative journalists have chronicled the savings and loan scandal of the 1980s. A few of the best are "S&L Hell: The People and the Politics Behind the $1 Trillion Savings and Loan Scandal," by Kathleen Day; "Trust Me: Charles Keating and the Missing Billions," by Michael Binstein and Charles Bowden; and "The Daisy Chain: How Borrowed Billions Sank a Texas S&L," by James O'Shea.

National Thrift News, New York City, is a valuable publication to read regularly.

More information on savings and loans is available from these sources:

- Office of Thrift Supervision (www.ots.treas.gov), Washington, D.C.
- The American Council of State Savings Supervisors (www.acsss.org), Leesburg, Va.

The Federal Home Loan Mortgage Corp. (Freddie Mac; www.freddiemac.com) is chartered by the U.S. Congress and owned by savings and loans to create a secondary market for conventional residential loans. The Federal National Mortgage Association (Fannie Mae; www.fanniemae.com) is a congressionally sanctioned private corporation that purchases mortgage loans from financial institutions.

Credit Unions

The federal government's National Credit Union Administration (www.ncua.gov) offers perspective on credit unions, as do the Credit Union National Association (www.cuna.org), Madison, Wis., the National Association of State Credit Union Supervisors (www.nascus.org), Arlington, Va., and the National Association of Federal Credit Unions (www.nafcunet.org), Arlington, Va.

Credit Card Companies

Many resources are available from the Office of the Comptroller of Currency (www.occ.treas.gov), the Federal Reserve Bank (www.federalreserve.gov), the Federal Trade Commission (www.ftc.gov), the office of the attorney general in each state, and other agencies that regulate financial institutions. In addition, various committees in the U.S. Congress are constantly scrutinizing the credit card industry. The HelpWithMyBank Web site (www.helpwithmybank.gov) from the Office of the Comptroller of the Currency is particularly good on consumer issues.

Investment Companies and Mutual Funds

The Investment Company Institute (www.ici.org), Washington, D.C., represents mutual funds. Perspective is also available from the Futures Industry Association (www.futuresindustry.org), Washington, D.C.

Investigating the Financial Issues

Perspective on how financial institutions are doing when it comes to insider transactions, lending diversity or many other measures can often be gained by reading reports from the Federal Financial Institutions Examination Council, Washington, D.C., especially its "Uniform Bank Performance Report."

Data on Small Business Administration–backed loans can be obtained from the National Institute for Computer-Assisted Reporting (www.nicar.org).

The newsletter Money Laundering Alert (www.moneylaundering.com), Miami, can help journalists understand the culture of money launderers. Books on money laundering include Ann Woolner's "Washed in Gold," Robert E. Powis' "The Money Launderers" and John P. Caskey's "Fringe Banking: Check Cashing Outlets, Pawnshops, and the Poor."

Insurance Resources

One of the first stops on the insurance beat is the National Association of Insurance Commissioners (www.naic.org), based in Kansas City, which does pricing surveys, profitability studies and consumer issue studies. A sharp critic of the industry is J. Robert Hunter, a former Texas insurance commissioner who runs the Consumer Federation of America. Joseph M. Belth, who is based at Indiana University, runs Insurance Forum, a publication that watches the insurance industry. An industry-supported organization for overview studies is the Insurance Services Office (www.iso.com) in New York City; the ISO Web site provides links to other relevant Web sites. For more possibilities, see journalist Randy Diamond's tip sheet, "Finding Investigative Riches," in the IRE Resource Center.

Consumer groups with insurance expertise include the Insurance Group of the Consumer Federation of America, Alexandria, Va., and Consumers Union, Mount Vernon, N.Y., publisher of Consumer Reports magazine.

Trade associations that will provide perspective include the Alliance of American Insurers, Schaumburg, Ill., and Insurance Information Institute (www.iii.org), New York City (both property/casualty); Independent Insurance Agents of America, Alexandria, Va.; Society of Chartered Property and Casualty Underwriters, Malvern, Pa.; and American Academy of Actuaries, American Council of Life Insurance, Mortgage Insurance Companies of America and Health Insurance Association of America, all headquartered in Washington, D.C.

Publications like Business Insurance, Chicago, abound. LexisNexis, among other online databases, has libraries devoted to insurance. Congressional hearings and reports, state legislative hearings and reports and studies from Congress's research division provide regular leads for investigations. A book from the National Conference of State Legislatures, "The State of Workers' Compensation," is helpful, as are General Accounting Office (www.gao.gov) reports.

A few other books can help immensely: "The Life Insurance Game," by Ronald Kessler; "The Invisible Bankers," by Andrew Tobias; and "Winning the Insurance Game," by Ralph Nader and Wesley J. Smith. Also useful are noncritical consumer guides like "The Guide to Buying Insurance: How to Secure the Coverage You Need at an Affordable Price," by David L. Scott.

Health and Disability Insurance

Joel Weissman and Arnold M. Epstein's book "Falling Through the Safety Net: Insurance Status and Access to Health Care" and Maggie Mahar's "Money-Driven Medicine: The Real Reason Health Care Costs So Much" are recommended.

Life Insurance

For an overview of life insurance issues, check the Web site (www.acli.com) for the American Council of Life Insurers.

Fraud

The Coalition Against Insurance Fraud (www.insurancefraud.org), a nonprofit organization in Washington, D.C., helps reporters who are looking into insurance fraud. The Fraud Defense Network (http://frauddefensenetwork.com) is an insurance industry–funded site that offers a daily news bulletin about insurance fraud schemes around the country. The National Insurance Crime Bureau in Palos Hills, Ill., can also provide perspective.

Companies and Their Finances

Ratings agencies study the financial condition of insurance companies, then grade them publicly. One such agency is A.M. Best (www.ambest.com), Oldwick, N.J., which also publishes the magazine Best's Review. The magazine has one edition covering property/casualty and another for life and health insurers. Other major agencies that rate insurance company finances are Moody's and Standard and Poor's, both New York City; Duff and Phelps, Chicago; and Weiss Research, West Palm Beach, Fla. Weiss Research seems to be the most skeptical of insurance company projections.

Before relying too heavily on ratings, journalists should ask which of the agencies require payment from insurers for a rating, which give advice to insurers on what they must do to achieve a better rating, which will not publish a rating contested by an insurer and which gave the highest rating to insurers that failed the same year.

Financial analysts at stock brokerages often track insurance company conditions as carefully as the ratings agencies do.

Andrew Tobias, one of the few journalists to write frequently about insurance in a clear way for a general audience, explains the financial shenanigans in a chapter of his book "The Invisible Bankers." The chapter's title tells a big part of the story: "By Popular Demand: A Very Short Chapter on Insurance Accounting and How to Take in $52 Million, Pay Out $6 Million and Report a Loss."

Government as Insurer

The FEMA Web site (www.fema.gov/business/nfip) offers more information on the National Flood Insurance Program.

The book "License to Steal: How Fraud Bleeds America's Health Care System," by Malcolm K. Sparrow, emphasizes how rarely those committing Medicare or Medicaid fraud get caught. The book "Prescription for Profit: How Doctors Defraud Medicaid," by Paul Jesilow, Henry N. Pontell and Gilbert Geis, examines one source of fraud in depth.

Journalists can get a quick understanding of how a state's Medicaid procedures compare with those of other states by consulting the U.S. Department of Health and Human Services, Health Care Financing Administration, Medicaid Bureau. One of many helpful reports is "Medicaid: Characteristics of Medicaid State Programs, Volume II, State-by-State Profiles." Sources to help ferret out Medicaid fraud can be found at the National Association of Attorneys General, Washington, D.C., and its affiliated organization, the National Association of Medicaid Fraud Control Units. Another resource is the National Association of State Medicaid Directors (www.nasmd.org).

16

Investigating Health Care

This chapter discusses how to investigate the many issues surrounding health care. It shows how to find documents and data that help measure the performance of doctors, hospitals, nursing homes and other organizations and programs. The chapter also outlines resources for reporting on pharmaceuticals, medical devices and medical labs.

The turn of this century proved to be a remarkable time for investigative journalism in the health care field. In 2000, The Orange County Register published a five-part series, "The Body Brokers," exploring how donated skin and bone had become the raw material for a $500 million industry. The series detailed how tissue banks were reaping large profits and regulators were failing to act as effective watchdogs. The same year, the Chicago Tribune revealed how unqualified or incompetent nurses were accidentally killing thousands of patients in U.S. hospitals. The Los Angeles Times also did a classic investigation into a local hospital and found malfeasance and malpractice leading to patient injuries and deaths.

During the same period, other news organizations looked deeply into racial disparity in treatment in hospitals and at profits for health maintenance organizations and hospitals. The Los Angeles Times, The Washington Post and The New York Times followed with major exposés on the pharmaceutical industry: The Los Angeles Times reported on how seven deadly drugs slipped through the regulatory system, The Post described how the industry was using destitute people in third-world countries as guinea pigs for drugs deemed too risky for testing in the United States and The New York Times showed how deadly counterfeit drugs were being distributed worldwide from China.

Americans spend more than a billion dollars each day for a health care system they fail to understand and that might fail them. Too often, the health care system is more "sick" than the patient seeking help.

The health care beat is filled with investigative potential on the international, national and local levels. Journalists who understand the system know how to judge the quality of care provided by local hospitals and how to look out for treatment based on federal reimbursements rather than on the patient's needs.

Many journalists have learned to probe HMOs, where patients are sometimes steered to incompetent doctors and where preventive medicine has been neglected for years. Meanwhile, news organizations in the past few years have used newly available federal data to reveal unnecessary deaths and faulty care in nursing homes. Doctors, too, have come under increasing scrutiny (see Chapter 13), as have insurance companies (see Chapter 15).

As the health care system has grown, so have the records and databases that explain it. Almost every procedure generates a record. Almost every provider of medical services is licensed or otherwise regulated by a government agency. Every patient is the subject of personalized files. A great deal of the documentation, in the aggregate, is public, although records on individual cases can be difficult to obtain unless the patient is dead, alive and cooperative, or involved in litigation. An array of secondary materials, primary documents and human sources can help to explain and clarify the technical language and the meaning of the documents.

Investigating Hospitals

Accreditation and Regulation

U.S. News and World Report magazine relies on a mix of sources to rank "America's best hospitals" each year, including death rates from all causes, as reported by the U.S. Center for Medicare and Medicaid Services, and many other informative ratios, such as hospital beds to registered nurses and various services and discharges.

A great deal of information about local hospitals is available from individual states. For example, the Missouri Bureau of Hospital Licensing and Certification monitors acute-care community hospitals, ambulatory surgical centers and abortion facilities. It checks not only quality of medical care but also fire safety, environmental hazards and dietary services. If the hospital accepts federal money for treating Medicare patients (and most do), the state agency helps monitor Medicare providers and suppliers: independent laboratories, physical and occupational rehabilitation facilities, end-stage renal disease services, portable X-ray centers, screening mammography operators, rural health clinics and hospital long-term-care units, among others.

What a journalist can find by searching files at the state agency overseeing hospitals is just the beginning. The Joint Commission on Accreditation of

Healthcare Organizations, Chicago, or the American Osteopathic Hospital Association, Washington, D.C., has probably paid a visit in the past three years. If so, the accreditation report will be rich with detail on defects in patient care and on how the institution compares with others.

If the commission has not visited, a journalist should find out why. Health care consumer advocates criticize the commission, saying it gives so much advance warning of an inspection that any hospital can mask its shortcomings temporarily, and then it almost always gives hospitals the benefit of the doubt, thus devaluing the meaning of accreditation. Furthermore, the commission's board has multiple slots reserved for members of the American Hospital Association, which pays more than half of the commission's budget. On the other hand, accrediting standards are often strict, and the details in an accreditation report are useful to journalists, even if overall the hospital receives unjustifiably high marks.

Accreditation may not be as rigorous as other surveys, though, especially when compared to the validation surveys by the Center for Medicare and Medicaid Services. Congress mandated the CMS surveys as a follow-up to accreditation by JCAHO. Despite being accredited, between one-fourth and one-third of the hospitals inspected by the center are found to be lacking in some aspect of their care for Medicare patients.

Quality of patient care is a major concern of the accrediting team. Their concern is shared by each state's quality-improvement organization, which used to be known as a peer review organization. The quality-improvement organizations are private contractors working for the CMS. There are 53 of them, one for each state and territory and the District of Columbia. They are to "work with consumers and physicians, hospitals, and other caregivers to refine care delivery systems to make sure patients get the right care at the right time, particularly patients from underserved populations." The organizations are supposed to do case reviews and determine whether diagnoses were coded incorrectly to justify overcharges, as well as investigate numerous other matters. They also deal with complaints and work on projects to provide better care. The quality-improvement organizations' reports can provide numerous tips and story ideas for journalists.

To reach their conclusions, organizations can calculate a hospital's performance according to each of the nearly 500 medical procedures identified by the government, known as a diagnostic-related group. The federal Medicare program has set payment schedules for each DRG. Because Medicare does not pay the full cost of care for some procedures, many hospitals release patients sooner than they should, which gave rise to the expression that patients are going home "quicker and sicker."

The Washington bureau of the former Knight Ridder newspaper chain was among the early news organizations to use statistics from the quality-improvement organizations. Reporters there performed an analysis of deaths apparently connected to coronary artery bypass surgery at hospitals nationwide. They discovered that 44 hospitals had death rates at least twice the national average. It appeared that as many as 1,000 Medicare patients in just one year suffered preventable deaths during or after surgery. The quality-improvement organizations can collect information more subtle than death rates—for instance, "adverse patient occurrences," which can include unplanned returns to the operating room, infections, unexpected cardiac or respiratory arrest and negative reactions to drugs.

Medical records of individual patients provide additional credibility for investigative projects, and journalists should ask patients, family members and lawyers representing patients for access to case histories, fees and correspondence with hospitals. Many individuals will provide this access. If a lawsuit is already filed, detailed individual medical records and hospital treatment studies are likely to be available.

Costs and Billing

Examination of any individual's hospital bill is bound to lead to questions. Experts are almost unanimous in agreeing that hospital bills of paying patients are routinely increased to subsidize nonpaying patients. Hospitals can be slow to correct their billing mistakes but fast to try to collect from patients when insurance companies reimburse less than the full amount.

Journalists should ask whether local hospitals use outside bill collection agencies. If so, do the bill collectors illegally resort to verbal threats or physical intimidation? Do local hospitals place liens on the residences of patients who have yet to pay or try to garnish their wages?

Life magazine provided a pictorial illustration of why bills are often so high, picturing the 105 hospital employees involved in a heart operation, for which the patient received a bill of $63,000. The total annual salary of the 105 employees equaled $3.6 million.

Some experts believe quality of care is tied to cost of care. Any hospital's budget is rich with details: the percentage of revenue coming from patient fees, the amount of write-offs for indigent care and uncollectible bills, the amount spent on new equipment and how the different departments within the hospital are faring. In Missouri, basic financial information on every hospital in the state is available from the Center for Health Statistics. Similar agencies in other states also generate hospital-by-hospital statistics. In many states, a hospital that wants to spend money on capital improvements must obtain a certificate of need from a state agency. In Missouri, that agency is the state Health Facilities Review Committee. If the hospital is owned by a for-profit corporation whose stock is publicly traded (see Chapter 13), financial information might be available from the U.S. Securities and Exchange Commission or from the state securities department. If the hospital operates on a nonprofit basis, it might have to disclose its finances to the Internal Revenue Service on Form 990.

Andrew Caffrey, formerly of WBUR-FM radio, Boston, routinely read tax returns of nonprofit hospitals. His accumulated knowledge led to a story about insider loans from hospital treasuries to senior executives and doctors. As Caffrey explained in the form accompanying his award-winning IRE contest entry, "The loans were often at interest rates several points below what an average consumer would get from a commercial lender. The story pointed up how well-paid top people in the nonprofit medical world were getting special perquisites . . . while consumers were footing the bills for ever-higher health-care costs."

Other hospital records critical to coverage are hospital discharge records, known as uniform billing records. They may be available from the state government or possibly from the National Association of Health Data Organizations. The records provide information on illnesses, length of stay, who pays, billing amounts and where patients are from.

Hospital Errors

A Chicago Tribune series on nurses and medical errors showed the range of people, documents and databases that can be found by an aggressive reporter like Mike Berens, who reported and wrote the series. Writing for The IRE Journal, Berens outlined his approach to the story: "At the heart of my reporting was the creation of a custom database compiled from a dozen state and federal sources, from databases at the Food and Drug Administration to files from the Centers for Medicare and Medicaid Services to disciplinary records from every state."

Berens began with MAUDE (Manufacturer and User Facility Experience) data, a Food and Drug Administration database that is used to spot machine-related problems and is available from the National Institute for Computer-Assisted Reporting. In the early 1990s, journalists used this database as a starting point for illuminating investigations into defective defibrillators and implants. Berens found deaths caused when nurses typed in wrong dosage amounts on infusion pumps, when nurses were not near enough to hear warning alarms when patients were dying and when groggy patients died when their heads were trapped in bed rails or strangled in postsurgical restraints. Berens pointed out that the data are neither conclusive nor reliable but pointed him in the right direction for talking to experts, which included the Institute for Safe Medication Practices in Pennsylvania and the Emergency Care Research Institute, a nonprofit research laboratory in Philadelphia. In his research, Berens also discovered that the National Council of State Boards of Nursing, based in Chicago, keeps a database of disciplinary actions against nurses. He also used federal Health Care Financing Administration lawsuits and death records.

When skilled journalists take the time to dig into any one aspect of hospital care, what they find is often alarming. Dave Davis and Ted Wendling of The (Cleveland) Plain Dealer had no idea how deep they would be digging when they received a daily assignment to cover a spill of radioactive phosphorus-32 at a Cleveland hospital. But their suspicions were aroused when hospital officials refused to identify a nearby music school that had been contaminated. As they began reading documents and asking questions about hospital radiation safety programs, Davis and Wendling started learning about deaths from radiation overdoses across the nation. They tapped into a computer database at the U.S. Nuclear Regulatory Commission on radiation overexposures and eventually identified more than 40 deaths attributable to radiation in hospitals, many of them followed by falsified records and other cover-ups.

Another common environment-related violation is burning medical waste and releasing residues into the air. Journalists should track the path of amputated limbs, scraped warts, blood, used bandages, syringes and scalpels, at the same time finding which state agencies license and regulate incinerators and landfill disposal.

Journalists can also investigate how well hospitals prevent drug thefts and other losses. Hospitals are supposed to report all such losses to the U.S. Drug Enforcement Administration. The local police department or the state narcotics agency might also know about specific instances of theft.

But even when drugs are all accounted for, there can be other types of trouble. At the Pittsburgh Post-Gazette, reporter Steve Twedt found that hospital patients sometimes died or were injured because they received the wrong medication or the wrong dose of the correct medication. Twedt wondered why the patterns showed up in hospital after hospital and concluded that the information network had failed: "Only a fraction of the errors are ever published in professional journals and even when they are, it is hard to know where to look. . . . There is no requirement for hospitals in most states . . . to share or analyze information on errors."

Like other top-notch investigators, Twedt found sources that others would have ignored. For example, he conducted a national survey of pharmacists who are employed by hospitals. The 250 respondents said that in just one year, they saw more than 16,000 medication errors, resulting in more than 100 deaths and more than 300 serious injuries. Transgressors rarely received punishment. Twedt wrote:

> Sometimes a medication error might be referred to a licensing board for discipline against a pharmacist, doctor or nurse. Or a coroner's office will be told about a death. But those agencies have narrow responsibilities, such as the revocation of a license or determination of criminality. It is not their job to look for patterns among errors. And even when mistakes are reported there is no central agency, governmental or private, that systematically seeks out and analyzes the information to alert other hospitals.

Like Berens, Twedt had to pull together information from a variety of sources:

> We checked civil lawsuit records. We went to the American Trial Lawyers Association. They could, in some cases, give us citations. We checked the professional journals. . . . You have an incident involving a drug. It could turn up in a nursing journal, it could turn up in an anesthesiology journal, it could turn up in a medical journal. We had to check all of these, one by one collect all these separate cases. Other sources we went to were medical boards. I contacted every medical board, nursing board and pharmacy board in every state and asked them for copies of any board actions involving a medication error. . . . We looked for newspaper clippings in a variety of databases, and we also had some record checking with the U.S. Food and Drug Administration's adverse drug reaction database. We used the newspaper accounts as kind of a signal that there was a case out there. We did not write about them unless we had some backup verification from the center where it happened or from someone who was directly involved.
>
>   We might have a copy of a three-paragraph newspaper account in the Midwest of someone who was accidentally given potassium chloride and died. And from that newspaper account, you just go through all the steps—you contact the hospital. You get the coroner's report. From the coroner's report you have names of family members and you follow that. . . . You try and track down names of practitioners involved and see if they would be willing to talk.

Indigent Care

In addition to budget documents, Medicare and Medicaid cost reports are a useful resource for journalists. These reports are required by federal and state governments that pay for treatment of elderly, low-income and disabled patients. The reports are kept by the hospital, the government agency paying the bills (at the federal level, usually the Center for Medicare and Medicaid Services, part of the Department of Health and Human Services) and the company administering the program day to day (often a nearby HMO plan). The latter decides which bills to pay in full and which to question.

In one investigation, The Chicago Reporter used financial statements and cost reports filed at the Illinois Health Facilities Planning Board to calculate the amount of indigent care provided by each hospital. Unsurprisingly, the reporter found that inner-city, public, nonprofit hospitals provided more indigent care than suburban, private, for-profit hospitals did. What surprised the reporter, though, were the huge variations in amounts spent among the nonprofit hospitals, leaving her the task of investigating whether the variations were accidents of geography or by design.

Health care facilities that have accepted federal government money for construction and modernization under the Hill-Burton Act agree to provide a reasonable amount of services to those who are unable to pay. Journalists should ask the Department of Health and Human Services which hospitals have filed an allocation plan and whether they are living up to their commitments to serve low-income patients. What happens in the community when the hospital has met its annual allocation? Does HHS allow some allocations to be set too low?

Minimal indigent care by nonprofit hospitals raises a legitimate question of whether hospitals have paid back the community adequately for property tax waivers and other special treatment. The situation is likely to worsen as hospitals treating only subacute patients or only head injuries spring up in a fragmented health care system. Those hospitals skim off the most profitable patients, leaving old inner-city hospitals to provide expensive, money-losing fundamental services like emergency rooms.

The federal Emergency Medical Treatment and Active Labor Act attempts to ban patient dumping, which occurs when a hospital inappropriately turns away an emergency case because the patient lacks health insurance or other ability to pay. A hospital receiving a patient dumped by another institution is supposed to notify HHS within 72 hours.

Journalists should request those notifications from the federal agency, then determine if any follow-up occurred. The Health Letter, a muckraking publication of Public Citizen Health Research Group, Washington, D.C., does an excellent job of tracking violators, listing every hospital and doctor or other health care professional cited by HHS. Hospital insiders warn, though, that what at first looks like dumping might be just sloppy paperwork.

Hospitals sometimes find themselves caught in a bind between the patient-dumping rules and insurance companies. Journalists should look for situations like this: A patient comes to a hospital emergency room because of sudden heart pains. The doctor on duty runs expensive but necessary tests to learn if a heart attack has occurred. If the tests had not been done or if the doctor had sent the patient elsewhere, it might have been a violation of the dumping law. But the insurer will not pay, because the patient's HMO does not have a contract with that hospital or that doctor. So either the patient pays the bill, or the hospital is not paid.

Ambulances and Other Emergency Medical Services

Ambulances and other emergency services are often tied closely to hospitals, which end up caring for the individuals transported. Journalists should determine which part of each county is covered by which ambulance service and then ask these questions:

- Are the ambulance companies so competitive that one service that has staked out a certain part of the county will fight off another service, even if the competitor can arrive more quickly?
- Are some portions of the county underserved because of their remoteness, poor roads, racial composition or high crime rate?
- Are some sick people refused a ride because they are uninsured?
- If the ambulance is owned by a hospital, do all riders end up at that hospital, even if some other facility is better suited to treat the patient?

Journalists should study ambulance response times. A study in one city found that nearly one-fourth of the ambulance runs did not begin until seven minutes after receipt of the emergency call. Generally, experts say critically ill people should be picked up within eight minutes 90 percent of the time. That standard, however, does not address what may happen to the other 10 percent of those needing assistance, particularly those who have suffered a heart attack and may need help within four minutes.

The Hartford Courant went further than calculating response times when reporter Jack Dolan matched the addresses in a response call database with the addresses in death records to see who might have died while waiting for an ambulance to arrive. The story found people who indeed had died waiting for an ambulance.

Journalists can also look at the qualifications of drivers to see if they have bad driving records, have a history of drug abuse or lack proper training. By checking court records and training requirements, several news organizations have found unqualified drivers, drug addicts and convicted felons driving ambulances.

WBRZ-TV, Baton Rouge, received a tip about slow response times by a public ambulance service. When its reporters had finished their research, they described their findings on an IRE awards entry form:

The public service, designed to treat on the scene and hand off noncritical patients to private ambulance companies, was now carrying noncritical patients so they could bill their insurance companies. While the ratio of transports rose, response times fell. The tax revenues were no longer sufficient, and city officials were breaking a promise not to send bills. Emergency room doctors were critical of the medical direction and were fighting over who controlled the service.

Journalists investigating ambulance services can explore these issues:

- What is the cost of an ambulance ride?
- Is it substantially higher or lower than in other cities?
- Does the city, county or state government regulate the rates ambulance services can charge?
- Does any government body license ambulance personnel, require certain equipment to be on board and require that the equipment pass regular inspections?
- When air ambulances (helicopters) are involved, is there any regulation over them other than through Federal Aviation Administration pilot licenses?
- If an air ambulance service contract is awarded by a hospital or a government entity to an outsider, is the award based solely on price? Or is the air ambulance service's safety record considered?

In Missouri, the state government's Bureau of Emergency Medical Services is a good place to start on the document and people trails. The agency handles ground and air ambulance licensing, emergency medical technician and paramedic licensing, poison control programs, trauma center inspections, plus head and spinal cord injury registries. In Missouri, in one year there were more than 200 ambulance services with 804 licensed vehicles. Advanced life support was provided by 185 services. Ten helicopter and eight fixed-wing air ambulance services were licensed to operate.

Investigating Other Care Providers

Veterans Administration Hospitals

Veterans Administration hospitals, operated by the U.S. Department of Veterans Affairs, constitute one of the largest health care networks in the world. But that size has not always been a blessing. VA hospitals are known for long waits, complicated paperwork and high death and medical malpractice rates, the consequences of which are paid for by U.S. taxpayers rather than individual malpractice insurance companies.

If examining the operation of an entire hospital is overwhelming, a journalist can concentrate on one aspect. That is what the (Fort Lauderdale) Sun-Sentinel did to produce a series on high death and injury rates in VA hospital heart surgery units. VA hospitals are supposed to be visited by accrediting teams every three years, just as private-sector hospitals are. If the local VA hospital withholds the accrediting report, a journalist should request it from the U.S. Department of Veterans Affairs, Washington, D.C. The agency's inspector general and the U.S. Government Accountability Office, an arm of Congress (see Chapter 9), audit VA hospitals from time to time. KTBS-TV, Shreveport, La., relied heavily on VA inspector general audits to tell viewers about shoddy medicine at the local hospital. Those audits might lead to congressional hearings by the appropriate committees in the U.S. House and Senate. Veterans' groups such as the American Legion, Washington, D.C., might have their own ratings of VA hospitals.

When trying to learn about individual cases, journalists might benefit from requesting a patient injury control report, contained on a routine form known as DVA Form 10-2633. PrimeTime Live, an ABC-TV news program, used patient records—some obtained from family members—to check tips from former VA doctors and nurses alleging inadequate care.

Nursing Homes

An investigative story on nursing homes by Gannett News Service, Washington, D.C., opened, "Thousands of violent criminals, thieves and bullies work in the nation's nursing homes, left to care for people too old, sick or disabled to care for themselves. . . . When their abusive natures surface, usually as scars on the frail bodies and psyches of patients, many aides move on to new nursing homes and, sometimes, new targets."

To conduct the investigation, a Gannett database editor asked state regulators for electronic registries of nursing home aides; federal law mandates that those registries be kept. Every state except Louisiana cooperated. Gannett then combined the registries to create a single list of aides designated as abusive. That list also pinpointed aides who were found to be abusive in one state and ended up with certification to work in a different state. The series suggested questions to ask about the staff of any nursing home:

- Are criminal record checks performed on every potential employee?
- Are references sought from previous employers?
- How many nurses and nursing aides per bed are on duty during a given shift?
- How closely are they supervised, and by whom?

- What is their hourly wage or annual salary?
- What is their turnover rate?
- How many positions are currently unfilled?

The Joint Commission on Accreditation of Healthcare Organizations and state regulation vary greatly in quality and quantity. But in recent years, federal and state legislation has created online reporting systems on nursing homes. A journalist now can check the Medicare Web site for making comparisons among nursing homes. Some states have other online reports or resources to check.

For example, nursing homes in Missouri are regulated by the Social Services Department's Division of Aging. It inspects and licenses adult day care centers, adult residential care homes, intermediate care and skilled nursing facilities. Journalists have access to complaint investigation forms, as well as the "Statement of Deficiencies and Plan of Correction." The agency also licenses nursing home administrators, rules on construction and equipment requests and establishes nursing home Medicare and Medicaid eligibility. City or county departments play a role too, checking kitchen sanitation, fire, electrical and other building codes.

News organizations have begun paying close attention again to nursing homes. At The Record in Hackensack, N.J., reporters started their investigation as the result of a telephone call about how residents at a nursing home were in danger of dying because the owner refused to fix an air conditioner during a heat wave. As The Record team searched obituary notices from the newsroom library, they noted people who had died at the nursing home in question, then contacted survivors and pulled death certificates. Checking for lawsuits turned up wrongful death allegations against the nursing home. As the reporters wrote in The IRE Journal:

> The lawyers in those cases had valuable medical records from the nursing home, such as schedules showing which hours nurses worked and patients' medical records. We scrutinized those records and found instances where nurses who were on the schedule as working were not the same nurses who allegedly signed patients' medical records. That finding supported our charges that records were falsified to cover up the fact that basic care was not given.

Journalists visiting nursing homes for themselves will walk away with useful impressions and promotional literature to compare with the reality, plus interviews with administrators, doctors, nurses, patients and family members.

Nursing homes are required to file certain reports similar to those filed by hospitals: U.S. Securities and Exchange Commission documents, if part of a publicly held company; IRS Form 990, if operating under certain tax-exempt sections of the law (many nonprofit nursing homes, a minority in the industry, belong to the American Association of Homes and Services for the Aging, Washington, D.C.); and Medicare and Medicaid cost figures.

State governments pay large portions of nursing home billings through Medicaid. With an increasing number of patients being moved from hospitals to nursing homes, states are trying to deal with the increased costs. As a result, state executive branch agencies and legislatures might be generating more studies and hearings than in the past.

Journalists should explore whether relatively well-to-do families are spending down their assets to qualify for Medicaid in nursing homes. They should check whether the spouse and children of a patient have to become impoverished before state Medicaid payments kick in. After the nursing home patient dies, journalists can check to see if the state government is going after the estate's assets to help pay off Medicaid costs. They can find out the average annual cost of nursing home care and see how much the cost varies in their area.

Mental Health Institutions

Deinstitutionalization altered the media's coverage of mental health forever. With more and more mentally disabled or emotionally unstable people working productively in the community—or living on the street or being jailed for being nuisances—journalists must cover mental health issues by not only visiting the state institutions for the mentally ill but also by getting out into the community and covering programs and clinics.

Many patients spend their lives going from mental hospital to inadequate community placement to the street and back to the hospital. Journalists should investigate how well the release of mental patients has worked locally, and they should ask these questions:

- How do outpatient treatment specialists at mental hospitals respond to broken appointments and failures to adhere to medication regimes?
- Are there enough supervised community residences locally?
- Do patients receive counseling?
- What are the qualifications of the supervisors and staff?
- Do private contractors charge too much?

In a stunningly written award-winning piece by Kate Boo, The Washington Post found more than 350 incidents of abuse, neglect, molestation and stealing in Washington group homes or day programs in the 1990s. (More on the story can be found at the Pulitzer Prize Web site.) At that time, the government did not levy a single fine against the homes, most of which were run on a for-profit basis by health care entrepreneurs.

While at The Charlotte Observer, Deborah Cenziper examined the shortcomings of the North Carolina mental health care system. She found that "from 1994 to mid-1999 at least 34 people under the care of N.C. mental care facilities have died suddenly or in circumstances that could raise questions about their care." Among the major findings were that North Carolina "allows individuals with little or no training to open mental health facilities" and that "the state offers little oversight." The series also explored "the lack of children's mental health care and how patients who can't afford care often seek a devastating loophole in the law: giving up custody of their children. The four state-run psychiatric hospitals provide only vague reports listing patient deaths. . . . N.C. law doesn't require private facilities to report deaths at all."

Journalists should also examine the more traditional mental health institutions. In Missouri, for example, the Department of Mental Health directs three state hospitals, nine mental health centers and three children's facilities and contracts with more than 20 private, nonprofit mental health agencies to help meet the needs of the population.

Some of these programs might not have enough beds or enough employees. Other centers might have an overabundance of beds, and so they bend the rules to accept patients involuntarily committed.

Finding current or former patients to interview can be difficult because of privacy considerations and doctor-patient confidentiality. Previous local newspaper articles or television features might mention specific names of patients who can later be contacted.

In one investigation, the St. Petersburg Times learned about "patient brokers" after receiving a tip that a local drug treatment center flew in pregnant addicts from states in the north. The center then enrolled the patients in Florida's Medicaid system so that taxpayers would absorb the costs of their care. In their IRE contest entry form, the reporters said that the patient brokers "can collect thousands of dollars per head in kickbacks for referring unsuspecting patients to drug treatment or psychiatric care they may not need. Patient referral services are run by ex-cons and drug addicts who use phony credentials to gain credibility. . . . Such patient brokers are completely unregulated; few states have laws banning the practice."

Some psychiatrists and other professional staff lack credentials altogether or come from the bottom of the employment barrel because the work is so draining and frustrating. Because mental illness is so difficult even to classify properly, poorly trained staff members complicate an already bad situation. The field's bible, "Diagnostic and Statistical Manual of Mental Disorders," compiled by the American Psychiatric Association, identifies about 300 conditions. Pinpointing the correct condition from all the possibilities and then treating it effectively is no job for the incompetent.

Home Health Care Companies

Home health care workers can be angels of mercy, allowing elderly or chronically ill patients to stay in their own homes instead of moving to unfamiliar nursing homes, or they can be workers from hell, abusing patients and stealing their belongings. Home health care is growing as Medicare administrators and private insurance companies push patients to shorten hospital stays. Journalists should inquire into whether problems are growing too.

At Scripps Howard News Service in Washington, D.C., reporters ran across high medical bills for in-home intravenous drug treatments, some of which were administered for the wrong disease. The reporters had heard the conventional wisdom that home health IV companies were transforming medical care in new, positive ways, but their suspicions led them to dig into the subject. As they said in their IRE awards contest entry, they "documented home charges four or five times greater than the highest hospital charges; found many IV companies using unskilled or undertrained nurses with some patients being seriously harmed; [and] uncovered massive kickbacks being paid to physicians who prescribed home IV for patients who did not have the illness being treated, such as Lyme disease."

In other cases, major home health care companies paid bribes to physicians to prescribe home IV therapy. Paying for legitimate referrals is permissible; what is inappropriate is treatment that occurs because of potential profit rather than medical necessity. The National Alliance for Infusion Therapy and the Home Health Care Association of America, both based in Washington, D.C., might be helpful in identifying the dishonest companies. When investigating home health care companies, journalists should ask whether they have submitted their services for national recognition from the Joint Commission on Accreditation of Healthcare Organizations. Then they should ask about state scrutiny.

In Missouri, for instance, the Bureau of Home Health Licensing and Certification is supposed to oversee 235 home health agencies and 33 hospices; that scrutiny is supposed to qualify the providers for billing the government under Medicare. Does the state collect financial information? A financially troubled home health care company might be cheating patients on the number of visits, paying minimum wage to unqualified nursing aides or taking other shortcuts.

Physicians, Nurses and Other Health Care Workers

Medical doctors are the most obvious subjects of journalistic inquiry because of their life-and-death powers, their wealth and their political influence. Their licensing, performance standards, ethics codes, discipline and professional associations all received attention in Chapter 13. In this chapter on the broader health care system, it is relevant to mention the claims to knowledge that split medicine.

The split sometimes is found along specialist lines. The professional interests and practice patterns of surgeons, pathologists and pediatricians occasionally diverge. Such divergence is played out starkly when in-hospital peer review panels suspend a physician's privileges. The physician might fight back, with the dispute resulting in legal action. The biggest splits are between the medical doctors (and increasingly the doctors of osteopathy) and others who usually call themselves doctors, especially chiropractors and homeopaths. As journalists try to explain which medical care works and which does not and why, they should explore alternative medicine too.

Journalists should be aware that some doctors are also businesspeople, and in those cases conflicts can arise. Some doctors refer patients to their own profit-making hospitals, infertility clinics, imaging centers and diagnostic laboratories. Journalists can document the self-referral by thinking of doctors as businesspeople and then running the corporate paper trails discussed in the first part of this book, as well as in Chapter 13.

Trying to profit from government medical care is another avenue for greed. Journalists can ask state government Medicaid administrators how much money any individual doctor earned the previous year and where that amount ranked statewide among doctors certified to see Medicaid recipients. The top earners might have stimulated the curiosity of the Medicaid fraud unit. One Michigan doctor brought unwanted attention to himself by billing Medicaid for 96,000 home visits over a two-year span. The Detroit News found that in a 21-month period, at least 30 Medicaid patients had died at least partly because their doctors had prescribed too many drugs because they could bill Medicaid for them.

On behalf of the federal Medicare program, the U.S. Health and Human Services Department inspector general publishes a list of doctors suspended from receiving Medicare payments. Journalists should check the list regularly for local names. Some of those same names might have already appeared on the investigations list of the state medical board, which the journalist should be monitoring regularly. But other names on the Medicare list might not be known to the state board.

PART III Investigating Business

Dentists, who need to be scrutinized separately because the dental insurance system is usually separate from the rest of health insurance, usually escape the attention of journalists. That is a mistake on the part of journalists.

In many medical settings, nurses play as important a role as doctors do. At the state level, journalists will find licensing and disciplinary boards and support agencies like the Missouri Bureau of Community Health Nursing. Groups like the American Nurses Association and the American College of Nurse-Midwives, both in Washington, D.C., can provide more information.

Investigating Suppliers and Services

Health Maintenance Organizations

Health maintenance organizations arose to encourage preventive care by charging a low flat fee for routine wellness visits, still one of their distinguishing features. But in an age of health care reform, HMOs have become the center of controversy over managed care. The issue is whether HMOs and insurance companies are cutting into the quality of health care as a way of cutting costs and increasing profits.

As journalists investigate HMOs, they should ask questions about accreditation. The National Committee for Quality Assurance, Washington, D.C., is an HMO-accrediting organization, but its coverage is not complete. Journalists should check to see when HMOs are inspected and how well they are inspected. In some states, health and insurance departments exercise jurisdiction over HMOs. If an HMO wants to be reimbursed for Medicare patients, it must be certified by the Office of Prepaid Health Care, part of the U.S. Health and Human Services Department.

Journalists can gather some data on their own:

- What is the ratio of doctors to patients at local HMOs? Many HMOs have high ratios. How does an HMO's ratio compare to that of private-practice doctors' offices?
- Do patients endure longer waits than in doctor's offices?
- Are they able to visit the same doctor every appointment if they so desire? If the HMO says patients can choose from among 500 doctors, a journalist should request the list. If 500 names appear, the journalist should verify their affiliation. If only 200 names are on the list, contrary to the HMO's advertising, that is automatically a story.
- If the list lacks specialists, how stingy will the HMO be about patients visiting outside specialists?

At the Sun-Sentinel in Fort Lauderdale, Fred Schulte and Larry Keller asked for information from the U.S. Health Care Financing Administration, eventually receiving "an obscure Medicare data set" called the Beneficiary Tracking and Information System. It allowed the reporters to "document more than 10,000 patient complaints filed against eight South Florida HMOs in recent years, grievances ranging from improper enrollments to failure to pay medical bills," as well as "rapid disenrollment rates at various HMOs, an indicator of patient dissatisfaction and perceived low quality." Some of the HMOs had dropout rates more than four times the national average. The Florida insurance department also yielded patient complaints. Schulte said, "We discovered hundreds of examples in which HMOs brazenly refused to pay legitimate medical bills, leaving patients to be hounded by collection agencies. We even found a few cases in which health plans hand-delivered letters to hospitalized patients directing them to check out by a set date or foot the bill themselves."

Some local patients choose a middle ground between HMOs and individual physicians, joining preferred provider organizations. Health care providers began PPOs in response to what they considered to be the HMO threat. For a monthly fee, PPOs offer more comprehensive benefits than traditional insurance, but less than HMOs, if subscribers are willing to visit only certain doctors and certain hospitals. If they visit doctors and hospitals outside the PPO network, they must pay extra. PPOs and physician-hospital organizations raise interesting regulatory questions:

- Should PPOs and PHOs be regulated as insurance companies, since they are offering insurance-type contracts?
- If they are not regulated, do they gain an unfair advantage over traditional insurance companies?
- What if a PPO or PHO has inadequate reserves to handle all payouts to its subscribers?
- Who provides a safety net similar to those provided by state insurance departments?

Medical Research and Journals

In recent years, more journalists have turned their attention to the issues surrounding medical research. David Armstrong of The Wall Street Journal did groundbreaking stories on medical journals that accepted articles from medical researchers who had conflicts of interest. He found that some researchers had been paid by pharmaceutical companies for the research they were reporting on, but that the journals did not know that.

Other journalists have looked at clinical reports filed by researchers with the Food and Drug Administration (posted on the FDA Web site) that raised questions about drugs that later received approval from the FDA.

And David Willman of the Los Angeles Times reported on the flaws in the approval of seven unsafe prescription drugs and the conflicts of interest that regulators had because they received money from pharmaceutical companies.

Pharmaceutical Companies

The U.S. Food and Drug Administration keeps records on premarket testing of specific medications, as well as any adverse reactions reported. The most egregious cases usually find their way into the government periodical FDA Enforcement Report. FDA clinical investigator files might help a journalist prove that the tests have been conducted by self-interested researchers at universities or supposedly independent private laboratories.

Sometimes the drug researchers are honest but their scientific methods are flawed. In any case, even the most upright drug companies tend to fund research that has the potential to find or increase a market for a product.

As for drug experience reports showing adverse reactions—which also might show up at the federal Centers for Disease Control and in state health departments—they are sporadic at best. When drug companies are forced by the FDA to add warnings to the package inserts, the serious consequences might be buried in a long list of trivial side effects. As a result, physicians might not know what they are seeing. Even if the warning is clear, physicians might not read it. Pharmacists, less beholden to drug manufacturers, are far more likely to contact the FDA about problems than physicians are. The Register-Guard in Eugene, Ore., started a project after a reporter saw a death notice for a seven-year-old boy in foster care. Curious, she requested the medical examiner's report, which pinpointed a prescription drug as the cause of death. FDA files indicated at least 80 similar child deaths, but the agency said it had never compiled the statistics in that way and so had missed the big picture.

Drug pricing has become not only a U.S. issue but an international concern. The industry says it needs money to develop new medicines, but high prices put essential drugs beyond the reach of the poor.

Some of the high prices can be attributed to promotion, advertising, lobbying and campaign contributions rather than development for the drugs. Much of the promotion budget for a drug goes to well-paid sales representatives who travel the nation calling on individual doctors; their primary goal is to sell the drugs, and the representatives may have no experience at all in medicine. Government regulations, however, have been put in place to limit what representatives can spend on doctors, such as lunches, speaking fees or covering travel to conferences. Some studies of drug company–paid advertisements in medical journals have shown that about one-third of the claims are misleading and that nearly half would lead to improper prescribing practices. Journalists can check FDA records and court records to learn which drug companies have been warned or sanctioned for misleading claims.

Journalists should always question claims about new drugs:

- Are studies purporting to validate the drug's effectiveness part of the official clinical trials submitted to the FDA?
- Did the drug affect people in the trial sample so that they dropped out before the final results were tabulated?
- Will the drug have even broader, more serious adverse effects if used in unapproved ways?

Pharmacies

All pharmacies must submit ownership information to the FDA. Here are some questions a journalist might consider when investigating local pharmacies:

- Are any local physicians on the list of officers and directors?
- If so, do they require their patients to use that particular pharmacy, even though a different pharmacy might have a different selection or better prices?
- And what financial inducements are offered to pharmacies by drug makers to stock certain medicines and to sway customers to those brands?

Medical Device Companies

In recent years, flawed medical devices have received more attention than ever. In 2005, the FDA issued recalls for defibrillators (heart pacemakers) made by Guidant. Later investigations alleged that Guidant knew several years earlier that the devices were flawed and could have prevented serious mishaps and patient deaths.

Journalists don't have to wait for this kind of medical fiasco. The existence of documents for any given medical device can be gleaned early in the process by regular reading of the Federal Register. The documents—clinical data, test results, labeling requirements, promotional materials, progress reports, adverse reaction data and correspondence—can be full of tips and story leads.

Journalists also can examine the database known as MAUDE, which contains reports by manufacturers of medical devices. Information about medical devices can also be found in the FDA adverse reaction reports. More can be learned by following lawsuits involving the manufacturers.

Medical Laboratories

A reporter at WRC-TV in Washington, D.C., knew that medical laboratories wanting federal payments for testing Medicare patients had to undergo periodic inspections, so he obtained inspection reports from the U.S. Health Care Financing Administration. They showed quality-control violations at 40 percent of the Washington-area laboratories. Because such violations often have troubling consequences, the reporter decided to look for lawsuits against the laboratories. He found them, including one filed by a teenager incorrectly diagnosed as having gonorrhea, a man falsely informed that he had AIDS, and a woman who had a hysterectomy because of an incorrect cancer test reading.

The Wall Street Journal found frequent incorrect readings of Pap smears by laboratories, resulting in women dying of cervical cancer who could have been saved through early detection. As the newspaper delved into the reasons, it found technicians paid by the number of slides they read per hour, leading to carelessness, low pay (despite the harried pace) and lack of supervision.

Only some states regulate laboratories. In states where they do, journalists should question whether labs in hospitals and physicians' offices are covered or exempt. If nobody is inspecting those labs, medical board complaints and lawsuits might lead to story ideas. In states that do provide regulation, journalists should study the inspection reports lab by lab. In states that do not regulate labs, journalists should ask why not.

Like many other types of Medicare providers, laboratories sometimes cheat the federal government by charging higher fees than they charge to hospitals, HMOs or private physicians. One technique is unbundling tests that are otherwise offered as a package for a flat fee. By charging the Medicare program separately for each unbundled test, the laboratory increases its profits. Some laboratories do no analysis, dumping blood and urine samples into a drain. The labs then charge the government as though they had performed sophisticated analyses.

Blood Banks

A Dateline NBC producer was analyzing a U.S. Food and Drug Administration recall database when he noticed a reference to a blood recall. Not knowing what that meant, he began asking questions. The result was a story about how blood banks frequently had to call back blood already released for use in transfusions because it had been taken from high-risk donors, had not been properly tested for diseases or had tested positively for HIV but had been circulated anyway.

The Philadelphia Inquirer began a project after a reporter's routine donation of blood. As the reporter lay still, he wondered where the blood would go after it left his body. How would it be processed? Who would decide where it got sent after processing? How much would it cost a patient receiving it during surgery? Eighteen months later, the newspaper published its unsettling series "The Blood Brokers." The reporter found that local blood shortages were caused by mismanagement, not donor reluctance. He discovered that blood banks with shortages were buying pints from overstocked banks, all without donor knowledge, government regulation or price controls.

⊃ CHECK IT OUT

✓ Go to the hospital quality site run by the Center for Medicare and Medicaid Services (www.cms.hhs.gov), and look at hospitals in your area. Try to identify the best and worst.

✓ Go to the Web site for comparing nursing homes sponsored by the U.S. Department of Health and Human Services (www.hhs.gov/resource/index .shtml), and look up nursing homes in your area. Go to your state's Web site, and see if the state has inspected local nursing homes.

✓ Go to your state's medical licensing board, and find out which doctors have lost their licenses and why.

PART III Investigating Business

RESOURCES FOR REPORTING

General Resources

The National Library of Medicine (www.nlm.nih.gov) is an excellent starting point for any investigation into health care. It contains Medline, which searches databases like the Index Medicus, which covers thousands of biomedical journals in print and online. The journals focus on nearly every health topic.

The National Institutes of Health (www.nih.gov), Bethesda, Md., is a federal agency consisting of subagencies that concentrate on specific diseases, including diabetes, allergies and arthritis. The federal government's publication Morbidity and Mortality Weekly Report covers the occurrence of disease and death from all causes in the United States. Every disease has its own interest groups, such as the American Cancer Society.

The Centers for Disease Control (www.cdc.gov) in Atlanta is another good starting place.

Independent publications, like medical journals, can help journalists understand what is considered acceptable medical theory and practice. The answers are not always clear-cut. Refereed journals tend to be the most dependable, but even they can have conflicts of interest.

The newsletter Public Health, Alexandria, Va., tries to track state legislative developments.

Books about health care in general, and specific aspects of it, abound. These are a few of the best:

- "The Social Transformation of American Medicine," by Paul Starr
- "Bitter Medicine: Greed and Chaos in American Health Care," by Jeanne Kassler
- "And the Band Played On," by Randy Shilts
- "Enemies of Patients," by Ruth Macklin
- "Health Care Finance: Economic Incentives and Productivity Enhancement," by Steven R. Eastaugh
- "Introduction to Reference Sources in the Health Sciences," by Fred W. Roper and Jo Anne Boorkman
- "Getting the Most for Your Medical Dollar: A Consumer's Guide to Affordable Health Care," by Charles B. Inlander and Karla Morales of the People's Medical Society, Allentown, Pa.

Hospitals

Organizations and agencies that can provide perspective include the following:

- Joint Commission on Accreditation of Healthcare Organizations (www.jcaho.org), Oakbrook Terrace, Ill.
- American Osteopathic Hospital Association (www.osteopathic.org), Chicago
- American Hospital Association (www.aha.org), Chicago

PART III   Investigating Business

- Centers for Medicare and Medicaid Services (previously known as the Health Care Financing Administration) (www.cms.hhs.gov), Baltimore, Md.
- Department of Health and Human Services' Hospital Compare Web site (www.hospitalcompare.hhs.gov)
- National Association of Health Data Organizations (www.nahdo.org), Salt Lake City, Utah

Two valuable books delving into hospitals include Walt Bogdanich's book "The Great White Lie: How America's Hospitals Betray Our Trust and Endanger Our Lives" and former hospital administrator Susan Garrett's "Taking Care of Our Own: A Year in the Life of a Small Hospital." Other valuable books are more narrowly focused, such as Lisa Belkin's examination of hospital ethics committees, "First, Do No Harm."

The Hospital Literature Index, compiled by the American Hospital Association, covers thousands of books and articles in every issue.

Ambulance and Other Emergency Services

Journalists investigating ambulance services should check out the National Transportation Safety Board (www.ntsb.gov) for crash records. The Federal Aviation Administration (www.faa.gov) is a starting place for records on air ambulances, as well as the National Transportation Safety Board (www.ntsb.org) for crash records.

Veterans Administration Hospitals

The agency's inspector general and the U.S. Government Accountability Office, an arm of Congress, audit VA hospitals from time to time. The U.S. Department of Veterans Affairs Web site is www.va.gov.

Nursing Homes

Nursing homes are regulated by the Social Services Department's Division of Aging. Groups like the American Association of Homes and Services for the Aging (www .aahsa.org), National Citizens Coalition for Nursing Home Reform (www.nccnhr .org), American Health Care Association (www.ahcancal.org), AARP (www.aarp .org) and Hospice Foundation (www.hospicefoundation.org), all based in Washington, D.C., can provide perspective and information. Journalists should browse publications like McKnight's Long-Term Care News and Assisted Living (www .mcknights.com) and consider books like Timothy Diamond's "Making Gray Gold: Narratives of Nursing Home Care," Nancy Foner's "The Caregiving Dilemma: Work in an American Nursing Home" and Mary Adelaide Mendelson's "Tender Loving Greed."

Mental Health

The following organizations provide useful information on mental health:

- American Mental Health Counselors Association (www.amhca.org), Alexandria, Va.
- National Association of State Mental Health Program Directors (www.nasmhpd.org), Alexandria, Va.
- National Alliance for the Mentally Ill (www.nami.org), Arlington, Va.
- American Psychiatric Association (www.psych.org), Washington, D.C.
- American Psychological Association (www.apa.org), Washington, D.C.
- Bazelon Center for Mental Health Law (www.bazelon.org), Washington, D.C.
- National Association of Psychiatric Health Systems (www.naphs.org), Washington, D.C.

Useful books include the following:

- "Bedlam: Greed, Profiteering and Fraud in a Mental Health System Gone Crazy," by Joe Sharkey
- "Under Observation: Life Inside a Psychiatric Hospital," by Lisa Berger and Alexander Vuckovic
- "9 Highland Road," by Michael Winerip, based on two years of immersion journalism in a state-financed group home for the mentally ill

The U.S. government publishes SAMHSA News, from the Substance Abuse and Mental Health Services Administration.

Home Health Care Companies

The National Alliance for Infusion Therapy and the Home Health Care Association of America, both of Washington, D.C., are helpful for identifying dishonest providers. When investigating home health care providers, journalists should ask whether they have submitted their services for national recognition from the Joint Commission on Accreditation of Healthcare Organizations.

Physicians, Nurses and Health Care Workers

Journalists should be sure to cultivate sources at each of the medical specialty organizations, such as the American College of Obstetricians and Gynecologists (www.acog.org).

The American Board of Medical Specialties and Marquis Who's Who (part of Reed Reference Publishing) compile The Official ABMS Directory of Board Certified Medical Specialists, covering most practices.

Organizations to consult for information or perspective include the following:

- American Dental Association (www.ada.org), Chicago, Ill.
- National Dental Association (www.ndaonline.org), Washington, D.C.

- National Association of Dental Laboratories (www.nadl.org), Alexandria, Va.
- American Chiropractic Association (www.amerchiro.org), Arlington, Va.
- National Center for Homeopathy (www. nationalcenterforhomeopathy.org), Alexandria, Va.
- American Academy of Physician Assistants (www.aapa.org), Alexandria, Va.
- American Medical Association (www.ama-assn.org), Chicago
- National Council of State Boards of Nursing (www.ncsbn.org), Chicago
- American Osteopathic Association (www.osteopathic.org), Chicago

The U.S. Health and Human Services Department inspector general publishes a list of doctors suspended from receiving Medicare payments.

HMOs

Organizations that can provide perspective include the following:

- National Committee for Quality Assurance (www.ncqa.org), Washington, D.C.
- Health Care Administrators Association (www.hcaa.org), Washington, D.C.
- American Association of Preferred Provider Organizations (www.aappo.org), Washington, D.C.

Blood Banks

The American Association of Blood Banks (www.aabb.org), Bethesda, Md., can provide perspective.

Pharmaceutical Companies

Barry Werth's book "The Billion-Dollar Molecule: One Company's Quest for the Perfect Drug" explains the industry well. "Inside the FDA: The Business and Politics Behind the Drugs We Take," by Fran Hawthorne, is a thorough look at the agency that is supposed to regulate the drug industry.

The Physicians' Desk Reference is probably the most comprehensive guide to prescription drugs. It is published by Medical Economics Data, of Montvale, N.J. The same company publishes companion guides to nonprescription drugs, drug interactions and side effects.

Pharmacies

The following are useful organizations:

- Pharmaceutical Manufacturers Association (www.phrma.org), Washington, D.C.
- American Pharmaceutical Association (www.pharmacist.com), Washington, D.C.
- National Community Pharmacists Association (www.ncpanet.org), Alexandria, Va.
- National Association of Chain Drug Stores (www.nacds.org), Alexandria, Va.

- Healthcare Distribution Management Association (formerly National Wholesale Druggists Association) (www.healthcaredistribution.org), Reston, Va.

- American Society of Health-System Pharmacists (www.ashp.org), Bethesda, Md.

Medical Device Companies

The Emergency Care Research Institute (www.mdsr.ecri.org) in Plymouth Meeting, Pa., a private organization, investigates medical device accidents and tracks litigation involving devices. Two industry groups, the Medical Device Manufacturers Association (www.medicaldevices.org/public), Washington, D.C., and the National Association for Medical Equipment Services, Alexandria, Va., can supply the industry's viewpoint.

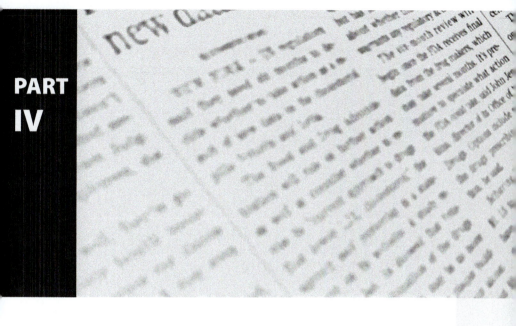

PART IV

Investigative Issues

17

Investigating Energy and Utilities

This chapter discusses how to investigate energy issues and the utilities that supply energy and other services. It outlines where to find documents on public and private electric, water, cable and communications companies. The chapter delves into sometimes complex and technical matters but also shows how to focus a story on energy and utilities issues that concern the public.

Over the past decade, journalists have become more sophisticated in reporting on and investigating utilities and energy issues, whether they are blackouts and brownouts, skyrocketing oil and natural gas rates, or financial malfeasance.

At the same time, the public wants to know why phone rates vary, why cell phone service is unreliable and holds many hidden costs, and why cable TV systems routinely raise their rates with little explanation. The public often asks where the regulators are.

Investigating Utilities

The terminology on the energy and utilities beat is often difficult, and regulation of utilities is complicated. Companies are often called "public utilities," implying that they are all government owned, even though some are private businesses owned by investors. In this book, all are referred to simply as "utilities." A utility is a business allowed to operate as a monopoly or near monopoly in exchange for offering its services to everybody in a defined geographic area for a reasonable price (reasonable to consumers and to the utility), subject to public review. In addition to opening their finances to public review, utilities undergo more scrutiny than the average business concerning the safety and adequacy of service.

But covering utilities can be about more than just electric transmission lines, gas lines, or cell phone towers. For starters, there are the multifaceted effects of these utilities on surrounding areas and on the people living there: There is the environmental impact, such as the pollution from local coal-fired electrical plants or the waste from a nuclear facility. There is the property impact, whether it is land condemned for rights of way or plummeting home values because of a utility's activities. There can even be disaster coverage, as when a dam owned by a utility suddenly collapses.

State Regulation

Utilities usually are regulated in the states where they do business, in addition to coming under scrutiny by one or more federal agencies. (The National Association of Regulatory Utility Commissioners in Washington, D.C., can provide a quick guide to which agency oversees which utilities.) In almost every state, one agency takes the regulatory lead. For example, the Missouri Public Service Commission regulates rates, service and safety for investor-owned electric, gas, telecommunications, sewer and water companies. It also has limited jurisdiction over rural electric cooperatives and municipally owned electric utilities. The five commissioners—appointed by the governor with state senate consent—and a professional staff frequently intersect with federal regulators, especially the Federal Energy Regulatory Commission and the Federal Communications Commission.

What residential and commercial customers must pay for their utilities is determined in part by the state public service commission. The process begins when a utility asks to raise its rates or the commission moves to decrease rates. Detailed hearings usually follow a rate increase or decrease petition. Utilities sometimes appeal decisions to state courts. Besides studying the big rate cases, journalists also should look at individual consumer complaints filed with the commission to see how the utility is falling short or to see if rates are beyond what the average consumer can pay.

In Missouri, the general public is represented at the commission by the Office of the Public Counsel, an independent agency. It is involved in every rate case but does not represent individual consumers with complaints. Similar offices in other states have banded together to form the National Association of State Utility Consumer Advocates, headquartered in Washington, D.C.

In a few states, like Kansas and Wisconsin, citizen utility boards represent the consumers. The boards consist of dues-paying members who have received authority from a legislature or regulatory agency to intervene routinely in utility cases. Furthermore, the boards are allowed to insert membership forms and informational literature in state mailings, such as motor vehicle registrations, tax forms and benefit payments.

Much of the regulatory structure of electric utilities has changed significantly under deregulation. Many states have passed legislation that allows customers to choose their electric supplier, much like they choose long-distance phone service. Under deregulation, utilities are no longer regulated monopolies relegated to serving particular areas; now companies can compete head to head.

This change brings new challenges in reporting on the industry. New players are emerging, such as companies and power marketers that don't own power plants or transmission lines but serve as electricity brokers. Some utilities may decide to sell their power plants and become "wire" companies—selling access to their transmission lines to other utilities.

The dangers of this new system were well reported during the Enron scandal in 2001 in which Enron employees caused rolling blackouts and drove up prices in California.

Deregulation is also changing how power plants and transmission lines are built. Currently, utilities must apply for a certificate of convenience and necessity to build a plant or power line. The company must prove to the state agency that regulates it that there is a compelling public local need. In a deregulated environment, these decisions could be made in other states or regions or even by the federal government.

The entire system of phone service and Internet service is changing too, as cable companies offer all-in-one packages: phone, television and Internet access.

Today, consumers need all the help they can get in understanding rates and services. They also need to know whether the sometimes cozy relationships between regulators and utility officials are failing to protect them.

Federal Regulation

The Federal Energy Regulatory Commission, part of the U.S. Department of Energy, rules on rates for the transportation and sale of natural gas and oil, the transmission and sale of electricity and the licensing of hydroelectric power projects. The federal government operates some of those power projects through regional administrations in Oregon, Georgia, Alaska, Oklahoma and Colorado. For example, the Tennessee Valley Authority is a regional government agency that acts as a wholesale power supplier for local municipal and cooperative electric systems in parts of seven states. When these electric power agencies lose money from operations and therefore receive subsidies, all federal taxpayers can be charged for low-cost energy that benefits a relative few.

FERC has a huge number of documents, data and records that reporters can mine for stories. Here are a few examples:

- FERC Form 714, Annual Electric Control and Planning Area Report, shows how much power is exchanged between control areas—that is, how much power one utility is selling to another. Utilities report sales of long-term contracts to other utilities on this form, not daily transactions.

- FERC Form 423 is a compilation of data for cost and quality of fuels delivered to electric power plants to be used for determination of electric rates.
- FERC Form 1 is the Electric Utility Annual Report. Reporters can use the online Records and Information Management System (RIMS) database to access records and documents filed with the commission.

Other bureaucracies within the Energy Department play a role in tracking utilities. The Energy Information Administration's Office of Coal, Nuclear, Electric and Alternate Fuels offers documents, such as Financial Statistics of Selected Publicly Owned Electric Utilities and Financial Statistics of Major Investor-Owned Electric Utilities, on its Web site. More general EIA information includes Annual Energy Review, Annual Energy Outlook, Petroleum Supply Annual, National Gas Annual and Electric Power Annual. EIA Forms 860 and 759 give information on electric generation.

An often overlooked but useful organization for reporters investigating the electric utilities industry is the North American Electric Reliability Council. Founded by the electric industry in 1965 after a massive blackout engulfed the East Coast, NERC promotes the reliability of the interconnected electric system in North America and coordinates planning and operation of the transmission system and power generation. There are 10 regional councils in NERC, each made up of regional power companies that oversee the reliability of the electric transmission system in their areas. NERC works with the Department of Energy on technical and policy issues concerning the industry.

Several NERC publications can be of use to reporters; chief among them is the Reliability Assessment: The Reliability of Bulk Electric Systems in North America. Published every year, this document gives an overview of the nation's generation capacity and transmission capacity for the next 10 years. It also points out where new power lines or plants might be needed because of increased demands for electricity. NERC also publishes summer and winter assessments of the generation and transmission system, as does each of the regional councils.

In an article in The IRE Journal, Tom McGinty of Newsday wrote about how he covers a local utility through databases and documents. (McGinty led the Newsday team that covered the 2003 blackout that hit the eastern U.S. and Canada and was a finalist for the Pulitzer Prize in breaking news.) McGinty writes,

> The first stop should be the U.S. Department of Energy's Energy Information Administration, which maintains dozens of databases with thousands of measurements of every facet of the electric industry. For example, the annual database cre-

ated from form EIA-826 contains monthly sales figures for most utilities in the nation. . . . Using that data, a reporter could quickly piece together the cost-per-kilowatt for his local utility over a decade and compare it to other trends for other utilities.

Other EIA databases include one that tracks utilities' conservation efforts (known as "demand-side management" in industry parlance) and another that documents the cost and quality of fuel burned in certain power plants. . . .

Another source of information on utilities are the so-called "system operators" that operate the energy markets created by deregulation and oversee the reliable flow of electricity on their territories' high-voltage power-lines. The New York Independent Operator maintains scores of public databases and documents everything from utility-level demand to bids and sales on the electric market.

The system operator's Web site also allows access to meeting materials of the various committees that oversee the system. . . . I used several presentations from one of those committees to document a flaw in New York City's energy market that allowed three large generating firms to keep prices artificially high.

McGinty said he also makes liberal use of state open-records laws to obtain payroll information, contracts and other documents. However, he noted,

Although FOI laws can help reporters gather information about government-run utilities, they're of no use to those who are writing about investor-owned utilities. Instead, [reporters] must turn to the numerous regulatory filings that utilities must submit even in the wake of deregulation.

. . . When it comes to rate cases in New York, my first stop for insights and tips is Gerald Norlander, executive director of the Public Utility Law Project, or PULP, an organization whose sole purpose is protecting the rights of low-income and rural utility customers. Norlander said a rate case is "like a little window into large corporations that we don't normally see. They have to leave tracks, and they have to come in and justify what they're doing. We get to ask questions."

For journalists outside metropolitan areas, the Rural Utility Service, part of the Agriculture Department, is a valuable source of information. The service assists rural electric and telephone utilities when they need financing. Some of its recipients are profit-making commercial enterprises; others are nonprofit consumer cooperatives or government units. The National Rural Electric Cooperative Association, Washington, D.C., can provide perspective.

Another great source of information on the nation's public utility holding companies is the Securities and Exchange Commission. The purpose of the holding companies for gas and electric services is to hold stock in companies that provide the services, and that means they are required to file with the SEC.

While privately owned utilities outnumber the public holding companies by about five to one, the small number of holding companies controls a significant amount of the nation's energy generation. The SEC becomes involved when the purchase or sale of a holding company's securities or assets is under consideration. Intrasystem transactions and service and management arrangements also might fall under SEC scrutiny.

Gas and Electricity

The U.S. electric power industry is a combination of electric utilities — some owned by profit-seeking private investors, some owned by governmental units, some owned by cooperatives consisting of consumers. There are far more government-owned and cooperative utilities than there are privately owned utilities, but the private companies have historically accounted for the vast majority of sales and revenues because they dominate in large urban areas.

Investor-owned utilities have traditionally participated in all three aspects of providing energy: generation, transmission and distribution. Federal laws and regulations have recently ended monopolies on power generation. Transmission has opened up to some extent, as utilities must now carry other utilities' electricity on their lines for a fee. That means that some consumers are able to negotiate with distant utilities for better rates, and those distant utilities now have a means to deliver their product. Some large business consumers are even building their own power plants.

The tradition of monopoly utilities has changed in the energy industry. There are numerous reasons. First, the monopoly status of utilities has been premised on government rate regulation. As the philosophy of deregulation took hold, it became clear that government would have to loosen its reins, giving competitors the potential to enter the field. Second, environmentalism led to questioning utilities that were using nonrenewable natural resources (coal, gas, uranium) to sell more power to make more money. Third, some utilities spent lots of money building nuclear power plants, thereby losing millions and requesting rate hikes that far exceeded inflation.

Here are just some of the questions investigative journalists should be asking about gas and electric utilities in their region:

- Are electric utilities changing rates on their own as they compete against alternative power sources that allow big manufacturers and other major customers to generate their own electricity?
- If they are cutting rates, are they laying off workers or executives or reducing salaries to stay profitable?
- If they are raising rates, what are the true causes? And how are the changes affecting day-to-day service in the average home and small business whose customers lack bargaining clout?

- Are regulators looking out for low-income households and the elderly by requiring lower rates for those with fixed incomes?
- Are regulators encouraging efficiency by requiring consumers to pay more for use at peak hours? The theory is that if consumption can be spread more evenly throughout the 24-hour cycle, utilities can refrain from building expensive, polluting plants merely to meet peak demand.
- Do regulators require utilities to offer and promote conservation measures to business and residential users to cut consumption at all hours?
- Is anybody pushing utilities to increase efficiency by storing excess electricity on site, to be retrieved as needed?

Electrical cooperatives also can be good sources of information. They are no longer solely institutions serving isolated farmers and ranchers who would lack electricity otherwise. Cooperatives that had received aid from the Rural Electrification Administration in the 1930s now serve suburbs of cities like Dallas and resort towns like Aspen.

Reporters investigating electric and gas utilities should also routinely check reports at the Government Accountability Office, which serves as Congress' auditing section. The GAO not only offers criticisms of energy and utility regulation but often explains clearly what a regulator is supposed to do and how the particular energy industry operates.

Nuclear Power

Nuclear power plants are often owned and operated by old-line utilities but are regulated separately from other utilities' operations because of their special characteristics.

The problems at the Three Mile Island nuclear plant in Pennsylvania in 1979 and the accident in Chernobyl in Russia in 1986 gave many the impression that nuclear power plants are especially dangerous, and this perception slowed the growth of the nuclear power industry. In fact, the state of Illinois, where nearly half the electricity is supplied by nuclear plants, banned any future construction.

But the industry is making a strong comeback in the light of recent energy shortages, and journalists need to increase their scrutiny of this energy source.

As Gary Lenton of The Patriot-News in Harrisburg, Pa., wrote in The IRE Journal: "Nuclear issues cut across several beats—environment, public safety, business and labor, to name a few. If you're not covering nuclear, now is a good time to start."

Lenton listed the issues that need attention. Most of the documents required for reporting are housed at a handful of agencies.

- *Relicensing of a nuclear plant.* Plants must seek relicensing from the Nuclear Regulatory Commission. Licenses last 40 years, but 20-year extensions can be granted. The relicensing process is described at the NRC Web site.
- *Aging of nuclear plants.* Lenton noted that no one knows how long a plant can run before it is "old." Lenton suggests looking at the NRC's Event Notification Reports, which are a daily listing of "reportable" events. An event report is supposed to be filed whenever an unusual occurrence takes place at a plant. Thousands are filed annually, but the NRC asks for remedial action only about 1 percent of the time. It classifies events from Level 1, the most serious, to Level 5, the least serious.
- *Security.* Since the Sept. 11 terrorist attacks in the United States, nuclear plants have invested hundreds of millions of dollars in security upgrades, but government auditors say security still falls short.
- *Public safety.* Lenton suggests reviewing emergency plans for a radiation release within 10 miles of a plant. That area is known as an Emergency Preparedness Zone. The plans are public documents and should be checked thoroughly.
- *Nuclear waste.* There is still not a permanent place to store nuclear waste, so nuclear plants must store their own. Reporters should find out how much storage space plants have, whether they will create more and who will cover those costs.

In 1987, Congress created the independent Office of Nuclear Waste Negotiator to seek a more stable, industrywide solution. The goal was to find a locale interested, for economic reasons, in serving as a waste repository site. Journalists can ask whether local nuclear utilities have been involved in that search. Transportation of nuclear waste off-site means hauling dangerous materials through populated areas that could be contaminated for decades if an accident occurs.

Much valuable information is online at ADAMS (Agencywide Document Access and Management System), which is the Nuclear Regulatory Commission's electronic document system and is available on the NRC's Web site. It covers more than electricity-generating plants run by utilities; the NRC also oversees research activities involving nuclear materials at universities, hospitals and industrial corporations.

Private-sector resources include the American Nuclear Energy Council, Nuclear Energy Institute and Nuclear Information and Resource Service, all in

Washington, D.C. ADAMS replaced NUDOCS, the previous online system, and is a public information system that allows wider and better access to NRC's publicly available documents. ADAMS permits full-text searching and is the same system as NRC employees use.

As on all beats, investigative journalists should find human sources. While at the Houston Chronicle, reporter Jim Morris was in contact with nuclear industry whistleblowers. They are everywhere, he says, because the industry has so many problems that it ignores or tries to cover up. A utility might lose $1 million a day if a nuclear plant must close for repairs because of problems reported by employees. In a talk at an Investigative Reporters and Editors annual conference, Morris made these observations:

> Covering nuclear power need not be limited to rewriting utility press releases and attending protests. . . . Reporters and editors are put off by the difficulties of the subject matter, the lack of cooperation by utility officials and the plodding pace of regulatory investigations. . . . The owners and operators of these plants, by and large, like it this way. . . . They want to tightly control . . . information . . . ostensibly to keep the public from panicking about "minor" incidents. Reporters who persist are forced to plow through dull inspection reports and interview engineers who talk like engineers. Rather than say "[the plant] damned near melted down last week," they will use cryptic terms like "unusual event," "turbine projectile" and "SALP report."
>
> There is another way. You can get a good sense of what is happening inside a plant by talking to whistleblowers. Initially, this may not seem appealing. Before . . . I thought of whistleblowers as disgruntled, somewhat eccentric people who hated their bosses and were looking for ways to get even. In some cases, this is true. After interviewing more than 50 of these people, however, I found that the vast majority were well-educated, conscientious utility or contractor employees who had devoted many years to the power industry and were strongly pro-nuclear. They merely wanted their bosses to follow the rules.

The Nuclear Regulatory Commission has a resident NRC inspector for each of the more than 100 nuclear plants in the United States. Journalists should seek out current and former inspectors as sources, but they should also try to determine how well current inspectors are performing their jobs.

Water

There are many potential investigations to do on water. Some stories center on water availability and pricing, especially in the dry Southwest and West. Other stories focus on sanitation and health.

Tens of thousands of water systems in the United States are owned by water districts, local governments or private developers. In recent years, the privatization of water has become of increasing concern in many communities.

In California, journalists found that tiny water districts spent about $10 million every month on construction and had an enormous influence on water allocation and price. Robert Gottlieb, a California freelance investigative journalist, said in his book "A Life of Its Own: The Politics and Power of Water" that the water industry is a combination of private interests and public agencies. The private groups, led by agriculture, have dominated over the years, with other contending parties — including recreation, mining and energy, navigation and, more recently, urban development interests — also playing critical roles. These groups are the beneficiaries of water development, taking advantage of its generous subsidies and extensive facilities.

The public agencies, on the other hand, predominate in supplying this most basic resource. They are organized in a variety of forms, from municipal water and sewer departments to county water authorities and irrigation districts (numbering in the hundreds in some states), each of which has varying powers, from levying taxes and charging user fees to making formal or informal land-use decisions. Water agencies, in fact, function at times as de facto land planners for their service areas.

In Madison, Wis., reporter Ron Seely started probing into the local Madison Water Utility after residents complained of discolored water. To his surprise, he found "an aging and decrepit water system that increased the perils of contamination, a renegade public utility that received little or no oversight from the city and managers who were less than forthright about everything from carcinogens and bacteria in the water to the security of wells and water towers."

To do his reporting, Seely did extensive interviewing and collected many documents, including test data for the presence of pollutants in the water system, complaint reports from the state Department of Natural Resources and consultant reports from the utility itself.

The Environmental Protection Agency also requires water suppliers to produce water-quality reports, which contain information on where the water comes from, what contaminants it contains, if any, and how it compares to standards set by regulatory agencies.

For more information on water pollution and resources, see Chapter 18 on investigating environmental issues.

Communications

At the Star Tribune in Minneapolis, a project about payoffs to state public utilities commissioners by the utilities they regulated began with a phone tip. The caller said that the utilities had provided commissioners with tickets to sports events. That brief story spawned more tips, until reporters couldn't ignore the possibility of a pattern. Eventually, the paper's team decided to examine whether the telephone company had received better rate treatment than companies in other states. The team devised 14 measures to help make comparisons valid, including basic residential rates, the percentage of utility requests approved by public utility commissioners and authorized profit levels. Only Minnesota came out above average on favorable treatment of phone companies on every measure.

In many states, the same underfunded agency regulating energy utilities also regulates rates charged by telephone companies for intrastate service. Telephone companies are divided into local and long-distance carriers, and both have the ability to provide video along with voice. Furthermore, cable television utilities, usually awarded a franchise at the city level rather than the state or federal level, can provide telephone service to accompany their pictures. Computer manufacturers supply components to both telephone and cable companies.

Journalists should check the Federal Communications Commission headquarters or its regional offices on any story, because its licensing, annual report, inspection and disciplinary files might provide insights into a regional utility — insights that may be unavailable in state capitals. The FCC can use any of nine enforcement methods when there is cause for concern:

- An admonishing letter asking for an explanation
- A consent order negotiated after an alleged violation is designated for hearing
- A cease-and-desist order
- A monetary fine
- Court action
- Conditional license renewal
- Short-term license renewal
- Denial of license renewal
- License revocation

State utility commissions, which handle individual consumer complaints, struggle to keep up with the changes in communications technology. They may impede efficient, innovative, affordable service by restricting the activities that local telephone companies can engage in and by refusing to drop old-fashioned rate-of-return regulation based on the past monopolistic system.

Because telephone service is available to just about anybody who desires it and because most incoming and outgoing calls are handled efficiently, price has become the focus. Journalists can examine phone bills, explaining how separate, and sometimes masked, charges for directory listings, operator-assisted calls, credit card calls, call-waiting, call-forwarding, separate lines and so on can baffle consumers. Long-distance calling from hotel rooms is especially confusing and expensive, as consumers often know nothing about the carrier owning and operating those phones. The charges are far more expensive than they would be if the callers had used access codes to connect to their usual long-distance service.

In rural and even some suburban areas, rural utility service telephone subsidies helped develop quality service, but taxpayers far away from the areas served also paid. Journalists can search for RUS subsidies to telephone companies that would be profitable in any case but that use access to government-backed funding to obtain low interest rates.

Telephone rates to households and businesses are based on many factors, including salaries of phone company officials, rents paid on phone company buildings and sometimes lavish advertising budgets. Journalists can examine which expenses state regulators allow and which, if any, they disallow when considering requests to hike rates. By doing just that, the Denver Business Journal discovered that a telephone company was paying millions of dollars above market rates to rent some of its buildings. The company planned to charge telephone users for the inflated rental costs.

The Wireless Telecommunications Bureau says it administers all FCC domestic wireless telecommunications programs and policies, except those involving satellite and public safety communications or broadcasting, including licensing, enforcement and regulatory functions. An extraordinary amount of information about cell phones can be found at the WTB Web site.

Cable

The FCC also regulates cable television, but local governments award licenses to cable companies that must abide by federal rules. Some state governments have created cable television commissions to promote uniform franchising requirements in every city where cable operators want to do business.

The National Cable Television Association and the Alliance for Community Media, both of Washington, D.C., and the Cable Telecommunications Association, Fairfax, Va., are among the most significant private-sector groups involved in the cable industry. The FCC also takes the lead in regulating interstate telephone service; state public utility commissions oversee intrastate service.

Journalists should check periodically to see how cable operators are raising rates and whether a cable operator is requesting modifications in its contract.

For instance, some cable companies have sought permission to convert public-access channels — free to citizens and nonprofit groups, including governments, to air their views — to for-profit channels after securing what is in effect a cable monopoly.

Renewal negotiations often begin several years before the contract actually expires. The FCC's involvement covers programming content, signal carriage, rates, service guarantees and ownership restrictions. The restrictions are meant to prohibit the same people from controlling a community's cable system while also controlling the telephone service, over-the-air television, multichannel-multipoint distribution services and satellite master antenna services.

Journalists who cover cable utilities should question the efficiency and availability of services as well as pricing. Some consumers lack access to cable television systems because the companies will not wire certain geographic areas and regulators cannot force them to do so.

When service is available, it is often difficult to obtain a hookup and begin service, which might itself be inept. As for rates, many customers become upset at complicated and sometimes hidden charges. When the cable company of one of the authors recently decided to charge an extra $1.16 per month for "expanded basic" service, its notice said, "You have the right to file a complaint with the FCC about any changes in service or price on the expanded basic tier within 45 days from the time these charges appear on your bill."

Regulation leads to situations such as cable operators petitioning the FCC to change its definition of "small" from systems with under 15,000 subscribers to the Small Business Administration standard of less than $11 million in annual revenue. Any cable operator gaining the "small" designation would be exempted from rate reductions of 17 percent mandated by the FCC.

With the packaging of so many services, including phone and Internet access, it has become more important to look into the operations of cable operators.

Writing in The IRE Journal, James Neff suggested ways to cover local cable television utilities more aggressively and meaningfully. Here are a few of his suggestions:

- *Rate increases*. Often viewers are gouged as rates rise faster than inflation. Compare the past five years of cable increases with inflation. What is the company's explanation? Today some cities are so strapped that elected officials just wink when companies raise rates because they know that franchise fee revenue will go up.
- *Renewal term*. Most franchises were awarded years ago. Now systems are coming up for renewal. Typically, terms had been for 15 years, but some

cities are moving to five-year renewals, which hold companies more accountable. Is your city asking for shorter contract terms? If politicians seem like pushovers, look for ties between the cable company principals and elected officials or their family members. Have the politicians benefited from campaign contributions from the cable owners?

- *Community programming.* Does anyone ever use the community-access studios other than elected officials? Why not? Are higher rates absorbing the costs of free studio time for elected officials?
- *The public file.* The public file, which is kept at the local cable company, should include complaints, correspondence between the FCC and the company and other public records required by the FCC. Other matters covered in the public file include finances and equal employment opportunity compliance.

⊃ CHECK IT OUT

✓ Find the documentation on electrical rates in your community for the past five years. See if rates have gone up. If they have, interview officials to find out why.

✓ Look up oversight inspection findings for a nuclear power plant in your state or another state by going to the Web site of the Nuclear Regulatory Commission's Reactor Oversight Process at www.nrc.gov/nrr/oversight/assess. Read a report on the nuclear plant that you selected.

✓ Find out what entity oversees your local water supply, and get its annual report and budget. Report on how much water rates have increased, if they have, and why.

RESOURCES FOR REPORTING

State Regulation

The state-by-state status on the degree of utility regulation and deregulation can be found at the Energy Information Administration Web site (www.eia.doe.gov/fuelelectric.html). The National Association of State Utility Consumer Advocates (www.nasuca.org) and the National Association of Regulatory Utility Commissioners (www.naruc.org), both in Washington, D.C., are good resources for journalists.

A textbook like "Accounting for Public Utilities," by Robert L. Hahne and Gregory L. Aliff, can help journalists determine whether companies are masking financial difficulties or outright fraud.

Federal Regulation

The following groups are good resources for journalists investigating federal regulation:

- North American Electric Reliability Corporation (www.nerc.com), Princeton, N.J.
- NERC's Regional Entities (www.nerc.com/regional)
- Federal Energy Regulatory Commission (www.ferc.gov), Washington, D.C.
- Energy Information Administration's Office of Coal, Nuclear, Electric and Alternate Fuels (www.eia.doe.gov/cneaf), Washington, D.C.

Gas and Electric Utilities

The following private-sector groups can provide perspective on electric power:

- Electricity Consumers Resource Council (www.elcon.org), Washington, D.C.
- Federal Energy Regulatory Commission (www.ferc.gov), Washington, D.C.
- American Public Power Association (www.appanet.org), Washington, D.C.
- Edison Electric Institute (www.eei.org), Washington, D.C.
- Electric Power Supply Association (www.epsa.org), Washington, D.C.
- Electric Power Research Institute (www.epri.com), Palo Alto, Calif.
- National Rural Electric Cooperative Association (www.nreca.org), Arlington, Va.
- USDA Rural Development Utilities Programs (www.usda.gov/rus), Washington, D.C.

Private-sector organizations supplying information on oil, coal and natural gas resources—the key fossil fuels used to make electricity—include the following:

- American Gas Association (www.aga.org), Arlington, Va.
- National Propane Gas Association (www.npga.org), Washington, D.C.
- American Coal Council (www.clean-coal.info), Washington, D.C.
- Natural Gas Supply Association (www.ngsa.org), Washington, D.C.

- Independent Petroleum Association of America (www.ipaa.org), Washington, D.C.
- American Petroleum Institute (www.api.org), Washington, D.C.
- Gas Technology Institute (www.gastechnology.org), Des Plaines, Ill.
- Association of Oil Pipe Lines (www.aopl.org), Washington, D.C.
- Interstate Natural Gas Association of America (www.ingaa.org), Washington, D.C.
- American Public Gas Association (www.apga.org), Washington, D.C.

  The following groups promote alternate energy sources:

- Solar Energy Industries Association (www.seia.org), Washington, D.C.
- American Wind Energy Association (www.awea.org), Washington, D.C.
- Renewable Energy Policy Project (www.crest.org), Washington, D.C.

McGraw-Hill's Energy and Business Newsletters division, New York City, covers virtually every power resource with one or more publications. "Public Utilities — From the State Capitals" is published by Wakeman/Walworth Inc., Alexandria, Va. The magazine Public Utility Fortnightly is also a good resource on the industry.

David Howard Davis' book "Energy Politics" explains how and why each type of fuel is regulated and delves into the regulation of electricity, which after all is the result of fuel use. "America's Electric Utilities: Past, Present and Future," written by Leonard S. Hyman, is a good primer on the industry.

Nuclear Power

Key resources in investigating nuclear power include the following:

- Nuclear Regulatory Commission (www.nrc.gov)
- NRC Electronic Reading Room (www.nrc.gov/reading-rm.html)
- ADAMS (www.nrc.gov/reading-rm.adams.html), a public information system that claims to provide wider information than NRC's publicly available documents
- Nuclear Energy Institute (www.nei.org), Washington, D.C.
- Nuclear Information and Resource Service (www.nirs.org), Takoma Park, Md.
- Union of Concerned Scientists (www.ucsusa.org), Cambridge, Mass.

Water Utilities

The Association of State Drinking Water Administrators has a link to state Web sites at www.asdwa.org/state.html. Local drinking water information from the EPA is available at www.epa.gov/safewater/dwinfo.htm. Another good source for reporters is the environmental group Environmental Defense Fund, which has a searchable database that identifies water-quality violations by geographic area at www.scorecard.org.

Robert Gottlieb's "A Life of Its Own: The Politics and Power of Water" and Marc Reisner's "Cadillac Desert" are good primers on the history and politics of water usage and rights in the United States.

Communication Utilities

The Web site of the Federal Communications Commission (www.fcc.gov) is a good starting point for journalists.

Leading private-sector groups include the U.S. Telephone Association, National Telephone Cooperative Association and Competitive Telecommunications Association, all in Washington, D.C.

Anne C. Roess' book "Public Utilities: An Annotated Guide to Information Sources" covers energy companies, their industry groups, their academic chroniclers and their regulators with admirable breadth.

Up-to-date rulings by regulatory authorities at every level are compiled in publications from Public Utilities Reports, Arlington, Va.

Cable Utilities

The Alliance for Community Media (www.ourchannels.org) and the National Cable and Telecommunications Association (www.ncta.org), both in Washington, D.C., are among the most significant private-sector groups involved in the cable industry.

18

Investigating the Environment

This chapter points to basic resources and databases that journalists can use to carry out investigations into environmental issues. The chapter includes starting points for investigating air, water and soil pollution and describes how to look at multiple documents and databases to get a clearer picture of environmental problems.

Investigations into environmental issues are among the most important in the 21st century. There is no shortage of both local and global topics, from the quality of drinking water coming out of home faucets to the impacts of global climate change.

Although covering environmental issues may require delving into sometimes complex science, there is an abundance of resources and guides to help journalists dig into such topics as hazardous waste, air pollution, and the dumping and cleanup of dangerous and cancer-causing chemicals into the soil.

Journalists also can probe how politics, lobbying and funding affect environmental legislation and scientific studies, and they can investigate the conduct of both industry and advocacy groups.

At an Investigative Reporters and Editors conference, journalist Michael Fabey discussed techniques that aid agricultural investigations, including environmental issues. Here are some excerpts:

> Do not try to cover the environment or agriculture from the office; you will never have a true idea of what is going on. You have to go out there and trod through the soil with a farmer as the planting season starts or choke on the dust during a summer drought. Meet the people, feel the dirt. These are beats about the outdoors and humankind's desire to use or misuse nature. Get out there. . . .
>
> Who is testing what and how are they doing it? Are the researchers' methods valid? When you refer to a study, make sure it has been published in a reputable journal and reviewed by the researchers' peers. Otherwise, the research may be suspect. . . .
>
> Get to know the history. Obtain and read all available reports — such as Environmental Impact Statements — on the topic. Go through the files of every agency involved. One time, I searched through a state agency's files and found a confidential EPA report the state folks had misfiled. It was a Page-One story. . . .

Keep it simple . . . that includes numbers, too. Take the phrase "parts per million." Most people have no idea what that means. It is a penny out of $10,000. It is a minute out of two years. It is an inch out of 16 miles. . . . Also remember that while these numbers may seem small, it may only take those minute amounts to do damage. You should tell your readers how the chemicals affect the environment and people. Which organs are affected? How much of a danger is there? Do the chemicals break down into other substances that are dangerous?

Regulation: The Environmental Protection Agency

Potential and actual polluters come under scrutiny from city, county, state and federal government agencies. A good place to start any investigation is at the government regulatory offices.

At the federal level, the first agency to go to for documents, databases and human sources is the Environmental Protection Agency. To find documentation for a story or to get story ideas, journalists can browse the EPA Web site and read the agency's annual and periodic reports. Journalists can research all forms of pollution in their communities, see what the latest regulatory issues are and download databases.

The National Law Journal documented the siting of hazardous waste dumps in low-income and minority neighborhoods because the reporters knew, as they said in their IRE Awards entry form, that

> for more than a decade, activists in both the environmental and civil rights movements have argued that minority communities have become a hazardous pollution dumping ground. Enough evidence emerged for the Environmental Protection Agency to admit that minority communities do bear a disproportionate share of pollution risks. Still lacking was scrutiny of what role, if any, the federal government played in creating this imbalance. The greatest journalistic challenge was to find a way to quantify in hard numbers whether EPA was culpable.

The reporters obtained a database of 1,177 toxic waste sites and 1,214 civil lawsuits brought by the EPA concerning those sites, among other information. After detailed analysis of the data combined with extensive interviewing, the reporters concluded that

> a community's color influences the way the federal government cleans up toxic waste sites and punishes polluters. When the EPA goes after violators in court, it gets as much as 500 percent more in money fines against polluters of white communities than those who have contaminated minority communities. In some regions, cleanup of the most serious abandoned hazardous waste dumps (so-called Superfund sites) begins three years later in minority areas than in white areas. In fact,

> minority communities wait a year longer than white communities for their toxic sites even to gain Superfund status. EPA fails to select the Superfund law's preferred clean-up method in minority areas, choosing more often merely to cap or isolate the pollution. In white areas, it more often attacks pollution directly, as the law requires.

This attention to the long-standing problem led to a White House executive order on environmental justice for minority and low-income populations.

In a more recent series, The Record in Hackensack, N.J., found that tons of paint sludge had been dumped in a low-income neighborhood and was still there despite an EPA Superfund site cleanup a decade before. The Record reported that 25 years after the Ford Motor Company had closed an assembly plant, toxic waste from the plant continued to pollute an area in which thousands of low-income families still lived—families that were suffering from numerous health problems.

As described in an article in The IRE Journal, The Record used numerous interviews with residents, lawyers, doctors, plant workers and investigators. The Record also searched through thousands of federal, state and local documents to reveal lax regulation, a shoddy cleanup of the site a decade before, and mob involvement in the dumping.

In addition, The Record commissioned its own testing and found the presence of cancer-causing chemicals at as much as 100 times the acceptable levels.

Other Federal Agencies

Besides the EPA, there are many other executive-branch agencies with some jurisdiction over environmental enforcement, including the Army Corps of Engineers, the Council on Environmental Quality and the Nuclear Regulatory Commission, as well as various bureaus and offices within the Agriculture, Energy and Interior departments. Also, the Securities and Exchange Commission is requiring publicly held companies under its jurisdiction to disclose environmental information.

The U.S. Fish and Wildlife Service can be a good source of information. The Times-Picayune in New Orleans did an award-winning story on the conditions that threaten the world's fish supply, using documents from the Fish and Wildlife Service, among other agencies.

Within the legislative branch, numerous House and Senate committees have jurisdiction over environmental matters. For example, the House Public Works and Transportation Committee holds hearings on relevant issues and publishes documents such as its "Compilation of Selected Water Resources and Environmental Laws." The General Accountability Office does dozens of studies a year on environmental issues. In the judicial branch, courts regularly decide environmental lawsuits, some of them argued by the Justice Department and some by the solicitor general.

At the state level, the lead executive-branch agency is usually called the Department of Natural Resources or the Department of Environmental Protection. It includes the divisions of environmental quality and state parks. In Missouri, the DNR generates reports like "Confirmed, Abandoned or Uncontrolled Hazardous Waste Disposal Sites in Missouri," which has a detailed narrative about each location. Many employees in these departments care deeply about their work and make excellent sources for stories.

State legislatures have multiple committees with environmental jurisdiction; the state courts, like their federal counterparts, hear environmental cases, some of them argued by the state attorney general.

Sometimes legislators, regulators and judges are part of the problem rather than part of the solution. The revolving door between public and private sectors can result in poor regulation. The Austin American-Statesman documented relationships between polluting industries and the state Air Control Board. Former board officials routinely went to work for companies interested in finding less costly ways to comply with or evade the rules.

Using the Toxics Release Inventory

Journalists can begin checking on their own communities by examining the Toxics Release Inventory kept by the EPA, as mandated by the Emergency Planning and Community Right-to-Know Act. Although it is a federal database, its usefulness for local stories cannot be exaggerated.

As noted in the IRE Beat Book "Covering Pollution," the annual TRI reports "are a reference for the day-to-day environmental beat, and in quick-hit stories, such as those that list the top toxic releasers in a community. But the TRI also can be a strong resource for in-depth environmental investigations."

In fact, USA Today did a story investigating pollution from mercury in cities and towns across the United States that used the TRI as a starting point. The newspaper documented how mercury, a poisonous metal, continues to come from

> the nearly 500 coal-burning power plants that supply half the nation's electricity. The $298-billion-a-year electric utility industry is the nation's largest source of mercury air emissions and the latest target of federal and state clean-air regulations.

Mercury emissions in the USA have been cut nearly in half since 1990 as municipal, medical and hazardous-waste incinerators closed or installed modern pollution controls. But mercury from coal-burning power plants has risen, largely because there have been no federal limits on such emissions.

In 2005, about 500 electricity-generating power plants emitted 48.3 tons of mercury, an increase of 1% since 2000, according to a USA Today analysis of the EPA's Toxics Release Inventory. Mercury emissions from all other industrial sources were collectively down 33% in the same period.

The TRI data include names and addresses of factories that manufacture, process or otherwise use any of hundreds of toxic chemicals and then discharge those chemicals into water, air and soil.

A journalist can search for his or her area by using the TRI Explorer on the EPA's Web site. (A tutorial on using the Explorer is included in the IRE Beat Book "Covering Pollution.") It is possible to search by report types (onsite or offsite "releases," for example) or by different categories, such as chemicals, industries, and facilities.

While the data are generally two years old and have other limitations, they can lead to many public-service stories. They also can be used in conjunction with information obtained through TOXNET, a superb site maintained by the National Library of Medicine. TOXNET has a cluster of databases on toxicology, hazardous chemicals and related areas. With the TRI, journalists can answer such questions as how much benzene industrial plants in their county released into a particular river, the names and addresses of steel plants importing lead and the amount of chlorine gas released by a company into the air.

The Hartford Courant used the TRI to uncover the following facts:

- Connecticut manufacturers had failed to report millions of pounds of emissions that the law required them to disclose.
- Of the emissions reported, ozone-eating Freon was on the increase, despite pledges by industries to cut back.
- Some factories were dumping toxic chemicals into city sewage treatment plants.
- The state environmental agency had inaccurately reported emissions to downplay the magnitude of the problem.

The Courant matched the TRI database with a state database on pollution from sewage-treatment plants, used the TRI for daily stories and for a longer story on ozone-eating chemicals, gave information from it to many bureau reporters, and analyzed transfers of chemicals to landfills and private disposal treatment companies.

Investigating Air Pollution

Under the federal Clean Air Act, EPA headquarters, its regional offices and state pollution agencies compile information about the locations of hazardous substances as well as emissions from specific work sites. But state and local agencies also have great authority to enforce the Clean Air Act.

In addition to the TRI, a good place to start is with the EPA's Aerometric Information Retrieval System and AIRS Facility Subsystem, where it's possible to search by several categories, including facility, geography and pollutant.

Journalists can also use the AirData search tool to gather information from the Air Quality System and the National Emission Inventory. Both datasets allow a journalist to see if communities are meeting the standards to lower air pollution.

Indoor air pollution can be a problem in homes, offices and public buildings. Since 1998, a series of Seattle Post-Intelligencer investigations have found that asbestos remained a bigger problem than previously thought.

Regulations from the Occupational Safety and Health Administration about indoor air pollution have spawned legal battles about whether building owners or tenants have responsibility for compliance.

Investigating Water Pollution

Throughout the United States, journalists have found that they don't have to venture far from home to find unsafe water.

In a startling investigation in 2006, The News & Observer in Raleigh, N.C., found that the state's efforts to ensure safe drinking water fell far short of protecting the public. The newspaper said its investigation revealed "a disregard for safety of private wells, weak regulation of public water systems and widespread problems with lead testing." Among the newspaper's findings were these:

- State law doesn't require that private wells be tested. More than 2 million North Carolinians get their water from private wells, many located in areas where arsenic and radiological contaminants might be present.
- When contamination is found in a private well, state officials aren't required to notify nearby well owners, whose water could also be contaminated.

- Only 14 counties have requirements for well testing.
- The state has standards for well construction but only eight employees to enforce them.

As with every other type of pollution, water coverage revolves to a large extent around sweeping federal laws, in this instance, the Clean Water Act and Safe Drinking Water Act. Factories, sewage-treatment plants and other facilities are supposed to report discharges into waterways. Documents generated by the process include national pollution discharge system permits, discharge monitor reports, quarterly noncompliance reports, violation warnings, violation notices and orders to cease. (See "Resources for Reporting" at the end of this chapter for online sources for the documents and databases mentioned below.)

When The (Fort Wayne) Journal Gazette received a tip about local companies discharging chemicals into the municipal sewer system without adequate government monitoring, a reporter found a list of companies tied into the system, their discharge permits, inspection reports by the city, court records of companies fined and the sewer department's annual reports. With that information in hand, he had his story.

The EPA's Office of Ground Water and Drinking Water is a good starting point. The site provides reports of the quality of local drinking water systems and provides links to state programs.

Among water-quality reports, the 305(b) report, a federally mandated inventory of water quality produced every two years, characterizes water quality, identifies widespread water-quality problems of national significance and describes various programs implemented to restore and protect water. As part of the 305(b) reporting process, states must compile a list of "impaired" streams and rivers. This is generally referred to as the 303(d) list and is available from state regulatory agencies.

Another database to pursue is the Water Discharge Permits database, which allows a journalist to look at water-discharge permits and violations. Like other EPA search tools, different categories can be selected, including geography and chemicals.

One of the hot topics today is total maximum daily load of contaminants. States are required, through the Clean Water Act, to establish TMDL levels for their water bodies. As the IRE Beat Book on covering pollution notes, "simply put, a TMDL is a cleanup plan for a particular body of water. A TMDL specifies the maximum amount of a pollutant that a body of water can receive from all sources . . . and still meet water quality standards." TMDL reports and lists can be accessed on the EPA Web site.

Another resource on water is the Safe Drinking Water Information System, which is a database of public water systems and their violations. USA Today discovered flaws in the database but still was able to use it for a major project on violations by thousands of water systems. A query form for this database allows a journalist to localize the data.

The EPA has tackled the problem of point-source pollution and has turned its attention to nonpoint-source pollution, a nebulous area of environmental protection, in which it is difficult to detect the origin of the pollution. It's also a big concern because of urban sprawl. Storm water is a big topic in the area of nonpoint-source pollution because new regulations that took effect in 2002 require local ordinances to protect against storm water pollution and erosion. The Maine Times found towns having trouble with sewer systems after heavy rains. Rainwater runoff was overflowing into streams and rivers without being treated first.

As water shortages reach many locales, some treat wastewater heavily and then use it as drinking water. If so, is the treatment process considered safe by relatively unbiased experts outside the locale? Has the citizenry been informed? Details and the National Pollutant Discharge Elimination System program are available on the EPA Web site.

Agricultural land close to home is sometimes the source of pollution, as pesticides, fertilizers and other chemicals applied to the soil run off into the water. Wetland areas, meant to filter water naturally, sometimes become the center of controversy because farmers want to use the land to plant and developers want to drain the land for apartments, offices or residential subdivisions. The National Conference of State Legislatures provides perspective in its publication "Wetlands Protection and the States." Pollution from corporate hog farms also has been well documented, beginning with a series in the 1990s by The News & Observer in Raleigh, N.C.

The operation of dams by the U.S. Army Corps of Engineers or other government entities is yet another possible cause of environmental degradation. Sometimes dams lead to new recreation areas. Journalists near water recreation areas can examine how much pollution comes from pleasure boaters, many of whom never think of themselves as polluters. The EPA has recognized pleasure boats as a source of water and air pollution.

Investigating Soil Pollution and Hazardous Waste

The term Superfund, mentioned earlier in the chapter, refers to a program created by Congress and implemented by the Environmental Protection Agency as part of the Comprehensive Environmental Response, Compensation and Liability Act of 1980. The purpose was to identify, seal off and clean up sites laced with toxic wastes. The identification process seems to work well, giving journalists the opportunity to find out about sites in their locales. But the sealing and cleaning tasks have been less successful.

The worst hazardous waste sites are placed on the National Priorities List, and there were more than 1,200 sites on the list at the beginning of the 21st century. The EPA devotes a whole section of its Web site to Superfund information.

Adam Berliant, then a Seattle freelancer, discussed how he went beyond federal TRI data to study state hazardous waste manifests meant to track toxic material shipped from an organization's premises. The Resource Conservation and Recovery Act requires shippers to complete a uniform hazardous waste manifest:

> Despite the name, there is no such thing as a standardized form. Some manufacturers actually generate their own forms. However, the law does specify reporting requirements. The manifest must not only describe hazardous material in superb detail, but also must specify who is transporting the material, where it is going (even if out of state), when the material is shipped and just about anything else you would want to know about the material's transport, delivery and disposal.

Many states have agencies that also track hazardous waste, and those agencies and their documents and databases should be checked.

Among the EPA databases to use when examining hazardous waste in your community are these:

- The Comprehensive Environmental Response, Compensation, and Liability Information System, widely known as CERCLIS, has information on all possible hazardous waste sites.
- The Record of Decision System, widely known as RODS, shows the justification for actions taken at Superfund sites.

A reporter at The Burlington Free Press in Vermont knew a barge canal site had been on the Superfund list for years and decided to check on the progress of the cleanup. She read documents at the EPA regional office and the state natural resources agency and conducted interviews. She found bungled scientific studies, inexplicable delays and cost estimates that had jumped from $3 million to $50 million.

Journalists should find out whether the EPA has asked site owners and managers to complete "information requests" to identify "potentially responsible parties" for cleanup costs. If a cleanup has begun, who won the contract, and how? Who is auditing that company's performance, and what auditing reports are available?

Beyond the Superfund sites, there are other dangers to the soil. Pesticides, insecticides and fertilizers used in agriculture often increase yields per acre, but the downside can be serious for the environment. Rachel Carson's 1962 book, "Silent Spring," still reverberates, as can be seen from the title of a congressional committee report: "Thirty Years After 'Silent Spring': Status of EPA's Review of Older Pesticides." Understanding the leading federal law, the Resource Conservation and Recovery Act, can help journalists sort through the issues; knowing state and local law is also important.

Soil might undergo long-term contamination, with consumers who eat the produce grown in that soil ingesting harmful substances that can cause or hasten a variety of ailments, including cancer. The Federal Insecticide, Fungicide and Rodenticide Act requires producers of the substances to file reports with the EPA. Another federal law, the Toxic Substances Control Act, triggers reporting requirements too. The cumulative effect is shown by no-till farming, which has cut back soil erosion by leaving the previous season's fields undisturbed and in turn has reduced pesticide runoff into nearby streams. But to increase crop yields in an untilled operation, farmers have started using more herbicides.

Because so much controversy exists over what is dangerous and at which levels, sometimes the best that journalists can do is report the various sides of the debate, making sure to consult a broad range of qualified sources, delving into their ulterior motives (if any) and evaluating the soundness of measurements used.

There is more than toxic material to monitor. Journalists can look at the solid waste disposal of nontoxic trash. Controversy exists about the appropriate location of landfills, whether incineration is effective, how much landfills pollute subsurface water and whether locales ought to have unrestrained access to dumping garbage across municipal, county or state lines.

Among the questions to pursue are these:

- Is the waste handled by government employees or private companies?
- Is it really less expensive if handled by a private company?
- Do the workers have the training to handle the waste in accordance with the law?
- Who monitors the transportation of the waste?

An investigation into waste disposal should involve spending time at the dump to see what really is discarded, how it is handled by the employees and how little space is left. Another technique is to follow waste from its source. WFAA-TV, Dallas, did that to document the illegal practices of waste disposal companies draining restaurant grease into sewers, dumping it on private property and mixing it with hazardous chemicals.

Military bases are exempt from some laws and regulations; even when they are subject to the rules, they often act as if they were not. Journalists near military bases should inquire who collects the toxic and nontoxic wastes generated there and where the wastes go. Then they should ask for ride-alongs to verify what they are told. The IRE Resource Center contains an entire section on military mishandling of wastes. Other federal lands are also polluted heavily, including mines, oil and gas wells, irrigation drainage canals and factories manufacturing radioactive materials.

Extracting natural resources such as coal, copper and gold from the ground causes its own brand of environmental degradation. Numerous mining laws and regulations are supposed to minimize long-term damage but sometimes are ineffective.

⊃ CHECK IT OUT

✓ Use the Toxics Release Inventory Explorer to find which facilities in your county emit the most pollutants and to find the highest amount of toxic chemicals emitted.

✓ Use the Air Data search tool on the EPA Web site to examine air pollution in your county and to find the biggest air polluter.

✓ Use the CERCLIS database to find any and all hazardous waste sites in your county. See if you can identify the worst site.

✓ Use the Safe Drinking database at EPA to examine the quality of the drinking water in your community. List other resources and databases you would use in an investigation into safe drinking water.

RESOURCES FOR REPORTING

General Resources

The IRE Resource Center is filled with environmental investigations. The Society of Environmental Journalists (www.sej.org), based in Philadelphia, has an extensive, targeted resource center, a strong Web site, an e-mail list for the latest tips and stories, a newsletter and a membership directory.

A complete list of organizations housing environmental experts would take many pages of this book. These are a few of the most useful:

- Energy Bar Association (www.eba-net.org), Washington, D.C.
- Friends of the Earth, United States (www.foe.org), Washington, D.C.
- American Council for an Energy-Efficient Economy (www.aceee.org), Washington, D.C.
- Worldwatch Institute (www.worldwatch.org), Washington, D.C.
- Environmental Law Institute (www.eli.org), Washington, D.C.
- The National Audubon Society (www.audubon.org), New York City
- Resources for the Future (www.rff.org), Washington, D.C.
- World Wildlife Fund (www.worldwildlife.org), Washington, D.C.
- Wilderness Society (www.wilderness.org), Washington, D.C.
- Sierra Club (www.sierraclub.org), San Francisco
- Union of Concerned Scientists (www.ucsusa.org), Cambridge, Mass.
- American Academy of Environmental Engineers (www.aaee.net), Annapolis, Md.
- Environmental Action (www.environmental-action.org), Boston, Mass.
- Izaak Walton League of America (www.iwla.org), Gaithersburg, Md.
- Natural Resources Defense Council (www.nrdc.org), New York City
- Environmental Defense Fund (www.edf.org), New York City

Many of these groups publish magazines that circulate widely beyond their membership. Other environmental magazines are not affiliated with activist groups, such as Grist, Garbage and E. Environmental newsletters abound, including those from the Bureau of National Affairs, Washington, D.C., and Business Publishers Inc., Silver Spring, Md. In-depth information on investigating environmental issues is available in "Covering Pollution," an IRE Beat Book.

In addition to the Society for Environmental Journalists, journalism organizations whose members specialize in environmental coverage include the Council for the Advancement of Science Writing and the National Association of Science Writers, both of Hedgesville, W.Va.

Strong nonfiction writing on environmental concerns has proliferated in the last decade. Here are just a few books that combine research and compelling writing:

- "Tracking the Vanishing Frogs: An Ecological Mystery," by Kathryn Phillips, which combines in-depth journalism with sound science
- "Collapse," by Jared Diamond
- "An Omnivore's Dilemma," by Michael Pollan, which attempts to trace the real cost of America's food
- "The World Without Us," by Alan Weisman

The Environmental Protection Agency

The federal government publishes Access EPA, available in hard copy and on-line, which explains how to find information within the EPA on every environmental topic. Because technology and general science knowledge are so vital to the environmental beat, journalists can broaden their base by consulting bibliographies like Information Sources in Science and Technology, by C.D. Hurt. Other useful reference works are The Environmentalist's Bookshelf: A Guide to the Best Books, by Robert Merideth, and Environmental Encyclopedia from Gale Research.

The Environmental Data Registry (www.epa.gov/edr) is a comprehensive source of reference information about the definition, source and uses of environmental data. The EDR catalogs the EPA's major data collections and helps locate environmental information of interest.

STORET (short for STOrage and RETrieval; www.epa.gov/storet) is a repository for water quality, biological and physical data and is used by state environmental agencies, the EPA and other federal agencies, universities, private citizens and many others.

Other helpful EPA Web pages include these:

- Air Data: Access to Air Pollution Data (www.epa.gov/oar/data)
- Local Drinking Water Information (www.epa.gov/safewater/dwinfo.htm)
- Emissions Monitoring (www.epa.gov/airmarkets/emissions)
- Envirofacts Data Warehouse (www.epa.gov/enviro)
- Monitoring and Assessing Water Quality: Mapping Tools (www.epa.gov/owow/monitoring/maptools.html)
- Polluted Runoff (Nonpoint Source Pollution) (www.epa.gov/owow/nps)
- National Pollutant Discharge Elimination System (http://cfpub.epa.gov/npdes)
- Office of Ground Water and Drinking Water (www.epa.gov/ogwdw)
- Superfund (www.epa.gov/superfund)
- Total Maximum Daily Loads (www.epa.gov/owow/tmdl)
- Toxics Release Inventory Database (www.epa.gov/tri)
- Monitoring and Assessing Water Quality (www.epa.gov/owow/monitoring)

Other Federal Regulatory Agencies

These other federal regulatory agencies or federal databases might prove useful:

- Army Corp of Engineers (www.usace.army.mil)
- Council on Environmental Quality (www.whitehouse.gov/ceq)
- Nuclear Regulatory Commission (www.nrc.org) and its Electronic Reading Room (www.nrc.gov/reading-rm.html)
- U.S. Fish and Wildlife Service (www.fws.gov)
- General Accounting Office (www.gao.gov)
- Toxicology Data Network (http://toxnet.nlm.nih.gov)

Using the Toxics Release Inventory

The Toxics Release Inventory kept by the EPA, as mandated by the Emergency Planning and Community Right-to-Know Act, is a sensible starting point for many pollution-related stories and can be found at www.epa.gov/tri.

Air Pollution

At the federal level, you can start with the EPA's Office of Air Quality Planning and Standards (www.epa.gov/air/oaqps/index.html). Other organizations helpful to journalists include the National Association of Clean Air Agencies (www.4cleanair .org) and Clean Air Watch (www.cleanairwatch.org), all of Washington, D.C.

Water Pollution

The EPA offers many helpful Web sites on water pollution:

- Ground Water and Drinking Water (www.epa.gov/ogwdw)
- Monitoring and Assessing Water Quality (www.epa.gov/owow/monitoring)
- National Assessment Database (www.epa.gov/waters/305b/index.html)
- Polluted Runoffs (Nonpoint Source Pollution) (www.epa.gov/owow/nps)
- Local Drinking Water Information (www.epa.gov/safewater/dwinfo.htm)

For local information, contact the State Drinking Water Administrators (www.asdwa.org), Arlington, Va. The Stormwater Authority offers information on its Web site at www.stormwaterauthority.org.

These are some of the many groups that can provide perspective on water-pollution stories:

- Clean Water Action (www.cleanwateraction.org), Washington, D.C.
- American Rivers (www.americanrivers.org), Washington, D.C.
- National Ocean Industries Association (www.noia.org), Washington, D.C.

- Association of Fish and Wildlife Agencies (www.fishwildlife.org), Washington, D.C.
- National Association of Water Companies (www.nawc.org), Washington, D.C.
- Water Environment Federation (www.wef.org), Alexandria, Va.
- National Fisheries Institute (www.aboutseafood.com), McLean, Va.
- Ducks Unlimited (www.ducksunlimited.com), Memphis, Tenn.
- Stormwater Authority (www.stormwaterauthority.org), Wilmot, N.H.
- Environmental Defense Fund, which has a searchable database that identifies water-quality violations by geographic area (www.scorecard.org)

Soil Pollution

The following sources may be useful:

- EPA's Superfund Web site (www.epa.gov/superfund)
- National Association of Conservation Districts (www.nacdnet.org), Washington, D.C.
- National Agricultural Biotechnology Council (http://nabc.cals.cornell.edu), Ithaca, N.Y.
- National Coalition Against the Misuse of Pesticides (www.beyondpesticides.org), Washington, D.C.
- National Pest Management Association, Inc., International (www.pestworld.org), Fairfax, Va.

The book "Circle of Poison," by David Weir and Mark Schapiro, demonstrates the dangers of exporting marginal pesticides for use by farmers with no training in handling them safely. "Global Dumping Ground," a collaboration between the Center for Investigative Reporting and Bill Moyers, exposes dangerous methods for disposing of trash that ought to be handled more responsibly. "Rubbish! The Archaeology of Garbage," by William Rathje and Cullen Murphy, explodes myths about solid waste. Also useful is Jennifer Seymour Whitaker's book "Salvaging the Land of Plenty: Garbage and the American Dream" and Elizabeth Royte's "Garbage Land: On the Secret Trail of Trash."

These groups can provide perspective on mining:

- American Coal Council (www.clean-coal.info), Washington, D.C.
- United Mine Workers of America (www.umwa.org), Fairfax, Va.
- National Mining Association (www.nma.org), Washington, D.C.
- American Petroleum Institute (www.api.org), Washington, D.C.
- American Forest Resource Council (www.amforest.org), Washington, D.C.
- Society of American Foresters (www.safnet.org), Bethesda, Md.

The book "Public Domain, Private Dominion: A History of Public Mineral Policy in America," by Carl J. Mayer and George A. Riley, is one of several primers on mining in the United States.

19

Investigating Transportation

This chapter offers guidelines and tips for covering transportation issues, ranging from safety to infrastructure to finances. The chapter reviews how to find the documents and sources to investigate crashes, security and deteriorating infrastructure.

Immediately following the collapse of a major interstate bridge between Minneapolis and St. Paul, Minn., in 2007 that killed 13 people, journalists throughout the United States hustled to examine the safety of the bridges and other infrastructure in their communities.

To do so, they used the federal database known as the National Bridge Inventory, an annually updated collection of data on nearly every bridge in every state. They interviewed transportation officials and engineering experts, and they went out into the field to photograph and observe local bridges firsthand.

In the following days and weeks, the reporters produced stories identifying a pattern of underfunding bridge maintenance in every region of the nation that resulted in structurally deficient and sometimes hazardous bridges going unrepaired.

"The highway bridge that collapsed into the Mississippi River on Wednesday was rated as 'structurally deficient' two years ago and possibly in need of replacement," wrote Dan Browning of the (Minneapolis) Star Tribune, just one day after the disaster. He noted that the rating was contained in the U.S. Department of Transportation's National Bridge Inventory database, which contained information that both state and federal officials had easy access to.

Other reporters went on to find that of the nearly 600,000 bridges in the national database, at least one-quarter were identified as structurally deficient or functionally obsolete. The Department of Transportation acknowledged that it needed at least $65 billion to upgrade U.S. bridges. Because of the spotlight that the reporting placed on the deteriorating bridges, repairs began on the worst bridges in many states.

As this example shows, some of the most compelling transportation investigations are about safety and often involve matters of life and death. In general,

PART IV Investigative Issues

449

there are two types of opportunities for conducting transportation safety investigations: after an accident in which injury or death occurred and before the tragedy strikes. The latter—the preventive investigation—is without question preferable.

Safety investigations can target any form of transportation—motor vehicles, trains, planes or boats—and there is a wealth of documents and data available for enterprising journalists.

In safety investigations, government reports and databases are invaluable, but simple day-to-day observations can also lead to questions like these:

- Which streets or highways have the highest accident rates?
- Which local railroad crossing is the most dangerous?
- Which airport has the highest rate of near misses between planes?
- On what lake do most boating accidents occur?

Compiling a list of the top ten locations where accidents occur in a community every month would itself be a public service, but an investigation into why they occur would be even more valuable.

Investigating Land Transportation

There are many investigations involving land transportation that go beyond crashes and collisions. Some transportation investigations probe fraud and other abuses, such as construction delays and cost overruns, unfair seizure of citizens' property for rights of way, and waste and abuse in highway projects. Newsrooms in Boston kept the pressure on highway contractors and state officials with their investigations into "the Big Dig," a problem-ridden project created to put extensive new highways and traffic tunnels in central Boston.

Some transportation investigations focus on design flaws not of highway infrastructure, but of vehicles or on the shortcomings of drivers. Others look at the dangers of what is being transported by truck or train and whether the material is hazardous or flammable.

Cars

Many transportation investigations focus on cars. After all, tens of thousands of people die every year in auto accidents.

Recently, many news organizations have started making use of the Fatal Accident Reporting System. FARS data detail fatal accidents on roads across the nation. In addition to traffic data and accidents by state, journalists can find the most dangerous intersections and roadways, measured in terms of both fatalities and accidents.

The safety of the cars being driven, including the tires, is monitored by the National Highway Traffic Safety Administration. The agency issues general standards, rates specific models for crashworthiness and fuel economy and tests tires for tread wear, temperature resistance and traction. If enough problems appear, the agency can order the manufacturer to take corrective action, often through a nationwide recall.

The Houston TV station KHOU-TV was the first news organization to call attention to the seriousness of Firestone tire defects in 2000. It began investigating car tires that lost their tread "after receiving viewer complaints and a tip from a local Houston lawyer." Through interviews with victims and lawyers, KHOU found 30 deaths that were connected to tread separation on ATX tires. It then expanded its investigation to other states and countries. As a result of the investigation, Firestone recalled 14.4 million tires.

Sometimes car manufacturers contest a recall within the executive branch or in court, and sometimes they quietly make the repairs without issuing a recall. As explained by Clarence Ditlow and Ray Gold in their book "Little Secrets of the Auto Industry," manufacturers sometimes authorize local dealers to make repairs, but only if consumers demand that the work be done.

The National Highway Transportation Safety Administration keeps a database of vehicle complaints, recalls, service bulletins and inspections. The database can be acquired easily from the National Institute for Computer-Assisted Reporting.

Car Inspections and Driving Records The (Raleigh) News & Observer compared local car inspection stations licensed by the state. At one, 90 percent of inspections led to approval. At another, two miles away, only 20 percent of inspections led to approval. Tire stores with inspection authority found tire problems more often than other inspection sites did. Muffler shops found muffler problems more frequently than other sites. Maybe the specialists spotted problems more often because of their expertise, or maybe they were hoping to increase sales.

By going to the state motor vehicles departments and by studying related laws and reports, journalists can come up with numerous topics to investigate. They can examine how easy it is to obtain a driver's license in their state and how stringently the requirements for obtaining a driver's license are enforced. Journalists can look at driving tests and see if the failure rate is low. They can look at accident reports from police to see how frequently the drivers involved are uninsured, and then return to the motor vehicles department with probing questions.

Some investigations have revealed the weak enforcement of license revocations. The Virginian-Pilot did an exposé in which they found that "thousands of drivers banned from the road chronically flout the law" and that "a recent study says they are four times more likely to kill than properly licensed drivers."

The newspaper reported that "from 2000 to 2004 in [the] Hampton Roads [region], 42,606 people were convicted of driving on a suspended or revoked license, according to an analysis of court records." Yet the newspaper reported that many of those continued to drive and cause accidents.

Furthermore, they said, "serial offenders are the most worrisome: In the same period, 4,605 were found guilty of driving with a suspended license three or more times. Dozens have convictions in the double digits. One man was convicted 24 times and arrested on a 25th charge." The newspaper said that those drivers "bounce in and out of court, often paying minimal fines with no jail time."

Journalists also can use state databases to examine driving records. At the Portland (Maine) Press Herald, reporters used a database they obtained through Maine's Freedom of Access Act to analyze about 160,000 motor vehicle crashes from 2003 to 2006. They also "examined hundreds of individual driving records; and interviewed scores of motorists, victims, traffic safety researchers, policymakers and law enforcement officials." They found that accidents involving suspended drivers "are six times more likely to be fatal, four times more likely to lead to an "incapacitating injury" and 10 times more likely to involve alcohol or drugs."

Drunken Drivers   Many investigations have focused on drunken drivers. The Dayton Daily News found a man convicted of drunken driving 19 times who was still driving. In another story, The Atlanta Journal-Constitution identified more than 83,000 offenders with at least three charges against them and 43 with at least 15 convictions.

Journalists should look at what steps states have taken to prevent drunken drivers from getting back on the road, whether it is confiscating the vehicles of drunken drivers or revoking license plates rather than merely suspending a driver's license temporarily. Reporters can also investigate how much legal liability bars and restaurants have if they serve customers who are drunk, knowing that the customers intend to drive home.

The Investigative Reporters and Editors Resource Center is filled with investigations about the failure of drunken driving prevention and enforcement campaigns, leading to thousands of deaths, tens of thousands of nonfatal injuries and millions of dollars in property damage.

Motorcycles and All-Terrain Vehicles

The risks of driving motorcycles either with or without helmets is another area that deserves investigation.

In a classic story that could be repeated on a state or local level, Thomas Hargrove of the Scripps Howard News Service used federal highway data in 2006 for an investigation called "A Fatal Freedom: Deaths in Motorcycle Crashes on Rise." Hargrove reported,

> Deaths in U.S. motorcycle crashes have nearly doubled in a decade, mounting to 4,000 annually, as more states have repealed mandatory helmet safety laws, according to a Scripps Howard News Service study.
>
> One federal analysis concludes that nearly 700 lives could have been saved in one year alone if all motorcyclists had worn helmets.
>
> Yet motorcyclists have become so passionately opposed to mandatory helmet laws that they've formed powerful state and national lobbies, persuaded Congress to muzzle federal highway safety experts and convinced lawmakers in 30 states to roll back their statutes.
>
> Nine of the 10 states with the worst motorcycle death rates don't require adults to wear helmets, according to the Scripps Howard study of records provided by the National Highway Transportation Safety Administration.
>
> Six states, including Florida and Texas, have relaxed their laws since 1997. Motorcycle fatalities quickly went up in all of them. Lawmakers in eight other states are considering rolling back their laws this year.
>
> . . . Those killed in wrecks are overwhelmingly white and disproportionately middle-aged and divorced men, according to federal death records.

By examining the state laws, the lobbyists and the highway accident data, any journalist can measure the effect of anti-helmet laws. Furthermore, journalists can look at the overall danger of operating a motorcycle compared with driving a car.

Other journalists have looked at all-terrain vehicles and found similar disturbing numbers. The (Portland) Oregonian reported that "the machines have soared in popularity, with 7.6 million in use. The result: Record numbers of riders end up in emergency rooms and morgues as accidents kill about 800 people a year and injure an estimated 136,700."

Trucks

Numerous investigations can be conducted of the trucking industry. Here are possible topics:

- Overworked, exhausted drivers
- Safety issues surrounding the transportation of hazardous materials
- Violations of weight standards and the resulting damage to roads and bridges

A journalist can investigate any local trucking company by using the Surface Transportation Board and state regulatory records, locating lawsuits, and developing human sources within the companies themselves.

The Orlando Sentinel found widespread falsification of drivers' logs at one local company, JDC. The Sentinel reported:

> Logbook falsification by truckers at the 589-driver firm was so widespread, federal auditors discovered last August, that the company was slapped with a $92,000 fine.
>
> That ranks among the largest fines against a trucking outfit in recent years, a Journal Sentinel analysis of federal records shows.
>
> Coming on top of $63,000 the firm was assessed for similar rule-breaking in 2004, the latest penalty put JDC in rare territory: Out of more than 50,000 truck and bus companies audited by the Federal Motor Carrier Safety Administration in the last six years, only six have been fined more.
>
> "It's absolutely outrageous," Gerald A. Donaldson, senior research director of Advocates for Highway and Auto Safety, said of JDC's record.
>
> Such behavior is "the tip of the iceberg" in trucking, he said, with more-ingenious drivers routinely flouting the regulations and knowing how to get away with it.

Trucking industry spokespeople said the violations were unusual, but other news organizations have found similar violations.

Andy Pierrotti of WCBD-Charleston examined South Carolina truck accident records that noted a fatigued or sleeping truck driver as a contributing factor and discovered a 75 percent increase in such crashes from 2001 to 2005. He found that the fatigued drivers contributed to 158 accidents that killed nine people and left more than 100 injured. "Despite property damage, loss of life, and injuries, only 42 percent of those tired truckers were ever ticketed," he reported.

The Los Angeles Times reported on truckers who avoided scrutiny of their equipment after a reporter rode with an independent trucker. The reporter observed the trucker swerve onto a gravel back road to avoid a weigh station. The trucker knew that if he had stopped at the weigh station, as required, he would have been fined for a missing mud flap, a blown tire, a log book that was many days behind and possession of an illegal radar detector.

Contributing to the problems is the Federal Highway Administration. The regulatory agency allows the biggest vehicles with the heaviest loads to travel without regard to state size and weight restrictions. Journalists can measure the effects of this by looking at safety issues or infrastructure issues like pavement damage.

In addition to the Fatal Accident Reporting System data, reporters investigating trucks can use such databases as the Department of Transportation's Truck Accidents, which contains information about accidents on U.S. roads involving a commercial vehicle weighing more than 10,000 pounds, including semi-tractor trailers, buses and hazardous material carriers. The DOT also has a truck census database that contains records on each company with commercial interstate vehicles weighing more than 10,000 pounds.

There are plenty of trucking incidents to investigate. WCCO-TV in Minneapolis received a tip from a truck driver who claimed that his employer made him operate unsafe vehicles. He reported the company to state regulators, but nothing happened. WCCO found that the problem was not isolated. As explained in an IRE awards entry, the series "showed that one out of three trucks inspected on Minnesota highways is so unsafe it should be pulled off the road; some truck companies tolerate shoddy maintenance, routinely allowing their trucks to operate with defective brakes, no lights and missing safety gear; trucks routinely dodge state inspections; judges and prosecutors have allowed companies and drivers that cause serious accidents to go virtually unpunished."

In a comprehensive 18-month investigation, The Dallas Morning News revealed many more safety problems in the industry. They used federal, state and local accident and inspection reports and databases, court records, criminal public records databases and interviews with truckers, company owners, law enforcement officers, lawyers, academics and safety experts.

One of the findings they reported was that truckers have one of the highest on-the-job death rates among U.S. workers.

Buses

Bus investigations include school buses, charter buses, and commercial buses on public routes. Stories about school bus safety and drivers' records are explored in Chapter 12.

The regulation of charter buses is often loose at best. After 21 elderly people died because their tour bus drove into a river, The Sacramento Bee found that lax state regulation combined with charter company greed led to unsafe vehicles operated by unfit drivers. The Bee used state and federal laws, driving records of individual operators obtained from the state motor vehicles department, inspection records from the state highway patrol, licensing records from the state public utilities commission and regulations from the Surface Transportation Board.

After an investigation into a Texas accident found similar problems, reporter Michael Grabell of The Dallas Morning News put together a tip sheet that listed the documents available to reporters. He wrote,

- Check the bus company's safety record on the Federal Motor Carrier Safety Administration's Web sites: SafeStat (http://ai.fmcsa.dot.gov/safestat/safestatmain.asp); SAFER (www.safersys.org/CompanySnapshot.aspx); and Passenger Carrier Safety (www.ai.fmcsa.dot.gov/Passenger/home.asp).
- Don't forget to check with your state department of transportation. Companies are regulated by the feds for interstate travel and by the state for intrastate travel.
- Make a federal public records request for the company's most recent Compliance Review from the Federal Motor Carrier Safety Administration.
- SafeStat has summary information on Accident Reports, Vehicle Inspections, Driver Inspections, and Citations. Request the full reports from the state or federal law enforcement agency that issued them.
- In addition to lawsuits, check for complaints with your state attorney general's office and the Better Business Bureau.
- Check for recalls with NHTSA's Office of Defects Investigation (www.odi.nhtsa.dot.gov/cars/problems/recalls).
- For vehicles, SafeStat's accident and vehicle safety pages will give you VIN numbers and license plates. Track registration and ownership records with your state DOT. In our situation, we had a bus that was operating in Texas, leased in Maryland and registered in Oklahoma by its owner in British Columbia. The bus had also operated for many years in Georgia, Ontario and Quebec.

As for commercial buses, intrastate companies tend to be watched less carefully than the interstate carriers, which are dominated by Greyhound. Among the areas to look at are these:

- Who is inspecting buses, and how often?
- Who licenses the drivers, and how frequently are they retested?
- Are drivers checked for alcohol- or drug-related arrests before they are hired? Are they rechecked periodically for drug use?
- How often does equipment fail?
- Where do bus companies provide service, and are illegal van services filling the gap?

Taxis and Limousine Services

In an excellent investigation that could be repeated at anytime, U.S. News and World Report looked at cabbie scams in 10 cities. By taking lots of cab rides and by interviewing drivers, fleet owners, dispatchers, taxi commissioners, police officers, hotel doorkeepers and airport officials, the team documented a host of problems:

- Rigged meters that ran faster than allowed by law or that added charges illegally
- Allegedly broken meters that were used as an excuse to charge flat fares far above the actual cost
- Impermissible baggage fees
- Drivers pretending to be lost while the meter ran
- Low-pressure rear tires that added revolutions per mile, making the meter rise faster than it should
- Drivers picking up passengers headed for different locations and then charging each the full fare, even though the second passenger to be dropped off should be charged the differential only
- Racial, ethnic, physical and geographic discrimination as drivers illegally refused to pick up passengers based on appearance, confinement to a wheelchair or destination

Because so many cab drivers are robbed, shot or in a hurry to transport the quickest, most lucrative-looking fares, their discrimination is justifiable in their own minds, but it is still illegal.

Other investigations have looked into the following:

- The requirements to obtain and retain a taxicab or limousine license
- Whether the procedures for complaints are easy to follow
- What fines are levied against taxi and limousine services that break the law

Roads

Road building at all levels of government is partly a story about contracts: who decides where the pavement should go and its design; who is willing to bid; whether contractors collude to rig bids, thereby spreading out the business (with designated "losers" later receiving subcontracts from the winner) and driving up costs to taxpayers; whether public officials awarding the contracts accept payoffs or steer awards to relatives or business partners.

The Independent Weekly in Durham, N.C., showed how campaign contributors to legislators ended up with the roads they sought. For example, one road bypassed a country club so that its wealthy members could play golf without the distracting noise of traffic. The series also documented how the governor's campaign contributors bought their way onto the state transportation board, which allocated several billion dollars of road money annually. Most of the board members had occupations that benefited directly from the roads they voted for themselves: land developers, contractors, bankers, lawyers, rock quarry owners, engineers, trucking company executives and automobile dealers.

Journalists can find stories by simply reading the state government manual, which explains the transportation agency's responsibilities on how multimillion-dollar contracts are awarded and how they are monitored.

Good investigations can also be done by watching the activities of the division of right of way in state transportation departments. By following what happens when the agency decides that residences, commercial buildings or productive farmland must be bought or destroyed to build roads, journalists can uncover waste and misdeeds.

The Orange County Register found that landowners were forced to sell their homes cheaply to the state and that the homes and land deteriorated while the projects were delayed or never went through.

In a story with the opposite finding, The Phoenix Gazette focused on the most expensive land purchases by the state transportation department to demonstrate how the agency was wasting taxpayer money by overpaying for property owned by speculators who had bought it to make a profit from road building. Abuses included the agency's paying $350,000 an acre for vacant land and more than $1 million an acre for desert brush in freeway corridors. Appraisers and county assessors had judged the land to be worth much less.

The St. Louis Post-Dispatch determined that Illinois highway officials frequently awarded contracts without competitive bidding, costing taxpayers millions of dollars annually in unnecessary expenses. The reporters made the discovery by analyzing Federal Highway Administration data on every highway construction project involving U.S. government money for five years. The data showed the location, date of contract award, completion date, estimated cost, final cost, name of contractor and number of bidders.

Private toll roads are being built in some areas, as investors see ways to make profits while governments struggle to pay for needed repairs, leaving new construction on the planning boards. Private roads might save taxpayer dollars and relieve traffic congestion, but the developers still need government approvals, which leads to the potential for bribes and other unsavory deals. Journalists should not become less vigilant in questioning these developments simply because the private sector is taking the lead.

Not all newsworthy decisions are made at the local and state levels. Journalists should ask how federal highway trust fund money is allocated by U.S. government officials in a local area. They can also track how local members of Congress are able to dip into the trust fund for pork-barrel highway projects that fail to meet the criteria of the interstate highway program.

Railroads

By reviewing federal railroad data and conducting numerous interviews, The New York Times won a Pulitzer Prize when it reported that dangerous railroad crossings across America were not being repaired or redesigned, leading to unnecessary deaths. A similar story can be done anywhere that railroads run. Railroad crossings are a problem in many locales, as poor markings (no flashing lights or warning bells), visual obstructions (such as untrimmed trees), inadequate restraints (such as no gates) and risk-taking drivers, bicyclists and pedestrians lead to death. When the Lansing State Journal in Michigan started investigating the death of a teenager at a railroad crossing, the reporter learned that the state was supposed to oversee about 5,500 crossings. The newspaper showed that recommendations from rail inspectors received no attention or met with delays lasting years.

Reporters from The Morning Call in Allentown, Pa., looked into railroad crossings in Lehigh Valley and found that of the 750 crossings, fewer than half were marked with signs. From 1989 to 1998, there were 76 accidents and 23 deaths at these unmarked crossings. The state transportation agency kept no priority list of dangerous crossings and frequently spent money earmarked for such improvements on other projects.

Meanwhile, WJLA-TV in Washington, D.C., revealed alarming evidence that America's largest railroad companies were running unsafe trains. The investigation documented trains leaving rail yards with defective equipment, improper train inspections, inadequate record keeping and a repeated pattern of safety violations on every major rail line. The stories also showed that federal regulators were well aware of these problems, but the information obtained from their files had never been made public.

Journalists who work in locales that depend on railroads for freight hauling, employment and passenger service ought to keep up with STB publications and develop human sources within the agency. The agency can provide information about the financial health of railroads, mergers, new construction and repair, abandonments that can leave a community without traditional shipping services, rates and attempts to begin or improve commuter and long-distance passenger service.

What should be a big story in many communities is the fate of short-line railroads, which can make or break small businesses that must ship goods medium or long distances. The STB has encouraged nonrailroad entrepreneurs to buy troubled short lines that major railroads threaten to abandon. But labor unions oppose sales to entrepreneurs because the STB refuses to protect union jobs in such circumstances. Those elements would make for interesting projects, yet many journalists are unaware of short-line railroads in their own backyards.

Sharing jurisdiction with the STB on some issues is the Federal Railroad Administration, which is supposed to concentrate on safety, including track maintenance, equipment standards and operating practices. Reporters should also consult the information and numerous databases available at the Federal Railroad Administration.

Hazardous Waste

One important railroad and trucking story involves the transportation of nuclear wastes from power plants and other producers. It is not always possible to route the dangerous waste through unpopulated areas, which means that residents will be put in danger if an accident occurs, and residents frequently have no idea such shipments are passing through their neighborhoods. Sometimes nuclear waste is shipped by truck, which means it might be passing through downtown and residential areas.

One such investigation, done by Phil Pitchford, David Danelski, Ben Goad and Mark Kawar of The (San Bernardino) Press-Enterprise, begins like this:

> A Union Pacific train hauling 28 cars of hazardous materials was headed north from the Colton switching yard when the crew felt the lead engine jerk and shudder to a stop.
>
> Behind them, two tank cars of deadly pressurized liquid chlorine and 12 other cars had jumped the tracks and now lay twisted and dented in the evening darkness. Residents a few hundred feet away were barely aware of the sudden danger facing their west San Bernardino neighborhood.
>
> More than 1.5 million Inland residents live close enough to railroad tracks to be at risk from a serious spill, according to a recent analysis using geographic information systems technology from Redlands-based ESRI.

The risk is growing, experts say. Rail traffic in the region is expected to double in 20 years, and more homes and businesses are being built near the tracks.

San Bernardino County already has more reported spills and other hazardous-materials incidents on trains than any other county in the nation, according to a computer analysis of federal Department of Transportation data from 1993 through 2004.

U.S. Transportation Department regulations require that heavily populated areas be bypassed whenever feasible. Journalists should check with local power plant operators and the U.S. Nuclear Regulatory Commission about the timing and routing of shipments.

To do their investigations, The (Cleveland) Plain Dealer and other newspapers used the Transnet database, developed by Sandia National Laboratories, Albuquerque, under contract with the U.S. Department of Energy. Transnet shows shipments and accidents in the transportation of radioactive materials; it also offers routing models that allow users to plan the safest highway and rail lines for shipping "hot" material. The Los Angeles Times used a different database, the U.S. Transportation Department's Hazardous Material Incident Reporting System, to cull compelling examples from the tens of thousands of shipments.

Mass Transit

Mass transit is another category worth investigating. In cities, suburbs and rural areas with subway or bus systems, the Federal Transit Administration pays a portion of construction and operating costs. Journalists should explore whether transit systems serve all neighborhoods equally or whether low-income or minority neighborhoods lack equal access. For instance, do routes in the wealthier sections of town get the newest equipment and the best trained and most courteous drivers? Are some neighborhoods bypassed altogether, as occurred in the Washington, D.C., subway system? Are there provisions to transport passengers in wheelchairs on the buses and subways?

Investigating Aviation

In a classic, award-winning series, Keith Epstein of The (Cleveland) Plain Dealer used National Transportation Safety Board reports, court records, cockpit recordings and other sources to examine delays in implementing agency recommendations meant to improve airline safety. He showed that minutes before takeoff, USAir Flight 405 from New York City to Cleveland had ice on its wings. The pilots knew a last de-icing would be useful, but there was pressure to take off on time and no regulator absolutely required a final de-icing.

As Epstein reported, the pilots "did not realize just how precarious their situation was. The federal government knew for seven years. U.S. safety officials repeatedly had pinpointed the cause of nine crashes of planes similar to that of Flight 405 — the wing's high vulnerability to trace amounts of ice. Yet Washington had done nothing to require simple, proven remedies advocated for years, such as checking the wings by hand or spraying with a stronger antifreeze just before takeoff." Twenty-seven people died when the plane crashed into Flushing Bay.

Journalists could serve the public interest simply by following up on recommendations from the NTSB, which investigates certain types of accidents, or on airworthiness reports issued by the Federal Aviation Administration. After a crash, journalists frequently find recommendations that might have helped prevent the accident, but manufacturers and regulators sometimes ignore or try to reverse NTSB or FAA recommendations.

One former NTSB chairman told Epstein, "We know when we investigate an accident we are going to see [the same cause] again." Summarizing his research, Epstein wrote, "Transportation experts describe a bureaucracy increasingly paralyzed by fear of lawsuits from regulated industries, hobbled by conflicts with other agencies, buffeted by meddling members of Congress and political appointees and crippled by weak leadership unable to choose priorities or stick to deadlines."

Dateline NBC investigated how the airline industry influences the FAA on costly safety issues. The series revealed that a large portion of the anti-collision lights on commercial jetliners failed to meet minimum safety standards; the FAA had known about the problem for years.

Some airplanes have design or manufacturing flaws. Consequently, journalists investigating safety must develop sources within companies that design and manufacture airplanes, be on the alert for litigation and check airworthiness certifications granted or denied by federal inspectors.

Many airlines are flying planes longer than intended by manufacturers. Journalists should interview manufacturers about the dangers associated with longer-than-expected usage, then check specific airlines and planes for reports of those dangers. Age-related cracks and corrosion can lead to aborted takeoffs, unscheduled landings and canceled flights. Landing gear, radar, hydraulic systems and cabin pressure are especially vulnerable to age-related problems. In 1997, The Seattle Times won a Pulitzer Prize for its coverage of rudder problems in Boeing 737s and caused repairs to be made more quickly.

Pilots and Flight Crews

There are many questions journalists should ask about pilots' training and experience:

- Is the pilot familiar with the airport where the plane will land, especially with any unusual local weather patterns?
- To what extent do pilots flying small private airplanes (many without two-way radios or transponders that transmit their altitudes) increase the danger for commercial airliners?
- Not all planes handle the same. Does the pilot have experience flying the type of airplane in service?
- Did the pilot have military flight experience before joining a commercial airline?

Journalists should inquire at the FAA about alcohol and drug prevention and testing programs for each airline. If no pilots or other crew have been sanctioned, then the reporter should probe more deeply. In the past decade, there have been well-publicized instances of pilots trying to board planes while drunk.

Journalists should also look for violations of federal rules concerning crew fatigue. Crews are supposed to be on the ground for a certain number of hours after flying for a certain number of hours. During that stretch on the ground, they are supposed to have the opportunity for adequate sleep.

Air Controllers and Ground Crews

Many air controllers are expected to retire in the coming years, and there is concern about replacing them. Journalists can do a public service by reviewing air traffic controller staffing and experience. At the same time, there is deep concern over the age of the radar and computer equipment that the controllers must use.

Years ago, The Plain Dealer found that a new radar system meant to help controllers worked poorly, despite its $1 billion cost to taxpayers. The newspaper relied on complaints filed by controllers with their union and with the FAA; the stories provided figures for individual airports. Journalists can use this approach to monitor how well the air traffic control system is working.

To see how serious the problems might be at a particular airport, journalists should check the FAA database on near misses. USA Today and other news organizations have done startling stories on near misses in the air and close calls on the ground, known as runway incursions. In Canada, CBC also reported on the alarming number of near misses.

Airlines

Airlines that are losing money tend to skimp on maintenance, so journalists concerned with safety need to study corporate bottom lines. Before federal airline deregulation, everything worked better, "Captain X" says in the book "Unfriendly Skies." Every system was checked and rechecked. As deregulation encouraged more competition based on price, profit margins eroded; so did ground maintenance, flight crew training and the overall safety cushion.

In 2008, the FAA threatened Southwest Airlines with a $10 million fine for flying planes that had not satisfactorily passed inspection. A week later, it grounded 43 of Southwest's planes after announcing that the airline had not inspected its older planes for cracks in the fuselage. That was followed by revelations by whistleblowers that many safety violations were sliding throughout the airline industry.

Security

Since 2001, airport security has been a high-profile issue. Before that, news organizations had been doing stories for years on poor airport security, but nothing had been done about it. In the late 1990s, Cincinnati's WCPO-TV "uncovered major holes in airport security, behind the scenes where the public can't see. [It] found [that] a Delta subcontractor called Intex Aviation, employing hundreds of people in high security jobs at the Cincinnati/Northern Kentucky International Airport, did not always do the required background checks. . . . [The undercover] investigation revealed that almost anyone could be hired, and once hired, it would be possible to sabotage a plane."

Before the devastating terrorist attacks, the FAA's inspector general had reported on problems in airport security, but, even more shocking, the inspector general, congressional investigators and journalists found major flaws even after the attacks, including the continued employment of convicted felons.

After September 11, journalists also discovered scathing General Accounting Office reports on airports' and airlines' consistent failure to keep passengers safe, an extensive database on FAA enforcement actions in response to security violations, a well-documented history of investigative stories and a history of problems going back more than 15 years.

Since then, investigative journalists have continued their vigilance in investigating airline security and have found further security failings in a system that the government had vowed to improve.

While the Department of Homeland Security has refused to release detailed reports on security lapses and attempts by passengers to circumvent security, many journalists have gotten the information from the records of local law enforcement agencies.

Commuter Planes, Cargo Planes and Government Flights

Private planes have some of the same safety problems as large commercial airliners, but sometimes journalists must raise different questions about manufacturing, maintenance, pilot competence, airport conditions and air traffic controller conduct than with large commercial airliners. Standards and training are more lax for aircraft that fly fewer than 30 passengers.

The pilots tend to be younger and less experienced and fly more hours per week (sometimes on schedules that allow for little sleep). They are not as well paid as pilots of large commercial carriers and may not receive as extensive training.

After a commuter airplane crashed in Minnesota, the St. Paul Pioneer Press found out that the pilot, who died in the crash, had failed six flight checks in a 13-year stretch, punched his first officer while in the air, sought turbulent pockets so passengers would complain to the airline he hated so much and verbally abused passengers. If journalists had checked pilot records routinely, they could have warned potential passengers before it was too late.

Airplanes operated for government officials also need close scrutiny: The planes and the pilots are exempt from some safety procedures that govern commercial and private aviation.

The operations of cargo planes should also continue to be examined. In a lengthy investigation involving the analysis of government documents, The Miami Herald discovered that 69 cargo planes had crashed during a five-year period, claiming the lives of 85 people, thus "making air cargo the nation's deadliest form of commercial aviation." The newspaper said that "pleas to apply more stringent safety regulations on cargo flights have been ignored. Worse yet, when these lax safety standards result in fatal crashes, the pilots are often saddled with the blame."

Helicopters also deserve more examination, especially when they are operated commercially as part of commuter and tourist services. Investigations after helicopter crashes have found shortcomings in rescue equipment and emergency procedures.

Journalists should routinely examine the safety records of local helicopter companies. They may discover unreported crashes and safety violations. In particular, scrutiny should be given to emergency medical helicopters that fly seriously injured patients to hospitals. Information about accidents involving medical helicopters is included in the NTSB's databases.

Airports

Publicly and privately owned airports are inspected by the aviation section within the state Division of Transportation to determine safety and efficiency. Journalists can routinely examine these reports for their investigations.

In addition to safety and security questions, investigative journalists can look at airport costs to travelers and to taxpayers. In many cities, airports are subsidized heavily by governments. Those airports might serve a relatively small number of travelers, but the federal and local governments sometimes operate an airport no matter how busy it is.

Journalists should be checking an airport's costs and benefits by studying budgets, calculating subsidies, conducting interviews with experts and seeing if it is part of the federal "essential air service" program. The program was created by Congress to appease locales in the wake of airline deregulation.

Because deregulation meant that market forces would eliminate air service to some small cities, Congress passed laws to keep local airports open. Some of the preserved routes benefited enough taxpayers to justify assessing everybody, but other routes were boondoggles. According to Martin L. Gross in his book "The Government Racket," "One 'essential' flight is from Washington, D.C., to the luxurious Homestead resort in Hot Springs, Va. The hotel, which charges $335 a day, has one of the richest clientele in the world, including businessmen, conventioneers, Washington politicians, lawyers and lobbyists." Without the subsidy, travelers would have to fly to a different airport and then drive 45 miles to the resort.

Another area to investigate is on-time service; many newsrooms have been using federal data to monitor increasing delays. In recent years, there has been a barrage of stories on the problems with delayed flights because reporters have been analyzing DOT databases on arrivals and departures.

Using Air Databases

Although FAA and other government databases can be incomplete and sometimes inaccurate, journalists should consult them as a standard part of their approach to gain tips, context and detail.

A good place to start is with "service difficulty reports," which can contain information about serious in-flight incidents—such as doors coming open—or flawed equipment.

Although FAA and other database reports can be incomplete, there are now routine data sets a journalist should check and analyze in any investigation. The National Institute for Computer-Assisted Reporting makes them available at low cost. In addition to service difficulty reports, there are the following:

- *FAA Accidents and Incidents.* A database of mainly U.S. flights where there was an accident or an incident, including crashes, collisions, deaths, injuries, major mechanical problems or costly damages.
- *NASA Air Safety Reporting System.* A database of anonymous reports of airplane safety submitted by pilots, flight attendants, air traffic controllers and passengers.
- *FAA Aircraft Registry.* A listing of all aircraft and aircraft owners registered in the United States. This data set also includes tables on registered aircraft dealers and individuals/companies that reserved the N-number for their planes, an alphanumeric string similar to a car license plate.

Investigating Water Transportation

Commercial Shipping

Commercial shipping receives little attention in daily reporting, so it is a fertile area to investigate.

The U.S. Maritime Administration helps commercial shipping by subsidizing private companies, collectively called the U.S. Merchant Marine. The Federal Maritime Commission, an independent agency, shares jurisdiction, with an emphasis on setting rates and licensing ocean freight businesses. Journalists in locales with large Merchant Marine employers can inquire about subsidies for construction and repair of private vessels, as well as the building and maintenance of port facilities.

Journalists in port cities also can monitor the ships that are coming and going. Many are staffed by international crews who know little about their rights, are cheated out of their wages, receive substandard food and may be badly treated by tyrannical captains. These ships may be owned by U.S. corporations, which means that they may have filed information with the Securities and Exchange Commission or with other financial regulatory agencies.

The U.S. Coast Guard

Investigative journalists would do well to give more attention to the Coast Guard. Besides serving as a law enforcement agency, the Coast Guard is charged with formulating, administering and enforcing safety standards for the design, construction, equipment and maintenance of U.S. commercial vessels and with enforcing safety standards on foreign vessels subject to U.S. jurisdiction. Investigations are conducted of reported marine accidents, casualties, violations of law and regulations, misconduct, negligence and incompetence occurring on commercial vessels subject to U.S. jurisdiction. The Coast Guard conducts surveillance operations and boardings to detect violations, and it administers a system for evaluating and licensing U.S. Merchant Marine personnel. This program develops safe staffing standards for commercial vessels.

The Coast Guard also maintains a valuable database on boating accidents, which many journalists have begun making effective use of.

The boating accident database contains information on recreational boating accidents in the United States, and the boat registration database contains information on registered recreational and commercial boats. The Northwestern newspaper in Oshkosh, Wis., found that inexperience and bad decisions are responsible for most of Wisconsin's boating accidents. The Kansas City Star reported that as boat traffic has increased in Missouri, so have accidents, arrests, injuries and deaths. The Star said Missouri is one of the most dangerous states for boaters, according to its analysis of U.S. Coast Guard data.

Journalists should also investigate the environmental damage resulting from boating accidents. The Coast Guard is responsible for enforcing the Federal Water Pollution Control Act and various other laws relating to the protection of the marine environment. U.S. and foreign vessels are prohibited from using U.S. waters unless they have insurance or other guarantees that potential pollution liability for cleanup and damages will be met.

The Coast Guard's other functions include providing a National Response Center to receive reports of oil and hazardous substance spills, investigating spills, initiating civil penalty actions when warranted, encouraging and monitoring responsible-party cleanups and, when necessary, coordinating federally funded spill-response operations. The program also provides a National Strike Force to assist federal on-scene coordinators in responding to pollution incidents.

The Coast Guard can become involved in accidents that appear to concern other agencies. For example, 47 people died as a National Railroad Passenger Corp. (Amtrak) train derailed on tracks that were out of alignment. The misalignment happened after a towboat accidentally rammed a railroad bridge while trying to pass under it. The National Transportation Safety Board investigated.

The U.S. transportation secretary proposed more stringent licensing requirements and route restrictions for towboat operators, as well as more Coast Guard inspections. The Coast Guard also planned to upgrade standards for radar and other navigational aids on towboats.

Regulatory Agencies

One good way to start an investigation is to look at the reports, audits and investigations done by the federal transportation agencies themselves. Numerous agencies are responsible for the oversight of transportation issues. Under the U.S. Department of Transportation, which establishes overall policy, are — among many others — the National Transportation Safety Board, Coast Guard, Federal Aviation Administration, Federal Highway Administration, Federal Railroad Administration, Federal Transit Administration, Maritime Administration, Office of Hazardous Materials Safety and Office of Pipeline Safety.

The Surface Transportation Board, a federal agency created by Congress to succeed the Interstate Commerce Commission, oversees surface transportation that crosses state lines, with an emphasis on trucks, railroads, buses, barges and some coal and chemical pipelines. NTSB programs and Transportation Department units overlap, so journalists frequently get different answers and findings from the various agencies.

In addition, state governments also oversee transportation and have their own laws to enforce, and cities and towns have their own budgets and programs. Going to several agencies can be advantageous to journalists because they can get documents and information from one agency when another denies access.

⊃ CHECK IT OUT

✓ Call or visit your local police department, and obtain reports and data on the most dangerous intersections with the highest rates of accidents. Through interviews and firsthand observation, find out why the rates are high and what is being done about the problems.

✓ Find out what hazardous waste passes through your community on trains or trucks and whether any hazardous waste is generated by your community.

✓ Get data on bridges in your area from the National Bridge Inventory, and determine whether any are structurally deficient. If so, what repair plans are under way?

RESOURCES FOR REPORTING

General Transportation Resources

The General Accounting Office (www.gao.gov) offers reports and testimony on transportation security at www.gao.gov/docsearch/featured/transportationsecurity .html.

Three general government agencies for transportation issues are the U.S. Department of Transportation (www.dot.gov), the Federal Transit Administration (www.fta.dot.gov) and the National Transportation Safety Board (www.ntsb.gov).

Cars

Individual companies and the following organizations can provide perspective:

- Association of International Automobile Manufacturers (www.aiam.org), Arlington, Va.
- National Automobile Dealers Association (www.nada.org), McLean, Va.
- National Institute for Automotive Service Excellence (www.ase.com), Leesburg, Va.
- Tire Industry Association (www.tireindustry.org), Bowie, Md.
- Center for Auto Safety (www.autosafety.org), Washington, D.C.
- Insurance Institute for Highway Safety (www.iihs.org), Arlington, Va.

The magazine Automotive News (www.autonews.com), Detroit, is among the publications covering the industry.

Clarence Ditlow and Ray Gold's book "Little Secrets of the Auto Industry: Hidden Warranties Cost Billions of Dollars" both warns and informs consumers about manufacturers' practice of repairing defects without issuing major recalls or informing the public of the problems.

Driver's Licenses and Inspections

The American Association of Motor Vehicle Administrators (www.aamva.org), Arlington, Va., can provide perspective, as can the American Automobile Association (www.aaa.org), Washington, D.C., and the Motorcycle Industry Council (www.mic.org), Irvine, Calif.

H. Laurence Ross' book "Confronting Drunk Driving: Social Policy for Saving Lives" looks at the big picture of drunken driving.

Trucks

Journalists who want to improve their understanding of the commerce and culture of long-distance trucking can contact the American Trucking Association (www.truckline.org), Arlington, Va., although the Web site is password-protected, or the Owner-Operator Independent Drivers Association (www.ooida.org), Grain Valley, Mo.

"Pedal to the Metal: The Work Lives of Truckers" is a study of the lives of truck drivers by sociologist Lawrence J. Ouellet, who was also a driver himself for 13 years.

Buses

Both the School Bus Manufacturers Institute, Bethesda, Md., and the American Bus Association, Washington, D.C., can answer questions. The National Association of State Directors of Pupil Transportation Services (www.nasdpts.org) includes the American School Bus Council (www.americanschoolbuscouncil.org), Chicago, Ill.

Taxis

The Taxicab, Limousine and Paratransit Association (www.tlpa.org), Rockville, Md., can provide perspective.

Roads and Bridges

The National Bridge Inventory (www.fhwa.dot.gov/bridge/nbi.htm) is a database put together by the Federal Highway Administration and also distributed by the National Institute for Computer-Assisted Reporting (www.nicar.org).

It may also be useful to consult the following organizations:

- Federal Highway Administration (www.fhwa.dot.gov), Washington, D.C.
- Insurance Institute for Highway Safety (www.iihs.org), Arlington, Va.
- National Highway Traffic Safety Administration (www.nhtsa.dot.gov), Washington, D.C.
- American Association of State Highway and Transportation Officials (www.transportation.org), Washington, D.C.
- American Road and Transportation Builders Association (www.artba.org), Washington, D.C.

Two useful government publications are the National Conference of State Legislatures' booklets titled "Traffic Congestion: A Never-Ending Problem" and "The State Surface Transportation Funding Crisis."

Railroads

The following agencies and organizations can provide information about railroads:

- Federal Railroad Administration (www.fra.dot.gov), Washington, D.C.
- Association of American Railroads (www.aar.org), Washington, D.C.
- American Short Line Railroad Association (www.aslrra.org), Washington, D.C.
- National Association of Rail Shippers (www.railshippers.org), Richardson, Tex.
- National Association of Railroad Passengers (www.narprail.org), Washington, D.C.

Hazardous Waste

The hazardous materials database is available from the National Institute for Computer-Assisted Reporting. The Office of Hazardous Materials Safety (http://hazmat.dot.gov) and the Office of Pipeline Safety (http://phmsa.dot.gov) are two government agencies with useful data.

The Council on Safe Transportation of Hazardous Articles (www.costha.com) offers a number of publications. Also, the National Conference of State Legislatures has published a booklet, "Spent Fuel Transportation: History, Status and State Involvement."

Mass Transit

Trade groups that can provide perspective include the American Public Transit Association (www.apta.org), Washington, D.C., the United Motorcoach Association (www.uma.org), Alexandria, Va., and the Association for Commuter Transportation (www.actweb.org), Washington, D.C.

Mass Transit magazine (www.masstransitmag.com), Melville, N.Y., covers most sectors of the industry.

Commercial Shipping

Paul K. Chapman's book "Trouble on Board: The Plight of International Seafarers" provides background on commercial shipping. Eric Nalder's book "Tankers Full of Trouble" concentrates on the perils of shipping oil. It demonstrates how some ship owners put profit first and safety and the environment last.

Private-sector sources abound. Todd & Associates maintains Maritime Information Systems (www.boatman.com/maritime.htm), documenting U.S. commercial vessels. The American Maritime Congress (www.americanmaritime.org), Washington, D.C., can provide perspective on issues facing U.S. flag carriers, as can the Shipbuilders Council of America (www.shipbuilders.org), Washington, D.C.

The union viewpoint is represented by the Seafarers International Union of North America (www.seafarers.org) and Marine Engineers Beneficial Association (www.d1meba.org). American Waterway Operators (www.americanwaterways.com), Arlington, Va., consists of commercial shipyard owners and operators of barges, tugboats and towboats. Those interests have some common ground with the American Association of Port Authorities (www.aapa-ports.org), Alexandria, Va. Recreational interests are represented by the Boat Owners Association of America (www.boatus.com), Alexandria, Va.

Boating Accidents

The National Conference of State Legislatures publishes a useful primer, "Recreational Boating Safety: State Policies and Programs."

The Federal Maritime Commission (www.fmc.gov) regulates oceangoing transportation of U.S. commerce. Through its Marine Safety Program, the U.S. Coast

Guard (www.uscg.mil) both regulates and inspects merchant vessels and licenses their crews.

Aviation

Investigative Reporters and Editors provides the Beat Book "Covering Aviation Safety" and many useful tip sheets in the IRE Resource Center.

Organizations to consult include the following:

- Aerospace Industries Association of America (www.aia-aerospace.org), Arlington, Va.
- Regional Airline Association (www.raa.org), Washington, D.C.
- Federal Aviation Administration (www.faa.gov), Washington, D.C.

The commercial Web site www.landings.com contains news, forums, organizations and resources.

Pilots and Flight Crews

The book "Unfriendly Skies: Revelations of a Deregulated Airline Pilot," written by an anonymous pilot identified only as Captain X (with assistance from author Reynolds Dodson), appears sensational at first, but it is a sober, informative look at getting from here to there at speeds that leave no margin for error. It will give a journalist points of reference when delving into airline safety. John J. Nance's book "Blind Trust" is especially useful in its explanation of how human error affects airline safety. "Collision Course: The Truth About Airline Safety," by Ralph Nader and Wesley J. Smith, is another useful book.

The FAA makes pilot license information available in the FAA Airmen Directory, but the database is now incomplete because, as of 2000, pilots may withhold their information. The database is available through the National Institute for Computer-Assisted Reporting (www.ire.org/datalibrary/databases).

The International Air Line Pilots Association (www.alpa.org), Washington, D.C., can provide perspective. In addition, reporters should monitor pilots' online discussion groups for tips.

Air Traffic Controllers and Airlines

The National Air Traffic Controllers Association (www.natca.org), Washington, D.C., can provide perspective. Aaron Bernstein's book "Grounded: Frank Lorenzo and the Destruction of Eastern Airlines" provides insights into airline economics, as does "Rapid Descent: Deregulation and the Shakeout in the Airlines," by Barbara Sturken Peterson and James Glab.

FAA Databases

In addition to collecting FAA information on CD-ROM, reporters should use Web sites for the latest information. Among the most useful are Web sites from the FAA (www.faa.gov) and the NTSB (www.ntsb.gov). Through its subscription, the National Institute for Computer-Assisted Reporting provides access to the following FAA databases:

- FAA Service Difficulty Reports
- FAA Accidents and Incidents
- FAA Aircraft Registry
- FAA Airmen Directory

Commuter, Noncommercial and Government Flights

The Air Transport Association of America (www.air-transport.org), Washington, D.C., represents scheduled airlines; the Regional Airline Association (www.raa.org), Washington, D.C., represents carriers operating planes with 60 or fewer seats. The Aircraft Owners and Pilots Association (www.aopa.org), Frederick, Md., represents those involved with smaller planes, often used for pleasure, and the Aeronautical Repair Station Association (www.arsa.org), Alexandria, Va., represents certified mechanics' garages. The Association of Flight Attendants (www.afanet.org), Washington, D.C., and the American Helicopter Society (www.vtol.org), Alexandria, Va., can also provide perspective.

Airports

James Kaplan's book "The Airport: Terminal Nights and Runway Days at John F. Kennedy International" provides useful information. The American Association of Airport Executives (www.aaae.org), Alexandria, Va., can provide perspective. The Airport Councils International-North American Chapter (www.aci-na.org) represents local, regional and state governing bodies that own and operate commercial airports in the United States and Canada.

20

Investigating Real Estate

This chapter explores how to report on the issues that concern every community: land, taxes and housing. It highlights government records that can be used to track property ownership, tax liens, mortgages and other real estate records. The chapter also provides guidance in detecting land fraud, misuse of public housing money and the impact of bad lending practices on homeowners.

Rising property taxes, escalating foreclosure rates, land fraud, bad loans, blighted properties, slumlords, shady developers, out-of-control suburban sprawl and manipulation of planning and zoning regulations: These are just a few of the investigative stories that require a solid knowledge of real estate records. And better yet, these are the kinds of stories that can emerge from a routine close examination of documents and the cultivation of real estate sources.

In most newsrooms, only a few journalists feel comfortable delving into property and tax documents, but those who master these documents will be able to do investigations that are at the heart of watchdog reporting that serves the taxpayer. The importance of covering real estate has been clearly shown in recent years as skyrocketing foreclosure rates and faulty lending practices have threatened to undermine the entire credit structure of the housing industry.

An investigation by Vikas Bajaj and Ron Nixon of The New York Times looked at the impact on minority homeowners who obtained subprime loans—high-interest-rate loans to those with shaky credit. They found that delinquencies and foreclosures soared as lenders increased the interest on the loans. That meant that people who thought they had finally been able to buy a house through a subprime loan were having their hopes dashed. At the same time, home values in neighborhoods were falling because of the foreclosures.

Reporters all around the country had similar findings as they examined federal data on home loans and interviewed homeowners and lenders. These revelations were followed by reports that lenders were on the verge of going bankrupt because of the bad loans they made.

Even without a lending crisis, investigative journalists should keep tabs on what is happening in the real estate and housing industries.

Good journalists should be constantly alert to the corruption and favoritism that sometimes accompany big developments, zoning changes and land purchases by public agencies. Such investigations yield important stories for communities and explain why, for example, a factory suddenly rises up next to a residential neighborhood when it should be in an industrial zone in another part of town.

Investigative reporters should also realize the need to examine the broader issues of land-use policies and patterns. These stories can begin with a tip from a real estate agent or property owner, but more often than not they begin with information from public records: ownership records, building permits, zoning files, inspection records and court cases.

The Document Trail: Finding Real Estate Records

Ownership Records

Finding the owner of a particular parcel of land might take minutes, days or even months. Sometimes the ownership is clear from looking up one record. Other times the land has been transferred from one person to another so many times that the trail is complex. In other cases, one person might have paid another to purchase it on his or her behalf to hide the property's true ownership for business reasons or criminal activities.

In searching for land ownership, a journalist often starts with only an address. In that case, he or she should go to the assessor's office, which maintains records on who receives the tax bill on every parcel in a county or city. A journalist can often get a name quickly by checking on computers in the assessor's office or by checking online at a county or city Web site. Sometimes, however, a journalist may need a "legal description of the property," which is kept by the recorder of deeds (sometimes known as the registrar of deeds).

If a legal description is needed, the journalist can visit the recorder of deeds or the planning or public works department to view plat maps. A parcel of land on the plat map might have a legal description like "Bluestone subdivision, Block 10, Lot 17." If the property is in an unincorporated area, the maps will probably consist of ranges, townships and sections, the units used to divide county land. The description might read: "The northwest quarter of the southwest quarter of Section 11, Township 41, Range 15." A section contains 640 acres. One-quarter of a section is 160; one-quarter of that is 40. So in addition to yielding the address, the legal description of some parcels will reveal the number of acres.

Sometimes investigative reporters want to document the history of ownership of a parcel: Who did the current owner buy from, when and at what price? The county recorder's office normally keeps information on every land purchase or sale the parties choose to file.

There is a double-entry system at the recorder's office that tracks the buyer and seller, referred to respectively as the "grantee" and the "grantor." After the filing of the legal document on transfer, the recorder furnishes the information to the assessor to keep the tax records current. An efficient way to trace a parcel's history is to obtain "the abstract." The abstract is not normally kept in a public repository, but a journalist can ask the holder of the mortgage, the title company that verified ownership or the landowner.

When the identity of the owner is unclear from documents in the recorder's office or assessor's office — or because the property is owned by a partnership that does not reveal the names of the partners — there are numerous other documents that may reveal ownership. They include building permits, fire safety or health inspections, Uniform Commercial Code forms (see Chapter 13 on for-profit business), lawsuits, federal or state tax liens, utility bills, doing-business-as filings, rezoning applications or bankruptcy records. Exterminators, lawn service crews, landscape architects, heating and air-conditioning services, plumbers, electricians, interior designers and tree trimmers, among others, might know who owns the property — or at least who does the hiring and pays the bills. When either residential or commercial buildings change hands, lawsuits sometimes result, especially concerning inadequate disclosure by the seller of a structure's defects. Journalists can track such lawsuits in local courts.

Government Documents

Most land records are easily accessible once a journalist knows how the system works. Many counties have put property assessment and tax records on their Web sites. For example, if you go to the Web site of Boone County, Mo., you can look up any individual's assessment and tax record in that county.

These records can be used not only on longer projects but on quick-breaking stories too. In a classic example at The (Portland) Oregonian, Dee Lane followed up on the story of the shooting of a 5-year-old boy by finding the owners of any house where a fire or shooting had taken place. "We're basically looking for slumlords," said Lane.

Using the county government's assessment and taxation database, Lane found the names of the owners of where the shooting occurred in a property database. She then searched for other properties owned by the same couple. She found 25, most in the same part of the city and acquired during a buying spree that lasted two years—clues that she might be dealing with landlords who had overextended themselves, letting their rental properties become slums. She checked the assessed valuation of the properties, finding they were on the low end of the scale.

Then she launched into other records, finding building code violations logged by city inspectors. At city hall, Lane found a letter issued to the owners under a local drug-house ordinance. The letter showed her that the owners were aware that illegal drugs had been dealt on the property where the fatal shooting occurred. Lane later learned that neighbors had complained to the owners about drug dealing and that police had arrested a gang member in the house's basement. Records showed that the owners evicted numerous tenants from their properties but never attempted an eviction from the house involved in the shooting.

Liens

A lien is a claim by one person or entity to a piece of property. Liens filed with the county recorder's office establish legal liability and name the owner responsible for satisfying the lien. If a property owner has failed to pay taxes, the appropriate government agency will file a tax lien against the property. A lien is basically a claim against the property. Potential buyers are reluctant to purchase a property until all claims against the property are paid off or resolved through negotiations with the agency. In some counties, you can look up tax liens online.

If a contractor hires a subcontractor to do work on a building, the subcontractor will likely file a mechanic's lien that stays attached to the property until all bills are paid. There is a reason for every lien. When a commercial property runs into financial difficulties, journalists should start asking questions. If there are enough failures in one area, a journalist can probe whether there is a pattern of poor business practices, city neglect or outright fraud.

Unpaid liens frequently lead to repossession of the property by the lender (often a bank) or to a government takeover by tax authorities. Such property foreclosures are important stories on their own and can be key evidence in a larger project.

In recent years, foreclosures have become big news, as noted earlier in this chapter. But foreclosures bear watching at all times because of the various scams that can take place.

The monitoring of foreclosures should include the auctioning off of the property by the county sheriff or another government agent. Foreclosures and auctions can happen not only because of default by borrowers on payments, but also because of failure to pay back taxes. More importantly, journalists should actually attend an auction to see who is there and what goes on. That fieldwork is a good way to find out who is truly involved in the bidding.

If there is a series of foreclosures involving a group of individuals or a particular company, an investigative journalist should see if illegal land flipping has occurred. Illegal land flipping occurs when the members of a criminal group transfer land and buildings among themselves. They sell the land and buildings at a higher price each time they transfer the property. The higher sales price—usually based on a fraudulent appraisal of the property's value—allows the conspirators to get higher bank loans. The conspirators then default on the property for which they have exorbitant mortgages and move on to another community.

The Asbury Park (N.J.) Press showed how the selling and reselling of real estate in a scheme to defraud lenders led to city blight. Longtime investigative journalists Rick Linsk and Dan Browning have written excellent IRE tip sheets on land records and how to use them to discover land flipping.

In some cases, you can look into whether the high bidder for property is a straw party for the previous owner (that is, the buyer does not actually have the money to buy the property but is using someone else's money to buy it for the previous owner).

To reduce such arrangements, some states require that property foreclosures be handled by a judge in a formal court setting. Journalists should know whether their state is a judicial or nonjudicial foreclosure jurisdiction.

Mortgage Documents

Mortgage documents often reveal ownership and price. Relatively few buyers of homes, commercial buildings or tracts of land pay the full cost up front. Instead, they borrow from a lender, who is supposed to disclose the terms before the papers are signed.

The lender records the loan for legal protection—that is, to protect the right to acquire the property if the borrower defaults on the loan. That paperwork should be filed in the county recorder's office. A journalist should never confuse the amount of the mortgage with the actual price of the property. The mortgage is generally lower than the purchase price. The amount might lead to a reasonable guess about total sales price, but then again people sometimes borrow more than the purchase price, if, for example, extensive renovation will be required.

It can be difficult to determine who actually owns the mortgage until it is paid in full. It used to be that a local lender owned the mortgage until the borrower had made all payments. But local lenders have entered the "secondary market," selling mortgages to investors around the nation. The secondary market, besides masking mortgage holders, influences how much money is available locally and at what rate.

One engine of the secondary market is the Federal National Mortgage Association, Washington, D.C., often called Fannie Mae. Chartered by the federal government, it is owned by stockholders and is listed on the New York Stock Exchange. It purchases mortgages for its own portfolio and issues and guarantees securities backed by mortgages. The Federal Home Loan Mortgage Corp. (Freddie Mac), McLean, Va., is also congressionally chartered. It purchases loans from financial institutions and then sells securities backed by those mortgages to investors.

The two corporations have standardized loan criteria, so investors in their securities anywhere in the nation believe the mortgages are good risks. Fannie Mae and Freddie Mac have no desire to own mortgages if the homes involved have problems, such as inadequate sewer systems. In places like Boone County, Mo., owners wanting to sell rural homes are pressured to replace environmentally unsound septic tanks with more effective, higher cost alternatives. The pressure is not coming from county inspectors or directly from local lenders; instead it is coming from the federally chartered organizations to which local lenders want to sell mortgages.

When mortgage rates drop, as they do cyclically, borrowers refinance at lower rates. Such refinancings generate documents that might help journalists track ownership. They may involve mortgage brokers, who help homeowners shop for the lowest rates among competing lenders.

It is worth looking at mortgage brokers because in many states they are unlicensed and unregulated. Some states do not even have a net worth requirement for entering the mortgage broker business. Some brokers are dishonest; some are just incompetent or so busy that they file documents too late to take advantage of the lower rates. As states move to regulate mortgage brokers, legislatures are requiring brokers to post a bond to pay customers who have been cheated.

Sales and refinancings can involve escrow companies, which hold cash as middlemen while the deal takes final shape. The Phoenix New Times documented fraud by an escrow company that left thousands of property buyers, sellers and refinancers holding worthless checks when the state banking department seized the company. The money had been embezzled rather than safely invested.

After a home loan is final, a different kind of escrow scam might kick in. The borrowers living in the home pay monthly fees to the mortgage company for property taxes. The mortgage holder often collects more than it needs for the escrow account, uses the excess without paying interest and might even be delinquent with the property tax payment, thus harming the borrowers' credit ratings and causing them difficulties on income tax returns. Yet government regulators almost never penalize mortgage lenders for escrow abuses.

Other kinds of fraud can involve selling land that does not exist, selling land owned by someone else or without clear title, or misrepresenting the value or utility of the land that is sold. Other swindles include selling desert land without adequate water or forest land miles from the nearest road or electric wires. Sometimes swindlers will persuade people to buy property based on artists' renderings of never-to-be-built swimming pools or golf courses.

Issues in Real Estate Investigations

Property Value and Tax Assessment

Determining the fairness of property tax assessments is a staple of investigative journalism. If certain individuals or institutions are receiving unwarranted favorable treatment, all individual taxpayers and organizations dependent on property tax revenue are hurt.

With the advent of computer-assisted reporting, these stories have become easier to do in a comprehensive way by analyzing the electronic assessment records. For example, a story by The Palm Beach Post documented that the homes of the wealthy tended to be assessed at a lower percentage of market value than the homes of the poor and middle class. That meant that the wealthy were paying less than their fair share for public schools, garbage pickup and other services paid for by property taxes.

Newsday, which has periodically reviewed assessments on Long Island, N.Y., found that "tens of thousands of homeowners in Nassau County — particularly those in predominantly minority communities — are paying disproportionately high property taxes, while most expensive homes in much wealthier North Shore areas are undertaxed."

Journalists can often find the sales price of a home by searching documents. In Illinois, for example, the sales price is listed in the assessor records, but in other states it can be much more difficult to locate. In some cases, an estate selling land might file a document attesting to the fair market value of the house. The sales price might or might not approximate market value. Perhaps, for example, the seller was under duress. When no such document exists, one route is to call real estate agents. They frequently know the sales price firsthand or can find out what it was with a call to a colleague or competitor.

Cross-referencing documents can be useful too. A Lexington (Ky.) Herald-Leader reporter found a hotel owner claiming a $3 million value in a lawsuit over damage caused by nearby blasting. But in a separate proceeding to reduce his property taxes, the hotel owner was claiming a $1.5 million value.

In Columbia, S.C., The State newspaper showed how officials gave up millions of revenue dollars by allowing developers to abuse a tax break meant to help farmers. No farming was taking place on the land, but developers called the tracts "farms," and nobody challenged the designation. Honest taxpayers— or those unaware of the loophole—ended up subsidizing the crafty ones.

Investigative journalists should also check if property tax assessors in the field are giving favorable treatment. If questions are raised about assessments, they should check the assessor's training and whether one assessor's valuations consistently are out of line with the judgments of colleagues.

Journalists should check on when reassessments are done and whether they are done every few years or only when a property changes owners. If assessments are only done when owners change, journalists may find nearly identical neighboring buildings with wildly varying taxes. Such a system operates to the advantage of longtime residents and merchants, as well as those able to hold their land for development.

When property owners think their assessments are too high, they go to a board of appeals or board of equity. An Ann Arbor News project looked at property owners asking for reductions based on some sort of hardship. It turned out that many of the requesters owned second homes, which did not indicate hardship.

An examination of assessment appeals can begin by finding out what the success rate for appeals is and who wins their appeals. The number of appeals in one locale can be compared to other cities or counties. You might also investigate the makeup of the board that decides the appeals. (This body is sometimes called the board of equalization.)

Another area to explore is properties exempt from property taxes. A journalist can examine tax exemptions to show how other property owners have carried the burden for that property. He or she also can examine applications for tax exemptions to determine if the information was truthful at the time and is still valid. For example, a church that obtained an exemption decades ago because its principal place of worship sat on a specific parcel might now be using the land for a profit-making subsidiary without notifying the assessor.

Landlords and Tenants

The most egregious violations of residential housing ordinances tend to occur in rentals. Landlords frequently take advantage of tenants, including overcharging on rent, repairs and utility bills; refusing to make repairs until after the tenant complains to government inspectors, a step that might place the complainer on a list of undesirable tenants kept by landlord associations; requiring deposits that are never refunded; revoking a lease without notice; holding inspections that violate tenant privacy; and refusing to rent to certain types of people.

Housing court records formed the backbone of a Buffalo News project identifying the most heavily prosecuted landlords and the streets with the highest percentages of substandard units. The stories established a link between poor conditions and absentee landlords. As for the housing court itself, its judges fined or jailed only 3 percent of defendants charged by government inspectors. In New York City, The Village Voice found a housing court judge soliciting bribes from landlords in exchange for guaranteed favorable verdicts on eviction cases.

Journalists should check for complaints of rental or sales discrimination at local, state and federal civil rights commissions, tenants' associations and courthouses. In addition to checking for existing complaints, news organizations can send journalists (or nonjournalists) of different races to real estate agents and property managers. Are prospective renters and buyers of different races but otherwise similar demographics treated similarly?

On the other side, tenants rip off landlords by lying about employment and income, damaging property or refusing to pay their rent or for needed repairs. Landlord-tenant disputes also occur in commercial buildings; news organizations pay too little attention to sleazy business district and shopping center landlords. How vigilant are city and county residential and commercial building inspectors? Do they conduct unannounced inspections? Or do they wait for complaints to arrive—complaints that tenants might be reluctant to file, knowing that their names will be revealed to landlords? Do inspectors look for dangerous lead paint, ventilation to avoid carbon monoxide poisoning from heating systems, violations of air pollution standards and compliance with fire safety codes? Are they screened and paid well enough that they turn down favors and bribes? Are they and their supervisors themselves landlords whose properties fail to measure up? How about when a government agency owns the properties? A Newsday investigation found a city government failing to meet its own housing code for apartment units that had come into its possession.

Mobile homes deserve special attention from inspectors and journalists alike. They are often dangerous, lacking fire-prevention devices and safeguards against high winds. Furthermore, mobile home park residents frequently have low incomes and are poorly educated about their rights, making them especially vulnerable to landlords and park managers.

Construction standards are especially important in commercial buildings that serve large numbers of people, as well as in hurricane and earthquake zones. The Miami Herald did a comprehensive examination of how much more severe hurricane damage was in its area than in other localities because of poor regulation on construction.

The rise of walled-in private housing developments with their own governing boards and security forces raises questions about the constitutional rights of the residents as the boards restrict what can be built, what can be displayed in yards and so on. Restricted entry to the developments raises constitutional questions for those on the outside.

Development, Zoning and Rezoning

Many zonings and rezonings are smart public policy. The same is true for building permits granted to structures that are out of character with their surroundings. But in other instances, rezoning property from residential to commercial can increase the value of property by thousand of dollars. The zoning change can result in shops, factories or malls to be built in or near residential neighborhoods, causing increased traffic and noise and driving down homeowners' property values.

As with many other potential projects, the experienced journalist asks early on who the winners and the losers are. Building permits and rezoning decisions often help the few to the detriment of the many, so there is temptation to bypass majority sentiment by greasing the process.

Zoning and rezoning have become a hot issue throughout the United States as journalists start to measure the effect of sprawl in their areas, such as an increase in traffic, industries and commercial zones placed next to residences, slow response times by ambulances to medical emergencies, and drainage problems.

When a zoning change doesn't make sense, it often means an elected politician or appointed member of the planning and zoning board is helping a friend. Sometimes there is some kind of benefit for the official who approves an unpopular application. However, just because officials vote for a rezoning, variance or building plan despite apparent widespread opposition does not automatically mean they are taking bribes. They may be voting for something that will benefit the whole community in the face of opposition from people who think only in terms of their own property. But a pattern of such rezonings is suspect, especially if they violate the community's master plan or alter previously approved subdivision plans submitted by developers.

Sometimes the bias in favor of developers is blatant. The Orlando Sentinel showed how local officials approved almost every development proposal from builders, leading to new schools that were overcrowded as soon as they opened, traffic jams, polluted rivers, visual blight, inadequate sewer systems, wholesale destruction of trees and poor or nonexistent utility service. When developers propose drastic changes, it is useful to determine if they live in the area and whether they plan to stay. When the developers are already local citizens, a journalist should document if they are former planning and zoning commissioners, attorneys or elected officials.

Sometimes developers' projects are controversial, as when they agree to build rental or owner-occupied units for low-income or moderate-income families in exchange for interest rate breaks from the government. When that happens, local zoning officials sometimes try to change the parcel's designation under pressure from longtime residents who stereotype the intended occupants.

If significant development is planned, journalists should ask whether the granting authority requires builders to pay for part of the infrastructure and the environmental mitigation and provide jobs to local workers. Such payments are referred to as "exactions." If the answer is no, then it is good to ask why not. If the answer is yes, do consumers end up paying higher prices for their homes because of the exactions? Does the government reduce or waive exactions if the developers promise to build housing for lower-income buyers? If not, why not?

The following methods illustrate the ways politicians and bureaucrats have been bribed for favorable votes on development plans, variances and rezonings:

- *Straight cash.* Cash is often the most effective method because it is tough to trace.
- *A collateral deal.* A member of the zoning board in, say, Minneapolis, at the suggestion of a Florida developer wanting to build up north, buys a piece of Tampa land for $10,000. The board member then votes favorably on the Minneapolis rezoning sought by the Florida developer. Two months later, through a well-disguised corporation, the developer buys the Florida land for $110,000. The board member thus receives a $100,000 bribe that can be reported as a capital gain on an income tax return.
- *Ownership.* The developer who wants the rezoning gives the board member stock in the corporation that owns the rezoned land or stock of equal value in one of the developer's other corporations.
- *Favorable business dealings.* The developer who wants the rezoning agrees to buy insurance, construction bonds, building supplies or engineering,

architectural drafting or design services from a firm owned by the board member or a relative.

- *Fringe benefits.* The developer provides the zoning board member with gifts or the use of a vacation condominium.

At The Detroit News, a suburban reporter decided to delve into the seemingly obvious: how suburban growth was draining people and wealth from the city. The findings were anything but obvious: Suburban public officials had hidden interests in real estate. They used their government positions to benefit themselves, their business partners and their family members. Developers made large contributions. A judge who was a land speculator used his authority to change the landscape to his benefit. The newspaper used computer databases to look for connections among thousands of corporations, licensed builders and real estate agents.

Sometimes zoning has nothing directly to do with lucrative development. Instead, it is used to keep out those deemed "undesirable"—for example, unpopular religious sects that want to build a church, halfway houses for ex-convicts, group homes for the mentally ill or housing for lower-income residents.

New Developments

Established residents in a neighborhood might only dream of cashing in when developers are considering building in their area, but those with inside knowledge can be assured of reaping profits. Fortunes can be made by those who have advance knowledge of designs affecting the value of land, such as master plans permitting new development or government plans for new highway exits.

Suppose, for example, that someone is tipped off that a new community master plan will allow high-rise apartments in a previously low-density residential area. He or she can buy the best land in the area quickly, and then sell it at many times the price to prospective builders when the master plan is made public. Or suppose the state wants to build a limited-access highway, with exits 15 miles apart, through what is now largely farmland. A land speculator is tipped off to the exact locations of the exits and then buys the land around them. The farmers who sell know nothing about the planned highway, so they accept a low price. When the highway is completed, the speculator makes a bundle selling or leasing the land around the exits for gas stations, motels and fast-food restaurants.

There are many questions to ask about new developments, for example: If the city plans to buy a tract of land for an airport or landfill, who currently owns that land? Who owns the adjacent land, which will increase or decreased in value once the new facility is built?

Especially in the American West, lots of land controversies revolve around low sales prices and rents paid by ranchers, miners and timber interests. Those low fees are granted by the federal government, in accordance with congressional policy, and carried out by the Bureau of Land Management. The reason behind the low fees seems to be political clout rather than sound economic or environmental policy. Richard Rhodes' book "Farm" identifies issues such as the abuse of farmland while raising crops and livestock; temporary loss of productive land to gain government payments for not growing crops; and permanent loss of productive land to build homes, office complexes, retail stores and factories.

Low-Income Housing

The least desirable residential sites in a geographic area tend to be chosen for public housing. Journalists do frequent articles about the poor quality of life in public housing projects. Many of the stories are marred by a lack of history and perspective and the assumption that public housing has to be that way.

In Kentucky, the Lexington Herald-Leader examined Lexington's unsafe low-rent housing, the lucrative industry behind it and the government regulators who not only allowed it to thrive but took part in running it. Reporters found houses with no running water, plumbing so fouled up that sewage backed up into the bathtubs, unsafe wiring and unsound floors. They also found that several staff members of the Lexington Division of Code Enforcement, who were supposed to be holding landlords accountable for meeting safety codes, had become landlords themselves. The newspaper found that those inspectors' houses violated the very codes the inspectors were supposed to be enforcing.

The Sun-Sentinel in Fort Lauderdale told of a housing inspector working with local contractors to fix bids on repairs to low-income homes in return for a cut of the inflated price. The money came from a $1 million annual government program to help low-income residents improve their living conditions. When a house needed work, the corrupt inspectors chose from a rotating list of six contractors who supposedly bid competitively. But a corrupt inspector was guiding the bidding, so the winner padded it by 10 percent, and then the inspector and the contractor split the overcharge.

Sometimes the story is much larger. Reporters dug into a Department of Housing and Urban Development scandal that continued for years in the 1980s, centered on well-connected presidential campaign contributors and friends of

Cabinet secretaries who won contracts for questionable projects. The first to publish some details was the trade publication Multi-Housing News, which was followed by metropolitan newspapers around the country.

Some journalists have found low-income housing scandals in their backyards. In a year-long investigation in 2006, The Miami Herald found rampant corruption at the Miami-Dade Housing Agency. The award-winning investigation, entitled "House of Lies," uncovered a system that operated like "an unchecked cash machine for developers and consultants and its own leaders and failed the families it was meant to serve." Such failings include millions being allocated for housing that was never built while developers kept the money. The agency also "diverted another $5 million—money earmarked by state law to build homes for the poor—to pay for a new office building complete with a $287,000 bronze sculpture of stacked teacups called Space Station that was shipped from Italy."

Journalists examining low-income housing should ask these questions:

- Who chose the site, and why?
- Who designed the project so poorly?
- Who won the building contract, and why? Were the bids competitive?
- Who holds the maintenance contract, and why?
- Are the volunteer board members conscientious and honest?
- Who chose them, and why?
- Why would they want such a seemingly thankless duty? Is there profit to be made somehow?
- Is the public housing security force composed of local police department rejects who are prone to brutality?
- Why does the housing authority manage the project the way it does?
- Has criticism from below (the tenants) and above (the U.S. Department of Housing and Urban Development regional office) been on target? Has anybody locally made any changes as a result?

A federal housing program called Section Eight is supposed to subsidize rentals of existing apartments by low-income tenants, but it has done less than promised partly because many landlords refuse to be subjected to federal inspections that might lead to costly and time-consuming repairs. In locales where few landlords participate, the number of qualifying affordable apartments fails to meet the demand.

Many states supplement federal efforts to provide affordable housing. In Missouri, for example, the state Housing Development Commission issues tax-exempt bonds to increase the availability of moderately priced residences. But the commission is not divorced from politics, consisting as it does of the governor, lieutenant governor, attorney general, treasurer and six gubernatorial appointees.

To supplement HUD programs, the U.S. Farmers Home Administration provides loans for rural housing. The agency is, unfortunately, also susceptible to dishonest contractors and speculators. FmHA is dependent on local offices in which farmers can influence who receives assistance.

⊃ CHECK IT OUT

✓ Go to the Web site of your local county office, and review what is available on the Web site concerning property. Report on whether it is possible to look up an assessment record, a property record, and a record of whether taxes were paid on a particular property.

✓ Pick a building in your community, and note its address. Using the address and public records, find out who owns the property and whether the owner is up-to-date on paying the taxes. Hint: You will need to use both assessor and tax collector records.

✓ For the same property, go to the recorder's office (sometimes known as the registrar's office), and track the ownership of the property back three owners (if there are that many). Hint: You will need to use grantor and grantee indexes.

RESOURCES FOR REPORTING

The IRE Resource Center contains land and building investigations under numerous categories, including Conflicts of Interest, Developers, Homeless Persons, Housing, Landlords, Property Taxes, Real Estate, Urban Renewal and Zoning.

Ownership

The American Land Title Association, Washington, D.C., can provide information about tracking land ownership, as can how-to books like Sally Light's "House Histories: A Guide to Tracing the Genealogy of Your Home."

- Federal National Mortgage Association (www.fanniemae.com), Washington, D.C.
- Federal Home Loan Mortgage Corp. (www.freddiemac.com), McLean, Va.
- American Society of Home Inspectors (www.ashi.org), Des Plaines, Ill.

The book "Who Owns Appalachia? Land Ownership and Its Impact," by the Appalachian Land Ownership Task Force, shows how much work is involved in tracking control of real estate—and how worthwhile that work can be.

Liens

The U.S. Internal Revenue Service's Web site (www.irs.gov) explains the system of federal tax liens that give the government claim to property. It also explains how liens can be released. You can generally find tax liens at the secretary of state's Web site in each state and at the county recorder's office.

The company Information Technologies maintains a database of federal and state tax liens throughout the United States that can be searched at www.inft.net/general/tax_liens.htm.

The commercial Web site www.searchsystems.net indexes all public records and links for a small fee to most county recorder's offices and also to databases of local tax liens.

Mortgage Documents

The federal government's Financial Institutions Examination Council hosts a Web page (www.ffiec.gov/hmda) listing public data authorized under Congress' Home Mortgage Disclosure Act.

Property Value and Tax Assessment

These organizations offer many resources for journalists investigating issues of property value and assessment:

- National Association of Realtors (www.realtor.org), Chicago, Ill.
- Society of Industrial and Office Realtors (www.sior.com), Washington, D.C.

- American Society of Appraisers (www.appraisers.org), Herndon, Va.
- National Society of Real Estate Appraisers (www.nsrea.org), St. Louis, Mo.
- International Association of Assessing Officers (www.iaao.org), Kansas City, Mo.

Landlords and Tenants

Useful books for examining landlord/tenant issues include the following:

- "Where We Live: A Social History of American Housing," by Irving Welfeld
- "The Suburban Racial Dilemma: Housing and Neighborhoods," by W. Dennis Keating
- "Community Versus Commodity," by John I. Gilderbloom

Perspective is available from these organizations:

- American Apartment Owners Association (www.american-apartment-owners-association.org), Westminster, Colo.
- National Apartment Association (www.naahq.org), Arlington, Va.
- American Society of Home Inspectors (www.ashi.org), Des Plaines, Ill.

When soundness of construction is an issue, the National Conference of States on Building Codes and Standards (www.ncsbcs.org), Herndon, Va., can help, as can the magazine Engineering News-Record, New York City. The books "House," by Tracy Kidder, and "Why Buildings Fall Down," by Matthys Levy and Mario Salvadori, both offer great background on the nuts and bolts of building construction.

Evan McKenzie discusses the dilemmas of homeowners' associations in his book, "Privatopia: Homeowner Associations and the Rise of Residential Private Government."

Development, Zoning and Rezoning

The Urban Land Institute (www.uli.org), Washington, D.C., is one of many organizations that can assist in answering the questions involved in development and zoning.

John Opie's "The Law of the Land: 200 Years of American Farmland Policy" is valuable, as is Richard Rhodes' book "Farm: A Year in the Life of an American Farmer."

Leonard Downie Jr. researched and wrote a classic investigative book, "Mortgage on America: The Real Cost of Real Estate Speculation."

The following are a few of the many helpful interest groups:

- Associated Builders and Contractors (www.abc.org), Arlington, Va.
- National Home Builders Association (www.nahb.org), Washington, D.C.
- American Institute of Architects (www.aia.org), Washington, D.C.
- American Resort Development Association (www.arda.org), Washington, D.C.

- National Trust for Historic Preservation (www.nationaltrust.org), Washington, D.C.
- Preservation Action (www.preservationaction.org), Washington, D.C.
- American Farm Bureau Federation (www.fb.org), Washington, D.C.
- National Farmers Organization (www.nfo.org), Ames, Iowa
- American Planning Institute (www.planning.org), Washington, D.C.
- National Roofing Contractors Association (www.nrca.net), Rosemont, Ill.
- Mechanical Contractors Association of America (www.mcaa.org), Rockville, Md.
- National Farmers Union (www.nfu.org), Greenwood Village, Colo.

The magazine Professional Builder and Remodeler, Newton, Mass., is one of many periodicals to consult. Richard F. Babcock's book "The Zoning Game" is a standard. Babcock, with Charles L. Siemon, also wrote "The Zoning Game Revisited." Terry J. Lassar's book "Carrots and Sticks: New Zoning Downtown" is another useful title.

New Developments

The Bureau of Land Management (www.blm.gov) offers much information on development and its environmental impact on federal land. The National Association of Industrial and Office Properties (www.naiop.org) keeps track of trends in commercial development throughout the United States. And the American Planning Association (www.planning.org) is a nonprofit organization of professional community planners that holds workshops, shares information on the latest issues in planning and grants certification to planners.

Low-Income Housing

The following organizations can provide guidance on issues of low-income housing and public housing. All are located in Washington, D.C.

- National Association of Housing and Redevelopment Officials (www.nahro.org)
- National Council of State Housing Agencies (www.ncsha.org)
- Public Housing Authorities Directors Association (www.phada.org)
- National Low-Income Housing Coalition (www.nlihc.org)
- U.S. Farmers Home Administration (www.fsa.usda.gov)

Irving Welfeld's insider book "HUD Scandals: Howling Headlines and Silent Fiascoes" tells part of the story about the HUD scandals during the Reagan administration. The Washington Post's Howard Kurtz relates the media's own lapses in investigating and reporting on the HUD scandals in his book "Media Circus."

HUD offers a Regulatory Barriers Clearinghouse (www.huduser.org/rbc) of state and local reform strategies that support affordable housing.

PART IV Investigative Issues

Land and Housing Fraud

Journalists can check the HUD Office of Housing Web site (www.hud.gov/offices/hsg/index.cfm) for an extraordinary amount of housing and lender information, including information about the Federal Housing Administration. The Web page of the Department of Veterans Affairs also details down payments if a warranty exists.

21

Investigating the World of the Disadvantaged

This chapter outlines ways to examine how the disadvantaged are exploited and the injustices they face. It shows how to examine government programs for the poor that fail to fulfill their goals. The chapter provides references to government reports and audits and offers strategies for pursuing stories on the disadvantaged.

In 2005, the U.S. Census Bureau estimated that 37 million people in the United States — or 13 percent — lived below the poverty line. About a fourth of all blacks and a fifth of all Hispanics were considered poor. A large percentage of the poor were foreign-born, children or in female-headed households.

Those figures gave a broad and abstract view of poverty in one of the world's wealthiest nations, but investigative journalists can focus and localize the impact of poverty by identifying the impoverished areas of their communities through a review of documents and databases and through aggressive fieldwork.

By doing that, a reporter will find numerous investigative stories. (Although this chapter focuses on poverty in the United States, resources for investigating international issues are listed at the end of the chapter.) These investigations generally fall into three areas. One set of stories exposes appalling living conditions and societal injustices. A second set shows how businesses or con men exploit the poor. A third set of stories uncovers fraud and waste in government programs intended to help impoverished families and children. Sometimes investigations may include elements of all of these different approaches.

Investigating the Issues

Having low or no income affects every part of a person's life — from housing to health care to environmental hazards to mistreatment within the court system. (Many of these areas are covered in other chapters, particularly in those chapters on law enforcement, the courts and health care.)

In a thorough series of stories entitled "The Black Belt," The Birmingham (Ala.) News showed just how widespread problems created by poverty were in 12 counties in Alabama:

> The state's Black Belt, sweeping across south-central Alabama with a history as rich and dark as the soil it is named for, is so stark a contrast to Birmingham and north Alabama that it stands out like a wound.
>
> Pick a statistic: Poverty. Infant deaths. Poor education. Births to single mothers. Unemployment. Gaps in health care. As Alabama and Mississippi lag the nation in most of those categories, this swath of counties trails the rest of the state.
>
> A person growing up in Wilcox County can expect to live about 69 years if he stays put in the Black Belt. That's a shorter life span than one could expect in Sri Lanka, Iran or Mexico, and a full six years less than a resident of Birmingham's suburban Shelby County.
>
> A child in the Black Belt is more likely to be born out of wedlock, more likely to come home to poverty, and more likely to die in the first year of life. A man in the Black Belt is more likely to drop out of school before the ninth grade, leave the mother of his children and die of heart disease.

For the story, the reporters gathered statistics from numerous agencies and institutions, including the U.S. Census Bureau; the Alabama departments of Public Health and Education; the U.S. Department of Labor; the Center for Demographic Research at Auburn University, Montgomery; and the Center for Business and Economic Research, University of Alabama.

But they also talked to officials and social scientists and traveled through the 12-county region, extensively interviewing those living in poverty and demonstrating the deep effect of poverty on individuals and families.

At The Columbus Dispatch, journalists did a series on poverty in the Appalachia region of Ohio and used similar reports and studies and traveled the region. But The Dispatch reporters focused on the failure of federal programs, noting that their investigation revealed that "billions of federal tax dollars dedicated to helping struggling residents of Appalachia have missed their mark in the core of the impoverished region."

Among the many topics an investigative journalist may look at are lack of access to health care, residential proximity to pollution and hazardous waste, lack of city or county services like police or street maintenance or public transportation, lack of sufficient food and nutrition for children, high frequency of crime and shortage of adequately paying jobs.

Special Challenges for Reporters

In the past, most U.S. newsrooms were staffed with white, college-educated reporters and editors who often had little street knowledge about impoverished communities. While there has been a substantial rise in the number of ethnic media newsrooms (newsrooms that cover a specific ethnicity in a non-English language), most journalists covering poverty still face the special challenge of going into unfamiliar areas where they are regarded with suspicion.

But like the editors and reporters at The Birmingham News and at The Columbus Dispatch, journalists can prepare themselves for investigations by researching the issues of poverty and reading government and nonprofit institute reports. Census Bureau and Government Accountability Office reports can provide not only numbers, but context and story ideas. State census data centers also can be helpful for getting a better idea of the local issues.

Among the many other valuable organizations to check are these:

- The Urban Institute, which has lots of research and discussion on its Web site
- The National Poverty Center at the University of Michigan
- The Institute for Research on Poverty at the University of Wisconsin
- The Southern Poverty Law Center in Atlanta
- The National Center for Children in Poverty at Columbia University in New York City

From there, an investigative journalist can start to reach out to human sources, whether it's an urban or rural story. Longtime investigative reporter Tom Brune shared his ideas for finding and contacting those sources in a tip sheet in the Investigative Reporters and Editors Resource Center. He suggested going to the following:

- Community organizations. These groups include the most active residents of an area. The activists in turn know people whose stories can illustrate your report.
- Legal aid groups, such as legal assistance foundations, public defenders, public guardians and public interest law firms. These groups have clients who often want to tell their stories.
- Local and federal court officials and the files they keep.
- Churches and church-based agencies like Catholic Charities, Lutheran Social Services and the Jewish Federation. They deal directly with people you might want to interview.
- Other charities, like the United Way, that provide direct services or are active in the issues of race and poverty.
- Social workers at welfare agencies. They have many cases to choose from if they want to provide information.

- Interest groups, such as organizations created to push for better housing.
- Human relations commissions, part of a local or state government structure.
- People who write letters to the editor of the local newspaper on poverty issues.
- Cold calls into a neighborhood based on names from the city directory or some other source.

The above combination of documents and sources can provide you with a direction for your investigation, but your reporting will be detached until you get out into the community and begin seeing poverty through the perspective of those who live it. Reporters who have not grown up in impoverished circumstances will need to think about how to present themselves and about what precautions they may need to take.

Previous editions of this book shared tips from journalist Robin Palley on investigating poverty issues in urban areas. Her tips also work, however, for rural areas. Here is a summary of her advice and warnings:

- Do anything not to look like the rich kid arriving in poverty land. Wear unassuming clothes, and don't drive higher priced cars.
- Don't look official. Don't drive company cars. Instead of a press badge, show a newspaper clipping or some other evidence of your work. Don't wear what police or social workers wear.
- Don't endanger yourself. Know where you are going, don't wear jewelry or watches, and try to have a "protector," someone who knows the neighborhood and will watch out for you. Ask around for the neighborhood grandmother or church lady, a beat cop, a youth worker or anyone who can put the word out that you are a reporter and can be trusted.
- Work in pairs, and make sure your newsroom knows where you are.
- Respect confidentiality if you have given it. You can destroy a person's welfare or threaten their safety by carelessly publishing or airing their name or address. Be sure, even more than usual, that the rules of what is on the record, off the record and on but not for attribution are clear.

Financial Exploitation

Although the poor by definition have less money than most, con men and businesses prey on them financially. Con men lure the poor into purchases they can't afford or small investments they can't recoup. Businesses charge them high prices or loan money at exorbitant rates.

Even state governments get into the game through their lottery systems, which some critics call another "tax" on the poor because it lures the poor into buying lottery tickets although they have a small chance of winning. (To see if this is happening in a particular state, journalists often compare the database of location of lottery ticket sales with census data on income levels in those areas.)

Previous chapters have covered subprime lending for housing and those insurance ploys in which salesmen get the poor or elderly to buy insurance policies for more than they will ever pay off. But there are numerous other financial areas to investigate.

Investigative journalists Ron Nixon and Holly Hacker put together a stellar tip sheet on the topic for IRE following a project they did for the (Minneapolis) Star Tribune. They wrote:

> Credit is the lifeblood of a community. It enables people to invest in their future by buying homes, send their children to college with the promise of a better life and it allows them, among other things, to purchase things such as furniture or a car.
>
> But for many moderate and low income Americans, credit can come at a steep price. For these residents, there is a two-tier economy, one made up of traditional banks and financial institutions and a second made up of what is known as the "fringe financial industry."
>
> This industry posts revenues in the billions of dollars each year mainly from customers who lack access to banks or other mainstream financial institutions.

They broke down the industry into these sections:

- *Payday lenders.* These lenders offer small loans backed by a postdated check. The consumer borrows a certain amount—typically between $150 and $500—until his or her next payday. In some states the amounts may be larger.
- *Car title lenders.* These lenders offer small loans where a vehicle is used as collateral against the loan. These loans are typically for a period of 30 days. The issuer of the loan will take possession of the car if the loan is not repaid in the time allotted. Car title loans are illegal in Minnesota, but many Wisconsin companies advertise the service there.
- *Check-cashing outlets.* Check-cashing outlets perform a variety of services, from cashing payroll and government checks to selling money orders or transferring funds. These stores usually charge about 3 percent to 10 percent of the face value of a check to cash it. Some of these stores also offer payday loans.
- *Pawnshops.* Pawnshops provide a small loan to customers in exchange for merchandise held for a period of time by the shop with the agreement

that the customer will reclaim the property in the future. The customer must also pay interest on the loan and a storage fee.

- *Rapid refund loans.* Although most people think of rapid refunds as tax refunds, they are actually loans made by national banks through companies like H&R Block for a fee in anticipation of a refund from the Internal Revenue Service.
- *Rent-to-own stores.* In these stores, customers rent furniture on a weekly basis. The stores cater mostly to low-income communities, where residents pay $25 or more a week for items like televisions.
- *Subprime loans.* These high-cost loans are usually intended for borrowers with poor credit, heavy debt or both. Subprime loans often carry interest rates of 8 percent to 20 percent and fees of 4 percent to 10 percent of the total loan. The high rates and fees are designed to protect the lender in the event that a borrower defaults on the loan.

Nixon and Hacker then suggested these steps for getting the story:

1. Know the law. Check the statutes that govern payday lenders, check cashers and others. In most states this is a largely unregulated industry. In states where the industry is regulated, the statutes will give you some idea of what information or data these industries have to provide for reporting purposes.
2. Check court filings. Court files are a rich source of information about the practices of the industry and can also point you to people who feel they have been wronged.
3. Get a firm understanding of how the fringe financial sector works. Several books can be helpful in understanding the business: John Caskey's "Fringe Banking," Robert Manning's "Credit Card Nation," Mike Hudson's "Merchants of Misery" and David Caplovitz's "The Poor Pay More." The Consumer Federation of America and an industry trade group, the Financial Services Center of America, can also provide information.
4. Get census data to study the demographics of the areas surrounding payday lenders, check-cashing stores, and so on. This data is especially important for mapping.
5. Get payday loan financial information. Some states like Minnesota require lenders to provide information on the number and amounts of loans, defaults and carry-over loans. Check with state regulators to see what is required.

Since the Star Tribune stories, many others have been done in which reporters in such states as New Hampshire, Missouri, Illinois and Washington have written about the high interest rates — often higher than 500 percent annually — being charged to low- and moderate-income people, including military personnel who could lose their security clearances because of large, high-interest debts.

Employment

Another area to investigate is how the poor are taken advantage of by employers in both urban and rural areas who pay low wages to the poor, whether they are immigrants, elderly or disabled.

Reporters from The Palm Beach Post investigated the conditions of migrant workers in Florida and found that they earn low pay while living in squalor. They even discovered five modern-day slavery cases that had been prosecuted in the past six years by the U.S. government. The reporters also found widespread Social Security fraud among the workers, often orchestrated by employers in the citrus industry.

In other states, particularly in the Midwest and South, journalists have exposed low pay and dangerous working conditions for illegal immigrants who work at food-processing plants in rural areas.

The Plain Dealer in Cleveland reported on companies employing inner-city people, mostly elderly, disabled or welfare recipients, to work in their homes putting together screws and washers for automobile manufacturers. The workers earn $1.50 for every 1,000 screws, less than $1 per hour. They kept the work hidden for fear of losing their welfare, and so the underground laborers were isolated from the Internal Revenue Service and the protections of federal law.

Other urban newsrooms have found workers, often illegal immigrants, toiling in factories, restaurants, and motels for low wages.

In a more general investigation, The Wall Street Journal explored the hardships of the working poor and found that those earning minimum wage often are worse off than those who receive welfare.

In "Nickel and Dimed," author Barbara Ehrenreich personalized that approach by posing as an unskilled worker and detailing the plight of America's working poor by taking low-skilled jobs for a month at a time. She worked as a waitress, a cleaning woman, an aide in a nursing home and an employee of Wal-Mart. She found that her income did not cover her expenses unless she worked two jobs seven days a week. Even then, paying for adequate housing was nearly impossible.

PART IV   Investigative Issues

Exploitative employment practices ensure that the poor are financially locked into poverty with little hope of getting out despite government programs created to alleviate or eliminate poverty. Indeed, these practices often increase the demand on government programs and undercut their potential successes.

Children and Families

Because children cannot provide for themselves, they sometimes suffer abuse and neglect at all income levels. Writing in Nieman Reports magazine, Carol Kreck of The Denver Post commented that abuse and neglect tend to be covered, death by death, by general assignment reporters; gangs and crack babies by urban affairs writers; infant mortality and AIDS babies by medical writers; deteriorating test scores by education writers.

Handed the children's beat, Kreck realized she had a blank check: "Played the right way, all the beats were mine — health care, courts, cops, the legislature, Congress, education, urban affairs. So were the big stories of our time. After all, AIDS is a children's issue, not to mention poverty, homelessness, welfare reform, gun control, prenatal drug abuse and foster care."

Over the past decade, the coverage of children and their families has increased tremendously, with much of the growth spurred by the Annie E. Casey Foundation, which supports the Journalism Center on Children and Families at the University of Maryland. Any journalist investigating these issues should bookmark its Web site and use its resources as a first step. The center also produces a magazine, The Children's Beat, twice a year that is full of ideas and tips.

In addition, the foundation grants the Casey awards each year to well-researched investigations on socially significant topics that "cut through 'compassion fatigue.'" In 2007, the awards showed how much investigative work can be done in the area. Here are summaries of just three of the winning entries:

- In "Bury Your Mistakes," The Philadelphia Inquirer documented the Philadelphia Department of Human Service's callous neglect of abused children it was charged with protecting. When officials refused to provide information on many cases, the reporters combed neighborhoods to give the stories scope and depth. The response was significant: Moved by the children's stories and nailed by the hard-nosed reporting, state legislators toughened laws and city officials had no choice but to clean house at the agency.
- In its story "Lethal Lapses," The Belleville (Ill.) News-Democrat documented how Illinois' Department of Children and Family Services mishandled cases involving 53 children who died in its care between 1998

and 2005. Reporters demonstrated great enterprise—scrutinizing Social Security Administration death records, coroner and police reports and countless other materials—to connect the dots and identify the child victims. They got beyond confidentiality laws that too often leave the state's most vulnerable wards insufficiently protected and unknown even in death.

- In "Failures by State, Caregiver Kept Secret in Child-Rape Case," The Seattle Times combined exhaustive investigation and skilled storytelling in a devastating account of systemic problems within Washington's child-welfare system. The story went beyond one terrible anecdote, giving it breadth and lasting impact. It was an increasingly rare example of a newspaper investing brawn and real resources in its watchdog role.

The IRE Resource Center also has many investigations on issues relating to families and children, including child abuse, juvenile justice, foster care and day care, with accompanying descriptions of how the stories were done. It also offers numerous tip sheets on doing these kinds of investigations.

Homelessness

No matter how much low-cost housing is available, most communities still have to deal with the problem of homelessness. Some homeless people are mentally ill, some are mentally sound but impoverished and others don't want to find shelter on their own.

Journalists can investigate how police and social welfare agencies deal with the homeless. They can check on what happens when a homeless person is arrested and where they are taken.

They also can check on the living conditions and financing of shelters and the ability of the shelters to meet the demand for emergency housing and to deal with the kind of clients they get. With the rise in home foreclosures in the United States, the potential need for shelters and other temporary housing will also rise.

Health Care

Another major issue facing the poor is health care. Tens of millions of Americans have no health care insurance and seek help at emergency rooms and local clinics when they become ill. Some hospitals will refuse care (which has led to successful class-action lawsuits). Some private hospitals will "dump" an uninsured patient on a publicly funded hospital by transporting the patient from their emergency room to the emergency room of the other hospital.

Investigations can also highlight the success stories. The San Francisco Chronicle profiled the Potrero Hill Health Center, which has successfully served the city's poor for more than 25 years. Reporter Mike Weiss used the perspective of one patient to showcase the center's successes.

Another burgeoning crisis is dental care. Many rural communities have no free or low-cost dental care, and poor people have no way to get to a larger community for help until their dental problems become critical.

Investigating the Programs

In 2007, the Government Accountability Office reported the following:

> Over the years, the policy approaches used to help low-income individuals and families have varied. For example, in the 1960s federal programs focused on increasing the education and training of those living in poverty. In the 1970s, policy reflected a more income-oriented approach with the introduction of several comprehensive federal assistance plans.
>
> More recently, welfare reform efforts have emphasized the role of individual responsibility and behaviors in areas such as family formation and work to assist people in becoming self-sufficient. Although alleviating poverty and the conditions associated with it has long been a federal priority, approaches to developing effective interventions have sometimes been controversial, as evidenced by the diversity of federal programs in existence and the ways in which they have evolved over time.

The report went on, in its understated style, to list a sample of programs intended to resolve the problems of poverty, each of which has had spotty success. Most of the programs highlighted have experienced withering audits by the GAO or by other government investigative agencies. The list provides a quick guide for journalists on which agencies to investigate:

- *Temporary Assistance for Needy Families*. Federal cash outlay: $10.4 billion. TANF permits a state to give ongoing basic cash aid to families that include a minor or a pregnant woman. Work and other requirements must be met.
- *Earned Income Tax Credit*. Federal cash outlay: $37.9 billion. EITC provides a refundable credit to workers with and without children.
- *Food Stamp Program*. Federal cash outlay: $27.2 billion. The program provides certain allotments to individuals to purchase food, based on the individual's level of eligibility and need.
- *Special Supplemental Nutrition Program for Women, Infants and Children*. Federal cash outlay: $4.5 billion. WIC provides benefits for low-income mothers, infants and children who are considered to be at "nutritional risk."

- *Medicaid.* Federal cash outlay: $176 billion. Medicaid provides payments to health care providers in full or via copay for eligible low-income families and individuals and for long-term care to eligible individuals who are aged or disabled.
- *State Children's Health Insurance Program.* Federal cash outlay: $4.6 billion. SCHIP provides federal matching funds for states and territories to provide health insurance to targeted low-income children.
- *Federal Pell Grant Program.* Federal cash outlay: $12 billion. The program provides assistance to undergraduate students who meet a certain needs test and are enrolled in an eligible institution of postsecondary education.
- *Head Start.* Federal cash outlay: $6.8 billion. Head Start provides comprehensive services to targeted low-income children. Services include educational, medical, dental, nutritional and social services.
- *Section 8 Low-Income Housing Assistance.* Federal cash outlay: $22.4 billion. The program provides rental assistance through vouchers or rental subsidies to eligible low-income families or single people.
- *Child Care and Development Block Grant.* Federal cash outlay: $6.9 billion. CCDBG provides funding to low-income parents for child care.
- *Social Services Block Grant (Title XX).* Federal cash outlay: $1.7 billion. SSBG provides funding to assist states in providing social services to eligible low-income individuals or families.
- *Job Corps.* Federal cash outlay: $1.5 billion. The program provides no-cost training and education to low-income individuals ages 16 to 24 while providing a monthly allowance.
- *Low-Income Home Energy Assistance Program.* Federal cash outlay: $1.9 billion. LIHEAP provides assistance to low-income home owners and renters to help meet energy needs, such as heating and cooling.

Some programs are funded entirely by the federal government, and some have been turned over to the states or are run by the states under contract to the U.S. Department of Health and Human Services. Other programs are largely paid for by the states without federal involvement.

Many programs are overseen by the Administration for Children and Families, under HHS, and information for each program can be found at its Web site (www.acf.dhhs.gov/programs).

Temporary Assistance for Needy Families

A major program, Temporary Assistance for Needy Families replaced the Aid to Families with Dependent Children and the JOBS programs in 1997. States and territories now run their own TANF programs; Native American tribes also can choose to run their own.

With TANF, states, territories and tribes each receive a block grant allocation. The block grant covers benefits, administrative expenses and services. States, territories and tribes determine eligibility, benefit levels and services provided to needy families, and there is no longer a federal entitlement.

Journalists who investigate local TANF programs often find that unqualified individuals are getting assistance or that the program is so confusing that qualified individuals do not get the help they need. In the pursuit of any stories of fraud or mismanagement, journalists should routinely check inspector generals' Web sites and reports of the relevant agencies.

Child-Support Enforcement

Contributing to the problems of the disadvantaged is the lack of support by parents who abandon their families and children.

Federal, state and local governments try to collect delinquent child-support payments on behalf of custodial parents, and laws have been strengthened to the point where deadbeat parents can be imprisoned.

Some states contract with county governments to handle enforcement and to locate the parent, establish paternity when necessary, set a payment level, monitor compliance and disburse any money collected.

To force payment, the government agency can garnish wages, intercept tax refunds, file tax liens on properties and refer the case to the local prosecutor for court action. Many custodial parents are TANF recipients.

Examining child-support enforcement procedures and the enforcers themselves can be worthwhile. When the St. Louis Post-Dispatch matched a database of state employees against a database of deadbeat parents, they identified some Illinois state employees who owed child support, including some whose job was to enforce child-support laws.

Food Stamps

The Agriculture Department's Food Stamp Program uses state welfare agencies to distribute stamps to needy families and individuals. Recipients can redeem their food stamps at authorized retail stores, which turn them into local banks, which exchange them at the Federal Reserve.

The U.S. House Government Operations Committee report said this about the Agriculture Department's handling of the Food Stamp Program, which serves tens of millions of people annually: "The program is losing at least $1 billion annually because the department and the states that administer the program have not prevented cheats from abusing it."

Fraud encompasses ineligible recipients, authorized retailers selling unauthorized nonfood items (from toilet paper to cocaine) for the stamps, retailers exchanging stamps for cash and individuals, working from a private residence, setting themselves up as "stores" to redeem stamps. Journalists can spend time at food stamp pickup points if they are interested in documenting fraud.

A San Francisco Bay Guardian reporter accompanied a recipient to a check-cashing store to pick up the monthly food stamp allotment. That same outlet was a regular site of food stamp–related criminal activity: Recipients were robbed of stamps as they left the store, they were offered cash for stamps at 50 cents on the dollar and stamps were traded for drugs.

After visiting distribution sites, journalists can walk down the street to retailers authorized to redeem stamps. The journalist can watch to see if food stamp recipients are offered cash, drugs or other commodities for stamps. Some states are trying to combat fraud by instituting an electronic benefits transfer program. Having recipients use a computerized card at the cash register leaves a paper trail and reduces street trafficking.

The GAO reported in 2007 that the national rate of food stamp trafficking declined from 2002 to 2005 and that trafficking occurred more frequently in smaller stores. But the GAO noted that despite the progress, "the Food Stamp Program remains vulnerable because retailers can enter the program intending to traffic and do so, often without fear of severe criminal penalties, as the declining number of investigations referred for prosecution suggests."

Journalists can find out what anti-fraud techniques are being tried in their jurisdiction and what prosecutions are being carried out.

Other Child and Family Nutrition Programs

While probing the Food Stamp Program, journalists can ask recipients whether the poor are able to use other assistance to feed their families nutritious meals every day. Often, the programs may not be coordinated, leading to confusion and ineffectiveness. All programs, many of which are run by the U.S. Department of Agriculture, are worth investigating individually or collectively.

The National School Lunch Program is supposed to provide balanced, nutritious, reduced-cost or free meals during the school day to children from low-income families. Journalists can look at how benefits are doled out and whether families are aware of them. They also can look at the quality of the food, as Dateline NBC did, and find numerous problems in its preparation. They can track where the food is coming from and see whether it is being processed at plants with unsanitary conditions.

Another program to examine is the Special Supplemental Nutrition Program for Women, Infants and Children. WIC is supposed to provide adequate nourishment for pregnant women and mothers and their young children.

Recipients receive vouchers for use on specific items at grocery stores and farmers' markets. Coverage extends beyond pregnancy for women and for children to age 5. The program contains an educational component about nutrition and limited health care.

Journalists can check to see how many needy women are being denied benefits because of funding limitations. Unlike many other hunger and poverty programs, WIC is dependent on annual appropriations, rather than serving everybody who meets objective requirements.

Most private-sector programs aimed at feeding the needy are well intentioned, and many are effective. But like other charitable organizations, they ought to be scrutinized by journalists. (See Chapter 14.)

Even if everybody working at food banks, food pantries, soup kitchens and food cooperatives is honest, at minimum journalists can show how their efforts are never enough, how for-profit businesses that could help instead do nothing or how a lack of public transportation prevents potential recipients from receiving available benefits.

They also can check out local food banks and observe the distribution process there. A journalist in San Diego discovered food bank operators who were taking donated food and selling it at local markets and stores.

Other Assistance Programs

When journalists do find trouble or fraud in welfare programs, they often find abuse of a related program, Supplemental Security Income. SSI was originally established to help elderly people who were ineligible for Social Security, but government bureaucracies have extended SSI eligibility to middle-aged and young people who claim mental disorders, including hard-to-prove (or disprove) anxiety attacks and depression. Using appeals filed at the Social Security Administration and word-of-mouth in neighborhoods, The (Baltimore) Sun produced a series following case histories of SSI recipients, complete with real names and specific income figures.

Other journalists have looked into whether adults have become foster parents in order to collect benefits rather than provide food and shelter for needy children. Many reporters have made it routine to run databases of foster care parents against databases of felons when the data are available.

Welfare Reform

In addition to investigating the flaws of the U.S. welfare system and fraud in federal and state programs, journalists can follow the history of welfare reform and the government's objective of moving the impoverished from welfare to jobs. Shortcomings of the new system as it develops have been looked at in several stories. Among the approaches used are these:

- A Kansas City Star investigation of the effects of the toughened welfare rules found that most Jackson County residents preferred to be off welfare but that many were unable to live without public funds. The three-part series focused on more than 200 families who had left the welfare system, more than a quarter of whom could not survive financially without welfare and eventually returned to the system.
- A routine inquiry by The City Paper into the progress of welfare reform in Baltimore revealed that promising statistics masked a questionable systemwide practice that favored the most competent cases, leaving the neediest far behind and gouging out a deep disparity.
- The Courier-Journal in Louisville, Ky., showed that former welfare recipients in Appalachia were unable to find jobs. As a way of humanizing the story, they told of the plight of a former welfare recipient who was trying to support four children on a $5.50 per hour bank job, while her ex-husband owed her $40,000 in child support.

One of the most effective and traditional ways to investigate the failings of a system is to combine documentation and interviews with officials and experts with the detailed story of a person trying to get help from the system.

Journalists can contact welfare recipients through social workers or employees at other charitable agencies or by simply approaching them outside public agency offices. After making contact and winning the trust of the recipients, journalists can accompany them through their day or week or month and record their frustrations.

Or, like Barbara Ehrenreich, the journalist can go underground as one reporter did while on assignment for the Los Angeles Times Magazine. Posing as an applicant for assistance, the reporter experienced firsthand the difficulties and hostilities of the welfare offices. He saw applicants lie on their applications and boast about it, and he witnessed agency employees who appeared burned out and fearful.

Investigating the world of the disadvantaged can be difficult, discouraging and sometimes dangerous. But it also can lead to some of the most important and rewarding work a journalist can do — the kind of work that can make an immediate difference in people's lives.

⊃ CHECK IT OUT

✓ Research poverty in your region by going to the U.S. Census Bureau Web site and using American Factfinder and the part of the site devoted to poverty.

✓ Pick an assistance program, such as WIC, and determine how much money from the program has come into your county for each of the last five years.

✓ Find out how many homeless people are in your county or region. Then determine how many beds are available in homeless shelters or in other temporary shelters and how that number of beds has changed over the past five years.

RESOURCES FOR REPORTING

General Resources

The National Poverty Center (www.npc.umich.edu) at the University of Michigan does research on the causes and consequences of poverty, evaluates and analyzes policies to alleviate poverty and trains the next generation of poverty researchers.

The Rural Poverty Research Center (www.rprconline.org), located at both the University of Missouri and Oregon State University, supports and conducts research into rural poverty issues.

The Southern Poverty Law Center (www.splcenter.org) in Montgomery, Ala., promotes civil rights and tolerance, fights all forms of discrimination and pursues legal cases concerning the poor and vulnerable members of society. It has extensive information on the poor and discriminated against.

The Urban Institute (www.urban.org) gathers and analyzes data, conducts policy research and evaluates programs and services in many areas, including poverty.

The U.S. Census Bureau (www.census.gov) collects data on many aspects of U.S. life, has a special section devoted to poverty, and offers a search tool called American Factfinder that allows people to easily create demographic profiles of their communities.

Investigating the Issues

The American Public Human Services Association (www.aphsa.org) is a nonprofit, bipartisan organization of individuals and agencies concerned with human services. Its members include all state and territorial human services agencies, more than 150 local agencies, and several thousand individuals who work in or otherwise have an interest in human services programs.

The Institute for Research on Poverty (www.irp.wisc.edu) at the University of Wisconsin does interdisciplinary research into the causes and consequences of poverty and social inequality in the United States. As one of three Area Poverty Research Centers sponsored by the U.S. Department of Health and Human Services, it has a particular interest in poverty and family welfare in the Midwest.

Financial Exploitation

The Consumer Federation of America (www.consumerfed.org) is an advocacy, research, education and service organization that offers information on unfair lending and other practices that take advantage of the poor.

Several books can be helpful in understanding the financial exploitation of the poor:

- "Fringe Banking," by John Caskey
- "Credit Card Nation," by Robert Manning
- "Merchants of Misery," by Mike Hudson
- "The Poor Pay More," by David Caplovitz

PART IV Investigative Issues

The industry trade group Financial Services Center of America (www.fisca.org) can also provide information.

Employment

Job Corps (http://jobcorps.dol.gov) is a free education and training program run by the Department of Labor to help young people ages 16 to 24 get better jobs.

Children and Families

The National Center for Children in Poverty (www.nccp.org) is a public policy center dedicated to promoting the economic security, health and well-being of America's low-income families and children. NCCP does research on policies and practices and promotes programs at federal and state levels.

The Child Welfare Information Gateway (www.childwelfare.gov) provides access to resources on children and families and is run by the Children's Bureau in the Administration for Children and Families.

The Journalism Center on Children and Families (www.journalismcenter.org) at the University of Maryland encourages and recognizes exemplary reporting on families and children and provides training and resources for journalists pursuing those kinds of stories.

Special Supplemental Nutrition Program for Women, Infants and Children (www.fns.usda.gov/wic) is run by the Food and Nutrition Service, under the Department of Agriculture, and provides health information and nutrition to pregnant women and children up to age 5.

Head Start (www.acf.hhs.gov/programs/hsb) promotes school readiness for children from disadvantaged families, giving grants to local preschools to encourage early reading and math skills.

Homelessness

More information on Section 8 Low-Income Housing Assistance is available from the Department of Housing and Urban Development (www.hud.gov).

Health Care

More information on Medicaid can be found at the Web site of the Centers for Medicaid and Medicare Services (www.cms.hhs.gov/home/medicaid.asp).

Investigating the Programs

Known as "the investigative arm of Congress" and "the congressional watchdog," the Government Accountability Office (www.gao.gov) helps improve the performance and ensure the accountability of the federal government. GAO's work includes oversight of federal programs and recommendations designed to make government more efficient, effective, ethical and equitable.

The Web site of the U.S. Department of Agriculture, Food and Nutrition Service (www.fns.usda.gov/fns) includes information about programs including food stamps, nutrition programs for women and infants, school meals and food recalls.

The U.S. Department of Health and Human Services (www.hhs.gov) runs and oversees many of the health and welfare programs available to U.S. citizens.

More information about the Earned Income Tax Credit is available from the Internal Revenue Service's Web site (www.irs.gov/individuals/article/0,,id =96406,00.html).

Other programs to investigate include these:

- State Children's Health Insurance Program (www.cms.hhs.gov/home/schip.asp)

- Federal Pell Grant Program (www.ed.gov/programs/fpg/index.html)

- Social Services Block Grant (www.acf.hhs.gov/programs/ocs/ssbg)

- Low-Income Home Energy Assistance Program (www.acf.hhs.gov/programs/ocs/liheap)

Temporary Assistance for Needy Families

The Office of Family Assistance runs the Temporary Assistance for Needy Families program (www.acf.hhs.gov/programs/ofa).

Child-Support Enforcement

The Office of Child-Support Enforcement (www.acf.hhs.gov/programs/cse) is run by the Administration for Children and Families at the Department of Health and Human Services. The office's Web site also offers links to state programs (www.acf.hhs.gov/programs/cse/extinf.html).

Food Stamps

More information on the Food Stamp Program can be found on the Department of Agriculture's Web site (www.fns.usda.gov/fsp).

Other Child and Family Nutrition Programs

The Administration for Children and Families (www.acf.dhhs.gov) at the Department of Health and Human Services (www.hhs.gov) is responsible for federal programs that promote the economic and social well-being of families, children, individuals and communities.

International Poverty

The Chronic Poverty Research Centre (www.chronicpoverty.org) in the United Kingdom is an international partnership of universities, research institutes and nongovernmental groups that studies the causes of chronic poverty and provides research, analysis and policy proposals.

PovertyNet at the World Bank (http://web.worldbank.org/poverty) provides information on poverty measurement, monitoring, analysis and poverty-reduction strategies for researchers and practitioners.

The United Nations Development Programme: Poverty Reduction Web page (www.undp.org/poverty) provides extensive research on ways to reduce poverty worldwide. It also sponsors pilot programs, brings together public and private groups and promotes the role of women in development programs.

The World Health Organization's Poverty page (www.who.int/topics/poverty/en) provides links to descriptions of the activities, reports, contacts and cooperating partners in the various WHO programs and offices working on poverty. It includes links to related Web sites and topics.

Index

abortion, 110–11, 389
absenteeism
    of government employee, 146
abstracts, 31
abuse of authority
    by law enforcement personnel, 242
    by school administrators, 265
accidents. *See also* aviation safety; traffic
        accidents
    boating, 61, 468
    commercial airlines, 462
    commuter airlines, 465
    databases on, 61, 62
    medical helicopters, 466
    safety investigations after, 449–50
    workplace, 317, 318
accountants, 68, 131, 312, 323, 326, 327, 328
accounting methods
    insurance companies and, 374
    nonprofit organizations and, 341, 343
accounting standards, 129
accreditation
    of colleges and universities, 281, 282–84
    of education, 271–72
    of health maintenance organizations, 404
    of hospitals, 389–91
    of law enforcement departments, 220
    of schools, 276
accuracy
    in journalism, 109, 115–16
    line-by-line check for, 115–16
accused persons. *See* suspects
adjunct family members, 289
administrative law judges, 143, 225, 315, 318
administrators
    college and university, 282, 286, 290
    nursing home, 399
    public, in probate court, 207
    school, 262, 265, 273, 274, 291
    workers' compensation and, 382
admission policies, colleges and universities, 284
adoption, 200, 320
advertising
    in newspapers, 23
    of prescription drugs, 406, 407

as source of information on businesses,
        310–11, 312
    on television, for candidates, 156
    for vocational schools, 280
advocacy groups, 434
affirmative action, 221, 223
affordable housing programs, 489–90
African Americans. *See* minority groups; racial
        discrimination
age, community data on, 63
age discrimination, 306
agenda of regulations, 126
agricultural land
    no-till farming and soil erosion and, 443
    soil pollution and, 443
    water pollution and, 441
    water supply and, 426
agricultural programs, 140
agriculture
    environment and, 434–35
    migrant and seasonal workers and, 319
AIDS, 196, 370, 408, 502
air ambulances, 397
air controllers, 463–64, 465
airlines. *See also* aviation safety
    deregulation of, 464, 466
    on-time service and, 467
airplanes. *See also* aviation safety; pilots
    air traffic controllers and, 463–64
    databases on, 61
    design or manufacturing flaws and, 462
    misuse of, by governors, 144
    registry of, 467
    safety issues in, 313, 461–67
air pollution, 439
    database on, 439
    government regulation of, 306
    indoor, 439
airports, 466–67. *See also* aviation safety
    databases on, 464
    maintenance crews and, 464
    on-time service and, 467
    safety issues and, 464, 465, 466–67
    security issues and, 464–65
air traffic controllers, 463–64, 465

alarm companies, 238
alcohol abuse
    drunk drivers and, 241
    by licensed professionals, 326
    parolee recidivism and, 197
    by police officers, 225
    by school bus drivers, 274
    in schools, 265–66
    workers and, 321
alcohol licenses, 307
alcohol tests, 241, 463
all-terrain vehicles, 453
alternative dispute resolution, 184
ambassadorships, 136
ambulances, 253, 396–97
ambush interviews, 112–13
analysis, database. *See* computer-assisted
    reporting (CAR)
anecdotal leads, 100
anecdotes, 84, 105
animals, research using, 290
annual reports, 6, 196, 302–3, 342, 427
annuities, 321, 367, 376
anonymous sources, 114–15, 134
appeals, 192–93, 202, 205, 210, 211, 418
appeals courts, 210, 211
appellate judges, 192–93
applications, job, 6
appropriations, 164–66, 168
arbitration
    in civil cases, 184
    of labor management disputes, 316–17
arbitrators, 182
archives
    of databases, 57
    National Archives system, 44–45
    of newspapers, 21, 69
arrests. *See also* crime
    bounty hunters and, 186
    clearance rate for, 250
    databases on, 62
    of juvenile offenders, 243
    lawsuits about conditions during, 194
    legal procedures following, 184–85
    motor vehicle violations and, 241–42
    narcotics-related, 235
    racial profiling and, 242
    records of, 60, 62, 220
    statistics on, 250
    of students, 265
arson, 239–40, 249, 373
arson rings, 240
articles of incorporation, 308
asbestos, 275
assault, 249, 264, 265, 288, 329

assessments
    appeals of, 483
    fairness of, 483
    land values and, 458
    reassessments, 483
    records, 59, 309, 478
assessor's office, 478
assistant prosecuting attorneys, 181, 202
associations, 23–24, 25. *See also* organizations;
    trade associations
athletes
    college, 26, 281, 286, 287–88
    secondary school, 270
attorneys
    assignment of cases to, 181–82
    campaign contributions and, 157, 181–82
    estate handling, 206–7
    fees for, 182
    judicial system and, 180, 181–82, 188
    labor, 312–13
    military, 210–11
    workers' compensation insurance and, 381
attorneys general, state, 243, 307, 340, 347
auctions, 23, 39, 128, 479–80
audit reports, 55
    campaign contributions and, 157
    at colleges and universities, 290
    contracting requirements for, 132
    court budgets and, 200
    executive branch and, 125
    by inspectors general, 138–40
    of jails, 185
    for nonprofit organizations, 339, 341
    of pension plans, 321
authorizations, 164–66
autobiographies, 25, 77
automobile insurance, 367, 371–72
    accident scams, 371
    documents in, 371–72
    fraud in, 372
    rate differentials in, 372
    redlining and, 368, 375
    uninsured drivers and, 372, 451–52
automobiles, 453–60. *See also* motor vehicles;
    traffic accidents
    inspections of, 451–52
    license plates on, 253, 452
    recalls, 451
    safety of, 450–53
    theft of, 239
    tire defects in, 451
autopsy reports, 230, 237, 247
aviation safety, 461–67
    air traffic controllers and, 463–64
    alcohol and drug testing programs and, 463

aviation safety *(continued)*
  cargo planes and, 464–66
  commuter airlines and, 464
  emergency air transport to hospitals and, 397, 466
  flight crew fatigue and, 463
  ground crew and, 464
  helicopters and, 465
  maintenance and, 464
  manufacturers and, 462
  pilots and, 462, 463
  private planes and, 464
  regulatory system defects in, 462
  security and, 464–65

background checks, of security personnel, 464
backgrounding, 7, 20, 34, 36–37, 70, 208
bail bondsmen, 185, 186
bail system, 185, 199
bankruptcies, 60, 113, 208–9, 320, 321, 341, 478
bankruptcy court, 181, 208–9
  judges in, 181
banks, 355–58. *See also* financial institutions
  annual reports of, 303
  capitalization of, 355–56
  competitors of, 359–60, 362
  documents on, 357–58
  executive branch conflicts of interest with, 136
  financial information from, 356–57
  government regulation of, 354, 355, 356, 362
  high-risk transactions in, 365–66
  inspection of, 356
  judicial branch conflicts of interest with, 201–2
  local communities and impact of, 354
  money laundering and, 366–67
  mutual funds and, 362
  newspaper stories on, 21–22
  probate court and, 207
  racial disparities in mortgage loans from, 353–54
  ratings of, 355–56
bar associations, 202
barges, 469
bar licenses, 325
bars, and drunk drivers, 452
bench trial, 188
bias, in textbooks, 267
bibliographies, 26, 30, 44, 168
bicycles, 459
bids
  bonds for, 132–33
  notices of, 23, 131, 139, 144, 200, 274, 277
  specifications and, 131–32

bidsplitting, 130
bill collection agencies, 391, 405
bill padding, 203
bills, legislative, 164, 166–67, 171
bingo games, 348
biographical dictionaries, 25
biographies, 25, 26, 30
birth certificates, 6, 36, 37
birth notices, 22
birth records, 25, 36, 37, 62
blackouts, 417, 419
blacks. *See* minority groups; racial discrimination
block grants, 505, 506
blogs, 71, 77, 325
blood-alcohol testing, 241
blood banks, 408–9
boards of directors, 55, 68, 136, 303, 304, 311, 365
boards of education, 145, 278
boards of regents, 290, 291
boating accidents, 61, 468
boats, paper trail on, 253
bombings, 240–41
bomb threats, 241
bond companies, 132
bonds
  bid and performance, 132–33
  government-issued, 128
  nonprofit organizations and, 338, 341, 343, 348
  as paper trail, 253
  school funding using, 277
booking of suspects, 185
books
  on investigative process, 16–18
  reference, as secondary sources, 25–26
  as secondary sources, 26–28
boot camps, for juvenile offenders, 195
bounty hunters, 186
bribery
  by home health care companies, 402
  lobbyists and, 153
  in local government contracts, 144
  by police officers, 225
  in school construction contracts, 278
bridges, 61, 449–50, 469
broadcast news programs, 23
brokerage houses, 310, 361, 364. *See also* investment companies
brownouts, 417
budgets
  authorizations and appropriations, 164–66
  of colleges and universities, 281
  executive branch and, 125, 126–28
  expenditures in, 126–27

budgets *(continued)*
  of hospitals, 391
  kinds of, 127
  law enforcement, 220, 250–51
  of licensing boards, 328, 330
  "off-budget" expenditures in, 126–27
  regulation of, 167–69
  revenues in, 126–27
  of schools, 62, 268, 275, 276–78
  software for analyzing, 54
  of state government, 144
  waste and fraud in, 126, 128, 165
building codes, 373, 479
building contractors, 134–35, 144, 183, 479
building inspectors, 61
building permits, 59, 478
buildings, and indoor air pollution, 439
bundling campaign contributions, 156
bureaucracy
  conflicts of interest and, 136–37
  corruption in, 124
  criminal justice and, 124
  financial disclosure statements and, 136
  legislative committees and, 167
  permanent, 140
  public affairs personnel and, 141–43
  schools and, 269
  top executive and, 135
burglary, 238–39, 249, 250, 373
bus drivers, 273–74, 323, 455–56
buses
  charter, 455–56
  safety issues and, 455–56, 469
  school, 274
business, 301–30. *See also* corporations;
    employees
  annual reports of, 302–5
  arbitration and, 316–17
  arson and difficulties in, 240
  bankruptcy of, 60, 321
  conciliation and, 316
  databases on, 59
  doctors running, 403
  federal regulatory agencies covering, 305–6
  government agency conflicts of interest with,
    136–37
  government employees hired by, 137, 437
  government-guaranteed loans to, 63, 305–6
  health insurance offered by, 369
  human sources on, 311–13
  insurance and, 367, 374
  labor lawyers and, 312–13
  labor relations boards and, 315–16
  labor unions and, 313–14
  licensing of, 59, 325
  mediation and, 316

  minority-owned, 38, 132, 139
  newspaper stories on, 21–22
  nuclear power and, 423
  organized crime and, 242
  paper trail in, 6, 7, 307–11
  parallel backgrounding and, 7
  pension plans and, 315, 320–21
  plant closings by, 322
  poor and, 498
  as powerful force, 301
  publicly traded stock, 302–5
  rationale for covering, 301–2
  relocation incentives for, 309
  safety and health and, 317–18
  school funding by, 268
  SEC documents and, 302–5
  state and local agencies on, 306–7, 380, 381
  unemployment compensation and, 321–22
  university-owned, 281
  wage enforcement and, 318–20
  warning signs of trouble in, 305
  Web sites on, 302, 349–50
  workplace directories in, 72–73
business associations, 311–12
business name records, 309
bylaws, 308, 314

cab drivers, 457
cabinet secretaries, 135–36
cable, 428–30
  availability of, 429–30
  community programming in, 429
  franchises in, 427
  news programs on, 23
  pricing in, 429
  rates in, 428
  sources of information on, 428, 429
  telephone and Internet packages from, 419,
    427, 428
cadging, 226
call reports, 356, 359
campaign finance
  analyzing, 54
  business contributions in, 306
  contribution limits and, 154, 155–56, 157
  contribution records and, 59, 136, 153–55
  corruption in, 123–34, 144, 146–47, 154–55
  databases on, 56, 59, 155
  executive branch and, 123–34, 136
  expenditures and, 59, 153, 155, 157
  housing contracts and, 489–90
  judicial candidates and, 181–82
  legislative branch and, 152, 153–57, 170
  legislative staff and, 162
  loans and, 157
  lobbyists and, 152

campaign finance *(continued)*
 local government and, 144, 170
 nonconstituents and, 155
 nonprofit groups (527 groups) and, 156
 pharmaceutical companies and, 406
 political action committees (PACs) and,
  156–57, 306, 338, 339
 reports on, 125
 road contracts and, 457–58
 special-interest groups and, 154, 181
 state government and, 146–47, 155
 violations, 155–57
 Web site on, 156
campus police, 291
cancer, and pollution, 436, 443
canine (K9) corps, 247–48
capital improvement budget, 127
capitalization, of banks, 355–56, 366
CAR. *See* computer-assisted reporting (CAR)
cargo planes, 465
cars. *See* motor vehicles; traffic accidents
case histories, 391
caseloads
 of defense attorneys, 190
 of probation officers, 196
 of public defenders, 190
case reviews, in hospitals, 390
cash payments, to informants, 236
catalogs
 library, 27
 university, 284, 287
cause, in jury selection, 189
cause-and-effect relationships, 103
CD-ROM databases, 29
cease-and-desist orders, 357–58, 427
cell phones, 428
censorship, 280
census data
 analyzing, 54
 databases, 62–63
 poverty line and, 495, 496, 500
 redlining and, 363, 364, 375
certification. *See also* accreditation; licensed
  professionals
 of health maintenance organizations, 404
 of police officers, 221, 222
 of teachers, 271
change orders, 133
Chapter 11 filings, 209
character, of legislators, 163
charitable remainder trusts, 345
charities, 337. *See also* nonprofit organizations
 analysis of money flow in, 55, 341
 annual reports of, 342
 defined, 338
 financial disclosure requirements, 340–41

foundation grants to, 345, 347
 fund-raising by, 338, 347
 legislators' honoraria donated to, 161
 Muslim-related, 349
 poverty programs and, 497, 509
 public, 339
 tax-exempt donations to, 339–40
 watchdog groups and, 342
charter buses, 455–56
charter schools, 270–71
chases, by police, 222–23
cheating, on school tests, 262
check-cashing outlets, 499, 507
chief executives, 135
child abuse, 115–16
 courts and, 199, 200
 in foster care homes, 508
child custody
 divorce court and, 6, 206
 family court and, 199
 missing children reports and, 237
 newspaper notices on, 23
child labor laws, 319
child molestation
 by priests, 348–49
 by school bus drivers, 274
children. *See also* juvenile offenders
 in divorce cases, 6, 23, 199, 206
 domestic violence and, 233, 265
 mental health care of, 401
 missing, 237
 nutrition programs, 504, 507–8
 pornography and, 236–37
 poverty and, 502–3
 sexual abuse of, 265, 348–49
 welfare system for, 502
child-support payments, 200, 506
chiropractors, 371, 383, 403
chop shops, 239
chronologies
 questions in interviews as, 82
 writing from, 95–96
churches, 483, 497. *See also* religious
  organizations
 tax exempt status, 340, 348, 349
circuit attorneys. *See* prosecutors
citation searches, 30
citizens' crime commissions, 158, 253
citizen utility boards, 418
city councils, 145, 169. *See also* local government
city directories, 72, 134
civil cases, 183–84
 appeals in, 192–93
 auto insurance scams and, 371
 class actions in, 184
 conflicts of interest of judges in, 201–2

civil cases *(continued)*
   criminal cases vs., 182–83
   docket sheets in, 183
   domestic relations, 206
   fraud in, 183
   juries and, 188
   public affairs personnel and, 142
   records of, 183
   settlement talks in, 184
   sources and, 181
civil rights, 248–49, 252, 484
civil service employees, 140–41
claims, insurance, 368, 370
class actions, 184
citizen review commissions, 225
class, and school placement and, 267, 269
classification of books, in libraries, 26–27
classified ads, 23
class size, 267, 277
clearance rate in arrests, 250
clemency, 211
clichés, 95
climate change, 434
clipping libraries, 5, 21
clubs, 69
coaches, 272, 287
coal
   mining of, 444
   pollution and, 417, 422
   transport of, 469
Coast Guard, 468–69
codes of ethics. *See* ethics
codes of professional responsibility, 328
code sheets, in databases, 56
cold-case police squad, 230
collateral, 486
collection agencies, 391, 405
college preparatory classes, 267
colleges and universities, 280–91. *See also*
   education; students
   accreditation of, 281, 282–84
   administrators at, 282, 290
   admission policies of, 284
   affirmative action at, 284–85
   athletes at, 26, 281, 286, 287–88
   budgets of, 281
   business information from, 311
   campus safety at, 288
   catalogs of, 284, 287
   credentials fraud and degrees from, 79
   crime on campus and, 251, 288
   criminal justice departments in, 253
   directories of employees of, 71, 72–73
   disabled at, 284–85
   diversity at, 284–85
   document trails in, 281
   donations to, 345
   endowments of, 281–82
   enrollment in, 284
   faculty at, 288–90
   financial aid at, 285
   fire safety at, 286
   governing boards of, 291
   graduation rates in, 26
   health services at, 286–87
   lobbyists used by, 158
   property owned by, 281, 286
   research at, 289–90
   retention of students at, 284
   support staff at, 290–91
   syllabuses on the Web at, 285–86
   tax-exempt, 342
   Web sites on, 251, 281, 287, 288
commercial buses, 456
commercial databases, 39–41
commercial insurance, 373–74
commercial litigation, 184
commercial shipping, 467–68
commissions, government, 125
committees, legislative, 43, 160, 163, 164,
   166–67, 171, 172
communications utilities, 426–27
communities, impact of financial institutions
   on, 354
community colleges, 281, 287
community databases, 57
community organizations, 497
community placement, 400
community policing, 245
community programming, 430
community relations, 248–49
community reinvestment, 363–64
commutation of sentences, 198
commuter airlines, 465
compensation programs, for victims, 252
competitive bidding
   contracting process and, 129, 130, 133
   in highway construction projects, 458
   in school building projects, 274
complaints
   against bus companies, 456
   against businesses, 307
   choosing a subject and, 4
   in civil cases, 183
   against credit card companies, 360–61
   against doctors, 380, 403
   under family leave law, 320
   against insurance companies, 368–69, 375, 377
   against legislators, 162
   against licensed professionals, 323, 324,
     326–27, 329
   against police officers, 225, 228, 251

complaints *(continued)*
    against prisons, 194
    safety inspections in response to, 317
    against utilities, 418, 427
    against vocational schools, 280
    wage issues and, 319
complication-tension-resolution model, 98–99
compulsory education. *See* education; schools
computer-assisted reporting (CAR), 53–63
    databases in, 55–58
    federal data sources in, 62–63
    local data sources in, 58–62
    property value and, 482
    redlining projects and, 364–65
    tools and software for, 54–55
    training in, 54
    Web sites for, 65–66
computers
    in schools, 268
    in white-collar crime, 243
conciliation, 316
conference proceedings, 44
confessions, illegal, 187–88, 204, 230
confidentiality, of juvenile crime records, 243
confirmation hearings, 136
conflicts of interest
    in business funding of schools, 268
    executive branch and, 125, 136–37
    of funeral directors, 247
    of governors, 144
    identifying, 59, 153
    of judges, 201–2
    legislative branch and, 160
    licensing process and, 324
    medical research and, 405, 406
    mutual fund managers and, 362
    stockbrokers and, 310
Congress, former members of, as lobbyists,
        158–59
congressional hearings, 40, 43
congressional publications, 43
Congressional Record, 42, 136, 166
consent, in research, 289–90
conspiracy, 153
construction
    of commercial buildings, 485
    of mass transit projects, 461
    of prisons, 193
    safety records in, 313
    of school buildings, 274–75, 278
construction contracts, 274, 278
construction permits, 307
consultants to government agencies, 68, 128–30
consumer complaints, 307
consumer protection divisions, 347
context in writing, 97, 100

continuing education, for police officers, 223
contracting process, 130–33
    audit requirements in, 132, 138–39
    bid and performance bonds, 132–33
    bid notices and specifications and, 131–32
    change orders and, 133
    competitive bidding and, 129, 130, 133,
        274, 458
    corruption in, 129–30, 131, 144
    cost estimates in, 130–31
    kickbacks and, 130
    minority contracting and, 38, 132, 139
    product preferences in, 131
    requests for proposals and, 130
    scams in, 130, 132–33
    schools and, 273, 274, 278
    state government and, 144
    waste and fraud in, 129–30
contractors to government agencies, 68, 128–30,
        137, 144, 183
contracts
    cable systems, 428–29
    civil cases on, 184
    colleges and universities and, 281
    executive branch and, 128–30
    law enforcement, 251
    legislative branch and, 152, 153
    no-bid, 278
    religious organizations and, 348
    road construction, 457–58
    school construction, 273, 274, 278
    with utilities, 421
controlled vocabulary search terms, 27
conventional wisdom, questioning, 8–9
convictions
    sealed, 323
    wrongful, 204, 236
cooperatives
    electrical utilities, 422, 423
    food, 508
copper mining, 444
coroners, 37, 230, 247, 253
corporations. *See also* business
    annual reports of, 302–5
    bankruptcy filings by, 209
    board of directors of, 55, 68
    commercial shipping and, 468
    corruption in government contracts and,
        134–35
    databases on, 61
    directories of employees of, 71
    document trails in, 6
    financial data on, 309–10
    government agency oversight of, 305–6
    political action committees (PACs) and,
        156–57, 306

corporations *(continued)*
  proxy statements of, 304
  public, 302–5
  school funding of equipment by, 268
  securities analysis of, 310
  social responsibility of, 305
corruption. *See also* fraud; misconduct
  arson and, 240
  campaign finance, 156–57
  contracts and, 129–30, 131
  coroners and, 247
  documenting, 111
  executive branch, 123–24, 134–35, 141, 143,
    146–47
  family court and, 199–200
  foundations and, 345–46
  government employees and, 141
  housing contracts and, 489–90
  insurance adjustors and, 374
  kickbacks and, 130
  labor unions and, 314
  law enforcement personnel and, 223, 226, 251
  lobbyists and, 152–53, 159
  local government and, 130, 144
  medical examiners and, 230, 247
  parole and pardons, 197
  prostitution and, 236
  real estate and, 477
  self-regulatory organizations and, 143–44
  state government and, 134, 146–47
  traffic violations and towing companies and,
    241–42
cost estimates, 130–31
cost reports, for Medicare and Medicaid, 394–95
counterfeit drugs, 388
court cases, 184–93. *See also* judicial system
  appeals in, 192–93
  assignment to judges in, 188
  auto insurance scam information and, 371
  backlogs in, 189–90, 205
  bail and, 185–86
  bringing charges, 203
  conviction rates in, 188
  court personnel and, 182
  databases on, 60
  discrimination in, 188–89
  files in, 180
  fines in, 127, 205
  first appearance in court, 186–87
  informants and changes in charges in,
    235–36, 250
  jury in, 188–89
  pleas in, 187
  politics and, 180–82
  pretrial hearings in, 187–88
  public affairs personnel and, 142

sentencing in, 191–92
  sources and, 51, 181
  transportation from jail to, 185
  victims of crime and, 190–91
court clerks, 183
courthouses, 200
court-martial, 210–11
Court of Appeals for the Federal Circuit, 210
courts. *See* court cases; judicial system
crank (methamphetamine), 251
creationism, 267
credentials fraud, 78–79
credit, in poor areas, 499
credit card companies, 360–61
  complaints against, 360–61
  government regulation of, 355
credit cards
  billing fraud and, 146, 278
  charges on, as document trail, 6
  scams with, 254, 360
credit checks, 252
creditors, in bankruptcy cases, 209
credit ratings, corporations, 309
credit reports, 309–10
credit unions, 340, 359–60
  competitors of, 359–60
  description of, 359
  financial information on, 359–60
  government regulation of, 355
  local communities and impact of, 354
  Web site on, 359
crime. *See also* arrests; *specific types of crime*
  arson as a way of hiding, 240
  bureaucracies and, 124
  at colleges and universities, 251, 288
  community policing and, 245
  databases on, 54, 58, 60, 62
  homeowners' insurance exclusion for, 373
  military courts and, 210–11
  probationers and, 197
  as a public health issue, 253
  real estate ownership and, 477
  statistics on, 60, 62, 249–50, 251
  teachers and, 272
  victimless, 236
  wiping out conviction records in, 203–4
crime laboratories, 245–46
crime scene
  coroners at, 247
  technicians at, 245–46
criminal behavior, legislative branch, 152
criminal cases, 182–83. *See also* court cases;
    judicial system
criminal justice departments, 253
criminal justice system. *See* court cases; judicial
    system; law enforcement personnel

criminal record checks, 398
cultural groups, newspapers form, 21
currency exchange shops, 367
"current" human sources, 6, 68–69, 81, 311
curriculum, in schools, 267
custodians, school, 274

dams, 53, 61, 441
Darwinism, 267
database analysis. See computer-assisted report-
    ing (CAR)
database managers, 54
databases, 53–63. See also government databases
    access to, 31, 35, 57–58
    acquiring, 56
    air pollution, 439
    airports, 464
    air safety, 467
    archiving of data on, 57
    ambulance response times, 396
    assessment and taxation, 478
    automobiles, 451
    boating accidents, 468
    building, 53–54, 57
    bus recalls, 456
    campaign contribution reports, 155
    on CD-ROMs, 20
    commercial, 39–41
    community, 57
    crime, 58
    demographic data, 62–63
    doctors, 327
    driving records, 452
    environment, 435
    felons, 508
    file size in, 56
    financial institutions, 354
    finding, 55–56
    format of data in, 56
    foster parents, 508
    full-text, 31
    gun dealers, 230
    hazardous materials, 442
    health care, 389, 392–93
    indexes to, 30
    on intranets for internal use, 56–57
    judges' opinions, 40–41
    in libraries, 28
    licenses, 52, 73
    local government, 58–62
    medical devices, 408
    motor vehicles, 274
    news programs, 23
    nuclear power, 424–25
    nuclear waste transport, 461
    online, 30–32

"outer integrity" check of, 56
    pawnshops on, 239
    pay services for, 38
    periodicals, 24
    pollution, 437, 439, 440
    press releases, 310
    primary documents on, 34, 37–38, 39–45
    record layout of, 56
    searching, 29, 31–32, 55–56
    secondary sources on, 28, 30–32
    state government use of, 49, 61
    Superfund sites, 436, 442
    teachers with criminal records, 272
    telephone directories, 72
    traffic stops, 242
    transportation, 61, 62, 449
    trucks, 455
    updating, 57
    utilities, 419–20
    vital records, 37–38
    voter registration records, 59
    water pollution, 440
    on the Web, 29, 31
    workplace directories, 73
day care workers, 323
day programs, for mental health patients, 400
death certificates, 230, 399
death records, 37, 38, 62
deaths
    in accidents, 62, 449–50, 453, 455–56, 459
    all-terrain vehicles and, 453
    arson and, 373
    bus accidents, 455–56
    cause of, 230, 247
    coroners on cause and manner of, 247
    drunk drivers and, 453
    fire-related, 240
    funeral notices on, 22
    in hospitals, 388, 389, 391, 392–93
    in jails, 195
    motorcycles and, 453
    in nursing homes, 389, 399
    prescription drugs and, 406
    probate courts and, 206–7
    railroad crossings, 459
    staged, 371
    transportation safety and, 449
    in the workplace, 317
debts, of legislators, 160
debt service budget, 127
deeds, 477
defendants
    bail system and, 185–86
    in civil cases, 182, 183
    confession of, 187–88
    in criminal cases, 182–83

defendants *(continued)*
  indigent, 182
  initial court appearance and, 184–85
  interviews of, 184–85
  multiple charges against, 203
  non-English speaking, 184–85
  plea bargaining by, 203
  release on own recognizance, 186
  representation of, 203–4
  sentencing of, 191–92
  in traffic court, 205
defense attorneys, 203–4
  bail setting and, 185
  bill padding and fraud by, 203
  caseloads of, 203
  investigating, 203
  jail conditions and, 185
  jury selection and, 188
  motions filed by, 203–4
  as sources, 185
  wiping out criminal records by, 203–4
  wrongful convictions and, 204
defense contractors, 137
defibrillators, 407
deinstitutionalization, 400
demographic databases, 54, 62–63
dental insurance, 404
dentists, 404
depositions, 183
depository libraries, 43
deregulation
  of airlines, 464, 466
  of utilities, 418, 419
derivatives, 366
descriptive leads, 99
desegregation, of schools, 269
"detached sources," 70
details, in writing, 94–95
developments, housing, 134–35, 477, 485
diagnostic-related groups (DRGs), 380, 390
dialogue, in writing, 102–3
diaries, 25
dietary services, hospital, 389
directories
  business information, 312
  city, 72, 134
  of college and university staff, 287
  finding sources through, 68, 71–73
  of foundations, 346
  membership, 21
  of outside experts, 70–71
  of periodicals, 24
  of prisons, 196
  in school districts, 276
  as secondary sources, 26

telephone, 72, 140
  workplace, 72–73
directors, nonprofit organizations, 338, 342–43
direct quotations, 96, 100, 104
disabilities, 269
  colleges and universities and, 284–85
  federal regulation of businesses and, 306
  schools and, 268–59
  workers' compensation and, 381, 383
disability insurance, 370, 383
disadvantaged. *See* disabilities; poverty; *specific types of disabilities*
disasters
  building standards and, 485
  insurance against, 367, 368, 372
  loans after, 63
discharge permits, and sewer systems, 440
discharge records, hospital, 392
discipline
  of chiropractors, in insurance fraud, 371
  of coaches, 272
  of college and university students, 286
  of doctors, 327, 403
  of insurance agents, 376
  of law enforcement officers, 224–27
  of lawyers, 323
  of licensed professionals, 324
  of nurses, 393, 404
  of prosecutors, 202
  of secondary school students, 264–65
disclosures. *See* financial disclosures
discovery materials, 183
discrimination, 306. *See also* ethnic discrimination; racial discrimination
  geographic, and taxis, 457
discussion groups, 71
dismissal of cases, 183
dispatchers, 244–45, 457
disposal treatment companies, 439
dispute resolution, 184
dissertations, 26
district attorneys. *See* prosecutors
diversity
  in colleges and universities, 284–85
  in schools, 269–70
divorce
  of public figures, 113
  records in, 6, 23, 26, 35, 37, 50
  students and, 265
divorce court, 206
divorce lawyers, 199, 327
divorced parents, 199
DNA analysis, 189, 204, 232, 246
docket sheets, 60, 183, 198, 208, 209
doctoral dissertations, 26

doctors, 403–4
    databases on, 327
    discipline of, 327, 403
    emergency room, 253
    health maintenance organizations and, 389
    licensing of, 323, 403
    malpractice insurance and, 373
    Medicaid and, 381
    Medicare complaints on, 380, 403
    misconduct by, 183
    pharmacies and, 407
    in prisons, 195
    professional organizations for, 328
    workers' compensation and, 383
documents, primary. *See* primary documents
"documents state of mind," 3, 5–6
document trails, 6, 7. *See also* paper trails
    colleges and universities and, 281
    judicial system and, 179–80
    nonprofit organizations and, 339, 340–42
dogs, police, 247–48
domestic relations cases, 199–200, 206, 233
domestic violence, 232–33, 265
dorm fires, 286
double jeopardy, 232
drinking water, 138, 434, 439–40
drive-by shootings, 229–30
drivers
    ambulance, 396
    bus, 455–56
    database of records of, 452
    drunk, 205, 241, 452–53
    racial profiling of, 242, 249
    railroad crossings and, 459–60
    speed traps and, 242
    taxi, 457
    traffic stops and, 241, 242, 249
    traffic violations and, 241–42
    truck, 455
driver's licenses
    automobile insurance and, 372
    of drunk drivers, 452
    records of, 25, 62, 73, 451, 452
    revocation of, 451
    suspension of, 452
dropout rates, secondary school, 262, 266, 276, 280
drug companies. *See* pharmaceutical companies
drugs, prescription
    counterfeit, 388
    errors, 393–94
    mental health care and, 401
    pharmaceutical companies and, 406–7
    pharmacists and, 406, 407
    prices of, 406–7

    testing, 388, 406, 407
    theft of, 393
    warnings about, 406
    wrong dose or use of, 393–94
drug tests, of police officers, 221
drug use and abuse, 233–36
    by airplane pilots and crews, 463
    drug raids in, 234
    law enforcement personnel and, 225, 251
    by legislators, 163
    by licensed professionals, 326
    money laundering and, 234, 367
    organized crime and, 242
    parolee recidivism and, 197
    pimps and prostitutes and, 236
    prosecution of, 202, 203
    by public figures, 113
    in rape cases, 231
    in schools, 265–66
    tactics in combating, 233
    tests for, 463
    workers and, 321
drunk drivers
    catching, 241
    legal liability of, 452
    licenses of, 452
    police officers at hearings of, 220
    prevention programs for, 452–53
    sentencing of, 205
    ticket-fixing for, 205
    traffic court and, 205
dumping of patients, 395–96, 503
dumps, and waste disposal, 444

"earmarks," 125
economic databases, 59, 62
economic interests, and parallel backgrounding, 7
education, 261–91. *See also* colleges and
    universities; schools; students; teachers;
    training
    charter schools and, 270–71
    class size and, 267
    continuing, for police officers, 223
    curriculum in, 267
    databases on, 60, 62
    desegregation and, 269
    funding in, 262, 276–78
    gender equity in, 270
    homeschooling, 279
    multiculturalism in, 269–70
    private schools and, 278–79
    quality of learning in, 261–62, 277
    school choice and, 270–71
    tracking in, 267

elections
  databases on, 62
  of judges, 181, 201
  in labor unions, 315
  of legislators, 152, 170
  violations of laws governing, 157
  voter registration records in, 6, 35, 36, 59
electric utilities, 422–23
  deregulation of, 418
  documents on, 419–20
  environmental impact of, 417–18
  government regulation of, 418–19
  holding companies for, 421
  nuclear power plants and, 423
  ownership of, 422
  rates for, 417
  rural systems of, 421
  transmission of, 417, 419, 422
Electronic Freedom of Information Act, 53,
  58
elementary schools. See education; schools
e-mail
  arranging interviews through, 68, 79
  finding sources through, 71, 72
embezzlement, 104, 377
emergencies
  air transport to hospitals in, 397, 466
  ambulances and, 396–97
  911 calls and, 244–45
  patient dumping and, 395–96
emergency medical services, 253, 368, 396–97
emergency rooms, 368, 503
employees. See also business; labor unions
  directories of, 71
  management relations with, 315–16
  safety and health regulation and, 317–18
  as sources, 68, 316
  wage enforcement and, 318–20
employers. See business; corporations
employment
  databases on, 61
  health insurance as part of, 369, 378
  lawsuits related to, 312
  poor people and, 501–2
  vocational training and, 279–80
employment agencies, 325
employment security departments, 321–22
endings
  in interviews, 84
  in writing, 99, 104–5
endowments, 281–82
energy
  blackouts and other issues in, 417, 419
enforcement records, 308
engineers, 328

enrollment
  at colleges and universities, 28
  in schools, 60
enterprise crime, 243
entitlement programs, 165, 168
entrapment, 111, 237
environment, 434–44
  agriculture and, 434–35
  air pollution and, 439
  asbestos and, 275
  complexity of, 434–35
  databases on, 54, 61–62
  documents on, 437–39
  government regulation of, 306, 435–37
  hazardous waste and, 442–44
  hospitals and hazards to, 389
  legal disputes and, 143
  mining and, 444
  nuclear power and, 423
  soil pollution and, 442–44
  solid waste disposal and, 443–44
  utilities and, 417–18, 422
  water pollution and, 138, 426, 439–41
  Web sites on, 435, 438
  white-collar crime and, 243
environmental claims, 209
erosion, 443
errors
  hospital care and, 392–94
  prepublication review and, 116–18
escrow companies, 481
estates
  in courts, 206–7, 208
  nursing home costs and, 400
ethical issues in journalism, 108–18
  accuracy and, 109, 115–16
  ambush interviews and, 112–13
  covertly obtaining information and, 110–12
  exposing public figures and, 113
  fairness, 109
  golden rule and, 110
  inside sources and, 253
  legality and, 109, 111–12
  prepublication reviews and, 116–18
  unidentified sources and, 114–15
  Web sites on, 119
ethics
  in bankruptcy court, 209
  doctors and, 403
  of executive branch, 136–37
  fairness and, 109
  of legislators, 162
  of licensed professionals, 326, 328
  of professional associations, 328
  workplace, 313

ethics codes, 108
ethnic discrimination, 188. *See also* racial
    discrimination
    federal regulation of businesses and, 306
    taxis and, 457
ethnic groups. *See also* minority groups
    colleges and universities and, 284–85
    jury selection and, 188
    newspapers for, 21
    school placement and, 267
ethnicity data, on prisoners, 60
evangelists, 348, 349
evidence
    analysis of, 246
    contamination of, 245–46
    court cases and, 186–87
    crime statistics and, 250
    in murder cases, 229, 230
    storage of, 246–47
    wrongful convictions and, 204
evidence rooms, 246–47
evolution theory, 267
exactions, 486
examinations
    of banks, 356, 357
    of teachers, 271. *See also* tests
excessive force, by police, 225, 226–27, 228, 254
exclusions, in insurance, 372, 373
executive branch, federal, 123–47
    agency missions in, 124–25
    budget and management watchdogs in, 133
    budgets and, 126–28
    cabinet secretaries in, 135–36
    civil service and, 140–41
    conflicts of interest and, 136–37
    consultants and contractors and, 128–30
    contracting process and, 130–33
    corruption in, 123–24, 134–35, 143
    databases and documents on, 124–25
    environmental enforcement and, 436
    Federal Register notices and, 125–26
    information collection in, 125–26
    inspectors general and, 138–40
    investigating, 134–44
    judicial appointments by, 208, 210, 211
    legislative oversight of programs of, 167
    permanent bureaucracy in, 140
    prosecutor appointments by, 202
    public affairs personnel in, 141–43
    public authorities and, 143–44
    school funding and, 277–78
    self-regulatory organizations and, 143–44
    top executive in, 135
executive branch, local, government employees
    in, 145–46

executive branch, state
    cabinet secretaries in, 135
    campaign finance corruption and, 146–47
    government employees in, 145–46
    governors and, 144–45
    state register in, 147
executive directors, nonprofit organizations, 338,
    342–43
executive orders, 135
experts, outside, 70–71
explosives, 241
exposure, of public figures, 113
expungement of criminal records, 190, 198, 323
extramarital affairs, 113

factories
    pollution and, 436, 438
    poor people working in, 501
faculty, 286, 288–90
fair market value, 482
fairness
    of assessments, 483
    of journalism, 109
    of property taxes, 277, 483
    unfair labor practices, 315–16
false identities, 79
family court, 199–200
family leave, 320
family members
    compensation programs and, 252
    domestic violence reporting by, 233
    of judges and court personnel, 182
    of legislators, 160, 170
    nepotism and, 22, 145
    nursing home costs and, 400
    poverty and, 502–3
    of prisoners, 194
    of school board members, 273, 274
    school violence and, 265
forensic pathology, 247
    as sources, 69
    of suspects, 219
federal appeals courts, 192
federal funds database, 63
federal government. *See* government and
    government agencies
federal government databases. *See* government
    databases
federal prisons, 196
federal prosecutors, 202
Federal Register, 125–26, 135, 137
fees
    attorneys and court cases and, 182
    budget revenue from, 127, 200
    for charter school management, 271

fees *(continued)*
   at colleges and universities, 281, 284
   from credit card companies, 361
   of foundations, 346
   insurance agents and, 376
   licensing, 127, 324, 329
   medical laboratories and, 408
   in prisons, 195
   in probate courts, 206–7
   of professional fund-raisers, 344
   taxi, 457
   for telephones, 427–28
   water systems and, 426
fee tables, mutual funds, 362
felons, 192, 197, 272, 323, 326, 327, 464, 508
fertilizers, 443
file size, in databases, 56
financial aid, at colleges and universities, 285
financial disclosures
   campaign finance, 147
   of corporations, 304
   of credit unions, 359–60
   executive branch and, 136
   of financial institutions, 355
   government employees, 59
   of hospitals, 391–92
   judges, 181, 201
   judicial candidates, 201
   labor unions, 314
   of legislators, 159–61, 170
   of mutual funds, 362
   of nonprofit organizations, 340–41
   savings and loans, 358, 359
financial holding companies (FHCs), 354
financial information
   municipal bond updates on, 128
   stock filings, 302–5
   UCC filings, 38
financial institutions, 353–83. *See also* banks;
      credit card companies; credit unions;
      investment companies; mutual funds;
      savings and loans
   community reinvestment and, 363–64
   government regulators and, 354, 355, 367
   high-risk transactions and, 365–66
   insider transactions and, 365
   loans to own directors in, 354
   loans to political candidates from, 157
   local communities and impact of, 354
   money laundering and, 354, 366–67
   redlining by, 353–54, 355, 363–65
   subprime lending crisis and, 354
   white-collar crime and, 243
financial statements. *See* financial disclosures
fines, 127, 200, 205, 238
fingerprints, 246

fire departments, 240, 241, 278
fire inspections, 240, 275, 307
fire marshals, 240
fire safety, 478
   arson and, 240
   in colleges, 286
   in hospitals, 389
   in schools, 275
fish supply, 436
fishing licenses, 6
527 groups, 156, 343
flashbacks, in writing, 103
flight crews, 463
flight engineers, 379
focus, in writing, 98–99
food assistance programs, 508
food banks, 508
food pantry, 508
food programs
   for poor people, 508
   in schools, 274, 278
food-server licenses, 6
food stamps, 138, 504, 506–7
footnotes, in annual reports, 303
foreclosures, 23, 476, 479
foreshadowing, in writing, 103
forfeiture laws, 233, 235
format, 508
   of database records, 56
"former" human sources, 6, 81
   in business, 311
   legislative branch, 162
   types of, 68–69
forms, and databases, 56
forums (online), 86
foster care, 200, 508
foundations, 338, 345–47. *See also* nonprofit
      organizations
   contributions to, 152
   defined, 345
   directories of, 346
   distribution requirements for, 346–47
   fees charged for services of, 346
   financial disclosure requirements, 345
   politicians linked to, 152
   purpose of, 345
   school evaluations by, 276
   transactions with disqualified persons by, 346
franchises, 307, 312, 427, 428
fraternal groups, 340
fraternities, 286
fraud. *See also* corruption; misconduct
   automobile accidents and, 372
   bankruptcy and, 209
   business, 305, 374
   in civil cases, 183

fraud *(continued)*
  at colleges and universities, 286
  in credentials, 78–79
  credit cards and, 360
  by defense attorneys, 203
  food stamps, 507
  government budgets and, 126
  government contracting and, 129–30
  government employees and, 145–46
  insurance and, 369, 370, 371, 372, 373, 374, 377
  land, 476, 481, 482
  licensed professionals and, 322–23
  lobbyists and, 153
  local government and, 144
  Medicaid and, 380
  military documents and, 36
  pension plans and, 321
  probate records and, 207
  school, 261, 267, 280
  by scientists, 125
  workers' compensation and, 146, 381, 383
freedom-of-information requests, 58, 281
friends, as sources, 69
fugitives, 186, 253
full-text databases, 31
functional story structure, 97
fund-raising
  legislative branch and, 156–57
  nonprofit organizations and, 339, 344, 347
funeral announcements, 22
funeral home directors, 247, 253, 323
funeral industry, 24–25, 323
fungicides, 443

gambling, 63, 209, 348
gang rape, 194
gangs, 230, 244, 251, 264
gas utilities, 422–23
  environmentalism and, 422
  government regulation of, 418, 419
  holding companies for, 421
  rates for, 417
gender equity
  in colleges and universities, 284–85
  in mortgage loans, 363
  in schools, 270
general operating budget, 127
geographic discrimination, and taxis, 457
gifted students, 267
gifts. *See also* bribery
  to colleges and universities, 345
  to governors, 144
  Tax Court and, 208
global climate change,
golden rule, in journalism, 110

gold mining, 444
go/no go decisions in, 12
governing boards, of colleges and universities, 291
Government Accountability Office (GAO), 167–69, 423, 504
government and government agencies
  agency liaisons and, 142
  agenda of regulations of, 126
  airplanes used by, 465
  bonds issued by, 128
  budgets of, 380, 382
  consultants and contractors to, 128–30
  contracting process and, 130–33
  corporations and, 129, 305–6
  corruption and, 129, 134–35
  depository libraries and, 43
  document trails in, 6
  financial institution regulation by, 355
  health services regulation by, 389
  information collection in, 125–26
  as insurers, 379–81
  legal notices posted by, 23, 144
  legislative oversight of programs of, 167
  libraries in, 28
  lobbyists used by units of, 158
  missions of, 124–25
  newspaper stories on, 21–22
  permanent bureaucracy in, 140
  pollution and, 306
  presentments against, 187
  public affairs personnel and, 141–43
  surplus equipment and, 127
  voter registration records, 59
  watchdogs and, 133
  water districts and, 425–26
  Web sites of, 55, 124, 126
government appointees, 144, 145
government databases, 42. *See also* databases
  accidents, 61
  agency records on, 41–42
  audit reports, 55
  availability of, 40
  business, 59
  courts, 60
  crime, 60
  demographic data, 62–63
  economic, 59
  education, 60
  environment, 61
  executive branch, 123–24
  finding, 42, 55, 61
  gun permits, 60
  indexes to, 55
  infrastructure, 61
  jails, 60

government databases *(continued)*
  local, 58–62
  municipal employees, 60
  politics, 59
  property records, 59–60, 478
  state, 61
  tax records, 59–60
  uses of, 42
  vendors, 61
government employees
  absenteeism and, 146
  biographical information on, 25
  civil service and, 140–41
  compiling list of, 125
  conflicts of interest and, 59
  contracts and, 129
  in executive branch, 145–46
  financial disclosure requirements for, 59
  fraud by, 145–46
  in judicial system, 180
  kickbacks and, 130
  in legislative branch, 161–62, 171, 172
  as lobbyists after leaving government
    employment, 137, 158–59
  nepotism and, 22, 145
  patronage and, 22, 145
  pensions of, 127, 165, 320
  permanent bureaucracy in, 140
  private-industry jobs and revolving door for,
    137, 437
  re-election campaigns and use of, 162
  state government appointments of, 144, 145
  whistleblowers among, 69
government-guaranteed loans, 63, 165, 305–6
government handbooks, 25
Government Printing Office, 41, 125
government regulation. *See* regulation
government subsidies
  to airports, 466
  for commercial shipping, 467
  to farmers, 22
  for housing, 134–35, 489
governors
  college and university appointments by, 291
  judicial appointments by, 182
  licensing board appointments by, 324–25
  road construction contracts and, 458
  role of, 144–45
  state insurance commissions and, 377
grading, in colleges and universities, 286
graduation rates
  in higher education, 26
  in secondary schools, 266
grand juries, 186–87
grants
  audits of, 139

to colleges and universities, 289
  corruption and, 125, 144
  executive branch and, 125
  by foundations, 345, 347
  to small businesses, 305–6
  state government and, 144
graphics, 90, 92–93
grievance arbitration, 316–17
ground crews, 464
group homes, for mental health patients,
    400–401
guardians, 182, 207
guardians ad litem, 200
guards, prison, 193, 194
guilty pleas, 187, 203, 323
guilty verdicts, 187
gun dealers, 60, 230, 253
guns
  evidence room storage of, 246
  handling, as evidence, 246
  murder and, 229
  paper trails with, 253
  permits for, 60
  police use of, 222
  in schools, 264
  security guards and training in, 227

habitual juvenile offenders, 244
hair braiders, 329
harassment. *See also* sexual harassment
  canine (K9) corps and, 247–48
harm, rule of, 110
hate crimes, 241
hazardous waste, 442–44
  databases on, 442
  government regulation of, 442
  marine oil spills and, 469
  mining safety violations and, 143
  sites for, 435–36
  Superfund cleanup sites and, 436, 442–43
  transport of, 460–61
hazing, 286
Head Start, 505
health
  cancer and pollution and, 436, 443
  databases on, 54, 62
  in the workplace, 317–18
health care, 388–409. *See also* hospitals; patient
    care
  blood banks and, 408–9
  databases for, 389, 392–93
  emergency medical services and, 396–97
  expenditures on, 388
  fraudulent pregnancy testing and, 110–11
  government regulation of, 389
  home health care companies and, 402

health care *(continued)*
  malpractice and, 327, 329, 367, 373, 388, 397
  medical device companies and, 407–8
  medical laboratories and, 408
  medical research and, 405–6
  mental health institutions and, 400–402
  nursing homes and, 398–400
  pharmaceutical companies and, 406–7
  pharmacies and, 407
  poor people and, 503–4
  in prisons, 195, 196
  Veterans Administration hospitals and, 397–98
  waste disposal in, 393
health departments, 278
health inspections, 307, 317–18
health insurance, 367, 369–70
  employment and, 369, 378
  financial reports in, 374
  government regulation of, 378
  uninsured persons and, 368, 369
health maintenance organizations (HMOs), 404–5
  accreditation of, 404
  doctors in, 389
  insurance and, 327, 370, 405
  racial disparities in treatment in, 388
health services, college and university, 286–87
hearings
  committee, 166
  court, 186–87, 205
hedge funds, 304
helicopters, 397, 466
helmet laws, 453
herbicides, 443
higher education. *See* colleges and universities; education
high fives story structure, 97
high-risk financial transactions, 365–66
high schools. *See* education; schools
highways
  accidents on, 61
  bridge safety and, 449–50, 469
  competitive bidding and, 458
  construction contracts for, 458–59
  databases, 61, 62
  toll roads, 458–59
  trucks and damage to, 455
Hispanics. *See* minority groups; racial discrimination
holding companies, 354, 355, 421
home health care companies, 126, 400
homelessness, 503
home loans. *See* mortgage loans
homeopathy, 403

homeowners insurance, 367, 372–73
  exclusions in, 372, 373
  fraud against, 373
  redlining and, 375
homeschooling, 268, 279
homicide. *See* murder
honoraria, for legislators, 161
hospices, 402
hospitals, 389–91
  accreditation of, 389–91
  admission records in, 6
  ambulances and, 396–97
  budget of, 391
  costs and billing in, 391–92
  deaths in, 388, 389, 391, 392–93
  emergency air transport to, 397, 466
  emergency rooms in, 368, 503
  environmental issues and, 393
  errors of care in, 392–94
  government regulation of, 307, 391–92
  indigent care and, 394–96
  information sources for, 389–90
  insurance and, 368
  licensing of, 389
  malpractice and, 327, 329, 367, 373, 388, 397
  medical records on, 391
  as nonprofit organizations, 340, 345, 392, 395
  patient dumping and, 395–96
  patient records in, 391
  pharmacies in, 407
  poor people and, 503
  quality improvement organization in, 389–91
  quality of patient care in, 390, 391
  racial disparity in treatment in, 388
  Veterans Administration, 397–98
hostages, 233
hotels
  long-distance telephone rates and, 428
  property stolen from, 238
hourglass story structure, 97
housing. *See also* real estate
  college students and, 286
  corruption in government subsidies to, 134–35
  databases on, 62
  emergency, for homeless, 503
  insider financial transaction and, 365
  low-income, 488–90
  religious organizations and, 348
  rental subsidies for, 489
  rural, 490
  Section 8 program in, 505
housing court, 484

human research subjects, 289–90
human sources, 67–85
    business information from, 311–13
    covertly obtaining information from, 110–12
    creditors in bankruptcies and, 209
    "currents," 6, 68–69, 311
    documents and records for locating, 73
    environment and, 435
    "formers," 6, 68–69, 162, 311
    identifying and evaluating, 68–71
    interviewing, 67, 68–69, 76–85
    investigative process and, 3, 6–7
    judicial system and, 179–80, 181, 193
    in law enforcement, 252–53
    legislative staff as, 162
    locating, 67–85
    mapping power structures among, 74–76
    for organized crime, 242
    outside experts as, 70–71
    parents as, in schools, 276
    payment for, 114–15
    personal habits of, 73
    poverty, 497–98
    prepublication review by, 93, 116–18
    primary document meaning and, 6–7
    professional associations as, 327–28
    in religious groups, 349
    students as, 276
    teachers as, 276
    tools for finding, 71–76
    trust with, 118
    unidentified, 114–15
    whistleblowers as, 69
    "working from the outside in" technique
        with, 3
    writing and attribution to, 102–3
human subjects
    background investigation of, 7, 20, 34, 208
    choosing, 4
    exposing, 113
    leads focusing on, 100–101
    in scientific research, 289–90
    in writing, 91–92
hunting licenses, 6
hypothesis development, 4–5

identity theft, 37
immigrants, illegal, 319–20, 501
imprisonment, of child support violators, 506
incident reports, 220
incinerators, hospital, 393
inclusion, in schools, 269
income
    data on, in communities, 63
    environmental issues and, 435
    hospital care and, 391–92

mass transit location and, 461
    outside, for legislators, 160, 161, 170
    school placement and, 269
    school spending and, 277
    school test scores and, 266
    toxic waste disposal and, 63
income taxes, 160. See also taxes
indeterminate sentencing, 191
indexes
    to bibliographies, 30
    to citations, 30
    to databases, 30, 31
    to government databases, 55
    to jail logbooks, 254
    key word searches using, 29–30
    to newspaper articles, 5
    to news programs, 23
    to outside experts, 70
    to periodicals, 24
    to property records, 49
    to reference books, 25
    to technical reports, 43–44
    to Web content, 29
indictments, 187, 231
indigent care, 391, 394–95
indigent defendants, 182
indirect backgrounding, 7
indoor air pollution, 439
informants, 204, 235–36, 250, 253
informational tax returns, of nonprofit
        organizations, 34, 342–43
infrastructure. See also bridges; highways
    databases on, 61, 62
    exactions in new construction for, 486
    trucks and damage to, 455
in-home intravenous drug treatment, 402
injuries
    from products, 305
    transportation safety and, 449
    workers' compensation and, 381–83
    workplace, 317–18
inmates. See prisoners
insecticides, 443
insider financial transactions
    loans, 356, 365
    trading, 304
inspection reports, 408
inspectors general, 138–40, 398
institutions. See also organizations
    directories of employees of, 71
    document trails of, 6
    licensing of, 325
    mapping power structures in, 74–76
insurance, 367–74
    automobile, 367, 371–72, 375
    automobile accident scams, 368, 371, 372

insurance *(continued)*
  boating, 468
  commercial and professional, 373–74
  deception in selling, 370–71, 377
  denial of claims in, 368
  dental, 404
  deposit, 358, 359
  disability, 370, 383
  disasters and, 367, 368
  government-provided, 379–81
  government regulation of, 369
  health, 369–70
  homeowners', 367, 372–73, 375
  life, 367, 370–71
  medical malpractice, 367, 373
  property, 372–73
  state regulation of, 369, 374, 375, 377–79
  statistics on, 378–79
  stolen property and, 239
  types of, 367
  unemployment, 367
  workers' compensation, 367, 381–83
insurance adjustors, 374
insurance agencies, 354
insurance agents, 322, 323, 324, 367, 371,
    376–77
insurance companies, 367
  accounting rules used by, 374
  annuities and pensions from, 321
  complaints against, 368–69, 375, 377
  financial reports of, 374
  fraud and, 369, 370
  fraud by, 369, 370, 371, 372, 373, 374,
    377
  government regulation of, 41, 307, 324, 354,
    369
  insolvencies of, 374, 379
  investigators in, 372
  lines of business operated by, unrelated to
    insurance, 375
  patient dumping and, 395–96, 503
  redlining and, 368, 375–76
  scams and, 375
integration, in schools, 269–70
intelligent design, 267
interest arbitration, 317
interior designers, 329
interlocking directorships, 346
internal affairs units, law enforcement, 220,
    224, 226, 236
Internal Revenue Service (IRS), 39, 60, 61,
    279, 288, 339, 340, 344, 347–48
international governments, and lobbyists, 159
Internet. *See also* Web sites
  finding sources through, 71
  pornography on, 236–37
  search techniques on, 29–32

secondary sources on, 30–32
  service providers for, 419, 429
interrogations, police, 222, 225
interstate buses, 456
interviews, 3, 76–85
  ambush, 112–13
  asking for documentation in, 84
  confidentiality of, 80
  credential fraud and, 78–79
  of "current" and "former" sources, 68–69, 81
  of defendants, 184–85
  document searches before, 34, 67, 78
  document trail and, 7
  ending, 84
  fairness of, 109
  following up, 85
  language of sources used in, 78
  lying in, 83
  mapping power structures using, 75
  of mental health personnel, 401
  motivations of the source in, 81–82
  on the record vs. off the record, 85
  of police, 219
  questions in, 75, 82–83
  reluctant interviewees, 78, 80
  research before, 77–78
  setting up, 79–80, 112
  silence in, 82
  structuring, 83–84
  with students, 265
  with suspects, 219
  taking notes during, 85
  tape-recording, 85, 94
  timing of, 80
  understanding human nature and, 67–68
  of witnesses, 252
intranets, for databases, 56–57
intrastate buses, 456
intravenous drug treatments, 402
inverted pyramid story structure, 96
investigations
  base building in, 12
  books about, 16–18
  choosing, 4
  "documents state of mind" in, 3, 5–6
  feasibility study in, 11–12
  go/no-go decisions in, 12
  human sources in, 3, 6–7
  organizing information in, 8
  planning, 12–13
  process of, 3, 4–9
  questioning conventional wisdom in, 8–9
  re-evaluation in, 13
  research hypothesis in, 4–5
  research techniques in, 7, 13
  sources of ideas for, 10–11

investigations *(continued)*
  Stith's version of Williams' approach to,
    14–15
  Williams' eleven-step approach to, 9–13
investment companies, 361–62
  documents on, 361–62
  government regulation of, 55, 361–62
  local communities and impact of, 354
Invisible Web, 29
irrigation districts, 426
Islamic charities, 349
issue briefs, 169

jails. *See also* prisons
  audits of, 185
  beatings and abuse of prisoners in, 185
databases on, 60
  deaths in, 195
  incarceration records (logbooks) in, 184, 185,
    254
  informants in, 204
  lawsuits against, 142, 185
  security measures in, 185
job applications, 6
Job Corps, 505
johns, 236
joint cost allocation, 343
journalistic writing. *See* writing
journals, 23, 30, 405–6
judges, 180, 201–2
  abuse of authority by, 201
  administrative law, 143, 225
  animosity between lawyers and, 201
  appeals and, 192–93
  appointment of, 181
  assigning cases to, 188
  attorneys assigned cases by, 181–82
  bail setting by, 185–86
  in bankruptcy court, 181, 209
  campaign contributions to, 181–82
  conflicts of interest and, 201–2
  databases of opinions of, 40–41
  divorce court, 206
  election of, 181, 201
  employees appointed by, 181
  environmental enforcement and, 436–37
  family court, 199, 200
  financial disclosures of, 201
  informants and, 236
  juvenile offenders and, 198, 199, 243
  leeway in sentencing by, 191–92
  in military courts, 210–11
  official investigation of, 202
  patronage and, 182
  prison overcrowding and, 190, 195–96
  probate, 206–7

  reversal rates of, 192
  small claims court, 207–8
  Tax Court, 208
  unfair labor practices and, 315
  work habits of, 200–201
"judge shopping," 188
judicial databases, 62
judicial system, 179–211. *See also* court cases;
    prisons; trials
  appeals in, 192–93
  attorneys and, 181–82
  budgets and court operations in, 200–201
  civil cases in, 182–84
  commutations in, 198
  crime victims and, 190–91
  criminal cases in, 182–83, 184–93
  databases on, 60, 62
  defense attorneys in, 203–4
  employees in, 180, 182
  environmental enforcement and, 437
  family court in, 199–200
  judges in, 180, 201–2
  juries in, 188–89
  juvenile cases in, 198–99, 243
  local, 202
  multifaceted aspect of, 180
  pardons in, 198
  parole in, 197
  patronage in, 182
  as a political system, 180–82
  probation in, 196–97
  prosecutors in, 202–3
  sentencing in, 191–92
  size of, 179
  sources in, 179–80, 181
  specialized courts in, 205–11
  state, 181, 182, 187, 205
  wrongful convictions in, 204
junkets, 162
juries, 188–89
  composition of, 188–89
  contacting members of, 189
  grand, 186–87
  police misconduct hearings and, 227
  selecting, 188–89
jury consultants, 189
jury pools, 189
jury verdicts, appeals of, 192
justice system. *See* court cases; judicial system;
    law enforcement personnel
juvenile courts, 198–99
juvenile crime, 243–44
juvenile offenders
  boot camps for, 195
  gangs and, 230, 244, 251
  as habitual offenders, 244

juvenile offenders *(continued)*
  judicial system and, 198–99
  records secrecy regarding, 195–96
  repeat, 198
  sealing of records of, 198
  trial as an adult, 243

key word searches, 30, 303
kickbacks, 130, 383, 401

labor databases, 62
labor lawyers, 312–13
labor liaisons, 318
labor union leaders, as source, 68, 69
labor unions, 313–14
  bankruptcy and contracts with, 209
  business information from, 312
  campaign contributions and, 306
  commercial shipping and, 467–68
  filings by, 314
  of law enforcement officers, 220
  licensed workers in, 328
  lobbyists used by, 158
  management relations with, 315–17
  as nonprofit organizations, 340
  nuclear power and, 423
  organizing, 315
  pension plan reports and, 321
  of prison guards, 193
  privatization and, 141
  racketeering by, 314
  railroads and, 460
  as sources, 314
landfills, 393, 439, 443
land flipping, 480
land fraud, 476, 481, 482
landlords, 476, 478, 483–85
land ownership. *See* property ownership
land planning, 426
land speculation, 458, 487
land-use policies, 477
larceny, 248
law enforcement, 218–54
  arson and, 239–40
  bombings and, 240–41
  budgets for, 250–51
  canine (K9) corps in, 247–48
  civil rights and, 248–49
  Coast Guard and, 468
  community relations and, 248–49
  crime laboratories and, 245–46
  crime statistics and, 249–50, 251
  domestic violence and, 231–32
  evidence room and, 246–47
  highway patrol and, 62
  internal affairs units in, 220, 224, 226, 236

  juvenile criminals and, 199
  missing persons and, 237, 252, 253
  murder and, 228–30
  narcotics and, 233–36
  organized crime and, 242–43
  paper trails in, 253–54
  people trails in, 252–53
  police brutality and, 236, 247
  police pursuit and, 222–23
  rape and, 231–32
  records divisions in, 251
  reform of, 252
  stolen property and, 238–39
  traffic patrol and, 241–42
  vice and, 236–37
  white-collar crime and, 243
law enforcement personnel
  abuse of authority by, 242
  airport security personnel and, 465
  arrests by, 184
  attitude toward women, 231–32
  barriers to journalists researching, 218–19
  campus police and, 291
  closing rank in, against outsiders, 219
  confessions after beatings by, 187–88, 230
  coroners working with, 247
  corruption in, 223, 226, 251
  court hearing appearances of, 220
  crime statistics collection by, 249–50, 251
  with criminal backgrounds, 221
  databases on, 218
  database use by, 58
  discipline of, 224–27
  dispatchers and, 244–45
  federal, 219
  as gang specialists, 244
  hostility toward journalists among, 219
  informants and, 204, 235–36, 250
  interrogations of suspects by, 225
  interviews of, 219
  justice system with, 219
  juvenile offenders and, 198
  licensing of, 323
  local, 219–44
  medical examiners working with, 247
  midnight police shift, 227, 229
  minority group attitudes toward, 248
  minority group members as, 221, 242
  misconduct by, 221, 224–27
  monitoring crimes by, 225–26, 227–28
  moonlighting by, 227
  911 officers and, 244–45
  overtime payments for, 250
  patrol officers, 245
  pensions for, 223
  physical conditioning of, 222

law enforcement personnel *(continued)*
  private detectives and, 252
  promotions of, 223
  public information officers and, 251
  public support for, 219
  racial profiling by, 242, 249
  raises for, 223
  recruitment of officers in, 221
  as sources, 252–53
  state, 219, 221–22
  techniques for monitoring police officers in, 220
  training of, 221–23, 232, 240, 241
  use of force by, 218, 222, 225, 226–27, 228
  vice officers in, 236–37
  as whistleblowers, 252
  workers' compensation claims of, 223
lawsuits
  against bus companies, 456
  against businesses, 304, 306, 307, 312
  auto insurance and, 372
  discrimination and, 306
  against government agencies, 143
  government contracts and, 131, 132
  hazardous waste dump siting and, 435–36
  health insurance and, 378
  homeowners' insurance and, 373
  against hospitals, 394
  against insurance companies, 370, 372, 373
  against jails, 142, 185
  against journalists, 109, 116
  against law enforcement personnel, 220, 226–27
  against licensed professionals, 326
  medical malpractice and, 373
  as primary documents, 35
  against prisons, 194
  against private schools, 279
  property value and, 482–83
  settlement terms in, 142–43
  state government and, 144
lawyers
  animosity between judges and, 201
  discipline of, 323
  fraud by, 322–23
  government contracting process and, 131
  as guardians ad litem, 200
  licensing of, 322, 323
  as lobbyists, 15
  professional organizations for, 328
  as sources, 68
leadership, 74–76
leading questions, 82
leads, in writing, 99–101
  composing, 99, 100–101
  effectiveness of, 101

tiebacks to, 104–5
  types of, 99–100
leaks, 85
leave, for family medical issues, 320
legal aid groups, 497
legal notices, 23, 144, 207
legislative branch, federal, 152–72
  authorizations and appropriations in, 164–66
  campaign contributions and, 153–55
  campaign finance records and, 155–57
  committees in, 43, 160, 163, 164, 166–67
  conflicts of interest and, 160
  "earmarks" used by, 152
  environmental enforcement and, 436–37
  expense records of, 162–63
  financial disclosures of legislators in, 159–61
  hearings in, 166
  honoraria paid to, 161
  investigative possibilities in, 153
  judicial appointments and, 181, 208, 210
  legislative process in, 163–64
  lobbyists and, 152–53, 157–59
  outside income for legislators, 160, 161
  oversight in, 166–67
  perquisites in, 161–63
  personal character of members of, 163
  pollution and, 434
  pork-barrel politics in, 165, 290
  prosecutor appointments and, 202
  re-election of, 162, 165
  research units of, 167–69
  resources of, 161–63
  scandals in Congress and, 152, 163
  school funding and, 277–78
  special interests and, 154, 161
  staff in, 161–62
  travel expenses of, 162–63
  voting records of, 165–66
legislative branch, local, 169–72
  annual personal financial disclosures and, 170
  campaign contributions and, 169–70
  campaign financial disclosures and, 170
  environmental enforcement and, 436–37
  financial disclosures of legislators in, 170
  government contracts and, 153
  outside income for legislators, 170
  travel advances for, 169
legislative branch, state, 169–72
  annual personal financial disclosures and, 170
  campaign contributions and, 169–70
  campaign financial disclosures and, 170
  college and university accreditation and, 283–84
  committees in, 171, 172
  comparative data by state on, 171
  conflicts of interest and, 153
  financial disclosures of legislators in, 170

legislative branch, state *(continued)*
    government contracts and, 153
    insurance regulation and, 377
    legislative process in, 171–72
    lobbyists and, 170–71
    staff in, 171, 172
letters
    arranging interviews using, 79, 112
    as sources, 25
letters to the editor, 22, 498
liability insurance, 368, 374
libel, 109, 367
librarians, 28, 29, 291, 314
libraries
    business reports in, 310
    city directories in, 72
    classification of books in, 26–28
    clipping, 5, 21
    database searching in, 28
    depository, 43
    finding information in, 26–28
    government agencies with, 28
    newspaper, 21
    presidential, 45
    secondary sources in, 28
    using librarians in, 28, 29
Library of Congress, 24, 28
Library of Congress subject headings, 27, 30
licensed professionals, 322–30
    bail bondsmen, 186
    bus drivers, 456
    complaints against, 326–27
    doctors, 323, 403
    gun dealers, 230
    hair braiders, 329
    individual fraud and misconduct by, 322–23
    insurance agents, 376, 377
    interior designers, 329
    interviewing, 68
    lawyers, 322, 323
    licensing process for, 325–26
    nurses, 404
    nursing home administrators, 399
    performance standards for, 326, 328
    pilots, 73, 323, 397
    police officers, 221
    professional associations for, 327–28
    real estate brokers and, 322, 323, 326
    records available for, 324
    state regulation of businesses and, 307
    towboat operators, 469
    Web sites on, 324
license plates, 253, 452
licenses
    bar, 325
    businesses, 307, 309
    catalogs in, 27

communications, 427
    databases on, 59, 73
    driver's, 62, 73, 297, 372, 451, 452
    fees for, 127, 324, 329
    fishing, 6
    food servers, 6
    hospital, 389
    hunting, 6
    limousine service, 457
    liquor store, 59, 325
    marriage, 6
    nuclear power plants, 424
    ocean freight, 467
    pet, 6, 73
    records of, 49, 73
    revocation of, 35, 329,
    suspension of, 329
    taxi drivers, 59, 325, 457
    wireless telecommunications, 428
licensing boards
    appointment to, 324–25
    complaint files, 324
    conflicts of interest and, 324
    databases on, 59, 62
    investigating, 328–30
lie detector tests, 221
liens, tax, 35, 39, 60, 307, 309, 478, 479–80,
        506
life insurance, 367, 370–71
    financial reports in, 374
    fraud in, 371
    types of, 371–72
limited partnerships, 308
limousine services, 457
line-by-line accuracy check, 115–16
liquor store licenses, 59, 325
listservs, 71
loans. *See also* mortgage loans; redlining
    campaign finance using, 157
    corruption and, 134–35, 138
    from credit unions, 360
    after disasters, 63
    government-guaranteed, 63, 165, 305–6
    high-risk transactions in, 365
    insider, to own directors, 354, 356, 365
    to legislators, 160
    to nonprofit organization executives, 338, 342
    payday, 499, 500
    as public records, 35, 38, 59
    rapid refund, 500
    rejection rates for, 55, 364
    special treatment in, 138, 157
    student, 285
    subprime, 354, 476, 500
lobbyists, 157–59
    for colleges and universities, 281
    for corporations, 158, 312

lobbyists *(continued)*
  corruption and, 152–53, 159
  crimes committed by, 153
  defined, 158, 170
  disclosure laws for, 59, 137
  former government employees as, 137,
    158–59
  foundations and, 347
  fund-raising and, 154–55
  insurance companies and, 360
  nonprofit organizations with, 338, 339
  pharmaceutical companies and, 406
  pollution and, 434
  public affairs personnel and, 142
  registered, 158, 159, 170–71
  scandals involving, 152–53
  stages to becoming, 157–58
  state government and, 145, 281
local communities, impact of financial institu-
    tions on, 354
local government
  airport security personnel and, 465
  campaign contributions and, 169–70
  corruption in, 131, 144
  crime statistics and, 249
  databases on, 58–62
  inspectors general in, 138
  kickbacks and contracts in, 130
  licensing boards and, 325, 329
  lobbyists used by, 158
  nonprofit organization regulation by, 347
  nursing home regulation by, 399
  property records and, 478–79, 480
  public records in, 36–37
  regulatory, 306–7
  watchdogs in, 144
  water districts and, 425–26
  water pollution and, 440
  workers' compensation and, 382
local government employees. *See* government
    employees
local newspapers, 21–22
locker searches, 265
logbooks, jail, 184, 185
logs, police, 218
long-distance telephone service, 428
loss control, 382
lotteries
  judge selection by, 188
  low-income persons and, 63, 277, 499
  school funding using, 277
low-income persons. *See also* poverty
  affordable housing programs for, 489–90
  community reinvestment and, 363
  developers and zoning and, 486
  hazardous waste dump siting and, 435–36

hospital care provided for, 391–92
  housing for, 488–90
  insurance sold to, 368
  in jails, 205
  lottery ticket purchases by, 63, 277, 499
  mortgage loan statistics and, 363
  rent subsidies for, 489
  schools for, 268, 269, 272
  student test scores and, 266
lying, in interviews, 83

Mafia, 242
magazines, 23–24
maiden names, 23, 73
mainstreaming, 269
malpractice, 327, 329, 367, 373, 388, 397
management
  of college funds, 282
  of schools, 273
management-worker relations, 314–15
mandatory sentencing, 192
manslaughter
  sentencing in, 191
  statistics on, 249
manufacturing
  airplanes and, 462–63
  discharge permits for sewer systems and, 440
  pollution and, 436, 438
mapping software, 54
marijuana, 235
marriage licenses, 6
marriage notices, 22
marriage records, 37
mass transit, 461
master's theses, 26
mechanic's lien, 479
mediation
  of civil cases, 184
  of labor-management disputes, 316
Medicaid, 367
  cost reports in, 394–95
  dental care, 404
  fraud and abuse in, 380
  government support for, 380–81, 400, 403
  indigent care and, 394–95
  nursing homes and, 399
  poor people and, 505
  purpose of, 380
medical care. *See also* health care; hospitals
  insurance and, 368
medical device companies, 407–8
medical examiners, 230, 247, 253, 406
medical facilities, 62. *See also* hospitals
medical helicopters, 397, 466
medical laboratories, 408
medical malpractice insurance, 367, 373

medical organizations, 25
medical records, 391
medical research, 405–6
medical waste disposal, 393
medical workers, in prisons, 194
Medicare, 367
  cost reports in, 394–95
  deaths of patients under, 391
  diagnostic-related groups (DRGs) in, 380, 390
  government regulation of, 378, 389
  government support for, 379–80
  health maintenance organizations (HMOs) and, 404, 405
  indigent care and, 394–95
  inspection reports for, 408
  lawsuits for abuse in, 378
  legislative support for, 165
  medical laboratories and, 408
  nursing homes and, 399
  providers and, 389
  purpose of, 379
medicine. *See* health care
membership directories, 21
memoranda, in court cases, 183, 191
mental health institutions, 400–2
mental health professionals, as guardians ad litem, 200
mental illness, of juvenile offenders, 199
mercury pollution, 437–38
methamphetamine, 234, 251
middle of stories, 101–3
migrant workers, 319
military bases, 444
military courts, 210–11
military personnel, 36
military records
  fraudulent, 36
  locating people with, 45
minimum wage, 318–19
mining, 143, 318, 444
minority groups. *See also* racial discrimination
  bail system and, 186
  civil rights issues and, 248
  community reinvestment and, 363–64
  contracting requirements and, 132, 139
  hazardous waste dump siting and, 435–36
  judicial appointments and, 181
  K9 dogs and, 247
  law enforcement personnel and, 248
  minority-owned businesses, 38, 132, 139, 101
  police officers from, 221, 242
  poverty and, 495
  racial profiling of, 242, 249
  redlining and, 353–54, 355, 363–65
  schools and, 269–70, 272, 276

  sentencing variations and, 191, 192
  students and, 269–70, 272
  wage issues and, 319
misconduct. *See also* corruption; fraud
  by coaches, 272
  by licensed professionals, 183, 322–23, 326
  by nonprofit organizations, 337–38
  by police officers, 221, 224–27
  by prosecutors, 202
  by scientists, 125
missing persons, 237–38, 252, 253
mission, of government agencies, 124–25
mobile homes, 484
money laundering, 234, 243, 327, 354, 366–67
monopolies, utilities as, 422
moonlighting, by police officers, 227
mortgage brokers, 354, 481
mortgage loans
  community reinvestment and, 363–64
  corruption in, 134–35
  documents in, 480–82
  insider transaction and, 365
  local community and impact of, 354
  property ownership and, 39, 476
  racial disparities in, 55, 63, 353–54, 355
  redlining and, 363–65
  refinancing, 481
  secondary markets and, 480–81
  subprime loans and, 354, 476, 500
motels
  illegal immigrants working in, 501
  property stolen from, 238
mother's maiden name, 73
motions, defense, 203
motorcycles, 453
motor vehicle departments
  accident reports in, 451–52
  databases in, 62
  driver's license data in, 73, 451
  inspections and, 451
  license plate data on, 253
motor vehicles. *See also* automobiles; traffic accidents
  all-terrain vehicles and, 453
  databases on, 50, 61, 62, 73
  drunk driving and, 241, 452–53
  homicides with, 230, 246
  motorcycles and, 453
  racial profiling of drivers of, 242, 249
  speeding and, 242
  traffic violations and, 241–42
multiculturalism, 269–70
municipal bonds, 128
municipal courts, 205
municipal employees, 60–61

murder, 228–30
    arson and, 240
    background investigation in, 20
        details about, 94, 230
    drive-by shootings and, 229–30
    guns and, 230
    illegal confessions in, 230
    informants in drug trafficking and, 236
    by juveniles, 198
    life insurance and, 371
    manslaughter and, 191
    murderers' records in, 203, 252–53
    pimps and prostitution and, 236
    police investigation into, 228–29
    pretrial hearings in, 189
    record-keeping and reports on, 228
    serial killers and, 19–20
    staged, 371
    statistics on, 249
    unsolved, 230
    vehicular homicide and, 230, 246
    wrongful convictions in, 204
murderers, as sources, 252–53
Muslim-related charities, 349
mutual funds, 304, 361–62

name change notices, 23
narcotics, 233–36
    arrests in, 235
    drug raids in, 235
    forfeiture laws and, 235
    informants in, 235–36
    in schools, 265–66
    tactics in combating, 233
narrative leads, 100
National Archives system, 44–45
National Labor Relations Board (NLRB), 315
national security, 72
natural gas, 417, 419. *See also* gas utilities
natural resource extraction, 444
neighbors, 68, 230, 240
neighborhoods
    crime statistics and, 250, 251
    hazardous waste dump siting in, 435–36
    mass transit and, 461
    newspapers in, 21
    redlining in, 353–54, 355, 363–65, 375–76
nepotism, 22, 145, 170, 224, 262
newsgroups, 71
newsletters, 23–24
newspapers
    access to articles in, 21
    archives of, 21, 69
    clipping libraries in, 5, 21
    on databases, 30–31

finding, 20–21
    indexes to articles in, 5
    legal notices in, 23, 144, 183, 207
    local, 21–22
    as secondary sources, 5, 20–23
    student, 280
    Web sites for, 20–21, 23, 31
news programs, 23
nicknames, 73
911 system, 244–45
no-bid contracts, 278
no-fault divorce, 206
nolo contendere pleas, 187
non-English-speaking individuals
    defendants, 184
    doctors in prisons, 195
nonpoint source pollution, 441
nonprofit organizations, 337–48
    affiliate groups of, 339–40, 343
    campaign contributions from, 156
    charities as, 338–48
    commercial ventures of, 338
    corporate profiles of, 343
    databases on, 62
    defined, 338
    distribution of funds by, 338
    document trails in, 6, 339, 340–42
    executive directors of, 338
    financial disclosure requirements for, 339,
        340–41
    foundations as, 338, 345–47
    fund-raising by, 339, 344, 347
    Gaul and Borowski model of, 340–42
    government regulation of, 347–48
    hospitals as, 340, 345, 392, 395
    judicial system and, 180
    mental health agencies as, 401
    misconduct by, 337–38
    nursing homes as, 400
    operating like for-profit businesses, 338
    parallel backgrounding and, 7
    school funding and, 278
    sources of information on, 339–40
    surpluses accumulated by, 338
    tax-exempt status of, 337, 338, 339–40, 347,
        348
    tax returns of, 340, 342–43, 392
    unrelated business income of, 341, 348
    utilities and, 421
    Web sites on, 340
note taking, in interviews, 85
"not guilty" pleas, 187
notice of bid, 131
notices, in newspapers, 22, 23
no-till farming, 443

nuclear power, 328, 423–25
  building of, 422
  documents on, 424
  waste from, 41, 418, 424, 460–61
  waste storage and, 424
  Web site on, 424–25
  whistleblowers on, 425
nurses
  errors in care and, 392
  hospital care and, 389
  licensing of, 323
  patient deaths and, 388
  roles of, 404
  as sources, 253
nursing homes, 398–400
  deaths in, 389, 399
  government regulation of, 307, 399
  Medicaid and costs of, 400
  registry of aides in, 398
  sources of information on, 126, 399–400
  violations in, 53, 91, 399
"nut" paragraph, 100
nutrition programs, 504, 507–8

obesity, in police officers, 222
obituaries, 22, 25, 399
observation, 11
Occupational Safety and Health Administration (OSHA), 317
ocean freight, 467
"off-budget" expenditures, 126–27
office allowances, 161
oil, 417, 419
oil companies, 181
online directories, 71
on-time service, 466–67
open-record laws, 53, 58, 226, 421
oral arguments, in appeals, 192
organic story structure, 97
organizations. See also institutions
  document trails of, 7
  lobbyists used by, 158
  mapping power structures in, 74–76
  parallel backgrounding and, 7
  workplace directories in, 72–73
organized crime, 183, 242
osteopathy, 403
"outer integrity" check, 56
outlines, writing from, 95–96
outside directors, 311
outside experts, 70–71
overcharging, by prosecutors, 203
overcrowding
  in prisons, 190, 195–96
  in schools, 275

oversight boards, 324
oversight hearings, legislative, 167
overtime wages, 319

pacing, in writing, 102
paid sources, 114–15
paper trails
  business information from, 307–11
  in civil cases, 183
  corruption in government contracts and, 134–35
  in criminal cases, 184
  in law enforcement, 253–54
Pap smear tests, 408
parallel backgrounding, 7
pardons, 193, 197, 198
parents
  divorce of, 199, 206
  government school program abuse by, 270
  homeschooling by, 279
  school-based management and, 273
  school choice and, 270–71
  school violence and, 265
  as sources on schools, 276
parking ticket databases, 66
parole, 190, 193, 197, 211
parole boards, 197
partnerships, 50–51, 62, 308, 478
part-time workers, 320
patent cases, 210
patient brokers, 401
patient care. See also health care
  in hospitals, 390–91
  nursing home abuse and, 399
patient dumping, 395–96, 503
patrol officers, 245
patronage, 22, 145, 182, 224
pawnshops, 239, 253, 499–500
payday loans, 499, 500
payments to sources, 114–15
payoffs
  in bankruptcy court, 209
  to fire inspectors, 240
  labor unions and, 314
  by utilities, 426
pedophiles, 236
peer review organizations, 390
Pell grants, 505
penalties, and budget revenue, 127, 200
pensions, 320–21
  bankruptcy and, 209, 321
  company plans in, 320–21
  corporations and, 304, 315
  federal employee, 165, 170
  government budgets and, 127

pensions *(continued)*
government employees and, 127, 165, 320
overfunding of, 321
of police officers, 223
tax court and, 208
people. *See* human sources
peremptory challenge, in jury selection, 189
performance bonds, 132–33
performance standards
for doctors, 403
for licensed professionals, 326, 328
for police officers, 220, 223
standardized tests in schools, 262–63, 279
periodical indexes, 24
periodicals, 23–24
permits
building, 59
gun, 60
perquisites (perks)
of foundation executives, 346
of legislators, 161–62
personal character, of legislators, 163
personnel records centers, 45
pesticides, 319, 443
petitions, 183
pet licenses, 6, 73
pharmaceutical companies, 388, 405, 406–7
pharmacies, 407
pharmacists, 323, 394, 406, 407
photographs, 229, 246
physical conditioning, of police officers, 222
physicians. *See* doctors
pilots
air ambulances and, 397
air traffic controllers and, 463–64
alcohol and drug prevention and testing
programs for, 463
licensing of, 73, 323, 397
planes for government officials and, 465
private planes and, 465
safety and, 462
pimps, 236
plagiarism, 286
plaintiffs, 183
plant closings, 322
playground supervisors, 274
plea-bargaining, 203
pleas, in court cases, 187
point of view, in writing, 103–4
point source pollution, 441
police. *See* law enforcement personnel
police academies, 221–23, 241
police boards, 225
police brutality, 236, 247
police chases, 222–23
police chiefs, 224

police dispatchers, 244–45
police dogs, 247–48
police logs, 218
police reports, 23
police stations, 224, 245, 252
political action committees (PACs), 55, 156–57,
306, 338, 339, 343
political committees, 339
politics
authorizations and appropriations and,
164–66
databases on, 59
insider financial transactions and, 365
judicial system and, 180–82
licensing boards and, 325
parallel backgrounding and, 7
pardons and, 198
pollution and, 434
schools and, 262, 277
pollution
agricultural land and, 441
air, 306, 439
cancer and, 436, 443
databases on, 62, 437
government regulation of, 306, 435–39
hazardous waste and, 442–44
mercury and, 437–38
military bases and, 444
mining and, 444
racial discrimination and, 435–36
soil, 442–44
Toxics Release Inventory (TRI) on, 437–39,
442
water, 46, 306, 426, 439–41
polygraphs, 246
poor people. *See* low-income persons; poverty
pork-barrel politics, 165, 290
pornography, 236–37
poverty. *See also* low-income persons
census on, 495, 496, 500
children and families and, 502–3
employment and, 501–2
financial exploitation of, 498–500
homelessness and, 503
human sources on, 497–98
problems created by, 496
school discipline and, 265
student behavior and, 265
poverty programs
child-support enforcement and, 506
food stamps and, 504, 506–7
health care and, 503–4
nutrition programs and, 504
temporary assistance and, 505–6
welfare and, 502–3
power structures, 74–76

preferred provider organizations (PPOs), 405
pregnancy
    fraudulent testing and, 110–11
    nutrition programs and, 508
prepublication reviews, 93, 116–18
prescription drugs. See drugs, prescription
presentencing reports, 191
presentments, 187
presidential libraries, 45
presidents
    of companies, 68
    in executive branch, 135
press releases, 69, 310
pretrial protective orders, 183
pretrial settlements, in tax disputes, 208
prevention programs
    for drunk drivers, 452–53
    of police, 220
preventive medicine, 389
primary documents, 34–51
    on commercial databases, 39–41
    database research and, 34
    depository libraries with, 43
    dissertations and theses as, 26
    "documents state of mind" on, 5–6
    example of techniques using, 45–48
    on executive branch, 125
    following trail of, 6, 7, 34–35
    government agency records as, 41–42
    on government databases, 42
    human sources and using, 6–7
    interview preparation and, 34, 67, 78
    liens as, 39
    limitations of, 67
    National Archives system and, 44–45
    public records and, 36–37
    sample investigation using, 48–51
    Social Security numbers as, 35–36
    tax records as, 39
    technical and scientific sources in, 43–44
    three I's of, 35
    types of, 35–39
    Uniform Commercial Code (UCC)
        statements as, 38
    verification of information in, 37
    vital records as, 37–38
    "working from the outside in" technique
        with, 3
principals, 272, 273
prisoners
    access to, 194
    appeals from, 193
    beatings and abuse of, 185, 187–88
    commutation of sentences of, 198
    complaints by, 194
    database on, 60
    death of, 195
    families of, 194
    lawsuits by, 142
    medical conditions of, 185
    pardons of, 198
    parole of, 197
    preparation for release of, 197
    rape of, 194
    records of, 60, 194
    rehabilitation of, 195
    transportation to courthouses of, 185
prisons, 193–96. See also jails
    access to, 193–94
    civil cases and, 183
    complaint files on, 194
    conditions in, 185, 194–96
    federal, 196
    fees in, 195
    guards in, 193, 194
    health care in, 195, 196
    industries and, 195
    juvenile offenders in, 199
    medical workers in, 194
    overcrowding in, 190, 195–96
    private companies running, 193, 195
    rape in, 194
    sources in, 194
    state, 196
    wardens in, 193, 194
privacy
    ethics and, 109
    law enforcement and, 218–19
    of licensed professionals, 327
private airplanes, 465
private companies
    government employees and revolving door to
        jobs in, 137, 437
    government operations awarded to, 141
    police officers as security guards at, 227
    prisons run by, 193, 195
private detectives, 252, 323
private foundations, 346
private investigators, 252
private practice defense attorneys, 203
private schools, 268, 278–79
private sector. See business; corporations
privatization, 141, 425
probate court, 35, 206–7
probation, 190, 193, 196–97
probation officers, 196–97
product liability claims, 209
product preferences, in government contracts,
    132
product safety, 183, 305
professional associations, 25, 158, 180, 324,
    327–28

professional fund-raisers, 344, 347
professional insurance, 373–74
professors, 282, 288–90
profilers, 229
promotion rates, in schools, 266
promotions, of law enforcement personnel, 223
property crimes, 238–39, 240
property insurance, 372–73
property ownership
    arson and, 230, 240
    bankruptcy and, 208
    by colleges and universities, 281, 286
    divorce and, 206
    by legislators, 160
    lender records on, 476
    locating owners in, 38, 49, 477–78
    by nonprofit organizations, 342
    by religious organizations, 348
    road construction and, 458
    tax liens and, 39, 60, 307, 309, 478, 479–80,
        506
property records, 35, 49
    databases on, 59–60, 478
property taxes
    assessments in, 59, 309, 482–83
    businesses and, 307
    escrow and, 481–82
    exemptions from, 483
    fairness of, 277, 483
    nonprofit organization exemptions for, 347,
        348
    reassessments in, 483
    records in, 39, 59, 476
    scams involving, 132–33, 481
    schools and, 277
prosecutors, 182, 202–3
    appointment of, 202
    bail setting and, 186
    domestic violence and, 233
    employees appointed by, 181
    federal, 202
    grand juries and, 186–87
    investigating, 202–3
    jury selection and, 189
    juvenile offenders and, 198, 243
    local, 202
    misconduct of, 202
    overcharging and undercharging by, 203
    performance measures for, 202–3
    plea-bargaining and, 203
    police misconduct and, 224, 226
    police-station-based, 245
    selection of, 181
    sentencing and, 191
    as sources, 252

prospectuses
    of bonds, 277
    of mutual funds, 361–62
prostitution, 10–11, 19, 231, 236
protective orders, 183
proxy statements, 304
psychiatric care, 401
psychiatrists, 253, 401
psychics, 229
psychological testing, of police officers, 221
psychologists, 200, 253, 323
public administrators, 207
public affairs personnel, 141–43
public authorities, 143–44
public charities, 339
public defenders, 190, 199, 203
public employees. See government employees
public figures, exposing, 113
public file, in cable companies, 430
public health, and crime, 253
public information officers, 70, 251
public opinion
    on crime, 221
    of police, 219
public policy, 165
public records, 36–37, 57–58
public relations firms, 158
public relations releases, 310
public schools. See schools
public service commissions, 418, 419
public utilities, 417. See also utilities
public utility commission, 421, 428
pyramid story structure, 97

quality
    of environment, and state parks, 437
    of learning, 261–62, 277
    of patient care, 390, 391
    of water, 440
quality control, in medical laboratories, 408
quality-improvement organizations, 390–91
questionnaires, 75, 189
questions
    in interviews, 82–83
    leading, 82
    phrasing of, 82, 84
    types of, 82
quotations, 96, 100, 104

race data
    on communities, 63
    on prisoners, 60
racial discrimination. See also minority groups
    bail system and, 186
    federal regulation of businesses and, 306

racial discrimination *(continued)*
fire departments and, 240
hazardous waste dump siting and, 435–36
home loans and, 55, 63
homeschooling and, 279
hospital treatment and, 388
jury selection and, 188–89
juvenile offenders and, 199
mortgage loans from banks and, 353–54, 355
nonprofit organizations and, 338
redlining and, 353–54, 355, 363–65
rental property and, 484
school boards and, 273
school placement and, 267
school test scores and, 266
sentencing and, 191, 192, 199
stereotypes and, 95
taxis and, 457
traffic violations and, 242
voting and, 63
race riots, 249
racial profiling, 242, 249
racketeering, 314
radiation, deaths from, 393
radioactive waste, 461
radon gas, in schools, 275
railroads, 459–60
crossings with, 459
databases on, 53, 61
safety issues and, 459–60, 469
raises, for law enforcement personnel, 223
rape, 231–32
at colleges and universities, 288
convictions for, 203
databases on, 60
DNA samples in, 232
insider financial transaction and, 365
in prison, 194
serial, 231–32
statistics on, 60, 231, 249, 250
rapid refund loans, 500
reading test scores, 262
real estate, 476–90. *See also* housing; property
taxes
broker licenses and, 322, 323, 326
corruption in government contracts in,
134–35
development in, 485–87
fair market value of, 482
foreclosure and auction notices on, 23, 39,
479–80
government documents in, 478–79
land fraud and, 476, 481, 482
landlord-tenant issues and, 483–85

land ownership and, 477–78
land values and, 482–83
liens and, 479–80
low-income housing and, 488–90
mortgage documents and, 480–82
new developments and, 485, 487–88
property value and tax assessment in, 482–83
records in, 308, 477–82
speculation in, 458, 487
tax-exempt, owned by nonprofit
organizations, 340
Web sites on, 477
zoning and, 485–87
reassessment, 483
recalls
automobiles, 451
blood banks and, 409
buses, 456
recidivism, 197, 200
recorder's office, 478, 480
record layout, in databases, 56
records, following trail of, 5. *See also* primary
documents
records divisions, in law enforcement, 251
recreational boating, 468
recreation areas, 441
recruitment, of police officers, 221
recusals, 201
redlining, 363–65
analysis techniques in, 364–65
documents on, 364
insurance and, 368, 375–76
mortgages from banks and, 353–54, 355,
363–65
re-election campaigns
judicial, 181
legislative, 162, 165
reference books, 25–26
reference librarians, 28
refinancing, 481
registration
of securities, 307
of sex offenders, 232
registries
of aircraft, 467
of nursing home aides, 398
regulation
airlines, 462
ambulances, 397
banks, 354
communications technology and, 427
credit card companies, 360
credit unions, 359
environment, 306, 435–39
equal opportunity and discrimination, 306

regulation *(continued)*
by federal agencies, 305–6
financial institutions, 354, 355
health insurance, 378
home health care companies, 402
hospitals, 389, 391–92, 393
incinerators and landfill disposal, 393
insurance companies, 41, 307, 324, 354, 369, 377–79
investment companies, 361–62
local government, 306–7, 347
low-income housing, 488
medical laboratories and, 408
military base exemption from, 444
motorcycles, 453
nonprofit organizations, 347–48
nursing homes, 399
pharmaceutical industry, 388
pollution, 435–39
railroads, 461
savings and loans, 354, 355, 358–59
self-regulatory organizations in, 143–44
state government, 306–7
transportation, 469
trucks and, 454
utilities, 418–22
wireless telecommunications, 428
workplace, 306
regulatory commissions, 141
rehabilitation, of prisoners, 195
relicensing, of nuclear power plants, 424
religion
homeschooling and, 279
in schools, 267
religious discrimination, and jury selection, 188
religious organizations, 337, 338, 348–49
molestation of children and, 348–49
newspapers for, 21
poverty programs and, 497
sources in, 349
tax-exempt status of, 349
textbook selection and, 267
relocation incentives, 309
rental properties
commercial buildings and, 484
housing subsidies and, 489
landlord-tenant relationships and, 483–85
rent-to-own stores, 500
repeat offenders, juvenile, 198
reputational model, 74–76
requests for proposals (RFPs), 131
research
college and university, 289–90
grants for, 289
on human subjects, 289–90
hypothesis development in, 4–5

indirect backgrounding, 7
investigative process with, 3, 7
by legislative branch, 167–69
medical, 405–6
parallel backgrounding, 7
social science and, 9
taking time for, 3
techniques in, 7
residence, place of, 36
residency requirements, for police officers, 221
resolution of tension, in writing, 98–99
response time
ambulance, 396–97
911 calls, 244–45
restaurant inspectors, 61
restaurants, and drunk drivers, 452
restitution payments, to victims, 190–91
restraint chairs, 194
résumés, 6
credentials fraud in, 78–79
of legislators, 163
of outside experts, 70
of police officers, 221
of superintendents, 273
verification of, 323
retention (keeping students) by
colleges and universities and, 284
schools and, 172–73
retention (repeating grades) of, 266–67
reversal rates, for judges, 192
reverse directories, 72
revictimization, 190
revocation of professional licenses, 328
riots, 249
risk management, 382
roads, 457–58
robbery, 236, 249, 250, 457
rule of harm, in journalism, 110
runaway children, 238
rural areas
housing in, 490
poverty in, 498
rural utilities
electric, 421
telephone, 421, 428

safety
airplanes, 464
airports, 466–67
all-terrain vehicles, 453
automobiles, 450–53
aviation, 461–67
bridges and, 449–50
buses, 455–56
business, 317–18
colleges and universities, 288

safety *(continued)*
  commercial shipping, 467–68
  commuter airlines, 465
  fire, 6, 240, 275, 286, 389
  hazardous waste, 460–61
  helicopters, 466
  helmet laws, 453
  inspections in, 317–18
  limousine services, 457
  mass transit, 461
  mining, 318
  motorcycles, 453
  nuclear power, 423
  railroads, 459–60
  roads, 457–59
  taxis, 457
  trucks, 454–55
  workplace, 306, 313
safety inspectors, 317–18
salaries
  of police officers, 223
  of school bus drivers, 273
  software for analysis of, 54
  of university personnel, 291
sales taxes, 341–42, 348
savings and loans
  competitors of, 359–60, 362
  financial information on, 358
  government regulation of, 354, 355, 358–59
  insider transactions in, 365
  local communities and impact of, 354
  SEC filing requirements for, 359
scams
  automotive insurance and, 368, 371, 372
  campaign finance corruption and, 146–47
  credit cards and, 254, 360
  escrow, 481
  financial, 183
  government contracts and, 132–33
  insurance, 368, 375
  taxi drivers, 457
scene setting, in writing, 101
school _____ gement, 273
_____ 273, 274, 275–76
_____ 73

_____ 268, 273, 276, 277

_____ 274, 278, 507
_____ udents; teachers

_____ istrators in, 262, 273, 291
alcohol and drug abuse in, 265–66

  approaches to investigating, 275–80
  budgets of, 62, 268, 275, 276–78
  buildings for, 273, 274–75, 278
  bureaucracy in, 269
  charter, 270–71
  choice in, 270–71
  class size in, 267
  college preparatory classes in, 267
  databases on, 60, 62
  desegregation in, 269
  discipline in, 264–65
  document trails in, 6
  dropout rates in, 262, 266, 276, 280
  enrollment in, 60
  evaluation of, 276
  fire safety in, 275
  funding of, 262, 276–78
  gender equity in, 270
  low-income families and, 268, 269, 272
  management of, 273
  overcrowding in, 185
  private, 268, 278–79
  racial diversity and multiculturalism in, 269–70
  religion in, 267
  staff in, 273
  state, 268
  teacher competency in, 271–72
  technology and corporate sponsorship in, 268
  test scores in, 60, 62, 261, 262–64, 266
  textbooks in, 267
  tracking in, 267
  violence in, 264–65
  vocational and trade, 279–80
scientific reports, 43–44
scientists, misconduct by, 125
scorecard, in college and university accreditation, 283–84
sealed convictions, 323
sealing juvenile records, 198
search engines, 55–56, 71
searches, in law enforcement, 254
searching, for data
  in bibliographies, 30
  for books, 26–28
  citations used in, 30
  in databases, 55–56
  help from librarians in, 29
  key words used in, 29–30, 303
  subject headings in libraries and, 27
  techniques in, 29–32
search warrants, 254
seasonal workers, 319
secondary market, 480–81
secondary schools. *See* education; schools

secondary sources, 19–32
  availability of, 5
  books as, 26–28
  broadcast and cable sources as, 23
  databases and, 19–20, 30–32
  defined, 20
  dissertations and theses, 26
  libraries and, 28
  limitations of, 67
  magazines as, 23–24
  newsletters as, 23–24
  newspapers as, 5, 20–23
  reference books as, 25–26
  search techniques for, 20–32
  verification of information in, 5, 21
  on Web sites, 30–32
  "working from the outside in" technique
    with, 3
secretaries of state, 62, 147, 308
Section 8 program, 505
sections story structure, 97
secular humanism, 279
securities, 302, 307, 345, 361, 366
Securities and Exchange Commission (SEC),
  302
security firms, 239, 354. *See also* investment
  companies
security guards, 227
security measures
  at airports, 464–65
  at colleges and universities, 288
  in jails, 185
  law enforcement restrictions and, 218–19
  for nuclear power plants, 424
  in schools, 264
  stolen property and, 238–39
segregation, in schools, 269
self-dealing, 346
self-employment, 322
self-referrals, by health care providers, 403
self-regulatory organizations, 143–44
self-study (accreditation), 282
semiannual reports, of inspectors general, 138
sensationalism, 113
sentencing, 191–92
  alternatives to, 191
  of drunk drivers, 205
  indeterminate, 191
  investigation before, 191
  juvenile offenders and, 199
  leeway in, 191–92
  mandatory, 192
  to probation, 196–97
  racial discrimination in, 191, 192, 199
  victims and, 190

serial murders, 19–20, 198
serial rape, 231–32
series of articles, 97–98
settlement talks, in civil cases, 183–84
sewage treatment plants, 438, 440
sewer systems
  regulation of, 418, 426
  storm water and, 441
sex crimes. *See* rape; sexual abuse
sexism, in fire departments, 240
sex offenders, registration of, 232
sexual abuse
  of children, 265, 348–49
  of drivers stopped for violations, 242
  by licensed professionals, 329
  pornography and, 236–37
  of spouses, 265
  of students, 290
sexual behavior, of legislators, 152, 163
sexual harassment, 152, 163, 242, 290, 322
sexual misconduct, by coaches, 272
shakedowns, 314
shelters, 503
shipping, commercial, 467–68
shock incarceration units, 195
short-line railroads, 460
signing statements, 135
silence, in interviews, 82
slumlords, 476, 478
small businesses, 305–6, 365–66, 460. *See also*
  business
small claims court, 207–8
sobriety checkpoints, 241
social network analysis, 55, 74–76
social organizations, 72
social registers, 25
social responsibility, 305
social science, 9, 496
Social Security numbers, 35–36
Social Security program, 165
social services
  child-support enforcement and, 506
  food stamps and, 504, 506–7
  nonprofit organizations and, 339
  nutrition programs in, 504
  temporary assistance in, 505–6
social welfare agencies, 200, 497, 503
social workers, 198, 323, 497, 509
soft money, 156
soil pollution, 443–44
  erosion and, 443
  government regulation of, 306
  Superfund sites and, 436, 442–43
solid waste disposal, 443–44
sororities, 286

soup kitchens, 508
sources. *See* human sources; primary docu-
    ments; secondary sources
"so what" paragraph, 100
special districts, 143–44
special interest groups
    campaign contributions from, 154, 181
    judges and, 181
    legislators and, 154, 161
    lobbyists used by, 158
specialized courts, 205–11
special libraries, 28
special-needs students, 268–69
specifications, in government contracts, 131–32
speculation, real estate, 487
speeding tickets, 242, 274
speed traps, 242
spin, 141–42
sponsors
    of legislative bills, 164
    of schools by businesses, 268
sports
    college, 26, 281, 286, 287–88
    gender equity in schools and, 270
    sexual misconduct by coaches in, 272
spousal abuse, 199
spreadsheet software programs, 54
standardized tests, 262–63, 279
state bar associations, 202, 312
state courts, appeals in, 192
state government
    affordable housing programs of, 489–90
    airports and, 466
    ambulance regulation by, 397
    budget of, 381
    cabinet secretaries in, 135–36
    cable systems, 428
    campaign contributions and, 155, 170
    child labor laws and, 319
    communications and, 427
    corruption in contracts from, 134–35
    databases on, 40, 49, 62
    depository libraries and, 43
    environmental responsibilities of, 437
    financial institution regulation by, 137, 355,
        359
    governors and, 144–45, 182
    hazardous waste and, 442
    health insurance regulation by, 378
    home health care companies and, 402
    hospitals and, 389, 391–92, 393
    incinerators and landfill disposal, 393
    inspectors general in, 138
    insurance company regulation by, 324, 369,
        374, 375, 376, 377–79
    legislatures in, 169–72, 181, 437
    licensed professionals and, 324, 328–29
    lobbyists and, 145, 170–71, 281
    lotteries of, 499
    Medicaid and, 380–81, 400
    medical laboratories and, 408
    motorcycle regulation and, 453
    motor vehicle regulation by, 451
    nonprofit organization regulation by, 61, 347
    nursing home regulation by, 399, 400
    prisons and, 196
    public employee relations boards and, 316
    railroad regulation and, 461
    regulatory agencies of, 306–7
    road construction contracts and, 457–58
    transportation and, 458
    truck regulation by, 454
    utilities regulation by, 418–19, 427
    vital records maintained by, 37–38
    whistleblowers and, 69
state government agencies, 144
state government employees. *See* government
    employees
state highway patrol databases, 61
state income tax returns, 160
state insurance departments, 370, 376, 377–79
state judicial system, 181, 182, 187, 205
state parks, 437
state registers, 147
state schools, 268
state transportation departments, 458, 461, 466
statistics
    on crime, 249–50, 251
    on health care, 391
    on insurance cases, 378–79
    on poverty, 496
    on rape reports, 231
    school test score analysis and, 264
    in scientific reports, 44
    software for, 55
stereotypes, in writing, 95
stockbrokers, 68, 304, 310, 323, 325
stock exchanges, 143–44, 302, 325
stocks, 159, 253, 302
    government regulation of, 355
    nonprofit organization ownership of, 338,
        343
stolen identity crimes, 37
stolen property, 238–39
storm water, 441
story structures, 96–105
student newspapers, 280
students. *See also* college and universities; edu-
    cation; schools
    alcohol and drug abuse by, 265–66

students *(continued)*
discipline of, 264–65
gender equity and, 270
homeschooling and, 279
loans to, 285
low-income, 268, 269
minority, 269–70, 272, 276
placement of, and test scores, 264, 266
retention (keeping students) of, 172–73
retention (repeating grades) by, 266–67
as sources, 276
special-needs, 268–69
suspension of, 265
test scores of, 60, 261, 262–64, 266
tracking, 267
violence in school and, 264–65
subcontracts, 457, 479
subject headings, in libraries, 27, 30
subjects. *See* human subjects
subpoenas, for witnesses, 187
subprime loans, 354, 476, 500
subsidies
to airports, 466
for commercial shipping, 467
to farmers, 22
for housing, 134–35, 489
substantial contributors, to foundations, 346
subway systems, 461
suicide, in jails, 195
summary judgments, 183
sunshine laws, 349
Superfund sites, 436, 442
superintendents, school, 273
suppliers, hospital, 389
support staff
at colleges and universities, 290–91
in executive branch, 135
in legislative branch, 161–62, 172
in schools, 273–74
suppression motion, 187
surgery, death after, 391
surplus government equipment, 127
surrogate's court. *See* probate court
surveillance, 112, 145, 233, 243, 468
suspects. *See also* defendants
bail payments by, 185–86
interviews with, 219
police interrogation of, 225
procedures following arrest of, 184–85
as sources, 252
suspension
of licenses, 329
of students, 265
SWAT teams, 209
syllabuses, 285–86
system operators, in utilities, 421

tape recording
fairness of, 109
of interviews, 85, 94
of 911 calls, 245
of police interrogations, 225
Tax Court, U.S., 208
taxes. *See also* property taxes
assessed value and, 59
budget revenue from, 127
business records on, 309
databases on, 59–60
delinquency records in, 60
disputes over, 208
document trails and, 6
government contracting process and, 131
legislative caps on, 168
liens and, 39, 60, 307, 309
lotteries as a type of, for low-income people,
499
payment in lieu of, 347
private schools and, 279
records on, 6, 59–60, 61, 208
refunds in, 506
school funding and, 277–78
special-interest groups and, 154
tax breaks for businesses and, 309
tax court and, 208
white-collar crime and, 243
tax-exempt status
bonds and, 341, 348
colleges and universities and, 342
nonprofit organizations and, 337, 338,
339–40, 347, 348
nursing homes and, 399
property, 483
of religious organizations, 340, 349
studies of, 341
taxis, 59, 325, 457
tax returns, of nonprofit organizations, 34,
342–43, 392
teachers, 271–72
accreditation of, 271
burnout of, 272
competency of, 271–72
criminal records of, 272, 323
licensing of, 323
quality of teaching by, 271, 272
school-based management and, 273
school violence and, 265
as sources, 276
training of, 271–72
teaching assistants, 289
technical conference proceedings, 44
technical reports
in depository libraries, 43
from government agencies, 43–44

telecommunications regulation, 418
telephone calls
  arranging interviews using, 68, 79
  fairness of tape-recording, 109
  to prisoners, 194
  solicitations using, 347
telephone directories, 72, 140, 312
telephone numbers, 79, 252
telephone service
  from cable companies, 419, 427, 428
  charges for, 146, 427–28
  documents on, 427
  long-distance, 428
  rural systems for, 421, 428
  wireless, 428
television
  cable, 428–30
  campaign spending on advertising on, 156
  evangelists on, 348, 349
  news programs on, 23
temporary assistance programs, 505–6
temporary workers, 320
tenants, 483–85
tension resolution, in writing, 98–99
tenure, 288, 289
term life insurance, 376–77
terrorism
  airport security and, 464–65
  bombings and, 240, 241
  Muslim-related charities and, 349
testing industry, 264
tests
  for drug use, 463
  of medical devices, 407
  in medical laboratories, 408
  pollution and cancer and, 436
  for pregnancy, 110–11
  of prescription drugs, 388, 406, 407
  psychological, of police officers, 221
  in schools, 60, 61, 262–63, 266, 279
  for sobriety, 241, 463
  of water systems, 426
textbooks, 267, 277
theft
  of drugs in hospitals, 393
  evidence rooms and, 246
  expungement of record of, 323
  in group homes for mental health patients,
    400–401
  of identity, 37
  by police officers, 225
  of property, 238–39
  statistics on, 249
therapists, and sex offenders, 231
tickets, traffic, 241–42
theses, 26

think tanks, 70, 311
"three I's," 35
ticket-fixing, 205
tips
  anonymous, 134
  choosing a subject and, 4
  ethics of using, 109
  examples of, 342, 426
tissue banks, 388
tobacco companies, 136, 166
toll roads, 458–59
tone, in writing, 104
total maximum daily load of contaminants
    (TMDL) levels, 440–41
towboats, 469
towing companies, 241–42
Toxics Release Inventory (TRI), 437–39, 442
toxic waste
  disposal of, 63, 437–38
  documentation of, 437–39
  storage sites for, 435–36
  Superfund cleanup sites and, 436, 442–43
tracings, 27
tracking, in schools, 267
trade associations, 25, 158, 312, 328, 340
trade schools, 279–80
traffic accidents, 241–42
  all-terrain vehicles and, 453
  automobile insurance scams and, 368, 371, 372
  buses and, 455–56
  databases on, 61, 242
  details about, 94
  fatal, 61
  motorcycles and, 453
  nuclear waste transport and, 460
  police pursuits and, 222–23
  railroad crossings and, 459
  staged, 183
  taxis and, 457
  trucks and, 454–55
  uninsured drivers and, 372, 451–52
  vehicular homicide and, 230, 246
trade journals, 23–24
traffic court, 205
traffic patrol, 241–42
traffic stops, 241, 242, 249
traffic tickets
  budget revenue from, 127
  fixing, 205
traffic violations, 241–42
training
  in fire departments, 240
  of police officers, 221–23, 232, 240, 241
  of security guards, 227
  of superintendents, 273
  of teachers, 271–72

trains
    hazardous waste transport on, 460–61
    safety of, 459–60
transitions, in writing, 102
transit systems, mass, 461
translators, 185
transmission lines, electric, 417, 419, 422
transportation, 449–69. *See also* airplanes; auto-
    mobiles; motor vehicles
    all-terrain vehicles, 453
    automobile inspections and, 451–52
    aviation safety and, 461–67
    boating accidents and, 468
    bombings and, 240
    buses and, 455–56
    commercial shipping and, 467–68
    databases on, 61, 62, 449
    of hazardous waste, 460–61
    labor unions in, 314
    limousine services and, 457
    mass transit and, 461
    motorcycles, 453
    railroads and, 459–70
    safety investigations in, 449–50
    taxis and, 457
    trucks and, 453–55
    water, 467–70
travel, by legislators, 162–63, 169
Treasury securities, 366
trial court judges, 181
trials. *See* court cases; judicial system
truck drivers, 455
trucks, 453–55, 469
trustees, 314
trusts, 345
tuition, college and university, 281, 284

UCC. *See* Uniform Commercial Code (UCC)
undercharging, by prosecutors, 203
undercover journalists, 111–12
undercover police officers, 222, 233
unemployment benefits, 322
unemployment compensation program, 165
unemployment insurance, 367
unfair labor practices, 315–16
unidentified sources, 114–15
uniform billing records, hospital, 392
Uniform Commercial Code (UCC), 38, 59,
    160, 307, 478
uninsured drivers, 372, 451–52
uninsured persons (health), 368, 369
unions. *See* labor unions
U.S. attorneys. *See* prosecutors
U.S. Bankruptcy Court, 208–9
U.S. Coast Guard, 468–69
U.S. Court of Appeals for the Federal Circuit, 210
U.S. Government Manual, 41

U.S. Marshals Service, 224, 235
U.S. Tax Court, 208, 341
United Way, 338, 345, 497
universal life insurance, 371
universities. *See* colleges and universities
unlisted telephone numbers, 252
unrelated business income tax (UBIT), 341, 348
unsecured creditors, 209
unsolved murders, 230
uranium, 422
utilities, 417–30
    cable systems, 428–30
    communication, 426–27
    as cooperatives, 422, 423
    databases on, 419–20
    defined, 417
    deregulation of, 418, 419
    documents on, 419–22
    electricity and, 422–23
    fees paid by, 127
    financial records of, 417, 421
    investor-owned, 422
    gas and, 422–23
    labor unions and, 314
    as monopolies, 417, 422
    multifaceted effect of, 417–18
    nuclear power and, 423–25
    state regulation of, 418–19, 427
    terminology in, 417
    water, 425–26
    Web sites on, 419

vandalism, 240
variable life insurance, 371
vehicular homicide, 230, 246
vendors, 61, 125, 144
verification
    of primary documents, 37
    of secondary sources, 5, 21
Veterans Administration hospitals, 397–98
veterans benefits, 165, 379
vice, 236–37, 242
vice officers, 236
victimless crimes, 236
victims of crimes
    compensation programs for, 252
    courtroom experience of, 190–91
    non-English speaking, 184–85
    restitution payments to, 190–91
    revictimization of, 190
    as sources, 252
    stereotypes of, in rape, 231
    uncooperative, 190
violence
    at colleges and universities, 288
    confessions after beatings by police and,
        187–88, 230

violence *(continued)*
    domestic, 232–33, 265
    in schools, 264–65
    statistics on, 250
    use of force by police and, 218, 222, 225
visiting team report (accreditation), 283
vital records, 37–38
    databases of, 62
vocational schools, 279–80
voir dire, 188
volunteer fund-raisers, 344
voter's registration records, 6, 35, 36, 63, 73
voting records
    databases on, 54, 59
    of legislative branch, 165–66
vouchers, in court cases, 182, 187

wages
    enforcement of laws on, 316, 318–19
    minimum, 318–19
    poor people and, 501
    overtime, 319
Wall Street Journal story structure, 97
wardens, 193, 194
wards of the court, 207
war on drugs, 233, 235
warrantless searches, 254
waste, government agency, 128, 129–30
waste disposal
    medical, 393
    military bases and, 444
    nontoxic trash and, 443–44
    Superfund sites and, 436, 442–43
    transport of, 460–61
wastewater treatment plants, 138
watchdogs and watchdog groups
    on charities, 342
    budgets and, 133
    executive branch and, 123
    local government and, 144
    school testing industry and, 264
    whistleblowers and, 69
water, 425–26
    agencies supplying, 425
    availability and pricing of, 425
    construction of new facilities in, 425–26
    drinking water quality, 434
    landfill use and, 443
water companies, 418
water districts, 425–26
Watergate exposé, 4, 114
water pollution, 439–41
    agricultural land and, 441
    dams and, 441
    documents on, 440
    drinking water and, 439–40
    government regulation of, 306, 440–41

inspectors general and, 138
    storm water and sewer systems and, 441
    testing for, 426
    total maximum daily load of contaminants
        (TMDL) levels and, 440–41
    utilities and, 426
    wells and, 439–40
water transportation, 467–60
    boating accidents and, 468
    commercial shipping and, 467–68
    oil and hazardous substance spills and,
        469
    U.S. Coast Guard and, 468–69
water treatment facilities, 441
water utilities, 425–26
    documents on, 426
    regulation of, 418
    shortages of water and, 441
    testing for pollutants in, 426
weapons. *See* guns
Web sites
    blogs on, 71, 77
    books, 27, 28
    campaign contributions, 156
    city directories, 72
    college and universities, 251, 281, 285–86,
        287, 288
    community reinvestment, 363
    computer-assisted reporting, 55, 65–66
    corporate filings, 302, 304–5
    credit unions, 359
    for databases, 29, 31
    for dissertations and theses, 26
    environment, 435, 438
    ethics, 119
    financial institutions, 363
    finding people through, 72, 73
    government agencies, 55, 124
    human sources, 106
    of inspector generals, 138
    legislative research reports, 167, 168
    legislative voting records, 165–66
    licensed professionals, 324
    listserv listings, 71
    medical research, 406
    Medicare, 399
    National Archives system, 44
    newspaper, 20–21, 23, 31
    nonprofit organizations, 340
    nuclear power, 424–25
    outside experts, 70
    personal, 71
    real estate, 477
    secondary sources, 30–32
    Securities and Exchange Commission, 302
    telephone and reverse directories, 72
    utilities, 419

wedding announcements, 22
weigh stations, 454
welfare system. *See also* poverty programs
  children and, 502–3
  homelessness and, 503
  reform of, 509
wells, 439
whistleblowers, 197, 313
  law enforcement personnel as, 252
  legal protection of, 313
  nuclear power industry and, 425
  as sources, 69
white-collar crime
  law enforcement and, 243
  prosecutors and, 202
whole-life insurance, 376
wills, 23, 206
wire companies, 419
wireless telecommunications programs, 428
witnesses
  arson and, 240
  crime lab personnel as, 246
  effective use of, 204
  grand juries, 187
  interviewing, 252
  for legislative committees, 166
  police misconduct hearings and, 227
  as sources, 252
  subpoenas for, 187
  in trials, 190
women. *See also* sexual abuse
  domestic violence and, 232–33
  gender equity in school sports and, 270
  judicial appointments and, 181
  nutrition programs and, 504
  as police officers, 221
  poverty and, 508
  pregnancy and, 515, 110–11
  rape and, 231–32
work habits, of judges, 200–201
"working from the outside in" technique, 3
workers' compensation insurance, 36, 367, 381–83
  fraud and abuse in, 146, 381
  newspaper stories on, 22
  police officers' claims for, 223
  purpose of, 381
workplace
  directories in, 72–73
  disability insurance and, 370
  ethics and, 313
  health in, 317–18
  illegal immigrants and, 501

  indoor air pollution and, 439
  injuries and workers' compensation in, 381–83
  newspapers aimed at, 21
  poor people in, 501–2
  regulation of, 306
  safety in, 306, 317–18
  whistleblower protection in, 313
  working conditions and, 313, 317–18
work programs, in prisons, 195
World Wide Web. *See* Web sites
writing, 89–105
  avoiding clichés in, 95
  avoiding stereotypes in, 95
  chronologically, 95–96, 103
  context in, 100
  details in, 94–95
  dialogue in, 102–3
  direct quotations in, 96, 100, 104
  endings of stories in, 99, 104–5
  focus in, 98–99
  foreshadowing in, 103
  flashbacks in, 103
  graphics and, 90, 92–93
  guidelines for writing effective stories in, 90–93
  leads in, 98, 99–100, 104–5
  middles of stories in, 101–3
  opening sentences in, 99–101
  outlines in, 95–96
  outrage expressed in, 91
  pacing in, 102
  people-oriented, 91–92
  point of view in, 103–4
  prepublication reviews by readers in, 93
  "reporters" vs. "writers" in, 89–90
  scene setting in, 101
  series of articles in, 97–98
  sources and, 102
  story structures in, 96–105
  talking to readers in, 92
  tension and resolution in, 98–99
  tips on, 90
  tone in, 91, 104
  transitions in, 102
written briefs, 193
wrongful convictions, 204, 236
wrongful death
  health insurance and, 378
  nursing homes and, 399

zoning, 485–97